What's HOT in This Edition!!

Coverage of the three top Linux distributions: Red Hat, Slackware 96, and Caldera Open Linux Base

- Although this book focuses mainly on the Red Hat distribution, we still provide coverage on how to install and configure the Slackware 96 distribution.

- All three distributions are available on the accompanying CD-ROMs!

DEC Alpha coverage

- See how to install Red Hat Linux on various DEC Alpha platforms.

How to go online with Linux

- Full coverage of ftp, telnet, and other Internet programs is included.

- See how to create World Wide Web documents with HTML, as well as manage an Internet Web server.

- Three chapters have been added that explain how to get Apache, the world's most popular Linux Web server, up and running.

- The complete text to Que's *Running a Perfect Web Site with Apache* is included in HTML on CD-ROM!

How to go GUI with X Windows

- See how to install and configure XFree86, the most popular X Windows server for Linux.

- Learn how to use several exciting X applications.

- Find X Windows resource files on CD-ROM!

Special Edition

USING
LINUX
THIRD EDITION

Special Edition

Using
Linux
Third Edition

Jack Tackett Jr. and David Gunter

Special Edition Using Linux, Third Edition

Library of Congress Catalog No.: 97-65022

ISBN: 0-7897-1132-x

99 98 97   6 5 4 3 2

Interpretation of the printing code: the rightmost double-digit number is the year of the book's printing; the rightmost single-digit number, the number of the book's printing. For example, a printing code of 97-1 shows that the first printing of the book occurred in 1997.

Credits

PRESIDENT
Roland Elgey

PUBLISHER
Stacy Hiquet

DIRECTOR OF MARKETING
Lynn E. Zingraf

PUBLISHING MANAGER
Fred Slone

SENIOR TITLE MANAGER
Bryan Gambrel

EDITORIAL SERVICES DIRECTOR
Elizabeth Keaffaber

ACQUISITIONS EDITOR
Tracy Dunkelberger

PRODUCT DIRECTOR
Rebecca J. Campbell

PRODUCTION EDITOR
Susan Shaw Dunn

EDITOR
Sherri Fugit

PRODUCT MARKETING MANAGER
Kristine Ankney

ASSISTANT PRODUCT MARKETING MANAGERS
Karen Hagen
Christy M. Miller

STRATEGIC MARKETING MANAGER
Barry Pruett

TECHNICAL EDITOR
Steven Burnett

TECHNICAL SUPPORT SPECIALIST
Nadeem Muhammed

SOFTWARE SPECIALIST
Brandon K. Penticuff

ACQUISITIONS COORDINATOR
Carmen Krikorian

SOFTWARE RELATIONS COORDINATOR
Susan D. Gallagher

EDITORIAL ASSISTANT
Andrea Duvall

BOOK DESIGNER
Ruth Harvey

COVER DESIGNER
Dan Armstrong

PRODUCTION TEAM
Jason R. Carr
Bryan Flores
Julie Geeting
Christy Hendershot
Sossity Smith

INDEXER
Ginny Bess

Composed in *Century Old Style* and *ITC Franklin Gothic* by Que Corporation.

To my wife, Peggy: I love and adore you.

—Jack Tackett Jr.

To my mother.

—David Gunter

About the Authors

Jack Tackett Jr. is a freelance writer and computer consultant in Research Triangle Park, N.C. He specializes in C/C++ and client/server development on various platforms. During his spare time, Jack enjoys traveling; writing; reading; and spending time with his friends, his family, and his family's two dogs and two cats in his new home in Cary, N.C. He invites your comments at **tackett@netwharf.com**.

David Gunter is an information technology consultant and author based in Cary, N.C. In addition to software development, he has been involved with supporting and managing diverse systems and networks for more than 10 years. David has a master's in computer science from the University of Tennessee. He has worked as both a lead and contributing author on 10 computer books, including the best selling *Special Edition Using Linux* series from Que. His publication credits include *Using Linux*, first, second, and third editions; *Using the Internet*, Third Edition; *Netscape Starter Kit*; *Using Netscape 3*; *Using Netscape 2*; *Client/Server Programming with RPC and DCE*; *Using UNIX*, Second Edition; and *Using Turbo C++ 4.5*. When not writing, consulting, researching, or surfing the Net, David spends as much time as possible with his wonderful wife, Lola, and their dog and two cats.

Contributing Authors

Lola Gunter is a technical consultant in Cary, N.C. She has worked in Web and multimedia software development as a computer consultant and as a manager of technical documentation. She has a bachelor's in computer science from the University of North Carolina-Asheville. Other than the Web and the Internet, her interests include working with stained glass, roughhousing with her German shepherd, and traveling.

Peggy Tackett is a software support specialist for Duke University. Webmaster for Duke University's Center for Aging and Human Development (**http://www.geri.duke.edu**), she teaches classes on using the Web. In her spare time, she enjoys gardening, working with dog-rescue groups, and traveling when she can pry her husband away from the computer.

Acknowledgments

From Jack Tackett:

First, I want to thank all the readers of the first two editions for their patronage and for their helpful and insightful comments. Your comments are important and make a difference; you have made this a better project!

I want to say thank you for the tremendous efforts put forth by the Linux developers scattered across the globe. I also want to acknowledge the fine contributions begun by Linus Torvalds and continued by so many others around the world—thanks for creating Linux and breathing life into such a monumental effort! Also, thanks to Matt Welsh, et al., for the work on the Linux Documentation project, and to Patrick Volkerding for the Slackware distribution. Also, a big thanks to the fine folks at InfoMagic for putting together such a great Linux CD combination and offer for our readers. Finally, I want to thank the staff at Red Hat for their help in preparing this edition.

Next, I want to express my regards for the people at the Que Continuum—never have I seen such professionalism in the publishing industry. Their efforts all revolve around one goal: creating a quality product through team effort. I especially want to thank Fred Slone and Tracy Dunkelberger for their help in getting this project off the ground and finished. I also want to thank Susan Dunn, Steve Burnett, Brandon Penticuff, and Becky J. Campbell for all their help.

To David V. Gunter, my partner in crime. :-) Third time's a charm, eh? Thanks for everything, Dave. Also to Lance Brown, Lola Gunter, and Margaret Tackett for all their help in preparing this book! Finally, thanks to Paul Barrett for his initial help with the research that eventually led to this book.

To my friends Paul Barrett, Keith E. Bugg, Gregg and Beckie Field, Dave and Lola Gunter, Kell and Joy Wilson, and Joe Williams: Thanks for the memories! Thanks to my combined family—the Tacketts and the Martins—for their support in all my endeavors. Also, a big thank you to the best cousins in the world—Bill and Hope Tackett Jr.

I'd like to thank my best instructor, Dr. Joe Daugherty of the University of North Carolina-Asheville. Also thanks to Myrtice Trent of the Blue Ridge Technical Community College. Thanks for the help and encouragement you provided.

Finally, to my wife Peggy, who has yet again put up with me spending endless hours at the computer writing yet another computer book. Thanks, sweetheart, and I love you!

From David Gunter:

First of all, I'd like to thank all the readers of the first two editions of this book. Your comments and suggestions have helped us continue to improve this book with each edition.

I'd like to thank all the folks at Que who worked on this project. Special thanks go to our acquisitions editor, Tracy Dunkelberger, for keeping her sanity while trying to work with me! Also, thanks go to Susan Dunn and Steve Burnett for their excellent editorial work.

Last, but most certainly not least, I would like to thank my wife, Lola, for putting up with the endless hours over the last three months while I worked on this revision!

We'd Like to Hear from You!

As part of our continuing effort to produce books of the highest possible quality, Que would like to hear your comments. To stay competitive, we *really* want you to let us know what you like or dislike most about this book or other Que products.

Please send your comments, ideas, and suggestions for improvement to

The Expert User Team
E-mail: **euteam@que.mcp.com**
CompuServe: **72410,2077**
Fax: (317) 581-4663

Our mailing address is

Expert User Team
Que Corporation
201 West 103rd Street
Indianapolis, IN 46290-1097

You can also visit our team's home page on the World Wide Web at

http://www.mcp.com/que/developer_expert

Your comments will help us to continue publishing the best books available in today's market.

Thank you,

The Expert User Team

Contents at a Glance

Table of Contents

6 Installing the X Windows System   159

III | Managing the File System

VI | Using the Internet

34   Managing an Internet Web Server   667

Appendixes

Introduction

What's new in the third edition of *Special Edition Using Linux*? Lots! First, we've revamped the book to highlight the Red Hat distribution—probably the most popular and easiest-to-install Linux distribution ever. You'll also find another CD-ROM containing a *lite* version of Caldera's Open Linux Base product. But we didn't forget Paul Volkerding's venerable Slackware distribution, so we also provide installation and usage information for Slackware 96. So you get not one, not two, but *three* complete Linux distributions for the price of a single book!

Next, we added an entire section of chapters on getting Apache—the world's most popular Web server software—up and running under Linux. In fact, on the accompanying CD-ROM you'll find the complete text to Que's *Running a Perfect Web Site with Apache*. As for the rest of the book, you'll find updates and new material throughout the chapters as we try to bring you the best introduction to Linux in the world.

However, if you're just tuning in, you might want to know just what the heck Linux is.

In 1991, Linus Torvalds, then a 23-year-old college student, began a personal project to expand the Minix operating system into a full-fledged clone of the UNIX operating system so popular on college campuses. The project is still evolving—Linux is continuously updated and expanded by literally hundreds of people spread around the world.

Well, Linux is a unique animal in the computer (r)evolution. It isn't a commercial product backed by a huge corporation; rather, it's an operating system born of frustration and built by a ragtag team of computer enthusiasts around the world. This team used Internet resources to communicate and build the operating system named Linux.

But don't think Linux is just a hobby for hackers around the world—it's not! Plenty of commercial products are being written specifically for Linux. In fact, several companies are porting their UNIX-based applications to Linux, such as Corel's WordPerfect. You'll also find many Fortune 500 companies using Linux for internal projects and mission-critical applications. Not bad for a product not controlled by any one organization.

You'll also find plenty of free applications and utilities for Linux. Since Linux's inception, almost the entire GNU library of utilities has been ported to Linux, and the X Windows GUI system— so popular on UNIX-type workstations—also has been ported. GNU (a recursive acronym for GNU's Not UNIX) is a project started by one man to make software available to anyone who wants access. The GNU General Public License in Appendix D describes the philosophy under which Linux and many other fine software packages are distributed. The accompanying CD-ROMs contain many of these packages.

This book provides you with enough information to use and enjoy Linux. The accompanying CD-ROMs contain the Red Hat 4.0 distribution and the Slackware 96 distribution, each of which use the 2.0.18 Linux kernel.

Probably the first order of business is to help you pronounce the word *Linux*. To most Americans, the pronunciation is LEN-nucks, with the short i sound. The official pronunciation is LIE-nucks, with the long i sound. ■

ON THE WEB

You can see and hear Linus pronounce Linux at the URL **http://www.cse.psu.edu/~drost/linus.html**.

N O T E If you don't understand what a Uniform Resource Locator (URL) is or how to use it, don't despair! This book will help you learn your way around the Internet by using Linux. ■

▶ **See** "Understanding URLs," **p. 557**

Who Should Use This Book?

Anyone interested in the Linux phenomenon can use this book as a guide to installing, configuring, and using Linux. Linux is often called a UNIX clone, but it's actually a POSIX-compliant multiuser, multitasking operating system for Intel 386 and later processors. POSIX is an international standard for operating systems and software detailing interoperability standards. Linux doesn't require MS-DOS or Windows to operate; in fact, Linux can replace those programs on your computer.

Because Linux is still evolving, it's imperative that you understand the possibility of losing existing data on your system. *Do not install Linux without first backing up your system.* It might be necessary to repartition your hard drive to make room for this new operating system, although it's possible to install Linux on top of MS-DOS or to repartition your hard drive without losing data. This book and the task of installing Linux aren't for the novice user. With the proper precautions, however, anyone can install and enjoy Linux.

N O T E The most current version of Linux is always available on the Internet, from sources listed in Appendix A, "Sources of Information." The accompanying CD-ROMs contain the latest possible versions of Linux, but due to the rapid development of this popular operating system and the chaotic process in which it's developed, it's impossible to provide the latest and greatest on a CD-ROM. In fact, although all efforts are made to keep the book and CD-ROMs in synch, that also is nearly impossible. Unlike commercial software, which changes infrequently and under controlled conditions, Linux and related software are perpetually dynamic. ▪

Because Linux is very close to UNIX, many of the operations and procedures necessary for using Linux also apply to many UNIX systems. By learning to use Linux, you also learn how to use most UNIX systems.

UNIX has evolved over the years to become the premier operating system used by hundreds of thousands of people throughout the world. This isn't an accident. Earlier versions of UNIX were harder to manipulate than other operating systems, but despite this, UNIX managed to amass a distinguished following in academic and scientific circles. These professionals realized not only what a powerful, flexible, and manageable operating system UNIX was, but also its potential to be the best operating system ever. Their efforts have culminated in the UNIX of today, with its marvelous utilities, bundled with the newest communications capabilities and graphical user interfaces (GUIs).

The UNIX of today promises again to revolutionize the personal computer industry, and perhaps redirect the industry's growth. UNIX has evolved from a minicomputer operating system to one that crosses all hardware platforms. There's no reason to think that this evolution will stop. UNIX may well become the standard for what most users dream of—complete standardization and compatibility of all computer systems eventually, regardless of size or power.

UNIX comes in several flavors from a variety of vendors, including versions for the Intel PC platforms, but most of these versions cost big bucks. Linux provides a relatively inexpensive—free if you have access to the Internet—solution to learning about UNIX-type procedures and commands, the X Windows GUI, and accessing the Internet via Linux.

Who Should *Not* Use This Book?

If you are a Linux kernel hacker or a UNIX guru, this book may not be your cup of tea. This book is a great resource for someone wanting to know more about Linux and UNIX who has never been involved with either operating system.

However, if you know how to install Linux and maneuver around in UNIX, you may still find this book of use, particularly if you are only a UNIX user and have never had the chance to perform system administration tasks. Several sections of the book explain the finer points of system administration and how to maintain a Linux/UNIX system. Typically, a normal UNIX user is never allowed to perform these system administration tasks, but with Linux you become king of the hill and ruler of the system, free to do whatever you want to do!

Now, if you don't have a clue what MS-DOS is or what a floppy disk looks like, you might want to brush up on some computer basics before tackling Linux. Linux isn't for the faint of heart—you must have some understanding of how a computer works. If the thought of repartitioning or reformatting your hard drive sends shivers down your spine, you probably should put off learning Linux for a while until you become more comfortable with your computer system.

Hardware Needed to Use This Book

Because Linux isn't a commercial software product, it hasn't gone through the rigorous quality assurance tests that most commercial software products endure. Also, most of Linux has been written across the Internet by computer *hackers* (not *crackers*, but people who truly enjoy writing software that accomplishes something)—thus, the hardware supported by Linux is the hardware owned by the various hackers. Table 1 is a brief list of the supported hardware. If you don't have the correct hardware, it's unlikely that you'll be able to boot Linux and productively use the system—forewarned is forearmed! Appendix C, "The Linux Hardware Compatibility HOWTO," provides a more in-depth listing of Linux-supported hardware.

Table 1   A Brief List of Hardware Supported by Linux

Item	Description
CPU	Intel 386 and later (and compatibles), DEC Alpha, Sun Sparcs, and PowerMacs.
Bus	ISA, EISA, VESA local bus, and PCI; the MicroChannel bus isn't fully supported yet.
RAM	Minimum of 2M of RAM; 4M is recommended.
Hard drive	AT standard hard drive controller; Linux supports controller MFM, RLL, ESDI, and IDE controllers. Linux also supports several popular SCSI drive and CD-ROM drive controllers.
Disk space	Minimum of 20M; 80M is recommended.
Monitor	Linux supports Hercules, CGA, EGA, VGA, and SVGA video cards and systems; X Windows has other requirements detailed in Chapter 6, "Installing the X Windows System."
Mouse	Any standard serial mouse (for example, Logitech, Microsoft, or Mouse Systems) or bus mouse from Microsoft, Logitech, or ATIXL.
CD-ROM drive	Any CD-ROM drive that uses a true SCSI interface works; some proprietary CD-ROM drives such as the SoundBlaster series are

Item	Description
	also supported. CD-ROM drives known to work with Linux include NEC CDR-74, Sony CDU-45, Sony CDU-31a, Mitsumi CD-ROMs, and Texel DM-3042.
Tape drive	Any SCSI tape drive works; other drives hosted from a floppy controller may also be supported. Now, the Colorado Jumbo 120 and 250 using the QIC 80 format are supported.
Printer	If you can access your parallel printer from MS-DOS, you should be able to access it from Linux; some fancy features might not be accessible.
Ethernet card	If you have access to an Ethernet network, Linux supports several standard Ethernet cards for accessing your network. Cards supported include 3Com's 3C503, 3C509, and 3C503/16; Novell's NE1000 and NE2000; and Western Digital's WD8003 and WD8013.

ON THE WEB

The Web site **http://glycerine.itsmm.uni.edu/mca/** provides more information on MicroChannel bus support.

How to Use This Book

You may prefer to read this book from cover to cover. The information progresses from simple to complex as you read through the various sections and their chapters. Because the information is separated into seven parts and four appendixes, each with its own particular emphasis, you can choose to read only those parts that appeal to your immediate needs. Don't, however, let your immediate needs deter you from eventually giving attention to each chapter. Whenever you have the time, you can find a wealth of information in them all!

Part I: Installing Linux

Part I, "Installing Linux," provides a detailed overview of the Linux system as well as instructions to get Linux up and running. It consists of seven chapters:

- Chapter 1, "Understanding Linux," introduces the Linux operating system.
- Chapter 2, "Overview of Features," provides a general overview of the various components that make up the Linux system and the various distributions. The chapter also covers some of the new commercial software available for Linux.
- Chapter 3, "Installing Red Hat," gives detailed instructions for installing the version of Red Hat provided on the accompanying CD-ROM.
- Chapter 4, "Installing Slackware 96," gives detailed instructions for installing the version of Slackware provided on the accompanying CD-ROM.

- Chapter 5, "Running Linux Applications," provides a basic introduction to the process of setting up your Linux system.

- Chapter 6, "Installing the X Windows System," provides you with the necessary information to get the X Windows system up and running under Linux. Under Linux, the X Windows system is called XFree86 and is similar to other GUI environments, such as Microsoft Windows or the OS/2 Workplace Shell.

- Chapter 7, "Using X Windows," provides you with information necessary to use the X Windows system under Linux.

Part II: Systems Administration

Part II, "Systems Administration," provides basic information on configuring and managing a typical Linux installation. It consists of six chapters:

- Chapter 8, "Understanding Systems Administration," provides a brief background of the processes and procedures needed to configure and maintain a Linux system.

- Chapter 9, "Booting and Shutting Down," details the various actions that happen when you boot up or shut down a Linux system, and explains why you can't simply switch off the power supply.

- Chapter 10, "Managing User Accounts," shows you how to add, delete, and manage user accounts on your machine.

- Chapter 11, "Backing Up Data," explains the necessity of backing up your data, as well as the procedures needed to back up your Linux system.

- Chapter 12, "Improving System Security," gives you a brief overview of system security on Linux systems and then explains the procedures needed to maintain a reasonably secure system.

- Chapter 13, "Upgrading and Installing Software," provides you with the information needed to install new software from the Internet, and also tells you how to patch existing programs.

Part III: Managing the File System

Part III, "Managing the File System," provides detailed knowledge of how to be more productive with various Linux features. Everything you learn in these three chapters can be transferred easily to other UNIX-type systems:

- Chapter 14, "Managing File Systems," provides an overview of creating, mounting, and using a file system under Linux.

- Chapter 15, "Understanding the File and Directory System," looks at subtle nuances of Linux command syntax, execution from the command prompt, parsing, command interpretation, and command feedback.

- Chapter 16, "Managing Files and Directories," details the Linux file system structure and organization, file-naming conventions, and directory hierarchy. The chapter also teaches you how to successfully navigate the Linux file system.

Part IV: Working with Linux

Part IV, "Working with Linux," increases your skill at working with the Linux command-line tools and utilities. Part IV consists of five chapters:

- Chapter 17, "Understanding Linux Shells," introduces you to the magical world of Linux shells, the powerful capabilities that exist through the use of shell scripting, and the different shells you may encounter with different versions of Linux.

- Chapter 18, "Managing Multiple Processes," explores the capabilities of Linux when you run more than one process at a time. You learn how to initiate and manage multiple processes, as well as how to control and stop them.

- Chapter 19, "Using the *vi* Editor," shows you how to use UNIX's visual editor. Although vi isn't the most productive editor in the world, every Linux/UNIX system has it, and sometimes it's the only editor available for use.

- Chapter 20, "Using the *emacs* Editor," teaches you how to use the ubiquitous UNIX editor written by GNU patriarch Richard Stallman.

- Chapter 21, "Printing," covers all the printing basics, from issuing print commands and checking printer status to canceling print jobs and dealing with common printing problems.

Part V: Network Administration

Part V, "Network Administration," provides a greater understanding of the procedures and processes necessary to administer a robust Linux system. Four chapters make up Part V:

- Chapter 22, "Understanding the TCP/IP Protocol Suite," provides an overview of the most common network transport protocol suite in use today on the Internet.

- Chapter 23, "Configuring a TCP/IP Network," shows you how to set up and configure TCP/IP on Linux.

- Chapter 24, "Configuring Domain Name Service," provides you with the necessary information to get your system up and running with Domain Name Service (DNS).

- Chapter 25, "Using SLIP and PPP," illustrates how to configure and use Serial Line Internet Protocol (SLIP) and Point-to-Point Protocol (PPP) lines to connect with the Internet.

Part VI: Using the Internet

The five chapters in Part VI, "Using the Internet," provide a basic overview of the Internet:

- Chapter 26, "Understanding the Internet," explains this network of networks that has become the information superhighway.

- Chapter 27, "Accessing the Network with *telnet*, *ftp*, and the *r-* Commands," provides you with information on how to use various programs such as telnet and ftp to access information around the world.

- Chapter 28, "Surfing the Internet with the World Wide Web," gives you an overview of using various Linux utilities to search for and retrieve information from the Internet, with emphasis on the Web.

■ Chapter 29, "Using Electronic Mail," gives you an overview of electronic mail (e-mail) and how to use it in Linux.

■ Chapter 30, "Surviving Usenet news," provides you with an explanation of Usenet newsgroups, and then provides you with instructions for accessing this global community of newsgroups.

Part VII: Setting Up a Web Site

Part VII, "Setting Up a Web Site," provides detailed information on setting up and running a Web server on Linux. Five chapters make up this part:

■ Chapter 31, "Creating Web Documents with HTML," tells you how to create home pages for the World Wide Web by using HTML for your Linux system.

■ Chapter 32, "Getting Started with Apache," gives you the basics so that you can get started with Apache. It covers compiling and installing Apache, and the basic configuration options.

■ Chapter 33, "Configuring Apache," discusses the major configuration options within Apache, including MIME types, indexing, server-side includes, image maps, and virtual hosts.

■ Chapter 34, "Managing an Intranet Web Server," discusses the various administrative concepts involved with managing a Web server, including controlling server child process, increasing server efficiency, managing log files, and dealing with security issues.

Appendixes

Appendix A, "Sources of Information," provides you with a detailed listing of books, magazines, Usenet newsgroups, and FTP sites dealing with Linux. Also, you get a brief glimpse of the myriad resources available to you as a Linux user.

Appendix B, "The Linux HOWTO Index," provides a list of all the main and mini HOWTOs available. HOWTOs provide information on *how to* accomplish a specific task with Linux. This HOWTO comes right off the Internet.

Appendix C, "The Linux Hardware Compatibility HOWTO," provides important details on the hardware supported by the current Linux distribution. This HOWTO also comes right off the Internet.

Appendix D, "The GNU General Public License," is the verbatim license for using GNU applications. It describes your responsibilities when using GNU programs.

Appendix E, "The Caldera Open Lite CD-ROM," provides a brief introduction to one of the most popular commercial products based on Linux—Caldera Open Linux Base.

Conventions Used in This Book

This book uses several special conventions that you need to become familiar with. These conventions are listed here for your reference.

Linux is a *case-sensitive* operating system; that means that when this book instructs you to type something at a command or shell prompt, you must type exactly what appears in the book, exactly as it is capitalized. This book uses a `monospaced typeface` for Linux commands to set them off from standard text. If you're instructed to type something, what you are to type appears in `monospaced bold`. For example, the book instructs you to do the following:

Enter `cat`.

You must press the letters <c>, <a>, and <t>, and then press the <Return> key.

Keys are sometimes pressed in combination; when this is the case, the keys are presented like this: <Ctrl-h>. This example implies that you must press and hold the <Ctrl> key, press the <h> key, and then release both keys.

N O T E   This book uses a convention for key names that may vary from what you are accustomed to. To avoid confusion in the case-sensitive UNIX environment, this book uses lowercase letters to refer to keys when uppercase letters may be the norm. For example, this book uses the form <Ctrl-c> instead of the form <Ctrl-C> (the latter form may make some readers wonder whether they should press <Ctrl> and <Shift> and <c>). ▩

Some example listings show a portion of the screen after you type a specific command. These listings show the command prompt or shell prompt—usually a dollar sign ($)—followed by what you type in **bold**. Don't type the dollar sign when you follow the example on your own system. Consider this example:

```
$ lp report.txt &
3146
$
```

You should type only what appears in **bold** on the first line (that is, type `lp report.txt &` and then press <Return>). The rest of the listing shows Linux's response to the command.

When discussing the syntax of a Linux command, this book uses some special formatting to distinguish between the required portions and the variable portions. Consider the following example:

```
lp filename
```

In this syntax, the `filename` portion of the command is a variable; that is, it changes depending on what file you actually want the `lp` command to work with. The `lp` is required because it's the actual command name. Variable information is presented in `italic`; information that must be typed exactly is not in italic.

In some cases, command information is optional—that is, it's not required for the command to work. Square brackets ([ ]) enclose optional parts of the command syntax. Consider the following example:

```
lp filename [device1] [abc]
```

Here, `lp` is the command name and is neither optional nor variable. The *device1* parameter is both variable and optional (it is in italic and enclosed in square brackets); this means that you can type any device name in place of *device1* (without the brackets), or type nothing at all for that parameter. The `abc` parameter is optional (you don't have to use it if you don't want to), but it's not variable; if you use it, you must type it exactly as it appears in the book—again, without the brackets.

Tips, notes, and cautions appear throughout the book in special formats to make the information they contain easy to locate. Longer discussions not integral to the flow of the chapter are set aside as *sidebars*, with their own heading.

The book also contains many cross-references to appropriate topics throughout the book. A typical cross-reference appears as follows:

▶ **See** "Using X Windows," **p. xxx**

Installing Linux

Understanding Linux

To understand Linux, you must first understand the question, "What is UNIX?" The reason is that Linux is a project initiated to create a working version of UNIX on Intel-based machines, more commonly referred to as IBM PC-compatible computers that most people are familiar with.

UNIX is arguably the most versatile and popular operating system found today on scientific and high-end workstations. This chapter explains why you may want to select the UNIX-like Linux instead of one of the other operating systems available for Intel platforms, such as MS-DOS, Windows 95, Windows NT, or OS/2. ■

What is Linux?

Linux is a freely accessible operating system.

Why use Linux?

This chapter briefly touches on the many uses you may have for Linux.

What are the different versions of UNIX?

UNIX comes in many flavors, each having a common base and—sometimes—ancestry. This chapter examines the history of this fascinating OS.

What are the features of Linux/UNIX?

This chapter provides a brief overview of the many features available to the user.

Who owns Linux?

This chapter discusses the oftentimes confused issue of who owns Linux.

What Is Linux?

Linux is an operating system for several types of computer platforms, but primarily Intel-based PCs. The system has been designed and built by hundreds of programmers scattered around the world. The goal has been to create a UNIX clone, free of any commercially copyrighted software, that the entire world can use.

Actually, Linux started out as a hobby of Linus Torvalds while a student at the University of Helsinki in Finland. He wanted to create a replacement for the Minix operating system, a UNIX-like operating system available for Intel-based PCs.

N O T E If some of the terms used in this chapter are unfamiliar to you, don't worry because we'll explain many of them within the chapter. ▪

Why Use Linux?

If you have a computer, you must have an operating system. An *operating system* is a complex set of computer codes that provides the operating process *protocols*, or laws of behavior. Without an operating system, your computer sits idly, incapable of interpreting and acting on your input commands or running a simple program. Most operating systems are commercial programs supported by major software companies. If you buy an operating system, you must be content with what that vendor offers. Because the program is a proprietary program, you can't modify or experiment with the operating system internals.

Application programs are software packages you purchase to perform certain activities, such as word processing. Each package is written for a specific operating system and machine. Again, you have little control on how modifications are made to the application program and when or if updates are ever performed.

You'll want to use Linux because it's the only operating system today that's freely available to provide multitasking, multiprocessing capabilities for multiple users on IBM PC-compatible hardware platforms. No other operating system gives you these same features with the power that Linux enjoys. Linux also separates you from the marketing whims of the various commercial providers. You aren't locked into upgrading every few years and paying outrageous sums to update all your applications. Many applications for Linux are freely available on the Internet, just as the source code to Linux itself is available on the Internet. Thus, you have access to the source code to modify and expand the operating system to your needs—something you can't do with commercial operating systems such as Windows NT, Windows 95, MS-DOS, or OS/2.

Freedom from commercial vendors is also a potential downside to using Linux. Because no one commercial vendor supports Linux, getting help isn't just a phone call away. Linux can be finicky and may or may not run properly on a wide range of hardware. The potential to damage or delete data files now residing on your system also exists because Linux is constantly changing and doesn't go through a rigorous testing process before being released.

Linux isn't a toy; it's a system designed to give users the feeling of tinkering with a new project, just like in the beginning of the PC revolution. However, Linux is relatively stable on many systems and thus provides you an inexpensive opportunity to learn and use one of the most popular operating systems in the world today—UNIX. Many CD-ROM vendors and software companies, such as Red Hat and Caldera, now support the Linux operating system. Linux is an alternative to other UNIX systems and can be used in place of those sometimes expensive systems. Thus, if you program on UNIX systems during the day, you can have a UNIX-like system at home. Are you a systems administrator of a UNIX system at work? You can perform some of your duties from home by using Linux. Don't have a clue as to what UNIX is? Well, then, Linux provides a low-cost introduction to one of the most popular operating systems in the world—UNIX.

Linux also provides you with easy access to the Internet and the rest of the information super-highway.

UNIX Versions

The name *UNIX* can mean many things. It's one of the most context-specific terms used in the computer industry today. To better understand what's meant when someone uses the word UNIX, you must know which version of the operating system is being referred to.

Now UNIX is a trademark of X/Open and must be licensed to be sold. Although versions of UNIX are offered by many different vendors, these versions fall into one of two major categories: System V or Berkeley Software Distribution (BSD). UNIX System V is the version developed by the creators of UNIX, AT&T Bell Laboratories. BSD UNIX is associated with the version of UNIX that was developed and proliferated by the University of California at Berkeley. The most popular version of BSD UNIX was sold by Sun Microsystems for its powerful workstations.

N O T E With UNIX System V Release 4, AT&T and Sun Microsystems merged their two versions of UNIX into UNIX System V. Because of this merger and the rallying of the industry around the UNIX System V standard, UNIX System V is now considered the standard UNIX system. ▪

Undoubtedly, the best thing to happen to the UNIX operating system was the development of System V, Release 4.2 (SVR4.2). Created and introduced by UNIX System Laboratories (USL, now owned by Nippon Santa Cruz, Inc., a wholly owned subsidiary of Santa Cruz Operation, Inc.), SVR4.2 combines the power and capabilities of UNIX with a "user-affectionate" graphical user interface (GUI). The result is an operating system that can be easily navigated by computer novices or radically customized by system administrators and other experts.

Before the release of SVR4.2, UNIX users saw only a command-line prompt (a simple dollar sign) after logging into the system. With no on-screen guidance evident, inexperienced users frequently were intimidated into forsaking UNIX in favor of other, easier-to-use operating systems. No doubt this (often) intimidating dollar sign prompt contributed to the UNIX reputation as an unfriendly operating system throughout its early years. Although experience and word of mouth dispelled some user reluctance, it was a reputation dying a slow death—until now.

An Overview of UNIX/Linux Features

The benefits derived from using the UNIX operating system, and hence Linux, stem from its power and flexibility. These are the result of the many features built into the system, ready for you to use as soon as you turn the system on. The following sections examine these features more closely.

Multitasking

The word *multitasking* describes the capability to seemingly execute multiple programs at the same time without hindering each application from running. Most UNIX variants provide a type of multitasking called *preemptive multitasking*. The name is based on the fact that each program is guaranteed a chance to run; each program executes until the operating system preempts it to allow another program to run. This type of multitasking is exactly what Linux does.

MS-DOS and Windows 3.1 don't support preemptive multitasking, but they do support a form of multitasking called *cooperative multitasking*. Under cooperative multitasking, programs run until they either voluntarily allow another program to run, or have nothing else to do for the time being.

To better understand Linux's multitasking capability, examine it from another view. The microprocessor in your computer can do only one thing at a time, but it can complete those individual tasks in periods of time so short they're difficult to comprehend. For example, typical microprocessors today operate at clock speeds of 75 to 300 MHz (megahertz) and faster. This means that they can transfer from 75 to 300 and more million bits per second. When processing a complete set of instructions, the speeds are much faster, typically 6 nanoseconds (billionths of a second). The human mind can't detect the difference between so short a delay and something occurring simultaneously. In short, it appears that tasks are performed at the same time.

Using a real-world example may further explain multitasking. Suppose that, while working in a spreadsheet application, you discover that the current month's information hasn't yet been merged from the database to the spreadsheet application. Typically, this takes some minutes to accomplish, so you start the process. Then you switch to another terminal window in Linux to work on a report you're preparing. Before you finish the report, you switch back to the original Linux virtual terminal to check on the progress of your spreadsheet merge process. Seeing that it's not yet complete, you switch back to the report terminal, only to realize that some of the information you want to include is located in a letter you wrote some time ago. So you open yet another window, select the file containing your letter, extract the information you need by using a copy utility, and return to the report, where you paste the copied information into place—all the while using the same word processor. Linux informs you that your merge process is now complete, so you close your word processing windows and return to the original spreadsheet window to finish your work there.

You can readily see the benefits of having preemptive multitasking capabilities. In addition to reducing *dead time* (time where you can't continue working on an application because a process hasn't yet finished), the flexibility of not having to close application windows before opening and working in others is infinitely more convenient.

Linux and other preemptive multitasking operating systems accomplish the preemptive processing by monitoring processes waiting to run, as well as those now running. The system then schedules each process to have equal access to the microprocessor. The result is that open applications appear to be running concurrently; in reality, there are delays of only billionths of a second between when the processor executes a set of instructions from one application and when it's scheduled by Linux to devote time to that process again.

It's the capability to allocate time to running applications from within a freely available operating system that sets Linux apart from other operating systems and environments available today, such as Windows 3.1 and Windows 95, MS-DOS, and commercial versions of UNIX. The other big feature of Linux is that you have access to the source code for the operating system. Thus, if you want to change how the system works and have the necessary capability to implement the change, you can modify the Linux operating system to your heart's content. Commercial vendors will never allow you access to their source code to modify their wares.

Multiuser

The concept of many users accessing applications or processing power from a single PC was only dreamed of a few short years ago. UNIX and Windows NT helped develop that dream into reality. Linux's capability of allocating microprocessor time to many applications at once naturally lent itself to serving many people at once, each running one or more applications. The truly remarkable feature of Linux and its multiuser, multitasking features is that more than one person can work in the same version of the same application at the same time, from the same or separate terminals. Don't confuse this with multiple users updating the same file simultaneously, a feature that's potentially confusing, potentially hazardous, and positively undesirable.

Again, a real-world scenario helps further your understanding of the multiuser feature. Imagine a company whose personnel are networked to a Linux system. While one employee places the finishing touches on outgoing correspondence, another produces a company roster. Still another uses the same word processing package to prepare a view-graph presentation by importing pictures from a graphics package; meanwhile, the boss extracts information from a database for a report he's preparing, using (you guessed it) the same word processing application.

Down the hall in accounting, three data-entry clerks are updating files in the same accounting database; in the mailroom, the supervisor updates the shipping file that simultaneously updates the accounting database. At the same time, the system administrator sets up an account for a new employee and deactivates a second system account for an employee who is away on an extended leave of absence.

Although it may be difficult to imagine this scenario, it's being repeated thousands of times each day in offices throughout the world that use the UNIX operating system. Linux is a freely available UNIX clone, and many systems are configured for scores of people to access; others are set up with only a few user accounts.

Programmable Shells

The *programmable shell* is another feature that makes UNIX, and hence Linux, what it is: the most flexible operating system available. Within the shell's framework is a whole new world available to those adventurous enough to master Linux's command syntax nuances.

Although you shouldn't be discouraged from attempting exciting forays into the Bourne, C, or bash shells, you should understand that, without proper guidance and preparation, shell programming can be a difficult lesson in frustration. Make sure that you have a reliable reference manual at hand (such as the one you're reading now) and that you have the phone number of a good system administrator or other Linux expert, in case you get bogged down.

▶ **See** " Understanding Shells," **p. 323**

For those of you who anticipate the rewarding experience of directing a powerful operating system such as Linux, the importance of command syntax in Linux can't be overstated. (*Syntax* is nothing more than the order and form of a command line.) The Linux shell scans each command line to determine whether the formation and spelling are consistent with its protocols.

The shell's scan process is termed *parsing*—the commands are broken down into more easily processed components. Each component is interpreted and executed, including those special characters that convey additional meaning to the shell. These special characters are further expanded into their proper command processes and executed.

Although many UNIX and Linux versions include more than one type of shell, they all function in essentially the same way. A shell works as the interpreter between the user and the kernel (the heart, or brain, of the Linux operating system). The primary difference among the three available shells lies in command-line syntax. Although it's not a severe limitation, you'll encounter difficulties if you try to use C shell commands or syntax in the Bourne or bash shells.

Perhaps the simplest of scenarios to help further your understanding of UNIX and Linux shell programming is that of *background processing*. For example, you should back up all or parts of your system files at one time or another for protection against accidental erasure or hardware problems. If those files and their associated directories are of substantial size, the backup process can take a considerable amount of time.

With a simple shell program consisting of a line or two of command arguments, a backup process can run concurrently with other operations you may want to do. After programming the shell and starting the backup process, you can simply open a different window to access the desired application and begin your work there. When the background processing is completed, UNIX signals that the job is finished.

Linux shell programming serves as many different functions as there are people willing to attempt it. Many use this programming feature to personalize their systems and make them more user-friendly. Others find it helpful in streamlining many of the applications they run by allowing them to perform a number of processes in the background so that they're free to work in others.

Some users go even further by devising programs that link processes or applications so that they can reduce their workload to perhaps a single session of data entry and have the system update numerous software packages at once. Only the user's imagination limits what can be done with Linux shell programming.

Device Independence Under UNIX

At first glance, whether your computer system's peripherals can operate on a stand-alone, or independent, basis, may not seem important. When you view these peripherals from a multiuser UNIX environment, however, device independence becomes fundamental to a productive workplace. To understand the importance of device independence, you must first understand how other systems view attached peripherals and how UNIX views them.

Until recently, computer systems could generally support peripherals such as printers, terminals, disk drives, and modems. The technology explosion has added other devices too numerous to list. Difficulties are encountered when the user can't utilize a peripheral because an operating system can't access the device. This incapability can be the result of incompatible system architecture, operating system addressing limitations, and so on.

UNIX sidesteps the problem of adding new devices by viewing each peripheral as a separate file. As new devices are required, the system administrator adds the required link to the kernel. This link, also known as the *device driver*, ensures that the kernel and the device merge in the same fashion each time the device is called on for service.

As new and better peripherals are developed and delivered to users, the UNIX operating system allows immediate, unrestricted access to their services as soon as the devices are linked to the kernel. The key to device independence lies in the adaptability of the kernel. Other operating systems allow only a certain number or a certain kind of device. UNIX can accommodate any number of any kind of devices because each device is viewed independently through its dedicated link with the kernel.

Device Independence Under Linux

Linux shares many of the same benefits of device independence as UNIX. Unfortunately, one of Linux's best features—freedom from a commercial entity—is also one of its biggest liabilities. Linux has been developed over the last few years by various programmers from around the world. These programmers don't have access to all the equipment created for the IBM PC and compatibles. In fact, Linux can't run on IBM PCs that support the MicroChannel bus. Linux does support a wide variety of PC hardware, as illustrated in Appendix C, "The Linux Hardware Compatibility HOWTO."

However, because Linux is a UNIX clone, it too has an adaptable kernel; as more programmers join the Linux project, more hardware devices are added to the various Linux kernels and distributions. As a last resort, because you have the source code to the kernel, you, or someone you hire, can modify the kernel to work with new devices.

Communications and Networking

UNIX's superiority over other operating systems is equally evident in its communications and networking utilities. Linux is no exception. No other operating system includes such tightly coupled networking capabilities, and no other operating system has the built-in flexibility of these same features. Whether you need to talk with another user through an e-mail utility or download large files from another system across the nation, Linux provides the means to do so.

Accessing the Internet is a hot topic today, and people are spending hundreds of dollars on software so that their PCs can hitch a ride on the information superhighway. With Linux, you get all that software for free! The Internet was created and thrives in the UNIX world and, thus, Linux is quite at home there. With Linux, you can communicate almost instantly with the rest of the world.

Next, you can accomplish internal messaging or file transfer through a number of Linux commands, including `write`, `call`, `mail`, and `mailx`, as well as `cu` and `uucp`. As an aid to understanding these capabilities, it's helpful to understand that information exchanged by users on the same system (also called *internal communications*) is accomplished by terminal-to-terminal communication, e-mail, and an automatic calendar that serves as a scheduler/information manager.

An extension of Linux communications is found in the `cu` and `uucp` commands (used for external communications). Not only does Linux allow for file and program transfer, it gives system administrators and technicians a window of access to other systems. Through this remote-access capability, one technician can effectively service many systems, even when those systems are located across great distances.

Networking in UNIX needs little explanation. The communications capabilities inherent in the operating system were designed to support many tasks and many users over many miles. UNIX quite naturally evolved in the professional marketplace as the operating system of choice, thanks to the same characteristics that gave it premier status in the scientific community and academia. Linux is set to follow that same route as a unique replacement for commercial UNIX systems.

Open Systems Portability

In the never-ending quest for standardization, many organizations have taken a renewed interest in the direction in which operating systems are developing. UNIX hasn't gone unnoticed. The drive to standardize UNIX stems from the many UNIX variants now available. You learn more about how those variants were developed in the following section.

Efforts have been made to combine, collate, and otherwise absorb all versions of UNIX into a single, all-encompassing version of the operating system. Initially, the effort met with guarded enthusiasm, and some effort was expended on coming to terms with blending the different versions. As with many noble efforts, this one was doomed to failure because developers weren't willing to sacrifice part of what they had already invested into their particular version. (Sad to say, many developers still feel that way.)

However, the continued existence of UNIX varieties isn't necessarily cause for alarm. Despite the different varieties, all are still inherently superior to all other operating systems available today because each contains the same elements described in the preceding pages.

Portability is merely the capability to transport an operating system from one platform to another so that it still performs the way it should. UNIX is indeed a portable operating system. Initially, UNIX could operate on only one specific platform—the DEC PDP-7 minicomputer. Today, the many UNIX variants can operate in any environment and on any platform, from laptops to mainframes.

Portability provides the means for different computer platforms running UNIX to communicate accurately and effectively with any of the other platforms without the addition of special, high-priced, after-market communications interfaces. No other operating system in existence can make this claim.

A Brief History of Linux

The history of Linux is tied to the history of UNIX and, to a lesser extent, a program called Minix. Minix was an operating system tutorial written by the well-known and respected computer scientist Andrew Tannebaum. This operating system became popular on several PC platforms, including MS-DOS-based PCs. But more on Minix later. First, a brief history of UNIX.

Although AT&T created the UNIX operating system, many other companies and individuals have tried to improve the basic idea over the years. The following sections examine a few of the leading variants in use today.

AT&T

Ken Thompson, a computer programmer for AT&T Bell Laboratories, and a group of people working under Ken's direction developed an operating system that was flexible and completely compatible with programmers' varied needs. Legend tells how Ken, who had been using the MULTICS operating system, dubbed this new product UNIX as he joked with others on his development team. He was lampooning the MULTICS multiuser operating system: UNIX was derived from *uni*, meaning *one* or *single*, followed by the homophone X. Perhaps the greater joke in this bit of folklore lies in the fact that MULTICS is remembered by few users today as a viable multiuser operating system, while UNIX has become the de facto industry standard for multiuser, multitasking operating systems.

BSD

Berkeley Software Distribution (BSD), University of California at Berkeley, released its first version of UNIX, based on AT&T's Version 7, in 1978. BSD UNIX, as it's known throughout the industry, contained enhancements developed by the academic community at Berkeley designed to make UNIX more user-friendly. The user-friendly "improvements" in BSD UNIX were an attempt to make UNIX appeal to casual users, as well as to advanced programmers who liked its flexibility in conforming to their changing demands. Despite being less than 100 percent compatible with AT&T's original UNIX, BSD did accomplish its goals: The added features enticed casual users to use UNIX.

BSD has become the academic UNIX standard. The original creators of BSD have since released a version for the Intel platform called, appropriately enough, BSD. This version too has a limited distribution on the Internet and via CD-ROM vendors. The authors also wrote several articles a few years ago in the computer magazine *Dr. Dobb's Journal* detailing the design and implementation of BSD386 or FreeBSD. Today BSDI, the commercial version of FreeBSD, is another popular operating system similar to Linux.

USL

UNIX System Laboratories (USL) was an AT&T spinoff company that had been developing the UNIX operating system since the early 1980s. Before Novell purchased it in 1993, USL produced the source code for all UNIX System V derivatives in the industry. However, USL itself didn't sell a shrink-wrapped product at that time.

USL's last release of UNIX was UNIX System V Release 4.2 (SVR4.2). SVR4.2 marked USL's first entry into the off-the-shelf UNIX marketplace. In a joint venture with Novell, which temporarily created a company called Univel, USL produced a shrink-wrapped version of SVR4.2 called UnixWare. With Novell's purchase of USL, Novell had shifted the focus of USL from source-code producer to UnixWare producer. Novell has now sold its version of UNIX to the Santa Cruz Operation (SCO).

Recently, SCO made a free single-user license available to the public for using SCO UNIX. The program, however, costs $19 for the distribution media, not unlike Linux. However, whereas SCO provides a copy of its operating system, it doesn't provide the source code. Some in the Linux community suspect Linux is giving the UNIX community—or at least the SCO community—some stiff competition.

XENIX, SunOS, and AIX

Microsoft developed its UNIX version, XENIX, in the late 1970s and early 1980s, during the peak of the PC revolution. Processing power available in PCs began to rival that of existing minicomputers. With the advent of Intel's 80386 microprocessor, it soon became evident that XENIX, which had been developed specifically for PCs, was no longer necessary. Microsoft and AT&T merged XENIX and UNIX into a single operating system called System V/386 Release 3.2, which can operate on practically any common hardware configuration. XENIX is still available today from Santa Cruz Operation (SCO), a codeveloper with Microsoft, whose efforts to promote XENIX in the PC market have made this version of UNIX one of the most commercially successful.

Sun Microsystems has contributed greatly to UNIX marketability by promoting SunOS and its associated workstations. Sun's work with UNIX produced a version based on BSD. Interestingly enough, AT&T's SVR4 is compatible with BSD, too—no doubt an offshoot of AT&T and Sun Microsystems' collaboration in UNIX System V Release 4.0.

IBM's venture into the world of UNIX yielded a product called AIX (Advanced Interactive Executive). Although AIX isn't as well known as some other UNIX versions, AIX performs well and has no problem holding its share of the operating system market. It's perhaps the old mindset that any UNIX version is an unfriendly, unforgiving operating system that has kept AIX from a better market reception.

Linux

Linux is the brainchild of a computer science student named Linus Torvalds. Linux began life as a hobby project in 1991 for Linus, then 23. He hoped to create a more robust version of UNIX for Minix users. Minix, as stated earlier, is a program developed by computer science professor Andrew Tannebaum.

The Minix system was written to demonstrate several computer science concepts found in operating systems. Torvalds incorporated these concepts into a stand-alone system that mimics UNIX. The program was widely available to computer science students all over the world and soon generated a wide following, including its own Usenet newsgroups. Linus Torvalds set out to provide a better platform for his fellow Minix users that could run on the widely available IBM PC. Linus targeted the emerging 386-based computers because of the task-switching properties of the 80386 protected-mode interface.

What follows are some of the announcements Linus made when announcing his Linux program.

N O T E These announcements are from the "Linux Installation and Getting Started Guide," by Matt Welsh (copyright 1992-94 by Matt Welsh, 205 Gray Street NE, Wilson, NC 27893, **mdw@sunsite.unc.edu**). They're used subject to section 3 of Matt's copyright.

You can obtain the complete "Linux Installation and Getting Started Guide" from the Linux Documentation Project's various archives sites. You can find this book on **sunsite.unc.edu** in the directory **/pub/ Linux/docs/LDP/install-guide**. For information on how to access archives and download files, refer to Chapter 28, "Surfing the Internet with the World Wide Web." ▪

"After that it was plain sailing: hairy coding still, but I had some devices, and debugging was easier. I started using C at this stage, and it certainly speeds up development. This is also when I started to get serious about my megalomaniac ideas to make 'a better Minix than Minix.' I was hoping I'd be able to recompile gcc under Linux some day….

"Two months for basic setup, but then only slightly longer until I had a disk driver (seriously buggy, but it happened to work on my machine) and a small file system. That was about when I made 0.01 available [around late August of 1991]: it wasn't pretty, it had no floppy driver, and it couldn't do much [of] anything. I don't think anybody ever compiled that version. But by then I was hooked, and didn't want to stop until I could chuck out Minix."

In a later announcement, made in **comp.os.minix** on Oct. 5, 1991, Linus introduced to the world Linux version 0.02, the first official version of Linux.

"Do you pine for the nice days of Minix 1.1, when men were men and wrote their own device drivers? Are you without a nice project and just dying to cut your teeth on an OS you can try to modify for your needs? Are you finding it frustrating when everything works on Minix? No more all-nighters to get a nifty program working? Then this post might be just for you."

"As I mentioned a month ago, I'm working on a free version of a Minix lookalike for AT-386 computers. It has finally reached the stage where it's even usable (though may not be depending on what you want), and I am willing to put out the sources for wider distribution. It's just version 0.02, but I've successfully run bash, gcc, gnu-make, gnu-sed, compress, and so forth under it."

Who Owns Linux?

IBM owns the rights to OS/2, Microsoft owns the rights to MS-DOS and MS Windows, but who owns the rights to Linux? First and foremost, Linux isn't public domain software; various components of Linux are copyrighted by many people. Linus Torvalds holds the copyright to the basic Linux kernel. Red Hat, Inc. owns the rights to the Red Hat distribution version, and Paul Volkerding holds the copyright to the Slackware distribution. Many Linux utilities are under the GNU General Public License (GPL). In fact, Linus and most Linux contributors have placed their work under the protection of the GNU GPL. You can find the license on each of the accompanying CD-ROMs in the root directory in the file named copying.

This license is sometimes referred to as the GNU Copyleft (a play on the word *copyright*). This license covers all the software produced by GNU (itself a play on words—GNU's Not UNIX) and the Free Software Foundation. The license allows programmers to create software for everyone. The basic premise behind GNU is that software should be available to everyone, and that if someone wants to modify the program to his or her own ends, that should be possible. The only caveat is that the modified code can't be restricted—others must have the right to the new code.

The GNU Copyleft, or GPL, allows a program's creators to keep their legal copyright, but allows others to take, modify, and sell the resulting new program. However, in doing so, the original programmers can't restrict any of these same rights to modify the program from the people buying the software. If you sell the program as is or in a modified form, you must provide the source code. That's why Linux comes with the complete source code.

From Here...

Linux is a viable alternative to UNIX on the desktop. The freely available source code and applications make Linux a reasonable alternative to other operating systems for PC-based platforms. For more information, check out the following:

- Chapter 3, "Installing Red Hat," provides information on putting the Red Hat distribution of Linux on your computer.
- Chapter 4, "Installing Slackware 96," provides information on putting Paul Volkerding's Slackware 96 distribution of Linux on your computer.
- Chapter 5, "Running Linux Applications," explains how to use some of the applications that come on the accompanying CD-ROMs.

## CHAPTER 2

Overview of Features

Linux represents a chance for you to explore a new world—the world of UNIX. Linux also provides superior performance when compared to other operating systems by providing a multiuser, multitasking, network-ready operating system you can use today. Thousands of applications are available for Linux from all over the world. Finally, Linux presents you with an inexpensive learning tool for a variety of subjects, from UNIX to software development. ■

The basic features

Linux provides a feature-rich set of services expected from a desktop operating system, including multitasking and full network access.

The various Linux distributions

Linux typically refers to the basic kernel, or *core*, of the operating system. Different organizations and people add other items, such as the GNU applications, GNU tools, and the Linux Documentation Project. This collection of items is referred to as a *Linux distribution*.

Advantages of using Linux

The many advantages to using Linux include its low cost, its abundance of utilities and GNU applications, and its excellent networking tools.

Disadvantages of using Linux

The major disadvantage is the inability to use applications you've already purchased for DOS, Windows, or the Mac. Other disadvantages include the lack of conventional technical support and lack of support for many hardware peripherals.

Commercial uses for Linux

Many startup Internet service providers use Linux as their primary operating system. Other companies use Linux to power their intranet Web servers.

Basic Features

Linux is a UNIX clone, which means that with Linux you get many of the advantages of UNIX. Linux multitasking is fully *preemptive*, meaning that you can run multiple programs at the same time and each program still seemingly continues to process. Other systems, such as Microsoft Windows 3.1, allow you to run multiple programs, but when you switch from one program to another, the first program typically stops running. Microsoft's Windows 95 and Windows NT are more like Linux because they allow preemptive multitasking. Linux allows you to start a file transfer, print a document, copy a floppy, use a CD-ROM, and play a game—all at the same time.

Linux is fully multiuser—more than one person can log in to and use the system at the same time. Although the multiuser feature may not be very useful at home, it gives many people in a corporate or university setting access to the same resources at the same time, without duplicating expensive machines. Even at home, you'll find the ability to log in to separate accounts on what are called *virtual terminals* very useful. Also from home you could provide your own personal online service by using Linux and several modems.

▶ **See** "Managing Users," **p. 119**

Linux is free—or nearly so. In fact, for the price of this book you've received three fully functioning distributions of Linux on the accompanying CD-ROMs. Everything you need to get Linux up and running is provided on the CD-ROMs, including hundreds of applications.

Linux provides a learning opportunity unparalleled today. Here you have a complete, working operating system, including source code, with which to play and learn what makes it tick. Learning what makes Linux tick is something you can't do in a typical UNIX environment, and definitely something you can't do with a commercial operating system, because no vendor is willing to just give away the source code.

Finally, Linux gives you a chance to relive—or perhaps experience for the first time—the chaos of the early PC revolution. In the mid-1970s, computers were the province of large organizations, such as the government, big business, and universities. The ordinary person had no access to these marvels. But with the introduction of the microprocessor and the first personal computers, things changed. At first, PCs were the province of the *hackers*—dedicated computer enthusiasts—who hacked the early systems because those systems could do very little in the way of productive work. But as the hackers experimented and became entrepreneurs, and the capabilities of PCs increased, PCs became commonplace.

The same is true today of system software (that is, operating systems). Linux represents a break away from a system controlled by large organizations that stifle creativity and enhancements in the name of market share. Although Linux is still the province of hackers, this is changing as Linux hackers become entrepreneurs to bring Linux to the masses.

Linux Distributions

Linux is distributed by many different organizations, each with a unique collection of programs, although each provides a core group of files that constitutes a Linux release. A release is identified by a series of numbers in the form of *A.BB.CC*, where *A* is either 0 or 1, and *BB* and *CC* are between 0 and 99. Higher numbers generally indicate newer releases. The current release of Linux on the accompanying CD-ROMs is kernel version 2.0.18. This distribution may also contain experimental kernels with drivers for unique hardware. You can find the various kernels used by the Slackware 96 distribution in the /kernels directory on the Slackware CD-ROM. Under Red Hat, the kernels are part of the Red Hat Package Management system (RPMs) and are installed as part of the system.

Luckily for you, the decision of which distribution to use is rather easy, because a complete version of both Red Hat's and Caldera's distributions (the companies' Internet versions, not the ones sold commercially) and a complete version of the Slackware 96 distribution are provided on the book's three CD-ROMs. However, other distributions are on the Net as well:

- MCC Interim Linux
- TAMU Linux
- LST
- SLS
- Debian Linux
- Yggdrasil Plug-and-Play Linux CD-ROM and the Linux Bible
- Trans-Ameritech Linux plus BSD CD-ROM
- The Linux Quarterly CD-ROM
- Caldera (this vendor uses Red Hat's distribution)
- Red Hat (Red Hat's commercial version includes a commercial X server called Metro X)

The Distribution HOWTO also provides an exhaustive listing of various Linux distributions. You learn later in this chapter how to access the various HOWTOs that accompany each Linux release.

Advantages of Using Linux

Using Linux has many advantages. Of the many operating systems available today, Linux is the most popular free system that's widely available. For the IBM PC, Linux provides a complete system with built-in multiuser and multitasking capabilities that take advantage of the entire processing power of your 386 and higher computer systems.

Linux comes with a complete implementation of the TCP/IP networking protocol. With Linux, you can connect to the Internet and the vast wealth of information it contains. Linux also provides a complete e-mail system to send messages back and forth through cyberspace.

Linux also has a complete graphical user interface (GUI), XFree86, that's based on the popular X Windows system. XFree86 is a complete implementation of the X Windows system that can be distributed free with Linux. XFree86 provides the common GUI elements you find on other commercial GUI platforms, such as Windows and OS/2.

Today, all of this is available for Linux, and basically for free. All you have to pay for is acquiring the programs from the Internet or via mail order from several different vendors. Of course, because you've purchased this book, you already have the entire Linux system on the accompanying CD-ROMs.

Applications

Using an operating system, although sometimes fun in and of itself, isn't the reason most people use a computer. Most people need to do productive work with their computers. Linux has literally thousands of applications available today, including programs for spreadsheets, databases, word processing, application development in a variety of computer languages, and telecommunications packages to get you online. Linux also comes with a wide range of games, both text- and graphics-based. When you need a break from the drudgery of the daily grind, Linux can provide a few minutes (or hours) of relaxation.

Advantages for Computer Professionals

If you're a computer professional, Linux provides a wealth of tools for program development. There are compilers for many of the top computer programming languages today, such as C, C++, and SmallTalk. If you don't like these languages, Linux provides you with tools, such as Flex and Bison, to build your own computer languages. These tools come with the accompanying CD-ROMs; their commercial counterparts can cost several hundred dollars each. If you want to learn one of the aforementioned languages but don't want to spend the hundreds of dollars for another compiler, Linux and its development tools are for you.

Linux also allows you to communicate with your company's office systems. And if you're a UNIX systems administrator, Linux can help you perform your duties from home. Although working from home is just in its infancy, perhaps some day you can use Linux to do your job at home, and then only occasionally visit the office for personal meetings.

Two of the industry's buzzwords are *open systems* and *interoperability*, which both refer to many different systems being able to communicate with each other. Most open systems specifications require POSIX (Portable Operating System Interface) compliance, which means some form of UNIX. Linux meets those standards today. In fact, Linux was designed for source-code portability, so if you have a corporate program running on one version of UNIX, you should be able to port that system relatively quickly to a system running Linux.

Corporations are insisting on these types of open systems so that they aren't locked into any single vendor. Remember the old adage "Don't put all your eggs in one basket"? Corporations today are becoming leery of systems controlled by single companies because those in control can dictate how the software behaves and what hardware systems the software supports. If that company chooses a direction that's not good for your corporation, tough luck. You're stuck with that company's decision whether you like it or not. With UNIX/Linux and open systems, however, you're in control of your own destiny. If the operating system doesn't have a feature you need, plenty of consultants are available who can make the necessary changes, especially given that you have the source code to your operating system.

Education

Students note that Linux provides you with editors to write your assignments and spell checkers to proof those assignments. With Linux, you should be able to log in to your school's computer network. Of course, with access to the Internet, you also have an instant tap into the limitless wealth of information there. You also have access to thousands of experts in a wide variety of subjects who can answer your questions. Linux can be useful, even if your major isn't computer science.

Linux provides such advantages for so little because of the spirit and philosophy of the community that built and continues to build Linux. Linux is a great experiment that took on a life of its own. Literally hundreds of computer hackers from around the world contributed to its development. Linus Torvalds first developed what became Linux for himself, and later released his brainchild to the world under the GNU copyleft.

▶ **See** "The GNU License," **p. 724**

Hackers

At the basic level, Linux is a system built by and for hackers. The popular definition of *hacker* has a negative connotation in today's society, but computer hackers aren't criminals by their definition of the word. Their definition deals with how one approaches any activity in life and not just when dealing with computers. Hackers feel a certain depth of commitment and an enhanced level of excitement at hacking a system. *Hacking* basically means learning all there is to know about a system, becoming immersed in the system to the point of distraction, and being able to fix the system if it breaks.

Hackers basically want to know how a system they find interesting works. They're not interested in making money or seeking revenge, although certain hackers do cross that line to become what the hacker community calls *crackers*. Computer hackers become outraged when they're compared with these vandals and criminals the popular media now calls *hackers* (instead of *crackers*). Hopefully, Linux gives you a feeling of what it's like to be a hacker, and ideally you shun becoming a cracker.

If you're simply the curious type and want to learn more about UNIX, Linux is for you. Here is a fully functional version of UNIX to which you have free, unrestricted access—something you seldom find in the real world. Most UNIX users are given accounts on UNIX machines that grant them only limited rights and privileges. There are some UNIX/Linux commands that a normal user can't use or experiment with. This isn't conducive to learning all about UNIX. With Linux, however, you have complete run of the place and can do what you want whenever you want. Of course, with this great power comes great responsibility; you must learn how to manage a real UNIX system, which can be fun in and of itself.

Disadvantages of Using Linux

Perhaps the biggest disadvantage of using Linux is the fact that no single corporate entity is in charge of its development. If something goes wrong or you have a problem, no toll-free technical support numbers are available to call for help. But do such numbers provide real support for current commercial systems? How often are you referred elsewhere—providing you get through to tech support—to have your question answered? How many times are you asked to post a question on an online service to get help? Well, with Linux, although there's no tech support number, there are literally thousands of users in the online communities to help answer your questions. (See Appendix A, "Sources of Information," for places to go for help.)

Lack of Technical Support

Having no source of technical support can be a problem with Linux, no doubt about it. The same goes for Linux applications; although there are a few commercial programs for Linux, most are developed by small groups and then posted to the world. Many developers, however, help out with questions.

N O T E　Many commercial companies are now building Linux applications that they sell. For people to use their applications, though, these companies typically provide a free copy of a Linux distribution along with their product and thus supply technical support for that version of Linux. ■

Hardware Problems

Another disadvantage is that Linux can be hard to install and doesn't work on all hardware platforms. Unlike a commercial program development operation, where a cohesive group spends months building and testing a program against a variety of conditions and hardware, Linux developers are scattered across the globe. There's no formal quality-assurance program. Developers release their programs when they feel like releasing them. Also, the hardware supported by Linux depends on the hardware each developer owns while writing that portion of the code. Thus, Linux doesn't work with all the hardware available for PCs today.

CAUTION

If your system doesn't have the hardware supported by Linux, you'll have problems installing and running the system. Chapter 3, "Installing Red Hat," Chapter 4, "Installing Slackware 96," and Appendix C, "The Linux Hardware Compatibility HOWTO," details the hardware you need to use Linux.

If you have the hardware that's supported, chances are you'll have no problem installing and using Linux. If you don't have the necessary hardware…well, Linux developers expect you to fix it—after all, this is a hacker's system.

Inability to Use Current Software

Another disadvantage is that your current applications for such operating systems as DOS and OS/2 more than likely won't work under Linux. Fortunately, those other systems can *coexist* with Linux; thus, although you can't use both operating systems at the same time, you can leave Linux and boot the other operating system to use your applications there.

Work is in progress on Linux emulators that run DOS and Windows programs, as well as the Executor project to run Macintosh programs under Linux. Although the DOS project is much further along than the Windows or Mac projects, all are in an early phase and not quite ready for prime time. But some day in the near future, Linux will be capable of running your Mac, DOS, and Windows applications.

Also, Caldera, Inc. has ported Sun's WABI (Windows Applications Binary Interface) product to Linux. WABI allows Windows 3.1 applications to run under X on Linux. Unlike many Linux applications, Caldera sells this product along with several other Linux applications. However, Caldera provides the Red Hat distribution of Linux free of charge to run the applications the company sells. Caldera is also at work on porting a version of DOS, called DR DOS, to Linux.

Part
I
Ch
2

To install Linux, you have to repartition your hard drive. *Repartitioning* means erasing part of your drive, thus wiping out your programs and data on that drive. Currently, there's no safe way of installing Linux without repartitioning. If you plan to install Linux, you should back up your disk (two or three backups is safest). Also, you might not have enough hard disk space to install Linux and keep your other software on the same disk, in which case you have to decide what goes and what stays. No matter what, you have to back up your system, repartition the drive, restore your old software, and then install Linux, which can be time-consuming and error-prone.

N O T E There are alternatives to repartitioning your hard drive. You can share space with Linux and DOS, or you can use a program that repartitions your drive without erasing files. These alternatives do work, but you still face the possibility of losing data while installing the system. Also, by repartitioning, you gain improved performance and better control over the amount of disk space used for Linux.

The amount of disk space you need to run Linux depends on the various applications you plan to install. You should have at least 120M free on the drive that you want to install Linux on, in addition to the programs and data you want to keep from your other operating systems. If you have 200M free, you should have more than enough space for a full installation of Linux. ■

Lack of Experience

Finally, unless you're already a UNIX guru, you must learn how to manage a Linux system. Unlike DOS, Windows, and OS/2, Linux and UNIX need to be managed. The manager, usually called the *systems administrator*, is responsible for maintaining the system and for performing such duties as adding and deleting user accounts, backing up the system on a regular basis, installing new software, configuring the system, and fixing things when they go wrong (which happens even on commercial versions of UNIX in use every day). Because UNIX doesn't run perfectly 100 percent of the time, the systems administrator must maintain the system. This presents a great opportunity for you to learn how to be a systems administrator on a UNIX system.

▶ **See** "Understanding Centralized-Processing Systems," **p. 204**

How to Overcome the Disadvantages

At first, you might think that using Linux puts you all alone in the world, making you survive by yourself. Part of this is true because Linux started life as a hacker's system, and hackers like to tinker and fix systems themselves. But today, as the popularity of Linux has grown, many sources of help are available.

Thousands of pages of documentation are provided with most distributions of Linux. You can find this information in the /DOCS directory on the accompanying Slackware 96 CD-ROM and in the /DOC directory on the Red Hat CD-ROM. There are magazines devoted to Linux, as well as plenty of online sources of information and online users willing to help with your questions. If you're a commercial entity and need a professional contractor, these too are available. After you install Linux, you'll also find a wealth of online help providing information on almost every Linux command and program available. Check out Appendix A, "Sources of Information," to see that you're not alone.

Disappearing Disadvantages

Although all the disadvantages discussed in the preceding sections still exist, many are slowly disappearing as new companies come into existence to build on Linux and offer new solutions. Two such companies are Red Hat and Caldera. We chose Red Hat as the primary distribution for this book because of its ease of use and installation. Caldera also uses the Red Hat distribution for its line of Linux applications. Both Red Hat and Caldera provide online, fax, and e-mail-based technical support for their products and their versions of Linux.

The Commercial Side of Linux

Linux is not just a "toy" OS anymore. Many companies use Linux as an inexpensive Web server for their intranets. Linux is also used for various network applications, such as DNS, routing, and as firewalls. Also, many Internet service providers (ISPs) use Linux as their main operating system. Many commercial programs are also available for Linux, which you can check out in the Commercial HOWTO.

Commercial Programs from Red Hat

Although Red Hat released one of the most popular distributions of Linux, the company also has produced several commercial programs. Red Hat has also created a Linux package manager, called RPM, which it released under the GPL for other distributions to use. Along with its GPL versions of Linux and RPM, Red Hat also provides an application framework called Applixware, which contains a word processor, a spreadsheet program, a presentation graphics program, a mail tool, and various development tools. Red Hat also provides a commercial version of Motif for developing and running X under Linux.

Commercial Programs from Caldera

Caldera originally provided a networking-based distribution based on Red Hat and technology from Novell, where many of Caldera's principals previously worked. Their second-generation product, Caldera Open Linux Base, is a low-cost UNIX-like operating system based on the Linux 2.0 kernel and the Open Linux distribution from Caldera. It includes a graphical user interface capable of managing system and networked resources, including client and server interaction with the Internet and all major networking systems. The menu-driven installation is provided in multiple languages. Caldera Open Linux Base is a non-dedicated gateway and includes all Internet client, server, and router protocols and services. Open Linux Base also includes a commercial X server from MetroLink and a fully licensed Linux version of the Netscape Navigator.

Caldera also provides Corel's WordPerfect for Linux, as well as an Internet office suite containing a bundle of complete business applications. These commercial programs, as well as dozens more, are available from Caldera on the company's Solutions CD. You can use Netscape to browse the catalog and then follow the instructions on the Ordering page to place an order.

ON THE WEB

You can see Caldera's catalog online at **http://www.caldera.com/solutionscd**.

Caldera also licensed and ported Sunsoft's WABI technology to allow end users to run the most popular Windows 3.1 applications on Linux-based system software.

From Here...

This chapter gave you an overview of the Linux system and the amount of software available. For more information, see the following chapters:

- Chapter 5, "Running Linux Applications," provides you with information on using various Linux applications and utilities. You learn how to maneuver your way around UNIX and Linux.
- Chapter 7, "Using X Windows," provides you with information on using X Windows.

Part

I

Ch

2

## CHAPTER 3

Installing Red Hat

This chapter gives you the information you need to install the Red Hat distribution of Linux. Remember, Linux isn't a commercial product, and you might find some problems. Although this book leads the way, you may find the need to use the resources, such as the various HOWTOs, provided on the Red Hat CD-ROM. However, Red Hat is one of the easiest distributions to install, so take heart! Although there are many advanced methods to installing Linux, this chapter focuses on installing from the CD-ROM.

The hardware you need to install Linux

Linux doesn't support all hardware components in all configurations. Check to make sure you have the necessary hardware.

How to prepare your system for the installation

Installing Linux requires some preparation, like formatting your hard drive. You must also plan the layout of your disk space for Linux's optimum performance.

How to partition your hard drives to make room for Linux

Linux requires certain partitions to work effectively, especially if swap space is required. You must also decide whether other operating systems will coexist with Linux and prepare for their installation as well.

How to install Red Hat Linux

After you prepare your system for installation, you must create your installation disks, select your installation media (the accompanying Red Hat CD-ROM), and begin the installation.

What to do if things go wrong

Because Linux has no formal technical support, you need to know what to do if you have problems with the installation.

N O T E This book assumes that you have a working knowledge of DOS and of such items as formatting your hard drive, partition tables, and sector sizes. If this information sounds like a foreign language, check out *Using MS-DOS 6.2*, Special Edition, or ask a computer guru buddy to help you through this. ■

T I P You're about to make major changes to your system, so be careful. It's a good idea to have paper and pen nearby to take notes just in case something does go wrong; besides, you'll need to jot down some numbers along the way.

Understanding Linux's Hardware Requirements

To be able to install Linux successfully, you need supported hardware. Choosing the right level of hardware for your Linux system depends on such factors as the number of users to be supported and the types of applications to be run. All this translates into requirements for working memory, hard disk storage space, the types of terminals needed, and so forth.

ON THE WEB

For current information on hardware that Red Hat 4.1 supports and doesn't support, see Red Hat's Web site at **http://www.redhat.com/support/docs/rhl-intel/rh40-hardware-intel.html**.

Most Linux systems today consist of PCs. These Linux installations are often for only a single user, although they may also be tied into larger Linux or UNIX systems.

> **CAUTION**
>
> Linux is a constantly evolving system, and hardware support is sporadically updated. The Red Hat distribution contained on the accompanying CD-ROM is relatively stable, but new hardware support may have been provided by the time this book is printed and the CD-ROM is created. Although many hardware components have clones or compatible replacements, not all may work with Linux. If you do have the hardware discussed in this chapter, the odds are excellent that Linux installs, boots, and operates properly. If you don't have the equipment listed, Linux may or may not operate properly, but the odds are against your getting a system up and running.

If you're using a version of Linux in a single-user configuration (the most likely configuration), you're the system administrator. It's your responsibility to understand the system well enough to perform the administrative duties required to keep it operating at an optimum level. These duties include keeping enough space on the hard drive, backing up regularly, ensuring that all devices attached to the system have the proper software drivers, installing and configuring software, and so forth.

Choosing the level of hardware you need depends heavily on the hardware used by the myriad people who programmed the Linux system. Unlike commercial software developers who can afford to test their systems on many different hardware configurations, Linux developers typically have access only to their personal computers. Luckily, because so many Linux developers exist, most of the standard hardware found in the PC world is supported.

The System's CPU

A basic system requires an IBM-compatible PC with an Intel 80386 or later CPU in any of the various CPU types, such as the 80386SX, 80486DX/2, and Intel's various Pentium processors. Other CPU clones, such as the 80386 clone chips made by Cyrix and Advanced Micro Devices (AMD), are also compatible with Linux.

The 80386 and 80486SX processors don't have math coprocessors built in, but Linux doesn't require a floating-point math coprocessor. Linux can emulate the coprocessor by using software routines, but at a significant reduction in execution speed. For a fast system, you should consider getting a CPU with a math coprocessor built in, such as an 80486DX or Pentium.

The System's Bus

The type of bus used to communicate with the peripherals is also important. Linux works only with the ISA and EISA buses. The MicroChannel Architecture (MCA) bus used on IBM's PS/2 isn't supported, although a port is in process. Some newer systems use a faster bus for such items as disk access and video displays, called the *local bus*. Linux does support the VESA Local Bus but may not support a non-VESA Local Bus architecture. Linux also supports the PCI (Peripheral Component Interconnect) bus found on many high-end Pentium systems.

Memory Needs

Linux requires surprisingly little RAM to run, especially when compared to comparable operating systems such as OS/2 and Windows NT. Linux requires at least 2M of RAM, although 4M is highly recommended. If you have less than 4M of RAM, you need to use what's called a *swap file*. The basic rule of thumb is that the more memory your system contains, the faster your system runs.

The next memory consideration for Linux is the use of the X Windows clone called XFree86. XFree86 is a version of X Windows that's freely distributable and is included with Linux for that reason. XFree86 is a GUI similar to Microsoft Windows.

▶ **See** "Installing the XFree86 System," **p. 163**

To productively use XFree86, your Linux system requires at least 16M of virtual memory. *Virtual memory* is the combination of physical memory and swap space on the hard drive. Again, the more physical memory contained on the system, the more responsive the system, especially when using XFree86.

Part

I

Ch

3

Disk Drives and Space Requirements

Although it's possible to run Linux from a floppy-drive-only system, running Linux from your system's floppy drive isn't recommended.

N O T E You can boot Linux from a floppy drive. *Booting a system* refers to the process of starting a computer system and loading the operating system into memory to start the system. The term is derived from the phrase *bootstrapping*. ▪

For a home-based system, you need a floppy drive—either 5 1/4 inch or 3 1/2 inch. You need a floppy drive even if you install and run Linux from your CD-ROM.

For better system performance, you want to install Linux on a hard drive. You must have an IBM AT standard drive controller. This shouldn't be a problem because most modern, non-SCSI controllers are AT compatible. Linux supports all MFM and IDE controllers, as well as most RLL and ESDI controllers. Linux may or may not support the newer, high-capacity IDE drives from older 8-bit IDE controllers.

Linux supports a wide range of SCSI hard-drive controllers. If your controller is a true SCSI controller—that is, not a proprietary version of SCSI—Linux can use your controller. Linux now supports SCSI controllers from Adaptec, Future Domain, Seagate, UltraStor, the SCSI adapter on the ProAudio Spectrum 16 card, and Western Digital. The following card types are supported:

Adaptec 152x/1542/1740/274x/284x/294X	Always IN2000
Buslogic	Pro Audio Spectrum 16
EATA-DMA (DPT, NEC, AT&T)	Qlogic
Seagate ST-02	Trantor T128/T128F/T228
Future Domain TMC-8xx, 16xx	UltraStor
Generic NCR5380	7000FASST
NCR 53c7, 8xx	

▶ **See** "Controllers (IO)," **p. 706**

If you have the proper drive controller, you must worry about disk space requirements. Linux supports multiple hard drives and can be installed across drives. Unlike other operating systems, Linux doesn't need to be installed on the same hard drive; pieces can be installed on different drives.

Disk Space   The one item to realize about disk space, however, is that Linux can't reside on the same partition as other operating systems, such as MS-DOS and OS/2. *Partitions* are areas of a disk drive specified during initialization of a drive and before formatting a drive. You typically use a program called `fdisk` to partition a drive. Some commercial products allow you to repartition a drive, and Linux provides a utility called FIPS to do the same. To use Linux efficiently, you should repartition your hard drive and allocate enough space for the Linux system files and your data files.

> **CAUTION**
>
> Unless you're installing Linux onto a brand-new hard drive, you'll need to repartition and reformat the drive. This destroys all information now stored on that portion of the drive. Thus, it's imperative to back up your files—twice—before installing Linux. If space permits, you can split a single hard drive into multiple partitions and copy your files back to one of the partitions.

The amount of disk space required depends on the software you install and the amount of data you expect that software will generate. Linux requires less disk space than most implementations of UNIX systems. You can run a completely functional Linux system, without X Windows support, in 20M. For a complete installation of everything in the distribution, 150M to 200M is recommended.

Swap Space   Finally, as mentioned earlier in the section "Memory Needs," if you have limited RAM, you need swap space. Whereas systems such as Microsoft Windows create a swap file that resides on your hard drive as any other file, Linux allows the swap file to reside on a separate swap partition. Most Linux installations use partitions rather than files. Because you can place multiple partitions on the same physical hard drive, you can place the swap partition on the same drive as Linux, but for better performance you should place the swap partition on a separate drive.

Linux allows up to eight swap partitions that can be no larger than 16M. A rule of thumb is to set the swap file size to twice the amount of physical RAM contained on your system. Thus, if you have 8M of physical RAM, your swap partition should be 16M in size.

Monitor Requirements

For text-based terminals, Linux supports all standard Hercules, CGA, EGA, VGA, and SuperVGA video cards and monitors. To take advantage of the color-coding directory listings available with Linux, you need a color monitor. So for text-based operation, any video/controller combination should work.

The big problems occur when you run the X Windows system distributed with Linux. To use XFree86, you need a video adapter that uses one of the chipsets listed in Table 3.1. *Chipsets* are a group of integrated circuits, or computer chips, used to take information from the computer and convert the data into a form displayable on a video monitor. To find out the chipset used by your video adapter, check the documentation included with your card to determine whether there are any problems using XFree86.

Part
I

Ch
3

Table 3.1   Video Chipsets Supported by Linux

Manufacturer	Chipset(s)
Tseng	ET3000, ET40000AX, ET4000/W32
Western Digital	WD90C00, WD90C10, WD90C11, WD90C24, WD90C30, WD90C31
Trident	TVGA8800CS, TVGA8900B, TVGA8900C, TVGA8900CL, TVGA9000, TVGA9000i, TVGA9100B, TVGA9200CX, TVGA9320, TVGA9400CX, TVGA9420
ATI	28800-4, 28800-5, 28800-a
NCR	77C22, 77C22E, 77C22E+
Cirrus Logic	CLGD5420, CLGD5422, CLGD5424, CLGD5426, CLGD5428, CLGD6205, CLGD6215, CLGD6225, CLGD6235
OAK	OTI067, OTI077
S3	86C911, 86C924, 86C801, 86C805, 86C805i, 86C928
Compaq	AVGA
Western Digital/ Paradise	PVGA1

N O T E   The release notes for the current version of XFree86 distributed with Linux should contain a more recent list of supported and non-supported chipsets. ▪

Some problems encountered by the XFree86 developers are caused by adapter manufacturers who don't provide the necessary information on programming the cards to display information. Without this information, developers can't support X Windows on those adapters. Also, some manufacturers provide this information but require either royalty payments or non-disclosure agreements for others to use the information. These types of restrictions make it impossible to support these adapters on a freely distributed system like the XFree86 system for Linux.

N O T E   The Diamond video cards haven't been supported in the past, due to restrictions the company had on giving out proprietary information. The Diamond company has now begun work with the XFree team to support the company's video systems specifically under Linux and XFree86. ▪

▶ **See** "Video Cards," **p. 700**

CD-ROMs

To install the Linux system included on the accompanying CD-ROM, you must have a CD-ROM drive supported by Linux. Because most CD-ROMs use a SCSI interface controller, any SCSI controller listed earlier in the section "Disk Drives and Space Requirements" should also work with a CD-ROM attached to the controller. Linux also now supports many of the new EIDE and ATAPI CD-ROMs available on the market.

Many of the CD-ROMs included with multimedia packages may or may not work with Linux, depending on whether the controller is a true SCSI adapter or a proprietary adapter. Proprietary adapters for the most part won't work. However, Linux does specifically support the Creative Labs SoundBlaster line of CD-ROMs and provides a specific installation configuration for their CD-ROMs. Other CD-ROMs known to work with Linux are as follows:

NEC CDR-74	Okano
Sony CDU-541	Wearnes CD with interface card
Sony CDU-31a or 33a	SoundBlaster, Panasonic Kotobuki, Matsushita, TEAC-55a, or Lasermate
Plextor DM-3024	Most IDE/ATAPI CD-ROMs
Aztech	Mitsumi CD-ROMs
Orchid	

▶ **See** "CD-ROM Drives Supported," **p. 712**

See "CD-ROM Drives Supported," p. 712

Network Access

You can connect a Linux system to the world in several ways, but the two most popular (and supported) methods are via network controller cards and modems. Network controller cards include Token Ring, FDDI, TAXI, and Ethernet cards. Most common business networks use an Ethernet controller card.

Network Access via Ethernet Ethernet, a protocol invented by Xerox, has gained immense popularity in the networking world. Although it's unlikely you'll connect Linux to an Ethernet network at home, many business and educational institutions are connected via Ethernet. Table 3.2 lists several of the Ethernet adapters supported.

Table 3.2   Ethernet Controller Cards Supported by Linux

Manufacturer	Interface Card
3Com	3c503, 3c503/16, 3c509
Novell	NE1000, NE2000
Western Digital	WD8003, WD8013
Hewlett-Packard	HP27245, HP27247, HP27250

Network Access via Modem   At home, you'll more than likely connect to the outside world via a modem and a communications protocol such as SLIP or PPP. Linux supports almost every type of modem on the market, internal and external. If you can access the modem from MS-DOS, you'll have no problem accessing the modem from Linux.

▶ **See** "Understanding the Requirements for SLIP and PPP," **p. 506**

Miscellaneous Hardware

The following sections list miscellaneous hardware supported by Linux, such as mice, tape drives, and printers. Although such hardware makes Linux easier to use and more robust, it isn't required.

Mice   Using text-based Linux doesn't require a mouse. Unlike many UNIX implementations, however, Linux does allow you to cut text from any area of the screen and paste it to the command line by using a mouse. If you intend to use the X Windows clone, XFree86, you must use a mouse.

Linux supports most serial mice, including the following mice:

- Logitech
- MM series
- Mouseman
- Microsoft
- Mouse Systems

Linux also supports the Microsoft, Logitech, ATIXL, and PS/2 bus mice. In fact, any pointing devices, such as trackballs and touch screens, which emulate the previously listed mice, should work with Linux.

Tape Drives   Tape drives provide a great deal of storage space for backing up your computer system. Linux supports several SCSI-based tape systems, as shown in Table 3.3. Linux also supports the popular Colorado Memory Systems tape drives (120 and 250 versions), which are plugged into a system's floppy-disk controller. The versions that plug into the printer port aren't now supported. Most drives supporting QIC-02 should also work with Linux.

Table 3.3   Tape-Backup Drives Supported by Linux

Manufacturer	Model
Exabyte	All SCSI models
Sanko	CP150SE
Tandberg	3600
Wangtek	5525ES, 5150ES, 5099EN

▶ **See** "Tape Drives—Supported," **p. 712**

Printers   Linux supports the complete range of parallel printers. Configuring Linux to support serial printers is tedious and error-prone. Serial printer support isn't well documented or supported by the basic Linux installation programs. If you have a serial printer, you may have problems using it under Linux. If you have a parallel printer, your biggest problem is most likely the *stair-step effect*:

```
This is line one.
            This is line two.
                        This is line three.
```

How UNIX, and hence Linux, treat carriage returns and line feeds produces the stair-step effect. Under most UNIX systems, the command to move the paper down one line (line feed) and then position the print head at the beginning of the line (carriage return) are represented by one control character. Under systems such as MS-DOS and Windows, however, each command is represented by a different control character. When you print a UNIX file under a printer configured for MS-DOS systems, you see the stair-step effect because the file contains only the line-feed control character and not the carriage-return control character.

▶ **See** "Knowing What You Need to Configure Printers," **p. 438**

Starting the Installation Process

To start the installation process, you need one or two (depending on the installation method) 3 1/2-inch 1.44M formatted floppy disks. These disks will be used to create a boot disk for the Linux installation.

Next, you should make sure that you have enough hard disk space to install Linux. Everything on the CD-ROM, if installed, requires about 300M of disk space, but you can get by with less, especially if you don't install the X Windows system. To decide on the amount of space, you should decide how much space you want for user accounts—that is, the space you want to provide to your users. On a single-user system, 30M is more than enough.

Next, decide how much swap space your machine needs. If your machine has 8M of RAM or less, you need a 24M swap space. If you have 16M or more, your swap space should equal the amount of RAM.

Finally, figure about 30M for your root directory. This is the main directory from which all other directories under Linux are accessed.

▶ **See** "Looking at Linux Standard Directories," **p. 297**

Again, a minimal installation should fit in 200M, whereas a full installation, with plenty of user space, should fit well on a 500M drive.

N O T E   You can also run part of the Linux file system from the CD-ROM without installing all the software. You can choose to do so during installation. ■

Part

I

Ch

3

If you decide to install and configure X (highly recommended), you should also write down what type of chipset your video card uses. If you have a serial mouse and modem, write down the serial port that each is using. You need this information later during the configuration process.

Understanding the Various Installation Methods

We, the authors, envision most of you installing Red Hat from the accompanying CD-ROM. However, you can use one of the following four methods to install Red Hat: from CD-ROM, via NFS, via FTP, or from a hard drive.

To install directly from CD-ROM, you need access to DOS. From the DOS prompt, execute the command

```
[cdrom-drive]:\dosutils\autoboot
```

where `[cdrom-drive]` is the drive letter for your system's CD-ROM.

> **CAUTION**
> This method will erase your hard drive. Back up any files you fear losing.

If you have another partition available, you can install Linux to coexist with your system without erasing what's already there. To do this, you need the CD-ROM, an empty partition, and a boot disk. You learn later in this chapter how to create the boot disk, as well as how to repartition your hard drive.

NFS (Network File System) provides a way to install Red Hat across a network. First, you must mount the CD-ROM drive on a machine supporting the ISO-9660 file system with RockRidge extensions, and then export the file system via NFS. You need to know the path to the exported file system and the IP number, or, if DNS is configured, the name of the system.

FTP (File Transfer Protocol) is a method for transferring files across the Internet. (Chapter 27, "Accessing the Network with *telnet*, *ftp*, and the *r*– Commands," explains FTP in more detail.) To install via FTP requires a boot disk and the supplemental disk described later in this chapter.

Installing Red Hat from a hard drive requires the same boot and supplemental disks used for an FTP installation. First, create a directory named RedHat. Then copy the corresponding directory from the CD-ROM, and all the subdirectories there, to the RedHat directory. You can use the following DOS commands to do this:

```
cd \RedHat
xcopy /s e:\RedHat
```

The `cd` command assumes that you're already on the installation hard drive; the `xcopy` command assumes that your CD-ROM drive is drive E.

No matter which method you use, you'll need at least the boot disk to proceed with installation. But first, you should gather some information.

Compiling Needed information

Before starting the installation, you need the following information about your system:

- The type of video card, chipset, and monitor used
- The serial port used by your mouse
- The serial port used by your modem
- The network information for your computer, if it's connected to a network (items such as its IP address, gateway, and domain name)
- The type of hard drive and CD-ROM drive in your system, and their controller type
- The name you intend to call your system

If you're connecting to the Internet, you can get most of this information from either your network administrator or from your Internet service provider.

If you intend to use other operating systems on the same computer (such as Windows 95, Windows NT, or OS/2), you'll need to create the necessary partitions for these operating systems. Typically, you need to use the operating system's partitioning software, because Linux can't handle these other partition types.

ON THE WEB

A product named System Commander, from V Communications, lets you install and switch between 32 different operating systems. You can find more information about this product at **http://www. v-com.com/**.

Next, you should check for any last-minute changes to the Red Hat distribution. The reasons are many, but the two major reasons are that Linux is constantly updated, and this chapter is being written at least a month before the CD-ROM is cut. In the interim, new material or bug fixes may have been released. You can contact InfoMagic, the manufacturers of the accompanying CD-ROM, for more information.

ON THE WEB

You can also check for updated material on the Web at **http://www.redhat.com/errata**.

If you're not installing directly off the CD-ROM, you next need to repartition your current hard drive to make room for Linux. This may cause problems, because repartitioning a hard drive destroys any data contained on the affected partitions. After making room for Linux, you need to boot the Linux system and create its new partitions and file systems. Typically, Linux systems need a primary partition to store the files on and a swap file partition, especially if you have a machine with 8M or less of memory.

Part

I

Ch

3

N O T E A file system is basically a section of your hard drive specially formatted to hold certain types of files. UNIX and Linux use file systems to represent entire sections of the directory tree. This is in contrast to MS-DOS, which places subdirectories in the directory tree on the same logical drive. UNIX systems use the directory tree format because placing subdirectories on different drives is safer. If one drive malfunctions, only the information on that drive needs to be replaced or fixed.

▶ **See** "Understanding File Systems," **p. 262** ■

After creating the file systems, you then install the Linux operating system, its support files, and various application packages distributed with the system. To install Linux, you must first boot a stripped-down version of the operating system. You do this by creating a boot disk and a supplemental disk set containing the stripped-down OS.

Creating the Boot and Supplemental Disks

You need to create the boot and supplemental disks by using the `rawrite` program. You can find this program on the accompanying CD-ROM in the /dosutils subdirectory. For this step, you need two formatted floppies: one labeled *boot*, the other labeled *supp*. Place the boot disk in the A drive and enter the following:

```
E:\dosutils>rawrite
```

```
Enter disk image source file name: e:\images\boot.img
Enter target diskette drive: A:
Please insert a formatted diskette into drive A: and press –ENTER–
```

If you want to abort the process, simply press <Ctrl-c> to stop. If `rawrite` fails, try a new formatted disk. If the problem persists, you should have your hardware checked for possible problems.

After writing the boot disk, you need to create the supp disk. Simply use the supp image file name (supp.img) as the source file name in the preceding command sequence.

Partitioning Your Hard Drive

After you back up your system and make the necessary boot and supplemental disks, you must prepare your system's hard drive for Linux.

> **CAUTION**
>
> This process is the most dangerous because maximum data loss is assured. If you haven't backed up your system, do so now. Although you can use an experimental program called FIPS and commercial programs such as Partition Magic to do non-destructive repartitioning, a full backup is recommended, just in case problems occur.

Understanding Partitions

In the early days of PCs, hard drives were few and far between. Most computers used floppies to hold the operating system, programs, and their data. With the introduction of the IBM PC XT, IBM introduced a 10M hard drive. Early operating systems such as DOS could access only a limited amount of space on hard drives. Then hard drive manufacturers kept expanding the space on their hard drives more quickly than the operating system's capability to access the additional space. The operating system got around this problem by letting the user split the hard drive into sections, called *partitions*. These partitions can hold program files, other operating systems, or data.

Typical MS-DOS systems have one partition, which is referred to as drive C. If you split the drive into partitions, these partitions are typically referred to in alphabetical order as D, E, and so on. MS-DOS also allows you to install multiple hard drives, so that the next drive in this chain might be referred to as F.

UNIX and Linux don't use drive letters to refer to partitions; instead, they use directory names to refer to partitions. Also, as indicated earlier, Linux users can place different directories on different partitions and even on different drives. You can also place different operating systems on different partitions.

Partitions are specified in a section of the hard drive referred to as the *boot record* in what's called a *partition table*. This table is used by the various operating systems to determine what operating system to boot and where their files can physically be found on the hard drive. The boot record is used to *boot*, or start up, the machine's operating system. Linux's boot program, LILO (which stands for LInux LOader), and other boot managers use this section of the hard drive, typically found on the first sectors of the drive, to control which operating system to start.

The partition table holds information about the locations and sizes of the various partitions on the hard drive. There are three kinds of partitions: primary, extended, and logical. DOS and some other operating systems must boot from primary partitions. Hard drives can contain only four primary partitions. An extended partition doesn't contain data itself; instead, it allows the user to define other, logical partitions on the drive. Thus, to get around the limit of four primary partitions, you can define an extended partition and then define other logical partitions within the extended partition.

Some operating systems, such as MS-DOS and versions of OS/2 before version 2.0, require that they be installed in a primary partition, but they can access logical drives in extended partitions. This is important to remember if you're going to have a DOS system and a Linux system reside on the same drive. DOS must go in a primary partition.

Using *FDISK*

Partitions are created, destroyed, and managed by a program usually called FDISK. Each operating system has its own version of FDISK, so be sure to use the correct one. If you're now using DOS or are planning to use DOS, you must first repartition the DOS drive by using DOS's FDISK. You later use the Linux version of fdisk to create the Linux partitions. If you're using OS/2, you also need to use the OS/2 version of FDISK to prepare the OS/2 partitions.

Partition Requirements   First, you should plan what partitions you need. DOS requires a primary partition; Linux and OS/2 can reside in other partitions. If you're using the OS/2 boot manager, which also works well with Linux, you must prepare for its use. You must also be aware that if you're shrinking a current DOS partition to make room for Linux, not all of your files can be restored to the new, smaller DOS partition.

N O T E   You can access DOS partitions from Linux, thus moving, saving, and editing DOS files under Linux. But you can't execute DOS programs under Linux.

Two experimental components of Linux allow you to emulate DOS under Linux and also install Linux under DOS. Both systems are still in the implementation stage and are, thus, more suited for Linux hackers. Also, one of the methods, UMSDOS, is incompatible with Red Hat, so you can't use this method at all. You can find plenty of information on these topics in the Linux world.

▶ **See** "Running DOS Programs Under Linux," **p. 139** ▪

Next, you should jot down the number of partitions you need and how much disk space to provide each with.

DOS Requirements   If you want to boot DOS, it must go in a primary partition. A bootable version of DOS doesn't require much space—just enough for the system files, COMMAND.COM, CONFIG.SYS, and any driver files needed to start your system. For example, I provide a 5M DOS partition on my first drive to boot DOS.

When DOS is loaded and running, you can access any of the other extended and logical drives on the system. Unfortunately, whereas Linux can access DOS files in a DOS partition, DOS can't access Linux files in a Linux partition.

OS/2 Requirements   OS/2 versions 2.0 and later don't need a primary partition. The OS/2 system can install and boot from an extended partition. Thus, you can install DOS on a primary partition and create an extended partition area for OS/2 and Linux. The space required for OS/2 is version- and feature-dependent; you should consult your OS/2 documentation for space requirements. You should also subtract 1M from available space if you intend to use the OS/2 boot manager.

Linux Requirements   As explained earlier, Linux stores files on file systems, and these file systems can reside on different partitions, basically as safety precautions. Linux requires one partition for each file system. The next consideration is for a swap partition. Linux, like most operating systems that use disk space for memory (called a *virtual memory configuration*), needs a swap file or a swap partition to simulate physical memory using disk space. Linux typically uses a swap partition.

The size of the swap partition depends on the amount of physical RAM your system contains. A rule of thumb is to make your swap partition twice the size of your amount of RAM. Thus, if you have 8M of RAM in your system, you should create a swap partition 16M in size. If you have 4M of RAM or less, you must activate a swap partition.

Linux swap partitions can be only 128M in size, so if you need more space, you have to create multiple swap partitions. Thus, if you have a Linux system that needs two partitions for Linux (one for the system files and one for user files), plus a swap partition, you need to define two Linux partitions and one 32M swap partition.

Repartitioning Your DOS Drive

This section assumes that you need to repartition a DOS drive. First, you execute FDISK by typing fdisk at the DOS prompt. The FDISK Options screen appears (see Figure 3.1).

FIG. 3.1

From the FDISK Options screen you can look at current partitions, create new partitions, and delete old partitions.

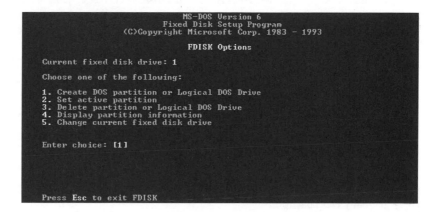

The screen shown in Figure 3.1 might look different depending on which version of MS-DOS you're using. Pick menu option 4, Display Partition Information. The Display Partition Information screen appears (see Figure 3.2). Write down the information in this screen. You need the current partition table information if you decide to abort the Linux installation and put your system back the way it was before you started.

FIG. 3.2

You can look at current partition information by using the Display Partition Information screen in MS-DOS 6.x

An Alternative to Repartitioning Your Hard Drive

You may not need to repartition your hard drive, although it's thought that repartitioning offers the best introduction to Linux. You can use FIPS to non-destructively repartition your hard drive.

FIPS stands for *First non-destructive Interactive Partition Splitting.* A program developed by Arno Schaefer as a result of the Linux project, FIPS is used to move around DOS partitions to make room for Linux partitions.

You can find the complete instructions for using FIPS in the document fips.doc located on the accompanying Red Hat CD-ROM in the /utils/fips directory. This program can help only if you have enough free space left on your drive to install Linux; otherwise, you need to delete unneeded files or use the process described earlier to repartition your hard drive.

Under Slackware Linux (whose installation is discussed in Chapter 4), you can install Linux on the same partition as DOS with UMSDOS. UMSDOS is a project to allow Linux to exist on DOS partitions. UMSDOS lets you create the Linux root file system under an existing DOS directory. Unfortunately, you can't use UMSDOS under Red Hat.

Deleting Partitions   Unfortunately, FDISK doesn't allow you to simply resize a partition; you must first delete the partition and then add it back with the desired size. From the FDISK Options screen, choose menu option 3, Delete Partition or Logical DOS Drive, which deletes the necessary partitions. The Delete DOS Partition or Logical DOS Drive screen appears (see Figure 3.3).

Pick the appropriate menu option for the type of partition you're deleting, such as a primary DOS partition. For example, option 1, Delete Primary DOS Partition, allows you to delete primary DOS partitions.

FIG. 3.3
Use the Delete DOS Partition screen to delete a specific partition or logical drive.

```
                    Delete DOS Partition or Logical DOS Drive

        Current fixed disk drive: 1

        Choose one of the following:

        1.   Delete Primary DOS Partition
        2.   Delete Extended DOS Partition
        3.   Delete Logical DOS Drive(s) in the Extended DOS Partition
        4.   Delete Non-DOS Partition


        Enter choice: [1]




        Press Esc to return to FDISK Options
```

Choose option 1 to display the Delete Primary DOS Partition screen (see Figure 3.4). The screen asks for a volume name of the partition and then a confirmation to see whether you really want to delete the partition. Because all information on the partition will be destroyed, FDISK wants to make absolutely sure that you want to delete the primary DOS partition.

FIG. 3.4

MS-DOS warns you when you try to delete a primary DOS partition.

```
                        Delete Primary DOS Partition
Current fixed disk drive: 1

Partition  Status  Type      Volume Label  Mbytes  System   Usage
  C: 1       A      PRI DOS   OPUS_DOS        5     FAT12     4%
     2              Non-DOS                   8               6%
     3              Non-DOS                 376             100%
     4              Non-DOS                 114              90%

Total disk space is  127 Mbytes (1 Mbyte = 1048576 bytes)



WARNING! Data in the deleted Primary DOS Partition will be lost.
What primary partition do you want to delete..? [1]
Enter Volume Label..............................? [OPUS_DOS  ]
Are you sure (Y/N)..............................? [N]

Press Esc to return to FDISK Options
```

Adding Partitions   After you delete all the necessary partitions, you must add the appropriate partitions for your DOS system by selecting the Create a DOS Partition menu item on the FDISK Options screen. Figure 3.5 shows the Create a DOS Partition or Logical DOS Drive screen.

FIG. 3.5

Most operating systems require a primary active partition to boot properly.

```
                    Create DOS Partition or Logical DOS Drive
Current fixed disk drive: 1

Choose one of the following:

1. Create Primary DOS Partition
2. Create Extended DOS Partition
3. Create Logical DOS Drive(s) in the Extended DOS Partition




Enter choice: [1]




Press Esc to return to FDISK Options
```

N O T E   You can't add the Linux or OS/2 partitions with the DOS FDISK program. Partitioning the hard drive for Linux is covered later in the section "Using the Linux *fdisk* Command." ■

Providing all the space available for the partition and making the partition the active partition are the FDISK defaults, as shown in Figure 3.6.

Part

I

Ch

3

FIG. 3.6
You can provide the all the disk space to one partition, or spread out the free space across several partitions.

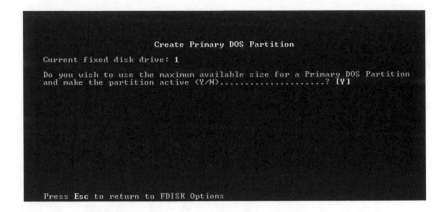

Active indicates that the partition is bootable. To boot DOS, you must specify the primary partition as active. Choose N (no) for this first selection so that you can specify the exact amount of disk space to provide to your DOS partition. Answering no to the question in Figure 3.6 displays the Specify Disk Space for the Partition screen. Specify the desired space for your DOS partition either in megabytes or in percentage of space available and press <Return>.

Next, you must set this partition as active. From the FDISK Options screen, choose menu option 2, Set Active Partition, and simply follow the instructions on the set active menu screen.

Formatting the Partition   After you repartition your hard drive, you need to prepare the new partition for DOS and restore the appropriate files back to the DOS partition. Reboot your computer with the boot disk you made earlier. Then format the appropriate drive and transfer the system files by using the following DOS command:

```
format c: /s
```

When the partition is formatted, you can restore your backup to the new drive. Remember, if you shrank the partition, not all the files will fit on the new drive. It might be necessary to place the files that don't fit on the new drive onto other DOS drives or partitions.

Installing the Linux System

To start the Linux installation, place the boot disk you created into your disk drive and reset your computer. The system displays the following prompt and then begins initializing the system:

```
LILO:boot:
Loading Linux....
```

Watch the messages as they appear, in case Linux can't recognize your hardware. If Linux can't, you may have to pass some extra parameters to Linux when it boots up. Record these parameters, enter them at the prompt, and press <Return>. You should then see a screen asking if you have a color monitor (see Figure 3.7).

FIG. 3.7

The Red Hat installation program can take advantage of screen colors on a color monitor.

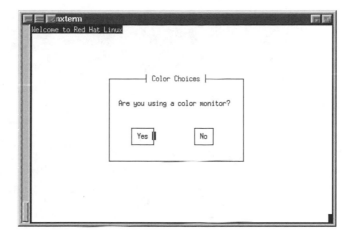

Select your choice by using the <Tab> key and then press <Return> to display the Welcome screen (see Figure 3.8).

FIG. 3.8

The Red Hat Linux Welcome screen.

Part

I

Ch

3

Press <Return> to continue. The next screen asks whether you need PCMCIA support for your system (see Figure 3.9). Select the appropriate answer with the <Tab> key and press <Return>.

N O T E Moving around in the dialog boxes is easy, and the installation program provides reminders at the bottom of most screens. To move from element to element (field), press <Tab> or <Alt-Tab>. Use the space bar if you need to select an item from a list or check a check box. To choose a button (typically OK or Cancel), just press <Return>. ■

The next dialog box (see Figure 3.10) asks you to select the installation method described earlier in the section "Understanding the Various Installation Methods." Select your installation method and press <Return>. The installation program asks you to insert the Red Hat CD-ROM into the CD-ROM drive. When you're done, simply press <Return> to continue.

FIG. 3.9
Red Hat Linux provides
optional support for
PCMCIA cards.

FIG. 3.10
Red Hat lets you install
the system by using a
variety of methods,
including NFS and ftp.

N O T E The rest of this chapter assumes that you're installing from the local CD-ROM drive. If you
select another method of installation, see the appropriate help topics or Red Hat's Web site
at **http://www.redhat.com**. ▪

Next, the program asks for your CD-ROM drive type (see Figure 3.11). You can select from

IDE (ATAPI)
SCSI
Other CDROM

FIG. 3.11

The Red Hat Linux installation program needs to know what type of CD-ROM used in your system.

The Other CDROM category includes such drives as those sold by Creative Labs (SoundBlaster) and other multimedia kit-based CD-ROMs, as well as

Aztech CD	Sanyo
Goldstar R420	Sony CDU-31A
Mitsumi	Sony CDU-5xx
Optics Storage 8000	SoundBlaster/Panasonic
Phillips CM206/CM260	

Depending on your selection, the installation program may ask for some parameters, such as IRQs or DMA addresses. Or the program may try to determined these values automatically by probing your hardware. It's best to let the program autoprobe first before providing parameters.

N O T E Any time the installation program probes the system's hardware, the system may hang. If that happens, you must reboot and redo the installation. Be sure to try to collect the needed information, such as IRQs and DMA addresses, before attempting to reinstall. ■

After detecting your CD-ROM type, the system starts its installation from the CD-ROM drive. First, it asks you whether you're installing a new system or upgrading an existing Red Hat system. Red Hat 4.0 easily upgrades over version 2.0, 2.1, or 3.0.3, but no Linux distribution easily upgrades over a different distribution version. So if you have a prior distribution version, such as Slackware, just performing a new install and blowing away your prior system is best—after backing up important data files, of course.

Next, the installation program displays the SCSI Configuration dialog box, where you tell the system whether you have any SCSI adapters in your system. Choose the appropriate button and continue.

If you have a SCSI adapter, the program displays the load module dialog box from which you can select from the following SCSI drivers:

Adaptec 152x	Iomega PPA3 (Parallel port Zip)
Adaptec 1542	NCR 5380
Adaptec 1740	NCR 53c406a
Adaptec 2740,2840, 2940	NCR 53C810/53C820 PCI
AdvanSys Adapters	Pro Audio Spectrum/Studio 16
Always IN200	Qlogic FAS
Buslogic Adapters	Qlogic ISP
DTC 3180/3280	Seagate ST01/02
EATA DMA Adapters	Trantor T128/T128F/T228
EATA PIO Adapters)	UltraStor 14F/34F
Future Domain TMC-885, TMC-950	UltraStor 14F/24F/34F
Future Domain TMC-16x0	Western Digital wd7000

Next, you must partition your disks—or at least select the partitions you've already created. You select the drive you want dedicated to Linux in the list box shown in the Partition Disks dialog box, and then press <Return> or choose the Edit button. This drops you into the fdisk program to partition the selected hard drive.

Using the Linux *fdisk* Program

At the fdisk prompt, type m for a list of commands. Table 3.4 lists the available commands.

Table 3.4   The Linux *fdisk* Commands

Command	Description
a	Toggles a bootable flag
c	Toggles the DOS compatibility flag
d	Deletes a partition
l	Lists known partition types
m	Displays this menu
n	Adds a new partition
p	Displays the partition table
q	Quits without saving changes
t	Changes a partition's system ID
u	Changes display/entry units

Command	Description
v	Verifies the partition table
w	Writes the table to disk and exits
x	Provides extra functionality for experts only

To begin the partitioning, select the p command (press <p><Return>) to display the current partition table, which should reflect the drive you partitioned earlier with the DOS FDISK program. Listing 3.1 shows a possible listing from the p command.

Listing 3.1   Example of a Current Partition Table

```
Disk /dev/hda: 15 heads, 17 sectors, 1024 cylinders
Units = cylinders of 255 * 512 bytes

Device      Boot    Begin   Start   End     Blocks   Id   System
/dev/hda1   *       1       1       41      5219     1    DOS 12-bit
FAT
dev/hda2            1024    1024    4040    384667+  51   Novell?
Partition 2 has different physical/logical endings:
phys=(967, 14, 17) Logical=(4096, 14.17)
```

N O T E   Your screen may appear different than what's shown in Listing 3.1, because the values are different for each drive type and the partitions already defined on that drive. ▓

Listing 3.1 indicates the various partitions already defined that it can detect, the start and ending locations of the partition, and how big it is in blocks. The listing also indicates the partition type. Table 3.5 shows all the different types of partitions you can define with the Linux fdisk program. The primary partition types you used are 83-Linux Native and 82-Linux Swap. You can get a similar listing with the l command.

Table 3.5   The Known Linux Partition Types

Reference Number	Type	Reference Number	Type
0	Empty	75	PC/IX
1	DOS 12-bit FAT	80	Old MINIX
2	XENIX root	81	MINIX/Linux
3	XENIX usr	82	Linux Swap
4	DOS 16-bit < 32M	83	Linux Native

continues

Table 3.5   Continued

Reference Number	Type	Reference Number	Type
5	Extended	93	Amoeba
6	DOS 16-bit >= 32M	94	Amoeba BBT
7	OS/2 HPFS	a5	BSD/386
8	AIX	b7	BSDI fs
9	AIX bootable	b8	BSDI swap
a	OS/2 Boot Manager	c7	Syrinx
40	Venix 80286	db	CP/M
51	Novell?	e1	DOS access
52	Microport	e3	DOS R/O
63	GNU HURD	f2	DOS secondary
64	Novell	ff	BBT

In Listing 3.1, Linux prints a note about the different physical and logical endings at the bottom of the screen. The difference is because on the system used to write this chapter, a prior partition containing the DOS D drive was left intact, whereas the C drive was repartitioned to a smaller C drive to make room for Linux. Thus, there's space between the C drive and the D drive. This is where the necessary partitions required by Linux will be created.

The begin, start, and end numbers from Listing 3.1 are very important and you should write them down. You'll need them in a later step to specify the necessary sizes of the partitions you'll add.

Adding the Necessary Partition

Because you've repartitioned the drive for DOS, you shouldn't have to delete any partitions for Linux. You only should have to add partitions. To add a partition, issue the n command, which displays

```
Command Action
e extended
p primary(1-4)
```

Press <p><Return>. fdisk then asks for the partition number; enter your selection and press <Return>. If you indicate a partition number already in use, fdisk reports this fact and asks you to delete the partition before trying to add it to the partition table. For this example, enter **3**, to add a third primary partition that's referred to as /dev/hda3.

Next, `fdisk` asks for the location of the first cylinder. This is usually the first available cylinder; in fact, `fdisk` displays a default range for your selection—for example,

```
First cylinder (42-1024) :
```

Notice that the first partition ends at cylinder 41 and that the next partition begins at cylinder 1024. Thus, the range supplied by `fdisk` here allows you to start the next partition anywhere in the range of 42-1024. It's a very good idea not to place partitions just anywhere throughout the disk, so choose the next available location, which in this case is cylinder 42. Enter **42** and press <Return>.

N O T E Linux can have trouble booting from partitions defined to start at cylinders above 1024. If you can create a Linux partition only in this range, you may have to boot Linux from a floppy. You learn how to create a boot floppy (different from the boot floppy used for installation) later in this chapter. The only downside is that it takes a little longer to boot Linux from floppy than from the hard drive. ■

Now `fdisk` wants you to specify how much space to allocate for this partition. You can express this size in number of cylinders or by the number of bytes (`+size`), kilobytes (`+sizeK`), or megabytes (`+sizeM`). Because you should already know the approximate size you need for the swap file, define this partition first, and then leave the rest of the disk space for the Linux program partitions. Thus, for this example, your machine has 8M of RAM, so you need to specify a 16M partition size by replying

```
Last cylinder or +size or +sizeM or +sizeK (42-1023): +16M
```

You should then use the `p` command to look at the new partition table you've defined. In this example, the new partition table looks like

```
Disk /dev/hda: 15 heads, 17 sectors, 1024 cylinders
Units = cylinders of 255 * 512 bytes

Device       Boot Begin Start  End   Blocks   Id   System
/dev/hda1     *    1     1      41    5219 1   DOS  12-bit FAT
/dev/hda2          1024  1024   4040  384667+ 51   Novell?

Partition 2 has different physical/logical endings:
phys=(967, 14, 17) Logical=(4039, 14.17)
/dev/hda3          42    42     170   16447+   83   Linux native
```

By default, `fdisk` made the new partition a Linux Native type. To change this to a swap partition, you need to use the `t` command. Enter **t** and then enter the partition number you want to change; in this example, enter **3**. `fdisk` then requests that you enter the hexadecimal value of the desired partition type from Table 3.5 (if you don't have the table handy, you can type **l** and get the list of codes). Because you want a swap partition, enter **82** at the prompt.

As you can see, `fdisk` reports the new partition type, but you can also use the `p` command to double-check that partition 3 is now a Linux Swap partition.

Now you can add your Linux partitions. For this example, add only one partition, but if you want to have multiple partitions for various reasons, you can also do so at this time. To add a partition, press <n>, specify p for another primary partition, and then specify the number for this partition (4). To keep from fragmenting different partitions across the drive, start the last partition where the other left off, at cylinder 171. For the last cylinder, because you want to use the rest of the space for the Linux system, you can specify the last cylinder instead of an exact byte count. Thus, enter **1023**, as shown here:

```
Command (m for help):n
Command action
e    extended
p    primary partition (1-4)
p
Partition number (1-4): 4
First cylinder (171-1024):171
Last cylinder or +size or +sizeM or +sizeK (171-1023):1023
```

Now use the p command to verify the new partitions. If you need to make any changes, do so now.

When you're satisfied with the layout of your partitions, you can use the w command to write the partition table information to the hard disk. None of your changes are permanent until you use the w command; thus, if you feel you've made some changes in error, you can use the q command to exit without altering the partition table. If you use the w command, Linux tells you the partition table has been altered and then resynchronizes the disks to match the new partition table. If your Linux system hangs at this point, reboot with the installation boot and root disks until you're back at the # prompt.

CAUTION

Don't use the Linux fdisk program to create or modify partitions for other operating systems. This could leave the hard drive in a useless state for both operating systems.

Creating the Swap Partition

Some distributions of Linux provide automatic creation and activation of the swap file during installation, so you don't have to worry about creating the swap file. However, if you're using a different distribution, you may need to create and activate the swap file before continuing with the installation.

NOTE If you get an "out-of-memory" type error during the installation procedures that follow, you should increase the size of your swap file. If you already have the maximum of 16M, you need to create and activate another swap partition by following these instructions. Remember, the Red Hat installation program creates only one swap partition.

To create the swap space, use the `mkswap` command and tell it which partition to use and how much size to use for virtual RAM. For example, to create a swap space on the /dev/hda3 partition that you previously defined, enter the following command at the # prompt:

```
# mkswap -c /dev/hda3 16447
```

The 16447 represents 16M and can be found in the blocks column of the `fdisk p` command output screen. The optional -c flag tells `mkswap` to check for bad sections on the partition.

Next, you need to activate the swap system with the `swapon` command:

```
# swapon /dev/hda3
```

Again, if you're using the accompanying Red Hat CD-ROM, you shouldn't have to worry about activating the swap system as long as you create the partition for one. During installation, the install program detects the swap partition and automatically starts the system for installation.

After creating your partitions on the various hard drives and returning to the Partitioning Disks dialog box, choose the Done button to continue with the installation.

Next, the system asks you to select the active swap space, which should be the partition you created and marked as type Linux Swap (82) in the preceding section. Select this partition and choose OK. The program then initializes the swap space.

After creating the swap space, the program displays the Select Root Partition dialog box. The root partition is your main file system for Linux where all the boot files are located. Select the device (hardrive) for your root partition from the list box and press <Return>. Now you can mount the other partitions, if any, from the Partition Disk dialog box. From here, you also can mount any DOS or OS/2 file systems so that you can access them from Linux. Select the partition to edit from the list box and press <Return>. From the Edit Mount Point dialog box, you can specify a mount point—that is, a directory—to which you want this partition mounted.

▶ **See** "Mounting and Unmounting File Systems," **p. 265**

After selecting the root and mount points for your various partitions, the program formats those you select. You select the partitions to format from the Format Partition dialog box.

Installing the Software Components

Congratulations! Your system is now prepped for Linux, but you're only halfway finished. Now you must select the various software components to install and then configure them.

The installation program displays the Components to Install dialog box, which allows you to select the various packages. Table 3.6 describes each package.

Table 3.6   The Installation Components

Component	Description
C Development	Provides the GNU gcc compiler and tools
Development Libraries	Provides various libraries needed by the various development tools, such as gcc and g++
C++ Development	Installs the GNU C++ compiler, gcc
Print Server	Allows your Linux box to act as a print server on your network
News Server	Allows your system to act as a news server (if you can get a news feed), thus providing news to your users
NFS Server	Allows your system to export and attach to other file systems on your network
Networked Workstation	Provides networking applications
Anonymous FTP/Gopher Server	Allows you to set up your system so that others may access it via anonymous FTP
Web Server	Includes the most used Web server software today, Apache
Network Management Workstation	Provides utilities and tools to help troubleshoot and monitor your network
Dialup Workstation	Allow you access to the Internet via dial-up lines—that is, via a modem
Game Machine	Provides your system with a variety of text and graphic games, including DOOM
Multimedia Machine	Allows you to play CDs and do other multimedia type actions from your computer
X Windows System	Provides the GUI for all UNIX—hence, Linux—workstations; X is a powerful GUI like Windows 95 and OS/2
X Development	Provides the tools, libraries, and miscellaneous items (such as fonts) needed to develop X applications
X Multimedia Support	Provides multimedia support for X
TeX Document Formatting	Provides a series of programs used to add formatting codes to documents
Emacs	Installs the ubiquitous editor for Linux (you can do anything with emacs, or so the emacs gurus say)
Emacs with X Windows	Provides an X front end to the powerful emacs editor

Component	Description
DOS/Windows Connectivity	Allows you to access DOS files, run DOS programs, and, with limited success, run some Windows programs
Extra Documentation	Provides the Linux documentation project containing the important HOWTOs, along with other helpful information
Everything	Installs everything on the CD-ROM; you need about 350M available, not counting free space for your data files

NOTE You can select individual packages by checking the appropriate check box in the dialog box, or you can install everything by selecting that list option. To select a package to install, simply move to the desired component and press the space bar. After you select all your components, tab to the OK button and press <Return>. ■

The next dialog box after installation informs you that you can see the files installed by viewing the file /tmp/install.log. Press <Return> to continue with the installation.

Now comes the hard part—waiting. Transferring and decompressing upward of 350M of programs can take a while. Setup firsts installs a file system on your indicated partitions and then starts installing software. The system informs you of its progress as it installs the various files you selected in the Install Status dialog box. Installation time varies depending on what you're installing and how fast your machine can process the information. Relax and order a pizza!

Configuring Your System

After installing the software, the installation program begins to configure your system. It first configures your mouse by displaying the Configure Mouse dialog box. Simply select the mouse type from the list box that best describes your mouse. Remember, many mice can emulate the Microsoft serial mouse if they have to. The Emulate 3 Buttons check box is there because many PC mice have only two buttons, and X Windows usually uses three buttons to maneuver and make program selections. By checking this box, the system will make clicking both mouse buttons at the same time the same as pressing the middle button on a three-button mouse. Make your selection and choose OK.

Next, you must specify the serial port that your mouse connects to. After making the selection from the list box, tab to the OK button and press <Return>. The program then asks you to select the type of video card in your system.

CAUTION

Try to select the correct video card, because of all things software-based, the only subsystem that software can easily destroy is your video card and monitor. If you make the wrong decision, you might fry your monitor! Although this is highly unlikely, there's still the slight possibility, so choose wisely, young Linux walker.

The system now tries to install the proper XFree86 server for your hardware.

▶ **See** "Installing the XFree86 System," **p. 163**

Next, you must select your monitor. Again, be as specific as possible. After selecting your monitor, the program asks for the amount of video memory your card contains. Make the appropriate selection and choose OK to continue.

Remember all those warnings about frying your monitor? Well, now you really have a chance to toast it, so be careful. The next screen asks you to select the clockchips located on your video card. These chips are used to drive the video signals through your card and into your monitor. If they're way out of synchronization, the signals can—you guessed it—fry your monitor (few actually explode, most just fizzle and smoke). Please be careful! If you have no clue as to what clockchips your card is using, take the default selection, No Clockchip Setting, and choose OK.

After selecting your clockchips (or lack thereof), the system can autoprobe and try to configure X. The autoprobe may hang your system, but as long as nothing is seriously wrong (for example, you selected outrageous clock speeds for your card), you can simply reboot and continue with the installation. You do have the option to skip the autoprobe and continue with the installation.

N O T E   I have installed Red Hat many times and have yet to have the installation software properly configure my X system. You may have better luck than me, so don't worry if your X installation fails. I've always been able to configure X with the Xconfig program described in Chapter 6, "Installing the X Windows System." Although the discussion centers on installing under Slackware, installing XFree86 is the same under most Linux distributions, including Red Hat.

▶ **See** "Configuring XFree86," **p. 167** ∎

If the autoprobe succeeds, the system displays an information screen on selecting the resolutions you want to use with your system. You can select more than one, as long as your video card and monitor can handle the resolutions. Finally, the program tells you on how to start and stop your X Windows system.

Configuring Your Network

After configuring X Windows, the installation program continues with your network. If your machine is or will be connected to the Internet and you installed the networking components, choose Yes and continue.

First, the system asks which Ethernet driver to use with the Load Module dialog box. Select the appropriate driver for your Ethernet card and choose OK.

Again, the installation program might try to autoprobe your hardware to determined certain values for the card. This probing can hang the system and force you to reboot. If this happens, hang in there. First make sure that you selected the correct driver. Then see whether you need to pass any special parameters to the device, such as IRQ or DMA address settings. You can do this by selecting the Specify Parameter option instead of the autoprobe option.

NOTE Ethernet is the most popular network interface for Linux today. Other technologies, such as Token Ring, ISDN, and ATM, have some support, but they're not ready for prime time yet under Linux. Many are still in alpha or beta stage and are dependent on vendor-specific hardware. ▥

If the system can detect your network card, it leads you through setting up your TCP/IP network.

Configuring the TCP/IP Network

The installation software uses the Configure TCP/IP dialog box to gather your system's TCP/IP information. Your network administrator or Internet service provider can provide the following information: your machine's IP number, netmask, network address, and broadcast address.

Next, the system must configure your network. It gathers information from the Configure Network dialog box. You must specify your network's domain name and your system's host name. The domain name is typically the last two parts of an Internet address. For example, if the name is www.netwharf.com, then netwharf.com is the domain name and www is the host name.

Next, your network administrator must give you the values for your system's default gateway and the primary name server. Your network may also have a secondary name server, too, so enter the value in the appropriate place.

NOTE Be careful what you name your host, because this name will appear on your default prompt line, in mail messages, and in log reports. Do you really want your boss to receive mail from uradork.netwharf.com? ▥

Configuring the Time

Next, you have to specify how your system will keep time and in what time zone it exists. This is done with the Configure Timezones dialog box. Check whether you want to use local time or GMT time, and then pick your time zone from the list box. After making your selections, choose OK.

Selecting Your Keyboard Settings

After configuring how your system tracks time, the installation program asks what type of keyboard you're using. Use the Configure Keyboard dialog box to select which country code you want to use and choose OK.

Selecting Your Root Password

Now you must select your root password. This is the ultimate key into your system, so some care should be given. The superuser, or root, on a Linux/UNIX system can do great things, and can also wreak awesome damage. Pick a secure password and be careful who you give it to. The Root Password dialog box lets you enter the password twice to confirm what you've typed. Although you can fix user accounts when they forget their password, if you forget the root password, you may be forced to reinstall the system. However, booting from a floppy and editing the password file may allow a recovery.

▶ **See** "Dealing with Password Security," **p. 239**

Installing LILO

LILO stands for LInux LOader. LILO is a program executed at system startup that lets you choose which operating system is used to boot the computer. You can use LILO to boot several different operating systems, such as Linux and MS-DOS. Press <Tab> to get a list of operating systems LILO can boot.

With LILO, you can specify a default operating system to boot and a default time limit before it boots that system. For example, if you had MS-DOS and Linux on your computer, you can configure LILO to boot either one. You could then tell LILO to boot MS-DOS if no one intervenes after 30 seconds. Before that 30 seconds is up, however, a user can specify another operating system to boot instead of the default. You can press the <Ctrl>, <Alt>, or <Shift> key to stop the timed process.

You specify all this information while configuring LILO. You can later directly edit the lilo.conf file located in the /etc directory. If you don't want to boot Linux automatically, you can select the Skip button to continue. Otherwise, select a hard drive to install LILO and press <Return> to edit the entry.

Congratulations! After you load LILO, your system is up and running—and, let's hope, problem-free.

Building a New Kernel

Sometimes a problem has only one solution—a new kernel. The kernel is the core operating system for Linux. Although not for the faint of heart, downloading a new kernel from the Net and build the kernel is sometimes necessary. If you have some programming experience and know your way around the C programming language, you should be able to build and install a new kernel. If not, you can skip this section.

You may have to install a new kernel for a few reasons:

- A new patch is provided to run new hardware.
- You want to remove features from the kernel you don't use, thus lowering the memory requirements for your system.

The starting point is to determine what kernel version you're now running. You can find out the kernel version with the following command:

```
uname -a
```

The response indicates which version of the kernel is now running and when it was created. The version numbers are in the form of

MajorVersionNumber.MinorVersionNumber.PatchLevel

Linus Torvalds is the official release point for new kernels, although anyone can modify Linux (due to the GPL). Linus as the official release point gives the Linux development and user community a common baseline from which to work and communicate.

N O T E Be sure to read the Kernel HOWTO for up-to-date information before actually trying to build and configure a new kernel. ■

To build a new kernel, you need to have the source files in the /usr/src/Linux directory. You also need to have the C compiler package loaded, which is disk set d. If you didn't install that package during installation, use RPM to do so now.

First, you must get the new kernel sources or patches. The new sources are usually found on the Internet; check **sunsite.unc.edu** for the latest and greatest kernels. (If you're modifying your current kernel, this step is, of course, unnecessary.) The source files are usually in a tar file and will need to be unarchived.

 T I P Making a backup copy of your current kernel with the following commands is a very good idea:

```
cd /usr/src
cp Linux linux.sav
```

These commands copy the entire Linux source directory to another directory called linux.sav.

Next, you should use the `patch` command to apply any patch files. After preparing the source files, you can configure and build your new system. Start by entering the following command from the /usr/src directory:

 # make config

The `make` command asks you various questions about the drivers you want to install or configure. Pressing <Return> accepts the default value for each question; otherwise, you must supply the answer. Some of the questions are shown in Table 3.7. You may have to answer other questions depending on the version of the kernel you're installing or the patches you've applied.

Table 3.7 Some Configuration Options

Configuration Option	Description
Kernel Math Emulation	Asks if the kernel should emulate a math coprocessor.
Normal Harddisk Support	Enables drivers for all standard hard drives.

continues

Part
I

Ch
3

Table 3.7   Continued

Configuration Option	Description
XT Harddisk Support	Applies only if your machine uses an XT class controller instead of an AT class controller.
Networking Support	If you answer yes, enables networking support within the kernel.
SCSI Support	Enables support for SCSI controllers.
CD_ROM Drivers	Asks a series of questions dealing with CD-ROMs, especially those not supported within the standard SCSI Support package.
Filesystems	Asks a series of questions dealing with file systems the kernel should support. If your kernel doesn't have support for the ISO9660 file system, you won't be able to use a CD-ROM.
Parallel Printer Support	Enables printer support via the parallel port.
Mouse Support	Enables support for bus mice from within the kernel.
Sound Card Support	Asks a series of questions about the hardware and software configuration of a sound card.

After you answer the various questions to configure your new kernel, you must compile it. The following commands will build the new kernel:

```
make dep
make clean
make
```

The build process can take anywhere from 15 minutes to many hours. So relax and order another pizza!

When the compilation is completed, you can create a new boot disk as discussed earlier in this chapter. You can copy this kernel to a new floppy disk, or use LILO to boot the new kernel.

Installing Red Hat Linux on DEC Alphas

Unlike other distributions, Red Hat also provides Linux for DEC Alphas. This distribution isn't included on the accompanying Red Hat CD-ROM, but it's available from Red Hat. For more information on getting this distribution, see Red Hat's Web site at **http://www.redhat.com/ products/rhl-alpha.html**. When you have the correct distribution, you can use the following instructions to install Red Hat Linux on an Alpha.

NOTE Red Hat also has a distribution for Sun's line of Sun Sparc processors. See Red Hat's Web site for more information. ▓

Before installing the distribution on an Alpha, you should read the installation instructions in the first part of this chapter, because many of the steps are the same. You'll also need access to a computer capable of reading and writing MS-DOS disks, because you must create an installation floppy.

Using Supported Alpha Hardware

Red Hat supports various Alpha hardware from both Digital Equipment Corporation (DEC) and other vendors. The following hardware is supported:

- AlphaPC64 (Cabriolet, Aspen Telluride)
- AxpPCI133 (Noname)
- EB64+ (Aspen Alpine)
- EB66 (NekoTek Mach 1)
- EB66+
- Jensen (DEC PC 150, 2000 model 300, Cullean)
- Universal Desktop Box (UDB, aka Multia)
- AlphaStation 200, 250,255,400 (Avanti machines)
- EB164 (Aspen Avalanche, Timerline, Summit)
- Kinetic's Platform 2000 machines
- PC164 (Durango)
- Alcor AlphaStations 500, 600 (Maverick, Brett)
- Alpha-XL
- Alpha-XLT (XL 300, XL 366)
- Mikasa AlphaServer 1000—the 1000A is NOT supported

All of these systems have SCSI systems supported by Red Hat Linux. The video systems should work too, although S3 support for the Jensen systems isn't included by default. To run X with a Jensen system, you need to download the X server from **ftp://ftp.azstarnet.com/pub/linux/axp/jensen**. Finally, all Ethernet solutions for these systems are supported, and the kernels for these machines also support Token-Ring adapters.

The hardware list changes frequently, so you should check the up-to-date list on Red Hat's Web site at http://www.redhat.com.

Creating the Boot and Root Disks

You need to create a boot and root floppy for an Alpha installation. The boot disk contains a program image allowing you to boot the system. The root floppy provides an image of the

Part I
Ch 3

Linux kernel for the system to use during installation. Just as for Intel machines, you use the `rawrite` program to create these disk images.

The boot disk image depends on the type of Alpha used. These images are located in the /images directory with a README file that provides more information on each image described in Table 3.8.

Table 3.8   Boot Images Available for DEC Alphas

Image	Description
cab.img	AlphaPC64, Cabriolet
noname.img	AxpPCI33, Noname, Universal Desktop Box (Multias)
eb64p.img	EB64+, Aspen Timberlines
eb66.img	EB66
eb66p.img	EB66+
jensen.img	Jensens
avanti.img	AlphaStation 200, 250, and 400
xl.img	Alpha XL
xlt.img	Alpha XLT
eb164.img	EB164-based machines
p2000.img	Platform 2000
alcor.img	Alcor-based machines
mikasa.img	Mikasa-based machines

To create a boot image for a Universal Desktop Box, you use the command

```
E:\dosutils\rawrite -f E:\images\noname.img -d a: -n
```

where E: represents the drive letter of your CD-ROM. After creating the boot disk, you must create the root disk, which contains the RAM disk image of the Linux kernel. You create the root disk with the following command:

```
E:\dosutils\rawrite -f E:\images\ramdisk.img -d a: -n
```

Installing the Main Red Hat Distribution

After you have your boot media ready, you can install Linux. The installation procedure is very much like the one outlined earlier in the section "Installing the Linux System." The installation program guides you through the process, asking you to make selections from a list of possible choices.

To begin, place your boot disk into the floppy drive and restart your system. At the prompt, enter the following command:

```
boot fd0:vmlinux.gz root=/dev/fd0 load_ramdisk=1
```

You may see several SCSI messages flash by on-screen. Don't worry about them unless you see a message such as `scsi0 : 1`, which indicates that you have a SCSI termination problem that needs to be fixed before continuing with the installation. If all goes well, you should see the message `VFS: Insert Root floppy to be loaded into ramdisk`. Insert the root disk you created and press <Return> to continue the installation process.

Going Back to the Beginning

After you complete the setup and configuration of your system, you should reboot the system so that all of your setup and configurations can take effect.

Rebooting Linux is more involved than rebooting DOS—you can't just turn off the power and turn the system back on. If you do so in Linux, you can damage the file structures and systems. Linux tries to repair itself on boot-up. Don't turn off the power while running Linux.

▶ **See** "Performing Backups and Restoring Files," **p. 230**

To exit Linux, use the following command:

```
shutdown [-r] time
```

The optional -r indicates that the system should reboot after shutting down, and *time* indicates the time that the system should shut down. You can use now in place of *time* to indicate immediate shutdown. Linux also recognizes the warm boot keys used by DOS to reboot the machine, <Ctrl-Alt-Delete>, which Linux interprets as the command

```
shutdown -r now
```

Make sure that you've removed the root disk from the drive and reboot your new Linux machine.

Troubleshooting Problems

After your machine reboots, the LILO prompt should appear. Make sure that you can boot to your old operating system if you left it on the hard drive. If that system was DOS, press <Shift> and then type the short word you used to identify the DOS partition when you installed LILO. If you enter an invalid word, press <Tab> to get a list of valid operating system types. If you're having problems at this point, place your DOS boot disk in the boot drive and reboot.

You should be able to boot from your boot disk. When your system is up and running under DOS, try the Linux boot disk you created during installation—not the ones you created to originally install the entire system. If that boot disk doesn't work, you may have to reinstall

Part
I
Ch
3

Linux. Potential problems to check initially are the kernels and your hardware. Before starting over, make sure that you have the appropriate hardware. If you made notes during the installation process, check which kernel you installed against what hardware you have. If you have a SCSI CD-ROM controller, did you install the idekern instead of the scsikern? But do make sure that you have hardware supported by Linux.

From Here...

When you have your system up and running, you can read the following chapters for further information about Linux:

- Chapter 5, "Running Linux Applications," gets you up to speed on the various programs you just installed.

- Chapter 6, "Installing the X Windows System," provides you with information on installing X if something went amiss during your Red Hat installation. Although designed for the Slackware distribution, the XFree86 software is the same for any Linux distribution version.

- Chapter 7, "Using X Windows," is interesting if you've installed the X system.

- Chapter 13, "Upgrading and Installing Software," provides instructions on how to reinstall packages you may have left out during the initial setup of your Linux system.

- Chapter 26, "Understanding the Internet," briefs you on the basics about how to get to the Internet.

## CHAPTER 4

Installing Slackware 96

This chapter gives you the information needed to install the Slackware 96 distribution of Linux. Remember, because Linux isn't a commercial product, you might find some problems. Although this book leads the way, you may find the need to use the resources provided on the CD-ROM. First, you must determine whether you have the appropriate hardware. After you determine that you have the necessary hardware, you must prepare for the installation. Following the steps provided in this chapter should ensure a smooth installation.

This book assumes that you have a working knowledge of DOS and of such items as formatting your hard drive, partition tables, and sector sizes. If this information sounds like a foreign language, check out Que's *Using MS-DOS 6.2*, Special Edition, or ask a computer guru buddy to help you through this. ■

How to prepare your system for the installation

Installing Linux requires some preparation, such as formatting your hard drive. You also must plan the layout of your disk space for Linux's optimum performance.

How to partition your hard drive to make room for Linux

Linux requires certain partitions to work effectively, especially if swap space is required. You must also decide whether other operating systems will coexist with Linux and prepare for their installation.

How to install the typical Slackware distribution

After preparing the system for installation, you must create installation disks, select your installation media (the accompanying Slackware CD-ROM), and begin installation.

What to do if things go wrong

Because Slackware, unlike Red Hat and Caldera, has no formal technical support, you need to know what to do if the installation goes wrong. Remember, unsupported hardware is the most typical reason for installation failure.

> **CAUTION**
> You're about to make major changes to your system, so be careful.

Understanding What You Need to Install Linux

First, you need a distribution of Slackware 96, which is supplied on the accompanying CD-ROM. To start the installation process, you need two formatted high-density floppy disks—either 3 1/2-inch disks or 5 1/4-inch disks.

You should also decide how you intend to boot Linux. You have two choices:

- You can boot Linux from a floppy disk, in which case you need an extra formatted disk—for a total of three disks.

- You can use a program called LILO, the LInux LOader. LILO allows you to specify which operating system to boot. Such programs as OS/2 and Windows NT provide similar functionality. (LILO is discussed later in this chapter.)

Next, you should make sure that you have enough disk space to install Linux. Most people can get by with 200M devoted to Linux—less if you plan not to use such applications as TeX and X Windows.

Having paper and pen nearby is a good idea, so you can take notes just in case something goes wrong; besides, you'll need to jot down some numbers along the way. For configuring XFree86, the X Windows program distributed with Linux, you should write down what type of chipset your video card uses. If you have a serial mouse and modem, write down the serial port that each is using. You need this information later during the configuration process.

Making the Preparations

If you have a brand-new system, or if you have an existing system but don't care what happens to the data already stored on the computer, you can skip most of the following sections and go directly to "Creating the Boot and Root Disks." If, however, you already have a system you're using and simply want to add Linux, you must do some planning because Linux is another operating system, not just a collection of programs.

In general, when you install Linux—a new operating system—you must do the following:

- *Create the Linux boot disks.* The boot disks consist of two floppies that you must create, because you need to bootstrap Linux onto the new system. (The term *bootstrap* comes from the old saying, "Pull yourself up by your bootstraps.")

- *Repartition the hard drive to make room for Linux.* Repartitioning a hard drive may cause problems because it destroys any data contained on the affected partitions.

- *Boot up Linux.* After making room for Linux, you need to boot the Linux system to gain access to the tools required to create its new partitions and file systems.

- *Create the Linux partitions.* Typically, Linux systems need a primary partition to store the files on and a swap file partition, especially if you have a machine with 8M or less of memory.

- *Create the file systems.* A *file system* is basically a section of your hard drive specially formatted to hold files. UNIX and Linux use file systems to represent entire sections of the directory tree. This is in contrast to MS-DOS, which places subdirectories in the directory tree on the same logical drive. UNIX systems use the file-system structure because placing subdirectories on different drives is safer. If one drive malfunctions, only the information on that drive needs to be replaced or fixed.

- *Install the Linux system and software applications.* After creating the file systems, you install the Linux operating system, its support files, and various application packages distributed with the system, such as the games and networking support packages.

Preparing Floppies and Backups for Installation

You must make a system disk for your PC. To install Linux, you need to repartition your hard drive to make room for the new operating system. Unfortunately, you just can't simply copy the files over to an MS-DOS, OS/2, or Windows NT file system.

Part I Ch 4

Creating an MS-DOS Boot Disk

When you repartition your hard drive, you should prepare for the worst—the trashing of your hard drive. If your drive crashes, you may not be able to boot up. Thus, you should create a boot floppy with the necessary boot files.

For MS-DOS, place a floppy into the disk drive and type **format a: /s** to create an MS-DOS boot floppy. Copy your current CONFIG.SYS, AUTOEXEC.BAT, and any driver files needed to start your computer. Also, copy FDISK.EXE and FORMAT.COM onto the floppy, because you'll be repartitioning your hard drive and will then need to reformat the hard disk. Keep this MS-DOS boot disk in a safe place.

N O T E If you're backing up your system (two backups are a good idea), also include the necessary file to restore your backup. ▦

You might want to record the various CMOS settings for your system. Most Intel-compatible computer systems allow you to access the setup information from the CMOS at startup.

N O T E If you're using OS/2, you need to see the OS/2 documentation on how to create an OS/2 boot disk. ▦

Backing Up Your System

Unless you're using a brand-new computer or a computer with a brand-new hard drive containing no software, take the time to make a backup; two backups is the wisest course of action. If you have a tape drive, use the program sold with your tape drive to back up the entire hard drive. If you don't have a tape drive, you can use the MS-DOS backup/restore programs to make a backup of your system. Make sure that you have plenty of floppy disks and use the following command syntax:

```
backup from to
```

For example, if you're going to back up all the files *from* the C drive *to* the A drive, enter **backup c: a:** and start swapping floppies. Of course, with the cost of large hard drives dropping, as well as the cost of tape backup units, you should consider doing a tape backup instead of backing up to floppies.

Creating the Boot and Root Disks

After you make your DOS boot disk and back up your system, you must create the boot disks for Linux. Two floppies are needed with Slackware: the boot and root floppies. You create these floppies with a set of MS-DOS programs provided with most Linux distributions—gzip and rawrite.

N O T E The boot images are decompressed on most major Linux CD-ROMs, including the Slackware CD-ROM that comes with this book. Also, the root images have new names compared with earlier versions of Slackware and are now compressed and *must remain compressed*; otherwise, you'll get a kernel panic because you shouldn't have decompressed the root image files. ■

gzip is a GNU program very much like PKWare's pkzip. gzip allows you to compress and decompress archived files. You need this program because many of the Linux files—especially those needed for installation—are compressed by using gzip.

rawrite is a program used to write the contents of a file directly to a floppy without regard to the format. After you unzip the boot images with gzip, you must use rawrite to transfer the images to the appropriate floppies.

Fortunately, most of the common boot and root disks can be found on the Slackware CD-ROM in decompressed format. All you have to do is use rawrite to transfer the files to floppy.

N O T E If you're having trouble creating your boot and root disks or getting Linux to boot, read the readme.txt and which.one files in the appropriate boot disk directory (/bootdsks.12 or /bootdsks.144) found on the Slackware CD-ROM. ■

You use the boot disk to start the Linux system for installation. It contains bare-bones device drivers and a basic version of the operating system. This boot disk is specific to the hardware and type of floppy drive your system uses to boot (usually the A drive under MS-DOS). Table 4.1 shows the various files. (These files may have been updated before the printing of this book. See the readme file in the /bootdsks.12 or /bootdsks.144 directory for details.) If the files are already decompressed (if they don't have the .gz extension), you don't have to use gzip to prepare that file.

For Slackware 96, also known as Slackware Linux 3.1.0, the Linux 2.0.0 series of kernels is used. All you have to do to create your boot disk is first select your kernel based on Table 4.1 for IDE drives or Table 4.2 for SCSI drives. Then issue the following command from the DOS prompt:

```
rawrite bares.i a:
```

Table 4.1   The IDE Boot Files

Name	Descriptions
aztech.i	CD-ROM drives: Aztech CDA268-01A, Orchid CD 3110, Okano/ Wearnes CDD110, Conrad TXC, CyCDROM CR520, CR540
bare.i	None, just IDE support
cdu31a.i	Sony CDU31/33a CD-ROM
cdu535.i	Sony CDU531/535 CD-ROM
cm206.i	Philips/LMS cm206 CD-ROM with cm260 adapter card
goldstar.i	Goldstar R420 CD-ROM (sometimes sold in a Reveal Multimedia Kit)
mcd.i	NON-IDE Mitsumi CD-ROM support
mcdx.i	Improved NON-IDE Mitsumi CD-ROM support
net.i	Ethernet support
optics.i	Optics Storage 8000 AT CD-ROM (the "DOLPHIN" drive)
sanyo.i	Sanyo CDR-H94A CD-ROM support
sbpcd.i	Matsushita, Kotobuki, Panasonic, CreativeLabs (SoundBlaster), Longshine, and Teac non-IDE CD-ROM support
xt.i	MFM hard drive support

Table 4.2   The SCSI Boot Files

Name	Descriptions
7000fast.s	Western Digital 7000FASST SCSI support
advansys.s	AdvanSys SCSI support
aha152x.s	Adaptec 152x SCSI support
aha1542.s	Adaptec 1542 SCSI support
aha1740.s	Adaptec 1740 SCSI support

continues

Table 4.2 Continued

Name	Descriptions
aha2x4x.s	Adaptec AIC7xxx SCSI support for these cards: AHA-274x, AHA-2842, AHA-2940, AHA-2940W, AHA-2940U, AHA-2940UW, AHA-2944D, AHA-2944WD, AHA-3940, AHA-3940W, AHA-3985, AHA-3985W
am53c974.s	AMD AM53/79C974 SCSI support
aztech.s	All supported SCSI controllers, plus CD-ROM support for Aztech CDA268-01A, Orchid CD-3110, Okano/Wearnes CDD110, Conrad TXC, CyCDROM CR520, CR540
buslogic.s	Buslogic MultiMaster SCSI support
cdu31a.s	All supported SCSI controllers, plus CD-ROM support for Sony CDU31/33a
cdu535.s	All supported SCSI controllers, plus CD-ROM support for Sony CDU531/535
cm206.s	All supported SCSI controllers, plus Philips/LMS cm206 CD-ROM with cm260 adapter card
dtc3280.s	DTC (Data Technology Corp) 3180/3280 SCSI support
eata_dma.s	DPT EATA-DMA SCSI support (boards such as PM2011, PM2021, PM2041, PM3021, PM2012B, PM2022, PM2122, PM2322, PM2042, PM3122, PM3222, PM3332, PM2024, PM2124, PM2044, PM2144, PM3224, PM3334)
eata_isa.s	DPT EATA-ISA/EISA SCSI support (boards such as PM2011B/9X, PM2021A/9X, PM2012A, PM2012B, PM2022A/9X, PM2122A/9X, PM2322A/9X)
eata_pio.s	DPT EATA-PIO SCSI support (PM2001 and PM2012A)
fdomain.s	Future Domain TMC-16x0 SCSI support
goldstar.s	All supported SCSI controllers, plus Goldstar R420 CD-ROM (sometimes sold in a Reveal Multimedia Kit)
in2000.s	Always IN2000 SCSI support
iomega.s	IOMEGA PPA3 parallel port SCSI support; also supports the parallel port version of the ZIP drive
mcd.s	All supported SCSI controllers, plus standard non-IDE Mitsumi CD-ROM support
mcdx.s	All supported SCSI controllers, plus enhanced non-IDE Mitsumi CD-ROM support
n53c406a.s	NCR 53c406a SCSI support
n_5380.s	NCR 5380 and 53c400 SCSI support

Name	Descriptions
N_53c7xx.s	NCR 53c7xx, 53c8xx SCSI support (most NCR PCI SCSI controllers use this driver)
optics.s	All supported SCSI controllers, plus support for the Optics Storage 8000 AT CD-ROM (the "DOLPHIN" drive)
pas16.s	Pro Audio Spectrum/Studio 16 SCSI support
qlog_fas.s	ISA/VLB/PCMCIA Qlogic FastSCSI! support (also supports the Control Concepts SCSI cards based on the Qlogic FASXXX chip)
qlog_isp.s	Supports all Qlogic PCI SCSI controllers, except the PCI-basic, which is supported by the AMD SCSI driver
sanyo.s	All supported SCSI controllers, plus Sanyo CDR-H94A CD-ROM support
sbpcd.s	All supported SCSI controllers, plus Matsushita, Kotobuki, Panasonic, CreativeLabs (SoundBlaster), Longshine, and Teac non-IDE CD-ROM support
scsi.s	A generic SCSI boot disk, with support for most SCSI controllers that work under Linux
scsinet.s	All supported SCSI controllers, plus full Ethernet support
seagate.s	Seagate ST01/ST02, Future Domain TMC 885/950 SCSI support
trantor.s	Trantor T128/T128F/T228 SCSI support
ultrastr.s	UltraStor 14F, 24F, and 34F SCSI support
ustor14f.s	UltraStor 14F and 34F SCSI support

Part
I

Ch
4

These boot files come in two flavors, depending on the size of your boot floppy. Luckily, the decompressed files are already available for you on the Slackware CD-ROM. If your A drive is a 1.2M (high-density) 5 1/4-inch drive, look in the /bootdsks.12 directory; if you have a 1.44M (high-density) 3 1/2-inch high-density drive, look in the /bootdsks.144 directory. If you use another distribution version, you need to copy the compressed files to a directory on your hard drive and use the `gzip` program to unzip them. Table 4.3 illustrates the commands for the `gzip` program, which uses the syntax

```
gzip [-acdfhlLnNtvV19] [-S suffix] [file ...]
```

Table 4.3 Flags for the *gzip* Command

Flag	Flag Name	Description
-a	ascii	ASCII text; converts end-of-line characters by using local conventions
-c	stdout	Writes on standard output, keeps original files unchanged

continues

Table 4.3 Continued

Flag	Flag Name	Description
-d	decompress	Decompresses
-f	force	Forces overwrite of output file and compresses links
-h	help	Gives a help listing
-l	list	Lists compressed file contents
-L	license	Displays software license
-n	no-name	Doesn't save or restore the original name and time stamp
-N	name	Saves or restores the original name and time stamp
-q	quiet	Suppresses all warnings
-S *suffix*	suffix *.suf*	Uses suffix *.suf* on compressed files
-t	test	Tests compressed file integrity
-v	verbose	Changes to verbose mode
-V	version	Displays the version number
-1	fast	Compresses faster
-9	best	Compresses better—that is, the file is smaller
file		Specifies file(s) to (de)compress; if none given, uses standard input

To create the images for a SoundBlaster installation, you unzip the sbpcd.gz file with the following command:

```
gzip -d sbpcd.gz
```

The result is a file called sbpcd, without the .gz extension. As stated earlier, the accompanying CD-ROM already contains the decompressed files in the appropriate boot directory.

Making the Root Disks   The Linux "root disk" contains the actual installation software. You use a boot disk to load it into your system and begin the installation. You'll probably want to use either the color or the UMSDOS disk image to install Linux, depending on whether you'll be installing it in its own partition. You need one of the image files listed in Table 4.4 for your system.

Table 4.4 Slackware 96 Root Images

File	Description
color.gz	The disk you'll want to use to install Linux onto its own partition.

File	Description
umsdos.gz	The disk used to install Linux into an existing MS-DOS partition (for example, into a C:\LINUX directory).
text.gz	A text-based disk that installs Linux into its own partition. This disk's text interface might be a little harder to use than the color disk, but better diagnostics are printed, and you can scroll back to look at messages with <Shift-Page Up>.
pcmcia.gz	A text-based root disk used to install Linux via PCMCIA Ethernet.
rescue.gz	A disk with an editor (vi), LILO, e2fsck, and other utilities useful for repairing a misconfigured Linux system. If you ever get locked out of your system for some reason, you can use this disk to mount your Linux partitions and fix the problems.

Creating the Disks with *rawrite* After you decompress the kernel image file, you can transfer the file to floppies. To do this, you need the rawrite program. You can find this program on the accompanying Slackware CD-ROM in the /install subdirectory.

For this step, you need the two floppies you formatted earlier. You must make sure that you write the current images to the floppy disks. Thus, you must write the images made for 1.44M disks to 1.44M disks. If you write the images from the 1.2M directories to a 1.44M disks, you won't be able to install Linux.

Label one disk the boot disk and place it in the disk drive. The following sequence assumes a 1.44M, 3 1/2-inch floppy disk drive, sbpcd.i(boot), and color144(root) installation disks (these commands create the boot and root disks):

```
E:\LINUX>RAWRITE sbpcd.i
Number of sectors per track for this disk is 18
Writing image to drive A:,  Press ^C to abort.
Track: 01  Head:  1 Sector: 10
```

rawrite displays progress information as the program writes the raw image to the disk, and then the program displays done when finished. If you want to abort the process, simply press <Ctrl-c>. If any errors occur during the operation, the program displays one of the error messages shown in Table 4.5.

Table 4.5   Possible *rawrite* Error Codes

Message	Description
Operation Successful	Not an error message; you want to see this message!
Bad command	Your hardware I/O system didn't understand a command sent by the program. Try a different version of rawrite from another distribution package.
Address mark not found	Try a different disk.

continues

Part

I

Ch

4

Table 4.5   Continued

Message	Description
Attempt to write on the write-protected disk	Remove the write protection from the disk.
Sector not found	Possibly a bad disk; try a different one.
Reset failed (hard disk)	Possible hardware problems; check hardware before continuing.
Disk changed since last operation	Don't remove the disk from the drive until the entire operation is complete.
Drive parameter activity failed	Possible hardware problems.
DMA overrun	Data was lost on transfer from memory to disk; try the operation again. This may indicate hardware or low memory problems.
Attempt to DMA across 64K boundary	Attempt by DMA chip to write beyond a 64K boundary. May indicate hardware or low memory problems.
Bad sector detected	Disk is bad; try a new one.
Bad track detected	Disk is bad; try a new one
Unsupported track	Possibly a bad disk; try a new one.
Bad CRC/ECC on disk read	Bad disk; try a new one.
CRC/ECC corrected data error	Possibly a bad disk or hardware.
Controller has failed	Major hardware problems.
Seek operation failed	Possibly a bad disk or hardware problem.
Attachment failed to respond	Check drive door; make sure that it's closed.
Drive not ready (hard disk only)	Possible major hardware problems.
Undefined error occurred (hard disk only)	Possible hardware problems.
Write fault occurred	Possibly a bad disk or hardware problems.
Status error	Undefined error—could be hardware or disk.
Sense operation failed	Possible bad disk or hardware problem.

If rawrite fails, try a new formatted disk. If the problem persists, you should have your hardware checked for possible problems. After writing the boot disk, you need to write the root disk to your other formatted disk. Simply use the root image file name as the source file name instead of the boot image file name:

```
E:\LINUX>RAWRITE color.gz
Number of sectors per track for this disk is 18
Writing image to drive A:,  Press ^C to abort.
Track: 01  Head:  1 Sector: 10
```

Partitioning Your Hard Drive

After you back up your system and make the necessary disks, you must prepare your system's hard drive for Linux.

> **CAUTION**
>
> This process is the most dangerous because maximum data loss is assured. If you haven't backed up your system, do so now. Although there's an experimental program called FIPS and commercial programs such as Partition Magic that do non-destructive repartitioning, a full backup is recommended (two backups are best), just in case problems occur.

Part

I

Ch

4

Understanding Partitions

In the early days of PCs, hard drives were few and far between. Most computers used floppies to hold the operating system, programs, and their data. With the introduction of the IBM PC XT, IBM introduced a 10M hard drive. Early operating systems such as DOS could access only a limited amount of space on hard drives. Then hard-drive manufacturers kept expanding the space on their hard drives more quickly than the operating system's capability to access the additional space. The operating system got around this problem by letting the user split the hard drive into sections, called *partitions*. These partitions can hold program files, other operating systems, or data.

Typical MS-DOS systems have one partition, which is referred to as drive C. If you split the drive into partitions, these partitions are typically referred to in alphabetical order as D, E, and so on. MS-DOS also allows you to install multiple hard drives, so that the next drive in this chain might be referred to as F.

UNIX and Linux don't use drive letters to refer to partitions; instead, they use directory names to refer to partitions. Also, as indicated earlier, Linux users can place different directories on different partitions and even on different drives. You can also place different operating systems on different partitions.

Partitions are specified in a section of the hard drive referred to as the *boot record* in what's called a *partition table*. This table is used by the various operating systems to determine which operating system to boot and where each OS's files can physically be found on the hard drive. The boot record is used to boot, or start up, the machine's operating system. LILO and other boot managers use this section of the hard drive—typically found on the first sectors of the drive—to control which operating system to start.

The partition table holds information about the locations and sizes of the various partitions on the hard drive. There are three kinds of partitions: primary, extended, and logical. DOS and some other operating systems must boot from primary partitions. Hard drives can contain only four primary partitions. An extended partition doesn't contain data itself; instead, it allows the user to define other, logical partitions on the drive. Thus, to get around the limit of four primary partitions, you can define an extended partition and then define other logical partitions within the extended partition. Some operating systems, such as MS-DOS and versions of OS/2 before version 2.0, require that they be installed in a primary partition, but they can access logical drives in extended partitions. This is important to remember if you're going to have a DOS system and a Linux system reside on the same drive. DOS must go in a primary partition.

Using *FDISK*

Partitions are created, destroyed, and managed by a program usually called FDISK. Each operating system has its own version of FDISK, so be sure to use the correct one. If you're now using MS-DOS or are planning to use MS-DOS, you must first repartition the DOS drive with DOS's FDISK. You later use the Linux version of fdisk to create the Linux partitions. If you're using OS/2, you also need to use OS/2's version of FDISK to prepare the OS/2 partitions.

> **CAUTION**
>
> Don't use the Linux fdisk program to create or modify partitions for other operating systems. This could leave the hard drive in a useless state for both operating systems.

Partition Requirements   First, you should plan out what partitions you need. MS-DOS requires a primary partition; Linux and OS/2 can reside in other partitions. If you're using the OS/2 boot manager, which also works well with Linux, you must prepare for its use also. You must also be aware that if you're shrinking a current MS-DOS partition to make room for Linux, not all of your files can be restored to the new, smaller MS-DOS partition.

You can access MS-DOS partitions from Linux, and move, save, and edit DOS files under Linux. However, you can't execute DOS programs under Linux.

N O T E   Two experimental components of Linux allow you to emulate DOS under Linux and also install Linux under DOS. Both systems are still in the implementation stage and thus are more suited for Linux hackers. You can also find plenty of information on these topics in the Linux world.

▶ **See** "Running DOS Programs Under Linux," **p. 139** ■

Next, you should jot down the number of partitions you need and how much disk space to provide each with.

DOS Requirements   If you want to boot DOS, it must go in a primary partition. A bootable version of DOS doesn't require much space—just enough for the system files, COMMAND.COM, CONFIG.SYS, and any driver files needed to start your system. For instance, I provide a 5M DOS partition on my first drive to boot DOS. As soon as DOS is loaded and running, you can access any of the other extended and logical drives on the system.

Unfortunately, whereas Linux can access DOS files in a DOS partition, DOS can't access Linux files in a Linux partition.

OS/2 Requirements OS/2 versions 2.0 and later don't need a primary partition; these versions can install and boot from an extended partition. Thus, you can install DOS on a primary partition and create an extended partition area for OS/2 and Linux.

The space required for OS/2 is version- and feature-dependent; you should consult your OS/2 documentation for space requirements. You should also subtract 1M from available space if you intend to use the OS/2 boot manager.

Linux Requirements As explained earlier, Linux stores files on file systems, and these file systems can reside on different partitions, basically as safety precautions. Linux requires one partition for each file system. The next consideration is for a swap partition. Linux, like most operating systems that use disk space for memory (called a *virtual memory configuration*), needs a swap file or a swap partition to simulate physical memory using disk space. Linux typically uses a swap partition.

The size of the swap partition depends on the amount of physical RAM your system contains. A rule of thumb is to make your swap partition twice the size of your amount of RAM. Thus, if you have 8M of RAM in your system, you should create a swap partition 16M in size. If you have 4M of RAM or less, you must activate a swap partition.

Linux swap partitions can be only 128M in size, so if you need more space, you have to create multiple swap partitions. For example, if you have a Linux system with 32M of RAM and want one partition for Linux system files and one partition for user files, you would create three partitions: one for the system files, one for user files, and one 32M swap partition.

Repartitioning the Drive

This section assumes that you need to repartition a DOS drive. First, you execute FDISK by typing **fdisk** at the DOS prompt, and you see the FDISK Options screen (see Figure 4.1).

FIG. 4.1
From the FDISK Options screen, you can look at current partitions, create new partitions, and delete old partitions.

```
                        MS-DOS Version 6
                     Fixed Disk Setup Program
              (C)Copyright Microsoft Corp. 1983 - 1993

                         FDISK Options

Current fixed disk drive: 1

Choose one of the following:

1. Create DOS partition or Logical DOS Drive
2. Set active partition
3. Delete partition or Logical DOS Drive
4. Display partition information
5. Change current fixed disk drive

Enter choice: [1]




Press Esc to exit FDISK
```

Part

I

Ch

4

The screen shown in Figure 4.1 might appear to look different, depending on which version of MS-DOS you're using. Pick menu option 4, Display Partition Information. The Display Partition Information screen appears (see Figure 4.2).

FIG. 4.2

The Display Partition Information screen in MS-DOS 6.x shows the current partition information.

```
                           Display Partition Information
Current fixed disk drive: 1

Partition  Status    Type     Volume Label  Mbytes    System    Usage
  C: 1       A      PRI DOS    OPUS_DOS         5      FAT12       4%
     2               Non-DOS                    8                  6%
     3               Non-DOS                  376                100%
     4               Non-DOS                  114                 90%

Total disk space is  127 Mbytes (1 Mbyte = 1048576 bytes)




Press Esc to continue
```

Write down the information on this screen. You need the current partition table information if you decide to abort the Linux installation and put your system back the way it was before you started.

Alternatives to Repartitioning Your Hard Drive

You may not need to repartition your hard drive, although it's thought that repartitioning offers the best introduction to Linux. You can either use FIPS to repartition your hard drive non-destructively, or install Linux on the same partition as DOS with UMSDOS.

FIPS stands for *First non-destructive Interactive Partition Splitting*, a program developed by Amo Schaefer as a result of the Linux project. It's used to move DOS partitions around to make room for Linux partitions. All instructions for using FIPS can be found in the fips.doc document in the /install/ fips directory on the accompanying Slackware CD-ROM. FIPS can help only if you have enough free space left on your hard drive to install Linux; otherwise, you either need to delete unneeded files or use the process described earlier to repartition your hard drive.

UMSDOS is a project to allow Linux to exist on DOS partitions. UMSDOS allows you to create the Linux root file system under an existing DOS directory. You learn more about using UMSDOS later in the section "Using UMSDOS Instead of Formatting Your Hard Drive."

Deleting Partitions   Unfortunately, FDISK doesn't let you simply resize a partition—you must first delete the partition and then add it back with the desired size. From the FDISK Options screen, choose menu option 3, Delete Partition or Logical DOS Drive, to delete the necessary partitions. If you press <Esc> at anytime, you are returned to the previous screen. The Delete DOS Partition or Logical DOS Drive screen appears (see Figure 4.3).

Pick the appropriate menu option for the type of partition you're deleting, such as a primary DOS partition. If, for example, you choose option 1 (Delete Primary DOS Partition), you see the Delete Primary DOS Partition screen (see Figure 4.4).

FIG. 4.3
Use the Delete DOS
Partition screen to
delete a specific
partition or logical drive.

```
                    Delete DOS Partition or Logical DOS Drive
Current fixed disk drive: 1

Choose one of the following:

1.   Delete Primary DOS Partition
2.   Delete Extended DOS Partition
3.   Delete Logical DOS Drive(s) in the Extended DOS Partition
4.   Delete Non-DOS Partition


Enter choice: [1]




Press Esc to return to FDISK Options
```

FIG. 4.4
MS-DOS warns you
when you try to delete a
primary DOS partition.

```
                       Delete Primary DOS Partition
Current fixed disk drive: 1

Partition   Status    Type     Volume Label   Mbytes    System    Usage
  C: 1        A      PRI DOS    OPUS_DOS          5      FAT12       4%
     2               Non-DOS                      8                  6%
     3               Non-DOS                    376                100%
     4               Non-DOS                    114                 90%

Total disk space is  127 Mbytes (1 Mbyte = 1048576 bytes)



WARNING! Data in the deleted Primary DOS Partition will be lost.
What primary partition do you want to delete..? [1]
Enter Volume Label.............................? [OPUS_DOS   ]
Are you sure (Y/N).............................? [N]

Press Esc to return to FDISK Options
```

The screen asks for a volume name of the partition and then a confirmation to see whether you
really want to delete the partition. Because all information on the partition will be destroyed,
FDISK wants to be absolutely sure that you want to delete the primary DOS partition.

Adding Partitions   After you delete all the necessary partitions, you must then add the appropriate partitions for your DOS system. You can't add the Linux or OS/2 partitions with the DOS
FDISK program (partitioning the hard drive for Linux is covered later in this chapter). Figure
4.5 shows the Create a DOS Partition or Logical DOS Drive screen.

Providing all the space available for the partition and making the partition the active partition
are the FDISK defaults (see Figure 4.6). *Active* indicates that the partition is bootable. To boot
DOS, you must specify the primary partition as active. Say no to this first question so that you
can specify the exact amount of disk space to provide to your DOS partition. Answering No to
the question in Figure 4.6 displays the Specify Disk Space for the Partition screen. Specify the
desired space for your DOS partition in megabytes or in percentage of space available and
press <Return>.

FIG. 4.5
To boot properly, most operating systems require a primary active partition.

```
                    Create DOS Partition or Logical DOS Drive
Current fixed disk drive: 1

Choose one of the following:

1. Create Primary DOS Partition
2. Create Extended DOS Partition
3. Create Logical DOS Drive(s) in the Extended DOS Partition


Enter choice: [1]




Press Esc to return to FDISK Options
```

FIG. 4.6
You can allot all the disk space to one partition, or spread out the free space across several partitions.

```
                       Create Primary DOS Partition
Current fixed disk drive: 1

Do you wish to use the maximum available size for a Primary DOS Partition
and make the partition active (Y/N).....................? [Y]







Press Esc to return to FDISK Options
```

Next, you must set this partition active. From the FDISK Options screen, choose menu option 2, Set Active Partition, and simply follow the instructions on the Set Active menu screen.

Formatting the Partition   After you repartition your hard drive, you need to prepare the new partition for DOS and restore the appropriate files back to the DOS partition. Reboot your computer by using the boot disk you made earlier. Then format the appropriate drive and transfer the system files by using the following command:

```
format c: /s
```

When the partition is formatted, you can restore your backup to the new drive. Remember, if you shrank the partition, not all the files will fit on the new drive. It might be necessary to place the files that don't fit on the new drive onto other DOS drives or partitions.

Using UMSDOS Instead of Formatting Your Hard Drive

UMSDOS is a full-featured UNIX file system Slackware Linux can use that resides on an MS-DOS partition, meaning that you don't have to repartition your hard drive. The name stands for *UNIX in MS-DOS*. UMSDOS acts within the constraints of the MS-DOS file system while still providing the long file names as well as other file system attributes known to the UNIX world. However, you can't use both your MS-DOS areas on the hard drive and your UMSDOS files at the same time. Of course, by using various Linux utilities and taking advantage of the advanced file system, Linux can access your MS-DOS areas. Under MS-DOS, you'll be able to see the Linux files, but some may not make much sense, because MS-DOS can recognize only 12-character file names (the eight-dot-three scheme) and can't handle multiple periods in a file name, likc Linux can do.

CAUTION

When you use MS-DOS, you can see a file named --linux-.---. *Do not erase this file!* This file maintains information used by Linux to handle such items as long file names and symbolic links. Deleting this file from MS-DOS will severely damage your Linux file system!

Windows 95 also allows long file names, but at this moment, Windows 95 and UMSDOS have problems working together. If you try to install UMSDOS under Windows 95, beware—you could trash your entire system!

To install the UMSDOS system, first create a Linux root disk containing the UMSDOS kernel. This is the umsdos.gz file, which works with 1.44M or 1.2M floppies. Follow the steps detailed earlier in the section "Making the Root Disks." Next, specify the MS-DOS partition table or an empty directory on an existing MS-DOS partition on which to install the UMSDOS file system.

▶ **See** "Understanding File Systems," **p. 262**

▶ **See** "File Types," **p. 289**

Part

I

Ch

4

Preparing the Hard Drive for Linux

After you repartition your hard drive and make the Linux boot and root disks, or after you prepare a UMSDOS file system, you need to install Linux. You must first boot Linux from the disks you've just created. Then you need to use the Linux version of fdisk to create the necessary Linux partitions. After preparing the hard drive for installation, you can run the Setup program to install and configure Linux to your taste.

Booting Linux

To use the boot and root disks you made, simply place the boot disk into the drive and reboot your system. The following screen appears:

```
Welcome to the Slackware 96 Linux (v.3.1.0) bootkernel disk!

If you have any extra parameters to pass to the kernel, enter them
at the prompt below. For instance, you might need something like
this to detect the hard drives on PS/1 and ValuePoint models from IBM:

ramdisk hd=cyl,hds,secs
 (where "cyl", "hds", and "secs" are the number of
cylinders, sectors, and heads on the drive.)
```

```
Also, in a pinch, you can boot your system with a command like:
mount root=/dev/hda1

On machines with low memory, you can use mount root=/dev/fd1 or
mount root=/dev/df0 to install without a ramdisk. See LOWMEN.TXT for Details.

If you would rather load the root/install disk from your second
floppy drive:
drive2

DON'T SWITCH ANY DISKS YET! This prompt is just for entering
extra parameters. If you don't need to enter any parameters,
hit ENTER to continue.
```

```
boot:
```

If you have any parameters to pass to the kernel before it boots, enter them at the boot: prompt. (For information on these parameters, see the BootPrompt HOWTO in /doc/ HOWTO.) If you don't have any parameters, press <Return> to continue the installation.

Linux then loads itself into a RAM disk and decompresses before running. While booting, Linux displays information to let you know what's happening, including what type of hardware it can detect and use. The system then checks the amount of memory available, which floppy drives are available, and what network protocols are available. Next, Linux checks the floating-point processor, if available, and how the two processors communicate. Linux then displays the identity, date, and time at which the Linux kernel was built. Then Linux does a partition check on the available partitions. Finally, because Linux was booted from the boot disk, it displays the following:

```
VFS: Insert root floppy disk to be loaded into ramdisk and press ENTER.
```

Replace the boot disk with the root disk and press <Return>.

The system starts by displaying information messages from the RAM disk, indicating how many bytes of information it's installing and what address it's using. When finished, the system displays the following information:

```
Welcome to the Slackware '96 Linux installation disk!, (v. 3.1.0)

###### IMPORTANT! READ THE INFORMATION BELOW CAREFULLY. ######
- You will need one or more partitions of type "Linux Native" prepared.
It is also recommended that you create a swap partition (type
"Linux Swap") prior to installation. Most users can use the Linux
"fdisk" utility to create and tag the types of all these partitions.
OS/2 Boot Manager users, however, should create their Linux partitions
with OS/2 "fdisk", add the bootable (root) partition to the Boot Manager
menu, and then use the Linux "fdisk" to tag the partitions as type
"Linux native".
- If you have 4 megabytes or less of RAM, you MUST activate a swap
partition before running setup. After making the partition with fdisk,
use: mkswap /dev/<partition> <number of blocks> ; swapon /dev/<partition>
- Once you have prepared the disk partitions for Linux, and activated a
swap partition if you need one, type "setup" to begin the installation
process.
```

```
- If you want the install program to use monochrome displays, type:
TERM=vt100
before you start "setup".

You may now login as "root".

Slackware login:
```

You're now ready to log in to a functioning Linux system. Unlike MS-DOS, UNIX doesn't boot directly to a system prompt. To gain access to UNIX, you must log in and let the system know you're using it. This is similar to how Microsoft Windows for Workgroups and Windows NT behave, except that you can't bypass this step.

At the moment, you don't have an account on your own Linux system. Later in this chapter, you learn how to add a simple user account, whereas Chapter 10, "Managing User Accounts," explains in detail how to manage Linux user accounts. Only one account is available—the one belonging to the *superuser*, also known as *root*. The root account has the highest privileges in the Linux system. When you log in as root, you can do anything you want. So until you add an account for yourself, type **root** and press <Return>.

▶ **See** "Adding a User," **p. 222**

The system responds with

```
Linux 2.0.0. (Posix)

If you're upgrading an existing Slackware system, you might want to remove
old packages before you run 'setup' to install the new ones. If you don't
your system will still work but there might be some old files left laying
around on your drive.

Just mount your Linux partitions under /mnt and type 'pkgtool'. If you
don't know how to mount your partitions, type 'pkgtool' and it will tell
you how it's done.

To start the main installation, type 'setup'

#
```

The # is the superuser prompt. This is similar to the command prompts found under MS-DOS. Linux is waiting for you to issue a command. The preceding information indicates that you should type **setup**, but before you can install the various programs, you must set up your partitions. To do this, you must run the Linux version of fdisk.

Partitioning the Drive for Linux

At the # prompt, enter **fdisk** to start the fdisk program, which displays

```
Using /dev/hda as default device!
```

```
Command (m for help)
```

Notice the first information line printed by fdisk—Using /dev/hda as default device! Remember that MS-DOS refers to most partitions and hard drives as a letter, such as C or D.

Part

I

Ch

4

Linux refers to them in a very different manner. Linux refers to drives as a file name, such as /dev/hda or /dev/hdb.

Linux and MS-DOS communicates with hardware via a series of programs called *device drivers*. Whereas MS-DOS device drivers usually have a .SYS extension and can reside anywhere on the system, Linux stores such device drivers in the /dev directory. The drivers Linux uses in installation were supplied by the boot disk you created. The important point to remember, though, is that because the hard drive, floppy drives, and CD-ROM drives are hardware, Linux uses device drivers in the /dev directory to access the drives. Linux also references these drives with the subdirectory name rather than by a letter. Table 4.6 displays a typical Linux device directory.

Table 4.6   Linux Devices

Device	Name
Floppy drive A	/dev/fd0
Floppy drive B	/dev/fd1
First hard drive	/dev/hda
First primary partition on hard drive A	/dev/hda1
Second primary partition on hard drive A	/dev/hda2
First logical partition on hard drive A	/dev/hda4
Second hard drive	/dev/hdb
First primary partition on hard drive B	/dev/hdb1
First SCSI hard drive	/dev/sda

Notice that the entire hard drive is referred to as /hd*letter*. The primary partitions are then given the next set of four numbers, followed by the logical partitions. Thus, logical partitions always start at /dev/hda4. SCSI hard drives and CD-ROMs follow the same convention, except the hd is replaced by sd.

Using the Linux *fdisk* Program

At the fdisk prompt, enter m for a list of commands. Table 4.7 provides a list of available commands.

Table 4.7   The Linux *fdisk* commands

Command	Description
a	Toggles a bootable flag
c	Toggles the DOS compatibility flag

Command	Description
d	Deletes a partition
l	Lists known partition types
m	Displays this table
n	Adds a new partition
p	Prints the partition table
q	Quits without saving changes
t	Changes a partition's system ID
u	Changes display/entry units
v	Verifies the partition table
w	Writes the table to disk and exits
x	Extra functionality (experts only)

To begin the partitioning, select the p command to display the current partition table, which should reflect the drive you partitioned earlier with the DOS FDISK program. Listing 4.1 shows a possible display from the p command.

Part
I
Ch
4

Listing 4.1 An Example of a Current Partition Table

```
Disk /dev/hda: 15 heads, 17 sectors, 1024 cylinders
Units = cylinders of 255 * 512 bytes

Device        Boot      Begin     Start     End       Blocks    Id      System
dev/hda2      1024      1024      4040      384667+   51        Novell?
Partition 2 has different physical/logical endings:
phys=(967, 14, 17) Logical=(4096, 14.17)
```

N O T E You may see different information than what's shown here, because the values are different for each type of drive and the partitions already defined on that drive. ■

The display in Listing 4.1 indicates the various partitions already defined, the start and ending locations of the partition, and how big each partition is in blocks. The display also indicates the partition type. Table 4.8 lists all the different partition types you can define with the Linux fdisk command. The primary partitions you used are 83-Linux Native and 82-Linux Swap. You can get a similar listing with the l command.

Table 4.8   The Known Linux Partition Types

Reference Number	Type
0	Empty
1	DOS 12-bit FAT
2	XENIX root
3	XENIX usr
4	DOS 16-bit < 32M
5	Extended
6	DOS 16-bit >= 32M
7	OS/2 HPFS
8	AIX
9	AIX bootable
a	OS/2 Boot Manager
40	Venix 80286
51	Novell?
52	Microport
63	GNU HURD
64	Novell
75	PC/IX
80	Old MINIX
81	MINIX/Linux
82	Linux Swap
83	Linux Native
93	Amoeba
94	Amoeba BBT
a5	BSD/386
b7	BSDI fs
b8	BSDI swap
c7	Syrinx
db	CP/M
e1	DOS access

Reference Number	Type
e3	DOS R/O
f2	DOS secondary
ff	BBT

Notice the note about the different physical and logical endings at the end of Listing 4.1. The difference is because on the system used to write this chapter, a prior partition containing the DOS D drive was left intact, whereas the C drive was repartitioned to a smaller C drive to make room for Linux. Thus, space is between the C drive and the D drive. This is where the necessary partitions required by Linux will be created.

The begin, start, and end numbers from the display are very important and you should write them down. You'll need them in a later step to specify the necessary sizes of the partitions you'll add.

Adding the Necessary Partition

Because you've repartitioned the drive for MS-DOS, you shouldn't have to delete any partitions for Linux. You only should have to add partitions. To add a partition, issue the n command, which displays

```
Command Action
e extended
p primary(1-4)
```

Press <p> and then <Return>. fdisk asks for the partition number; enter your selection and press <Return>. If you indicate a partition number already in use, fdisk reports this fact and asks you to delete the partition before trying to add it to the partition table. For this example, enter **3** to add a third primary partition that's referred to as /dev/hda3.

Next, fdisk asks for the location of the first cylinder. This is usually the first available cylinder. In fact, fdisk displays a default range for your selection; for example,

```
First cylinder (42-1024) :
```

From this example, you can infer that the first partition ends at cylinder 41 and that the next partition begins at cylinder 1024. Thus, the range supplied by fdisk allows you to start the next partition anywhere in the range of 42 to 1024. It's a very good idea not to place partitions just anywhere throughout the disk, so choose the next available location, which in this case is cylinder 42.

N O T E Linux can have trouble booting from partitions defined to start at cylinders above 1024. If you create a Linux partition starting above 1024, you may have to boot Linux from a floppy. You learn how to create a boot floppy (which is different than the boot floppy used for installation) later in this chapter. The only downside is that booting Linux from a floppy takes a little longer than booting from the hard drive. If you have an IDE drive with more than 1024 cylinders, read the /help/big_ide file on the Slackware 96 CD-ROM. ▪

Part

I

Ch

4

Now fdisk wants you to specify how much space to allocate for this partition. You can express this size in number of cylinders or by the number of bytes (+*size*), kilobytes (+*size*K), or megabytes (+*size*M). Because you should already know the approximate size you need for the swap file, define this partition first, and then leave the rest of the disk space for the Linux program partitions. Thus, for this example, your machine has 8M of RAM, so you need to specify a 16M partition size by replying as such

```
Last cylinder or +size or +sizeM or +sizeK (42-1023): +16M
```

You should then use the p command to look at the new partition table you've defined. In this example, the new partition table looks like

```
Disk /dev/hda: 15 heads, 17 sectors, 1024 cylinders
Units = cylinders of 255 * 512 bytes

Device      Boot Begin Start  End   Blocks  Id    System
/dev/hda1    *     1     1     41    5219 1  DOS   12-bit FAT
/dev/hda2         1024  1024  4040  384667+ 51    Novell?

Partition 2 has different physical/logical endings:
phys=(967, 14, 17) Logical=(4039, 14.17)
/dev/hda3          42    42    170   16447+  83    Linux native
```

Note that by default, fdisk made the new partition a Linux native type. To change this to a swap partition, you need to use the t command. Enter **t** and then enter the partition number you want to change; in this example, enter **3**. fdisk then requests that you enter the hexadecimal value of the desired partition type (refer to Table 4.8). If you don't have Table 4.8 handy, you can enter **1** to get the list of partition type codes. Because you want a swap partition, enter **82** at the prompt.

As you can see, fdisk reports the new partition type, but you can also use the p command to double-check that partition 3 is now a Linux swap partition.

Now you can add your Linux partitions. For this example, add only one partition, but if you wanted to have multiple partitions for various reasons, you could do so at this time. To add a partition, press <n> and specify p for another primary partition, and then specify the number for this partition, which is 4. To keep from fragmenting different partitions across the drive, start the last partition where the other left off, at cylinder 171. For the last cylinder, because you want to use the rest of the space for the Linux system, you can specify the last cylinder instead of an exact byte count. Thus, enter **1023**, as follows:

```
Command (m for help):n
Command action
e    extended
p    primary partition (1-4)
p
Partition number (1-4): 4
First cylinder (171-1024):171
Last cylinder or +size or +sizeM or +sizeK (171-1023):1023
```

Now use the p command to verify the new partitions. If you need to make any changes, do so now. When you're satisfied with the layout of your partitions, you can use the w command to write the partition table information to the hard disk.

None of your changes are permanent until you use the w command; thus, if you feel you've made some changes in error, you can use the q command to exit without altering the partition table. If you use the w command, Linux tells you that the partition table has been altered and then resynchronizes the disks to match the new partition table. If your Linux system hangs at this point, reboot with the install boot and root disks until you're back at the # prompt.

Creating the Swap Partition

Some distributions of Slackware, including the one on the accompanying CD-ROM, provide automatic creation and activation of the swap file during installation, so you don't have to worry about creating the swap file. However, if you're using a different distribution version, you may need to create and activate the swap file before continuing with the installation.

▶ **See** "Creating a Swap File," **p. 285**

N O T E If you get an "out of memory" type error during the following installation procedures, you should increase the size of your swap file. ■

To create the swap space, use the mkswap command and tell the program which partition to use and how much space to use for virtual RAM. For example, to create a swap space on the /dev/hda3 partition that you defined earlier, enter the following command at the # prompt:

```
mkswap -c /dev/hda3 16447
```

The 16447 represents 16M and can be found in the blocks column of the fdisk p command output screen. The optional –c flag tells mkswap to check for bad sections on the partition.

Next, you need to activate the swap system with the swapon command:

```
# swapon /dev/hda3
```

Again, if you're using the accompanying Slackware CD-ROM, you shouldn't have to worry about activating the swap system as long as you create the partition for one swap file. During installation, the install program detects the swap partition and automatically starts the system for installation.

Installing the Linux System

Now that the system is partitioned for Linux, you can install the various packages described in Chapter 2, "Overview of Features." The install package allows you to specify what you want to install. It also detects any DOS partitions and can make them visible to Linux, if you want. To start the installation, type **setup** and press <Return>. Be careful throughout the installation, because the Slackware Setup program doesn't recover well from mistyped or extraneous keys.

If you have a color monitor and have installed the color root disks, you should next see a color display titled Slackware Linux Setup (version FD-2.2.0). The screen provides the menu selections shown in Table 4.9.

Part

I

Ch

4

Table 4.9　The Slackware Linux Setup Screen

Menu Item	Description
HELP	Reads the Slackware Setup Help file
KEYMAP	Remaps your keyboard if you're not using a U.S. keyboard
MAKE TAGS	Experts may customize tagfiles to preselect packages
ADDSWAP	Sets up your swap partition(s)
TARGET	Sets up your target partitions
SOURCE	Selects source media
DISK SETS	Selects disk sets to install
INSTALL	Installs selected disk sets
CONFIGURE	Reconfigures your Linux system
EXIT	Exits Slackware Linux Setup

You can navigate through the menu by using the <↑> and <↓> keys, the <+> and <–> keys, or the key corresponding to the first letter of the menu item previously listed. After you select an option, pressing the space bar or <Return> activates the selection—that is, performs the tasks associated with that menu item. Your first selection should be to review the help file for the Setup program (the HELP menu option). After you review the help file, the recommended sequence for installing Slackware is ADDSWAP, SOURCE, TARGET, DISK SETS, INSTALL, and CONFIGURE.

Setting Up a Swap Partition

Although you can go through the various commands outlined earlier in the section "Creating the Swap Partition" to set up your swap partition, it's easier to allow the Setup program to do this work for you. You can set up and configure your swap partition by selecting the ADDSWAP menu item. This command displays a screen titled SWAP SPACE DETECTED and provides the following information:

```
Slackware Setup has detected a swap partition:

Device    Boot   Begin   Start   End     Blocks    Id    System
/dev/hda3          42      42     170     16447+    82     Linux Swap

Do you wish to install this as your swap partition?
You have two options: yes or no. Choose yes, using the arrow keys, to continue
the installation process. Linux Setup gives the following warning:
IMPORTANT NOTE: If you have already made any of your swap partitions
active (using the swapon command), then you should not allow Setup to
use mkswap on your swap partitions, because it may corrupt memory pages
that are currently swapped out. Instead, you will have to make sure
```

that your swap partitions have been prepared (with mkswap) before they
will work. You might want to do this to any inactive swap partitions
before you reboot.

▶ **See** "Using Swap Files and Partitions," **p. 284**

Choose OK to continue. Setup asks whether you want to use mkswap. If you haven't prepared the swap files, choose yes and continue. Setup next asks whether you want to make the swap partitions active with the swapon command. Choose yes to continue the installation. After the program configures and activates your swap partitions, Setup shows you information that will be added to the /etc/fstab file.

Choose OK to continue with the installation. Next Setup asks,

```
Now that you've set up your swap space, you may continue on
with the installation. Otherwise, you'll be returned to the
main menu. Would you like to continue the installation and
set up your TARGET drive(s)?
```

Choose yes to set up your TARGET partitions on your hard drive.

Selecting a Target Partition for Installation

Again, the Setup program displays a screen with the partition information. If you've used fdisk to create multiple partitions, each partition is displayed, and Setup asks you to select one to use for installation. Because this example uses only one partition, the information for the one partition is all that's displayed, as shown here:

```
Device     Boot    Begin    Start    End       Blocks   Id     System
/dev/hda4   171      171     1023    108757+     83     Linux native
```

Next, Setup asks you to choose a file system. You have two choices: ext2 and xiafs. Setup displays the following message and asks for a selection:

```
There are two main filesystem types that are used for Linux.
These are the xiafs filesystem, and the second extended
filesystem (ext2). Ext2 seems to be the current standard.
Xiafs hasn't really been changed in quite some time. Ext2 has one
really nice feature that xiafs doesn't have: an ext2 partition is
unmounted, a clean bit is written to it. When the machine is rebooted,
checking is skipped for any partitions that have the clean bit on them.
Xiafs may be a better choice for machines with low memory, however, so
it's still supported. What filesystem do you plan to use on your root
partition (/dev/hda4 ), ext2fs or ziafs?
```

Installing the ext2 file system is recommended, so choose ext2 and choose OK. You're then asked to format the partition:

```
If this partition has not been formatted, you should format it.
NOTE: This will erase all data on it. If you are trying to upgrade
an existing Linux partition, you should use setup from your hard drive,
not from the boot/root disk. (The versions of setup supplied on the
hard drive and the boot/root disk differ.) Would you like to format
this partition?
```

Part

I

Ch

4

You have three options: Format, to provide a quick format with no checks for bad blocks; Check, which is slower but checks the hard drive for bad blocks; and No, to bypass formatting the partition. Choose Check and then OK to format this partition.

N O T E Checking for bad spots on your hard drive probably isn't necessary for newer (that is, IDE) drives, because the drives take care of remapping bad spots. ▪

Next, the Setup program asks about inode density. Inodes are explained in Chapter 15, "Understanding the File and Directory System," but basically you need one inode for each file on your Linux system. If you're going to have many small files, you need many inodes. The Setup program displays the following screen:

```
SELECT INODE  DENSITY

Ext2fs default to one inode per 4096 bytes of drive space. If you're
going to have many small files on your drive, then you may need more
inodes (one is used for each file entry). You can change the density
to one inode per 4096 bytes, or even per 1024 bytes. Select '2048' or
'1024', or just hit enter to accept the default of 4096 bytes.
NOTE: If you are going to run from CD using a small (<60MB) partition,
use 1024 to be safe. Each link uses an inode and it's easy to run out
of space.
```

▶ **See** "Directories and Physical Disks," **p. 291**

Select the second entry, 4096, and choose OK. The Setup program then displays an information screen indicating the formatting choices you've made.

CAUTION

Watch the drive in-use light. Don't press any keys until the program displays the next screen with an option you can select. If you press any keys during an operation, the Slackware installation program will use these keys as your next selection when the next screen appears. Thus, you may inadvertently make a selection you didn't mean to make.

Next, if Setup detects any DOS or OS/2 High Performance File System (HPFS) partitions, Setup asks whether you want to make these partitions visible to Linux. If you have any such partitions on your drive, answering yes is a good idea because you can access the files on these partitions from Linux. Make your choice (yes or no) to continue.

If you choose yes, the CHOOSE PARTITION screen appears, listing the various partitions you can select. In the entry box, type the name of the partition you want to make visible to Linux and press <Return>. If you have more than one partition available, the Setup program continues to ask for a choice until you enter <q>.

After you enter the name, Setup asks for a place in the directory tree to mount the partition. What this means is that the entire partition is accessed as though it were a subdirectory. You must specify where this subdirectory starts. The following information appears:

```
SELECT MOUNT POINT

Now this new partition must be mounted somewhere in your directory tree.
Please enter the directory under which you would like to put it. For
instance, you might want to reply /dosc, /dosd, or something like that.
NOTE: This partition won't actually be mounted until you reboot.

Where would you like to mount /dev/hda1?
```

In the entry box, enter the directory where you want to mount the partition. If this is a DOS partition, use /dosc for drive C, /dosd for drive D, and so on. If you're mounting an OS/2 partition, you can respond with /os2c, /os2d, and so on. Also, make sure that you specify the correct slash mark in directory names—/ (forward), not the DOS backslash (\).

After entering the mount point, the Setup program displays an information screen called CURRENT DOS/HPFS STATUS to let you know which partitions will be mounted. After dismissing this screen by choosing OK, you're returned to the CHOOSE PARTITION screen.

If you have other partitions to mount, you can repeat the preceding procedure until all desired partitions are mounted. When all are processed, press <q> to move on to the next phase of installation, selecting what media to install from.

Choosing from Where to Install Linux

After formatting and mounting your directories, the Setup program asks you to continue with installation with the SOURCE selection. This selection lets you pick from where you'll install the Slackware distribution. If you're using the accompanying CD-ROM, that choice is CD-ROM. If you have the distribution on floppies, you use the floppy drive to install. Choose yes to display the SOURCE MEDIA SELECTION screen:

```
SOURCE MEDIA SELECTION
Where do you plan to install Slackware Linux from?
1     Install from a hard drive partition
2     Install from floppy disks
3     Install via NFS
4     Install from a pre-mounted directory
5     Install from CD-ROM
```

If you're using the CD-ROM, select choice number 5 and choose OK, which displays the Installing from CD-ROM screen:

```
INSTALLING FROM CD-ROM

In order to install Slackware from a CD-ROM, it must contain the
distribution arranged beneath a source directory in the same way
as if you were to install it from a hard drive or NFS. The source
directory must contain subdirectories for each floppy disk. Your
CD-ROM should be compatible with this format if it contains a mirror
of the Slackware FTP site.

What type of CD-ROM drive do you have?
```

```
1    SCSI [/dev/scd0 or /dev/scd1]
2    Sony CDU31A [/dev/sonycd]
3    Sony 535 [/dev/cdu535]
4    Mitsumi [/dev/mcd]
5    Sound Blaster Pro (Panasonic) [dev/sbpcd]
```

Select your CD-ROM drive from those provided and choose OK.

N O T E If you have problems getting the installation program to detect your CD-ROM, you may have
to abort the installation and create a new root disk with another kernel. See The CDROM-
HOWTO in the /doc/HOWTO directory for more information on using CD-ROMs. ■

You now need to look up the source directory you saved in the section "Repartitioning the
Drive" earlier in this chapter. The Setup program displays the SELECT SOURCE DIRECTORY
screen.

N O T E The following screens may appear differently because Linux changes so rapidly. Every effort
has been made to assure that this book is in step with the accompanying CD-ROMs, but
this isn't always possible. ■

```
SELECT SOURCE DIRECTORY

Now we need to know which directory on the CD contains the Slackware
sources. This location may vary depending on the cd you have. There
are default selections for the Slackware Professional CD (including
an option to run mostly from the CD), InfoMagic CD, TransAmeritech CD,
and the Linux Quarterly CD-ROM. There may be other directories
containing other versions - enter a custom directory name if you like.
Which option would you like?
```

If you're using the accompanying Slackware CD-ROM, immediately select the type of install—
slackware, slaktest, and so on. Make your selection and continue. The next screen asks you to
pick the packages to install on your system.

N O T E If you enter the wrong directory or don't remember the directory name, the Setup program
alerts you and prompts for the correct directory name. If you're using the accompanying
CD-ROM, the /slackware directory is the correct directory on the CD-ROM. If you're using another
installation media or CD-ROM and forgot the directory name, you need to exit Setup and look on the
media to find the directory. You can usually recognize the directory structure because the subdirectories have names similar to the package names—for example, /a, /ap, /oop, and so on. ■

Selecting the Series to Install

After you specify the installation media and source directory, the Setup program displays the
SERIES SELECTION screen:

```
SERIES SELECTION
```

```
Use the spacebar to select the disk sets you wish to install.
You can use the UP/DOWN arrows to see all the possible choices.
Press the ENTER key when you are finished. If you need to install
a disk set that is not listed here, check the box for custom
additional disk sets.

CUS    Also prompt for CUSTOM disk sets
A      Base Linux system
AP     Various Applications that do not need X
D      Program development (C, C++, Lisp, Perl, etc)
E      GNU Emacs
F      FAQ lists, HOWTO documentation
K      Kernel sources
N      Networking (TCP/IP, UUCP, Mail, News)
Q      Extra Linux kernels with UMSDOS/non-SCSI CD drivers
T      TeX
TCL    Tcl/Tk/TclX, Tcl language, and Tk toolkit for X
X      XFree-86 2.1.1 X Window System
XAP    X Applications
XD     XFree-86 2.1.1 X11 Server Development System
XV     XView 3.2 release 4. (OpenLook window Manager, apps)
Y      Games (that do not require X)
```

Simply move through the list with the arrow keys and mark the desired packages with the space bar. When you make a selection with the space bar, an x appears next to the selection. When you've made all your selections, press <Return> to continue.

Your selections are based on personal preference and the type of hardware you have—that is, if you don't have the hardware to run XFree86, you shouldn't install the packages that require X (iv, x, xap, xd, and xv). You must install package A, the base Linux system. Also, if you're interested in programming, you should install the various programming packages, such as d, oop, tcl, and xd. If you aren't interested in programming, you really don't need these packages. If you want to access the Internet, you want to install package n. Installing the f package, which contains FAQ lists and HOWTO documentation, is strongly recommended, because the package contains a wealth of information you'll need about Linux.

For each package you select, you're led through a series of screens for each package, and each package has programs that it must add, programs that it highly recommends you add, and programs you can skip. Simply follow the instructions on each screen to install the system. For this example, you install the following packages: a, ap, d, e, f, n, t, tcl, x, xap, and y.

After you select the desired packages, choose OK to continue. A simple screen appears telling you that you're about to enter the INSTALL section and that if you haven't made all the appropriate selections, you're returned to the main selection menu. Choose yes to continue with the Setup process.

Installing Your Selections

The Setup program next prompts you for the type of prompting you want to have while Setup goes through each package, installing programs. Each package contains a set of tagfiles that indicate how the file should be treated. For a first-time install, select the HELP mode indicated in the SELECT PROMPTING MODE screen, to help you decide which mode to use.

Part

I

Ch

4

```
SELECT PROMPTING MODE
Now you must select which type of prompting you would like to use while
installing your software packages. If you're not sure which to use,
read the help file.

Which type of prompting would you like to use?

Normal    Use the default tagfiles
Custom    Use custom tagfiles in the package directories
Path      Use tagfiles in the subdirectories of a custom path
None      Use no tagfiles - install everything
HELP      Read the prompt mode help file
```

After reading the HELP file, select the Normal prompting mode and choose OK. Then choose INSTALL.

N O T E   The HELP file indicates a Prompting mode, but as you can see from the menu selections, there's no such item. Normal is the closest matching item, which is why you should use that selection for the installation procedure. ▨

At this point, the Setup program is on autopilot and goes through each package you selected earlier to install the various programs. Programs marked as ADD in the tagfiles are automatically added. Setup displays a screen indicating what package it's installing and a brief message about what the package is. You can't stop the Setup program from installing a program marked as ADD in the tagfile.

When the Setup program comes across a program marked as OPT, REC, or SKIP, it displays a screen telling you what it's about to install, whether it's recommended that you install the program, how much space is required to install the program, and then a list of choices. The choices—accessible with the arrow keys—are usually yes, no, or an option to abort the entire program. Usually, the default selection is yes, install package *xxx*, where *xxx* is the name of the package being installed.

N O T E   Be careful with your answers. If you make an incorrect choice, you can't go back and change that choice. If you accidentally install a package you didn't want, things aren't so bad; you may lose some disk space and gain another program to experiment with. However, if you don't install a package you need, the best you can do is write down the missed package and then later run pkgtool, explained in Chapter 13, "Upgrading and Installing Software," to install the desired package. You can also abort the current installation and start over, but that's a rather harsh and time-consuming option.

▶ **See** "Using *pkgtool*," **p. 253** ▨

Configuring Your System

The Setup program has finished loading all the software components you specified. Now it must configure your system. The Setup program displays

CONFIGURE YOUR SYSTEM

```
Now it's time to configure your Linux system. If this is a new system,
you must configure it now or it will not boot correctly. Otherwise,
you can back out to the main menu if you're sure you want to skip this
step. If you've installed a new kernel image, it's important to
reconfigure you system so that you can install LILO (the Linux Loader)
or create a bootdisk using the new kernel. Do you want to move on to
the CONFIGURE option?
```

Because this is your first time through, you need to configure your system. Choose yes to continue. The next screen asks you to make a boot disk. You should create a boot disk, even if you use LILO. The screen displayed is as follows:

MAKE BOOT DISK

```
It is HIGHLY recommended that you make a standard boot disk for your
Linux system at this time. Such a disk can be very handy if LILO is
ever improperly installed. Since the boot disk will contain a kernel
that is independent of LILO and the kernel on your hard drive, you'll
still be able to use it to boot your system no matter what you do to
LILO or your hard drive kernel. Would you like to make a standard
boot disk?
```

Be sure to have a formatted floppy ready, choose yes, and press <Return>. Setup displays the BOOT DISK CREATION screen. Simply put the formatted floppy into the drive and choose yes to create the boot disk. If you skip boot disk creation, Setup displays this warning message:

SKIPPED BOOT DISK CREATION

```
Boot disk creation skipped. I hope you already have a boot disk.
If you don't, you have to install LILO if you haven't already,
or you'll have a hard time booting your machine. :^)
```

It's highly recommended that you create a boot disk. If anything goes wrong with the preceding installation or the following configuration—especially when installing the Linux Loader, LILO—you'll have an extremely hard time booting your system. In fact, you should also make a boot disk for any other operating systems you may have resident on your system. Typically, with a boot disk you can boot from a floppy if things go bad and correct the problem.

Configuring Your Modem

Next, Setup asks you to configure a modem. You should do this now, even if you don't plan to use a modem at this time. Setup displays the following screen if you want to configure your modem:

MODEM CONFIGURATION

```
This part of the configuration process will create a link in /dev from
your callout device (cua0, cua1, cua2, cua3) to /dev/modem. You can
change this link later if you put you modem on a different port.
```

Choose yes to continue. Next, you need to specify the serial port that your modem is hooked to. You do this via the SELECT CALLOUT DEVICE screen. The items cua0-3 represent your serial ports, with cua0 representing COM1, cua1 being COM2, and so on. Select the appropriate COM port and the choose OK.

Configuring the Mouse

You next go through a similar process to configure your mouse. If you have a mouse with your system, you should go ahead and configure it at this time. Choose yes from the MOUSE CONFIGURATION screen to continue. You're then presented with a screen containing six selections. If you have a mouse that's Microsoft-compatible and not listed in the choices in Table 4.10, you can select option 1 and have a good chance of your mouse working.

Table 4.10   Mouse Types Supported by Linux

Option	Description
1	Microsoft-compatible serial mouse
2	C&T 82C710 or PS/2 style mouse (auxiliary port)
3	Logitech bus mouse
4	ATI XL bus mouse
5	Microsoft bus mouse
6	Mouse Systems serial mouse

If you select a mouse that requires a serial port, Setup requires you to specify the port. Like modems, Linux refers to the serial ports with a different name than COM1, COM2, and so on. Linux refers to the ports as ttyS0 through ttyS3. Select the appropriate serial port from the SELECT SERIAL PORT screen and then choose OK to continue with the installation.

Configuring Linux to Use *ftape*

Setup detects whether you loaded the ftape package and asks whether you want to start the program as soon as Linux boots. It doesn't hurt to start the program at boot time, so if you loaded the ftape package, you should have Setup start the program at boot time. Choose yes from the FTAPE CONFIGURATION screen to continue.

Configuring Your Modem's Baud Rate

Next, if you installed the gp9600 package, the Setup program displays the SET YOUR MODEM SPEED screen. Simply select the appropriate baud rate and choose OK. If you don't see a rate high enough for your modem needs, you can later use the setserial program to set the baud rate to whatever value you require.

Installing LILO

LILO stands for the LInux LOader. LILO is a program executed at system startup that lets you choose which operating system is used to boot the computer. You can use LILO to boot several different operating systems, such as Linux and MS-DOS. With LILO, you also can specify a default operating system to boot and a default time limit before it boots that system. For example, if you had MS-DOS and Linux on your computer, you can configure LILO to boot either one. You could then tell LILO to boot MS-DOS if no one intervenes after 30 seconds. Before that 30 seconds is up, however, a user can specify another operating system to boot instead of the default. You can press the <Ctrl>, <Alt>, or <Shift> keys to stop the timed process. Press <Tab> to get a list of operating systems LILO can boot.

You specify all this information while configuring LILO. Although you can directly edit the lilo.conf file located in the /etc directory, the LILO INSTALLATION screen provides a better interface for editing the file.

After you configure your system, Setup lets you install LILO. Setup displays

```
LILO INSTALLATION

LILO (the Linux Loader) allows you to boot Linux from your hard drive.
To install, you make a new LILO configuration file by creating a new
header and then adding at least one bootable partition to the file.
Once you've done this, you can select the install option, Alternately,
if you already have an /etc/lilo.cfg, you may reinstall using that.
If you make a mistake, you can always start over by choosing 'Begin'.
Which Option would you like?

Begin       Start LILO configuration with a new LILO header
Linux       Add a Linux partition to the LILO config file
OS/2        Add an OS/2 partition to the LILO config file
DOS         Add a DOS partition to the LILO config file
Install     Install LILO
Recycle     Reinstall LILO using the existing lilo.conf
Skip        Skip LILO installation and exit this menu
View        View your current /etc/lilo.cfg
Help        Read the Linux Loader Help file
```

To begin, you should select the Help option to read the help file. After reading the help file, you should start at the beginning—the Begin option. If you don't want to install LILO at this time but instead want to use a boot floppy, you can select the Skip menu option.

CAUTION

If you skip installing LILO, you must have a bootable floppy. If you skipped creating a boot floppy earlier, you should install LILO or, when back at the main menu, re-enter the configuration selection and create a boot floppy. If you do leave Setup without a way to boot your system, you're forced to configure your system at a later time with the boot and root disks you originally created.

Configuring the Kernel with the *append*= Parameter

You have the option to pass the Linux kernel command-line flags to configure the kernel before execution begins. The extra flags might be needed with certain SCSI hard drives and IBM motherboards. LILO allows you to specify these command-line flags via the append= parameter. If you need to pass any command-line parameters, enter them in the edit box of the displayed screen. If you have no parameters to pass, press <Return> to continue.

Setting a Target Location

Next, you must choose where to place the LILO program. You can place the program in the master boot record of your first hard drive, in what's called the *superblock* of your root Linux partition, or on a floppy disk. If you choose the Floppy Disk option, you need to place a formatted floppy in the drive. You should probably use the master boot record for LILO.

Setting the Delay Option

The next screen lets you set the amount of time LILO waits before booting the default operating system. Select one of the following options and then choose OK:

Option	Description
None	Don't wait at all—boot straight into the first operating system
5	5 seconds
30	30 seconds
Forever	Present a prompt and wait until a choice is made

Choosing Your Default Operating System and Adding All Partitions

When you return to the main LILO INSTALLATION screen, you must choose your default operating system. This is the first operating system located in the lilo.conf file. If you want Linux to be the default operating system, for example, you should select the Linux menu option; if you want MS-DOS to be the default, select the DOS menu option.

After you select the default OS, the installation program presents a screen consisting of all the possible partitions that you can boot from. Enter the name of the partition just as it appears under the Device column heading on the SELECT *XXX* PARTITION, where *XXX* indicates the type of partition you're using. For example, if you had selected DOS as your default operating system, the screen reads SELECT DOS PARTITION and displays all available bootable DOS partitions. After you enter the correct device name, choose OK to continue.

Next, you must choose a short name to help identify the operating system when someone presses the <Tab> key at the LILO prompt. This is the name a user must enter to select that operating system as the boot operating system from LILO. Examples of names are DOS, LINUX, OS/2, and so on. The name must be a single word.

After selecting your default operating system, you can continue to add various operating systems to LILO by using the Linux, OS/2, and DOS menu options. Just remember to add Linux.

After you add all the appropriate operating system partitions, you should use the View option to examine your current /etc/lilo.conf file. For this example, assume that you've specified DOS as the default operating system and have added an entry for Linux. You also specified a 30-second delay before booting into DOS. In that case, your lilo.conf file looks like

```
# LILO configuration file
# generated by 'liloconfig'
#
# Start LILO global section
boot = /dev/hda
#compact          # faster, but won't work on all systems.
delay = 300
vga = normal      # force sane state
ramdisk = 0       # paranoia setting
# End LILO global section
# Linux bootable partition config begins
image = /vmlinuz
root = /dev/hda4
label = linux
# Linux bootable partition config ends
# DOS bootable partition config begins
other = /dev/hda1
label = dos
table = /dev/hda
# DOS bootable partition config ends
```

After you add all the needed partitions, select the Install option to configure LILO.

Uninstalling LILO

If you're running LILO version 0.14 or newer, you can uninstall LILO with the following command:

```
opus:~# lilo -u
```

If you have a previous version, you must remove or disable LILO from its primary partition. You can use Linux's or MS-DOS's FDISK program to make another partition active.

If you placed LILO within the MBR (master boot record), you must replace it with another MBR from another operating system. With MS-DOS 5.0 or above, the command

```
c:\>fdisk /mbr
```

restores the MS-DOS MBR.

When LILO is removed from the active partition or the MBR, you're free to remove the files from /etc/lilo.

▶ **See** "Removing Files or Directories," **p. 307**

Configuring Your Network   Next, Setup allows you to configure your network. You may not have all the information available yet, but go ahead and configure as much as possible. The Setup program tries to configure your system, but if it can't (which is very likely the first time),

Part

I

Ch

4

you can configure the network later with the netconfig command. Choose yes to start the configuration, and choose OK on the NETWORK CONFIGURATION screen to begin.

The first item you need is a name for your machine. This is a personal name, and you can be as creative as you want. At the ENTER HOSTNAME prompt, enter your selected name and press <Return>.

N O T E It's a good idea to stick with lowercase letters, because UNIX and Linux are case-sensitive and most commands and interactions are done with lowercase letters. ■

The next prompt asks for something called a *domain name*. If you understand this term and have one available, enter the domain name for your system. If you don't have a domain name yet or don't understand what one is, don't worry. (Later chapters of this book, such as Chapter 26, "Understanding the Internet," explain what an Internet domain name is and how to configure your network with one.) If you don't have a domain name, enter the following as a placeholder:

`tristar.com`

▶ **See** "Internet Names," **p. 525**

N O T E You must enter a domain name to continue the installation process. ■

The next question deals with using *TCP/IP* through *loopback*. (If you don't understand these terms, check out Chapter 23, "Configuring a TCP/IP Network," for this information before returning to this section.) By answering yes to the Only use loopback? prompt, you can skip several layers of configuration. Answering yes to this question and configuring your network later is a good idea. If you choose yes, the network configuration is complete and you can continue with the rest of the configuration.

▶ **See** "The/etc/hosts File," **p. 474**

▶ **See** "Configuring the Software Loopback Interface," **p. 478**

Using the *selection* Program   If you have a mouse, you can use the selection program to cut and paste commands from your terminals. This screen asks whether you want to start the selection program automatically at boot time. If you have a mouse, you should start selection at boot time by answering yes at this screen. However, if you have a bus mouse, there are potential problems using selection and XFree86. If you have a bus mouse, you shouldn't start selection automatically.

If you don't choose to start selection at boot time, you can execute the program at any time with the following command:

`selection -f &`

Configuring *sendmail*   Next, Setup asks you to choose a configuration file for sendmail. Chapter 29, "Using Electronic Mail," provides more information on using e-mail, but for starters you might want to preload one of the supplied sendmail configuration files. If you know how you're connecting to the Internet with PPP, via Ethernet and so on, you can choose the SMTP-BIND or SMTP menu option. If you plan to use a modem and UUCP, select the UUCP menu option. If you don't plan on using a network, select the SKIP menu option. If you're unsure, the SKIP menu option is a good choice because you can reconfigure the system at a later time.

▶ **See** "Understanding E-Mail," **p. 570**

Selecting a Time Zone   Next, Setup requires you to select a time zone that Linux uses to keep track of the date and time. Look through the list of available time zones and choose the most appropriate one. If you're in the United States, several selections begin with US. The same applies for Australia, Canada, and those systems that use Greenwich Mean Time or Universal Time. Select your time zone and press <Return>.

Replacing /etc/fstab   /etc/fstab is a file-system table that represents each of your partitions. If you modify the table—with LILO, for example—while using the Setup program, it may ask you to replace the old one with the new one. This screen appears only if, for some reason, you stop and restart the Setup program or the configuration process. If you've made no changes to the partition table, answer no to this question; otherwise, answer yes.

Modifying the Kernel with *rdev*

When configuration is complete, you can rerun Setup to add new items, or you can use the pkgtool program to view, add, or delete packages.

▶ **See** "Using *pkgtool*," **p. 253**

You might have to change items germane to your kernel, such as the video mode used. One solution is to reinstall Linux—a major undertaking, as you've just seen. Or you can recompile and build a new kernel from scratch, but that's not for the novice. Another option is to modify the current kernel, which, fortunately, Linux allows you to do with the rdev program. rdev is found in /sbin and should be used only when you're logged in as root.

For a complete listing of options, invoke rdev with the \h or \? parameter.

Your kernel file—that is, the actual software—is found in a file named vmlinuz. The reason for this name is historical; most UNIX systems store the kernel in a file named vmunix, and Linux is based on UNIX. Note the installed kernel is vmlinuz, where the z signifies a compressed kernel. When a kernel is built, the decompressed version is made and called vmlinux; however, the decompressed version isn't bootable. A parameter to rdev is usually this file name. You can use rdev to fix problems such as root and swap partitions and video modes.

Building a New Kernel

Sometimes a problem has only one solution—a new kernel. The Linux kernel is the core operating system for Linux. Although not for the faint of heart, sometimes downloading a new kernel from the Net and building it is necessary. If you have some programming experience

Part
I

Ch
4

and know your way around the C programming language, you should be able to build and install a new kernel; if not, you can skip this section.

You may have to install a new kernel for various reasons:

- A new patch is provided to run new hardware.
- You want to remove features from the kernel you don't use, thus lowering the memory requirements for your system.

The starting point is to determine what kernel version you're now running. You can find out the kernel version with the following command:

uname -a

The response indicates which version of the kernel is now running and when it was created. The version numbers are in the form of

MajorVersionNumber.MinorVersionNumber.PatchLevel

Linus Torvalds is the official release point for new kernels, although anyone can modify Linux (due to the GPL). The fact that Linus is the official release point gives the Linux development and user community a common baseline from which to work and communicate.

N O T E Be sure to read the Kernel HOWTO before actually trying to build and configure a new kernel! The Kernel HOWTO is in /doc/HOWTO. ▉

To build a new kernel, you need to have the source files in the /urs/src/linux directory. You also need to have the C compiler package loaded, which is disk set d. If you didn't install that package during installation, use pkgtool to do so now.

First, you must get the new kernel sources or patches. The new sources are usually found on the Internet (check out **sunsite.unc.edu** for the latest and greatest kernels). The source files are usually in a tar format and will need to be unarchived. If you're modifying your current kernel, obtaining the new sources is, of course, unnecessary.

N O T E It's a *very* good idea to make a backup copy of your current kernel with the following commands:

cd /usr/src
cp linux linux.sav

These commands copy the entire linux source directory to another directory called linux.sav. ▉

Next, you should use the patch command to apply any patch files. After preparing the source files, you can configure and build your new system. Start by entering the following command from the /usr/src directory:

make config

This command asks you various questions about the drivers you want to install or configure. Pressing <Return> accepts the default value for each question; otherwise, you must supply the answer. Table 4.11 shows some of the questions; you may have to answer other questions depending on the version of the kernel you're installing or the patches you've applied.

Table 4.11   Some Config Questions

Configuration Option	Description
Kernel Math Emulation	Asks if the kernel should emulate a math co-processor.
Normal Hard disk Support	Enables drivers for all standard hard drives.
XT Hard disk Support	Applies only if your machine uses an XT class controller class instead of an AT controller.
Networking Support	Answering yes enables networking support within the kernel.
SCSI Support	Enables support for SCSI controllers.
CD_ROM Drivers	A series of questions dealing with CD-ROMs, especially those not supported within the standard SCSI Support package.
Filesystems	A series of questions dealing with file systems the kernel should support. If your kernel doesn't have support for the ISO9660 file system, you won't be able to use a CD-ROM.
Parallel Printer Support	Enables printer support via the parallel port.
Mouse Support	Bus mice need their own support from within the kernel.
Sound Card Support	A series of questions about the hardware and software configuration of a sound card.

Part

I

Ch

4

After you answer the various questions to configure your new kernel, you must compile it.

N O T E   The build process can take anywhere from 15 minutes to many hours. So relax and order a pizza! ▪

The following commands will build the new kernel:

```
make dep
make clean
make
```

When compilation completes, you can create a new boot disk as discussed earlier in the section "Creating the Boot and Root Disks." You can copy this kernel to a new diskette, or use LILO to boot the new kernel.

Upgrading from a Previous Version of Slackware

The current version of Slackware (version 3.0) contains the Linux files in a special format, called Executable and Linking Format (ELF). Earlier versions of Slackware were in a format called a.out. You can't mix these types of executables on the same system, so if you plan to upgrade from an earlier version, you must reinstall from scratch to be on the safe side. This is especially important when dealing with the A and N packages. The pkgtool program can uninstall programs as well as install them, but the safest route is to back up your important configuration files and reinstall Linux from scratch.

If you're upgrading from similar formats—that is, from an ELF-based distribution to an ELF-based distribution—you can use pkgtool to remove those packages you want to update, and then use the tool to install the newer versions.

▶ **See** "Using *pkgtool,*" **p. 253**

Going Back to the Beginning

After you complete the setup and configuration of your system, the Setup program returns you to the main menu. From there, you can choose the EXIT option to leave Setup. If you want to change options, you can do so here. But Chapter 13, "Upgrading and Installing Software," provides information on updating and installing software after your initial installation. Choose EXIT to leave the Setup program.

Choosing EXIT returns you to the system prompt, indicated by the # sign. You're now in Linux and can issue simple commands, such as ls for a directory listing of files. At this time, though, you should reboot the system so that all your setup and configurations can take effect.

Rebooting Linux is more involved than rebooting DOS. You can't turn off the power and turn the system back on. If you do so in Linux, you can damage the file structures and systems. Linux tries to repair itself on bootup. Don't turn off the power while running Linux. To exit Linux, use the following command:

shutdown [-r] *time*

The optional –r flag indicates that the system should reboot after shutting down. *time* indicates the time that the system should shut down; you can use now in place of *time* to indicate immediate shutdown. Linux also recognizes the warm-boot keys used by DOS to reboot the machine, <Ctrl-Alt-Delete>, which Linux interprets as the command

shutdown –r now

▶ **See** "Shutting Down Linux" **p. 218**

Make sure that you've removed the all floppy disks from the drive and reboot your new Linux machine.

Resolving Problems

After rebooting your machine, the LILO prompt should appear. Make sure that you can boot to your old operating system if you left it on the hard drive. If that system was DOS, press the <Shift> key and then type the short word you used to identify the DOS partition when you installed LILO. If you enter an invalid word, press <Tab> to get a list of valid operating system types. If you're having problems at this point, place your DOS boot disk in the boot drive and reboot.

You should be able to boot from your boot disk. When your system is up and running under DOS, try the Linux boot disk you created during installation—not the ones you created to originally install the entire system. If that boot disk doesn't work, you may have to reinstall Linux. Potential problems to initially check are the kernels and your hardware. Before starting over, make sure that you have the appropriate hardware. If you made notes during the installation process, check which kernel you installed against what hardware you have. If you have a SCSI CD-ROM, did you install the idekern instead of the scsikern? But do make sure that you have hardware supported by Linux.

From Here...

After you have your system up and running, you can read the following chapters for further information about Linux:

- Chapter 5, "Running Linux Applications," gets you up to speed on the various programs you just installed.
- Chapter 7, "Using X Windows," is interesting if you've installed the X system.
- Chapter 13, "Upgrading and Installing Software," provides instructions of how to reinstall packages you may have left out during the initial setup of your Linux system.
- Chapter 26, "Understanding the Internet," briefs you on the basics about how to get to the Internet.

## CHAPTER 5

Running Linux Applications

Now that you've installed your Linux system, this chapter presents a brief introduction to setting up a user account for you to use and some basic commands to get you moving around your new system. This is your very own multitasking, multiuser system; experimenting is encouraged, so go ahead and play with your system. You may never get this type of opportunity on a typical UNIX system.

However, just playing with an operating system is no fun; it doesn't get your daily job done. After all, you don't use DOS all day, right? You use applications. Linux provides access to literally thousands of applications from around the world. You've installed several from the Slackware or Red Hat distribution from the accompanying CD-ROMs. There are plenty more where they came from, too. Programs that rival those costing hundreds of dollars for the PC platform are readily available for Linux. ■

Using basic file and directory commands

Like UNIX, Linux makes extensive use of files, so you need to know how to work with files.

Adding new users and executing programs

Like Windows NT, Linux allows many different users to access the system at the same time. To gain access, new users must be added to the system.

Using the *minicom* modem communications program

minicom, a communications program available with Red Hat and Slackware, is similar to the DOS-based PROCOMM program.

Playing the various games available

Linux provides various text-based and graphical games for your enjoyment.

Using emulators that let you run DOS and Windows programs under Linux

Linux doesn't exist in a vacuum, and the myriad developers realize plenty of DOS and Windows programs are out there that users simply don't want to abandon. So several groups are working on emulators with which you can use your DOS and Windows programs under Linux.

Maneuvering Through Linux

After installing Linux and rebooting, you're faced with a system prompt based on the name you gave your system during installation. The prompt looks similar to

```
Red Hat Linux release 4.0 (Colgate)
Kernel 2.0.18 on an I486
web login:
```

The prompt may indicate a different version of Linux, however, because Linux is an evolving system.

You must now supply a user name and a password. A user name identifies you to the operating system because Linux can support many different users, both at different times and concurrently. An account also provides each user with a default directory, called the *home directory*. Many accounts are also set up to restrict users to certain directories on the system and to prevent them from using certain commands, primarily to protect the files of one user from the prying eyes of another.

Entering Commands

You enter commands in Linux much as you do in DOS and other command-line-oriented operating systems. Linux, like UNIX, is case-sensitive; if Linux doesn't know a command, make sure that you've spelled it correctly and that you've entered it in the proper case. Most commands are executed after you press <Return>.

Recalling Command History

Linux also provides a history function to recall previous commands. This history is kept across sessions, too. You can press the <↑> key to recall previous commands, and then press <Return> to activate that command. To get a complete listing of all the prior commands you've entered, you use the history command:

```
[tackett@web~]$ history
1 clear
2 adduser
3 history
```

When you have the preceding history list, you can repeat the command by using the <↑> key and cycling through the commands until the proper one appears on the command line, or you can press <!> (the *bang* character) and enter the number of the command you want to re-execute. For example, if you wanted to repeat the adduser command in the previous list, enter

```
[tackett@web~]$ !2
```

The number of entries in the history list is user-defined in the user account's .profile configuration file. See Chapter 17, "Understanding Linux Shells," for more information on the .profile configuration file.

N O T E Linux provides many different command shells, some of which don't provide the history functions. ■

Making Selections

If you have a mouse with your system and installed the `selection` program, you can also use your mouse to copy text from other areas of your screen to the command line. To select the text, simply move the mouse cursor (which appears as soon as you click the left mouse button) by holding down the left mouse button as you drag the cursor across the desired text, and then press the right mouse button to copy the text to the command line. This is useful if you need to enter a long file name on the command line.

Completing Commands

Linux also offers another nice feature when entering commands. You can start to type a file name and then press <Tab>. Linux searches the directory for a file beginning with the same letters you've typed and completes the file name it finds. If Linux can't find a unique file name, it beeps and completes the file name to the last common character. For example, if you wanted to copy a file called todo_monday to todo_today, you type **cp to** at the prompt and then press <Tab>, Linux beeps and fills out the command line like so:

```
[tackett@web~]$ cp todo_
```

If you now typed an **m** and pressed <Tab>, Linux would place the entire todo_monday file name on the command line.

Managing Users

On many systems, the person responsible for maintaining the user accounts is referred to as the *systems administrator*. The systems administrator sets up user accounts and performs other duties. For more information on the various aspects of systems administration, check out the chapters in Part II, "Systems Administration." On your Linux system, you're the systems administrator, so it's your responsibility to set up accounts for yourself, family, and friends.

To add an account for yourself, you must create that account as the systems administrator. Systems administrators are also sometimes referred to as *superusers* because they have so much control over the system. To begin your trek through Linux, you must first log in as the superuser via the root account.

Logging In and Out

To log in as root, enter **root** at the login prompt. Linux asks for a password.

By using a password, you prevent unauthorized users from logging in to any account. Linux wants to make sure that the user name is in fact the correct user. You shouldn't share your passwords with just anyone. Linux protects the password you type by not *echoing*—that is, not displaying—the letters on screen, so make sure that you enter the correct password.

If you enter an invalid user name or password, Linux gives the following error message and starts the process over:

Part

I

Ch

5

```
web login: jack
Password: password
Login incorrect

web login:
```

Because this is your first time logging in to the system since installation, the root account has no password set, so after entering **root**, you're presented with a command prompt. You now can enter Linux commands. Most commands are entered in the same way as in DOS: Type the command with any needed parameters and press <Return>.

N O T E The default installation of the Slackware distribution provides a small "fortune cookie" message every time someone logs in to the system. This message displays a short— sometimes amusing, sometimes not—adage about life. You can also get a fortune at any time by using the `fortune` command, provided that you've installed the text-based games.

The Red Hat distribution doesn't provide this functionality by default. To get a fortune cookie under Red Hat, type **/usr/games/fortune**. ▇

To log out, enter **logout**. This command returns you to the login prompt. If this command doesn't work, try the `exit` command.

Adding Users Under Slackware

After you log in as root, you should add an account for yourself. To add an account, enter the following command and follow the prompts:

```
[root@web~]# adduser

Adding a new user. The user name should be not exceed 8 characters
in length, or you many run into problems later.

Enter login name for new account (^C to quit):
```

Look at this screen for a second. Notice the command prompt after which you entered the command. The prompt begins with the host name of the computer. This is the name you entered while installing the n package of disks. The next item is the ~ (tilde) character. Linux uses this character to refer to the account's home directory (described later). Here, it represents the directory the user is now located in. If you issued the `adduser` command from the /usr/bin directory, the prompt reads

```
[root@web~]#/usr/bin#
```

The next character is the pound sign (#). This prompt, by convention, belongs to any superuser account. A normal user account usually has $ (dollar sign) as a prompt.

Next, you may have noticed the misspellings and improper grammar in the prompts—that is, `should be not` and `you many run`. These errors don't affect the performance of the system, but they help highlight the fact that Linux, while fully functional and a great system, isn't a commercial venture.

Now enter a user name of up to eight characters and press <Return>. An example session to create an account for Jack Tackett follows:

```
Enter login name for new account (^C to quit): jack

Editing information for new user [jack]

Full Name: Jack Tackett, Jr.
GID[100]:<Return>

Checking for an available UID after 500
501...
First unused uid is 502

UID [502]:<Return>

Home Directory [/home/jack]:<Return>

Shell [/bin/bash]:<Return>

Password: opus

Information for new user [jack]:
Home directory: [/home/jack] Shell: [/bin/bash]
Password: [opus] uid: [502] gid: [100]

Is this correct? [y/N] :y

Adding login [jack] and making directory [/home/jack]

Adding the files from the /etc/skel directory:
./ .kermc -> /home/jack/ ./ .kermc
./ .less -> /home/jack/ ./ .less
./ .lessrc -> /home/jack/ ./ .lessrc
./ .term -> /home/jack/ ./ .term
./ .term/termrc -> /home/jack/ ./ .termrc
./ .emacs -> /home/jack/ ./ .emacs

[root@web ~]#
```

As you move through the process, you must enter a full name for the user to help identify the user account further. Next, you're asked to enter a group ID and a user ID. Don't worry about these items at this time. Linux uses them to determine the directories and files that you have access to by default. You can safely accept the default values (within the brackets) by simply pressing <Return> after each request.

Next, you're asked to enter a home directory for the user. This is where the user is automatically placed when he or she first logs in. This is the user's account area for storing files and for working storage. Linux provides a default directory based on the user's name. If this default directory is acceptable, press <Return>; otherwise, enter a directory and press <Return>. Accept, for now, the defaults offered by the adduser command.

Part
I

Ch
5

You're now asked to specify a shell for the user. The shell is a command interpreter much like COMMAND.COM is for DOS. The shell accepts the input and runs specified commands. You've been using a shell called bash since installing Linux. For the time being, simply accept the default bash option.

▶ **See** "Understanding Shells," **p. 325**

The final parameter is the password for the account. It's highly recommended that you provide every account with a password. Linux then displays all the information entered and asks whether it's correct. If the information isn't correct, enter **n** (or simply press <Return>, because No is the default choice); you must go back and correct the errors. If everything is correct, enter **y**.

Linux displays a series of files it copies from a skeletal user account located in the ./etc/skel directory to the new user's home directory. These files are configuration files for such items as the user's terminal and how such programs as emacs and less run from their accounts. The users can modify these files at any time to change the default behavior of the programs.

After adding the account, you can verify its existence in one of two ways; the quickest is to use a utility called finger to see whether the user has an account. The general form of the command is finger *name*. For example, you can test for the account you just created by entering

```
[root@web ~]#finger jack

Login: jack   Name Jack Tackett, Jr.
Directory: /home/jack   Shell: /bin/bash
Never logged in.
No Mail.
No Plan.
[root@web ~]#
```

If the user has an account, the appropriate information is displayed; otherwise, a message indicating no such user has an account is displayed.

The next way to verify the account is to actually log in to the account to see whether Linux will let you. You can do this in one of several ways:

- You can log out and then log in as the new user.
- You can use the su command, which stands for *switch user*.
- You can use the login command.
- You can use one of the six virtual terminals provided by Linux to log in to a new account. Remember, Linux is multiuser.

Table 5.1 presents an overview of each method.

Table 5.1   Logging In to a Newly Created User Account

Command	Description
logout	Logs you out of the root account and brings you back to the login prompt. You no longer have access to the root account until you log in as root.
su *username*	Logs you out of the account, doesn't ask for the user name to log in as, and then prompts you for the password. If you don't specify *username*, su assumes that you're trying to log in as root and expects you to enter the root password.
login *username*	Almost the same as su, except that leaving off *username* merely places you at the normal login prompt.
<Alt-F*x*>	Lets you use the virtual terminals. You can access a virtual terminal by pressing the <Alt> key and one of the function keys (F1 through F6). This takes you to another login screen, where you can log in as the new user. The best feature of using the virtual terminals is that you're still left in the other account and can swap back and forth by using the <Alt-F*x*> keys; you aren't logged out of the other account.

N O T E If you try to add a user later from the account you now create, you may not be able to use the command adduser because certain commands can be entered only by the superuser, adduser being one of them. If you have trouble adding a user to the system, make sure that you're logged in as root. ■

Adding Users with Red Hat

Red Hat Linux automates many of the adduser functions. To add a new user from the command line, enter the following command:

```
[root@web /root]#adduser jack
```

This command is a shell script located in /usr/sbin. You must be the superuser—that is, root—to issue this command.

▶ **See** "Working with Shell Scripts," **p. 350**

The script, which is just an ASCII file, creates the necessary directories and files needed by the new user. The only thing left is to set the user's password when he or she first logs in. Changing passwords is discussed later in the section "Changing Passwords."

▶ **See** "Viewing the Contents of a File," **p. 309**

Part
I

Ch
5

Using Red Hat's Control Panel to Manage Users

If you installed XFree86 with your Red Hat installation, you can use the Control Panel's User/
Group Manager configuration window (see Figure 5.1) to add users, modify user settings, and
delete or deactivate users. To manipulate a user's account, simply select the user in the dialog
box and click the appropriate button. Table 5.2 describes each button's function.

FIG. 5.1

The RHS Linux User/
Group Manager dialog
lets you see the
information stored in
/etc/passwd as well
as manipulate the
information.

Table 5.2 The RHS Linux User/Group Manager Buttons

Button	Description
Add	Displays the Add User dialog box, which lets you set the various required attributes for a user, such as home directory and password.
Deactivate	Allows you to deactivate the account of a user who you know will need the account again in the future. You may want to deactivate an account for a user who's on sabbatical or is being disciplined for some infraction. You can choose to compress the user's files to save space on your system until you reactivate that user later.
Reactivate	Allows you to reactivate a user's account.
Remove	Deletes a user from your system. The user's various files and directories will be removed. You may want to back up these files before deleting them.
Edit	Allows you to edit user accounts for such items as passwords (if they forget their password), their groups, or the shell they want to use.
Exit	Exits the RHS Linux User/Group Manager.

Clicking the Add button displays the Add User dialog box shown in Figure 5.2. You can set up
the user's account from this dialog box by filling in the information for the various fields. Table
5.3 describes the fields and their function.

FIG. 5.2
Red Hat's graphical admin tools make adding new users a breeze.

Table 5.3   The Options of the Add User Dialog Box

Field	Description
Username	The name the user uses to log in to your system.
Password	The user's password. To give the user a password, you must use the combo box arrow and choose Edit from the menu. This displays a new dialog box that lets you enter a new password for the user. The password combo box also lets you blank out the password field by selecting the "none" value, or lock the password.
UID	A field generated by the system. For more information on UIDs and groups, see Chapter 10, "Managing User Accounts."
Primary Group	The primary group to which the user belongs. Groups allow you to put users into similar groupings, all having the same permissions.
Full Name	The user's full name.
Home	The user's home directory. Typically, it's located in a directory under /home or /usr/home.
Shell	The default shell the user's account starts with. This combo box allows you to select any shell offered by the Red Hat system for the user.

▶ **See** "Working with Groups," **p. 225**

Changing Passwords

In the future, you may want to change your password or add a password to an account that doesn't have one, such as the current root account. You should always password-protect the root account.

To change a password under any version of Linux or UNIX, you use the `passwd` command, specify the old and new password, and then verify the new password. If you don't have (or—worse—don't remember) the old password, you can't use the `passwd` command to change your password. The typical sequence for `passwd` follows:

Part

I

Ch

5

```
[tackett@web ~]$ passwd
Changing password for jack
Enter old password: password
Enter new password: new-password
Re-type new password: new-password
```

If you make an error, Linux informs you that the password hasn't been changed. Linux also requires at least six characters for a valid password, and this minimum is enforced.

> **CAUTION**
>
> *Don't forget your passwords!* If you forget a user password, you must change the account information. If you forget the root account password, you must use the boot floppy created during installation to boot the system and change the password. Typically, you can set the password to empty by selecting none in the RHS Add/Edit User dialog box, and then let the user set a new password with the passwd command. You can also edit the /etc/passwd file and remove the emncrypted password from the user's record.

▶ **See** "Setting User Passwords," **p. 223**

Using Basic Commands

You need to know some basic commands to get around the system. The following sections provide some of the commands you need to use your Linux system. Finally, many of the "commands" presented in the following sections are actually utility programs that Linux uses to extend its command set. These programs are found in the /bin, /sbin, and /usr/bin directories.

Getting Help for Commands with *man*

To get online help for each of the various Linux commands, you can type man. Linux then displays, a screen at a time, any information it has on the command. If you aren't sure of what command to use, you can try the -k parameter and enter a simple keyword that represents the topic of interest. man then searches through its help files (called man, or manual, pages) for a topic that contains the keyword. Linux also provides an alias for this command, called apropos.

If you enter the command man ls, Linux provides help on the ls command, including all its parameters. The command man -k cls provides a listing of commands that have the word cls in the help file; the command apropos cls is the same as man -k cls.

Using Directory-Manipulation Commands

Linux provides many commands to work with directories. Like other operating systems you may have used, Linux allows you to create, delete, and move directories, as well as display information about the directory.

Changing the Current Working Directory with *cd*   Linux, like DOS and other operating systems, stores files in a tree structure called a directory. You can specify a file via a path from the root directory, specified with the / character, to the file itself. Thus, the configuration file for emacs for the user jack can be exactly specified like so:

```
/home/jack/.emacs
```

If you're familiar with the DOS limits of eight characters for a file name and three characters for an extension, you'll be pleasantly surprised to learn that Linux has no such limit on file names.

▶ **See** "Understanding File and Path Names," **p. 288**

Linux also uses the concept of a home directory, which is specified when an account is added to the system. A user's home directory is usually specified with the ~ (tilde) character. You can use the tilde in place of the directory name, where the user wants to copy a file from the current directory \usr\home\jack to his or her home directory:

```
cp .emacs ~
```

To move around the Linux directory structure, you use the change directory command, cd. If you enter **cd** without any parameters, Linux immediately returns you to your home directory. To move from one directory to another directory, you use the cd command much as you do in DOS—that is, cd *new-directory*. Linux also uses the single . (dot) to represent the current directory and the .. to represent the parent directory. In fact, it's DOS that emulates UNIX, not UNIX/Linux emulating DOS.

> **N O T E**   Be careful how you specify the directory separator. DOS uses as its directory separator the \ (backslash) character, which Linux uses as the character for continuing a command on another line. To separate directory names in Linux, you must use the / (forward slash) character.
>
> Also, although DOS doesn't mind if you fail to use spaces when specifying the . and .. parameters, Linux does. Linux doesn't understand cd.., but it understands cd ... Linux needs the space separating the command and the parameter. ▪

Displaying Information About Files and Directories with *ls*   ls stands for *list* and is used by Linux to display a list of files. This command is the counterpart to the DOS DIR command. (Linux also accepts the dir command to list files in a directory.) Under Linux, the ls command displays all the main files in a directory in color. By default, blue indicates directories and green indicates executable programs. You can change the default colors by modifying the file /etc/DIR_COLORS.

▶ **See** "Listing Files," **p. 302**

ls takes many parameters to specify not only how to display a file but what files to display. The most common parameter is -la, which tells ls to display information in a long format for every file in a directory.

The command `ls -la` lists all information about every file in the current directory. The command `ls .emacs` lists the file .emacs, whereas `ls -l .emacs` lists all information about the file .emacs.

Creating New Directories with *mkdir*   Because Linux's file system is based on directories, Linux provides the `mkdir` command so users can create new ones. Unlike DOS, which has an alias for the `mkdir` command called MD, Linux requires that the full `mkdir` command be spelled out. You must specify a name for each new directory, as shown in the following example:

```
mkdir backup
```

> **N O T E**   Linux does provide a way, via the command shell, to make aliases for command names;
> thus, if you simply can't live without the DOS MD command and hate typing **mkdir**, you
> can alias md to the `mkdir` command.
>
> ▶ **See** "Aliasing Commands," **p. 349** ◼

Deleting Directories with *rmdir*   The `rmdir` command deletes Linux directories. The command takes the name of the directory to delete. This directory must be empty—otherwise, Linux can't remove it.

For example, if the /backup directory had two directories within it, the command `rmdir /backup` fails. The command `rmdir /backup/jack/*` removes all files in the /backup/jack directory, and then `rmdir /backup/jack` removes the now-empty /backup/jack directory.

> **CAUTION**
>
> You can't delete a directory that contains files with the `rmdir` command. Instead, you can use the `-r` flag to the `rm` command. For example,
>
> ```
> rm -r *
> ```
>
> deletes everything from the current directory and every directory below the current directory. Be very careful using this command, because the moment you delete a directory, you can't recover the directory or the files that were located in the directory. Make backups.

Using File-Manipulation Commands

Because Linux treats directories and files similarly, it provides similar commands for manipulation.

Copying Files with *cp*   The `cp` command is similar to the DOS COPY command. You use this command to copy one or more files from one directory to another directory. The syntax of `cp` is

```
cp from-filename to-filename
```

You must supply a *from-filename* and a *to-filename* for the files to be copied. If you want to preserve the file name, use the dot (.) as a placeholder for the *to-filename* parameter. This is in contrast to DOS, where you could leave off the *to-filename*.

The command cp fred1 fred1.old copies the file fred1 to a backup file named fred1.old, whereas the command cp ~fred1.old /backup/jack copies the file fred1.old from the home directory to the /backup/jack directory. (The ~ character represents the user's home directory.)

Moving Files with *mv* The mv command, which is similar to the DOS MOVE command, allows you to move files from one directory to another directory. When you move a file, it has the same effect as if you had copied the files to a new directory and then deleted the files in the old directory. mv doesn't make a copy of the files.

The syntax of the mv command is identical to the cp command:

```
mv from-filename to-filename
```

The command mv fred1 fred1.old copies the file fred1 to a backup file named fred1.old and deletes the old fred1 file, whereas the command mv ~fred1.old /backup/jack moves the fred1.old file from the home directory to the /backup/jack directory.

Deleting Files with *rm* To delete files under Linux, you use the rm command. The rm command is dangerous because as soon as a file is deleted, you can never recover it. For safety reasons, you should use the following form of the rm command:

```
rm -i filename
```

The -i parameter tells the command to query, or inquire, the user to see if that's the file they really want to remove. For example, the command rm fred1 removes the file named fred1, whereas the command rm -i fred1 deletes the fred1 file after asking whether the user really wants to remove this file.

> **CAUTION**
>
> As soon as you delete a file under Linux, that file is gone. You can't undelete a file or directory under Linux like you can with DOS. If you delete a file, your only hope is a backup copy.

Displaying File Contents with *more* The more command displays a screen of a text file. You can look through a text file without invoking an editor, printing the file, or trying to pause the terminal as it displays the file. To display the contents of your emacs configuration file, for example, you can type the following:

```
more .emacs
```

N O T E If you try to pass a binary data file to more, you could have some unpleasant effects—for example, your terminal can lock up. If your terminal does lock up, try pressing <Ctrl-q> or <Ctrl-s>. ▪

Part

I

Ch

5

A disadvantage with more is that you can't back up to see a screen of information once it passes. But the command discussed in the following section overcomes that problem.

Using *less*—a Better *more*   less displays information a screen at a time on your terminal. The program's name is a play on words for the program it's meant to replace—more. Like more, less can display a screen of information in a text file, but unlike more, less allows you to page back and forth within the file. You can use the following command to browse through the readme file located in the info directory:

```
less /info/readme
```

Clearing the Screen with *clear*   Sometimes after filling your terminal screen with information, you want a blank screen while you sit and contemplate your next action. Under DOS, you can use the cls command, but under Linux, you must use the clear command.

Dealing with DOS Files Under Linux

During installation, you were given the chance to make any DOS partitions you had available visible to Linux. These partitions were then placed in a directory you specified during configuration—for example, /dosc.

▶ **See** "Repartitioning the Drive," **p. 85**

If you want to copy these files to a floppy, using the cp command may cause problems because UNIX and Linux treat text files a little differently than DOS, especially when dealing with carriage returns and line-feeds. To overcome this problem, a group of programs were developed to help deal with MS-DOS files under a UNIX environment. These are the m- commands, which include such commands as mcopy and mdir. mcopy works just like the DOS COPY command, and mdir provides a directory listing. As you may notice, they resemble their DOS counterparts, except that they begin with the letter m, hence the name "m- commands." The m- commands are part of the mtools package, which is a collection of public-domain programs that allows UNIX to interact with DOS files much more easily.

These commands also make copying files to floppy disks much easier because you can use the DOS designation, like A, rather than the Linux designation /dev/fd0. For more information on the m- commands, enter

```
man mtools
```

Table 5.4 provides a brief listing of the various m- commands.

Table 5.4 The *m-* Commands

Command	Description
mattrib	Displays the file attributes for the specified file(s)
mcd	Changes directory to the specified path
mcopy	Copies the files specified to the new path

Command	Description
mdel	Deletes the specified files
mdir	Provides a directory listing
mformat	Formats a floppy
mlabel	Labels the DOS file system
mmd	Makes a directory
mrd	Removes a directory (must be empty, just as in DOS)
mren	Renames an existing DOS file
mtype	Displays the text contents of a DOS file

N O T E Although you can see a DOS file with Linux and even do some editing on text files in DOS partitions that Linux can see, you can't execute DOS or Windows programs under Linux. However, projects are under way across the Internet to supply such emulation for Linux. Although the prospects look very good for such emulators in the future, at this time DOS and Windows emulation isn't fully available. You'll have a brief introduction to both items later in this chapter. ▪

Shutting Down Linux

When you're finished using a DOS machine, you can typically just turn off the power and walk away. You could also do the same under Windows, although there's a great possibility for file damage. Under Linux, there are even more chances for damaging your system, both to hardware and file systems, by simply turning off the power. You must shut down Linux in an orderly fashion, or you might corrupt the operating system to the point where it can't boot the next time you try.

Linux keeps a lot of information about itself and files in memory, in areas called *buffers*, before writing the information to disk. This process helps improve system performance and control access to the hardware—something a multitasking operating systems needs to maintain so that one user doesn't try to use a hardware device that another user is using. If you turn off the power, this information is lost and you can corrupt your file system.

▶ **See** "Shutting Down Linux," **p. 218**

Because Linux is a multiuser and multitasking operating system, it must make sure that every user stops processing gracefully and save any work in progress before shutting the system down, to prevent data loss and file damage. This also gives each user logged in to the system time to log out. To shut down Linux in an orderly fashion, you must use the shutdown command. The shutdown command syntax is

```
shutdown [-r] time-to-shutdown [message]
```

The optional -r flag indicates that Linux should immediately reboot after it shuts down. This is useful if you want to quit Linux and boot to another operating system.

time-to-shutdown indicates when the system should shut down. The time is specified on a 24-hour clock, so you can tell the machine to shut down at 11 p.m. by entering

`shutdown 23:00`

The *message* parameter is a message sent to each user logged in to the system. This message is displayed on their terminals. You can use this message to tell users why you're shutting down the system. For example, if you needed to do weekly backups, you can use the following message to make sure that everyone logs out of the system:

`[root@web /root]# shutdown -r 23:00 Shutting down at 11:00pm for system maintenance`

Remember, don't simply turn off the computer or press the reset button to exit Linux.

CAUTION

On some systems, Linux traps the <Ctrl-Alt-Del> reboot keystroke and executes an orderly shutdown as though the user had typed the `shutdown` command. However, on some systems Linux can't detect this keystroke combination and reboots immediately.

If you do accidentally turn off your system and damage the file structure, you can use the `fsck` command to try and repair the file system.

▶ **See** "Using the *fsck* Command," **p. 275**

Running Linux Programs

When you're familiar with moving around Linux and executing basic commands, you can try several applications installed when you set up the system. These applications cover a broad range of utilities, from a calculator to full-featured C and C++ compilers. Some of these programs cost hundreds of dollars; thanks to the GNU philosophy, however, many are readily available, and the only monetary outlay is the cost of getting the program from the Internet.

Luckily, many programs for Linux are also available on local bulletin boards, which you can reach via the telecommunications program included with the Slackware and Red Hat distributions of Linux. Also, many CD-ROM vendors supply CD-ROMs with hundreds of UNIX programs in source code. You can retrieve these programs from the CD-ROM and, by using the gcc and g++ compilers distributed with Linux, get those programs up and running on your PC—even if you've never compiled a program before.

Finally, these programs are text-based and don't require the X Windows system to operate; thus, they may not have flashy graphics, but they work with most Linux installations.

Using the *workbone* CD Player

workbone is installed with the Slackware distribution. workbone is a text-based CD player written by Thomas McWilliams. If you have a CD-ROM capable of playing audio CDs, you should give it a try.

McWilliams wrote the program for his own enjoyment by hacking an X Windows-based program. Because he did this for his own enjoyment, workbone may not work correctly with every CD-ROM drive.

The program uses the numeric keypad to control the CD, so make sure that you have the <Num Lock> key engaged. Table 5.5 lists the various controls used.

Table 5.5   *workbone* Commands

Key	Description
0	Exits workbone and leaves music playing
DEL	Displays the help screen
1	Goes backward 15 seconds
2	Aborts workbone and stops music
3	Goes forward 15 seconds
4	Goes to the Previous selection
5	Restarts the current selection
6	Goes to the next selection
7	Stops
8	Pauses/resumes
9	Plays

As workbone plays, the display updates the time and current selection. If you want to continue working while your CD plays, you have two choices:

- You can exit workbone and leave the music playing (key 0).
- If you want to keep the display up and running, you can simply switch to another virtual terminal via the <Alt> key and log in to another account. When you want to check on the display, you can switch back to the proper virtual terminal and check on the status of the CD.

You can also stop the CD with the 0 key and then later simply re-execute the program to see what tracks are playing. For more information, check out the man page by typing **man workbone**.

Part

I

Ch

5

Using the *sc* Spreadsheet Calculator

Do spiffy computers sell software, or does software sell computers? This is an age-old question whose answer tends to side with the concept that the proper application can sell thousands of computers. When the program called VisiCalc entered the market, PC use in business exploded. Why? Because for years, business people had played what-if games with their businesses on pieces of paper called ledgers, or spreadsheets. VisiCalc was an electronic version of the paper spreadsheet; it revolutionized how business did its forecasting and planning. Today, the successors of VisiCalc, such as Microsoft Excel and Lotus 1-2-3, still carry on the legacy started by VisiCalc. In the world of Linux, sc carries on that same legacy.

sc is a spreadsheet calculator containing rows and columns of cells. Each cell can contain a numeric value, a label string, or an expression or formula that evaluates to a numeric value or label string. These label strings can also be based on other cells to form complex relationships across a multiple collection of information.

If you've worked with other spreadsheet programs, you should have no problem getting up to speed on using sc. If you do need help, you can run a tutorial program to help you learn by entering

```
sc /usr/lib/sc/tutorial.sc
```

This tutorial provides an excellent introduction to using sc. If you need a quick reference card, you can print one by entering

```
scqref ¦ lpr
```

The solid bar is referred to as a *pipe* because you're piping, or passing on, the results of one command, scqref, to another command, lpr.

N O T E   Check out Chapter 21, "Printing," if you have any problems printing with Linux. The biggest problem you may face, besides the possibility of not being able to print at all, is a bad case of the *jaggies*, which are the stair-step effects caused by how UNIX/Linux treats carriage returns and line feeds versus how MS-DOS treats them when printing text files containing these characters. ■

For online help about sc, simply type **man sc**.

Using the *bc* Calculator

bc is a command-line calculator for those quick-and-dirty calculations. bc is actually a sophisticated programming language that allows you to evaluate arithmetic expressions interactively.

When executed, bc responds with a short copyright notice and then leaves you at the command prompt, a blank line. You can then enter simple addition and subtraction functions. You can also perform division and multiplication—however, the version of bc distributed with Linux truncates the result of division and multiplication operations. (This is one of the hazards to be aware of when dealing with GNU software.) bc is great for simple calculations, as long as you're aware of the possible problems with its division and multiplication operations.

Another great feature is bc's capability of storing values from one operation to the next with a simple syntax, *variable-name = expression*. The following example calculates the value of 125 * 5 and stores the result in the var1 variable. To see what the results of the calculation are, you can type the name of the variable and bc prints the value on the next line, as shown in the example. Next, the example sets the variable var2 to the contents of var1 divided by 5.

```
var1 = 125 * 5
var1
625
var2 = var1 / 5
var2
```

Using the *minicom* Telecommunications Package

Let's hope, after having read the chapters in Part V, "Network Administration," that you can get your Linux system up and running on the Internet, the global Information Superhighway so much in the news today. Until then, you can still connect with the rest of the world if you have a modem and a telecommunications package. Linux supplies the package, called minicom, so all you have to do is supply the modem connected to one of your serial ports.

minicom, like a lot of Linux software, was written by a single person with help from many people on the Internet. The main author of minicom is Miquel van Smoorenburg. minicom is a very robust application that rivals many other commercial applications. With it you can connect to various bulletin-board services, maintain a list of numbers to dial, and download and upload files as soon as you connect. Help for most of minicom's functionality is available on the man page.

The first item to remember is that minicom uses the key sequence <Ctrl-Shift-a> to access the various functions, such as auto-dial and file downloading. To get help at anytime while in minicom, simply press <Ctrl-a><z> to display a brief command summary screen. Table 5.6 lists a few of those commands.

Table 5.6 *minicom* Command Summary

Key	Description
D	Dialing directory
S	Sends files
P	Communication parameters
L	Toggles on or off capturing the session to a file
F	Sends a BREAK to the other terminal
T	Sets terminal emulation between vt100, Minix, or ANSI
W	Toggles line wraps on or off

continues

Part

I

Ch

5

Table 5.6 Continued

Key	Description
G	Runs a `minicom` script file
R	Receives a file
A	Adds a line-feed character to the end of lines
H	Hangs up the phone line
M	Initializes the modem
K	Runs the Kermit protocol
E	Toggles on or off local echo
C	Clears the local screen
O	Allows you to configure `minicom`
J	Jumps to a new command shell
X	Quits and resets the modem
I	Cursor key mode
Z	Displays the help screen
B	Scrolls back through the terminal window

While in the help window, you can simply press the appropriate letter to execute the command. From the `minicom` program, however, you must preface the appropriate letters with <Ctrl-a>.

`minicom` has four file-transfer protocols: zmodem, ymodem, xmodem, and kermit. If possible, you should try to use zmodem because of its superior error-recovery capabilities. If zmodem isn't available on the other system you're dialing, you should try each of the protocols in the order given. This isn't to say kermit is a bad protocol (it's not)—it's just slower than most of the others. The upside to using kermit is that more than likely almost any system you log in to supports kermit.

The next area you should be aware of is that `minicom` takes advantage of some commands that gives it access to the same type of power controlled by the superuser; thus, anyone running `minicom` has access to certain features of Linux that you may not want them to have.

▶ **See** "Handling File Security," **p. 242**

Playing Games

If you installed the y package, you have access to myriad games. Most are text-based, so you don't need the X Windows system up and running to enjoy a few minutes of fun. To get an idea of the variety of games, check out the /usr/games directory. By listing the files, you can see the available games. If you don't know what a game is or does, you can try to get help on the game with the man command. Of course, if you're adventurous, you can simply start the game and explore. Have fun!

Tetris

Tetris originated in the former Soviet Union. In the game, various shapes drop from the sky and pile up at the bottom of the screen. The object of the game is to eradicate those shapes building up and keep the game area from filling. You accomplish the elimination by completely filling a row across the playing field. When you connect one wall of the playing field with the other so that there are no gaps, that row disappears and all the shapes above it fall down to take up the vacated row. The catch to this strategy is that the shapes fall in a variety of patterns. To fill a row, you must decide how to orient a shape and then where to place it before it touches another block. When a shape touches another block, it remains at that position.

This game has been ported to most platforms, so if you've played the game on other systems, you should have no problem playing Tetris under Linux.

This version of the game is meant to be played only from the terminal, so don't expect fancy graphics. Also, the biggest pain is that on other systems you can position and orient the falling shapes with the keyboard arrow keys—not so with this version of Tetris. You must use the keys listed in Table 5.7 for positioning and orienting the various blocks.

Table 5.7 Tetris Command Keys

Command	Key
Move left	<,>
Move right	</>
Rotate	<.>
Drop	Space bar
Pause	<s>
Quit	<q>
Refresh the screen	<Ctrl-l>

Part

I

Ch

5

Dungeon

Dungeon is a text adventure based on the ancient Adventure text games, but instead of caves, you deal with dungeons. You interact with this text-based world in search of treasures and adventure; if you've played other text adventures, this one is very similar. If you've used only glittery graphics, sit back and use the brain. You interact with the game by issuing commands and requests in the form of verbs and nouns. For instance, at the beginning of the game it tells you that you're in an open field west of a big, white house with a boarded front door. There's a small mailbox here. At the prompt, you can issue the following command to read whatever is in the box:

```
There is a small mailbox here.
> open box
Opening the mailbox reveals:
a leaflet.
> read leaflet
```

The game then provides a brief overview of the game and the talented programmers who built it. The last line of the information in the leaflet tells you to get assistance by entering the command help or info.

Trek

Trek is a text-based game based on the popular TV series *Star Trek*. Your goal is to survive the bloody battles with the Klingons and rid your star sector from their scourge. When you start the game by typing **trek**, you're asked a series of questions to set up the game:

- You're asked for the length of the game you want to play.
- You can restart a saved game from a logfile. To do so, you specify a logfile on the command line. This file name then becomes the name of the game saved.
- You're asked what skill level you want to play.
- You can enter a password so that others can't claim your glory. No, really—you need a password so that no one but you can blow up your ship.

At any point—during setup or while playing—you can type a question mark to get help on the possible answers and actions available to you. Table 5.8 lists some of the possible actions.

Table 5.8   Trek Commands

Command	Description
abandon	Quits Trek
damages	Lists the damages your starship has sustained
impulse	Goes to impulse power
ram	Ramming speed
srscan	Short-range scan
undock	Leaves starbase
capture	Captures the Klingons
destruct	Self-destructs
lrscan	Long-range scan

Command	Description
dump	Who knows?
visual	Looks at the Klingons' position
cloak	Cloaks the ship
dock	Enters starbase
move	Plots and follows course
rest	Rests for a while
terminate	Quits
Warp	Engages warp engines
computer	Finds out some information
help	Calls a starbase for help
phasers	Fires phasers
shields	Shields up
torpedo	Fires torpedoes

The game begins by telling you how many Klingons are in your sector and how many starbases are here and their location. Docking at a starbase can replenish and repair your ship. Unfortunately, the game doesn't tell you where the nasty Klingon warships are located. Make sure that you pay attention to energy use; otherwise, you're in for some bad surprises.

Although this text-based game has no glitzy graphics, you can get a short-range scan with the srscan command, which displays your sector and all known objects at their respective coordinates. srscan also provides you with valuable information on the condition of your ship. All coordinates refer to a Cartesian matrix that you can maintain on paper—better yet, graph paper—so you don't have to remember from one srscan command to the other.

Running DOS Programs Under Linux

After you have enough of running various Linux applications, you occasionally might want to run some of your DOS or Windows programs. Although not yet a complete reality, work is progressing to allow you to do just that, by emulating the various operating systems under Linux. DOSEMU is a program that lets programs based on MS-DOS (and variants such as PC-DOS) run under Linux. DOSEMU stands for DOS EMUlator.

Also, a project is under way to allow users access to Windows programs under Linux. This project, called Wine, and is discussed later in "Running MS Windows Programs under Linux."

Part

I

Ch

5

Installing DOSEMU

You can find the current version of DOSEMU on the accompanying Slackware CD-ROM under the name /contrib/dosemu_0.000 and contrib/dosemu_0.060. This file archive and its files need to be placed in the /usr/src directory and then unzipped and untarred by using the following commands:

```
[root@web src]# gzip -d dosemu_5.tgz
[root@web src]# tar -xvf dosemu_5.tar
```

Next, you must build the various files by using the following commands:

```
[root@web src]#make config
[root@web src]#make depend
[root@web src]#make most
```

These commands should install the DOSEMU files in the /var/lib/dosemu directory. You must be logged in as root and have at least 10M of virtual memory available for the build.

N O T E You must have installed package d, the program development package. You need the various compilers and tools within this package to build the DOS emulator. ▪

Configuring DOSEMU

After the emulator is built, you must configure the system. To start, make a bootable DOS disk and copy the following DOS files on the disk: command.com, fdisk.exe, and sys.com.

Next, copy the following DOSEMU files from the dosemu subdirectory onto the floppy: emufs.sys, ems.sys, cdrom.sys, and exitemu.com. You can use the m- commands mentioned earlier in "Dealing with DOS Files Under Linux" to copy the files from the Linux partitions to the floppy drive.

 If you have trouble finding the Linux files, you can use the find command to locate the necessary files—for example,

```
find -name emufs.sys -print
```

This command will display the location of the file on your system, providing that it exists.

DOSEMU requires a configuration file, dosemu.conf, to operate correctly. You must customize this file for your system. You can find an example file in the examples directory on your system with the name config.dist. Listing 5.1 shows config.dist. Remarks are indicated with a pound symbol (#), and most options take the form of *parameter value*. If a parameter has more than one value, the values are placed within braces ({}).

Listing 5.1   A Sample dosemu.conf File

```
# Linux dosemu 0.51 configuration file.
# Updated to include QuickStart documentation 5/10/94 by Mark Rejhon
# James MacLean, jmaclean@fox.nstn.ns.ca, 12/31/93
```

```
# Robert Sanders, gt8134b@prism.gatech.edu, 5/16/93
#
# NOTICE:
#  - Although QuickStart information is included in this file, you
#    should refer to the documentation in the "doc" subdirectory of the
#    DOSEMU distribution, wherever possible.
#  - This configuration file is designed to be used as a base to make
#    it easier for you to set up DOSEMU for your specific system.
#  - Configuration options between lace brackets { } can be split onto
#    multiple lines.
#  - Comments start with # or ; in column 1. (beginning of a line)
#  - Send Email to the jmaclean address above if you find any errors.


#************************ DEBUG ********************************************
#
# QuickStart:
#  This section is of interest mainly to programmers. This is useful if
#  you are having problems with DOSEMU and you want to enclose debug info
#  when you make bug reports to a member of the DOSEMU development team.
#  Simply set desired flags to "on" or "off", then redirect stderr of
#  DOSEMU to a file using "dos 2>debug" to record the debug information
#  if desired. Skip this section if you're only starting to set up.
#
debug { config off    disk  off    warning off    hardware off
port  off    read  off    general off    IPC    off
video off    write off    xms   off    ems    off
serial off    keyb off    dpmi off
printer off    mouse off
}

#************************ MISCELLANEOUS ************************************
#
#  Want startup DOSEMU banner messages? Of course :-)
dosbanner on
#
#  timint is necessary for many programs to work.
timint on

#************************ KEYBOARD *****************************************
#
# QuickStart:
#  With the "layout" keyword, you can specify your country's keyboard
#  layout. The following layouts are implemented:
#    finnish        us        dvorak    sf
#    finnish_latin1 uk        sg        sf_latin1
#    gr          dk        sg_latin1 es
#    gr_latin1      dk_latin1 fr        es_latin1
#    be          no        fr_latin1
#  The us-layout is selected by default if the "layout" keyword is omitted.
#
#  The keyword "keybint" allows more accurate keyboard interrupts,
#  It is a bit unstable, but makes keyboard work better when set to "on".
#
#  The keyword "rawkeyboard" allows for accurate keyboard emulation for
```

continues

Part
I
Ch
5

Listing 5.1 Continued

```
#  DOS programs, and is only activated when DOSEMU starts up at the
#  console. It only becomes a problem when DOSEMU prematurely exits
#  with a "Segmentation Fault" fatal error, because the keyboard would
#  have not been reset properly. In that case, you would have to reboot
#  your Linux system remotely, or using the RESET button. In reality,
#  this should never happen. But if it does, please do report to the
#  dosemu development team, of the problem and detailed circumstances,
#  we're trying our best! If you don't need near complete keyboard
#  emulation (needed by major software package), set it to "off".
#
keyboard { layout us keybint on rawkeyboard on }
# keyboard { layout gr-latin1 keybint on rawkeyboard on }
#
#  If DOSEMU speed is unimportant, and CPU time is very valuable to you,
#  you may want to set HogThreshold to a non-zero value. This means
#  the number of keypress requests in a row before CPU time is given
#  away from DOSEMU. A good value to use could be 10000.
#  A zero disables CPU hogging detection via keyboard requests.
#
HogThreshold 0


#*************************** SERIAL ************************************
#
# QuickStart:
#  You can specify up to 4 simultaneous serial ports here.
#  If more than one ports have the same IRQ, only one of those ports
#  can be used at the same time. Also, you can specify the com port,
#  base address, irq, and device path! The defaults are:
#    COM1 default is base 0x03F8, irq 4, and device /dev/cua0
#    COM2 default is base 0x02F8, irq 3, and device /dev/cua1
#    COM3 default is base 0x03E8, irq 4, and device /dev/cua2
#    COM4 default is base 0x02E8, irq 3, and device /dev/cua3
#  If the "com" keyword is omitted, the next unused COM port is assigned.
#  Also, remember, these are only how you want the ports to be emulated
#  in DOSEMU. That means what is COM3 on IRQ 5 in real DOS, can become
#  COM1 on IRQ 4 in DOSEMU!
#
#  Also, as an example of defaults, these two lines are functionally equal:
#  serial { com 1 mouse }
#  serial { com 1 mouse base 0x03F8 irq 4 device /dev/cua0 }
#
#  If you want to use a serial mouse with DOSEMU, the "mouse" keyword
#  should be specified in only one of the serial lines. (For PS/2
#  mice, it is not necessary, and device path is in mouse line instead.)
#
#  Uncomment/modify any of the following if you want to support a modem
#  (or any other serial device).
#serial { com 1 device /dev/modem }
#serial { com 2 device /dev/modem }
#serial { com 3 device /dev/modem }
#serial { com 4 device /dev/modem }
#serial { com 3 base 0x03E8 irq 5 device /dev/cua2 }
#
```

```
#  If you have a non-PS/2 mouse, uncomment/modify one of the following.
#serial { mouse com 1 device /dev/mouse }
#serial { mouse com 2 device /dev/mouse }
#
#  What type is your mouse? Uncomment one of the following.
#  Use the 'internaldriver' option with ps2 and busmouse options.
#mouse { microsoft }
#mouse { logitech }
#mouse { mmseries }
#mouse { mouseman }
#mouse { hitachi }
#mouse { mousesystems }
#mouse { busmouse }
#mouse { ps2 device /dev/mouse internaldriver }
#  The following line won't run for now, but I hope it will sometime
#mouse { mousesystems device /dev/mouse internaldriver cleardtr }

#************************* NETWORKING SUPPORT ****************************
#
#  Turn the following option 'on' if you require IPX/SPX emulation.
#  Therefore, there is no need to load IPX.COM within the DOS session.
#  The following option does not emulate LSL.COM, IPXODI.COM, etc.
#  NOTE: MUST HAVE IPX PROTOCOL ENABLED IN KERNEL !!
ipxsupport off
#
#  Enable Novell 8137->raw 802.3 translation hack in new packet driver.
#pktdriver novell_hack

#************************* VIDEO *****************************************
#
# !!WARNING!!: A LOT OF THIS VIDEO CODE IS ALPHA! IF YOU ENABLE GRAPHICS
# ON AN INCOMPATIBLE ADAPTOR, YOU COULD GET A BLANK SCREEN OR MESSY SCREEN
# EVEN AFTER EXITING DOSEMU. JUST REBOOT (BLINDLY) AND THEN MODIFY CONFIG.
#
# QuickStart:
#  Start with only text video using the following line, to get started.
#  then when DOSEMU is running, you can set up a better video configura-
#  tion.
#
# video { vga console }     # Use this line, if you are using VGA
# video { cga console }     # Use this line, if you are using CGA
# video { ega console }     # Use this line, if you are using EGA
# video { mda console }     # Use this line, if you are using MDA
#
# Even more basic, like on an xterm or over serial, use one of the
# following :
#
#  For Xterm
# video { vga chunks 25 }
#  For serial at 2400 baud
# video { vga chunks 200 }
#
# QuickStart Notes for Graphics:
#  - If your VGA-Bios resides at E000-EFFF, turn off video BIOS shadow
```

continues

Listing 5.1 Continued

```
#   for this address range and add the statement vbios_seg 0xe000
#   to the correct vios-statement, see the example below.
#   - Set "allowvideoportaccess on" earlier in this configuration file
#     if DOSEMU won't boot properly, such as hanging with a blank screen,
#     beeping, or the video card bootup message.
#   - Video BIOS shadowing (in your CMOS setup) at C000-CFFF must be dis-
#     abled.
#
#   *> CAUTION <*: TURN OFF VIDEO BIOS SHADOWING BEFORE ENABLING GRAPHICS!
#
#   It may be necessary to set this to "on" if DOSEMU can't boot up properly
#   on your system when it's set "off" and when graphics are enabled.
#   Note: May interfere with serial ports when using certain video boards.
allowvideoportaccess on
#
#   Any 100% compatible standard VGA card _MAY_ work with this:
#video { vga console graphics }
#
#   If your VGA-BIOS is at segment E000, this may work for you:
#video { vga console graphics vbios_seg 0xe000 }
#
#   Trident SVGA with 1 megabyte on board
#video { vga console graphics chipset trident memsize 1024 }
#
#   Diamond SVGA
#video { vga console graphics chipset diamond }
#
#   ET4000 SVGA card with 1 megabyte on board:
#video { vga console graphics chipset et4000 memsize 1024 }
#
#   S3-based SVGA video card with 1 megabyte on board:
#video { vga console graphics chipset s3 memsize 1024 }

#*************************** MISCELLANEOUS ********************************
#
# QuickStart:
#   For "mathco", set this to "on" to enable the coprocessor during DOSEMU.
#   This really only has an effect on kernels prior to 1.0.3.
#   For "cpu", set this to the CPU you want recognized during DOSEMU.
#   For "bootA"/"bootC", set this to the bootup drive you want to use.
#   It is strongly recommended you start with "bootA" to get DOSEMU
#   going, and during configuration of DOSEMU to recognize hard disks.
#
mathco on        # Math coprocessor valid values: on off
cpu 80386        # CPU emulation valid values: 80286 80386 80486
bootA            # Startup drive valid values: bootA bootC

#*********************** MEMORY ********************************************
#
# QuickStart:
#   These are memory parameters, stated in number of kilobytes.
#   If you get lots of disk swapping while DOSEMU runs, you should
#   reduce these values. Also, DPMI is still somewhat unstable,
```

```
#  (as of early April 1994) so be careful with DPMI parameters.
#
xms 1024      # XMS size in K, or "off"
ems 1024      # EMS size in K, or "off"
dpmi off      # DPMI size in K, or "off". Be careful with DPMI!

#********************** PORT ACCESS **************************************
#
# !!WARNING!!: GIVING ACCESS TO PORTS IS BOTH A SECURITY CONCERN AND
# SOME PORTS ARE DANGEROUS TO USE. PLEASE SKIP THIS SECTION, AND
# DON'T FIDDLE WITH THIS SECTION UNLESS YOU KNOW WHAT YOU'RE DOING.
#
# ports { 0x388 0x389 } # for SimEarth
# ports { 0x21e 0x22e 0x23e 0x24e 0x25e 0x26e 0x27e 0x28e 0x29e } # for
# jill

#****************** SPEAKER *********************************************
#
# These keywoards are allowable on the "speaker" line:
#  native   Enable DOSEMU direct access to the speaker ports.
#  emulated  Enable simple beeps at the terminal.
#  off      Disable speaker emulation.
#
speaker native    # or "off" or "emulated"

#****************** HARD DISKS ******************************************
#
# !!WARNING!!: DAMAGE MIGHT RESULT TO YOUR HARD DISK (LINUX AND/OR DOS)
# IF YOU FIDDLE WITH THIS SECTION WITHOUT KNOWING WHAT YOU'RE DOING!
#
# QuickStart:
#  The best way to get started is to start with a boot floppy, and set
#  "bootA" above in the configuration. Keep using the boot floppy
#  while you are setting this hard disk configuration up for DOSEMU,
#  and testing by using DIR C: or something like that.
#  If you want DOSEMU to be able to access a DOS partition, the
#  safer type of access is "partition" access, because "wholedisk"
#  access gives DOSEMU write access to a whole physical disk,
#  including any vulnerable Linux partitions on that drive!
#
#  !!! IMPORTANT !!!
#  You must not have LILO installed on the partition for dosemu to boot
#  off.
#  As of 04/26/94, doublespace and stacker 3.1 will work with wholedisk
#  or partition only access. Stacker 4.0 has been reported to work with
#  wholedisk access. If you want to use disk compression using partition
#  access, you will need to use the "mkpartition" command included with
#  dosemu to create a partition table datafile for dosemu.
#
#  Please read the documentation in the "doc" subdirectory for info
#  on how to set up access to real hard disk.
#
#  "image" specifies a hard disk image file.
#  "partition" specifies partition access, with device and partition
```

Part

I

Ch

5

continues

Listing 5.1 Continued

```
#    number.
#    "wholedisk" specifies full access to entire hard drive.
#    "readonly" for read only access. A good idea to set up with.
#
#disk { image "/var/lib/dosemu/hdimage" }   # use diskimage file.
#disk { partition "/dev/hda1" 1 readonly }  # 1st partition on 1st IDE.
#disk { partition "/dev/sda2" 1 readonly }  # 1st partition on 2nd SCSI.
#disk { wholedisk "/dev/hda" }              # Entire disk drive unit


#******************** DOSEMU BOOT*********************************************
#
#  Use the following option to boot from the specified file, and then
#  once booted, have bootoff execute in autoexec.bat. Thanks Ted :-).
#  Notice it follows a typical floppy spec. To create this file use
#  dd if=/dev/fd0 of=/var/lib/dosemu/bdisk bs=16k
#
#bootdisk { heads 2 sectors 18 tracks 80 threeinch file /var/lib/dosemu/#bdisk }
#
#  Specify extensions for the CONFIG and AUTOEXEC files. If the below
#  are uncommented, the extensions become CONFIG.EMU and AUTOEXEC.EMU.
#  NOTE: this feature may affect file naming even after boot time.
#  If you use MSDOS 6+, you may want to use a CONFIG.SYS menu instead.
#
#EmuSys EMU
#EmuBat EMU


#******************** FLOPPY DISKS *****************************************
#
# QuickStart:
#  This part is fairly easy. Make sure that the first (/dev/fd0) and
#  second (/dev/fd1) floppy drives are of the correct size, "threeinch"
#  and/or "fiveinch". A floppy disk image can be used instead, however.
#
#  FOR SAFETY, UNMOUNT ALL FLOPPY DRIVES FROM YOUR FILESYSTEM BEFORE
#  STARTING UP DOSEMU! DAMAGE TO THE FLOPPY MAY RESULT OTHERWISE!
#
floppy { device /dev/fd0 threeinch }
floppy { device /dev/fd1 fiveinch }
#floppy { heads 2 sectors 18 tracks 80
#     threeinch file /var/lib/dosemu/diskimage }
#
#  If floppy disk speed is very important, uncomment the following
#  line. However, this makes the floppy drive a bit unstable. This
#  is best used if the floppies are write-protected.
#
#FastFloppy on


#******************** PRINTERS ********************************************
#
# QuickStart:
#  Printer is emulated by piping printer data to a file or via a unix
#  command such as "lpr". Don't bother fiddling with this configuration
#  until you've got DOSEMU up and running already.
#
```

```
#printer { options "%s" command "lpr" timeout 20 }
#printer { options "-p %s" command "lpr" timeout 10 }  # pr format it
#printer { file "lpt3" }
```

You must then use a text editor to change the settings from the example configuration file to match your system. Such items as processor type and video cards must match.

N O T E You can also boot DOSEMU from a hard drive partition, instead of from a floppy. To access a hard drive, simply configure a drive/partition in the dosemu.conf file. ▨

Running DOSEMU

To run DOSEMU, simply type **dos** at any Linux prompt. To exit, use the exitemu command from the prompt. Table 5.9 provides a listing of command-line options you can pass to DOSEMU. You also can use -? to get a complete, up-to-date listing of command-line parameters.

Table 5.9   DOSEMU Command-Line Parameters

Parameter	Description
-A	Boot from the A drive
-C	Boot from the hard drive
-c	Optimize video performance from virtual terminals
-D	Set debug options
-e	Specify the amount of EMS memory
-F#	Number (#) of floppies to use from dosemu.conf
-f	Flip the definition of the A and B floppy drives
-H#	Number (#) of hard disks to use from dosemu.conf
-k	Use the raw keyboard console defined in the rawkeyboard parameter of dosemu.conf
-P	Copy the debug information to a file
-t	Deliver the time interrupt 9
-V	Activate VGA emulation
-x	Specify the amount of XMS memory
-?	Display summary help for each command
-2	Emulate a 286
-3	Emulate a 386
-4	Emulate a 486

Part
I

Ch
5

From the DOS prompt supplied by DOSEMU, you can run most DOS programs except those that require DPMI (DOS Protected Mode Interface) support. Simply type the name of the program and—providing that DOSEMU can find the program in your path—DOSEMU will load and run the program.

Table 5.10 shows some of the programs known to operate under Linux, but more are added every day (check the file EMUsuccess.txt, in the directory where DOSEMU was installed, for an up-to-date listing). Table 5.11 lists some of the programs that don't work with Linux.

Table 5.10   Programs Known to Run with DOSEMU

Name	Function	Success Story Posted by
1st Wordplus	GEM word processor	jan@janhh.hanse.de
4desc	4dos desc editor	piola@di.unito.it
4DOS 4.2	Command interp.	rideau@clipper.ens.fr
4dos 5.0c	Command interp.	J1MCPHER@VAXC. STEVENS-TECH.EDU
ack3d	3-D engine	martin5@trgcorp. solucorp.qc.ca
ACU-COBOL	Compiler	fjh@munta.cs.mu.OZ.AU
Alite 1.10		ph99jh42@uwrf.edu
AmTax 93 & 94	Tax software	root@bobspc.canisius.edu
ansi.sys	Screen/keyboard driver (display functions)	ag173@cleveland. Freenet.Edu
arj v2.41a	[Un]archiver	tanner@winternet. mpls.mn.us
As Easy As 5.01	Spreadsheet	ph99jh42@uwrf.edu
Autoroute Plus	Route planner	hsw1@papa.attmail.com
Axum	Sci. graphics	miguel@pinon. ccu.uniovi.es
battle chess	Chess game	jvdbergh@wins.uia.ac.be
Binkley 2.50eebd	Fidomailer	stub@linux.rz.tu-clausthal.de
Blake Stone_	Game	owaddell@cs.indiana.edu
bnu 1.70	Fossil (Fido)	stub@linux.rz.tu-clausthal.de

Name	Function	Success Story Posted by
Borland C++ 2.0	86/286 C/C++ IDE	**rideau@clipper.ens.fr**
Boston Business EDT+		**keegstra@csdr2.fsfc. nasa.gov**
Cardbox Plus	Database	**hsw1@papa.attmail.com**
Castle Wolfenstein	3-D game	**gt8134b@prism.gatech.EDU**
Checkit diagnostics		
clipper 5.1	dBASE compiler	**jvdbergh@wins.uia.ac.be**
COMPRESS	Compressed fs	**rideau@clipper.ens.fr**
CCM (Crosstalk)	Modem program	
cshow 8.61	Picture viewer	**jvdbergh@wins.uia.ac.be**
cview	Picture viewer	**lotov@avarice.ugcs. caltech.edu**
d86/a86		
DataPerfect 2.1	Database	**fbennett@uk.ac.ulcc.clus1**
Dbase 4		**corey@amiganet.xnet.com**
Derive 1.2	Math package	**miguel@pinon.ccu. uniovi.es**
Disk Freedom 4.6	Disk utility	
diet 1.45f	File compression	**stub@linux.rz.tu- clausthal.de**
dosnix 2.0	UNIX utilities	**miguel@pinon.ccu. uniovi.es**
Dosshell task	Swapper	**jmaclean@fox.nstn.ns.ca**
dtmm	Molecular models	**miguel@pinon.ccu. uniovi.es**
Dune 2	Game	**COLIN@fs1.in.umist.ac.uk**
dviscr	EMTEX dvi preview	**ub9x@rz.uni-karlsruhe.de**
Easytrax	Layout editor	**maehler@wrcd1.urz. uni-wuppertal.de**
Elvis	vi clone	**miguel@pinon.ccu. uniovi.es**

continues

Part

I

Ch

5

Table 5.10 Continued

Name	Function	Success Story Posted by
Epic Pinball	Game	krismon@quack.kfu.com
ETen 3.1	Chinese terminal	tyuan!root@mp.cs.niu.edu
Eureka 1.0	Math package	miguel@pinon.ccu.uniovi.es
Falcon 3.0	Fighter simulator	rapatel@rockypc.rutgers.edu
FastLST 1.03	FidoNdlstcompiler	stub@linux.rz.tu-clausthal.de
FormGen II		root@bobspc.canisius.edu
freemacs 1.6d	Editor	ph99jh42@uwrf.edu
Frontier (Elite II)	Game	COLIN@fs1.in.umist.ac.uk
FW3		Sebastian.Bunka@vu-wien.ac.at
MS Flight Simulator 5	Game (runs *slow*!)	newcombe@aa.csc.peachnet.edu
Foxpro 2.0	Database	
Framework 4		corey@amiganet.xnet.com
Freelance Graphics 2.1	Graph/drawing application	jwest@jwest.ecen.okstate.edu
GEM/3	GUI	jan@janhh.hanse.de
GEM Draw	GEM drawing app	jan@janhh.hanse.de
GEM Paint	GEM painting app	jan@janhh.hanse.de
gmouse	Mouse driver	tk@pssparc2.oc.com
God of Thunder	Game	ensor@cs.utk.edu
Gravity	Simulation package	miguel@pinon.ccu.uniovi.es
GWS for DOS	Graphic file conv	bchow@bchow.slip
Gzip 1.1.2	File compression	miguel@pinon.ccu.uniovi.es
Harpoon	Game	wielinga@physics.uq.oz.au

Name	Function	Success Story Posted by
Harvard Graphics 3.0	Graph/drawing package	**miguel@pinon.ccu. uniovi.es**
Hero's Quest I	Game	**lam836@cs.cuhk.hk**
Hijaak 2.0	Graphic file conv	**bchow@bchow.slip**
hocus pocus	Apogee game	**kooper@dutiws.TWI. TUDelft.NL**
Image Alchemy Pro (-v doesn't work)	Graphic file conv	**J1MCPHER@VAXC. STEVENS-TECH.EDU**
Incredible Machine	Game (slow)	**sdh@po.cwru.edu**
Key Spreadsheet Plus	Spreadsheet (on non-doublespaced disks)	**jwest@jwest.ecen. okstate.edu**
Lemmings		**sdh@po.cwru.edu**
less 1.7.7	More than more	**miguel@pinon.ccu. uniovi.es**
LHA	File compression	
Lotus Manuscript	Word processor	**miguel@pinon.ccu. uniovi.es**
Managing Your Money	Financial	**newcombe@aa.csc. peachnet.edu**
Manifest	(dies during memory timings)	**hsw1@papa.attmail.com**
Mathcad 2.01	Math package	**root@bobspc.canisius.edu**
MathCad 2.06	Math package	**miguel@pinon.ccu. uniovi.es**
mcafee 9.23 v112	Virus scanner	**jvdbergh@wins.uia.ac.be**
Microemacs	Editor	**hjstein@MATH.HUJI.AC.IL**
MicroLink Yaht 2.1		**root@bobspc.canisius.edu**
Microsoft C 6.0	Compiler	**ronnie@epact.se**
Microsoft Assembler 5.0	Assembler	**ronnie@epact.se**
Microsoft Library 2.0		**root@bobspc.canisius.edu**

Part
I

Ch
5

continues

Table 5.10 Continued

Name	Function	Success Story Posted by
Microsoft Make	make	ronnie@epact.se
MicrosoftMouse Drv 8.2	Mouse driver	hsw1@papa.attmail.com
MoneyCounts 7.0	Accounting package	raeburn@cygnus.com
mscmouse	Mouse driver	tk@pssparc2.oc.com
nnansi.com	ANSI driver	mdrejhon@undergrad. math.uwaterloo.ca
Netzplan	GEM project mgr	jan@janhh.hanse.de
NHL Hockey	Game	krismon@quack.kfu.com
NJStar 2.1	Chinese word proc	aab2@cornell.edu
Norton Utils 4.5	Disk utils	rideau@clipper.ens.fr
Norton Utils 7.0	Disk utils	rideau@clipper.ens.fr
PAF	Geneology package	geek+@CMU.EDU
Paradox	Database	hp@vmars.tuwien.ac.at
PC Paintbrush IV	Paint program	bchow@bchow.slip
PCtools 4.20	Disk utils	rideau@clipper.ens.fr
pcwdemo		vinod@cse.iitb.ernet.in
PC-Write 3.0	Word processor	
pcxlab 1.03	PCX viewer	miguel@pinon.ccu. uniovi.es
peachtree complete 6.0	Accounting	stjeanp@math.enmu.edu
Pinball Dreams	Game	ronnie@lysator.liu.se
PKzip/unzip	File compression	
pklite 1.15	File compression	stub@linux.rz.tu-clausthal.de
Pong Kombat	Game	ensor@cs.utk.edu
PrintShop	Greeting card pkg	geek+@CMU.EDU
Procomm Plus 2.0	Communication	newcombe@aa.csc. peachnet.edu

Name	Function	Success Story Posted by
Procomm 2.4.3	Communication	**hsw1@papa.attmail.com**
Pspice 5.0	Circuit sim.	**root@bobspc.canisius.edu**
Q&A	Word proc/database	**newcombe@aa.csc.peachnet.edu**
Qbasic/edit (from DOS 5.0)	Interpreter	
Qedit	Editor	
QuickC	Compiler	**martin@trcsun3.eas.asu.edu**
Quicken 4.0 for DOS	Accounting pkg	**juphoff@nrao.edu**
Quicken 6.0 for DOS	Accounting pkg	
Quicken 7.0 for DOS	Accounting pkg	**juphoff@astro.phys.vt.edu**
Railroad Tycoon		**juphoff@astro.phys.vt.edu**
Red Baron	Game	**wielinga@physics.uq.oz.au**
RM/COBOL	compiler	**fjh@munta.cs.mu.OZ.AU**
Rpro 1.6		**root@bobspc.canisius.edu**
scan109	Antivirus	**miguel@pinon.ccu.uniovi.es**
scan112	Antivirus	**piola@di.unito.it**
Scorch	Tank game	**geek+@CMU.EDU**
Shez94	Arcer-Shell	**stub@linux.rz.tu-clausthal.de**
sled	Editor	**piola@di.unito.it**
Space Quest IV	Game	**lam836@cs.cuhk.hk**
Spell Casting 301		**mancini@phantom.com**
SPSS/PC+4.0	Statistical pkg	**jr@petz.han.de**
Squish 1.01	Fido Scan/Tosser	**stub@linux.rz.tu-clausthal.de**

Part
I

Ch
5

continues

Table 5.10 Continued

Name	Function	Success Story Posted by
Stacker 3.1	Compressed fs	**mdrejhon@undergrad math.uwaterloo.ca**
Stacker 4.00	Compressed fs	**J1MCPHER@VAXC. STEVENS-TECH.EDU**
StatPhys	Simulation pkg	**miguel@pinon.ccu. uniovi.es**
STSORBIT	Orbit simulation	**troch@gandalf.rutgers.edu**
Stunts	Game?	**gt8134b@prism.gatech.EDU**
Superstor	Compressed fs	**rideau@clipper.ens.fr**
TAG 2.02	Polish word proc	**rzm@oso.chalmers.se**
TASM 2.51	MACRO assembler	**rideau@clipper.ens.fr**
Telix	Modem program	**jou@nematic.ep. nctu.edu.tw**
THelp from BC++2.0	Popup help	**rideau@clipper.ens.fr**
TimED/beta	Fido MSGeditor	**stub@linux.rz.tu-clausthal.de**
TLINK 4.0	LINKER	**rideau@clipper.ens.fr**
Topspeed Modula-2	Compiler	**mayersn@hermes. informatik.uni-stuttgart.de**
Turbo Debugger 2.51	Realmode debugger	**rideau@clipper.ens.fr**
Turbo Pascal 5.5	Compiler	
Turbo Pascal 6.0	Compiler	**t2262dj@cd1.lrz- muenchen.de**
Turbo Pascal 7.0	Compiler	**mdrejhon@undergrad. math.uwaterloo.ca**
Turb-opoly 1.43		**root@bobspc.canisius.edu**
Ultima 6	Game	**msphil@birds.wm.edu**
Vpic 6.1		**root@bobspc.canisius.edu**
warlords II	Game	**buckel@cip. informatik.uni-wuerzburg.de**
Warrior of Destiny	Game	**msphil@birds.wm.edu**
WITWI Carmen	Game	**tillemaj@cae.wisc.edu**

Name	Function	Success Story Posted by
Sandiego		
Windows 3.0	Windows (real mode)	**cjw1@ukc.ac.uk**
Wolf3d	Game	**owaddell@cs.indiana.edu**
WordPerfect 5.1	Word processor	**sdh@po.cwru.edu**
WordPerfect 6.0	Word processor (needs >1M RAM)	**lujian@texmd.minmet. mcgill.ca**
Xtpro 1.1	Disk util	**root@bobspc.canisius.edu**
XWing	Game (very slow)	**ronnie@lysator.liu.se**
Zarkov 2.6	Chess	**a-acero@uchicago.edu**
zoo	File compression	

Table 5.11 Programs Known *Not* to Run with DOSEMU

Name	Function	Posted By
4D-box	Boxing game	**jvdbergh@wins.uia.ac.be**
Apple][emulator	Emulator	**ph99jh42@uwrf.edu**
Borland C++ 3.1 IDE	Compiler	**juphoff@uppieland. async.vt.edu**
brief	Editor	**bchow@bchow.slip**
Chuck Yeager Aircombat	Flight simulator	**jvdbergh@wins.uia.ac.be**
CIVILIZATION	Game	**miguel@pinon.ccu. uniovi.es**
DesqView 2.51 (Alt key doesn't work)		**hsw1@papa.attmail.com**
doom	Game	**rideau@clipper.ens.fr**
dpms from Stacker 4.0		**J1MCPHER@VAXC. STEVENS-TECH.EDU**
dxma0mod.sys	Token-ring driver	**adjihc4@cti.ecp.fr**
dxmc0mod.sys	Token-ring driver	**adjihc4@cti.ecp.fr**
ELDB	Economics database	**hjstein@math.huji.ac.il**

Part
I

Ch
5

continues

Table 5.11   Continued

Name	Function	Posted By
FIPS 0.2.2	Disk util (hdimage FAT problem)	
Howitzer	Tank game	**geek+@CMU.EDU**
Lahey Fortran	Fortran compiler	**hjstein@math.huji.ac.il**
Maple V2	Math package	**ralf@ark.btbg.sub.de**
MSDOS 5/6 QBASIC/EDIT	Editor	**bchow@bchow.slip**
NORTON UTILITIES 7.0	Disk utils	**bchow@bchow.slip**
Quattro Pro 4.0	Spreadsheet	**jwest@jwest.ecen. okstate.edu**
Raptor	Game	**ensor@cs.utk.edu**
Silent Service II	Submarine game	**jvdbergh@wins.uia.ac.be**
thunderByte scan	Virus scanner	**jvdbergh@wins.uia.ac.be**
Ventura Publisher 3.0	Desktop pub	**niemann@swt.ruhr- uni-bochum.de**
wildunix	Wild cards	**miguel@pinon.ccu. uniovi.es**
Windows 3.1		**juphoff@uppieland. async.vt.edu**

Running programs under DOSEMU has several problems, mostly because the computer is emulating DOS and the underlying machine instead of actually running DOS. Emulation slows down the system. The slowdown can become annoying, especially when you're also running other Linux programs in other virtual terminals. Video updates are also rather slow under DOSEMU.

Many DOS programs hog the CPU, because they believe they're the only program running. This prevents other Linux programs from receiving access to the CPU. To alleviate this problem, Thomas G. McWilliams wrote a program called garrot to release access of the processor back to Linux from DOS-hogging programs. You can find garrot on the **sunsite.unc.edu** FTP site in the /pub/linux/alpha/dosemu directory.

Running Windows Programs Under Linux

DOSEMU can't run Microsoft Windows programs, so the Linux community has embarked on creating a program that will allow Linux users to run such programs. This Windows emulator is called Wine. Wine isn't a standard acronym; it can stand as WINdows Emulator or, because Wine can be built as a static library instead of an emulator, Wine Is Not a Windows Emulator. Both acronyms are from the Windows FAQ.

The Windows FAQ is required reading if you want to experiment with Wine, because Wine isn't as far along in development as DOSEMU. Thus, it's very experimental and error-prone. Also, not many Windows programs are supported. In fact, to use Wine, you must have Windows installed on a partition accessible to Linux, because Wine still relies on many parts of Windows to work. Wine also requires the X system to be installed and operational.

To experiment with Wine, you'll need the following:

- A Linux kernel, version 99.13 or above
- Source code for Wine, because it's available only in source code format
- The d package installed for the compiler tools to build the source code
- At least 8M of RAM and at least a 12M swap drive
- At least 10M of disk space
- X Windows installed and configured
- A pointing device such as a mouse
- Microsoft Windows installed on a partition accessible to Linux

Because Wine is under heavy development, new versions are released almost weekly. The newest source code is located at **sunsite.unc.edu** (and other major FTP sites) in the /pub/Linux/ALPHA/wine/development directory. The file is named after the date of its release—for example, wine-961201.tar.tgz.

▶ **See** "Using FTP for Remote File Transfer," **p. 540**

Because Wine is changing so fast and is so unstable, it's not included on the accompanying CD-ROMs. If you want to experiment with Wine, feel free to download the newest files and read over the FAQs and HOWTOs. These documents are located on the CD-ROM in the /docs directory and provide the information needed to compile, install, configure, and use Wine.

Installing Wine is very similar to installing DOSEMU, with the exception that you can place the source tar file anywhere. Use the tar command to unarchive the file in the directory—for example,

```
[root@web wine]# gzip -d 950606.tar.gz
[root@web wine]# tar -xvf 950606.tar
```

Building Wine is a little more involved than building DOSEMU—in fact, it's more like building a new kernel. You must answer several questions to configure the build process. The Wine HOWTO explains the full process in detail.

Next, you must answer several questions to configure Wine with runtime parameters. These configuration parameters are stored in a file named /usr/local/etc/wine.conf. Although you can edit this file by hand, it's best to use the supplied configure program to do so.

After you configure the compilation files and the runtime parameter file, you can build Wine with the simple command make. This process takes several minutes. To use Wine, you invoke the emulator and provide the path name to a Windows executable file—for example,

```
[tackett@web ~]
```

```
$wine /dosc/windows/winmine.exe
```

The programs now supported by Wine are calc.exe, clock.exe, notepad.exe, and winmine.exe. This list is continuously expanding, so check the FAQ and HOWTO for current programs supported by the Windows emulator.

N O T E MS-DOS and Microsoft Windows aren't the only operating systems emulated under Linux. There are also emulators for the old Apple II, CPM, and the newer Macintosh operating systems. You can generally find these emulators on FTP sites in the \pub\Linux\system\emulators directory. ▩

From Here...

This chapter has just lightly touched on getting started with Linux and the various application programs available. For more information, see the following chapters:

- Chapter 7, "Using X Windows," deals with the graphical user interface provided with Linux, XFree86.
- Chapter 13, "Upgrading and Installing Software," explains how to install new software from CD-ROM or the Internet.
- Chapter 19, "Using the *vi* Editor," and Chapter 20, "Using the *emacs* Editor," discuss two of the more popular text editors for Linux.

Installing the X Windows System

For any operating system to compete for space on today's desktops, it must have an easy-to-use, graphical interface. The most popular systems today are Windows, Macintosh, and OS/2. Although these applications have gained great popularity, they can't run graphical applications across a heterogeneous network.

Linux provides the capability to run windowed applications across a heterogeneous network by incorporating the XFree86 implementation of the X11 standard of X Windows created at the Massachusetts Institute of Technology (MIT). This system is much more than a graphical interface used to run applications—it's a very powerful client/server system that allows applications to be run and shared across a network. Although XFree86 is meant to run in a networked environment, it runs fine on a single machine. You don't need a network to run XFree86 or X Windows applications.

To install, configure, and use XFree86, you need to know some basic Linux commands, such as how to execute programs, move through directories, and copy, view, and delete files. You may even need to modify some of the files with a text editor. If you come across a topic you don't fully understand, this chapter tries to give you the command you need to perform the operation and then a reference to another chapter to learn, in more detail, how to perform the operation.

What are X Windows and XFree86?

Everyone seems to enjoy graphical user interfaces (GUIs). GUIs are staples of modern operating systems such as Windows, OS/2, and the Macintosh Finder. The GUI of choice for Linux is XFree86, a GPL version of X Windows.

How to install XFree86

XFree86 isn't a single program, but a series of programs that interact with each other and with your hardware. The system must be properly installed to work well with Linux.

How to configure the XFree86 system

When installed, XFree86 needs to be tailored to your specific hardware. Be careful—a misconfigured system could damage your hardware!

Like most parts of Linux, XFree86 also has a HOWTO document. This document is located in the /howto directory on the accompanying Slackware CD-ROM and in the /X11 directory when installed under Linux. The XFree86 HOWTO is maintained by Matt Welsh at **mdw@ sunsite.unc.edu**.

> **CAUTION**
>
> Typically, you don't have to worry about software damaging your hardware. Unfortunately, however, any software that deals directly with your video system—either the card or the monitor—can cause physical damage, especially if you try to use XFree86 under Linux with an unsupported video card. Make sure that you have the necessary hardware before trying to run XFree86. Reading the documentation that comes with the XFree86 system, located in the /usr/X386/lib/X11/etc directory under Linux and the XFree86 HOWTO by Helmut Geyer in /usr/doc/faq/howto/XFree86-HOWTO, is strongly suggested.

Understanding X Windows

The X Windows system is a powerful graphical operating environment that supports many applications across a network. The X Windows system was developed at MIT and can be freely distributed. The version of X Windows discussed in this chapter is X11R6. However, Linux and XFree86 are moving targets, and a newer version of X may be available on the Net.

▶ **See** "Using FTP for Remote File Transfer," **p. 540**

XFree86, the version used by Linux, is the X11R6 standard ported to Intel-based systems. XFree86 supports a wide range of standard PC hardware.

The X Windows system grew out of a cooperative effort between two sections at MIT: the section responsible for a networking program called Project Athena, and a section called the Laboratory for Computer Science. Both used large quantities of UNIX workstations and soon realized they were each reinventing the wheel when it came to programming graphical user interfaces (GUIs) for UNIX workstations. To cut down on the amount of code both groups were writing, they decided to create one robust, extensible windowing system—X Windows.

In 1987, several vendors—in hopes of creating a single windowing system for UNIX workstations—formed an organization called the *X Consortium* to promote and standardize X Windows. Thanks to this effort, open computing is a reality. The X Consortium is composed of entities such as IBM, Digital Equipment, and MIT. This group of large organizations oversees the construction and release of new versions of X11.

XFree86 is a trademark of the XFree86 Project, Inc. The original programmers who ported X Windows to the 80386 platform decided to found the project in order to gain membership in the X Consortium. By becoming a member of the X Consortium, the XFree86 Project gained access to works in progress and could thus port the new features to XFree86 while the features were being implemented for X Windows, rather than wait until after the official release to make the port. As of January 1, 1997, the X Consortium turned over X to the Open Group.

X Windows is actually a series of pieces working together to present the user with a GUI:

- The base window system is a program providing services to the X Windows system.
- The next piece is a protocol for communicating across the network—the X Network Protocol.
- On top of the program implementing the X Network Protocol is the low-level interface, named Xlib, between the network/base system and higher level programs. Application programs typically use functions in the Xlib rather than the lower-level functions.
- Tying these pieces all together is a window manager. The window manager is an X Windows application whose purpose is to control how windows are presented to users.

Different from most other window systems, the base window system doesn't provide user interface objects, such as scroll bars, command buttons, or menus. The user interface items are left to the higher-layer components and the window manager.

X Windows applications include not only window managers, but also games, graphics utilities, programming tools, and many other tidbits. Just about any application that you need has either been written for or ported to X Windows. The setup and use of several of the standard X Windows applications is covered in more detail in Chapter 7, "Using X Windows."

X Windows implements a windows manager to handle the task of creating and controlling the interface that makes up the visual portion of the X Windows system. This isn't to be confused with the OS/2 Presentation Manager or the Microsoft Windows Program Manager. Although the window manager for X Windows does control the behavior and position of the windows, you won't find a system setup icon or control panel for maintaining your Linux system settings.

For the not-so-faint-of-heart, XFree86 also includes programming libraries and files for programmers who want to develop their own applications under XFree86. The topic of programming or any of the caveats involved in creating X Windows applications is beyond the scope of this book, but ample documentation is available on any number of Internet distribution sites, such as **prep.ai.mit.edu**, and on many CD-ROM distributions to help you gain the foothold necessary to create applications for XFree86.

What Is a Client/Server System?

X Windows is a client/server system controlled by two individual pieces of software with one piece running on the client and the other running on the server. The client and server pieces of this puzzle can be on different systems or, as is the case with most personal computers, both pieces can reside on the same machine.

Client/server is one of the major buzzwords used in the computer industry today. Like most basic concepts in the industry, client/server has been overplayed and overused to the point of confusing the average computer user. In the traditional sense, a *server* is a machine that just provides resources—disk drive space, printers, modems, and so on—to other computers over a network. A *client* is the consumer of these services—in other words, a client uses the disk space, printer, or modems provided by a server.

In the world of X Windows, this relationship is the opposite of what you've come to know in the present PC world. The accepted, or more common, notion of a server is that it provides services to a client who uses them. In the most basic form, a client displays the application that's running on the server.

Under X Windows, the server displays the application that's running on the client. This may seem a bit confusing at first, but it'll make sense when you become more intimate with the X Windows system.

In X Windows, a client is the resource that provides the programs and resources necessary to run an application—what in the traditional sense would be called a server. The resources reside on the client system (remember that the client and server systems can be on the same machine), whereas the application is displayed and interacted with on the server system.

The capability of an X Windows application, which is the client, to run under a server located on either the same computer or on another computer is called *network transparency*. Thus, an X application doesn't care whether it runs on a local or remote machine. This capability can be used to run time-consuming tasks on another server, leaving the local client unencumbered to perform other tasks.

Output Capabilities

The base window system provides X Windows with plenty of bitmapped graphical operations. X Windows and X Windows applications use these operations to present information graphically to the users. XFree86 offers overlapping windows, immediate graphics drawings, high-resolution bitmapped graphics and images, and high-quality text. Whereas early X Windows systems were mostly monochrome-based, today X Windows and XFree86 support a wide range of color systems.

X Windows also supports the multiprocessing capabilities of UNIX; thus, XFree86 supports the multiprocessing capabilities of Linux. Each window displayed under X Windows can be a separate task running under Linux.

User Interface Capabilities

The X Consortium left out the standard rules for user interfaces. Although this seems somewhat shortsighted today, at the time very little research had been done on user interface technology, so no clear interface was considered the best. In fact, even today, unilaterally declaring one interface the best can alienate many people. The preferred look and feel presented by the user interface is a very personal decision.

The X Consortium wanted to make X Windows a standard across UNIX workstations, which is one reason X Windows is available freely on the Internet. By making X Windows freely available, it fosters interoperability, which is the cornerstone of open systems. Had the X Consortium dictated a user interface, X Windows may not have gained its current level of popularity.

Input Capabilities

Systems running X Windows typically have some form of pointing device, usually a mouse. XFree86 requires a mouse or a device, such as a trackball, that emulates a mouse. If you don't have such a device, you can't use the XFree86 system with Linux. X Windows converts signals from the pointing device and from the keyboard into events. X Windows then responds to these events, performing appropriate actions.

> **CAUTION**
>
> If your mouse or other hardware pointing device isn't among those supported by Linux, you'll have problems using XFree86 and the `selection` program.

▶ **See** "Making Selections," **p. 119**

Installing the XFree86 System

Hopefully, you installed the XFree86 system while installing the entire Linux Slackware package from the accompanying CD-ROM. The X Windows system is contained in the `x` and `xap` distribution packages. If you didn't install the X Windows system at that time, you can use Slackware's `pkgtool` program to install X Windows.

▶ **See** "Using *pkgtool*," **p. 253**

N O T E The Red Hat distribution also installs X as part of the installation process. ■

Installing the Software

Under Slackware, `pkgtool` is the easiest way to install XFree86, and later in the section "Installing the X System with *pkgtool* for Slackware" are the instructions for installing X using `pkgtool`. But if you need to install the files manually (when upgrading to a newer system, for example), you need to know that the files are located on the Slackware CD-ROM in the /slakware/x# directories: /slakware/x1 through x16.

X consists of several large archived files. The current version of XFree86 for Linux is 3.1.1, which is located on the CD-ROM. Table 6.1 shows the main files. You should log in as the superuser (root) and copy the necessary files to /usr/x386. If this directory doesn't exist, create it with the `mkdir` command, as follows:

```
opus#: mkdir /usr/x386
opus#: cd /usr/x386
opus#: cp -r /cdrom/slakware/x1 .
```

These commands also copy all the files from the CD-ROM mounted at /cdrom to the current directory.

Part

I

Ch

6

Table 6.1   XFree86 Main Distribution Files

File Name	Description
x3270.tgz	IBM 3270 terminal emulation
x_8514.tgz	IBM 8514 server
x_mach32.tgz	Mach32 chip-based server
x_mach8.tgz	Mach8 chip-based server
x_mono.tgz	Monochrome monitor server
x_s3.tgz	S3 chip-based server
x_svga.tgz	Server for most SVGA cards (a good basic setup)
_vga16.tgz	EGA/VGA 16-color server
xconfig.tgz	Sample Xconfig configuration files (a must-have)
xf_bin.tgz	Basic binary files required for X (clients)
xf_cfg.tgz	XDM configuration and FVWM programs
xf_doc.tgz	Documentation for XFree86
xf_kit.tgz	Linker kit for XFree86 (1 of 2)
xf_kit2.tgz	Drivers for Linker kit (2 of 2)
xf_lib.tgz	Dynamic link libraries and configuration files
xf_pex.tgz	PEX distribution
xfileman.tgz	File manager program
xfm.tgz	The xfm file manager
xfnt.tgz	X Window fonts
xfnt75	75 point fonts for X
xfract	The xfractint program for displaying fractals
xgames	Games to play under X
xgrabsc.tgz	The Xgrabsc and Xgrab programs (Xgrab was used to create most of the images in this book)
xinclude.tgx	Programming header files for X Windows programming
xlock.tgz	The xlock screen password-protection program
xman1.tgz	Man pages for X
xman3.tgz	More man pages for X
xpaint.tgz	The Xpaint program for drawing under X

File Name	Description
xpm.tgz	The Xpm libraries, both shared and static
xspread.tgz	The Xspread spreadsheet program
xstatic.tgz	Static libraries for X
xv.tgz	The XV image viewer
xxgdb.tgz	The X Window front end for the GNU debugger

To extract these files, use the following command:

```
opus: gzip -d filename.tgz
opus: tar -xvf filename.tar
```

N O T E The CD-ROM included with this book is as up-to-date as possible, given the time lag
necessary for the production of the book. Nonetheless, a newer version of XFree86 may be
available on the Internet by the time you read this, so check the necessary archive sites—this may save
some headaches down the road.

▶ **See** "Using FTP for Remote File Transfer," **p. xxx** *(Ch 27)* ■

Ensuring Hardware Support for XFree86

Make sure that you have the proper hardware to run X Windows, the proper amount of
memory, and the necessary disk space.

You need about 21M of disk space to install the XFree86 system and the X Windows applications
provided. You need at least 16M of virtual memory to run X Windows. *Virtual memory* is
the combination of the physical RAM on your system and the amount of swap space you've
allocated for Linux. You must have at least 4M of physical RAM to run XFree86 under Linux,
thus requiring a 12M swap file. The more physical RAM you have, the better the performance
of your XFree86 system.

▶ **See** "Creating the Swap Partition," **p. 60 and 97**

Next, you need a video card containing a video-driver chipset supported by XFree86. According
to the March 15, 1995, release of Matt Welsh's XFree86 HOWTO, the video cards with the
chipsets listed in Tables 6.2 and 6.3 are supported by XFree86.

Part

I

Ch

6

Table 6.2   Non-Accelerated Chipsets Supported by XFree86

Manufacturer	Chipsets
ATI	28800-4, 28800-5, 28800-6, 28800-a
Advance Logic	AL2101
Cirrus Logic	CLGD6205, CLGD6215, CLGD6225, CLGD6235
Compaq	AVGA

continues

Table 6.2   Continued

Manufacturer	Chipsets
Genoa	GVGA
MX	MX68000, MX680010
NCR	77C22, 77C22E, 77C22E+
OAK	OTI067, OTI077
Trident	TVGA8800CS, TVGA8900B, TVGA8900C, TVGA8900CL, TVGA9000, TVGA9000i, TVGA9100B, TVGA9200CX, TVGA9320, TVGA9400CX, TVGA9420
Tseng	ET3000, ET4000AX, ET4000/W32
Western Digital/ Paradise	PVGA1
Western Digital	WD90C00, WD90C10, WD90C11, WD90C24, WD90C30
Video 7	HT216-32

Table 6.3   Accelerated Chipsets Supported by XFree86

Manufacturer	Chipsets
Cirrus	CLGD5420, GLGD5420, CLGD5422, CLGD5424, CLGD5426, CLGD5428
Western Digital	WD90C31
ATI	Mach8, Mach32
S3	86C911, 86C924, 86C801, 86C805, 86C805i, 86C928

Installing the X System with *pkgtool* for Slackware

To install X Windows, you need to log in as the superuser—that is, as root. Then you should record the location of the X Windows packages you want to install. These files are located on the accompanying Slackware CD-ROM in the /slackware directory. To access the X Windows packages from the enclosed CD-ROM, look in the following directories: /cdrom/slackware/x1, /cdrom/slackware/x2, and so on. Make sure that you remember where these files are located.

N O T E   Because Linux mounts the CD-ROM in a directory, the files are relative to that mount point.
So a typical Linux installation usually places or *mounts* the CD-ROM in a directory under the root directory named cdrom.

▶ **See** "Mounting and Unmounting File Systems," **p. 265** ■

Next, enter `pkgtool` from the command prompt. This command activates the Slackware package tool program that allows you to delete old packages or install new ones. For X Windows, these packages are the x and xap packages contained with the Slackware distribution. A menu with the following options appears:

Menu Item	Description
Current	Installs packages from the current directory
Other	Installs packages from some other directory
Floppy	Installs packages from floppy disks
Remove	Removes packages that are now installed
View	Views the list of files contained in a package
Exit	Exits package tool

Press <Shift-o> or use the arrow keys to select the Other menu line and press <Return>. `pkgtool` asks for the source directory. Enter the directory you recorded earlier for the first x package directory, normally x1. Hence, you would enter **/cdrom/slackware/x1**.

After supplying the initial directory, `pkgtool` first seeks the X server for your graphics card. You can install only one server, so as you go from screen to screen, wait until you reach the required X server before choosing Yes.

▶ **See** "Using *pkgtool*," **p. 253**

Remember that you have to install the appropriate programs from each package. Although not all packages are required, if you're installing XFree86 after installing Linux, you should review the full details on the packages to install. If you have the 21M needed for a full installation, go ahead and install each package, with the exception of the X server; install only one X server for your chipset.

N O T E If you've previously installed X Windows, you should first back up important configuration files and then delete the currently installed x and xap packages. ■

Configuring XFree86

After installing XFree86, you must then configure it for your system. XFree86 expects to find a file named XF86Config in one of the following directories:

- /etc/XF86Config
- /usr/X11R6/lib/X11/XF86Config.*hostname*
- /usr/X11R6/lib/X11/XF86Config

N O T E Configuring XFree86 is the same under most Linux distributions, including Red Hat, Slackware 96, and Caldera. ■

Part

I

Ch

6

You can find the configuration file information in the /etc/X11/etc directory. Before configuring your system, you should check out the files labeled README.Config and README.Linux. If you have the standard, supported equipment listed earlier in the section "Ensuring Hardware Support for XFree86," you should check out the sample Xconfig files from the x3 package. These files are stored in the /usr/X11/lib/X11/Sample-Xconfig-files directory. Check out the Xconfig.Index file to see whether your video card is listed. You can do so by using the following commands:

```
cd /usr/X11/lib/X11/Sample-Xconfig-files
less Xconfig.Index
```

> **CAUTION**
>
> You should never use an Xconfig file from someone else, or even one verbatim from this book or any other source, *without* looking the file over for improper values. For example, driving your monitor at unsupported frequencies may damage your equipment.

If your video card is listed, copy the corresponding Xconfig.number file from the sample directory to the /usr/X11/lib/X11 directory. You can use the following command to do this (just substitute the number from the Xconfig.Index file for the number shown here):

```
cp Xconfig.number /usr/X11/lib/X11/Xconfig
```

These sample configuration files might work for standard hardware. You can test the configuration file by starting X Windows (enter **startx**). If the X Windows system starts and runs, congratulations! If for some reason the configuration file isn't correct, Linux reports an error. Reboot your system if it just hangs. After a start failure, you need to create a configuration file yourself when you return to the command prompt.

> **N O T E** If something does go wrong (and your monitor doesn't explode), pressing <Ctrl-Alt-Backspace> should terminate the X server and return you to a shell prompt. ■

Running the SuperProbe Program

If the preceding installation procedures don't work, you can run a program to configure your system. Slackware provides a program called xf86Config to help you configure your XFree86 system, but this program requires you to answer several questions. These questions deal with the type of hardware you have on your system, and incorrect information can cause X to damage that hardware.

You should read several document files located in the /usr/X11R6/lib/X11/doc directory: HOWTO.Config, README.Config, and configxf.doc. You can use the following command to read the files:

```
less filename
```

You should also gather any manufacturer's manuals for your video card and monitor.

Next, run the SuperProbe utility:

/usr/X11R6/bin/SuperProb

This utility scans your system, trying to identify the installed video hardware. You should write down the information reported for later use with the xf86Config program. You should also double-check the information generated by SuperProbe with your hardware's documentation. The SuperProbe program will generate information that will be placed in the various sections of the XF86Config file.

Understanding the XF86Config Sections

The XF86Config file is a normal ASCII text file read by XFree86 and used to configure the X server to run properly under your hardware system. The file is formatted into the following sections, as shown in Table 6.4.

Table 6.4   XF86Config File Sections

Section	Description
Files	Lists directories for the font and rgb files.
ServerFlags	Specifies special flags for the X server.
Keyboard	Describes the type of keyboard.
Pointer	Describes your pointing device, typically your mouse.
Monitor	Provides detailed descriptions about your monitor. *This section is very important because incorrect information can severely damage the monitor.*
Device	Describes your video card.
Screen	Uses the information from the Monitor and Device sections to describe your physical screen area, including such items as number of colors and size of the screen in pixels.

Each section in the file has the following general form:

```
Section "Name"
data entry values
data entry values
more values as needed...
#this is a comment line and is ignored by XFree86
EndSection
```

You should build such a configuration file using a text editor such as vi, following the examples given. After creating the file, you run the xf86Config program to generate an XF86Config file for comparison. Finally, you run the X server in a special mode to probe for your system's settings, which you may not be able to determine from the examples, the generated file, or the documentation. These precautions are necessary because of the real threat of damage to your system.

▶ **See** "Using *vi*," **p. 393**

Part

I

Ch

6

The *Files* Section   This section lists the various fonts installed on your system in the /usr/ X11R6/lib/X11/fonts directory. Each font series will have its own subdirectory here, so you can use the following command to determine which ones are loaded:

```
ls /usr/X11R6/lib/X11/fonts
```

Each directory listed should have a corresponding entry in the `Files` section.

Depending on your selections during installation, your font files should go into standard directories, and your `Files` section will appear as in the sample section here:

```
Section "Files"
RgbPath     "/usr/X11R6/lib/X11/rgb"
fontPath    "/usr/X11R6/lib/X11/misc/"
fontPath    "/usr/X11R6/lib/X11/Type1/"
fontPath    "/usr/X11R6/lib/X11/speedo/"
fontPath    "/usr/X11R6/lib/X11/75dpi/"
fontPath    "/usr/X11R6/lib/X11/100dpi/"
EndSection
```

The *ServerFlags* Section   You'll rarely need to edit the default `ServerFlags` section. This section controls three flags used by the X server to control its operation. These flags are as follows:

Flag	Description
NoTrapSignals	An advance flag that causes the X server to "dump core"—create a debugging file—when an operating system software signal is received by the X server
DontZap	Disables the use of the <Ctrl-Alt-Backspace> key combination to terminate the X server
DontZoom	Disables switching between various graphics modes

The sample section is shown as follows with each flag commented out and thus disabled:

```
Section "ServerFlags"
#NoTrapSignals
#DontZap
#DontZoom
EndSection
```

The *Keyboard* Section   The `Keyboard` section lets you specify several options for your keyboard, such as key mappings. The minimal `Keyboard` section is

```
Section "Keyboard"
Protocol "Standard"
AutoRepeat 500 5
ServerNumLock
EndSection
```

Many more options are available, as shown in Table 6.5, but many aren't required for proper operation of your keyboard. Type **man XF86Config** at a shell prompt to see a full description of the various parameters for each section of the XF86Config file.

Table 6.5 *Keyboard* **Section Options**

Option	Parameter/Description
Protocol	Is Standard or Xqueue (Standard is the default)
AutoRepeat *delay rate*	Sets the *delay* before repeating the key at the specified *rate*
ServerNumLock	Tells the X server to handle the response to the NumLock key internally
VTSysReq	Specifies that the X server will handle switching between virtual terminals by using the <SysRq> key instead of the <Ctrl> key

Typically, you use the <Alt-F*x*> method to switch between the various virtual terminals under Linux (where F*x* indicates any function key). But when in X, you must use <Ctrl-Alt-F*x*> to access the virtual terminal. Of course, if you're questioning the need for virtual terminals when running a GUI, consider what happens if your X session locks—you can then use a virtual terminal to kill your X session.

▶ **See** "Logging In," **p. 324**

The *Pointer* Section   The Pointer section deals with your mouse or other pointing device. XFree86 uses the information here to configure your mouse for use under X. Minimally, you should specify the protocol used by your mouse and the device type. If you have a serial mouse, the device will be the serial port used by the mouse. A sample Pointer section follows:

```
Section "Pointer"
Protocol    "Microsoft"
Device      "/dev/mouse"
EndSection
```

The various protocols supported by Linux are

BusMouse	Mouse Systems
Logitech	Mouse Systems
MM Series	Xqueue
Mouseman	PS/2
Microsoft	

Some of the other options available in the Pointer section are shown in Table 6.6, but you shouldn't add them to your XF86Config file unless you're absolutely sure what effect they'll have on your system.

Table 6.6 *Pointer* **Section Options**

Option	Description
BaudRate *rate*	Specifies the baud rate for a serial mouse.
SampleRate *rate*	Needed by some Logitech mice.
ClearDTR or ClearRTS	Required by some mice using the MouseSystem protocol.
ChordMiddle	Needed by some Logitech mice.
Emulate3Buttons	Allows a two-button mouse, such as Microsoft mice, to emulate a three-button mouse. The third button is emulated by pressing both buttons at once. Many X applications need a three-button mouse for proper operation.

N O T E If you have a Logitech mouse, especially one that doesn't emulate a Microsoft mouse, you may have to experiment with some of the options in Table 6.6. ■

The *Monitor* Section   The Monitor section is probably the most important section of the XF86Config file—and probably the most dangerous. Misinformation in this file can cause catastrophic damage to your system, so be careful!

The SuperProbe program and your manufacturer's documentation will help greatly in creating this section. You can also use the files /usr/X11R6/lib/X11/doc/modesDB.txt and /usr/X11R6/lib/X11/doc/monitors to search for information on your particular monitor.

A typical Monitor section follows:

```
Section "Monitor"
Identifier   "Sanyo 1450 NI"
VendorName   "Sanyo"
ModelName    "My 14 inch monitor"
Bandwidth    60
HorizSync    30-60
VeriRefresh  50-90
#Modes:    Name      dotclock   Horizontal Timing     Vertical Timing
ModeLine   "640x480"   25       640 672 768 800       480 490 492 525
ModeLine   "800x600"   36       800 840 912 1024      600 600 602 625
ModeLine   "1024x768i" 45       1024 1024 1224 1264   768 768 776 816
EndSection
```

Your Monitor section can have more than one monitor defined, so for each monitor you must supply the information shown in Table 6.7.

Table 6.7 *Monitor* Section Options

Option	Description
Identifier *string*	Monitor identifier.
VendorName *string*	Identifies the manufacturer.
ModelName *string*	Identifies the make and model.
Bandwidth *value*	The monitor's bandwidth.
HorizSync *range*	The valid horizontal sync frequencies (in kHz). This can be a range if you have a multisync monitor, or a series of single values for a fixed-frequency monitor.
VertRefresh *range*	Specifies the vertical refresh frequencies. They can be listed as a range or a series of single values, like the HorizSync value.
Gamma *value*	The gamma correction value for your monitor.
ModeLine *values*	Specifies a series of values for each resolution to be displayed on the monitor.

For each resolution you'll need a ModeLine entry in the Monitor section. The entry has the following format:

```
ModeLine "name" dotclock    Horizontal Freq Vertical Freq
```

The horizontal and vertical frequencies are a series of four values expressed in kHz. You can get most values from running the xf86Config program (discussed later in the section "Running the *xf86Config* Program") or from the various documentation files included with the XFree86 package. For your initial test, it's best to enter a standard configuration from the documentation and then let X probe your system for more appropriate values.

The *Device* Section   The Device section describes the system's video card to XFree86. The Device section for Standard VGA is as follows:

```
Section "Device"
Identifier    "SVGA"
VendorName    "Trident"
BoardName     "TVG89"
Chipset       "tvga8900c"
VideoRam      1024
Clocks        25.30 28.32 45.00 36.00 57.30 65.10 50.40 39.90
Option        ...
EndSection
```

The only values that might be hard to come by are the clock values. You video card uses these values to generate the clock signals that in turn provide the various frequencies needed to display information on your monitor. If you get these values really wrong, you can blow your monitor! You can get this value by running X with a special parameter, –probeonly, which allows X to scan your system without much chance of physical damage to your system (–probeonly is discussed later in this chapter). X then generates a report with most of the values needed for your configuration.

Part

I

Ch

6

Your server may also require optional parameters. These optional entries in the `Device` section are detailed in the appropriate man page for your server.

The *Screen* Section Your XF86Config file can contain many monitor and device entries. These entries are tied together in the `Screen` section to create your X desktop for your X server. A sample `Screen` section follows:

```
Section "Screen"
Driver     "vga2"
Device     "SVGA"
Monitor    "Sanyo 1450 NI"
Subsection "Display"
Depth      8
Modes      "1024x768" "800x600" "640x480"
ViewPort   0 0
Virtual    1024 768
EndSubsection
EndSection
```

The `Screen` section uses the identifier names from the `Device` and `Monitor` sections. The `Driver` value tells what X server you're running and can have one of the following values:

- Accel
- SVGA
- VGA16
- VGA2
- Mono

Within the `Screen` section are display subsections, which describe the various modes available for a particular resolution. Each `Mode` value refers back to each `ModeLine` value defined in the `Monitor` section.

X starts up at the position specified by the `ViewPort` value. A value of `0,0` tells X to start with position 0,0 in the upper-left corner of the display.

With the `Virtual` value, you can define a virtual screen that's larger than your physical screen. If you specify a larger screen, X will automatically scroll the screen as needed when you move the pointer to positions outside the range of your physical screen.

Many programs found on the Internet assume a 3-button mouse and a screen size of 1152×900. This screen size is a typical screen size found on a Sun workstation. So to emulate such a system, you would need to specify the `Emulate3Buttons` in the `Pointer` section and a `Virtual 1152 900` in a `Display` subsection of the `Screen` section.

Running the *xf86Config* Program

After running SuperProbe and building a basic XF86Config file, you then can run the `xf86Config` program to generate a config file for your system. First, make sure that you aren't in the /usr/X11R6/lib/X11 directory, because this is where X looks for the XF86Config file first, and you don't want to overwrite the file you just created. To run the xf86Config program, issue the following command:

```
/usr/X11R6/bin/xf86Config
```

The xf86Config program asks many questions about your system, which it uses to fill in the various sections of the XF86Config file. After the program finishes, you must check to make sure that the values are similar to the ones you collected while creating your version of the file. The only items you'll need help with are the clock values for your monitor. You can get X itself to help with those values.

Running X in *-probeonly* Mode

By running X in a special mode, the program generates a file with information about your entire system. You can use the information in this file to complete your XF86Config file. To run X in the special probe-only mode, simply enter this command:

```
X -probeonly > /tmp/x.value 2>&1
```

The command redirects the output of X into a file named /tmp/x.value. This is an ASCII file you can edit with any ASCII editor, such as vi. You can cut the clock information from this file and paste the information into your XF86Config file, thus completing your configuration file for X.

▶ **See** "Copying, Cutting, and Pasting," **p. 408**

Now copy the file you've created into one of the directories XFree86 looks through. More than likely you can copy the file with this command:

```
cp XF86Config /usr/X11R6/lib/X11/
```

You're now ready to start up your X server with the startx command.

Using the X Windows Resource Files

To operate and use X, you need at least a startup file named .xinitrcm, which provides default settings used by X when running. To override the defaults, you can use a personal file named .Xresources that you place in your home directory. Linux provides a default .xinitrc in /etc/X11/xinit/xinitrc, although you may find the file in /usr/lib/X11/xinit/xinitrc. See the man pages for startx and xrdb for more information on these files.

From Here...

In this chapter, you learned about the XFree86 implementation of the X Windows XR11R6 standard. You've seen the difference between client and server applications and how they vary from other PC-based client/server applications. The following chapters provide more information:

■ Chapter 3, "Installing Red Hat," explains how to install the Red Hat Linux distribution, which installs X Windows as part of the installation process.

■ Chapter 4, "Installing Slackware 96," explains how to install Linux, which you need to do before installing X Windows. Without a base system, XFree86 is useless.

■ Chapter 13, "Upgrading and Installing Software," shows you how to use the `pkgtool` program to install new software systems onto your Linux box. This program is useful for installing X if you didn't install it with the base Linux system.

■ Chapter 19, "Using the *vi* Editor," shows you how to use `vi`. You need to edit your X configuration file, XF86Config, to provide X with the proper information to run on your specific hardware. `vi` is the perfect editor to use for editing the various files needed by X.

■ Chapter 20, "Using the *emacs* Editor," shows you how to use the `emacs` editor.

Using X Windows

If you're familiar with other GUIs, such as Microsoft Windows or the Macintosh user interface, you shouldn't find many differences in X Windows. X Windows presents to the user several windows, each showing the output of an X Windows application, called a *client*. The client can be running on the user's PC, which is more than likely with Linux, or on another workstation on the network.

How you move around in X Windows very much depends on window managers. Most windows use an on-screen pointer called a *cursor* to indicate where you're working. The cursor can take on many shapes, depending on what you're doing and what window manager you're running. ■

How to use X

If you're familiar with other popular GUIs, such as Windows or the Macintosh Finder, you'll have little difficulty in learning to use X. Most differences you'll encounter deal with the various window managers available under X.

How to use virtual terminals

Linux provides not only the X Windows GUI, but also several virtual terminals that you can use simultaneously. Moving among the terminals takes a little practice, however.

The different window managers

X Windows derives much of its look and feel from the window manager. The various Linux distributions provide several window managers, so experiment to find the one you most enjoy.

The X applications available for Red Hat and Slackware

What good is a GUI without applications? No matter what distribution of Linux you install, all provide many X-related applications. You also can find plenty of games to play under X too, such as Id Software's popular DOOM.

Navigating X Windows

X Windows, like most GUIs, allows input from the keyboard and the pointing device, usually a mouse. Typically, for a window to accept input, it must be the active window. An active window normally has a different appearance (for example, a highlighted border) than inactive windows.

Making a window active depends on the window manager. Some window managers allow the window to become active by merely moving the cursor into the window; others require you to click the window with the mouse, like you do in Microsoft Windows.

Using Menus

Many GUIs on PCs today provide drop-down and pop-up menus. Again, such items depend on the window manager, including the types of menu choices provided. Most X Windows window managers don't have a main menu bar across the top of the monitor; instead, they use a floating menu. You typically invoke this floating menu by clicking over an empty area of the desktop. You hold down the mouse button and drag the cursor through the various menu selections. When you find the desired menu choice, simply release the button, which is very much like how you navigate menus on a Macintosh and very unlike how you navigate menus under Microsoft Windows.

Using Virtual Terminals in X Windows

Your X server runs on a virtual terminal assigned by Linux. This terminal is assigned to the seventh virtual terminal, which you can reach with the <Ctrl-Alt-F7> key from a character terminal. From X Windows you can reach the other terminals with the <Ctrl-Alt-Fx> key combination, where x represents the number of the virtual terminal you want to access. Although accessing the other virtual terminals can be handy, X Windows does allow you to start character terminal emulators, called *xterm sessions*.

NOTE   If your X server is running, you must use the <Ctrl-Alt-Fx> combination to move from the X server to a virtual terminal. You can still use the <Alt-Fx> combination to move among the virtual terminals.

Using Window Managers for Linux

As stated earlier in the chapter, X Windows doesn't specify a window manager. The look and feel of X Windows is left up to the user. In this spirit, Linux doesn't provide just one window manager for X Windows, although the default installation of Red Hat and Slackware installs fvwm as the default window manager. Table 7.1 lists the various window managers Linux provides.

Table 7.1   Window Managers Available for Linux

Name	Description
twm	Tom's window manager
fvwm	Virtual window manager for X11
mwm	Motif window manager
olwm	Openlook's window manager, based on Sun's Open Look
olvwm	Openlook's virtual window manager

twm

The twm window manager for the X Windows system provides title bars, shaped windows, several forms of icon management, user-defined macro functions, click-to-type and pointer-driven keyboard focus, and user-specified key and mouse button bindings. This program is usually started by the user's session manager or startup script. When used from xdm or xinit without a session manager, twm is frequently executed in the foreground as the last client. When run this way, exiting twm causes the session to be terminated (that is, logged out).

By default, application windows are surrounded by a "frame," with a title bar at the top and a special border around the window. The title bar contains the window's name, a rectangle that's lit when the window is receiving keyboard input, and function boxes known as *title buttons* at the left and right edges of the title bar. Clicking Button1 (usually the leftmost button on the mouse, unless it has been changed with xmodmap) on a title button invokes the function associated with the button. In the default interface, windows are *iconified* (minimized to an icon) by clicking the left title button, which looks like a dot. Conversely, windows are *deiconified*, or maximized, by clicking the associated icon or entry in the icon manager.

Windows are resized by clicking the right title button (which resembles a group of nested squares), dragging the pointer over the edge that's to be moved, and releasing the pointer when the outline of the window is the desired size. Similarly, windows are moved by clicking the title bar, dragging a window outline to the new location, and then releasing when the outline is in the desired position. Just clicking the title bar raises the window without moving it.

When new windows are created, twm honors any size and location information requested by the user. Otherwise, an outline of the window's default size, its title bar, and lines dividing the window into a three-by-three grid that track the pointer are displayed. Each mouse button performs a different operation:

■ Clicking Button1 positions the window at the current position and gives it the default size.

■ Clicking Button2 (usually the middle mouse button) and dragging the outline gives the window its current position but allows the sides to be resized as described above.

Part

I

Ch

7

■ Clicking Button3 (usually the right mouse button) gives the window its current position but attempts to make it long enough to touch the bottom of the screen.

fvwm

The fvwm window manager for X11 is a derivative of twm, redesigned to minimize memory consumption, provide a three-dimensional look to window frames, and provide a simple virtual desktop. Memory consumption is estimated at about a half to a third the memory consumption of twm, due primarily to a redesign of twm's inefficient method of storing *mouse bindings* (associating commands to mouse buttons). Also, many of the configurable options of twm have been removed.

XFree86 provides a virtual screen whose operation can be confusing when used with the fvwm virtual window manager. With XFree86, windows that appear on the virtual screen actually get drawn into video memory, so the virtual screen size is limited by available video memory.

With fvwm's virtual desktop, windows that don't appear on-screen don't actually get drawn into video RAM. The size of the virtual desktop is limited to 32,000×32,000 pixels. It's impractical to use a virtual desktop of more than five times the size of the visible screen in each direction.

N O T E   Memory usage with the virtual desktop is a function of the number of windows that exist. The size of the desktop makes no difference. ■

When becoming familiar with fvwm, it's recommended that you disable XFree86's virtual screen by setting the virtual screen size to the physical screen size. When you become familiar with fvwm, you may want to re-enable XFree86's virtual screen.

fvwm provides multiple virtual desktops for users who want to use them. The screen is a viewport onto a desktop that's larger than (or the same size as) the screen. Several distinct desktops can be accessed. The basic concept is one desktop for each project, or one desktop for each application when view applications are distinct. Because each desktop can be larger than the physical screen, windows that are larger than the screen or large groups of related windows can be viewed easily.

The size of each virtual desktop must be specified at startup; the default is three times the physical size of the screen. All virtual desktops must be the same size. The total number of distinct desktops doesn't need to be specified but is limited to approximately 4 billion total. All windows on the current desktop can be displayed in a pager, miniature view, or the current desktop. Windows that aren't on the current desktop can be listed, with their geometries, in a window list, accessible as a pop-up menu. (The term *geometries* specifies the coordinates and number of pixels needed for the window under an X window manager.)

Sticky windows are windows that transcend the virtual desktop by "sticking to the screen's glass." They always stay put on-screen. This is convenient for things such as clocks and xbiffs, so you need to run only one such utility, and it always stays with you.

N O T E The xbiff application notifies you when new mail arrives. ■

Window geometries are specified relative to the current viewport—that is, xterm-geometry +0+0 always appears in the upper-left corner of the visible portion of the screen. It's permissible to specify geometries that place windows on the virtual desktop but off-screen. For example, if the visible screen is 1,000×1,000 pixels, the desktop size is three-by-three, and the current viewport is at the upper-left corner of the desktop, invoking xterm-geometry +1000+1000 places the window just off the lower-right corner of the screen. It can be found by moving the mouse to the lower-right corner of the screen and waiting for it to scroll into view. You can map a window only onto the active desktop, not an inactive desktop.

A geometry specified as xterm-geometry -5-5 generally places the window's lower-right corner five pixels from the lower-right corner of the visible portion of the screen. Not all applications support window geometries with negative offsets.

olwm

The olwm window manager for the X Windows system implements parts of the Openlook graphical user interface. It's the standard window manager for Sun's Open Windows product, but it works properly with any X11 system, including XFree86. The only requirements for running olwm are that the server have the OPEN LOOK glyph and cursor fonts available, which should be the case if you installed all the available fonts for X Windows.

Using X Applications in Red Hat

Red Hat spared nothing in creating a distribution well tuned to X. In fact, the commercial version of the Red Hat distribution contains a one-user licensed copy of a commercial X server called Metro-X. When you start X under Red Hat with the command

```
startx &
```

you see a screen very reminiscent of Microsoft's Windows 95 environment (see Figure 7.1).

The Start button contains menu items for many useful Linux programs, system commands, and processes. As in most X installations, you can get to these same commands by clicking your left and/or right mouse buttons over the desktop. Figure 7.2 shows the Start menu items, and Table 7.2 provides a description of each.

Part
I

Ch
7

FIG. 7.1
Shades of Windows 95, X under Red Hat bears a striking resemblance to the popular Microsoft user interface.

FIG. 7.2
Red Hat Linux provides an easy access location for many services through the Start menu.

Table 7.2 The Start Menu Items

Item	Description
New Shell	Provides the user with a new command shell window—that is, an xterm window.
Applications	Provides access to various applications, such as pine (e-mail), xpaint (graphics), and irc (chatting).

Item	Description
Utilities	Provides utilities such as a calculator, a calendar, a color `xterm`, and access to man pages.
Multimedia	Provides an audio CD player and an audio mixer.
Games	Provides arcade games such as Tetris and graphical adventure games such as DOOM.
Hosts	Provides graphical access to other hosts on your network or on the Internet.
System Utilities	Provides access to utilities for accessing the system as root and for proper window management.
Window Operations	Provides menu items for closing, killing, and moving windows around the desktop.
Preferences	Allows you to customize your X desktop as you like.
Screensaver	Provides you with a choice of images for your screen saver, which activates after a period of inactivity.
Lock Screen	Provides you with a selection of screen patterns to use when you lock your screen. Locking your screen happens when you select one of the patterns. To unlock your screen, just enter your password.
About Fvwm	Displays a dialog box with information on the `fvwm` window manager.
Help Fvwm	Displays an HTML browser with help for `fvwm`.
Exit Fvwm	Allows you to quit X and return to the terminal that launched X, or to restart the X server.

nxterm

Selecting the New Shell menu item starts an `xterm` session, which under Red Hat Linux is called a *nxterm session*. `xterm` is a common X Windows application that simulates a common video terminal such as the DEC vt100. When you start an `xterm` session, you can run any command-line program or execute any Linux command just as you do on any of the virtual terminals supplied by Linux. Figure 7.3 illustrates an `xterm` session.

xv

xv is a screen-capture program provided by Red Hat. Unlike most Linux applications, this program is shareware. Figure 7.4 shows the main dialog box for the xv application.

Part

I

Ch

7

FIG. 7.3

Starting a new command-line shell is easy under X.

FIG. 7.4

xv provides a complete screen capture and graphic file format conversion program under X.

N O T E *Shareware programs* are programs that you can download for free, but if you find the programs useful after a certain time period, you are asked to pay the creator of the program. The cost of shareware programs is usually fairly inexpensive. ▪

The buttons along the right side of the main dialog box are the most useful. Table 7.3 describes their functions. The main file list provides the file names of each graphic file now available to the program.

Table 7.3 xv's Command Buttons

Button	Description
Next	Selects the next file in the file list box.
Prev	Selects the previous file in the file list box.
Load	Loads a file from disk into the program.
Save	Saves the currently captured image to a disk file. You can choose from the following image types: GIF, JPEG, TIFF, PostScript, PBM (raw), PBM (ASCII), X11 bitmap, XPM, BMP, Sun raster file, IRIS RGB, Targa (24-bit), Fits, and PM.
Print	Prints the currently selected image file.
Delete	Deletes the currently selected image file.

The Grab button in the lower right corner of the dialog box allows you to capture any area of the desktop. Clicking this button brings up the xv grab dialog box (see Figure 7.5).

FIG. 7.5
You can use a variety of methods to grab any part of the screen under xv.

You use the mouse to select on-screen the object that you want to capture. To capture a window, you can click the Grab button and then click the left mouse button in the window you want to capture. You can also set a delay value, click the AutoGrab button, and then position the mouse cursor in the window. Either way, xv captures the image and displays it in a window of its own. You can then use the main dialog controls to manipulate and save the image.

Using X Windows Applications with Slackware 96

There are plenty of applications for X Windows on the Internet. The following sections provide a brief overview of several of the X applications furnished either with the Slackware distribution or in the /contrib directory of the Slackware CD-ROM. Several are also included with the Red Hat distribution or are available for download from your favorite GNU Web site.

Part
I

Ch
7

xterm

Slackware's `xterm` is the same program as Red Hat's New Shell command (`nxterm`). `xterm` is a common X Windows application that simulates a common video terminal such as the DEC vt100. When you start an `xterm` session, you can run any command-line program or execute any Linux command just as you do on any of the virtual terminals supplied by Linux. Figure 7.6 illustrates an `xterm` session.

FIG. 7.6

`xterm`s provide convenient access to a command-line shell.

The `xterm` program is a terminal emulator for the X Windows system. It provides terminals compatible with DEC vt102 and Tektronix 4014 for programs that can't use the window system directly. If the underlying operating system supports terminal resizing capabilities, `xterm` uses the facilities to notify programs running in the window whenever it's resized.

The vt102 and Tektronix 4014 terminals each have their own window, so you can edit text in one and look at graphics in the other at the same time. To maintain the correct aspect ratio—the height of the screen in pixels divided by the width of the screen in pixels—Tektronix graphics are restricted to the largest box with a Tektronix 4014 aspect ratio that fits in the window. This box is located in the upper-left area of the window.

Although the text and graphics windows may be displayed at the same time, the window containing the text cursor is considered the "active" window for receiving keyboard input and terminal output. The active window can be chosen through escape sequences, the vt Options menu in the vt102 window, and the Tek Options menu in the 4014 window.

Emulations   `$TERMCAP` entries that work with `xterm` include `xterm`, `vt102`, `vt100`, and `ANSI`. The `$TERMCAP` environment variable specifies the type of terminal your system emulates. `xterm` automatically searches the termcap database file in this order for these entries and then sets the `TERM` and `$TERMCAP` environment variables.

N O T E   For more information on the termcap entries and the escape sequences supported, see the man page for termcap. ■

Many of the special `xterm` features may be modified under program control through a set of escape sequences different from the standard `vt102` escape sequences.

The Tektronix 4014 emulation is also fairly good. Four different font sizes and five different line types are supported. The Tektronix text and graphics commands are recorded internally by `xterm` and may be written to a file by sending the Tektronix `COPY` escape sequence.

Other *xterm* Features   `xterm` automatically selects the text cursor when the pointer enters the window and deselects it when the pointer leaves the window. If the window is the focus window, the text cursor is selected no matter where the pointer is.

In vt102 mode are escape sequences to activate and deactivate an alternate screen buffer, which is the same size as the display area of the window. When activated, the current screen is saved and replaced with the alternate screen. Saving lines scrolled off the top of the window is disabled until the normal screen is restored. The `termcap` entry for `xterm` allows the visual editor `vi` to switch to the alternate screen for editing and to restore the screen on exit.

In vt102 or Tektronix mode are escape sequences to change the name of the windows.

Mouse Usage with *xterm*   When the vt102 window is created, `xterm` lets you select text and copy it within the same or other windows.

The selection functions are invoked when the pointer buttons are used with no modifiers, and when they're used with the <Shift> key. The assignment of the functions to keys and buttons may be changed through the resource database.

Mouse Button1 (usually the left button) is used to save text into the cut buffer. Move the cursor to the beginning of the text and then press the button while moving the cursor to the end of the region and then release the button. The selected text is highlighted and saved in the global cut buffer. This selected text is then made the primary selection when the button is released. Double-clicking selects entire words, triple-clicking selects lines, quadruple-clicking goes back to characters, and so on.

Mouse Button2 (usually the middle button) pastes the text from the primary selection, if any. Otherwise, text is inserted from the cut buffer, inserting it as keyboard input.

By cutting and pasting pieces of text without trailing new lines, you can take text from several places in different windows and form a command to the shell, for example, or take output from a program and insert it into your favorite editor. Because the cut buffer is shared globally among different applications, you should regard it as a file whose contents you know. The terminal emulator and other text programs should be treating the cut buffer as if it were a text file—that is, the text is delimited by new lines.

The scroll region within the window displaying the `xterm` displays the position and amount of text now showing in the window relative to the amount of text actually saved. As more text is saved (up to the system-determined maximum), the size of the highlighted area decreases.

Part

I

Ch

7

Clicking Button1 with the pointer in the scroll region moves the next line to the top of the display window. Clicking Button2 moves the display to a position in the saved text that corresponds to the pointer's position in the scrollbar. Clicking Button3 moves the top line of the display window down to the pointer position.

Unlike the vt102 window, the Tektronix window doesn't allow text to be copied. It does, however, allow Tektronix GIN mode, in which the cursor changes from an arrow to a cross. Pressing any key sends that key and the current coordinate of the cross cursor. Clicking Button1, Button2, or Button3 returns the letters l, m, and r, respectively. If the <Shift> key is pressed when a button is pressed, the corresponding uppercase letter is sent. To distinguish a pointer button from a key, the high bit of the character is set.

xcalc

Figure 7.7 shows xcalc, a scientific calculator desktop accessory that emulates a TI-30 or HP-10C calculator. Operations may be performed with mouse Button1 or, in some cases, with the keyboard.

FIG. 7.7

X provides various calculators, including TI (pictured) and HP emulations.

Many common calculator operations have keyboard accelerators. To quit, click the AC key of the TI calculator with mouse Button3 or click the OFF key of the HP calculator with mouse Button3. In TI mode the number keys; the +/− key; and the +, −, *, /, and = keys all do exactly what you expect them to.

N O T E   The operators obey the standard rules of precedence. Thus, entering **3+4*5=** results in 23, not 35. You can use the parentheses to override operator precedence. For example, entering **(1+2+3)*(4+5+6)=** results in 90 (6*15). ▪

The entire number in the calculator display can be selected for pasting the result of a calculation into text. Table 7.4 lists the various functions for TI emulation.

Table 7.4 TI Emulation

Key/Function	Description
1/x	Replaces the number in the display with its reciprocal.
x^2	Squares the number in the display.
SQR	Takes the square root of the number in the display.
CE/C	When clicked once, clears the number in the display without clearing the state of the machine, allowing you to re-enter a number if you make a mistake. Clicking it twice clears the state. (Clicking AC also clears the display, state, and memory.) Clicking CE/C with Button3 turns off the calculator, exiting xcalc.
INV	Inverts function. See the individual function keys for details of their inverse function.
sin	Computes the sine of the number in the display, as interpreted by the current DRG mode (see DRG). If inverted, it computes the arcsine.
cos	Computes the cosine. When inverted with the INV key, computes the arccosine.
tan	Computes the tangent. When inverted, computes the arctangent.
DRG	Changes the DRG mode, as indicated by DEG, RAD, or GRAD at the bottom of the calculator display. When in DEG mode, numbers in the display are assumed to be degrees; in RAD mode, numbers are in radians; in GRAD mode, numbers are in grads. When inverted, the DRG key has a feature of converting degrees to radians to grads and vice versa. For example, put the calculator into DEG mode and enter **45 INV DRG**. xcalc displays .785398, which is 45 degrees converted to radians.
e	The constant e, which is 2.7182818.
EE	Used for entering exponential numbers. For example, to get –2.3E–4, you enter **2 . 3 +/- EE 4 +/-**.
log	Calculates the log (base 10) of the number in the display. When inverted, it raises 10.0 to the number in the display. For example, entering **3 INV log** results in 1000.
ln	Calculates the log (base e) of the number in the display. When inverted, it raises e to the number in the display. For example, entering **e ln** results in 1.
y^x	Raises the number on the left to the power of the number on the right. For example, entering **2 y^x 3 =** results in 8, which is 2^3.
PI	The constant π, which is 3.1415927.

continues

Part

I

Ch

7

Table 7.4 Continued

Key/Function	Description
x!	Computes the factorial of the number in the display. The number in the display must be an integer in the range 0-500; depending on your math library, however, it might overflow long before that.
(	Left parenthesis.
)	Right parenthesis.
/	Division.
*	Multiplication.
–	Subtraction.
+	Addition.
=	Performs calculation.
STO	Copies the number in the display to the memory location.
RCL	Copies the number from the memory location to the display.
SUM	Adds the number in the display to the number in the memory location.
EXC	Swaps the number in the display with the number in the memory location.
+/–	Negate; change sign.
.	Decimal point.

In RPN, or HP, mode, the numbered keys; CHS (change sign); and +, –, *, /, and ENTER keys all do exactly what you expect. Many of the remaining keys are the same as in TI mode. The differences are detailed in Table 7.5.

Table 7.5 HP Emulation

Key/Function	Description
<	A backspace key that can be used if you make a mistake while entering a number; erases digits from the display. If you invert backspace, the x register is cleared.
ON	Clears the display, state, and memory. Clicking it with the Button3 turns off the calculator, exiting `xcalc`.
INV	Inverts the meaning of the function keys. This is the f key on an HP calculator, but `xcalc` doesn't display multiple legends on each key. See the individual function keys for details.
10^x	Raises 10.0 to the number in the top of the stack. When inverted, it calculates the log (base 10) of the number in the display.

Key/Function	Description
e^x	Raises e to the number in the top of the stack. When inverted, it calculates the log (base e) of the number in the display.
STO	Copies the number in the top of the stack to a memory location. There are 10 memory locations. The desired memory is specified by following this key with a digit key.
RCL	Pushes the number from the specified memory location onto the stack.
SUM	Adds the number on top of the stack to the number in the specified memory location.
x:y	Exchanges the numbers in the top two stack positions, the x and y registers.
R v	Rolls the stack downward. When inverted, it rolls the stack upward.
(blank keys)	These keys were used for programming functions on the HP-10C. Their functionality hasn't been duplicated in xcalc.

xspread

The program xspread, shown in Figure 7.8, is a public domain spreadsheet that runs under X Windows. It's installed with the Slackware distribution, and you must be using an X Windows terminal to be able to run this program. (The creators of xspread are working on making it use the ASCII screen if it can't find an X Windows display to use.) The xspread Reference Manual gives complete documentation for the program. The LaTeX source copy for this manual is in the file xspread.tex.

FIG. 7.8

xspread under XFree86 provides familiar spreadsheet capabilities for Linux users.

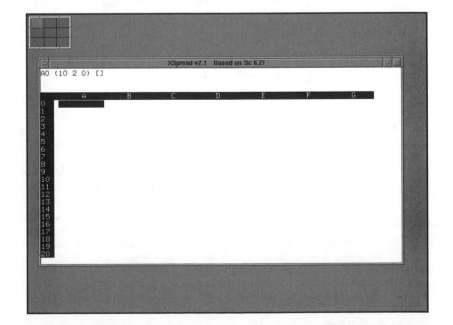

Part

I

Ch

7

xspread supports many standard spreadsheet features, including the following:

- Cell entry and editing
- Worksheet size: 702 columns with unlimited rows
- File reading and writing
- File encryption
- Absolute and relative cell references
- Numeric and label (that is, character string) data in cells
- Left or right justification for labels
- Row and column insertion and deletion
- Hiding and unhiding of rows and columns
- Range names
- Manual or automatic recalculation
- Numeric operators (+, −, *, /, ^, %)
- Relational operators (<, <=, >, >=, =, !=)
- Logical (or Boolean) operators (&, ¦, ~)
- Function references
- Graphs (XY, bar, stack bar, pie, and line graphs)
- Matrix operations (transpose, multiply, add, subtract, and inversion)
- Cursor positioning with mouse
- Menu item selection with mouse
- References to external programs, which are called *external functions*

The structure and operation of the spreadsheet is similar to—but not identical with—popular spreadsheets such as Lotus 1-2-3 and its clones. Like other spreadsheets, the workspace is arranged into rows and columns of cells. Each cell can contain a number, a label, or a formula that evaluates to a number or label.

You can start the program with or without specifying a file to be read. This file must be a saved worksheet. If a file is specified on the command line, xspread attempts to locate and read the file. If it's successful, xspread starts with the file's contents in the workspace. If it's unsuccessful or no file is specified on the command line, xspread starts with the workspace empty.

For a tutorial of the spreadsheet program, run one of the demo files—demo, demo_math, or demo_matrix—and see the file Sample_Run in the doc directory.

Seyon

Seyon, as shown in Figure 7.9, is a complete full-featured telecommunications package for the X Windows system. Some of its features are as follows:

- A dialing directory
- Terminal emulation
- A scripting language
- A variety of download protocols, including Zmodem
- Various translation modes

FIG. 7.9

Although accessing the Internet is important today, many users still need access to bulletin boards via their modems.

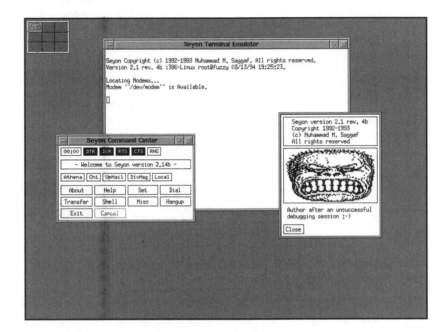

Dialing Directory   The dialing directory supports an unlimited number of entries. The directory is fully mouse-driven and features call-progress monitoring, dial timeout, automatic redial, multinumber dialing, and a circular redial queue. Each item in the dialing directory can be configured with its own baud rate, bit mask, and script file. The dialing directory uses a plain ASCII text phone book that you can edit from within Seyon. Seyon also supports manual dialing.

Terminal Emulation   Terminal emulation supports DEC vt102, Tektronix 4014, and ANSI. Seyon delegates its terminal emulation to xterm, so all the familiar xterm functions—such as the scroll-back buffer, cut-and-paste utility, and visual bell—are available through Seyon's terminal emulation window.

Using xterm also means that Seyon has a more complete emulation of vt102 than any other UNIX or DOS telecommunications program. You also can use other terminal emulation programs with Seyon to suit the user's need; for example, color xterm can be used to provide emulation for color ANSI (popular on many BBS systems), and xvt can be used if memory is a bit tight.

Part

I

Ch

7

Scripting Language   You can use scripting language to automate tedious tasks such as logging in to remote hosts. Seyon's script interpreter uses plain-text files and has a syntax similar to that of sh, with a few extra additions. It supports many familiar statements such as conditional branching by if...else and looping by goto. Scripts may be assigned to items in the dialing directory for automatic execution after a connection is made.

File Transfers   Seyon supports an unlimited number of slots for external file transfer protocols. Protocols are activated from a mouse-driven transfer console that uses a plain ASCII text file, editable from within Seyon, for protocol configuration. Seyon prompts the user for file names only if the chosen protocol requires file names or if the transfer operation is an upload for which Seyon also accepts wild cards. Multiple download directories can be specified for the different transfer slots.

Seyon detects incoming Zmodem signatures and automatically activates a user-specified Zmodem protocol to receive incoming files. Zmodem transfers are thus completely automatic and require no user intervention.

Translation Modes   Seyon can perform useful translations with the user's input. For example, Seyon can translate <Backspace> to <Delete>, a new-line marker to a carriage-return marker, and meta-key translation—that is, you can switch your <Esc> meta key to the <Alt> key. The latter mode simulates the meta key on hosts that don't support 8-bit-clean connections and makes possible the use of the meta key in programs like emacs.

Other Seyon Features   Seyon allows you to interactively set program parameters, online help, software (XONN/XOFF) and hardware (RTS/CTS) flow control; capture a session to a file; and temporarily run a local shell in the terminal emulation window.

Seyon is intended to be simple yet extensively configurable. Almost every aspect of Seyon can be configured via the built-in resources to suit the user's taste.

xgrab

xgrab is an interactive front end for xgrabsc, an X Windows image grabber. xgrab was written by Bruce Schuchardt (**bruce@slc.com**) and many other people, who retain a loose copyright on the program. xgrab lets you grab arbitrary rectangular images from an xserver and writes them to files or commands (such as lpr) in a variety of formats.

Read the man page for xgrabsc for a description of the options presented by xgrab. After selecting options from the various categories presented, click OK to have xgrab run xgrabsc to let you grab an image from the screen. After you click OK, xgrab's window disappears, and xgrabsc gains control until the grabbing process is finished. Afterward, the xgrab window reappears.

xgrab responds to the standard application options, such as -_display. See the man page for X Windows for a complete list. You can also override the default xgrab settings in your .Xdefaults file. See the "Examples" section for instructions.

Resources The xgrab resource file, XGrab.ad, contains a complete specification of the resources of all the widgets used in the xgrab window. *Widgets* are resource specifications for such items as buttons and menus. Global resources, such as default font and color, are at the bottom of the file.

Examples The ToCommand output option may be used to pipe xgrabsc output to programs. The most common commands are lpr for PostScript output and xwud for X Windows Dump output. Programs that don't accept piped input shouldn't be used with ToCommand.

 You can also get fancy and pipe the output through more than one command, such as tee screen.dmp ¦ xwud, to store the grabbed image and get a preview window.

Default settings for xgrab can be made in your .Xdefaults file. For the Athena toolkit version of xgrab, toggle buttons can be set or unset through their .state attribute, and text-field strings can be set through their *string attribute. For the Motif toolkit version, which has diamond-shaped buttons for radio buttons, toggle buttons can be set or unset through their .set attribute and text-field strings can be set through their *value attribute. For example, to set the default paper size for PostScript output, put these lines in .Xdefaults (use xrdb to load them into the server):

```
XGrab*.pageWidthText*string: 8.5
XGrab*.pageHeightText*string: 11.0
```

or

```
XGrab*.pageWidthText*value: 8.5
XGrab*.pageHeightText*value: 10.0
```

To set the default output type to XWD, put these lines in .Xdefaults:

```
XGrab*.ps.state: 0
XGrab*.xwd.state: 1
```

xlock

Patrick J. Naughton (**naughton@eng.sun.com**) wrote xlock and released it to the world. The xlock program locks the local X Windows display until the user enters their password at the keyboard. While xlock is running, all new server connections are refused, the screen saver is disabled, the mouse cursor is turned off, and the screen is blanked and a changing pattern is put on-screen. If a key or a mouse button is pressed, the user is prompted for the password of the user who started xlock.

If the correct password is entered, the screen is unlocked and the X server is restored. When you're typing the password, <Ctrl-Shift-u> and <Ctrl-Shift-h> are active as kill and erase commands, respectively. To return to the locked screen, click the small icon version of the changing pattern.

Part

I

Ch

7

Having Fun with DOOM for Linux

The best is always saved for last. Why run XFree86 under Linux? Because ID Software, Inc. has made a version of their shareware game DOOM available. DOOM is an enthralling shoot-'em-up adventure game still played the world over. Using realistic 3-D graphics, you're a space marine going into an unholy, terror-filled space colony located on one of the moons of Mars. You must find your way through the labs and various sites, looking for your lost comrades. All you find instead are hideous monsters and other space marines who have turned against you.

The X Windows version supplied on the accompanying Slackware CD-ROM in the /contrib directory is a complete shareware version. (The Red Hat distribution automatically installs the game during installation.) Although this version runs on 386 computers, it was built to run on high-end 486 systems. If you run DOOM on a 386 with a small amount of physical RAM, be prepared to be disappointed; the game will be too slow to be enjoyable. You need lots of horse-power to play DOOM under Linux.

Installing DOOM

DOOM is installed by default with the Red Hat distribution and can be started by selecting xdoom from the Games menu from the taskbar/Start menu.

Under Slackware, DOOM is stored in a series of archived files under the ///slackware/y2 directory. If you chose to install the games package while installing Linux, DOOM should already be installed. If not, you can use pkgtool to install it now, or you can perform the following steps:

▶ **See** "Using *pkgtool*," **p. 253**

1. Copy the archived files under the ///slackware/y2 directory to an area on your hard drive.

2. Change the directory to the base directory you want to use. The archives will extract the files to the usr/games/doom directory, so you may as well copy all the files in the doom directory on the accompanying Slackware CD-ROM to /usr with the following commands:

```
cd /usr
cp /cdrom/contrib/linuxdoom/* .
```

3. Decompress each file in the directory with

```
gzip -d filename
```

where *filename* is the name of each file in the directory. This command creates two tar files.

4. Unarchive each file with the tar command to create the necessary directories and files:

```
tar -xfv archive-file
```

▶ **See** "Using *tar*," **p. 231**

Starting DOOM

To play DOOM, you must first have X Windows running, so enter **startx**. When X Windows is running, you can start an `xterm` session or use the <Ctrl-Alt-F*x*> key sequence to access one of the virtual character terminals; then enter `linuxxdoom`. If this doesn't work, Linux can't find the DOOM program—that is, it's not located in your path. If this occurs, simply change the current directory to the directory where you installed DOOM. Then enter the DOOM command again.

If you started DOOM from a virtual terminal, you need to return to the X Windows session by pressing <Ctrl-Alt-F7>. If you started DOOM from an `xterm` session, you should see the DOOM introduction screen in a few seconds.

While DOOM loads, notice a series of messages. One might indicate that DOOM and Linux can't start the sound system; thus, you might have to play DOOM without sound. Sound still isn't fully supported in this port of DOOM; such is the life of an evolving system such as Linux. For instructions on playing DOOM, see the README.Linux file.

From Here...

Plenty of programs are available for Linux out on the Net. You can also use X Windows to multitask different Linux programs easier by using `xterms` rather than the virtual terminals available from the character screens. You can check out the newsgroups **comp.windows. x.apps** and **comp.windows.x.intrinsics** for various information about X Windows in general. The following chapters also provide more information:

- Chapter 3, "Installing Red Hat," explains how to install the Red Hat distribution of Linux, which includes installing X under Red Hat.
- Chapter 4, "Installing Slackware 96," explains how to install the Slackware 96 distribution of Linux.
- Chapter 6, "Installing the X Windows System," explains how to install the XFree86 version of X for Linux, which you need to do before installing X Windows.
- To learn how to access the Internet with Linux, check out Chapter 27, "Accessing the Internet with *telnet*, *ftp*, and the *r*- Commands."
- For surfing the Net, check out Chapter 28, "Surfing the Internet with the World Wide Web."

Part
I

Ch
7

Systems Administration

Understanding Systems Administration

A Linux system should have at least one person designated as the systems administrator to manage the system and oversee its performance. The systems administrator is responsible for seeing that the system is functioning properly, knows who to call if things can't be fixed locally, and knows how to provide software and hardware facilities to current and new users.

A Linux system requires initial configuration and continuous attention to ensure that the system remains effective, trustworthy, and efficient for all users. The systems administrator is the person responsible for attending to the Linux system's needs. As such, this person is responsible for many different tasks.

This chapter discusses some of the major tasks and issues confronting a systems administrator in a networked multiuser environment. Assuming that you bought this book to learn about and install Linux, you'll probably find yourself in the role of a systems administrator almost immediately. Some of the topics in this chapter are geared to systems administration in a larger organization. However, even if you're a single user who wants to play with Linux at home, you should read about the topics discussed in this chapter so that you can be aware of the larger issues involved in systems administration.

Why Linux administration is needed

Learn about the most common tasks associated with systems administration, and the tasks required to set up and maintain a Linux network.

The different computer processing models

Learn about the concepts and elements of centralized processing and distributed processing.

User support issues

Learn how to provide users with access to your system and support their needs.

In many cases, your Linux system is networked with other computers that aren't running Linux. These other computers might be running other types of UNIX, or they might be running a different operating system entirely. Because Linux is a specific flavor of UNIX, much of the information in this chapter is applicable to Linux *and* UNIX. In some places in this chapter, UNIX and Linux are referred to interchangeably. ■

Understanding the Importance of Proper Administration

All UNIX systems are different in one way or another, and each is unique in the way it must be administered. Linux is no exception. Your administrative duties vary, based on variables such as the number of users you manage, the kinds of peripherals (printers, tape drives, and so on) attached to the computer, networking connections, and the level of security you require.

A systems administrator, alone or with a support staff, must provide a secure, efficient, and reliable environment for system users. The administrator has the power and responsibility to establish and maintain a system that provides effective and dependable service. In a multiuser environment, a number of competing purposes and priorities exist. The administrator exercises the power and responsibility necessary to provide a well-functioning system.

Delegation of administrative responsibilities varies from system to system. On large systems, administration tasks can be divided among several people. Conversely, some small systems don't even require a full-time administrator; such systems simply designate a certain user to act as systems administrator. If you work in a networked environment, your system may be administered over the network by a network administrator.

Each Linux system has a single user who can perform virtually any operation on the computer. This user is called the *superuser* and has a special login name called *root*. The home directory for the root user when logged in to the system is typically / (the root directory of the file system) or a specific home directory, such as /home/root.

The systems administrator logs in as the superuser to perform tasks that require special access privileges. For normal system work, the systems administrator logs in as an ordinary user. The superuser's login name—root—is used only for limited, special purposes. The number of users who can log in as root should be kept to a minimum (at most, two or three). When any person logs in to the system as root, that person is a superuser and has absolute power on the system. With this privilege, the superuser can change the attributes of any file, stop the system, start the system, back up the system's data, and perform many other tasks.

The administrator must be aware of many of the technical aspects of the computer system. Also, the administrator must be aware of the users' needs as well as the system's primary purpose. Any computer system is a finite resource; policies regarding its use must be established and enforced. Thus, the administrator has a technical role as well as a policy role to play. That policy role, combined with the power to perform virtually any possible action, requires a responsible, skillful, and diplomatic person in the role of administrator.

The precise job description of the systems administrator often depends on the local organization. As systems administrator, you might find yourself involved in a wide variety of activities, from setting policy to installing software to moving furniture. However, all systems administrators have to perform or manage a number of tasks, as follows:

- *Manage users.* Add users, delete users, and modify users' capabilities and privileges.
- *Configure devices.* Make available and share devices such as printers, terminals, modems, tape drives, and so on.
- *Make backups.* Schedule, make, and store backups for possible restoration if the system's files are lost or damaged.
- *Shut down the system.* Shut down the system in an orderly manner to avoid inconsistencies in the file system.
- *Train users.* Provide or obtain effective training for users so that they can use the system effectively and efficiently.
- *Secure the system.* Keep users from interfering with each other through accidental or deliberate actions.
- *Log system changes.* Keep a log book to record any significant activity concerning the system.
- *Advise users.* Act as the "local expert" to aid the system's ordinary users.

Understanding Multiuser Concepts

A multiuser system employs two main concepts: multitasking and multiuser services. Linux has the apparent capability to execute multiple tasks concurrently—transparent to the user. For example, you can read your e-mail while compiling a program.

Each task—whether it's a simple command you enter on the command line or a complex application—starts one or more processes. Everything running on a Linux system is associated with a process; hence, because Linux is running many processes simultaneously, Linux is a multitasking operating system.

You can connect to a computer running UNIX (referred to as a *server*) in many ways. You can use a terminal or a computer; you can be located physically near the server, connected with a cable, or you can be on the other side of the planet connected with high-speed data lines or ordinary phone lines. Whether you're using a terminal or computer and how you're connected to the server determine if the computer's resources are considered to be distributed or centralized.

A single-user computer operating system, such as DOS, is designed to be used by one person at a time. All the processing is done on one computer that has sole access to resources, such as printers, storage, and processing.

Multiuser systems use the centralized- and distributed-processing models to accommodate many users simultaneously:

- In a *centralized-processing environment*, many users (large systems can have hundreds of users) access the resources of one computer; storage, printer, memory, and processing tasks are all performed by that one computer.

- In the *distributed-processing environment*, processing can occur on the user's own workstation, and the central processor is used to distribute applications and data. Printers and storage can be connected to the user's workstation or to the main server.

Understanding Centralized-Processing Systems

As technology during the 1950s and '60s advanced, operating systems began to allow multiple users to share resources from separate terminals. By using a batch-processing sequence, two users could execute two sets of instructions while sharing a processor, storage, and output.

With the advent of a switched telephone network, computers began to use telephone resources to extend computer resources geographically. In this model, each processor used communications-processing resources to connect with remote terminals. This created a need for computers and terminals to communicate in a better way. The result was the development of *front-end processing* for communications tasks and the centralized-processing model.

Until personal computers became inexpensive, powerful, and ubiquitous, most UNIX systems used the centralized-processing model. With centralized processing, mainframe computers handled all the processing. Users connected to the mainframe shared its resources. This model is used less and less today, although it's still appropriate for computing sites where users are separated geographically.

For example, your bank may have one main processing center, yet all the bank's branches can access the data center regardless of their locations. On each user's desk is a terminal, including a keyboard, a monitor, and a direct connection to the mainframe so that the terminal can access the centralized resources: processing, printing, and storage (see Figure 8.1). The centralized-processing model is usually made up of many elements, such as the server, front-end processors, terminals, modems, and multiport adapters.

As a user requests data, the request is processed by the computer in the bank's main office. Results of the processing are sent back to the terminal in the branch office. All data is processed and stored by the mainframe computer.

FIG. 8.1

This figure shows the centralized-processing model of a computing environment.

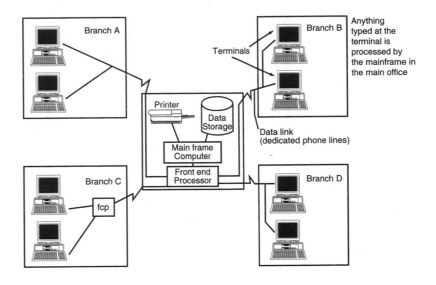

Elements of the Centralized-Processing Model

To make the centralized-processing model work, you need many elements, including the server, front-end processors, terminals, modems, and multiport adapters.

A *server* can be defined as any computer set up to share its resources (processing power, storage, printers, and so on). For example, you can use an IBM-compatible PC as a server as long as it has enough hard disk space and RAM.

A *front-end processor* connects the communication channels and the server. It handles the details of communication so that the server is free to process its data.

Two popular types of terminals are used today: *dumb terminals* and *smart terminals*. Traditionally, UNIX is used with dumb terminals, which have keyboards and monitors, but nothing else. The most important thing to realize about dumb terminals is that they have no local processing power. The communications port on the terminal is connected—directly or through a modem—to the server. When you type at a dumb terminal, each keystroke is transmitted to the server, where it's processed.

Smart terminals can complete minimal processing at the local site. Cash registers and other point-of-sale devices are examples of smart terminals, as are the familiar automated teller machines (ATMs). The local device stores the transaction request and transmits the entire request rather than transmit each keystroke as a dumb terminal does.

To connect your terminal to a telephone line, use a modem. Modems translate the digital signals of terminals and computers into analog signals required by telephone lines. Modems are always used in pairs. The first one connects your terminal to the telephone line; the second connects the server to the telephone line. To make the connection, you dial out on the terminal. When the modem on the other end (the one connected to the server) answers, your terminal can communicate with the server.

To expand the number of ports available that users can connect to, install a multiport adapter. For example, a PC typically has only two serial ports: COM1 and COM2. If you want to use a PC as a server for more than two users, you need more ports. The multiport adapter, in this case, consists of a card that you install inside the computer, a small box with eight or more connectors, and a cable that connects the box and the card. Software is supplied with the adapter to permit the added connectors to function as additional serial ports.

Understanding Distributed-Processing Systems

In distributed processing, the terminal is replaced by a workstation, which is itself a computer usually running DOS or UNIX. Programs can be located and run from the server or from your workstation. Similarly, files can be located on either system. If you process a file on your workstation, you store it on the server so that others can access it. You can print on local printers connected to your workstation or on printers connected to the server.

Since workstations are in common use, your bank probably uses a distributed-processing system instead of the centralized system described in the preceding section. Figure 8.2 shows the same bank with a distributed-processing system.

FIG. 8.2
This figure shows the distributed-processing model of a computing environment.

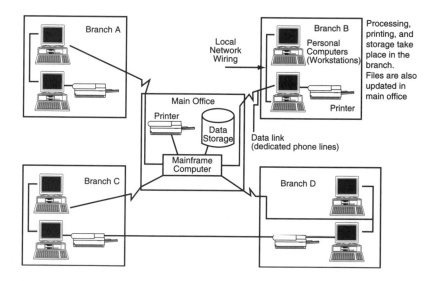

Elements of the Distributed-Processing Model

Distributed processing uses file servers, workstations, network interface cards, hubs, repeaters, bridges, routers, and gateways. The purpose of the file server is to distribute files and segments of programs to workstations, print from a central location, and control flow on the connection between workstations. More than 90 percent of processing occurs at the workstation level, leaving 5 to 10 percent of the load at the file server for administrative tasks.

Workstations   In addition to using it as a file server, you can use a personal computer as a Linux workstation. Linux was designed to run in a very minimal hardware configuration. In fact, you can run Linux with a 386SX microprocessor and 4M of RAM! Because most current systems are more powerful than Linux's minimum requirements, you should have no problem with computing power. The amount of hard drive space required depends on how much software you want to install. If you want to run entirely off CD-ROM, you need only about 5M of hard disk space. A minimal hard-disk installation takes 10M to 20M of space; a full installation takes more than 100M.

Generally, resources should be applied to the workstation level, where most of the processing occurs. The amount of additional resources depends on the types of tasks you plan on doing. For example, word processors take minimal resources (hard drive, RAM, quality of monitor) compared with graphics-intensive tasks, such as multimedia and computer-aided design (CAD) programs. For applications involving CAD, you need very large hard disks (1 gigabyte or more), a lot of RAM (16M, 32M, or even 64M), and high-resolution monitors and video cards (1,280×1,024 or higher). You might even want a tape drive for backup and a CD-ROM drive for loading large applications.

Network Interface Cards   A network interface card (NIC) attaches to a slot on the motherboard and is the physical link between the computer and the cabling for the network. Network interface cards are generally available for coaxial or twisted-pair cabling.

Hubs   The hub serves as a connecting point for network cables, such as 10BaseT Ethernet, and can be passive or active. A passive hub usually has four connectors. An active hub usually has at least eight ports and amplifies or relays the signal.

Repeaters   Repeaters amplify or regenerate the signal over the network so that you can extend the normal distance limitations of network cabling.

Bridges   Use a bridge when you need to connect two similar network types.

Routers   Routers are used in large, complex networks where there are many paths for network signals to travel to the same destination. The router determines and sends the signal along the most effective route.

Gateways   Use a gateway when you need to connect dissimilar network types, which use different protocols. The gateway performs the necessary protocol conversions so that the two networks can communicate. For example, an SNA network connected to a TCP/IP network would require a gateway.

Topologies

Topology refers to how workstations and file servers are connected in a network. The names of various topologies are derived from the pattern the cables make after you connect the various terminals, workstations, and file servers. The most common topologies are *star*, *bus*, and *ring*. When more than one topology is used in a network, it's referred to as a *hybrid network*.

Star Topology   With the star topology, all workstations are connected to a central file server or hub (see Figure 8.3). You can have passive or active hubs in this scheme.

FIG. 8.3

All workstations connect to a central file server in a star topology.

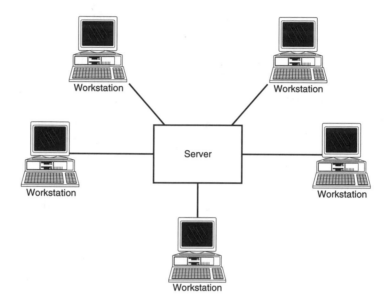

A passive hub is simply a connecting point for the workstations. An active hub also offers amplification of the signal. AT&T's StarLan is an example of a network using star topology.

Bus Topology   In a bus topology (see Figure 8.4), all workstations and file servers share a common pathway. They are, in fact, connected directly together. The bus topology is the foundation for Ethernet and token bus.

FIG. 8.4

All workstations and file servers share a common pathway in a bus topology.

Ring Topology   A ring topology looks like a wagon wheel without the hub (see Figure 8.5). The server is connected to the workstations in bus fashion, except that the last items along the network are connected to make a closed loop. Ring topologies use a repeater, which IBM refers to as a Multistation Access Unit (MAU). The IBM Token-Ring Network is an example of a ring topology.

FIG. 8.5
A ring topology has the server connected to the workstations in bus fashion.

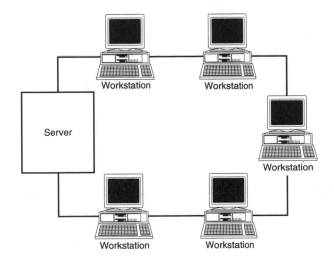

Hybrid Topology   In the 1970s and '80s, firms with decentralized purchasing departments experienced the growth of different topologies on their networks. For example, the accounting department used a bus network; the purchasing department installed Token-Ring machines; manufacturing used an Ethernet bus; and administration relied on mainframe technology. This combination of networks planted the seeds for enterprise computing and hybrid wide area networks. The integration of these networks linked dissimilar topologies, such as rings, stars, and buses.

Understanding the Client/Server Model

The result of the development of distributed processing is the *client/server model*. Today, Linux can be used in this model as the client, the server, or both.

To understand a client/server setup, assume that several Linux workstations (the clients) are connected in a bus topology to a server (a high-end PC with lots of disk space, also running Linux). The server has directories for each client where important files can be stored and backed up with the server's nightly backup. The server also has directories from which clients can share files. Connected to the server is a fast laser printer that everyone can access and a tape drive suitable for backing up the large hard disks. Also, several of the clients have their own slower, less expensive laser printers connected locally.

> **N O T E**   The server in this example is a PC running Linux—just like the clients' PCs, although the
> server is more powerful. There's no reason why the server can't act like a client at times and
> share resources from the clients. In other words, any Linux system can be a client and a server. ■

Performing Administration in a Networked Environment

A UNIX network usually takes the form of many computers, large and small, tied together over directly connected wires or common telephone lines. Administering the network is usually the task of a person or persons located at one of the sites in the network.

Most people can learn Linux and administer a network. In a production environment, it would be nice to find a qualified person right away; however, such people are somewhat rare—and usually well paid. With practice and patience, even people with limited backgrounds in computers can learn how to administer a corporate UNIX/Linux computer.

Defining the Role of the Network Administrator

Any time you have more than a few UNIX/Linux systems connected in a network, you should probably have a dedicated network administrator. Some expertise is needed to decide how systems are connected (LANs or modems), the level of security needed, and how shared peripherals (printers, tape backups, and so on) are distributed. On a day-to-day basis, the administrator maintains lists of system names, network addresses, and user access, and generally makes sure that the network is running properly.

Corporations with networks of hundreds of computers can afford to have several administrators with extensive training in selected topics. This can be a necessity if you have complex printing needs, for example. Printers and printing, as an administrative topic, can require extensive knowledge of specific printers and how to interface that equipment to Linux.

Understanding Hardware and Software Issues

If, as systems administrator, you're required to choose the networking software and hardware for the computers under your control, you should consider several things. As with most things in life, you balance what you need with what you can afford.

If your systems are close together in the same building, a local area network is a low-cost, high-speed means of networking your computers. Put an Ethernet board in each Linux system and use TCP/IP as the networking protocol software. TCP/IP is a standard component of Linux distributions.

To connect over greater distances, you can use modems for lower-speed transmissions and Point-to-Point Protocol (PPP) or Serial Line Internet Protocol (SLIP) to provide asynchronous

TCP/IP connections. You also can use UUCP software for e-mail, news, and file transfers, although UUCP has limitations. For higher speeds over long distances, you can use ISDN or get leased lines from the telephone company.

Don't buy just any old networking hardware. Although many off-the-shelf networking hardware products come with drivers needed to make them work with DOS, the same isn't true with Linux. As a result, Linux systems have many standard networking drivers built in. Table 8.1 shows some of the Ethernet cards now supported by Linux. Check the Ethernet HOWTO for updates to this list (see Appendix A for information about HOWTOs).

Table 8.1 Some Ethernet Cards Now Supported Under Linux

Manufacturer	Cards
3Com	3c503, 3c503/16, 3c509, 3c579
SMC (Western Digital)	WD8003, WD8013, SMC Elite, SMC Elite Plus, SMC Elite 16 ULTRA
Novell Ethernet	NE1000, NE2000, NE1500, NE2100
D-Link	DE-600, DE-650, DE-100, DE-200, DE-220-T
Hewlett-Packard	27245A, 27247B, 27252A, 27247A, J2405A
Digital	DE200, DE210, DE202, DE100, DEPCA (rev. E)
Allied Telesis	AT1500, AT1700
PureData	PDUC8028, PDI8023

Applications that aren't integrated with networking products can be used in a network environment. For example, you can install an application on a Linux system and have many users from other computers use the application by running the remote execution commands built into UNIX. Or you can share an application by remotely mounting the file system that contains the application and then running it from the local system.

Performing Common Networking Administrative Tasks

Administration of a network takes on several dimensions. Most networks don't just occur; typically, they evolve. In the ideal situation, the administrators are involved with the purchase of the computers and software so that they know what's expected of them as administrators and what the users are getting.

Setting Up the System   Network software should be installed and ready to connect on site. If you're using Ethernet for your Linux network segment, it's a good idea to have the continuity tests completed. If you're using telephone lines, have them tested. Wiring and terminals for users also should be tested and ready. Installation should be "plug and play," but it never is—there are always connection problems.

The advantage of buying a computer for a situation in which the operating system isn't yet installed is that you can set up file systems to accommodate your specific needs. You must know what software is going on the computer, the number of users who will be using the system, and the intensity of their usage.

 TIP   You've invested time and money in setting up the network to this point. Immediately back up the configuration files you've set up.

When the system is fully functional, the application software should be installed. Software on a Linux computer is often more complex than on a single-user system, so anticipate that installing, tuning, and making the software fully operational will take time. This task can take from a couple of hours to several days—or longer.

You're now ready to start adding users to the system, although you're still not on site. Add login IDs for a few key users and put in a common startup password, such as *temp01*. This provides some initial security and gives you a chance to get key people onto the system and operational right away when you install the system.

After installation, the computer should be attached to the network. Make sure that you can communicate from any point in the network to any other point. Test communications by moving large and small files from one computer to another. Electronic mail should be directed to and from other nodes in the network. All computers must "know" this new computer in the network. This means that you need to add it to your host name database that's used by any other computers on your network. If you use Domain Name System (DNS) locally, you must add it to the DNS name database. If you aren't using DNS, add it to the /etc/hosts files on your other systems.

Handling Peripherals   Printers can be a major issue to an administrator. Monitoring and maintaining printers is a significant task and can take a lot of an administrator's time. Understanding the spooling of print jobs, interface tools, and equipment peculiarities requires time and patience.

Modems are the cheapest way to link a network that spans long distances. Modems and PPP or UUCP are tools that can make it practical for a small staff to administer many computers. As with printers, however, modems have some problems that require time to get them running right. Choose one or two brand names and really learn their idiosyncrasies.

Monitoring the System   When the installation is complete, you can set up UNIX tools to monitor this new system. The administrators should start getting a feel for how the system is performing.

Monitoring running systems in a network is an ongoing process, but the administrative load should stabilize after a while if you aren't constantly adding peripherals or software. Occasionally, something fails or tweaking may be necessary. A good administrator learns to determine whether the problem is related to hardware or software.

Coping with Software Upgrades   Some software packages are constantly being updated. Although this is a concern with commercial UNIX, it's a special issue under Linux because much of the software is publicly available over the Internet and is continually modified. The good news might be that a bug is fixed. The bad news might be that each system in the network has to be updated. Expect a new challenge with each update.

The best advice isn't to immediately put all new versions on your systems, but to test the upgrade or patch on one non-critical system. When you're sure that the new version is okay, upgrade the other systems. A good administrator learns how to install these patches or new versions without going to the other sites in the network. This sounds impossible at first, but you'll find that many UNIX tools facilitate the installation of patches and upgrades.

Training the Administrator

Training in most organizations is very hit or miss. Perhaps the person has some computer background in some computer topic, but little is done to formally train that person to administer the system. Administration requires attention and a solid knowledge of the following topics:

- *Linux/UNIX design and usage.* The administrator has to have a thorough understanding of such issues as redirection, pipes, background processing, and so on.

- *The vi editor.* The vi editor is on virtually every credible UNIX computer put out during the last 10 years, including Linux. Many people criticize it, and many people substitute other editors for their own use, but it's advisable to have an administrator learn and become proficient in the use of vi because it's the "common denominator" among UNIX editors.

- *Shell script programming.* Many of the key programs used to administer UNIX are written in shell script language and might require modification for your specific needs. Many of the tools outlined in this chapter require knowledge of how to put together and use a shell program. Almost every user has a favorite shell.

  bash, the Bourne Again shell, is a Bourne shell clone that's the default shell under Linux. Also, the Z and T shells are available in the distribution. You should, however, stay with the common Bourne shell until you master this shell language. Also, virtually all the shell programs written by the Linux creators are written in the Bourne shell. You should also investigate the Perl system administration language. It provides a very robust set of tools for systems administration in one programming environment.

- *Communications.* Communications training is generally not very good as of this writing. To set up computer networking effectively, knowledge of TCP/IP and the related protocols is essential. Similarly, you'll want to understand PPP if you're going to set up an asynchronous Internet connection. Ideally, these protocols should be taught in a laboratory environment with the many options available. Attend classes or at least buy manuals on the subject, but accept that you'll be spending much time experimenting.

■ *UNIX conventions.* UNIX conventions aren't taught or even mentioned in many UNIX classes, and you'll probably have to pick them up by observing as you go through training. For example, the bin directories, such as /usr/bin, /bin, and /usr/local/bin, are where binary executable programs are generally located. You can put your own executable programs in /usr/local/bin. The lib directories, such as /usr/lib, are used for library files. You can put your own libraries in a directory such as /usr/local/lib. Understanding and following standard Linux/UNIX conventions such as these can save time in finding and fixing problems.

Several reputable companies, perhaps including the company that you bought your computer from, offer training on all these topics. However, this training is probably not specific to Linux. A few vendors sell various distributions of the Linux operating system and offer classes on selected topics. You should also look for user groups in your area and check the **comp.os. linux** newsgroup hierarchy on Usenet news on the Internet.

Training is best done in small pieces. You should take a course and then come back and use what you learned right away on your network. Linux has an elaborate set of tools that will probably never be completely mastered, but you have to know where to find information in manuals.

From Here...

You can find more information about system administration topics in the following chapters:

■ Chapter 9, "Booting and Shutting Down," discusses proper procedures for starting and stopping the Linux system.

■ Chapter 10, "Managing User Accounts," describes how to create and manage user accounts under Linux.

■ Chapter 14, "Managing File Systems," shows how to create, update, and manage your file systems.

Booting and Shutting Down

Two of the most common tasks that you encounter when administering a Linux system are booting the system and shutting it down. As you might have guessed, booting and shutting down Linux are operations that require special consideration.

To use Linux, you must boot the operating system. Although this sounds pretty straightforward, you need to consider that most people run at least one additional operating system on their PCs other than Linux. This means that you must have some way to specify which operating system you want to boot when you start the system. You can do this in two basic ways: you can boot Linux from a floppy or you can boot from your hard drive by using a boot manager. ■

Booting Linux

You can boot Linux in several different ways. Look here to learn about those different ways.

Booting from the LILO boot manager

Learn how you can use the LILO boot manager to boot multiple operating systems.

Shutting down a running Linux system

Learn the proper way to shut down a running system, and why you should never just turn the power off.

Booting Linux from a Floppy

Many people use a boot floppy to start Linux. This boot floppy contains a copy of the Linux kernel that points to the root Linux file system on the appropriate hard drive partition. The Red Hat and Slackware Linux installation programs give you the opportunity to create a bootable floppy during the installation process.

> **CAUTION**
>
> You should make a bootable Linux floppy disk during the installation, even if you intend to install a boot manager on your hard drive. If your hard disk should crash, the bootable floppy might be the only way to boot your system!

Booting from a Boot Manager

Another way to boot Linux is to use a boot manager program. Linux comes with a boot manager known as LILO, which stands for LInux LOader. This program modifies the master boot sector of your boot hard disk and allows you to choose which operating system you want to boot when you turn on your computer.

Boot Managers

Using a boot manager has its advantages and disadvantages. With a boot manager, you don't need a floppy disk to boot your system. Also, you can choose to boot different operating systems from a menu at boot time, or have the system default to a given operating system.

As for the disadvantages, a boot manager adds another level of complexity to the boot process. It must be modified or possibly reinstalled if you add, delete, or upgrade a version of any of the operating systems on your disk. It modifies the master boot record of your hard disk, so if something goes wrong, you might not be able to boot with anything other than a floppy disk until you reformat your hard drive. Also, the boot manager that you choose might not be compatible with some operating systems.

You should consider your own computing needs carefully before deciding on a floppy or boot manager for booting Linux.

It's also possible to set up LILO so that it can be started from the OS/2 boot manager.

Understanding LILO, the Linux Loader

LILO is a boot manager that comes bundled as part of the Red Hat and Slackware Linux distributions. It can be installed in the master boot record, on a formatted floppy disk, or on the boot partition's super block for booting OS/2.

▶ **See** "Installing LILO," **pp. 66** and **107**

When LILO is installed, you can use the master boot record to select from a set of different operating systems at boot time. Depending on its configuration, LILO counts to a timeout value and then boots a default operating system.

The easiest way to install LILO is to do it via the Red Hat or Slackware Linux installation program, which takes you through a menu-driven system that automates much of the installation process.

> **CAUTION**
>
> It's highly recommended that you install LILO from the Red Hat or Slackware installation program. Installing a boot manager is an inherently dangerous process; you can easily corrupt data on your hard disk if the installation isn't done correctly.

Configuring LILO

LILO reads a configuration file, /etc/lilo.conf, and uses it to figure out what operating systems are installed on your system and where their boot information is located. The /etc/lilo.conf file starts with some information that tells LILO how to operate in general. It then contains several sections that list the boot information specific to each operating system that LILO can boot. LILO is configured to boot one section for each operating system on your Linux system.

Two sections from a LILO configuration file follow:

```
# Section for the Linux partition
image=/vmlinuz
label=Linux
root=/dev/hda1

# Section for MS-DOS
other=/dev/hda3
table=/dev/hda
label=msdos
```

The first section gives the boot information for Linux. The `image` line tells LILO where the Linux kernel is located. The `label` lines that appear in both sections give the name of the operating system that appears in the LILO boot menu. The `root` line specifies the location of the Linux root file system.

In the MS-DOS section, the `other` line indicates that the partition for an additional operating system is located on the disk partition hda3. The `table` line tells LILO where to find the partition table for /dev/hda3.

Using LILO

When you install LILO, you typically want to set a default timeout value and a default operating system to boot. This allows you to have a certain amount of time to select another operating system at boot time. In the event that you don't select an operating system, LILO boots the one that you've set as the default at the end of the timeout count.

When you boot your computer with LILO installed, you get a prompt that reads `LILO:`. At this point, you have several options. You can wait and have Linux boot your default operating system, or you can press <Ctrl>, <Alt>, or <Shift> to have LILO boot the default operating system immediately. You can also type the name of one of the operating systems to have LILO boot the one you specify. Finally, you can press <Tab> to have LILO display a list of the different available operating systems.

Shutting Down Linux

With a Linux system, you have to be careful when you shut the system down. You can't simply turn the power off. Linux maintains file system I/O information in memory buffers. If you just power down a Linux system, file system corruption can result.

> **CAUTION**
>
> You should never turn off a Linux system without shutting down properly. The file systems need to synchronize properly when the system is shutting down. You can cause severe damage to the Linux file system if you just power the system off.

The best way to shut down a Linux system is with the `shutdown` command. The syntax of the command is

`/sbin/shutdown [flags] time [warning-message]`

`[warning-message]` is a message sent to all users that are now logged on, and `time` is the time that the shutdown is to occur. The `time` argument can have a couple of different formats:

- It can be specified as an absolute time in the format *hh:mm*, where *hh* is the hour (in one or two digits) and *mm* is the minute of the hour. The *mm* value must be specified with two digits.

- The `time` value can also be given in the format *+m*, where *m* is the number of minutes to wait before the shutdown. You can substitute the word `now` for *+0*.

Table 9.1 lists the flags that can be used with the `shutdown` command.

Table 9.1   Command-Line Flags for the *shutdown* Command

Flag	Description
`-t sec`	Wait *sec* seconds between sending the warning and the kill signal to all processes. This delay gives processes time to finish any shutdown processing that they have to do.
`-k`	Don't really shut down the system; just send the warning message to all users.
`-r`	Reboot after shutdown.

Flag	Description
-h	Halt after shutdown.
-n	Don't synch disks before rebooting or halting. *Use with caution, as it can cause your data to be corrupted.*
-f	Do a "fast" reboot. This creates the /etc/fastboot file. The rc boot script should check for this file and not do an fsck if it's found.
-c	Cancel an already running shutdown. With this option, it's not possible to specify the *time* argument.

Part
II

Ch
9

The shutdown command prevents any users from logging on, notifies all users on the system that the system will be shut down, waits until the time that you specify, and then sends a SIGTERM signal to all processes so that they can exit cleanly. shutdown then calls halt or reboot, depending on your command-line choice in the shutdown command.

> **CAUTION**
>
> It's possible to halt or reboot the system by entering **halt** or **reboot** directly. However, no warning is given to the users, and the system goes down immediately. These commands should be used only if you're the only user on the system.

From Here...

Obviously, there's more to systems administration than just booting and shutting down the system. You can find more information about systems administration in the following chapters:

- Chapter 8, "Understanding Systems Administration," provides an overview of the various tasks that the average system administrator faces.
- Chapter 10, "Managing User Accounts," shows how to create and maintain user login accounts on your Linux system.
- Chapter 14, "Managing File Systems," discusses how to manage and maintain file systems properly.

Managing User Accounts

As the systems administrator, you're in charge of managing users. Managing involves adding users so that they can log in to the system, setting user privileges, creating and assigning home directories for users, assigning users to groups, and deleting users when necessary. In this chapter, you explore the various tools and techniques for user account management. ■

Adding and removing user accounts

One important aspect of managing a Linux system is adding and deleting user accounts. This chapter shows you how.

Managing user passwords

After you add a user account to the system, you need to set a password for that account.

Working with groups

This chapter introduces you to groups and explains how to assign users to groups for maximum benefit.

Managing home directories

Finally, this chapter provides some tips for managing home directories and file systems.

Working with Users

Every user should have a unique login name. Login names make it possible to identify each user and avoid the problem of one user deleting another's files.

Each user also must have a password. About the only exception to having a password is when only one user is on a system, and the system has absolutely no connection by modem or network to any other computer.

▶ **See** "Dealing with Password Security," **p. 239**

When there's no real reason for a person to have access to your system, you must make sure that individual can't log in. That person's login name should be removed, along with any files that your remaining users no longer need.

Adding a User

When you add a user, the result is an entry for the user in the password file, /etc/passwd. That entry has the following form:

```
login_name:encrypted_password:user_ID:group_ID:user_information:
➥login_directory:login_shell
```

In this syntax, fields are separated by colons. Table 10.1 lists the fields.

Table 10.1   Fields in an /etc/passwd File Entry

Field	Description
login_name	The name used to log in.
encrypted_password	The password required to authenticate the user—the primary line of defense against security violations.
user_ID	A unique number the operating system uses to identify the user.
group_ID	A unique number or name used to identify the primary group for this user. If a user is a member of multiple groups, he or she can switch group membership to another group if permitted by the administrator.
user_information	A description of the user, such as the user's name or title.
login_directory	The user's home directory (where the user ends up after logging in).
login_shell	The shell used by a user when logging in (for example, /bin/bash if using the bash shell).

The adduser command is used to add a user to your Linux system. You invoke the command with the name of the user that you want to add.

Using the *adduser* Command

When you add a user, you simply use the `adduser` command and provide the name of the user you want to add (see Listing 10.1).

Listing 10.1   An Example of an *adduser* Session

```
# ./adduser jschmoe

Looking for first available UID... 508
Looking for first available GID... 508

Adding login: jschmoe...done.
Creating home directory: /home/jschmoe...done.
Creating mailbox: /var/spool/mail/jschmoe...done.

Don't forget to set the password.
#
```

The `adduser` command also copies the files whose names begin with . (dot) from the /etc/skel directory into the user's home directory. The /etc/skel directory should contain template files you want every user to have. These typically include "personal" configuration files, such as .profile, .cshrc, and .login for shell configuration; .mailrc for e-mail setup; .emacs for your users using `emacs` as an editor; and so on.

The `adduser` command is a Bourne shell script located in the /usr/sbin directory. As such, you can customize this script if you need to perform some additional actions when you create a user account. A common modification is to have `adduser` prompt for the user's full name, rather than hard-code a default user name into the password file. If you don't change the script so that it asks for the user's name, you'll have to change it by hand with the `chfn` command—for example,

```
# chfn jschmoe
Changing finger information for jschmoe.
Name [RHS Linux User]: Joseph A. Schmoe
Office []:
Office Phone []:
Home Phone []:

Finger information changed.
#
```

The `adduser` command doesn't set the password for the account. You'll have to do that via the `passwd` command.

Setting User Passwords

You set a user's password by using the `passwd` command. You should set a password for each user added to the system; users can then change their passwords when they log in. Use `passwd` as follows:

Part
II

Ch
10

1. Type the command and login name (for example, **passwd jschmoe**) and press <Return>.

2. At the New password: prompt, enter the password (you don't see the password on-screen).

3. You're prompted to type the password again. Enter the password again:

   New password (again): *newpassword*

The password is encrypted and put into the /etc/passwd file. It's important that you take the time to enter passwords that follow the rules for choosing a password, as follows:

- Passwords should be at least six (preferably eight) characters long.

- Passwords should contain upper- and lowercase letters, punctuation symbols, and numerals.

  ▶ **See** "Dealing with Password Security," **p. 239**

When you're adding a number of users, you'll be tempted to enter short, easy passwords. Don't fall for it. Good passwords are your first line of defense against intruders. Be sure to tell your users why you've assigned that type of password. Further, it's a good idea to change passwords regularly, but remember to educate system users about the choice of good passwords.

After a user is assigned a password, the file entry looks something like this:

jschmoe:Zoie.89&^0gW*:123:21:Joseph A. Schmoe:/users/jschmoe:/bin/bash

The second field is the password—not as it was typed, but in encrypted form.

N O T E   Users occasionally forget passwords. It isn't possible for you to tell users their own
passwords. You can delete a forgotten password by editing the /etc/passwd file and
deleting the second field in the user's file entry. You can then set the user's password with the passwd
command. Have a procedure in place to deal with this situation, and let your users know about it. ■

Removing a User

There are several different degrees of user removal. Removing a user from the system doesn't need to be a final, irrevocable act. Here are some possibilities:

- Remove only the capability to log in. This is useful if the user is away for a while and needs to be reinstated some time in the future. The user's directory, files, and group information are kept intact. Edit the password file (/etc/passwd) and put an * in the second field of the user's entry, as follows:

  jschmoe:*:123:21:Joseph A. Schmoe:/users/jschmoe:/bin/bash

- Remove the user from the password file but keep the user's files on the system. This is useful if the files are used by others, or a new person will be taking over the duties of the old user. Delete the user's entry from the password file or files. You can do this by using an editor or the userdel *login_name* command. You then can change the ownership and location of the deleted user's files by using the chown and mv commands.

■ Remove the user from the password file and remove all files the user owns. This is the ultimate and complete form of deleting a user. You must delete the user's entry from the password file and delete the user's files from the system. You can do this by using the find command:

```
find user's-home-directory -exec rm {} \;
```

Then remove the directory with rmdir user's-home-directory, and remove the appropriate entry from the password file or files.

N O T E If you use other configuration files at your site, such as e-mail alias files, you'll also have to remove the user from these files. ■

Working with Groups

Each user is a member of a group. You can give different types of groups different capabilities or privileges. For example, it's reasonable to give a group of users who use the system to analyze the company's sales data access to a different set of files than a user group whose main function is researching new products.

The password file contains information for a single user. Information about groups is kept in the /etc/group file. The following is a sample entry:

```
sales::21:tuser, jschmoe, staplr
```

The group name is sales, the group ID number is 21, and the members are tuser, jschmoe, and staplr. Files and directories have permissions associated with them for the owner, group, and others. A user can be a member of more than one group, and you can change group memberships.

Adding a Group

You create a new group by editing the /etc/group file directly and entering the new group information.

Each group in the /etc/group file has a unique group ID number associated with it. Linux pays attention to the number that you assign, not to the name. Hence, if you assign two groups with the same number, they will behave as though they're the same group.

Deleting a Group

You delete a group by editing the /etc/group file and removing the entry for the specific group that you want to delete. Also, you should reassign all files that have that associated GID to a different group. An easy way to do this is with the find command, as in

```
find / -gid group-id find users-home-directory -exec chgrp newgroup {} \;
```

Managing Home Directories

You should give some thought to grouping your home directories logically if you plan to have a lot of users on your system. In general, you should try to place all the home directories on a given machine under one single top-level directory. That way, they can be grouped according to whatever arrangement makes sense for your needs.

▶ **See** "Mounting and Unmounting File Systems," **p. 265**

For example, you can specify that /home be the top-level directory for user directories. Under /home, you can group users by department. The sales users would have accounts under /home/sales, development under /home/develop, and so on. Your user home directories would then fall under these directories or under another set if additional grouping is needed. Because user directories can use a lot of disk space, you could consider placing logical groups of users on different physical file systems. As you need additional space, you can simply create an additional category for home directories and mount it on a file system as a mount point under /home.

From Here...

As the systems administrator, you're responsible for managing and supporting the users that log in to your system. Proper user management procedures can help simplify creating and deleting accounts. Linux provides a complete set of tools for managing user account and group information. It's important to understand how user accounts can be grouped logically. By considering how to set up their directory structures so that they reflect this grouping, you can make the most out of limited disk space and make file system maintenance a less taxing job.

You can find more information about systems administration in the following chapters:

- Chapter 8, "Understanding Systems Administration," gives an introduction to common systems administration tasks.
- Chapter 11, "Backing Up Data," discusses how to plan and implement plans for data backups.
- Chapter 14, "Managing File Systems," describes how to set up and manage file systems on your Linux system.

Backing Up Data

Various kinds of problems can result in loss of data: files get accidentally removed, hardware fails, important information stored in files is no longer available. Users should feel confident that, in such cases, they can access a timely backup of the "lost" files.

Your company's future—and your future with your company—may depend on making those backup files available. At such times, you and others will be thankful that you've taken the time and effort to copy files to some sort of storage media according to a regular, rigorous, and well-documented schedule. Backing up files isn't very glamorous, but no administrator can ignore the process. ■

Planning for backups

Learn the issues involved in planning for and developing an effective backup system.

Making a backup schedule

This chapter provides information on different types of backups and scheduling procedures that you can use.

Using *tar* and *cpio*

To create backups and archive files, you use the commands `tar` and `cpio`, which this chapter explains how to use.

Considering Backup Issues

The following are several issues to consider in backing up a system:

- *Full or incremental backups.* A *full backup* copies every file. Is it necessary to do that every day? A full backup usually requires a good deal of time and enough media to hold all the files on the system. An *incremental backup* copies the files that have changed since the last full backup.

- *File systems to back up.* Naturally, active file systems must be backed up regularly. Others can be backed up less frequently. Make sure that you have current copies of all the file systems.

- *Types of backup media.* Depending on the devices on your system, you may be able to use nine-track tape, 1/4-inch cartridge tape, 4mm or 8mm DAT tapes, or floppy disks. Each has advantages over the other in terms of sheer bulk, storage capacity, and cost for devices and media. Choose the backup medium to fit your budget, remembering that the least expensive medium may be the most time-consuming.

- *Effect of backups on users.* Performing a backup operation increases the load on a system. Will that be an unreasonable burden on users? Also, files that are changed during the backup process may not be backed up, which can merely be an inconvenience or a very important consideration if you're backing up an active database. Should you perform backups when the system is quiet?

- *Commands to use for backups.* Some relatively simple, time-honored commands are available for creating backups, such as `tar` and `cpio`. Are they sufficient?

- *Documentation of the backed-up files.* You must label all backed-up material so that you can use it to recover files when necessary. Some procedures and commands allow you to prepare a table of contents or list of the material that has been backed up.

From an administrator's view, the file system should be backed up according to some automated process with as little operator intervention as possible. It should also be done when the system is relatively quiet so that the backup is as complete as possible. This consideration must be balanced with convenience and costs. Should an operator or administrator have to stay until midnight on Friday to perform a full backup? Is it worth $2,000 for a DAT tape drive so that the entire system can be backed up automatically at 3 a.m. with no operator intervention?

Consider the alternatives, determine the true costs, and make a decision or recommend a course of action. It's generally a lot cheaper and always easier to restore well-managed backup information than to re-create it or do without it.

Considering Backup Tips

The purpose of performing backups is being able to restore individual files or complete file systems as rapidly and easily as possible. Whatever you do about backups should be focused on that central purpose.

Set up a backup plan. Include the files to be backed up, how often they'll be backed up, and document how the files are to be restored. Let all users know the backup schedule and how they can request restoration of files. Be sure to stick with the plan.

Be sure to verify your backups. This could include reading a table of contents from the backup medium after it's stored, or restoring an arbitrarily chosen file from the medium. Remember that it's possible for the backup medium—disk or tape—to have flaws.

Make backups so that files can be restored anywhere on the file system or on another computer system. Use backup or archive utilities that create archives that can be used on other Linux or UNIX computer systems.

Be sure to label all media—tapes, disks, whatever—used in a backup. If you have to use multiple tapes or disks, make sure that they're numbered sequentially and dated. You must be able to find the file or files you need.

Plan for a disaster. Have copies of the files on your system so that the entire system can be restored in a reasonable amount of time. Store copies of backup tapes or disks off-site. You should also have a complete hardware list so that you can reorder identical parts should a disaster occur.

Plan to re-evaluate your backup procedures periodically to make sure that they're meeting your needs.

Several tools are available that can help automate your backup procedure. Check out the Linux archives on **sunsite.unc.edu** for more information. Also, Linux supports the FTAPE extensions. FTAPE lets you perform backups to QIC-80 magnetic tape units that run off a floppy controller on your system. For detailed information, refer to the FTAPE HOWTO guide.

Part

II

Ch

11

Planning a Backup Schedule

It's important to come up with a backup schedule that meets your needs and makes it possible to restore recent copies of files. After you decide on a schedule, stick to it.

The ideal situation is to be able to restore any file at any time. Taken to an extreme, that's not possible, but you should be able to restore files on a daily basis. To do this, you use a combination of complete and incremental backups. A *complete backup* is one that contains every file on the system. An *incremental backup* is one that contains files that have changed since the last backup. Incremental backups can be at different levels—incremental to the last complete backup or incremental to the last incremental backup. It's convenient to think of backups as occurring at different levels:

- Level 0: full backup
- Level 1: incremental to the last complete backup
- Level 2: incremental to the last level 1 backup

The following are some sample backup schedules:

■ *Full backup one day, incremental other days:*

Day 1	Level 0, complete backup
Day 2	Level 1, incremental backup
Day 3	Level 1, incremental backup
Day 4	Level 1, incremental backup
Day 5	Level 1, incremental backup

If you create and save an index of each backup, you should need only one day's backup to restore an individual file and only two days' backup (day 1 and another day's) to completely restore the system.

■ *Full backup once a month, weekly incremental, and daily incremental.* This example is built around Tuesday but can be any day of the week:

First Tuesday	Level 0, complete backup
Any other Tuesday	Level 1, incremental backup
Any other day	Level 2, incremental backup

To restore an individual file under this schedule, you may need the complete backup if the file wasn't changed during the month, the level 1 backup if the file was changed the previous week but not this week, or the level 2 backup if the file was changed this week. This schedule is more complex than the previous example, but backups take less time per day.

You also might want to consider keeping backup files for an extended period, in case you need to restore an older version. A common schedule is to keep one weekly copy of a full backup for four weeks. For periods of longer than four weeks, you might consider keeping a biweekly backup for about three months.

Performing Backups and Restoring Files

Several different utilities are available for backing up and restoring files in a Linux system. Some are simple and straightforward; others are more complex. The simple methods have their limitations. Choose the one that meets your needs.

Because backing up and restoring files is very important, a number of available software systems are dedicated to that task. The following sections present two of them:

■ `tar`   Tape archive utility available on every Linux or UNIX system. This easy-to-use Linux version can use several tapes or disks.

■ `cpio`   General-purpose utility for copying files available on every UNIX system. Easy to use, more robust than `tar`, and can use several tapes or disks.

Using *tar*

The UNIX `tar` utility was originally designed to create a tape archive (to copy files or directories to tape and then to extract or restore files from the archive). You can use it to copy to any device. It has the following advantages:

- It's simple to use.
- It's reliable and stable.
- Archives can be read on virtually any Linux or UNIX system.

It also has a few disadvantages:

- For some versions of `tar`, the archive must reside on one disk or tape, which means that if a portion of the medium fails—from a bad sector on a disk or bad block on a tape, for example—the entire backup may be lost.
- `tar` can't back up special files, such as device files.
- On its own, `tar` can perform only complete backups. If you want to do incremental backups, you have to do a little shell programming.

  ▶ **See** "Working with Shell Scripts," **p. 350**

Table 11.1 lists some of the commonly used options for `tar`. You can use many additional command parameters with `tar`; refer to the man page for a complete list.

Table 11.1 Common Options for the *tar* Command

Option	Description
c	Creates an archive.
x	Extracts or restores files from the archive that's on the default device or on the device specified by the f option.
f *name*	Creates the archive or reads the archive from *name*, where *name* is a file name or a device specified in /dev, such as /dev/rmt0.
Z	Compresses or decompresses the tar archive.
z	Compresses or decompresses the tar archive with `gzip`.
M	Creates a multivolume tar backup.
t	Creates an index of all files stored in an archive and lists on stdout.
v	Uses verbose mode.

Consider some examples of the use of `tar` in backing up and restoring files. The following command copies the directory /home to the floppy drive /dev/fd0:

```
tar -cf /dev/fd0 /home
```

In this case, the f option specifies that the archive is created on the floppy drive device /dev/fd0. The following command also archives the directory /home:

Part II Ch 11

```
tar -cvfzM /dev/fd0 /home ¦ tee homeindex
```

The v option indicates verbose mode, the z option indicates that the archive should be compressed to save space, and the M option tells tar to create a multivolume backup. When one floppy disk is full, tar prompts you for another. A list of the copied files is directed to homeindex. It's a good idea to look at that file to see what was copied.

The find command is useful for locating files that have been modified within a certain time period so that they can be scheduled for incremental backups. The following example uses the command find to create a list of all files that have been modified in the last day:

```
find /home -mtime -1 -type f -print > bkuplst tar cvfzM /dev/fd0
➥`cat bkuplst` ¦ tee homeindex
```

To use the list as input to the tar command, place the command cat bkuplst in back quotes (backward, single quotation marks, also known as *grave accents*—`cat bkuplst`). This tells the shell to execute the command as a subshell and place the output from the command on the command line in the location of the original back-quoted command.

The following command restores the /home/dave/notes.txt file from the device /dev/fd0 (note that you have to give the complete file name to restore it):

```
tar xv /usr2/dave/notes.txt
```

 T I P You can automate any of these commands by putting them in root's crontab file. For example, the following entry in the root's crontab file performs a backup of /home every day at 1:30 a.m.:

```
30 01 * * * tar cvfz /def/fd0 /home > homeindex
```

If you need to do more complicated backups, you can create shell scripts to control your backups. These shell scripts can also be run via cron.

▶ **See** "Scheduling Commands with *cron* and *crontab*," **p. 374**

You also can use the tar command to create archive files in the Linux file system rather than write to a backup device. This way, you can archive a group of files along with their directory structure in one file. To do this, simply give a file name as the argument to the f option, instead of a device name. The following is an example of archiving a directory and its subdirectories with the tar command:

```
tar cvf /home/backup.tar /home/dave
```

This creates the file /home/backup.tar, which contains a backup of the /home/dave directory and all files and subdirectories below /home/dave.

 N O T E The tar command by itself doesn't perform any file compression. To compress the resulting tar file, either specify the z option with the tar command or use a compression program, such as gzip, on the final tar file. ■

When you're using tar to make archive files, it's usually a good idea to try to make the top-level entry in the tar file a directory. This way, when you extract the tar file, all the files in it are placed under a central directory in your current working directory. Otherwise, you could end up with hundreds of files in your directory if you extract a tar file in the wrong place.

Suppose that you have below your current directory a directory named data, which contains several hundred files. There are two basic ways to create a tar file of this directory. You can change directories to data and create the tar file from there:

```
$ pwd
/home/dave
$ cd data
$ pwd
/home/dave/data
$ tar cvf ../data.tar *
```

This creates a tar file in /home/dave that contains just the contents of data without containing an entry for the directory. When you extract this tar file, you don't create a directory to put the files in—you just get several hundred files in your current directory.

Another way to create the tar file is to start from data's parent directory and specify the directory name as the thing to archive. For example,

```
$ pwd
/home/dave
$ tar cvf data.tar data
```

still creates an archive of the data directory, but it puts the directory entry as the first thing in the archive. This way, when the tar file is extracted, the first thing that's created is the directory data, and all the files in data are placed in the data subdirectory.

N O T E   When creating a tar file of all the files in the directory, specifying a different location for the tar file other than the current directory is good practice. That way, if you try to archive all the files in the current directory, tar won't get confused and try to add its tar file recursively to the tar that it's creating. ■

Using *cpio*

cpio is a general-purpose command for copying file archives. You can use it to create backups by using the -o option, or to restore files by using the -i option. It takes its input from standard input and sends its output to standard output.

The advantages of cpio are as follows:

- It can back up any set of files.
- It can back up special files.
- It stores information more efficiently than tar.
- It skips bad sectors or bad blocks when restoring data.
- Its backups can be restored on almost any Linux or UNIX system.

Some people find cpio's syntax to be a bit more confusing than tar's syntax. Also, to perform incremental backups, you have to do some shell programming.

Table 11.2 lists the commonly used options for cpio. See cpio's man page for a complete description of the options you can use with this command.

Table 11.2 Commonly Used Options for *cpio*

Option	Description
-o	Copy out. Creates an archive on standard out.
-B	Blocks input or output at 5,120 bytes per record. Useful for efficient storage on magnetic tape.
-i	Copy in. Extracts files from standard input. This is typically used when the standard input is the result of a copy-out action of another cpio command.
-t	Creates a table of contents of the input.

Consider some examples of cpio in backing up and restoring files:

- The following command copies the files in the directory /home to the device /dev/fd0:

  ```
  ls /home ¦ cpio -o > /dev/fd0
  ```

- The following example extracts the files on the device /dev/fd0 and creates an index in the bkup.indx file:

  ```
  cpio -it < /dev/fd0 > bkup.indx
  ```

- The following example uses the find command to create a list of all files in /home that have been modified in the last day:

  ```
  find /home -mtime 1 -type f -print ¦ cpio -oB > /dev/fd0
  ```

  The output of that command is piped to cpio, which creates an archive on /dev/fd0, where the data is stored at 5,120 bytes per record.

- The following command restores the file /home/dave/notes.txt from the device /dev/fd0:

  ```
  echo "/home/dave/notes.txt" ¦ cpio -i < /dev/fd0
  ```

N O T E You must give the complete file name to restore a file with cpio.

T I P You can automate any of these commands by putting them in root's crontab file. For example, the following entry in the root's cron file performs a backup of /home daily at 1:30 a.m.:

```
30 01 * * * ls /home ¦ cpio -o > /dev/fd0
```

If you need to do more complicated backups, you can create shell scripts to control your backups. You also can run these shell scripts via cron.

▶ **See** "Scheduling Commands with *cron* and *crontab*," **p. 374**

From Here...

You can find more information about systems administration in the following chapters:

- Chapter 8, "Understanding Systems Administration," gives an overview of the duties of a systems administrator.
- Chapter 10, "Managing User Accounts," shows how to create and manage user access to your Linux system.
- Chapter 14, "Managing File Systems," discusses the ins and outs of file systems and the various issues that you need to consider.

Part
II

Ch
11

## CHAPTER 12

Improving System Security

Unless your system is locked in a closet, you're the only one with a key, and you keep the key on a chain around your neck at all times, you should be concerned about system security. This really isn't a joke. If there are multiple users, if the system is connected to the outside world by modems or a network, or if there are times when the system isn't attended, there's the real risk that someone may gain unauthorized access to it.

Sometimes, unauthorized access is benign—but it can still be unnerving. If someone takes the time to gain access to your system, that person probably has the skill to copy information you want to keep confidential, make unauthorized use of your system's resources, and modify or delete information.

In most organizations, the systems administrator has the responsibility for system security. You don't have to be paranoid about it, but you should be aware of the risks and be able to take steps to keep your system secure. Be assertive and professional when addressing security issues.

This chapter discusses ideas and policies for increasing computer security, as well as actual techniques that you can use to make your system more secure. Some of these ideas are of little use to the home computer user and tend to apply to larger installations. Other points in this chapter are very applicable to home users.

Physical security

This chapter explains why you should physically protect your computer equipment.

Password security

In this chapter, you see how to implement a secure password policy.

File security

In this chapter, you learn about setting file permissions and how to look for permissions that can be security loopholes.

Social engineering threats

Social engineering is about convincing people to do what you want, either by playing on their assumptions or behavior, or by misrepresenting themselves and lying. You need to know how to educate your users to prevent intruders from using social engineering to tap into your system.

NOTE Over the past several years, the mass media has changed the meaning of the word *hacker* from "a computer enthusiast" to "someone who breaks into computers." In the computer community, the commonly accepted term for someone who breaks into computers is *cracker*. This is the term used throughout this chapter. ▪

Handling Physical Security

With all the mass media hype about viruses, computer break-ins, and diabolical computer crackers with their modems and network connections, too little attention is paid to the physical security of computer systems. Computer equipment is fairly sensitive to various environmental conditions.

Fire and smoke can obviously mean a quick end for your computing equipment. If you have any sort of business computer installation, you should consider installing smoke detectors, automatic fire extinguishers, and a fire alarm system.

In addition to fire and smoke, dust can wreak havoc with computer equipment. Dust is abrasive and can shorten the life of magnetic media and tape and optical drives. Dust can collect in ventilation systems and block the airflow, letting computers overheat. Also, dust can be electrically conductive and can cause circuit boards to short out and fail.

Electricity poses a special threat to computer equipment. Computers are very sensitive to surges in electrical current. All computer equipment should be connected to surge suppression equipment to reduce the chances of damage. This includes modems connected to telephone lines. Many areas suffer from "dirty power" that fluctuates in current and voltage.

NOTE Although surge suppressors can help protect against spikes in the electrical current, they're virtually worthless against any kind of lightning strike. If lightning hits an incoming line to your house or business, simple surge suppressors are unlikely to save your equipment. In the case of a severe thunderstorm, it's best to unplug your surge suppressor and wait it out. ▪

Computers are also common targets for theft. Many computer components are small and expensive. As a result, they're easily stolen and sold. You should evaluate how secure your computers are and try to protect them against theft as you do any valuable possession.

Another aspect of physical computer security is preventing access by unauthorized persons. If someone can walk into your computer room, sit down at a console, and start working unchallenged, you have a problem. By controlling access to your computers, you make it more difficult for someone to steal or damage data or equipment. Establish access policies for your computing facilities, and educate your users as to these policies.

The following are some steps you can take to improve the physical security at your installation:

▪ Don't leave a system, tape drives, disk drives, terminals, or workstations unattended for a prolonged period of time. It's a good idea to have some restrictions regarding access to the rooms that house your primary system and associated tape and disk drives. A lock on the door goes a long way in providing security. An unauthorized person can remove backup media—disks or tapes—from an unlocked area.

- Don't leave the system console or other terminal device logged in as root and unattended. If users know the system, they can easily give themselves root privileges, modify important software, or remove information from the system.

- Educate system users about physical security risks. Encourage them to report any unauthorized activity they may witness. Feel free to courteously challenge someone you don't recognize who is using the system.

- If possible, don't keep sensitive information on systems that have modem or network connections.

- Keep backups in a secure area, and limit access to that area.

Dealing with Password Security

The first line of defense against unauthorized access to a system is password protection. This is also often the weakest link in the chain. This section describes some steps you can take to keep passwords secure.

The reality is that users want simple, easy-to-remember passwords. They don't want to change their passwords. They like to write them down so that they can reference them. Unfortunately for you, the systems administrator, these are all bad approaches from a computer security standpoint. Password security requires almost constant attention.

The root password is special. Anyone who knows it can access anything on your system and perhaps other systems that your computer is connected to through a network. Change the root password often, choose it wisely, and keep it secure. It's best committed to memory. In most organizations, it's a good idea for two people to know it—but no more than that!

Passwords should be at least six characters long; however, only the first eight characters in any password are recognized. This means that your password is truncated to eight characters if you enter one that's longer than eight characters.

It's not too difficult to write a program that can attempt to guess a password. If the password-guessing program is trying to guess a random password, it will take longer to be successful if the password itself is longer.

Computers are very good at doing the same thing over and over, such as encrypting every word in a dictionary and comparing it to your password to try to break into your system. You should never choose a password that's a dictionary word. Also, try not to choose a password that's easily associated with you. Your name, address, spouse's name, child's name, pet names, phone number, driver's license number, and so on are all obvious targets for a cracker.

So how do you pick a good password if all the easy ones are also easy to guess? One technique is to pick two random short words and connect them with a punctuation character. This makes an almost random sequence of characters as far as a password guesser is concerned, but is fairly easy for a user to remember. The following are a few examples of passwords that use this technique:

joe&day

car!pan

modem!at

Another method for picking passwords is to take a phrase that you'll remember and use the first letter from each word for the password. This results in a random sequence of characters, but one that you can easily recall. For example, the phrase "Ladies and Gentlemen, Elvis has left the building" translates into the password L&GEhltb.

The crucial point is that the password should be remembered. It shouldn't be written down anywhere. If your users feel they must write down their password at all, give them a tip to disguise it in some type of list or sentence. For instance, if your password is modem!at, a note on a small piece of paper saying "Don't forget to pick up modem! At computer shop for repairs" looks like an ordinary reminder in case another person sees the paper, but the password is well disguised.

Developing Login Security

Each account on your Linux system is a door into your computer. All someone needs is the right key—the password. If you've instituted good password-management practices, you already have a head start toward developing a more secure system. One aspect of computer security that goes hand in hand with password security is login or account security.

Login or account security involves looking for accounts on your system that may be potential security problems and dealing with them. Login security can pose several different kinds of problems.

Accounts Without Passwords

Many computer crackers succeed in breaking into a computer by simply finding an account that doesn't have a password. You should check your password file regularly for such accounts and disable them. The password is stored in the second field of the password file under Linux. You can check for a blank password field with several tools, such as grep, awk, or perl. You can disable logins to an account by editing the password file and changing the password field to a * character. This prevents anyone from logging in with that login ID.

▶ **See** "Setting User Passwords," **p. 223**

Unused Accounts

If a login name won't be used any more, you should delete the account so that it can't be compromised. At the very least, you should edit the password file and set the password to the * character, which will prevent anyone from logging in to the account. If you choose to delete the account, you should use the `find` command to locate all files owned by the account and then change their ownership or delete them.

▶ **See** "Removing a User," **p. 224**

N O T E If you use other configuration files, such as system mail alias lists, you'll have to remove the account from those files as well. ■

Default Accounts

Linux comes with several standard login IDs that are required for the operating system to work correctly. For example, the root account has no password when Linux is first installed. You should check the password file when you've finished your installations to make sure that all your default accounts have good passwords or have been disabled by setting the password field to a * character.

Some software packages automatically create accounts on your system during their installation processes. Remember to disable them or set their passwords accordingly.

Guest Accounts

It's not uncommon for computer centers to provide some type of guest access accounts for visitors so they can use the local computers temporarily. These accounts usually don't have passwords or have passwords that are the same as the login ID. For example, the login *guest* might not have a password or has a password of guest. As you might guess, these are security disasters waiting to happen.

Because these accounts and passwords are probably widely known, an intruder could use one to gain initial access to your system. When a cracker has broken into your system, the intruder can then try to get root access from the inside or use your system as a waypoint from which to attack other computers over a network. Tracing an attack back to an open, public account makes it much harder to find the true source of the attack.

Guest or open accounts really aren't a good idea on any system. If you really must use one, keep it disabled until it's needed. Randomly generate a password for the account when it needs to be used and, when you can, disable it immediately. Remember not to send the password via e-mail.

Part

II

Ch

12

Command Accounts

It's common for computers to have several *command accounts*—login IDs that run a given command and then exit. For example, finger is an account that has no password. When a user logs in as finger, the `finger` program is run, showing who is on the system, and then the session terminates. Other such accounts may be sync and date, which typically don't have passwords. Even though they don't run a shell and run only one command, they can still pose a security risk.

If you allow command accounts on your system, you should ensure that none of these commands accepts command-line input. Also, these commands shouldn't have any type of shell escape that can allow a user to get to an interactive shell.

A second reason for not using these types of accounts is that they can give away information about your system that can be useful to an intruder. Using programs such as `finger` or `who` as command accounts can allow intruders to get the login IDs of users on your system. Remember that the login ID/password combination protects your accounts. If an intruder gets the login ID of a user, that person now has half the information that's needed to log in to that account.

Group Accounts

A group account is an account for which more than one person knows the password and logs in under the same ID. You guessed it—a bad idea. If you have an account shared by several people that is broken into and is being used as a base to attack other computers, finding the person who gave out the password is difficult. If you have an account that's shared by five people, it may in fact be shared by 25. There's no way to know.

▶ **See** "Working with Groups," **p. 225**

Linux allows you to provide file access based on group membership. This way, a group of people who need access to a set of files can share them without needing to share an account. Rather than create group accounts, make wise use of groups under Linux. Stay with the "One Login ID, One Person" philosophy.

Handling File Security

The file system under Linux is a tree structure that's built from files and directories. Linux stores several types of information about each file in its file system, including the following:

- The file name
- The file type
- The file size
- The file's physical location on disk
- Various access and modification times
- The owner and group ID of the file
- The access permissions associated with the file

If a user can modify some of the file information on certain files, security breaches can occur. As a result, the file system plays a very important role in system security.

Permissions

Linux file permissions control which users can access which files and commands. These permission bits control access rights for the owner, the associated group members, and other users. By using the `ls -l` command, you can generate a file list that shows the permissions field. The leftmost field shown by `ls -l` specifies the file permissions. For example, this field may look like `-rw-r--r--`. The first - in the field shows the file type. For regular files, this field is always -.

▶ **See** "Displaying Information About Files and Directories with *ls*," **p. 127**

The next nine characters represent the file access permissions for the owner, group, and world, respectively. Each category takes up three characters in the permissions field, consisting of the characters r (for read permission), w (for write permission), and x (for execute permission). Any or all of these characters may be present.

If one of the permissions has been granted, the corresponding character is present. If permission isn't granted, there's a - instead. For example, if a file has a permission field that looks like `-rw-r--r--`, this indicates that the file is a regular file (the first character is -), the owner has permissions rw- (which means read and write, but no execute), and the other group members and the world at large both have permissions r-- (which means read permission but no write or execute access). File permissions are changed via the `chmod` command.

▶ **See** "File Permissions," **p. 293**

N O T E You can specify the permissions to the `chmod` command as octal values instead of the rwx symbolic values. Simply treat the three characters in a permission field as bits in an octal number—if the character is present, count it as a 1. So, the permissions `-rw-r--r--` are represented numerically as 644. ■

SUID and SGID Programs

Two additional permission bits are associated with a file: the SUID and SGID bits. SUID stands for *Set User ID*, and SGID is *Set Group ID*. Programs with these permissions behave as though they were owned by different UIDs when they're run. When an SUID program is run, its effective UID is set the same as the user that owns the program on the file system, regardless of who is actually running the program. SGID is similar except that it changes the group ID instead.

Although the SUID/SGID feature can be useful, it can present a big security hole. SUID programs are generally used when a program needs special permissions, such as root permission, to run.

Programmers usually go to great lengths to ensure that their SUID programs are secure. Most security holes in SUID programs occur when the program executes a command line, activates a shell, or runs a file that users can change to contain their own commands. Although some SUID programs are necessary, you should try to keep them to a minimum. You should also regularly scan your file systems to check for new SUID programs by using the `find` command (refer to the man page for the exact syntax).

Avoiding Social Engineering Threats

With all the different security features available on a Linux system, the biggest security hole is typically your users. After all, your users already have valid accounts.

But what does this have to do with social engineering? What is social engineering, anyway? *Social engineering* is about convincing people to do what you want, either by playing on their assumptions or behavior, or by outright misrepresentation and lying. People, in general, want to be helpful. And, if given the opportunity, they usually try to help out as much as possible. Crackers with good social engineering skills play on this characteristic.

Assume that you have a computer user named Mr. Jones. He's just your average user—not a guru at all. One day, Mr. Jones gets a call at the office that goes something like this:

Mr. Jones:	Hello?
Caller:	Hello, Mr. Jones. This is Fred Smith in tech support. Due to some disk space constraints, we're going to be moving some user home directories to another disk at 5:30 this evening. Your account will be part of this move and will be temporarily unavailable.
Mr. Jones:	Uh, okay. I'll be home by then, anyway.
Caller:	Good. Be sure to log out before you go. I just need to check a couple of things. What was your login ID again—jones?
Mr. Jones:	Yes, it's jones. None of my files will get lost during the move, will they?
Caller:	No sir. But I'll check your account just to make sure. What was the password on that account so I can get in to check your files?
Mr. Jones:	My password is tuesday.
Caller:	Okay, Mr. Jones. Thanks for your help. I'll be sure to check your account and verify that all the files are there.
Mr. Jones:	Thank you. Bye.

So what just happened here? Someone called one of your users on the phone and managed to get both a valid user name and password in the course of the conversation. And you guessed it—if Mr. Jones calls tech support tomorrow, he'll probably find that no Fred Smith is working there!

How do you prevent things like this from happening? Educate your users. Your users should never give out a password over the phone to a caller. They should never leave one on e-mail or voice mail. Crackers use social engineering by convincing users to give them what they want; they don't even have to try to break into your system.

Recording Use of the *su* Command

Linux verifies your identity by your login ID/password combination. As you log in, your process is tagged with an ID that identifies you to the system. It's this UID that's checked for file and directory access.

Linux offers the capability to switch to another UID while you're working. When users use the su command, they can become root or another user. They must know the password of the user that they're changing to. For example, for a user to change user ID to that of user ernie, the command is

```
su ernie
```

The user is then prompted for the password associated with the login ID ernie.

To change to root, the command is

```
su root
```

The user is then prompted for the root password.

Typically, all attempts at using su are automatically logged in a system logfile, such as /var/adm/syslog. Examine this file periodically to check on this sort of activity.

Developing a Secure System

Along with power comes responsibility. If not handled carefully, Linux's power to share information, processing resources, and peripherals can leave your system open to abuse. Your job is to set up system security so that only the right users and systems can connect to yours, and that they can use only the parts of your computer you want to share.

Security Threats

You can monitor your system for security threats. To determine who is using your system and the type of work they're doing, use the ps command.

Be wary of jobs that seem to be running a very long time or users who seem to be using more resources than normal. These can be an indication that a login has been compromised and an unauthorized user is running a program to guess passwords.

Controlling the Root

The root login is reserved for your administrators. The person who logs in as the root has the power to erase any file, restrict use by any person on the network, and quite literally to cause havoc among users. That's the downside of the picture. Linux was designed to give the people having root access the tools to do their jobs better than in other environments.

Many proprietary operating systems have blockages established by the creators to avoid accidental damage to files and other operating factors on the system. The creators of UNIX and Linux took a different attitude toward the administrator. You'll find tools that permit you to connect almost any computer device. You'll find software that monitors the performance of the computer. You can create an endless array of software and adapt it to just about any business environment.

Part
II

Ch
12

Also, you can force your users to do only specified things on the computer, or you can give them limited rights until they grow in their knowledge. The root user, the administrator, has the power to do these things.

N O T E Because access to the root is so important, some companies restrict use to a select few. ■

Controlling Modems and Crackers

Allowing access from a common modem, similar to those that people have at home, can permit someone to "crack" the system and destroy important data. As a result, many companies insist that the computer have elaborate security mechanisms, which can make these computers almost impossible to work with. Some companies put a dial-back option on the computer so that you must dial the computer and then wait for a return call before you can interact with the system.

Most of the time, a traditional UNIX/Linux approach is recommended. Make sure that all your user logins have passwords. Restrict the systems that can connect to your system. Keep permissions closed on sensitive files. Be careful of set UID bit programs (those that give the user who runs the program the permissions to run as another user). Most break-ins occur because someone left the door open.

N O T E Ultimately, security is a problem with people rather than systems. You can't allow passwords to be etched in the wall near a terminal or have DOS computers with root passwords embedded in communication programs. ■

Preventing Idle Terminals

Users should log out or use some kind of terminal lock program when they leave at the end of the day. Most UNIX systems have such a program that shuts down terminals left on beyond a prescribed length of time.

Enforcing Security

Security in defense firms is clearly understood. Companies that have highly sensitive products in the design cycle understand the need for security. But employees in a small distributor of plumbing parts may have a hard time understanding what everybody is so concerned about. Security in this example isn't an issue until you can't figure out who removed a file that included a key proposal.

Employees should have a quick lesson about the sensitivity of data on your computer. A business has a significant investment in the data on the computer. Loss of data can be a distraction or it can mean chaos. Employees who are unwilling to participate in securing a computer should understand that this can be cause for dismissal.

For an administrator, the task becomes apparent. If you're the chief security officer for the network, how can you be sure that files and directories are adequately secured? Fortunately, there are many tools to help you, such as umask, cron, and Linux itself.

Permissions seem to be a significant source of worry for most administrators. New administrators typically tighten up permissions and then field calls from people saying they can't gain access to a file they need or can't execute a program on the system. After a while, these administrators loosen up the permissions so that anybody can do anything. The balancing act of securing the computer while permitting the proper people the tools to do their jobs is sometimes frustrating.

Handling Security Breaches

Security on a computer can require a little detective work. For example, look at the following:

```
# who -u
root    tty02   Jan 7 08:35    old    Ofc #2
martha ttym1d  Jan 7 13:20    . Payroll #1
ted     ttyp0   Jan 7 08:36   8:25   Warehouse
margo   ttyp2   Jan 7 07:05   9:45   CEO Ofc
root    ttyp4   Jan 7 08:36    . Modem #1
# date
Tue Jan 7 19:18:21 CST 1997
```

Suppose that you know that Martha left the office at 5 p.m. Has someone found her password, or did she leave the terminal on when she left? You can see that she logged in at 13:20 today. It's now 19:18, and somebody is active on the system using her login. Do you dispatch security?

But what do you do if someone does break into your system? First, try to determine whether you really do have an intruder. Many times, what you notice may just be the result of human error. If you do have an intruder, you have several options. You need to decide whether any damage was done, and the extent of the damage. Do you prosecute those responsible if you can catch them? If so, you should start trying to gather and protect evidence.

You must decide how to go about securing your system and restoring any damage from your backups. Probably the most important thing of all is to document what you do. Start a log immediately. Sign and date any printouts showing evidence of intrusion; these may be useful as evidence. Your log may be invaluable in helping you figure out what you've done when you have to change or restore files.

Two other preventive measures that you should take are to make printouts of your basic system configuration files, such as /etc/fstab, and establish a site security policy. You must make sure that your users are aware of your site policy, and that they're reminded frequently.

Another area of concern is when an employee leaves the company. When an employee leaves, for whatever reason, personnel should contact the computer staff to retire the login.

With all the different security considerations, how much security is enough? Can you have too much? You may be surprised to learn that yes, you can have too much security. In general, if the cost of recovering from a security breach is less than the cost of security, you should reduce the security level for your systems. Note that these cost factors include much more than monetary costs. Among other things, you should take into consideration the content of your files, the amount of time and money that it will take to replace them, any lost productivity time that an attack would produce, and the effect that publicity of a computer security problem will have on your organization.

Performing Backups

Few issues that the typical Linux administrator deals with are as important as the backup or archiving of a system. An administrator can be fired or a company can literally fail because of the loss of valuable data. The disk or disks on a computer are electromechanical devices, and they will fail at some time.

Most new hard disks are rated at around 150,000 hours mean time between failures—more than five years. But the mean-time statistic can be deceptive. Your disk could fail at the 50,000 hour mark or it might last for more than 10 years (highly unlikely). You're gambling if you back up your systems only occasionally, and you take an even greater chance if you aren't checking your backup tapes regularly.

▶ **See** "Planning a Backup Schedule," **p. 227**

From Here...

You can find more information about security issues in the following chapters:

- ▓ Chapter 10, "Managing User Accounts," discusses the issues relating to creating and maintaining user accounts on Linux.

- ▓ Chapter 11, "Backing Up Data," describes how to set up and maintain backups of your system.

Upgrading and Installing Software

Using *pkgtool*

Slackware Linux provides the
pkgtool program to help you install
software.

Installing other software

For software packages that aren't
installed by pkgtool, this chapter
explains how to perform the installations.

Upgrading kernels

Along with software upgrades, new
versions of the kernel sources are
released regularly. This chapter
discusses concerns and methods
for upgrading your Linux system.

The base Linux system initially contains only a core set of
utilities and data files. The system administrator installs
additional commands, user application programs, and
various data files as required. Applications get updated
frequently. System software changes as new features are
added and bugs are fixed. The system administrator is
responsible for adding, configuring, maintaining, and
deleting software from the Linux system.

The word *installing* means copying the associated program files onto the system's hard disk and *configuring* the
application (assigning resources) for proper operation
on a specific system. The configuration of a program instructs it as to where parts of the application are to be
installed and how it is to function within the system environment in general.

The Slackware distribution of Linux eases the pain of
installing and upgrading software by including the
pkgtool command. However, you'll also find yourself
installing software that isn't in pkgtool format. Many of
the software packages available on the Internet are in
compressed tar format.

On large systems, an administrator usually installs applications because most users don't have access to the tape or floppy drives. Administrative permission is also often needed to install components of the applications into system directories. Components may include shared libraries, utilities, and devices that need to go into directories that a normal user can't access. ■

Understanding Key Terms Used in This Chapter

As you may have surmised if you read the introduction to this chapter, the installation of applications involves an expanded vocabulary. Table 13.1 lists some terms and definitions that you should become familiar with.

Table 13.1   Terms Related to Application Installation

Term	Definition
superuser	The highest privileged user on the system. Also called the *root user*.
system administrator	The person in charge of keeping the Linux system optimized and properly running. The system administrator has superuser privileges and can install new software onto the system.
installing applications	The initial installation or update of a program for a UNIX system. The process usually requires superuser privileges and access to the computer's tape or floppy disk drive.
configuring	The act of setting up an application to work with your particular system. Configuring can include setting up the application for many users to use, putting it in accessible directories, or sharing it with the network.

Understanding the Politics of Upgrading

What software should you upgrade? How often should you upgrade? The answers to these questions are largely determined by the purpose of your system—personal or business—and the demands of your users. Software versions are changing all the time. Various parts of the Linux system are constantly being updated. You wouldn't have time to use your system if you tried to keep up with each and every upgrade that comes out.

Typically, you shouldn't have to reinstall the entire Linux system when you upgrade your system software. Usually, only a tiny portion of the system software changes with a new release. You may have to upgrade your kernel or upgrade your system libraries, but you probably won't have to do a full reinstall. However, when you upgrade software packages, you quite often have to completely install a new version, especially if you're several versions behind when you upgrade.

N O T E Making a current backup of your system before upgrading software is a good idea. That way, if something goes wrong, you can always get back to your original system. ▪

▶ **See** "Considering Backup Tips," **p. 228**

In general, you should upgrade your system if a new version of either system or application software becomes available that either fixes a serious problem or adds functionality that you need. It's up to you to determine what constitutes a serious problem. If a new release of a software package fixes something that has caused problems on your system or fixes a bug that could damage your system, it's probably worth the time it takes to install it.

N O T E Don't try to keep up with every release of every piece of software; upgrading for the sake of upgrading takes too much time and effort. With a little research, you can keep your system working in good condition and update only the parts that need upgrading as you go along. ▪

Installing Software

Installing a major program onto a Linux system is more complicated than installing a similar program on a single-task operating system, such as MS-DOS or Apple Macintosh System 7.6. The multiuser nature of Linux means that every application on the system sometimes receives simultaneous calls for access.

To further complicate installation, most application programs—with the exception of very simple ones—require configuration to your specific system before they can be used. It's up to the system administrator installing the software to identify items specific to the system's configuration when prompted during an application's configuration process.

For example, one user may have only an older character-based terminal, whereas another has a fancy new X Windows terminal. The superuser must make sure that the application responds correctly to the older terminal, sending only ASCII characters—that is, letters and numbers— and that the X Windows terminal receives full advantage of the application's colors and graphics. The system administrator manages the system and has the responsibility of keeping it optimized (all programs up to current versions, proper user accounts assigned, and so forth).

As already stated, loading a program onto a Linux system is more complicated than doing so on single-user operating systems. The system administrator who's installing an application may have to create new directories to house the files associated with a particular program. Some software packages call for the configuring or reconfiguring of system devices. Although the end user worries only about learning the new program's features and operating commands, the superuser must make sure that system resources are properly allocated, configured, and maintained for the program (while, of course, not messing up any already installed applications).

Installing software by using menus or commands is outwardly a relatively simple task; to the system itself, however, the task is complex. Applications for single-user operating systems, such as DOS programs, usually run only one copy of themselves at a time and have no competing programs. In even a simple Linux installation with only one user logged in, many processes

Part
II
Ch
13

can be running at the same time. Multiply this activity by several users all running programs—including some users who utilize the same application—and the complexity increases dramatically.

The Linux operating system excels at juggling a multitude of processes, programs, users, and peripherals simultaneously. To live in a Linux environment, an application must be properly loaded. An ill-behaving application, or one improperly installed, can cause a system *crash* (when a process or program goes wild and locks the CPU, causing it to lose control of all the currently running programs). The system shuts down, all users are kicked off, and their programs are interrupted. There's often much wailing and gnashing of teeth from frustrated persons in the midst of some complicated task.

As the one loading a new application, the system administrator or superuser is responsible for making sure that the application is compatible with the system and to test the application after it's installed. Understanding the loading of software onto a Linux system first requires a basic knowledge of the responsibilities and privileges of the system administrator.

Understanding the System Administrator's Job

If you use Linux on a small system, you're probably your own system administrator. You install and run your applications. It's your responsibility to keep a current backup of files, maintain a proper amount of free space on the hard disk, make sure that the system runs optimally through memory management and other means, and do everything else required in the administration of an efficient and productive system. If you're a user in a larger system environment, a specific person probably handles system administration. The following list briefly summarizes what the system administrator does:

- Starts and stops the system, as needed
- Makes sure that there's enough free disk space and that file systems are free of error
- Tunes the system so that the maximum number of users have access to the system's hardware and software resources, and so that the system operates as fast and as efficiently as possible
- Protects the system from unauthorized entry and destructive actions
- Sets up connections to other computer systems
- Sets up or closes user accounts on the system
- Works with software and hardware vendors, and with those with training or other support contracts for the system
- Installs, mounts, and troubleshoots terminals, printers, disk drives, and other pieces of system and peripheral hardware
- Installs and maintains programs, including new application programs, operating system updates, and software-maintenance corrections

Using *pkgtool*

Some Linux software, especially software included with a distribution such as Slackware, is bundled into a special package format. Slackware Linux provides the pkgtool program, which installs software in this special format. If you've installed the Slackware distribution of Linux, you're already familiar with pkgtool. It's called by setup, the program that you ran to install Linux on your system.

N O T E The Red Hat distribution of Linux doesn't include the pkgtool command. ▪

pkgtool knows how to install the various software packages that make up the full Slackware distribution. These packages are bundled in disk sets, with each set represented by some letter code. A complete disk set may contain several different software components, but they're usually related, such as in the disk sets for networking or the disk sets for games. Each disk set also contains a file known as a *tagfile*, which tells pkgtool what software sets to install for a particular package.

If you run pkgtool without any arguments, you get an interactive menu system that allows you to select source and destination directories and the various disk sets that you want to install. In addition to running pkgtool from the menu system, you can also run pkgtool with command-line arguments that specify the various arguments for pkgtool. You'll probably want to run pkgtool from the menu system most of the time. But if you ever need to run it with command-line arguments, Table 13.2 lists the various options available.

Table 13.2   Command-Line Arguments for the *pkgtool* Command

Option	Description
-sets *setlist*	Tells pkgtool which disk sets to install. The *setlist* argument is a list of disk set labels separated by # characters, as in -sets #A#C.
-source_mounted	Tells pkgtool not to unmount and remount the source device with each disk.
-ignore_tagfiles	Causes pkgtool to ignore the instructions in the tagfiles and install every software component that it finds in a given disk set.
-source_dir *dir*	Gives the directory where the subdirectories for each disk are found, if you're installing multiple packages from disk sets. Not used for installing from floppy.
-target_dir *dir*	Specifies where the target directory is located.
-source_device *dev*	Specifies the source device to install from, usually a floppy drive. Not used with the source_mounted option.

Part

II

Ch

13

Installing Non-Linux Software

Most of the different software packages that you'll find aren't in the same form that the software components from the Linux installation were in. Typically, these packages are downloaded via anonymous FTP from some archive site.

The process of installing software can range from extremely simple to almost impossible. It all depends on how well the software authors wrote their installation scripts and how good their installation documentation is.

Deciphering Software Package Formats   The software packages that you get via anonymous FTP will virtually all be in the form of a compressed tar file. These files can be created in a couple of different ways. Typically, a directory tree containing source files, libraries, documentation, executables, and other necessary files are bundled into a tar file by using the tar program. This tar file is then usually compressed to save space.

The software package will probably have an extension at the end of the file name that tells you what format it's in. If the file ends in .gz, it was compressed with the GNU gzip program. This is the most common file-compression format for Linux software packages. If the archive name ends with a .Z, it was compressed with the compress program. For example, the software package foo.tar.gz is a tar archive that has been compressed with gzip.

N O T E   Sometimes, a tar file that has been compressed with gzip is written with the .tgz extension instead of .tar.gz. ▪

▶ **See** "Using *tar*," **p. 231**

Installing the Package   The next thing that you have to do after you figure out the package format is figure out where you want to place the source files so that you can build the software package. Some software packages are fairly large, so it's a good idea to place them on a file system that has a good bit of free space. Some people create a separate file system for sources and mount it under a directory, such as /usr/local/src or /src. Wherever you decide to build your software packages, make sure that you have enough disk space so that the software can be compiled successfully.

Now, you can go ahead and move the software package to the source tree that you've set up and decompress it and expand the archive. If a file is compressed with gzip, you can decompress it with the gzip -d command. For example, the command

```
gzip -d foo.tar.gz
```

expands the compressed file foo.tar.gz and replaces it with the tar archive named foo.tar. For files that have been compressed with the compress command, use the uncompress command to expand them. The command

```
uncompress foo.tar.Z
```

expands the compressed file foo.tar.Z and replaces it with the tar archive named foo.tar.

After you expand the compressed file, you need to expand the tar file into a directory tree. You want to put the sources for each separate package in its own directory in your source tree. Before untarring the file, you should look at its tar listing to see whether it was created with a directory as the first entry. Use the command

```
tar -tvf tarfile-name ¦ more
```

to see whether the first entry in the tar file is a directory. If so, the tar file creates the directory when it's expanded. If there's no directory entry at the top level of the tar file, all the files at the top level are extracted into the current directory. In this case, you need to make a directory and move the tar file into it before you expand it.

N O T E   Always check for a top-level directory before expanding a tar file. It can be quite a mess if the tar file expands and places a few hundred files in the current directory instead of in a subdirectory.

When you have the tar file where you want to expand it, you can use the command

```
tar -xvf tarfile-name
```

to expand the source tree in the tar file.

The next step depends on how the software package that you're installing was written. Typically, you change directory to the top-level directory of the software sources and look for a file named something like README.1ST. There should be a few documentation files in the top-level source directory that explain the installation process.

N O T E   On most versions of Linux, you can decompress a tar file "on the fly" as you extract it. Simply add the z flag to the tar command, as in `tar -zxvf foo.tar.gz`.

The typical installation process involves editing the file named Makefile to edit the destination directories where the software places its compiled binaries. You then usually run `make` followed by `make install`.

The `make` process probably varies with each package that you install. For some packages, some sort of configuration shell script may ask you questions and then compile the software for you. Make sure that you read the documentation files that come with the package.

Reviewing File Permissions

Setting permissions for a software package usually occurs automatically during installation. The installation script that comes with your application usually installs each file with the proper ownership and permissions. Only when something goes wrong and a user who should be able to access the program can't do so are you required to find the directory the application was copied to and check the permissions.

Typically, the executable file that you run to start the application is installed with permissions that let any user run the file; however, only the superuser can delete or overwrite it. The application usually is installed in a directory with read and execute permissions, but no write permissions.

▶ **See** "File Permissions," **p. 293**

Solving Problems

A well-written and well-supported application installs onto your system with minimal requests for information from you. It sets permissions properly so that all you have to do is test the program and inform your users—often through e-mail—that the application is now available. But things can and do go wrong in the installation of programs and their subsequent operation (or non-operation). If, for whatever reason, the program doesn't complete the loading process or fails to operate correctly after installation, it's your responsibility to determine why and to fix the problem.

If a program doesn't install completely, your troubleshooting efforts often require no more than reading the documentation and README files supplied with the application and looking for a list of exceptions or problems and their solutions. However, no one expects you to possess expertise and familiarity with the scores of software packages available for Linux. Occasionally, you'll require outside help.

If you can't solve the problem by using the information that came with the package, you should try looking on Usenet news to see whether there's any discussion of the package in question. A question posted in the appropriate Linux group on Usenet can solve a lot of problems. If you can't find help on the Net, you can try to contact the application developer, usually via e-mail. Remember, Linux is free, and so are most of the software packages that exist for Linux. Don't expect shrink-wrapped manuals and 24-hour technical support lines. But if you weren't the adventurous type, you wouldn't be using Linux—right?

Removing Applications

If an application is superseded by a better package or is no longer used by any user on the system, removing it is a good idea. Disk space is always precious; you certainly don't want old, unused programs to hog space required by new applications.

Like installation, removal of a program on a Linux system is more complicated than for single-user operating systems. It's sometimes not enough just to erase the application's files and remove its directory. Drivers and other software connections must be disconnected to avoid future problems. By taking notes and capturing the installation messages to a logfile, you can usually figure out what was changed when the software was installed. You can then deduce what files to remove and which files to change in order to successfully delete a package.

Upgrading Your Kernel

Along with upgrades for other software, new versions of the kernel sources are released regularly. These versions may fix bugs or add new functionality. Alternatively, you may decide to upgrade your kernel because you need to reconfigure it or add new device drivers. In any case, the process is fairly straightforward. You should make sure that you have a backup of your system software and a Linux boot floppy before you start so that you can recover if you should damage your system. For a complete description of how to rebuild the Linux kernel, see the installation chapters: Chapter 3, "Installing Red Hat," and Chapter 4, "Installing Slackware 96."

▶ **See** "Building a New Kernel," **pp. 66** and **111**

The process for upgrading your kernel is detailed in the Kernel HOWTO document, which is regularly posted to the Linux newsgroups on the Internet and is available on the various Linux FTP sites, including **sunsite.unc.edu**. Be sure to get a copy of this HOWTO and read it thoroughly before you start your kernel upgrade.

The first step in the basic process of upgrading your kernel is getting the new kernel sources, which are available via anonymous FTP from the various Linux archive sites. When you have the sources, you need to preserve your current kernel sources. To do so, move your /usr/src/ linux directory to another name, such as /usr/src/linux.old. Unpack the kernel sources in the /usr/src directory, which creates the linux subdirectory in the process. At that point, change to the linux directory and look at the documentation and the README files. Things may change as new kernels are released, so be sure to read the documentation.

From here, the process may vary a bit. Typically, you enter `make config`, which runs a configuration script and asks you questions about your system. If the configuration phase completes successfully, you then enter something similar to `make dep`. This checks for all the file dependencies to make sure that the new kernel finds all the files it needs to compile.

After the dependency check is complete, you typically enter `make clean` to delete any old object files that are left lying around in the kernel source directory. If everything has gone okay up to this point, you can enter `make` to compile the new kernel. After it compiles, you can install it with the LILO boot manager, and off you go.

Again, be sure to read the Kernel HOWTO before trying to do this. It goes into deep detail on setting up your kernel and will probably save you hours of frustration. Also, it may keep you from trashing your current Linux system in the process.

From Here...

You can find more information about installing and upgrading software in the following chapters:

- Chapter 3, "Installing Red Hat," provides a detailed discussion about how to install and set up the Red Hat distribution of the Linux operating system.
- Chapter 4, "Installing Slackware 96," provides a detailed discussion about how to install and set up the Slackware 96 distribution of Linux.
- Chapter 5, "Running Linux Applications," provides a basic introduction to setting up your Linux system.
- Chapter 11, "Backing Up Data," looks at the process for making system backups.

Part

II

Ch

13

Managing the File System

## CHAPTER 14

Managing File Systems

File systems form the basis for all data on a Linux system. Linux programs, libraries, system files, and user files all reside on file systems. Proper management of file systems is critical because all your data and programs exist on top of file systems.

Many of the steps outlined in this chapter are performed automatically when you install Linux. However, you should learn to manage your file systems so that you can create, manage, and maintain your Linux system. Understanding file system management is critical to successful systems administration. Your file system must work properly for your Linux system to work at all. ■

Understanding file systems

File systems are directories created on hard drives, floppies, or CD-ROMs. File systems can also be available over the network.

Mounting and unmounting file systems

To access a file system, you must make its existence know to Linux by mounting the file system to a mount point.

Working with the Network File System (NFS)

NFS allows Linux to access file systems on remote machines as though they were on the local hard drive.

Maintaining file systems

Over time, Linux file systems can become stale or corrupted, and thus need to be maintained.

Creating and formatting file systems

You must create and format file systems as new hard drives are added.

Using swap files and partitions

To take advantage of virtual memory, Linux needs *swap space*—disk space the system uses as memory when physical RAM is exhausted.

Understanding File Systems

Under Linux, the file space that's visible to users is based on a tree structure, with the root at the top. The various directories and files in this space branch downward from the root. The top directory, /, is known as the *root directory*. Figure 14.1 gives a graphical example of a tree structure.

FIG. 14.1

Picture the Linux file system as an upside-down tree, with the root at the top and the branches and leaves spreading downward.

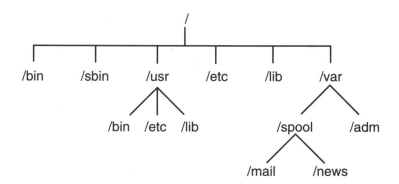

To users, this directory tree looks like a seamless entity—they just see directories and files. In reality, many of the directories in the file tree are physically located as different partitions on a disk, on different disks, or even on different computers. When one of these disk partitions is attached to the file tree at a directory known as a *mount point*, the mount point and all directories below it are referred to as a *file system*.

The Linux operating system is made up of several directories and many different files. Depending on how you selected your installation, these directories may be different file systems. Typically, most of the operating system resides on two file systems: the root file system, known as /, and a file system mounted under /usr (pronounced as "user").

If you change directories to the root directory with the cd / command and ask for a directory listing, you see several directories. These make up the contents of the root file system and provide the mount points for other file systems as well.

The /bin directory contains executable programs, known as *binaries.* (In fact, the directory named /bin is short for *binary.*) These programs are essential system files. Many Linux commands, such as ls, are actually programs found in this directory.

The /sbin directory is also used to store system binary files. Most files in this directory are used for system administration purposes.

The /etc directory is very important, containing many of the Linux system configuration files. Essentially, these files give your Linux system its "personality." The password file, passwd, is found here, as is the list of file systems to mount at startup, fstab. Also, this directory contains the startup scripts for Linux, the list of hosts with IP addresses that you want permanently recorded, and many other types of configuration information.

The shared libraries that programs use when they run are stored in the /lib directory. By using shared libraries, many programs can reuse the same code, and these libraries can be stored in a common place, thus reducing the size of your programs at run time.

The /dev directory contains special files known as *device files*, which are used to access all the different types of hardware on your system. For example, the /dev/mouse file is for reading input from the mouse. By organizing access to hardware devices in this way, Linux effectively makes the interface to a hardware device look like any other piece of software. This means that you, in many cases, can use the same syntax that you use with software to perform operations on computer hardware devices. For example, to create a tape archive of your home directory on a floppy drive, you can use the following command:

```
tar -cdf /dev/fd0 ~tackett
```

Many of the devices in the /dev directory are in logical groups. Table 14.1 lists some of the most commonly used devices in the /dev directory.

Table 14.1 Some of the Most Commonly Used Devices in the /dev Directory

Device File	Description
/dev/console	The *system console*, which is the computer monitor physically connected to your Linux system.
/dev/hd	The device driver interface to IDE hard drives. The /dev/hda1 device refers to the first partition on hard drive hda. The device /dev/hda refers to the entire hard disk hda.
/dev/sd	The device driver interface for SCSI disks. The same conventions for SCSI disks and partitions apply as they do to the IDE /dev/hd devices.
/dev/fd	Device drivers that provide support for floppy drives. /dev/fd0 is the first floppy drive and /dev/fd1 is the second floppy drive.
/dev/st	The device driver for SCSI tape drives.
/dev/tty	Device drivers that provide different consoles for user input. The name comes from when terminals known as *teletypes* were physically hooked to a UNIX system. Under Linux, these files provide support for the virtual consoles that can be accessed by pressing <Alt-F1> through <Alt-F6>. These virtual consoles provide separate simultaneous local login sessions.
/dev/pty	Device drivers that provide support for pseudo-terminals, which are used for remote login sessions such as login sessions using Telnet.
/dev/ttyS	The serial interface ports on your computer. /dev/ttyS0 corresponds to COM1 under MS-DOS. If you have a serial mouse, /dev/mouse is a symbolic link to the appropriate ttyS device that your mouse is connected to.
/dev/cua	Special call-out devices used with modems.

Part

III

Ch

14

continues

Table 14.1	**Continued**
Device File	**Description**
/dev/null	A very special device—essentially a black hole. All data written to /dev/null is lost forever. This can be very useful if you want to run a command and throw away the standard output or the standard error. Also, if /dev/null is used as an input file, a file of zero length is created.

The /proc directory is actually a virtual file system. It's used to read process information from memory.

The /tmp directory is used to store temporary files that programs create when running. If you have a program that creates a lot of large temporary files, you may want to mount the /tmp directory as a separate file system rather than just have it as a directory on the root file system. If /tmp is left as a directory on the root file system and has lots of large files written to it, the root file system can fill up.

The /home directory is the base directory for user home directories. It's common to mount this as a separate file system so that users can have plenty of room for their files. In fact, if you have many users on your system, you may need to separate /home into several file systems. To do so, you could create subdirectories such as /home/staff and /home/admin for staff members and administrators, respectively. Mount each of these as different file systems and then create the users' home directories under them.

The /var directory holds files that tend to change in size over time. Typically, various system log files are located below this directory. The /var/spool directory and its subdirectories are used to hold data that's of a transitory nature, such as mail and news that's recently received from or queued for transmission to another site.

TIP

You can create other mount points under the / directory if you want. You might want to create a mount point named /cdrom if you routinely mount CD-ROMs on your system.

The /usr directory and its subdirectories are very important to the operation of your Linux system. It contains several directories with some of the most important programs on your system. Typically, subdirectories of /usr contain the large software packages that you install. Table 14.2 discusses some of the /usr subdirectories. The /usr directory is almost always mounted as a separate file system.

Table 14.2	**Important Subdirectories in the /usr File System**
Subdirectory	**Description**
/usr/bin	This directory holds many of the executable programs found on your Linux system.
/usr/etc	This directory contains many miscellaneous system configuration files.

Subdirectory	Description
/usr/include	Here and in the subdirectories of /usr/include is where you find all the include files for the C compiler. These header files define constants and functions and are critical for C programming.
/usr/g++-include	This directory contains the include files for the C++ compiler.
/usr/lib	This directory contains various libraries for programs to use during linking.
/usr/man	This directory contains the various manual pages for programs on your Linux system. Below /usr/man are several directories that correspond to the different sections of the man pages.
/usr/src	This directory contains directories that hold the source code for different programs on your system. If you get a package that you want to install, /usr/src/*packagename* is a good place to put the source before you install it.
/usr/local	This directory is designed for local customizations to your system. In general, much of your local software is installed in this directory's subdirectories. The format of this directory varies on almost every UNIX system you look at. One way to set it up is to have a /usr/local/bin for binaries, a /usr/local/etc for configuration files, a /usr/local/lib for libraries, and a /usr/local/src for source code. The entire /usr/local directory tree can be mounted as a separate file system if you need a lot of room for it.

Mounting and Unmounting File Systems

By now, you should have a good feel for what a file system is. So how do you set up a directory as a separate file system?

To mount a file system in the Linux directory tree, you must have a physical disk partition, CD-ROM, or floppy disk that you want to mount. You also must make sure that the directory to which you want to attach the file system, known as the *mount point*, actually exists.

Mounting a file system doesn't create the mount point directory. The mount point must exist before you try to mount the file system. Suppose that you want to mount the CD-ROM in drive /dev/sr0 under the mount point /mnt. A directory named /mnt must exist, or the mount fails. After you mount the file system under that directory, all the files and subdirectories on the file system appear under the /mnt directory. Otherwise, the /mnt directory is empty.

Part
III

Ch
14

TIP Use df . if you need to know on which file system the current directory is located. The command's output shows the file system as well as the free space available.

Mounting File Systems Interactively

As you may have guessed by now, Linux uses the `mount` command to mount a file system. The syntax of the `mount` command is

`mount device mountpoint`

`device` is the physical device that you want to mount; `mountpoint` is the point in the file system tree where you want it to appear.

> **N O T E** The `mount` command can be used only by superusers. This is to help ensure system security. Several software packages are available that allow users to mount specific file systems, especially floppy disks. ▪

`mount` accepts several command-line arguments in addition to the two mentioned above (see Table 14.3). If a needed command isn't given, `mount` attempts to figure it out from the /etc/fstab file.

Table 14.3 Command-Line Arguments for the *mount* Command

Argument	Description
`-f`	Causes everything to be done except for the actual mount system call. This "fakes" mounting the file system.
`-v`	Verbose mode; provides additional information about what `mount` is trying to do.
`-w`	Mounts the file system with read and write permissions.
`-r`	Mounts the file system with read-only permission.
`-n`	Mounts without writing an entry in the /etc/mtab file.
`-t type`	Specifies the type of the file system being mounted. Valid types are `minux`, `ext`, `ext2`, `xiafs`, `msdos`, `hpfs`, `proc`, `nfs`, `umsdos`, `sysv`, and `iso9660` (the default).
`-a`	Causes `mount` to try to mount all file systems in /etc/fstab.
`-o list_of_options`	When followed by a comma-separated list of options, causes `mount` to apply the options specified to the file system being mounted. Many options are available here; for a complete list, refer to the `mount` man page.

> **N O T E** Several forms of the `mount` command are very common. `mount /dev/hdb3 /mnt` mounts the hard-disk partition /dev/hdb3 under the directory /mnt. `mount -r -t iso9660 /dev/sr0 /mnt` mounts the SCSI CD-ROM drive /dev/sr0, which is read-only and of the ISO 9660 file format under the directory /mnt. `mount -vat nfs` mounts all the NFS file systems listed in the /etc/fstab file. ▪

TIP If a file system doesn't mount correctly, use the command mount −vf *device mountpoint* to see what mount is doing. This gives a verbose listing and tells mount to do everything except mount the file system. This way, you can fake out the mount command and get a lot of information about what it's trying to do.

Mounting File Systems at Boot Time

Under most circumstances, the file systems that your Linux system uses won't change frequently. For this reason, you can easily specify a list of file systems that Linux mounts when it boots and that it unmounts when it shuts down. These file systems are listed in a special configuration file named /etc/fstab, for *file system table*.

The /etc/fstab file lists the file systems to be mounted, one file system per line. The fields in each line are separated by spaces or tabs. Table 14.4 lists the different fields in the /etc/fstab file.

Table 14.4   Fields in the /etc/fstab File

Field	Description
File system specifier	Specifies the block special device or the remote file system to be mounted.
Mount point	Specifies the mount point for the file system. For special file systems such as swap files, use the word none, which makes swap files active but not visible within the file tree.
Type	Gives the file system type of the specified file system. Now, the following types of file systems are supported:
	• minix, a local file system supporting file names of 14 or 30 characters
	• ext, a local file system with longer file names and larger inodes (this file system has been replaced by the ext2 file system and should no longer be used)
	• ext2, a local file system with longer file names, larger inodes, and other features
	• xiafs, a local file system
	• msdos, a local file system for MS-DOS partitions
	• hpfs, a local file system for OS/2 High Performance File System partitions
	• iso9660, a local file system used for CD-ROM drives
	• nfs, a file system for mounting partitions from remote systems

Part
III

Ch
14

continues

Table 14.4   Continued

Field	Description
	• swap, a disk partition or special file used for swapping
	• umsdos, a UMSDOS file system
	• sysv, a System V file system
Mount Options	A comma-separated list of mount options for the file system. At a minimum, it must contain the type of mount for the file system. See the mount man page for more information on mount options.
Dump Frequency	Specifies how often the file system should be backed up by the dump command. If this field isn't present, dump assumes that the file system doesn't need to be backed up.
Pass Number	Specifies in what order the file systems should be checked by the fsck command when the system is booted. The root file system should have a value of 1. All other file systems should have a value of 2. If a value isn't specified, the file system won't be checked for consistency at boot time.

TIP It's recommended that you mount your file systems at boot time via the /etc/fstab file instead of by using the mount command. Remember, only superusers can use mount.

The following is a sample fstab file:

```
# device       directory    type     options
/dev/hda1      /            ext2     defaults
/dev/hda2      /usr         ext2     defaults
/dev/hda3      none         swap     sw
/dev/sda1      /dosc        msdos    defaults
/proc          /proc        proc     none
```

In this sample file, you can see several different file systems. First, notice that comments in the file are prefixed by a # character. In this fstab file, two normal Linux file systems are mounted—the disk partitions /dev/hda1 and /dev/hda2. These are listed as being of type ext2 and are mounted under the root directory, / and /usr respectively.

The entry defaults listed under the options field indicates that this file system should be mounted by using a common set of default options. Specifically, the file system is mounted read/write enabled, it's to be interpreted as a block special device, all file I/O should be done asynchronously, the execution of binaries is permitted, the file system can be mounted with the mount -a command, the set UID (user ID) and set GID (group ID) bits on files are interpreted on this file system, and ordinary users aren't allowed to mount this file system. As you can see, it's a lot easier just to type **defaults** for the option instead.

▶ **See** "Creating the Swap Partition," **pp. 60 and 97**

The partition /dev/hda3 is a swap partition that's used for kernel virtual-memory swap space. Its mount point is specified as none because you don't want it to appear in the file system tree. It still has to be in the /etc/fstab file, so the system knows where it's physically located. Swap partitions are also mounted with the option sw.

The /proc file system is a virtual file system that points to the process information space in memory. As you can see, it doesn't have a corresponding physical partition to mount.

 TIP For full information on all options available in the /etc/fstab file, refer to the man page for fstab.

MS-DOS file systems can also be mounted automatically. The partition /dev/sda1 is the first partition on the SCSI hard drive sda. It's mounted as an MS-DOS partition by specifying msdos as the type and by giving /dosc as its mount point. You can place the mount point for the MS-DOS file system anywhere—there's no requirement that it be under the root directory.

Unmounting File Systems

Now that you know all sorts of stuff about mounting file systems, it's time to look at how to unmount. You use the umount command to unmount file systems. You would want to unmount a file system for several reasons: so that you can check/repair a file system with fsck, unmount NFS-mounted file systems in case of network problems, or unmount a file system on a floppy drive.

N O T E This command is umount, not "unmount." Make sure that you type it correctly. ▪

There are three basic forms of the umount command:

umount *device* ¦ *mountpoint*

umount -a

umount -t *fstype*

device is the name of the physical device to unmount; *mountpoint* is the mount point directory name (specify only one or the other). The umount command has only two command-line parameters: -a unmounts all file systems, and -t *fstype* acts only on file systems of the type specified.

CAUTION

The umount command doesn't unmount a file system that's in use. For example, if you have some file system mounted under /mnt and you try

cd /mnt

continues

Part
III

Ch
14

> *continued*
>
> `umount /mnt`
>
> you get an error telling you that the file system is busy. You have to change to a different directory in another file system to unmount the file system mounted under /mnt.

Understanding the Network File System

The Network File System (NFS) is a system that allows you to mount file systems from a different computer over a TCP/IP network. Under NFS, a file system on a remote computer is mounted locally and looks just like a local file system to users. The illusion of being mounted locally has numerous uses. For example, you can have one machine on your network with a lot of disk space acting as a file server. This computer has all the home directories of all your users on its local disks. By mounting these disks via NFS on all your other computers, your users can access their home directories from any computer.

NFS has three essential components:

- The computers with the file systems that you want to NFS mount must be able to communicate with each other via a TCP/IP network.

- The computer with the file system that you're interested in as a local file system must make that file system available to be mounted. This computer is known as the *server*, and the process of making the file system available is known as *exporting the file system*.

- The computer that wants to mount the exported file system, known as the *client*, must mount the file system as an NFS file system via the /etc/fstab file at boot time or interactively via the `mount` command.

The following sections discuss exporting the file system and mounting it locally.

Exporting an NFS File System

For clients to mount an NFS file system, this file system must be made available by the server. Before the file system can be made available, you must ensure that it's mounted on the server. If the file system is always going to an NFS exported file system, you should make sure that you have it listed in the /etc/fstab file on the server so that it automatically mounts when the server boots.

When you have the file system mounted locally, you can make it available via NFS. This is a two-step process. First, you must make sure that the NFS daemons `rpc.mountd` and `rpc.nfsd` are running on your server. These daemons are usually started from the startup /etc/rc.d/init.d/nfs script. Usually, all that's needed is to make sure that the following lines are in your script:

```
daemon rpc.mountd
daemon rpc.nfsd
```

N O T E As RPC-based programs, the `rpc.mountd` and `rpc.nfsd` daemons aren't managed by the `inetd` daemon but are started up at boot time, registering themselves with the `portmap` daemon. You must be sure to start them only after `rpc.portmap` is running. ▪

Second, you must enter the NFS file system in a configuration file named /etc/exports. This file contains information about what file systems can be exported, what computers are allowed to access them, and what type and level of access is permitted.

Understanding the /etc/exports File

The /etc/exports file is used by the `mountd` and `nfsd` daemons to determine what file systems are to be exported and what restrictions are placed on them. File systems are listed in /etc/exports, one per line. The format of each line is the name of the mount point for a local file system, followed by a list of computers that are allowed to mount this file system. A comma-separated list of mount options in parentheses may follow each name in the list. Table 14.5 lists the mount options available in the /etc/exports file.

Table 14.5 Mount Options Available in the /etc/exports File

Option	Description
insecure	Permits non-authenticated access from this machine.
secure	Requires secure RPC authentication from this machine.
root_squash	Maps any requests from root, UID 0 on the client, to the UID NOBODY_UID on the server.
no_root_squash	Doesn't map any requests from UID 0 (default behavior).
ro	Mounts the file system as read-only (default behavior).
rw	Mounts the file system as read-write.
link_relative	Converts absolute symbolic links (where the link contents start with a slash) into relative links by prefixing the link with the necessary number of `../` characters to get from the directory containing the link to the root on the server.
link_absolute	Leaves all symbolic links as they are (normal behavior for Sun NFS servers). This is the default behavior for Linux.
map_daemon	Maps local and remote names and numeric IDs by using an `lname/uid` map daemon on the client where the NFS request originated. Used to map between the client and server UID spaces.
all-squash	Maps all uids and gids to the anonymous user. This option is useful for NFS-exported public directories, such as those housing FTP and news.

continues

Part
III

Ch
14

Table 14.5 Continued

Option	Description
no-all-squash	The opposite of the all-squash option. This is the default option for Linux.
squash-uids	Specifies a list of uids subject to anonymous mappings. A valid list of ids looks like this: squash_uids=0-15,20,25-50
squash-gids	Specifies a list of gids subject to anonymous mappings. A valid list of ids looks like this: squash_gids=0-15,20,25-50
anonuid	Sets the uid for the anonymous account. This option is useful for PC/NFS clients.
anongid	Sets the gid for the anonymous account. This option is useful for PC/NFS clients.
noaccess	Used to exclude certain subdirectories from a client. Makes everything below the directory inaccessible to the client.

Here is a sample /etc/exports file:

```
/home                   bill.tristar.com(rw) fred.tristar.com(rw)
➥george.tristar.com(rw)
/usr/local/bin          *.tristar.com(ro)
/projects               develop.tristar.com(rw) bill.tristar.com(ro)
/pub                    (ro,insecure,root_quash)
```

In this example, the server exports four different file systems. /home is mounted with read/write access on three different computers: bill, fred, and george. This indicates the directory probably holds user home directories because of the directories' names. The /usr/local/bin file system is exported as read-only with access allowed for every computer in the tristar.com domain.

The /projects file system is exported with read/write access for the computer develop.tristar.com but with read-only access for bill.tristar.com.

For the /pub file system, there's no list of hosts that are allowed access. This means that any host is allowed to mount this file system. It has been exported as read-only, non-authenticated access allowed, and the server remaps any request from root on a remote machine that accesses this file system.

Mounting NFS File Systems

Mounting an NFS file system is similar to mounting any other type of file system. You can mount NFS file systems from the /etc/fstab file at boot time or interactively via the mount command.

CAUTION

You must be sure to separate the host name and file/system/path portions of the remote file system name with a colon, such as

```
mailserver:/var/spool/mail
```

when using the mount command or when making an entry in /etc/fstab. If you don't separate the host name from the directory, your system won't mount the remote directory correctly.

Mounting NFS File Systems via /etc/fstab   When you specify an NFS file system in the /etc/fstab file, you identify the file system with the format

hostname:/file/system/path

hostname is the name of the server where the file system is located; */file/system/path* is the file system on the server.

The file-system type is specified as nfs in the mount options field of the file system entry. Table 14.6 lists the most commonly used mount options.

Table 14.6   Commonly Used Options for NFS Mounts

Option	Description
rsize=*n*	Specifies the datagram size in bytes used by the NFS clients on read requests. The default value is 1,024 bytes.
wsize=*n*	Specifies the datagram size in bytes used by the NFS clients on write requests. The default value is 1,024 bytes.
timeo=*n*	Sets the time, in tenths of a second, that the NFS client waits for a request to complete. The default value is 0.7 seconds.
hard	Mounts this file system by using a hard mount. This is the default behavior.
soft	Mounts this file system by using a soft mount.
intr	Allows signals to interrupt an NFS call. This is useful for aborting an operation when an NFS server doesn't respond.

Hard Mounts vs. Soft Mounts

Hard mounts and *soft mounts* determine how an NFS client behaves when an NFS server stops responding. NFS file systems are hard-mounted by default. With either type of mount, if a server stops responding, the client waits until the timeout value specified by the timeo option expires and then resends the request (this is known as a *minor timeout*). If the requests to the server continue to time out and the total timeout reaches 60 seconds, a *major timeout* occurs.

If a file system is hard mounted, the client prints a message to the console and starts the mount requests all over again by using a timeout value that's twice that of the previous cycle. This has the

Part

III

Ch

14

continues

continued

potential to go on forever. The client keeps trying to remount the NFS file system from the server until it gets it. Period.

Soft mounts, on the other hand, just generate an I/O error to the calling process when a major timeout occurs. Linux then continues on its merry way.

Typically, important software packages and utilities that are mounted via NFS should be mounted with hard mounts. This is why hard mounts are the default. You don't want your system to start acting strange if the Ethernet gets unplugged for a moment; you want Linux to wait and continue when the network is back up. On the other hand, you might want to mount non-critical data, such as remote news spool partitions, as soft mounts so that if the remote host goes down, it won't hang your current login session.

A typical NFS file system entry in the /etc/fstab file might look like this:

```
mailserver:/var/spool/mail   /var/spool/mail    nfs timeo=20,intr
```

This entry mounts the /var/spool/mail file system located on the host mailserver at the local mount point /var/spool/mail. It specifies that the file system type is nfs. Also, it sets the timeout value to 2 seconds (20 tenths of a second) and makes operations on this file system interruptible.

Mounting NFS File Systems Interactively   NFS file systems can be mounted interactively, just like any other type of file system. However, you should be aware that the NFS mount command isn't very pretty due to all the options that you can specify on the command line.

By using the previous example, the interactive mount command that you use to mount the /var/spool/mail file system becomes

```
# mount -t nfs -o timeo=20,intr mailserver:/var/spool/mail   /var/spool/mail
```

If you need to specify datagram sizes and timeouts, interactive mount commands can become very complex. It's highly recommended that you place these mount commands in your /etc/fstab file so that they can be mounted automatically at boot time.

Maintaining File Systems

As the systems administrator, you're responsible for maintaining the integrity of the file systems themselves. Typically, this means checking the file systems periodically for damaged or corrupted files. Linux automatically checks file systems at boot time if they have a value greater than 0 specified in the pass number field of the /etc/fstab file.

N O T E   The ext2 file system commonly used under Linux has a special flag known as a *clean bit*. If the file system has been synchronized and unmounted cleanly, the clean bit is set on the file system. If the clean bit is set on a file system when Linux boots, it's not checked for integrity. ■

Using the *fsck* Command

It's a good idea to check your file systems occasionally for damaged or corrupt files. Under the Slackware distribution of Linux, you use the fsck (file system check) command to check your file systems. The fsck command is really a "front end" for a series of commands that are designed to check specific file systems. The syntax for the fsck command is

```
fsck [-A] [-V] [-t fs-type] [-a] [-l] [-r] [-s] filesys
```

However, the most basic form of the command is

```
fsck filesys
```

Table 14.7 describes the command-line options for the fsck command.

Table 14.7 Command-Line Arguments for *fsck*

Argument	Description
-A	Goes through the /etc/fstab file and tries to check all file systems in one pass. This option is typically used during the Linux boot sequence to check all normally mounted file systems. If you use -A, you can't use the filesys argument as well.
-V	Verbose mode. Prints additional information about what fsck is doing.
-t fs-type	Specifies the type of file system to be checked.
filesys	Specifies which file system is to be checked. This argument can be a block special device name, such as /dev/hda1, or a mount point, such as /usr.
-a	Automatically repairs any problems found in the file system without asking any questions. Use this option with caution.
-l	Lists all the file names in the file system.
-r	Asks for confirmations before repairing the file system.
-s	Lists the superblock before checking the file system.

The fsck command is actually a front-end program that calls the command to check the file system that matches the type you specify. To do so, Linux needs to know the file system type that it's checking. The easiest way to make sure that fsck calls the right command is to specify a file system type with the -t option to fsck. If you don't use the -t option, Linux tries to figure out the file system type by looking up the file system in /etc/fstab and by using the file type specified there. If fsck can't find the file type information in /etc/fstab, it assumes that you're using a Minix file system.

Part

III

Ch

14

> **CAUTION**
>
> The fsck command assumes that the file system you're checking is a Minix file system if you don't tell it differently—either with the −t argument or by listing the type in /etc/fstab. Because your Linux file systems are probably of type ext2 and not Minix, you should be careful and make sure that fsck knows the correct type. This is especially important if you're checking a file system that isn't listed in the /etc/fstab file.

It's a good idea to unmount a file system before checking it. This ensures that none of the files on the file system are in use when they're being checked.

N O T E Remember, you can't unmount a file system if any of the files on it are busy. For example, if a user is now in a directory on a file system that you try to unmount, you get a message saying that the file system is busy. ■

Trying to check the root file system presents an additional problem. You can't directly unmount the root file system, because Linux must be able to access it in order to run. To check the root file system, you should boot from a maintenance floppy disk that has a root file system on it, and then run fsck on your real root file system from the floppy by specifying the special device name of your root file system. If fsck makes any changes to your file system, it's important that you reboot your system immediately. This allows Linux to reread important information about your file system and prevents your file system from further corruption.

> **CAUTION**
>
> Be sure to reboot your computer immediately after you run fsck if any changes were made to your file system, to prevent further corruption to your file system. Use the shutdown −r command or the reboot command to reboot.

Creating and Formatting File Systems

When you add a new hard disk to your computer or want to change the partition information on an old hard disk, you go through the steps of creating a file system from a raw disk. Assuming that you've added a new hard disk to your system, you must set the disk partition information and then create the actual file systems on the disk before Linux can use the disk. To change disk partition information, you use the fdisk command. After you partition the hard drive, you need to create the file systems by using the mkfs command.

Using *fdisk* to Create Disk Partitions

The fdisk command is used to create disk partitions and set the attributes that tell Linux what type of file system is on a particular partition. If you installed Linux from scratch on an

MS-DOS system, you had to run `fdisk` to change the disk partition information before you could install Linux.

> **CAUTION**
>
> Using `fdisk` on a disk can destroy all data on the disk. Because `fdisk` completely rewrites the file table on the disk, all your former files may be lost. Make sure that you have a complete, current backup of your disks before using `fdisk`.

You should always run the `fdisk` command on an unmounted file system. `fdisk` is an interactive, menu-driven program, not just a single command. To start `fdisk`, type

```
fdisk [drive]
```

`drive` is the physical disk drive that you want to work on. If you don't specify a disk, the disk /dev/hda is assumed. For example, to run `fdisk` on the second IDE hard drive in your system, enter

```
fdisk /dev/hdb
```

at the superuser command prompt. Because `fdisk` is a menu-driven program, several different commands are available when you're using `fdisk`, as summarized in Table 14.8.

Table 14.8 Commands Available from the *fdisk* Menu

Command	Description
a	Toggles the bootable flag on a partition
c	Toggles the DOS compatibility flag on a partition
d	Deletes a partition
l	Lists partition types known to `fdisk`
m	Displays a menu listing all available commands
n	Adds a new partition
p	Prints the partition table for the current disk
q	Quits without saving any changes
t	Changes the file system type for a partition
u	Changes display/entry units
v	Verifies the partition table
w	Writes the table to disk and exits

Part
III

Ch
14

continues

Table 14.8   Continued

Command	Description
x	Lists additional functions for experts:

- b   Moves the beginning location of data in a partition
- c   Changes the number of cylinders
- d   Prints the raw data in the partition table
- e   Lists extended partitions on disk
- h   Changes number of heads on disk
- r   Returns to main menu
- s   Changes number of sectors on disk

fdisk can set the file system type of a disk partition to any of several different types. Only use Linux fdisk to create partitions used under Linux. For MS-DOS or OS/2 partitions, you should use the fdisk tool that's native to that operating environment, and then use Linux's fdisk to tag the partitions as Linux native or Linux swap.

Table 14.9 lists the partitions supported by Linux fdisk. Each partition type has an associated hexadecimal code that identifies it. You must enter the appropriate code in fdisk when you want to set a partition type.

Table 14.9   Partition Codes and Types in Linux *fdisk*

Hex Code	Partition Type
0	Empty
1	DOS 12-bit FAT
2	XENIX root
3	XENIX usr
4	DOS 16-bit file system, less than 32M
5	Extended
6	DOS 16-bit file system supporting more than 32M
7	OS/2 High Performance File System (HPFS)
8	AIX
9	AIX bootable
a	OS/2 Boot Manager
40	Venix 80286

Hex Code	Partition Type
51	Novell?
52	Microport
63	GNU HURD
64	Novell NetWare
65	Novell NetWare
75	PC/IX
80	Old MINIX
81	Linux/MINIX
82	Linux swap, used for swap files under Linux
83	Linux native, common Linux file system type
93	Amoeba
94	Amoeba BBT
a5	BSD/386
b7	BSDI file system
b8	BSDI swap file system
c7	Syrinx
db	CP/M
e1	DOS access
e3	DOS R/O
f2	DOS secondary
ff	BBT

The following sections show how to use fdisk. Here is an example of how to use fdisk to set up the partitions on a hard disk for use by Linux. Assume that you want to configure the first IDE drive in your system for Linux. Make sure that you have a backup of your data. All data on your hard disk is destroyed in the process. The name of the first IDE hard disk is /dev/hda, which is the default device for Linux.

Running *fdisk*   You run fdisk with

```
# fdisk
```

fdisk responds with

```
Using /dev/hda as default device!
Command (m for help):
```

This tells you that fdisk is using disk /dev/hda as the device that you're working with. Because this is what you wanted, you're fine. You should always check to make sure that you're

Part

III

Ch

14

really on the disk that you think that you're on. Linux then displays the `fdisk` command prompt.

Displaying the Current Partition Table The first thing you want to do is display the current partition table. This is done with the p command:

```
Command (m for help): p
Disk /dev/hda: 14 heads, 17 sectors, 1024 cylinders
Units = cylinders of 238 * 512 bytes

Device     Boot   Begin   Start    End   Blocks   Id    System

Command (m for help):
```

This listing shows that the current disk, /dev/hda, has a geometry of 14 heads, 17 sectors, and 1,024 cylinders. The display units are in cylinders of 238 * 512 (121,856) bytes each. Because there are 1,024 cylinders and each cylinder is 121,856 bytes, you can deduce that the disk can hold 1,024×121,856 = 124,780,544 bytes, or about 120M. You can also see that /dev/hda has no partitions.

Creating a New Partition Assume that you want to create a 100M Linux file partition for user home directories and a 20M swap partition. Your next step is to use the n command to create a new partition:

```
Command (m for help): n
Command action
e   extended
p   primary partition (1-4)
p
Partition number (1-4): 1
First cylinder (1-1023):  1
Last cylinder or +size or +sizeM or +sizeK (1-1023):   +100M
```

Using the n command to create a new partition displays another menu. You must choose whether you want to create an extended partition or a primary partition. You typically want to create a primary partition unless you have more than four partitions on a disk. `fdisk` then asks you for the partition number that you want to create. Because this is the first partition on the disk, you answer 1. You're then prompted for the first cylinder for the partition. This determines where on the disk the data area starts. Again, because this will be the first partition on the disk, you can start the partition at cylinder 1.

The next line asks you how large you want the partition to be. You have several options as to how to answer this question. `fdisk` accepts either a number, which it interprets as the size in cylinders, or the size in bytes, kilobytes, or megabytes. The size in bytes is specified as +*bytes*, where *bytes* is the size of the partition. Similarly, +*size*K and +*size*M set the partition size to size kilobytes or size megabytes, respectively. You know that you want a 100M partition, so the easiest answer to the prompt is **+100M**.

Rechecking the Partition Table Now you should check the partition table again to see what `fdisk` has done:

```
Command (m for help): p
Disk /dev/hda: 14 heads, 17 sectors, 1024 cylinders
Units = cylinders of 238 * 512 bytes

Device    Boot    Begin   Start    End     Blocks    Id    System
/dev/hda1                1     1    861     102400    81    Linux/MINIX
Command (m for help):
```

The partition table shows that you have 1 partition, /dev/hda1, that goes from cylinder 1 to cylinder 861 and uses 102,400 blocks. It's listed as being type 81, Linux/MINIX.

Creating the Swap Partition   Now you need to create the 20M swap partition by using the remaining disk space. This is just like creating the first partition:

```
Command (m for help): n
Command action
e    extended
p    primary partition (1-4)
p
Partition number (1-4): 2
First cylinder (862-1023):  862
Last cylinder or +size or +sizeM or +sizeK (862-1023): 1023
```

TIP   It's usually better to go ahead and enter the size of the last partition in cylinders to make sure that you use all the disk space.

Here you specified partition number 2 for the second partition. When fdisk prompts for the first cylinder, notice that it gives a range of 862 to 1023. This is because the first partition takes up everything before cylinder 862. So enter **862** as the starting cylinder for the second partition. You want to use all the remaining space on the disk for the swap partition. You should have about 20M left, but if you specify the size in megabytes, the internal fdisk calculations could leave you with a couple of unused cylinders. So you enter **1023** for the last cylinder on the size prompt.

N O T E   You might see an error similar to

```
        Warning: Linux cannot currently use the last xxx sectors of this
partition.
```

where *xxx* is some number. Such an error can be ignored. It's left over from the days when Linux couldn't access file systems larger than 64M. ▪

Making Sure the Sizes Are Correct   At this point, you've created both partitions that you wanted to create. You should take a look at the partition table one more time to check that the sizes are correct:

```
Command (m for help): p
Disk /dev/hda: 14 heads, 17 sectors, 1024 cylinders
Units = cylinders of 238 * 512 bytes

Device    Boot    Begin   Start    End     Blocks    Id    System
/dev/hda1                1     1    861     102400    81    Linux/MINIX
```

Part

III

Ch

14

```
/dev/hda2                862    862    1023    19159    81    Linux/MINIX
Command (m for help):
```

As you can see, /dev/hda1 uses cylinder 1 through cylinder 861 with a size of 102,400 blocks, which is approximately 100M. Partition /dev/hda2 goes from cylinder 862 to cylinder 1023 with a size of 19,156 blocks, or almost 20M.

Changing the Partition Type   The next thing that you need to do is change the partition type for each partition. To change the partition type, use the t command at the fdisk command prompt. The most common choice for a standard Linux file system partition is to set it to partition type 83, Linux native. Swap partitions should be set to partition type 82, Linux swap.

```
Command (m for help): t
Partition number (1-4): 1
Hex code (type L to list codes): 83
Command (m for help): t
Partition number (1-4): 2
Hex code (type L to list codes): 82
```

When you use the t command, you're prompted for the partition number that you want to change. You're then prompted for the hex code for the file system ID that you want to set the partition to. Typically, Linux file systems are set to type 83 for normal file systems, and type 82 for swap partitions. You can type l at this point to see a list of file systems, if you want.

Finishing Up   Now that you've created the partitions and labeled them, you should take one last look at the partition table before you exit just to make sure that everything is okay.

```
Command (m for help): p
Disk /dev/hda: 14 heads, 17 sectors, 1024 cylinders
Units = cylinders of 238 * 512 bytes

Device     Boot   Begin   Start   End    Blocks    Id    System
/dev/hda1            1       1    861    102400    83    Linux native
/dev/hda2          862     862   1023    19159     82    Linux swap
Command (m for help):
```

As you can see, the partitions are in the right place, they're the right size, and the file system types are set correctly. The last thing that you need to do is use the w command to write the partition table to disk and exit:

```
Command (m for help):  w

#
```

None of the changes that you make during an fdisk session take effect until you write them to disk with the w command. You can always quit with the q command and not save any changes. This said, you should still always have a backup of any disk that you want to modify with fdisk.

After you make changes to a disk with fdisk, you should reboot the system just to make sure that Linux has the updated partition information in the kernel.

Using *mkfs* to Build a File System

After you create a file system partition with fdisk, you must build a file system on it before you can use it for storing data. This is done with the mkfs command. Think of building a parking lot. If you think of fdisk as physically building the parking lot, mkfs is the part of the process that paints the lines so that the drivers know where to park.

Just like fsck is a "front-end" program for checking different types of file systems, mkfs actually calls different programs to create the file system, depending on what file system type you want to create. The syntax of the mkfs command is

```
mkfs  [-V] [-t fs-type] [fs-options] filesys [blocks]
```

where filesys is the device of the file system that you want to build, such as /dev/hda1.

> **CAUTION**
>
> The mkfs command also accepts the name of a mount point, such as /home, as the file system name. You should be extremely careful about using a mount point. If you run mkfs on a mounted "live" file system, you might very well corrupt all the data on that file system.

Table 14.10 lists the various command-line parameters that you can specify with mkfs.

Table 14.10 Command-Line Parameters for the *mkfs* Command

Option	Description
-V	Causes mkfs to produce verbose output, including all file system-specific commands that are executed. Specifying this option more than once inhibits execution of any file system-specific commands.
-t fs-type	Specifies the type of file system to be built. If the file system type isn't specified, mkfs tries to figure it out by searching for filesys in /etc/fstab and using the corresponding entry. If the type can't be deduced, a MINIX file system is created.
fs-options	Specifies file system-specific options that are to be passed to the actual file system-builder program. Although not guaranteed, the following options are supported by most file system builders: ● -c Checks the device for bad blocks before building the file system ● -l file-name Reads a list of the bad blocks on the disk from file-name ● -v Tells the actual file system builder program to produce verbose output

Part
III

Ch
14

continues

Table 14.10	Continued
Option	Description
`filesys`	Specifies the device on which the file system resides. This parameter is required.
`blocks`	Specifies the number of blocks to be used for the file system.

Although -t *fs-type* is an optional argument, you should get in the habit of specifying the file system type. Just like `fsck`, `mkfs` tries to figure out the type of the file system from the /etc/fstab file. If it can't figure it out, it creates a MINIX file system by default. For a normal Linux file system, you probably want an `ext2` partition instead.

Using Swap Files and Partitions

Swap space on your Linux system is used for virtual memory. A complete discussion of all the issues involved with virtual memory is beyond the scope of this book. Any good general computer operating system text book discusses the issue in detail.

Linux supports two types of swap space: swap partition and swap files. A *swap partition* is a physical disk partition with its file system ID set to type 82, Linux swap, and is dedicated for use as a swap area. A *swap file* is a large file on a normal file system that's used for swap space.

You're better off using a swap partition instead of a swap file. All access to a swap file is performed through the normal Linux file system. The disk blocks that make up the swap file are probably not contiguous and, therefore, performance isn't as good as it is with a swap partition. I/O to swap partitions is performed directly to the device, and disk blocks on a swap partition are always contiguous. Also, by keeping the swap space off a normal file system, you reduce the risk of corrupting your regular file system if something bizarre happens to your swap file.

Creating a Swap Partition

To create a swap partition, you must have created a disk partition by using `fdisk` and tagged it as type 82, Linux swap. After you create the swap partition, you have two additional steps to follow to make the swap partition active.

First, you must prepare the partition in a manner similar to creating a file system. Instead of `mkfs`, the command for preparing the partition is `mkswap`. The syntax of the `mkswap` command is

```
mkswap [-c] device size-in-blocks
```

device is the name of the swap partition, such as /dev/hda2, and *size-in-blocks* is the size of the target file system in blocks. You can get the size in blocks by running `fdisk` and looking at the partition table. In the example earlier in the section "Making Sure the Sizes Are Correct," the size of /dev/hda2 was 19,159 blocks. Linux requires that swap partitions be between 9 and 65,537 blocks in size. The -c argument tells `mkswap` to check the file system for bad blocks when creating the swap space, which is a good idea.

Following the example in "Making Sure the Sizes Are Correct," the command for setting up a swap partition on /dev/hda2 is

```
mkswap -c /dev/hda2 19159
```

After you run mkswap to prepare the partition, you must make it active so that the Linux kernel can use it. The command to make the swap partition active is swapon. The syntax for the swapon command is

```
swapon filesys
```

filesys is the file system that you want to make available as swap space. Linux makes a call to swapon -a during boot, which mounts all available swap partitions listed in the /etc/fstab file.

N O T E Remember to put an entry for any swap partitions or swap files that you create into the /etc/fstab file so that Linux can automatically access them at boot time. ▪

Creating a Swap File

Swap files can be useful if you need to expand your swap space and can't allocate disk space to create a dedicated swap partition. Setting up a swap file is almost identical to creating a swap partition. The main difference is that you have to create the file before you can run mkswap and swapon.

To create a swap file, you use the dd command, which is used for copying large chunks of data. For a full description of this command, see the man page for dd. The main things that you have to know before creating the file are the name of the swap file you want to create and its size in blocks. A block under Linux is 1,024 bytes. For example, to create a 10M swap file named /swap, enter

```
# dd if=/dev/zero of=/swap bs=1024 count=10240
```

of=/swap specifies that the file to be created is named /swap, and count=10240 sets the size of the output file to be 10,240 blocks, or 10M. You then use mkswap to prepare the file as a swap space:

```
# mkswap /swap 10240
```

Remember that you have to tell mkswap how big the file is. Before you run swapon, you need to make sure that the file is completely written to disk by using the /etc/sync command.

Now you're ready to make the swap file active. Like with the swap partition, you use the swapon command to make the file active; for example,

```
# swapon /swap
```

If you need to get rid of a swap file, you must make sure that it's not active. Use the swapoff command to deactivate the swap file, as in

```
# swapoff /swap
```

You can then safely delete the swap file.

Part

III

Ch

14

From Here...

In this chapter, you've looked at many different aspects of the Linux file system, from a tour of the basic directory structure to mounting and unmounting file systems. You've explored accessing remote file systems with NFS and looked in detail at how to create file systems and prepare them for use. Finally, this chapter discussed the creation of swap partitions and swap files.

You can find more information about systems administration in the following chapters:

- Chapter 8, "Understanding Systems Administration," introduces you to common systems administration tasks.
- Chapter 10, "Managing User Accounts," describes how to set up and manage user accounts on your Linux system.
- Chapter 11, "Backing Up Data," discusses how to plan and implement plans for data backups.

## CHAPTER 15

Understanding the File and Directory System

The term *Linux file system* has two different and often conflicting meanings: the file system of disks and mechanisms of the disks, and the logical file system that the user sees and manipulates. This chapter is about the logical Linux file system you see and manipulate. Also, if you're familiar with PC operating systems such as MS-DOS and OS/2, you'll find many of the following topics familiar because the file structures of MS-DOS from version 2.0 onward were modeled on those of UNIX, which is the file structure used by Linux.

Every physical and logical entity in Linux is represented as a file in the Linux file system. The physical entities include disks, printers, and terminals; logical entities include directories and, of course, ordinary files—the kind that store documents and programs. ■

What constitutes a valid Linux file name

All operating systems allow only certain characters and certain patterns to be used in naming a file. This chapter explains the valid file names used in Linux.

The various types of Linux files

Linux is washed in a variety of file types. In fact, almost everything is a file to the operating system, from devices such as the screen and disk drive to "real files" such as binary programs and text files.

How to read and set file permissions

Unlike operating systems such as MS-DOS and Windows 3.1, Linux allows users to specify who can access a file and what they can do with the file when they gain access.

The Linux directory structure

Many Linux operations, such as booting, mail, and printing, rely on the existence of certain key directories. Also, by tradition, many directories are expected to be in certain locations in the UNIX community.

Understanding File and Path Names

In Linux, just as in other operating systems such as MS-DOS, you must distinguish between a file name and a path name. A *file name* consists of a simple series of contiguous letters, numbers, and certain punctuation marks. File names can't contain spaces or any character that represents a field separator. For example, the file name *johns.letter* is valid; *johns letter* isn't.

A file name shouldn't contain any characters that have special meaning to the shell. These special characters are as follows:

! @ # $ % ^ & * ( ) [ ] { } ' " \ / ¦ ; < > `

Also, the file name can't contain the / character, because this character is used to indicate path names. (Path names are discussed later in this section.)

> **N O T E**   Actually, you can use any of these characters by placing double quotations around the file name—for example, `"! johns.letter"`—but you'll have a hard time accessing the file with most programs, and the file isn't very portable to other UNIX systems. ▪

Most early versions of UNIX, on which Linux is based, limited file names to 14 characters; however, Linux allows 256 characters in a file name. Some recent UNIX versions, such as the Berkeley version (BSD), allow 64-character file names, but only the first 14 are significant. Because one of the goals of Linux is portability, in the interest of writing portable programs and shell scripts, you might want to limit yourself to 14-character file names.

A path name can be any number of characters. In Linux, files don't exist in a vacuum; they exist in a directory. The highest directory in Linux is called the *root* and is symbolized by the slash character (/). If a file named fred exists in the root directory, its absolute path name is /fred. When you add a user to the system with the adduser command, users are assigned a home directory. By convention, this home directory is usually found under root in a directory named, appropriately enough, home. If a user named Fred is assigned a directory named /home/fred, all files that Fred creates are attached to the directory /home/fred. An absolute path name for one of Fred's files might be /home/fred/freds.file. An absolute path name specifies exactly where in the file system you can find a file.

Another kind of path name is a *relative path name*, which unambiguously points to a file relative to the current directory. If Fred is in his home directory, the file name freds.file is also a relative path name, relative to his current directory. To find out which directory is your current directory, use the command pwd (print working directory). You can also check the contents of the $PWD environment variable with the command echo $PWD to see which directory is the current working directory.

You can define a file anywhere in the Linux file system with relative path names by using the two pseudonyms found in all directories. The single dot (.) refers to the current directory; the double dot (..) refers to the parent directory. MS-DOS and OS/2 use this same convention.

If Fred is in /home/fred, he can point to /fred by using ../../fred. The second double dot points to /home (the parent directory of /home/fred); the first double dot points to the parent directory of /home—namely, the root.

The pseudonym for the current directory, the single dot, comes in handy if you want to move files. If Fred wants to move /fred to his current directory, he can do so with absolute path names by using this command:

```
mv /fred fred
```

Alternatively, Fred can use the pseudonym for the current directory by using this command:

```
mv /fred .
```

Most Linux commands operate on path names. In most cases, the path name you use is the name of a file in the current directory. The default path name points to your current directory. If Fred is in his home directory, /home/fred, all three of the following are equivalent:

```
command freds.letter
command /home/fred/freds.letter
command ./freds.letter
```

N O T E   Although a difference exists between file names and path names, directories are files, too. When naming directories, remember that they have the same name limitations as ordinary files.

Also note that unlike many PC-based operating systems, Linux doesn't have the concept of disk-drive letters, only directory paths. The only time Linux deals with disk-drive letters is while dealing with MS-DOS file systems on floppies with the m– commands, such as mcopy.

▶ **See** "Understanding File Systems," **p. 262** ■

File Types

There are just four basic types of files: ordinary files, directories, links, and special files. There are several kinds of ordinary files, links, and special files and a large number of standard directories. Each is described in the following sections.

You can use the command file to determine the type of a file. file can recognize whether the file type is executable, text, data, and so on. Many UNIX commands are only shell scripts, or interpreted programs similar to MS-DOS batch files, and file can be used to report whether a UNIX command is a binary executable program, or simply a shell script. It's also useful to determine whether the file is text-based or not and, therefore, whether it can be viewed or edited. The syntax is

```
file [-vczL] [-f namefile] [-m magicfile] filelist
```

Table 15.1 explains the arguments for the file command.

Table 15.1 *file* **Command Arguments**

Argument	Description
-c	Prints out the parsed form of the *magic file* (/usr/lib/magic), which is a number in the first part of a binary file that identifies the file type. This is usually used with -m to debug a new magic file before installing it.
-z	Looks inside a compressed file and tries to figure out the file type.
-L	Causes symbolic links to be followed.
-f *namefile*	Tells file that the list of files to identify is found in *namefile*, a text file. This is useful when many files must be identified.
-m *magicfile*	Specifies an alternative file of magic numbers to use for determining file types. The default file is /usr/lib/magic.
filelist	Lists space-delimited files whose type you want to know.

Ordinary Files

Ordinary files are what you spend most of your time manipulating. Ordinary files can contain text, C language source code, shell scripts (programs interpreted by one of the Linux shells), binary executable programs, and data of various types. As far as Linux is concerned, a file is a file. The only difference that Linux knows about is files marked as executable. Executable files can be executed directly—provided, of course, that the file contains something to execute and that it's in your search path. Basically, the search path is a list of path names you've specified that Linux searches to find an executable file.

▶ **See** "Understanding Shells," **p. 325**

Executable files are binary files—that is, files that execute machine code and shell scripts. The Linux file command discussed in the preceding section looks at the data in a file and makes a reasonable guess as to what's inside. If you type **file ***, you might see something similar to this:

```
INSTALL:       symbolic link to /var/adm
ghostvw.txt:   ascii text
linux:         symbolic link to /usr/src/linux
mbox:          mail text
mterm.txt:     English text
seyon.txt:     English text
xcalc.txt:     English text
xclock.txt:    English text
xeyes.txt:     English text
xgrap.txt:     English text
xlock.txt:     English text
xspread.txt:   English text
xtris.txt:     empty
```

All the files named in the first column are ordinary files that contain different kinds of data. All the files are located within the directory where the file command was executed.

Directory Files

Directories are files that contain the names of files and subdirectories, as well as pointers to those files and subdirectories. Directory files are the only place that Linux stores names of files. When you list the contents of a directory with the ls command, all you're doing is listing the contents of the directory file. You never touch the files themselves.

When you rename a file with the mv command and that file is in the current directory, all you're doing is changing the entry in the directory file. If you move a file from one directory to another, all you're doing is moving the description of the file from one directory file to another—provided, of course, that the new directory is on the same physical disk or partition. If not, Linux physically copies each byte of the program to the other disk.

Directories and Physical Disks

Every file in a Linux system is assigned a unique number called an *inode*. The inode is stored in a table called the *inode table*, which is allocated when the disk is formatted. Every physical disk or partition has its own inode table. An inode contains all the information about a file, including the address of the data on the disk and the file type. File types include such things as ordinary files, directories, and special files.

The Linux file system assigns inode number 1 to the root directory. This gives Linux the address on disk of the root directory file. The root directory file contains a list of file and directory names and their respective inode numbers. Linux can find any file in the system by looking up a chain of directories, beginning with the root directory. The contents of the root directory file might look like this:

```
1      .
1      ..
45     etc
230    dev
420    home
123    .profile
```

Notice that the files . (dot) and .. (double dot) are represented in the directory. Because this is the root directory, . and its parent directory, .., are identical. The contents of the /home directory file are different:

```
420    .
1      ..
643    fred
```

Notice that the inode of the current directory, ., matches the inode for /home found in the root directory file and that the inode for the parent directory, .., is the same as that of the root directory.

Linux navigates its file system by chaining up and down the directory file system. If you want to move a file to a directory on another physical disk, Linux detects this by reading the inode table. In such a case, the file is physically moved to the new disk and assigned a new inode on that disk before being deleted from its original location.

As with the `mv` command, when you delete a file with the `rm` command, you never touch the file itself. Instead, Linux marks that inode as free and returns it to the pool of available inodes. The file's entry in the directory is erased.

▶ **See** "Moving and Renaming Files," **p. 307**

Links

Ordinary links aren't really files at all. They're simply directory entries that point to the same inode. The inode table keeps track of how many links there are to a file; only when the last directory reference is deleted is the inode finally released back to the free pool. Obviously, ordinary links can't cross device boundaries because all the directory references point to the same inode.

Linux, as well as most modern versions of UNIX, has another kind of link called a *symbolic link*. For such a link, the directory entry contains the inode of a file that is itself a reference to another file somewhere else in the logical Linux file system. A symbolic link can point to another file or directory on the same disk, another disk, or to a file or directory on another computer. One major difference between an ordinary link and a symbolic link is that with ordinary links, every link has equal standing (that is, the system treats every link as though it were the original file) and the actual data isn't deleted until the last link to that file is deleted. With symbolic links, when the original file is deleted, all symbolic links to that file are also deleted. Symbolically linked files don't have the same standing as the original file.

Other than these subtle differences between links and files, links are treated and accessed exactly as though you were accessing the file directly.

You can tell a file is a link with the `ls -l` command because the response shows the local file name and then an indication of the linked file:

```
lrwxrwxrwx  1 root   root   4 Oct 17 15:27 Info -> info/
```

The file permission flags begin with an `l` to indicate that the file is a linked file.

Special Files

Every physical device associated with a Linux system, including disks, terminals, and printers, are represented in the file system. Most, if not all, devices are located in the /dev directory. For example, if you're working on the system console, your associated device is named /dev/console. If you're working on a standard terminal, your device name might be /dev/tty01. Terminals, or serial lines, are called *tty devices* (which stands for *teletype*, the original UNIX terminal). To determine what the name of your tty device is, type the command **tty**. The system responds with the name of the device to which you're connected.

Printers and terminals are called *character-special devices*. They can accept and produce a stream of characters. Disks, on the other hand, store data in blocks addressed by cylinder and sector. You can't access just one character on a disk; you must read and write entire blocks. The same is usually true of magnetic tapes. This kind of device is called a *block-special device*. To make life even more complex, disks and other block-special devices must be able to act like character-oriented devices, so every block-special device has a matching character-special device. Linux makes the translation by reading data being sent to a character device and translating it for the block device. This happens without you doing anything.

You might run into at least one other type of special device—a FIFO (first-in-first-out buffer), also known as a *named pipe*. FIFOs look like ordinary files; if you write to them, they grow. But if you read a FIFO, it shrinks in size. FIFOs are used mainly in system processes to allow many programs to send information to a single controlling process. For example, when you print a file with the `lp` command, `lp` sets up the printing process and signals the `lpsched` daemon by sending a message to a FIFO. A *daemon*, sometimes called a *demon*, is a system process that acts without a user requesting an action.

One device-special file is very useful—the bit bucket, /dev/null. Anything you send to /dev/null is ignored, which is useful when you don't want to see the output of a command. For example, if you don't want to see any diagnostic reports printed on the standard error device, you can pour them into the bit bucket with the following command:

```
ls -la> /dev/null
```

File Permissions

File permissions mean more in Linux than just what permissions you have on a file or directory. Although permissions determine who can read, write, or execute a file, they also determine the file type and how the file is executed.

You can display the permissions of a file with the long form of the listing command, `ls -l`. The -l flag tells the `ls` command to use the long listing. If you type **ls -l**, you might see a directory listing that looks like this:

```
drwx------  2 sglines  doc     512 Jan  1 13:44  Mail
drwx------  5 sglines  doc    1024 Jan 17 08:22 News
-rw-------  1 sglines  doc    1268 Dec  7 15:01  biblio
drwx------  2 sglines  doc     512 Dec 15 21:28 bin
-rw-------  1 sglines  doc   44787 Oct 20 06:59 books
-rw------   1 sglines  doc   23801 Dec 14 22:50 bots.msg
-rw-r----   1 sglines  doc  105990 Dec 27 21:24 duckie.gif
```

This listing shows virtually everything that can be known about a file from the directory entry and the inode of the file. The first column shows the file permissions, the second column shows the number of links to a file (or extra blocks in a directory), and the third column shows who owns the file. (In Linux, ownership has three possibilities: the owner, the owner's group, and everyone else. Ownership is detailed later in this chapter.) The fourth column shows the group to which the file belongs. The fifth column shows the number of bytes in the file, the sixth column shows the date and time of creation, and the seventh column shows the name of the file itself.

The permissions field (the first column) is broken into four subfields:

```
- rwx rwx rwx
```

The first subfield defines the file type. A normal file has a hyphen (–) as a placeholder; directories are marked with a d. Table 15.2 shows the permissible values for the file-type subfield.

Table 15.2   Valid Entries for the File-Type Subfield

Character	Meaning
–	Ordinary file
b	Block-special file
c	Character-special file
d	Directory
l	Symbolic link

The next three subfields show the read, write, and execute permissions of the file. For example, an rwx in the first of these subfields means that the file has read, write, and execute permission for the owner. The next three subfields show the same information for the group ownership of the file; the third set of subfields shows the permissions allowed for everyone else.

These permission fields can show more information; in fact, several attributes are packed into these three fields. Unfortunately, what these attributes mean is determined by the version of Linux you use and whether the file is executable.

N O T E   Normally, a running program is owned by whoever ran it. If the user ID bit is on, the running program is owned by the owner of the file. This means that the running program has all the permissions of the owner of the file. If you're an ordinary user and the running program is owned by the root user, that running program has automatic permission to read and write any file in the system regardless of your permissions. The same is true of the set group ID bit. ▪

The *sticky bit* can also be set in these subfields. The sticky bit tells the system to save a copy of a running program in memory after the program completes. If the program is used often, the sticky bit can save the system a little time because the program doesn't have to be reloaded into memory from disk each time someone runs it.

You can change permissions on any file you have write permission for by using the chmod command. This command has two different syntaxes: absolute and relative. With absolute permissions, you define exactly what the permissions on a file will be in octal, or base 8. An octal number can have a value from 0 to 7. UNIX was originally created on a series of DEC minicomputers that used the octal numbering system, hence the current use of octal numbers. The octal numbers are added together to arrive at a number that defines the permissions. Table 15.3 lists the valid octal permissions.

Table 15.3 Absolute Octal Permissions Used with the *chmod* Command

Octal Value	Permissions Granted
0001	Execute permission for the owner
0002	Write permission for the owner
0004	Read permission for the owner
0010	Execute permission for the group
0020	Write permission for the group
0040	Read permission for the group
0100	Execute permission for all others
0200	Write permission for all others
0400	Read permission for all others
1000	Sticky bit on
2000	Group ID bit on if the file is executable; otherwise, mandatory file locking is on
4000	User ID bit on if the file is executable

Group and user IDs refer to who has permission to use, read, or execute a file. These initial file permissions are granted by the systems administrator when the user's account is first created. Only users of an indicated group can access files in a group, and only if the user has given group members permission to those files.

To give a file read and write permissions for everyone, you must add the required permissions together, as in the following example:

0002	Write permission for the owner
0004	Read permission for the owner
0020	Write permission for the group
0040	Read permission for the group
0200	Write permission for all others
0400	Read permission for all others
0666	Read and write permission for everyone

To give a file these permissions, use the following command:

```
chmod 666 file
```

Relative permissions use a slightly different format. With relative permissions, you must state the following:

- Who you're giving permissions to
- What operation you intend (add, subtract, or set permissions)
- What the permissions are

For example, if you type `chmod a=rwx file`, you give read, write, and execute permission to all users. The commands are summarized in Table 15.4.

Table 15.4   Relative Permissions Used with the *chmod* Command

Value	Description
Who	
a	All users (the user, their group, and all others)
g	Owner's group
o	All others not in the file's group
u	Just the user
Operator	
+	Adds the mode
–	Removes the mode
=	Sets the mode absolutely
Permission	
x	Sets execute
r	Sets read
w	Sets write
s	Sets user ID bit
t	Sets sticky bit

If a file has been marked as having the user ID bit on, the permissions displayed by the `ls -l` command look like this:

```
-rws------ 1 sglines    3136 Jan 17 15:42 x
```

If the group ID bit is added, the permissions look like this:

```
-rws--S--- 1 sglines    3136 Jan 17 15:42 x
```

If you then turn on the sticky bit for the file, the permissions look like this:

```
-rws--S--rws--S--T 1 sglines    3136 Jan 17 15:42 x
```

Note the use of uppercase S and T to indicate the status of the user ID bit and the sticky bit, respectively.

Looking at Linux Standard Directories

You're already familiar with the concept of directories. When you log in, the system places you in your home directory. The PATH environment variable is set to point to other directories that contain executable programs. These other directories are part of the standard Linux directory structure.

There is the classic set of directories for UNIX and what can be called the "emerging standard set of directories," which Linux basically follows. Both are described in the following sections.

Classic UNIX Directories

Before UNIX System V Release 4 (for example, UNIX System V Release 3.2 and earlier), most versions of UNIX settled on a regular system of organizing the UNIX directories that looked like this:

```
/
        /etc
        /lib
        /tmp
        /bin
        /usr
                /spool
                /bin
                /include
                /tmp
                /adm
                /lib
```

The /etc directory contains most of the system-specific data required to boot, or bring the system to life. It contains such files as passwd and inittab, which are necessary for the proper operation of the system.

The /lib directory contains a library of functions needed by the C compiler. Even if you don't have a C compiler on your system, this directory is important because it contains all the shared libraries that application programs can call. A shared library is loaded into memory only when the command calling it is run. This arrangement keeps executable programs small. Otherwise, every running program contains duplicate code, requiring a lot more disk space to store and a lot more memory to run.

The /tmp directory is used for temporary storage. Programs that use /tmp generally clean up after themselves and delete any temporary files. If you use /tmp, be sure to delete any files before logging out. Because the system automatically deletes the contents of this directory periodically, don't keep anything you might need later in it.

The /bin directory keeps all the executable programs needed to boot the system and is usually home for the most commonly used Linux commands. Note, however, that an executable program doesn't have to be binary (which the name *bin* implies). Several smaller programs in /bin are, in fact, shell scripts.

The /usr directory contains everything else. Your PATH variable contains the string /bin:/usr/bin because the /usr/bin directory contains all the Linux commands that aren't in the /bin directory. This arrangement has a historical precedence. In the early days of Linux, hard disks weren't very big. Linux needs at least the /etc/tmp/ and /bin directories to *bootstrap* (that is, start executing) itself. Because the disks of the early Linux era held only those three directories, everything else was on a disk that could be mounted after Linux was up and running. When Linux was still a relatively small operating system, placing additional subdirectories in the /usr directory wasn't much of a burden. It allowed a moderately sized Linux system to exist with just two disks: a root disk and a /usr disk.

The /usr/adm directory contains all the accounting and diagnostic information needed by the system administrator. If both system accounting and diagnostic programs are turned off, this directory is effectively empty.

The /include directory contains all the source code used by #include statements in C programs. You'll have at least read permission for this directory because it contains all the code fragments and structures that define your system. You shouldn't modify any of the files in this directory because they were crafted (carefully, you can assume) by your system vendor.

The /usr/spool directory contains all the transient data used by the lp print system, the cron daemon, and the UUCP communications system. Files "spooled" to the printer are kept in the /spool directory until they're printed. Any programs waiting to be run by cron, including all the crontab files and pending at and batch jobs, are also stored here.

The /usr/lib directory contains everything else that's part of the standard Linux system. In general, the /usr/lib directory represents the organized chaos hidden beneath the relatively well-disciplined Linux system. This directory contains programs called by other programs found in /bin and /usr/bin as well as configuration files for terminals and printers, the mail system, cron, and the UUCP communications system.

The /usr directory contains all the subdirectories assigned to users. The general convention is this: If your login ID is mary, your home directory is /usr/mary.

This directory arrangement made a lot of sense when disks were small and expensive, but with the advent of very large disks at (relatively) inexpensive prices, there are better ways of organizing Linux, as evidenced by the new directory structure discussed in the next section.

Linux Directories

One problem with the classical structure of UNIX is that backing up your data files is difficult with a fragmented /usr directory. Three different levels of backup generally are required in a system: the basic system itself, any changes to the tables that define the basic system for a specific site, and user data.

The basic system should be backed up only once with changes to the controlling tables backed up when there are changes. User data changes all the time and should be backed up frequently. The typical Linux directory structure is shown as follows, but your structure might be a little different, depending on what packages you installed:

```
/
      /etc
            /passwd        (user database)
            /rc.d          (system initialization scripts)
/sbin
/bin
/tmp
/var
/lib
/home
      / <your user name here>    (user accounts)
/install
/usr
      /bin
/proc
```

The /bin, /etc, and /tmp, directories have the same function as they do in the classic structure. System definition tables are moved into the /var directory so that whenever the operation of the system changes, you can back up only that directory.

What's new is that all system programs are moved into the /sbin directory. All the standard Linux programs are in /usr/bin, which is linked to /bin. For compatibility, all the classic directories are maintained with symbolic links. The /usr directory, which no longer contains user data, has been reorganized to make sense from the chaos that once was the /usr/lib directory.

From Here...

In this chapter, you examined how Linux uses files and directories and how the file permission system protects your data. You learned how to change the permissions on files and directories and what the meaning of a special file is. Finally, you looked at the purpose and names of the most common directories found in Linux. For more information, see the following chapters:

- Chapter 8, "Understanding Systems Administration," explains how to set up new users with file permissions.
- Chapter 14, "Managing File Systems," discusses the concept of file systems and how they're organized.
- Chapter 16, "Managing Files and Directories," discusses how to organize and use your files and directories.

Managing Files and Directories

The vast majority of Linux commands manipulate files and directories. Indeed, Linux shell scripts are particularly adept at manipulating files and directories. File manipulations that are difficult in a conventional language (even in C) are made easy from within a shell, largely because of the rich selection of file-manipulation commands available in Linux.

Listing files

Before doing anything with a file, you need to know what files are on your system, who owns them, and what file operations you can perform. Linux provides you with a rich set of commands to list lots of information about a file.

Viewing the contents of a file without an editor

Linux gives you the ability to look at the contents of a file without invoking an editor. You can examine ASCII text files as well as binary files, such as data files and executables.

Compressing files

Although hard drives are increasing in size and decreasing in cost, space is always at a premium. Linux provides several tools to compress files to save space.

Manipulating files with the Xfilemanager

If you're using XFree86, you can manipulate files much as you would under Windows 95 or Windows NT. The Xfilemanager program provides the same functionality as Microsoft's File Manager.

File-manipulation commands can be grouped roughly into two categories:

- Commands that manipulate files as objects
- Commands that manipulate the contents of files

This chapter concentrates on commands that manipulate files as objects—commands that move, rename, copy, delete, locate, and change the attributes of files and directories. This chapter also takes a quick look at commands that manipulate the contents of files. ■

Listing Files

The basic command to list files is ls. The way ls displays files depends on how you use the command. If you use the ls command in a pipe, every file is displayed on a line by itself. This is also the default for some versions of UNIX, such as SCO UNIX. Other versions of UNIX list files in several columns. For most uses, the columnar format is more convenient; systems that list files one per row often have an alternative command, usually lc, for lists in column format.

The ls command's behavior is modified with the use of flags that take the form -abcd. In general, versions of the ls command fall into two categories: versions of ls derived from Linux System V and those derived from Berkeley. Because the Berkeley Linux systems are slowly giving way to Linux System V, this chapter concentrates on the flags used by System V. If you're in doubt about which version of ls you have, consult the manuals for your system or try the command man ls.

NOTE Most man pages for commands in this chapter are no longer being maintained and may be inaccurate or incomplete under Red Hat Linux as the system is moved to more graphical-based systems such as HTML and Texinfo. However, for the time being, this information is accurate for this release of Red Hat Linux 4.0. ■

Flags used with the ls command can be concatenated or listed separately. This means that the following commands are effectively identical:

```
ls -l -F
ls -lF
```

Table 16.1 lists in alphabetical order several of the flags used with ls and their uses.

Table 16.1   Flags for the *ls* Command

Flag	Description
-a	Lists all entries. In the absence of this or the -A option, entries whose names begin with a period (.) aren't listed. Linux has a way of "hiding" files; all files that begin with a period by default aren't listed because they're generally files used to customize applications. For example, .profile is used to customize the Bourne and Korn shells; .mailrc is used to

Flag	Description
	customize your system-wide e-mail configuration file. Because almost every major command you use has a startup file, your home directory looks cluttered if the ls command lists all those startup files by default. If you want to see them, use the -a flag.
-A	Same as -a, except that . and .. aren't listed. Recall from Chapter 15, "Understanding the File and Directory System," that . is a pseudonym for the current directory and .. is a pseudonym for the parent directory. Because these file names begin with a period, the -a flag lists them. If you don't want to see these pseudonyms, use the -A flag instead.
-b	Forces printing of non-graphic characters to be in octal \ddd notation. -b is more useful than the -q flag because it allows you to figure out what the characters are.
-c	Uses time of last edit (or last mode change) for sorting or printing. Linux maintains three time and date stamps on every file: the file creation date, the date of last access, and the date of last modification. Normally, files are listed in *ASCII order* (alphabetical order, except that capitals are sorted before lowercase letters).
-C	Forces multicolumn output with entries sorted down the columns. This is the default format of ls when output is to a terminal.
-d *filename*	If the argument is a directory, this flag lists only its name (not its contents); often used with the -l flag to get the status of a directory. Normally, the contents of a directory are listed if a directory name is explicitly listed or implied with the use of a wild card. Thus, the simple command ls lists just the directory names themselves, but ls * lists files, directories, and the contents of any directories encountered in the current directory.
-F	Marks directories with a trailing slash (/), executable files with a trailing asterisk (*), symbolic links with a trailing at sign (@), FIFOs with a trailing bar (¦), and sockets with a trailing equal sign (=).
-i	Prints each file's inode number (*inodes* are described in Chapter 15, "Understanding the File and Directory System") in the first column of the report. If you list linked files, notice that both files have the same inode number.
-l	Lists directory entries in long format, giving mode, number of links, owner, size in bytes, and time of last modification for each file. If the file is a special file, the size field instead contains the major and minor device numbers. If the time of last modification is greater than six months ago, the month, date, and year are shown; otherwise, only the date and time are shown. If the file is a symbolic link, the path name of the linked-to file is printed, preceded by the characters ->. You can combine -l with other options, such as -n, to show user and group ID numbers instead of names.

Part **III**

Ch **16**

continues

Table 16.1 Continued

Flag	Description
-n	Lists the user and group ID numbers, instead of names, associated with each file and directory. Usually, only the names are listed. If you're setting up networking products, such as TCP/IP, it's useful to know ID numbers when you're setting up permissions across several systems.
-q	Displays non-graphic characters in file names as the character ?. For ls, this is the default action when output is to a terminal. If a file has accidentally been created with non-printable characters, the -q flag displays the file.
-r	Reverses the sort order to show files in reverse alphabetical or oldest-file-first order, as appropriate.
-s	Gives the size of each file, including any indirect blocks used to map the file, in kilobytes. If the environment variable POSIX_CORRECT is defined, the block size is 512 bytes.
-t	Sorts by time modified (latest first) rather than by name. If you want to see the oldest file first, use the -rt combination.
-u	Uses time of last access, instead of last modification, for sorting (with the -t option) or printing (with the -l option).
-x	Forces multicolumn output with entries sorted across rather than down the page.

If you installed the Slackware distribution of Linux, you'll find ls also provides color output for each file type. The color definitions are defined in the configuration g»le DIR_COLORS in the /etc directory. The default configuration highlights executable files in green, directories in blue, and symbolic links in cyan. To customize the colors, you must copy the DIR_COLORS file to your home directory and change its name to .dir colors. Table 16.2 provides the color definitions available; see the man pages and the DIR_COLORS file for more information.

N O T E For the Red Hat distribution, you must type **ls --color** to get the color effect. ▦

Table 16.2 DIR_COLORS Values to Create Color Highlighting

Value	Description
0	Restores default color
1	For brighter colors
4	For underlined text
5	For flashing text

Value	Description
30	For black foreground
31	For red foreground
32	For green foreground
33	For yellow (or brown) foreground
34	For blue foreground
35	For purple foreground
36	For cyan foreground
37	For white (or gray) foreground
40	For black background
41	For red background
42	For green background
43	For yellow (or brown) background
44	For blue background
45	For purple background
46	For cyan background
47	For white (or gray) background

There are more options than those shown here, so consult the man pages for ls.

Organizing Files

There are no fixed rules for organizing files in Linux. Files don't have extensions (such as .EXE for executables) as they do in MS-DOS. You can (and perhaps should) make up your own system of naming files, but the classic system of organizing files in Linux is with subdirectories.

More and more, however, Linux applications that have come from the DOS world are bringing their conventions to Linux. Although they may not require it, vendors encourage you to name files that you use with their applications with certain extensions.

If you're going to write your own commands, a useful way to organize your directories is to mimic Linux's use of the /bin, /lib, and /etc directories. Create your own structure of subdirectories with these names, perhaps under your /home directory, and follow the Linux tradition of placing executable commands in your /bin directory, subsidiary commands in your /lib directory, and initialization files in your /etc directory. Of course, you aren't required to do this, but it's one way of organizing your files.

You create directories with the mkdir command. Its syntax is simple:

```
mkdir directory-name
```

In this syntax, *directory-name* is replaced by the name you want to assign to the new directory. Of course, you need write permission in the directory before you can create a subdirectory with mkdir, but if you're making a subdirectory within your home directory, you should have no problem.

Suppose that you've written three programs called prog1, prog2, and prog3, all of which are found in $HOME/bin. Remember that $HOME is your home directory; if you want your private programs to run as though they were a standard part of the Linux command set, you must add $HOME/bin to your PATH environment variable. Do this with the following command in the Bourne or Korn shell:

```
PATH=$PATH:$HOME/bin;export PATH
```

In the C shell, you use this command:

```
setenv PATH "$PATH $HOME/bin"
```

N O T E   Remember that $HOME is the placeholder for the complete path that refers to your home directory. If your home directory is /home/ams, $HOME/bin is interpreted as /home/ams/bin. ■

If your programs call subsidiary programs, you may want to create subdirectories within your $HOME/lib directory. You can create a subdirectory for each program. The private command pgm1 can then explicitly call, for example, $HOME/lib/pgm1/pgm1a.

Similarly, if your command prog1 requires a startup table, you can name that table $HOME/etc/pgm1.rc; your data can be in your $HOME/data/pgm1 directory.

Copying Files

The command for copying files is cp *from to*. You must have read permission for the file you're copying from, and write permission for the directory (and the file if you're overwriting an existing file) you're copying to. Other than that, there are no restrictions on your ability to copy files.

You need to watch for a few things as you copy files:

- If you copy a file and give it the name of a file that already exists and that you have write permission for, you'll overwrite the original file.
- If you give the name of a directory as the destination of the cp command, the file is copied into that directory with its original name. For example, if you type the command **cp *file directory***, the file is copied into *directory* as *directory/file*.
- You can copy a list of files into a directory with the command cp *file1 file2 file3 ... directory*. If the last item in the list isn't a directory, an error message appears.

Likewise, if any element in the list other than the last item is only a directory, an error message appears.

■ Be careful when you use wild cards with the cp command, because you can copy more than you intend to.

N O T E Because many Linux users also have MS-DOS files on their systems and usually make the DOS file system accessible from Linux, most of the Linux commands recognize when a file is being copied to or from a DOS partition. Thus, Linux can handle the necessary file translation when copying files. This translation is required because most DOS files embed the carriage return/line feed characters into an ASCII file to indicate a line break. Most Linux and UNIX systems embed only a line-feed character, called *newline*, in the file to indicate a line break. ■

Moving and Renaming Files

In Linux, moving and renaming files are accomplished with the same command: mv. The syntax and rules are the same for mv as they are for the copy command, cp. That is, you can move as many files as you want to a directory, but the directory name must be last in the list and you must have write permission to that directory.

One thing you can do with mv that you can't do with cp is move or rename directories. When you move or rename a file, the only thing that happens is the entry in the directory file is changed. Unless the new location is on another physical disk or partition, the file and the contents of the directory are physically moved.

If you try to use rm (for *remove*) or cp without options on a directory, the command fails and displays a message telling you that the item you're dealing with is a directory. To remove or copy directories, you must use the -r flag (for *recursive*) with rm and cp. The mv command, however, moves directories quite happily.

Removing Files or Directories

The command to remove a file is rm. To delete a file you don't own, you need read and write permission. If you own the file, you're allowed to delete it, provided that you haven't closed off your own permission to the file. For example, if you turn off write permission to a file by typing **chmod 000 *file***, you must open permission again with the chmod command (by typing **chmod 644 *file***) before you can delete it.

If you accidentally type **rm ***, you delete all the files you have permission to delete in the current directory; you don't delete the subdirectories. To delete subdirectories, you must use the recursive option (-r).

Some versions of rm stop and ask whether you really want to delete files that you own but don't have at least write permission for. Other versions of rm prompt you for any files marked for removal with wild cards. Indeed, you can write a macro or shell script that gives you a second chance before actually deleting a file.

If your version of rm balks at removing files you own but don't have write permission for, you can partially protect yourself from accidentally deleting everything in your directory by following these steps:

1. Create a file named 0. In the ASCII string sequence, the number 0 is listed before any files that begin with letters.

2. Remove all permissions from the file named 0 by typing the command **chmod 000 0**. This command removes read, write, and execute permissions for everyone, including yourself.

3. If you type the command **rm ***, the file named 0 is the first file that rm attempts to remove.

If your version of rm balks at removing the 0 file when you type **rm ***, you have the chance to think about what you just did. If you didn't intend to delete everything in your directory, press <Del> or <Ctrl-c> to kill the rm process. To test this out, try removing just the file named 0. Don't use rm *, because if your version of rm doesn't stop at the file 0, you'll erase all the files in your directory.

A better way to protect yourself from accidentally deleting files is to use the -i flag with rm. The -i flag stands for *interactive*. If you give the command rm -i *filename*, you're asked whether you really want to delete the file. You must answer yes before the file is actually deleted. If you type the command **rm -i ***, you must answer yes for every file in your directory. This should give you enough time to think about what you really want to do.

> **CAUTION**
>
> Think before you delete files. When you delete a file (in most versions of Linux), it's gone and the only way to recover a lost file is from a backup. You did make a backup, didn't you?

▶ **See** "Performing Backups and Restoring Files," **p. 230**

If you use the rm -i command frequently, you can implement it in two ways: by writing a shell script or by creating a shell function. If you write a shell script, remember that the shell searches for commands in the directories listed in your PATH variable in the order in which they're listed. If your $HOME/bin directory is listed last, a shell script named rm will never be found. You can place your $HOME/bin directory first in the PATH variable's list or create a new command, such as del. If you create a shell script called del, you must mark it as executable with the chmod command before the shell can recognize it. When you create your del command, you need to give it only one command: rm -i $*. If you then type the command **del ***, the shell translates it into rm -i *.

▶ **See** "Editing and Aliasing Shell Commands," **p. 348**

Another way to accomplish the same task is with an *alias*, which takes precedence over commands that must be looked up. You can think of an alias as an internal shell command (similar to the doskey commands introduced in MS-DOS version 5.0).

To add an alias if you're using the C shell, you must edit the file named .cshrc. You can use any text editor, such as `vi` (see Chapter 19, "Using the *vi* Editor"), to edit this file. For the C shell, add the following lines to the top of your .cshrc file:

```
rm ()
{
/bin/rm -i $*
}
```

To add an alias to the Korn shell, add the following line to your $HOME/.kshrc file:

```
alias rm 'rm -i $*'
```

If you try to delete a directory with the `rm` command, you're told that it's a directory and can't be deleted. If you want to delete empty directories, use the `rmdir` command, as with MS-DOS.

Linux offers another way to delete directories and their contents, but it's far more dangerous. The `rm -r` command recursively deletes any directories and files it encounters. If you have a directory named ./foo that contains files and subdirectories, the command `rm -r foo` deletes the foo directory and its contents, including all subdirectories.

If you give the command `rm -i -r`, each directory that the `rm` command encounters triggers a confirmation prompt. You must answer yes before the directory and its contents are deleted. If you left any files in the directory you were attempting to delete, `rm` balks, just as it does if you attempt to remove the non-empty directory with the `rm` command with no options.

N O T E You don't have to issue each flag individually for a Linux command. If the flag doesn't take an argument, you can combine the flags together. Thus, `rm -i -r` can be issued as `rm -ir`. ▪

Viewing the Contents of a File

Almost every Linux command prints to the standard output device, typically your screen. If the command takes its input from a file after manipulating the file in some way, the command prints the file to your screen. The trick in choosing a Linux command depends on how you want the file displayed. You can use three standard commands: `cat`, `more`, and `less`.

N O T E Linux, as all UNIX systems do, opens four system files at startup: standard input, standard output, standard error, and AUX. These files are actually physical devices:

Name	Alias	Device
Standard input	standard in(stdin)	The keyboard
Standard output	standard out(stdout)	The screen
Standard error	standard err(stderr)	The screen
AUX	auxiliary	An auxiliary device ▪

Using *cat* to View a File

For displaying short ASCII files, the simplest command is cat, which stands for *concatenate*. The cat command takes a list of files (or a single file) and prints the contents unaltered on standard output, one file after another. Its primary purpose is to concatenate files (as in cat *file1 file2>file3*), but it works just as well to send the contents of a short file to your screen.

If you try to display large files by using cat, the file scrolls past your screen as fast as the screen can handle the character stream. One way to stop the flow of data is to alternatively press <Ctrl-s> and <Ctrl-q> to send start and stop messages to your screen, or you can use one of the page-at-a-time commands, more or less.

Using *more* to View a File

Both more and less display a screen of data at a time. Although they both do roughly the same thing, they do it differently. more and less determine how many lines your terminal can display from the terminal database and from your TERM environment variable.

The more command is older than less, and it's derived from the Berkeley version of UNIX. It proved so useful that, like the vi editor, it has become a standard. This section covers just the basics of the command.

The simplest form of the more command is more *filename*. You see a screen of data from the file. If you want to go on to the next screen, press the space bar. If you press <Return>, only the next line is displayed. If you're looking through a series of files (with the command more *file1 file2 ...*) and want to stop to edit one, you can do so with the e or v command. Pressing <e> within more invokes whatever editor you've defined in your EDIT shell environment variable on the current file. Pressing <v> uses whatever editor has been defined in the VISUAL variable. If you haven't defined these variables in your environment, more defaults to the ed editor for the e command and to the vi editor for the v command.

▶ **See** "Setting the Shell Environment," **p. 330**

The more command has only one real drawback—you can't go backward in a file and redisplay a previous screen. However, you can go backward in a file with less.

Using *less* to View a File

One disadvantage to the less command is that you can't use an editor on a file being displayed. However, less makes up for this deficiency by allowing you to move forward and backward through a file.

The less command works almost the same way that more does. To page through a file, type the command **less** *filename*. One screen of data is displayed. To advance to the next screen, press the space bar as you did with the more command.

To move backward in a file, press the <b> key. To go to a certain position expressed as a percentage of the file, press <p> and specify the percentage at the : prompt.

Searching Through a File and Escaping to the Shell

The `less` and `more` commands allow you to search for strings in the file being displayed. The `less` command, however, allows you to search backward through the file as well. Use the search syntax `less /string` to search backward through the file. With the `less` and `more` commands, if a string is found, a new page is displayed with the line containing the matching string at the top of the screen. With `less`, pressing the <n> key repeats the previous search.

The `more` and `less` commands also allow you to escape to the shell with the `!` command. When you escape to the shell with the `!` command, you're actually in a subshell; you must exit the subshell just as you do when you log out from a session. Depending on which shell you're using, you can press <Ctrl-d> or enter `exit` to return to the same screen in `more` or `less` that you escaped from. If you press <Ctrl-d> and get a message to use `logout` instead of <Ctrl-d>, use the `logout` command.

Part
III

Ch
16

Viewing Files in Other Forms

Other commands display the contents of files in different forms. For example, if you want to look at the contents of a binary file, display it with the `od` command, which stands for *octal dump*. The `od` command displays a file in octal notation, or base 8. By using various flags, `od` can display a file in decimal, ASCII, or hexadecimal (base 16).

Octal, Decimal, and Hexadecimal Notation

Representing binary data is an intriguing problem. If the binary data represents ASCII, you have no problem displaying it (ASCII is, after all, what you expect when you look at most files). If the file is a program, however, the data most likely can't be represented as ASCII characters. In that case, you have to display it in some numerical form.

The early minicomputers used 12-bit words. Today, of course, the computer world has settled on the 8-bit byte as the standard unit of memory. Although you can represent data in the familiar decimal (base 10) system, the question becomes what to display—a byte, a word, or 32 bits? Displaying a given number of bits compactly requires that base 2 be raised to the required number of bits. With the old 12-bit systems, you could represent all 12 bits with four numbers (represented by 2^3, which was the octal or base 8 format). Because early UNIX systems ran on these kinds of minicomputers, much of the UNIX—and, thus, Linux—notation is in octal. Any byte can be represented by a three-digit octal code that looks like this (this example represents the decimal value of 8):

`\010`

Because the world has settled on an 8-bit byte, octal is no longer an efficient way to represent data. Hexadecimal (base 16 or 2^4) is a better way. An 8-bit byte can be represented by two hexadecimal digits; a byte whose decimal value is 10 is represented as 0A in hexadecimal.

The `od` command lets you choose how to display binary data. The general form of the command is

`od [option]... [file]...`

or

```
od --traditional [file] [[+]offset [[+]label]]
```

Table 16.3 summarizes the flags you can use with od.

Table 16.3 The *od* Command Flags

Short Flag	Full Flag	Description
-A	--address-radix=*radix*	Decide how file offsets are printed
-N	--read-bytes=*bytes*	Limit dump to *bytes* input bytes per file
-j	--skip-bytes=*bytes*	Skip *bytes* input bytes first on each file
-s	--strings[=*bytes*]	Output strings of at least *bytes* graphic chars
-t	--format=*type*	Select output format or formats
-v	--output-duplicates	Don't use * to mark line suppression
-w	--width[=*bytes*]	Output *bytes* bytes per output line
	--traditional	Accept arguments in pre-POSIX form
	--help	Display this help and exit
	--version	Output version information and exit

The pre-POSIX format specifications in Table 16.4 may be intermixed with the commands in Table 16.3, and their effects accumulate.

Table 16.4 Pre-POSIX Format Specifications for *od*

Short Flag	POSIX Equivalent	Description
-a	-t a	Select named characters
-b	-t oC	Select octal bytes
-c	-t c	Select ASCII characters or backslash escapes
-d	-t u2	Select unsigned decimal shorts
-f	-t fF	Select floats
-h	-t x2	Select hexadecimal shorts
-I	-t d2	Select decimal shorts
-l	-t d4	Select decimal longs
-o	-t o2	Select octal shorts
-x	-t x2	Select hexadecimal shorts

For older syntax (second-call format), *offset* means -j *offset*. *label* is the pseudoaddress at first byte printed, incremented when the dump is progressing. For *offset* and *label*, a 0x or 0X prefix indicates hexadecimal. Suffixes may be . (dot) for octal and may be multiplied by 512. The *type* parameter is made up of one or more of the specifications listed in Table 16.5.

Table 16.5   Type Parameters

Parameter	Description
a	Named character
c	ASCII character or backslash escape
d[*size*]	Signed decimal, *size* bytes per integer
f[*size*]	Floating point, *size* bytes per integer
o[*size*]	Octal, *size* bytes per integer
u[*size*]	Unsigned decimal, *size* bytes per integer
x[*size*]	Hexadecimal, *size* bytes per integer

In Table 16.5, *size* is a number and also may be C for sizeof(char), S for sizeof(short), I for sizeof(int), or L for sizeof(long). If *type* is f, *size* may also be F for sizeof(float), D for sizeof(double), or L for sizeof(long double).

N O T E   sizeof is a C language function that returns the number of bytes in the data structure passed as the parameter. For example, you would use the following function call to determine the number of bytes in an integer on your system, because the number of bytes in an integer is system-dependent:

sizeof(int);

radix in Table 16.3 stands for number system and is d for decimal, o for octal, x for hexadecimal, or n for none. *bytes* is hexadecimal with a 0x or 0X prefix; it's multiplied by 512 with a b suffix, by 1,024 with k, and by 1,048,576 with an m suffix. -s without a number implies 3; -w without a number implies 32. By default, od uses -A o -t d2 -w 16.

Searching for Files

If you can't find a file by looking with the ls command, you can use the find command. The find command is an extremely powerful tool, which makes it one of the more difficult commands to use. The find command has three parts, each of which can consist of multiple subparts:

- Where to look
- What to look for
- What to do when you find it

If you know the name of a file but don't know where in the Linux file structure it's located, the simplest case of the `find` command works like this:

```
find / -name filename -print
```

Be careful when searching from the root directory; on large systems, it can take a long time to search every directory, beginning with the root directory and continuing through every subdirectory and disk (and remotely mounted disk) before finding what you're looking for.

It may be more prudent to limit the search to one or two directories, at most. For example, if you know that a file is probably in the /usr or /usr2 directory, use the following command instead:

```
find /usr /usr2 -name filename -print
```

You can use many different options with `find`; Table 16.6 lists just a few. To see all the available options, use the `man find` command.

Table 16.6   A Sample of the *find* Command Flags

Command	Description
`-name file`	The *file* variable can be the name of a file or a wild-carded file name. If it's a wild-carded file name, every file that matches the wild cards is selected for processing.
`-links n`	Any file that has *n* or more links to it is selected for processing. Replace *n* with the number you want to check.
`-size n[c]`	Any file that occupies *n* or more 512-byte blocks is selected for processing. A c appended to *n* means to select any file that occupies *n* or more characters.
`-atime n`	Select any file that has been accessed in the past *n* days. Note that the act of looking for a file with `find` modifies the access date stamp.
`-exec cmd`	After you select a list of files, you can run a Linux command that uses the selected files as an argument. You use two simple rules with `-exec`: the name of a selected file is represented by `{}`, and the command must be terminated by an escaped semicolon, which is represented by `\;`. Say that you've created a user directory while logged in as root; thus, all the files are owned by root, but the files should be owned by the user. You would issue the following command to change the owner of all the files in /home/jack and all subdirectories from root to jack: `find /home/jack-exec chown jack {} \;`
`-print`	This instruction, the most often used, simply prints the name and location of any selected files.

The `find` command allows you to perform many logical tests on files as well. For example, if you want to find a selection of file names that can't be collectively represented with wild cards, you can use the *or* option (`-o`) to obtain a list:

```
find /home ( -name file1 -o -name file2 ) -prin
```

You can combine as much selection criteria as you want with the find command. Unless you specify the -o option, find assumes that you mean *and*. For example, the command find -size 100 -atime 2 means find a file that's at least 100 blocks in size and that was last accessed at least two days ago. You can use parentheses, as in the above example, to prevent ambiguous processing of your criteria, especially if you combine an and/or selection criteria.

Changing File Time and Date Stamps

Each Linux file maintains three time and date stamps: the date of the file's creation, the date of the file's last modification, and the date of the last access. The file creation date can't be changed artificially except by deliberately copying and renaming a file. Whenever a file is read or opened by a program, the file's access date stamp is modified. As mentioned in the preceding section, using the find command also causes the access date to be modified.

If a file is modified in any way—that is, if it's written to, even if the file is actually not modified—the file modification and file access date stamps are updated. The date stamps on a file are useful if you need to back up selectively only files that have been modified since a given date. You can use the find command for this purpose.

If you want to modify the date stamps on a file without actually modifying the file, you can do so with the touch command. By default, touch updates the access and modification date stamps on a file with the current system date. By default, if you attempt to touch a file that doesn't exist, touch creates the file.

You can use touch to fool a command that checks for dates. For example, if your system runs a backup command that backs up only files modified after a particular date, you can touch a file that hasn't been changed recently to make sure that it's picked up.

The touch command has the following three flags that you can use to modify its default behavior:

-a   Updates only the file's access date and time stamp

-m   Updates only the file's modification date and time stamp

-c   Prevents touch from creating a file if it doesn't already exist

The default syntax for touch is touch -am *filelist*.

Compressing Files

If space is tight on a system or you have large ASCII files that aren't used often, you can reduce the size of the files by compressing them. The standard Linux utility for compressing files is gzip. The gzip command can compress an ASCII file by as much as 80 percent. Most UNIX systems also provide the command compress, which typically is used with tar to compress groups of files for an archive. A file compressed with the compress command ends with a .Z extension—for example, archive1.tar.Z. Red Hat's distribution also provides the zip and unzip programs for compressing and archiving lists of files.

TIP   Compression is a good thing to do before you mail a file or back it up.

If a file is successfully compressed with the command `gzip filename`, the compressed file is named *filename*.gz and the original file is deleted. To restore the compressed file to its original components, use the `gunzip filename` command.

N O T E   You don't have to append the .gz to the file name when you uncompress a file. The .gz extension is assumed by the `gunzip` command. ▓

If you want to keep the file in its compressed form but want to pipe the data to another command, use the `zcat` command. The `zcat` command works just like the `cat` command but requires a compressed file as input. `zcat` decompresses the file, and then prints it to the standard output device.

▶ **See** "Connecting Processes with Pipes," **p. 341**

For example, if you've compressed a list of names and addresses stored in a file named namelist, the compressed file is named namelist.gz. If you want to use the contents of the compressed file as input to a program, use the `zcat` command to begin a pipeline, as follows:

```
zcat namelist ¦ program1 ¦ program2 ...
```

`zcat` suffers from the same limitations as does `cat`—it can't go backward within a file. Linux offers a program called `zless` that works just like the `less` command, except `zless` operates on compressed files. The same commands that work with `less` also work with `zless`.

The `compress` command's legal status is in limbo; someone has claimed patent infringement. The compression program of choice for Linux is the freely distributed compression utility `gzip`. The `gzip` command has none of the potential legal problems of `compress`, and almost all the files installed by Linux that are compressed were compressed with `gzip`. `gzip` should work with most compressed files, even those compressed with the older `compress` program.

For those of you familiar with PKWARE's PKZIP line of products, you can use the `zip` and `unzip` programs provided with the Red Hat distribution. The `zip` command compresses several files and stores them in an archive, just like PKZIP. The `unzip` command extracts files from an archive. See the man pages for `zip/unzip` for more information.

Manipulating Files with XFree86's GUI

If you're using the Slackware distribution of XFree86, chances are you're working with its graphical user interface (GUI). All the file manipulation you do with commands from the shell can be done with mouse actions from the GUI. If you didn't install the XFree86 X Windows system, you can skip this section. The program used is called Xfilemanager by Ove Kalkan. (See the application's Copyright menu item for information about the program.) Xfilemanager is similar to Windows 3.x's File Manager or Windows 95's Explorer.

To activate the Xfilemanager application, you must press the left mouse button over an open area of the desktop. This action displays the X Windows Utilities menu. Move the cursor to the Applications selection to activate the application's pop-up menu. You then see the Xfilemanager command. Select this command to activate the program.

N O T E Using the mouse under X Windows is different than under MS-DOS and Microsoft Windows. The mouse behaves more like a mouse on the Macintosh. For example, to select a menu item, you must continuously hold down the mouse button, move the cursor to the desired entry, and then release the mouse button. For more information on using X Windows, see Chapter 7, "Using X Windows." ▧

Part

III

Ch

16

The X Windows application Xfilemanager displays the contents of your directories in windows that look like folders. These folders represent your directories. This section is concerned with how you manage the files, directories, and applications that appear in your folder windows. Managing these items includes listing, copying, deleting, and moving.

Figure 16.1 shows an example of a Linux folder window named MyFile that exists in your home folder. Note that you can get to this same folder (although you call it a directory) from the command line by typing **cd $HOME/MyFile**. Remember, $HOME refers to your home directory, and all file names are case-sensitive under Linux.

FIG. 16.1

The Xfilemanager name folder window lists the various files and directories in the user's home directory.

The buttons across the top of the application provide access to a command menu. The first button, File, allows you to switch directories and exit the application. The Move button allows you to move files, whereas the Copy button lets you copy files. The Delete button allows you to delete files. The Make Directory button lets you create a new directory. The File Information button provides information on the selected file, and the final item is a simple clock.

Listing Files with the GUI

You can list the files located in a subdirectory by clicking the folder. This displays a new window (see Figure 16.2). The new window has a similar set of buttons as the window in Figure 16.1, and each button performs the same actions. The first button, with the bomb icon, immediately exits the application.

FIG. 16.2

Click a folder to list the files in a subdirectory.

You can display and modify the various file permission settings by highlighting a file and clicking the File Information button, which displays the File-Information dialog box (see Figure 16.3). To change a file permission, simply move the mouse to the appropriate box and click. A filled box indicates that a permission is set; an empty box indicates that the permission isn't set. After you changed the permissions, you must click the Apply button for the changes to be made.

FIG. 16.3

The File-Information dialog box lets you display and modify file permission settings.

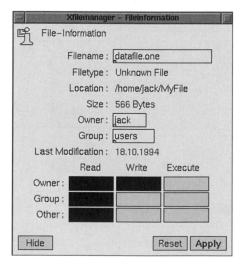

Copying Files in the GUI

To copy files from one folder to another, click the Copy button, which displays the Copy File dialog box (see Figure 16.4).

FIG. 16.4

The Copy File dialog box lets you copy a designated file to another location.

The currently selected file name appears in the From text box. You must supply the destination path and file names in the To text box. To cancel the operation, click Cancel. To execute the command and actually copy the file, click OK.

Moving and Renaming Files in the GUI

To rename a file or move a file from one folder to another, you can select a file and then click the Move button, which displays the Moving & Renaming Files dialog box (see Figure 16.5). Its operation is very similar to the Copy File dialog box. Simply fill in the desired information, and click OK to rename or move the file.

FIG. 16.5

The Moving and Renaming Files dialog box allows you to copy and rename the designated file.

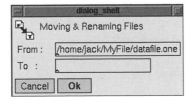

Removing Files and Folders

To remove or delete a file or folder from a folder window, select the file from the file listing dialog. After selecting the desired file or folder, click Delete, which displays the Remove File dialog box (see Figure 16.6). Clicking OK removes the selected file(s).

FIG. 16.6

The Remove File dialog box lets you remove a file or a directory (folder).

Part III

Ch 16

CAUTION

Be careful. Just as with the command-line method of deleting files, if you delete a file by mistake, you can't recover the file except from a backup. Linux—and any UNIX system, for that matter—doesn't have utilities to "undelete" a file because of the way UNIX systems maintain their file systems. Under MS-DOS, a deleted file only has an entry in the FAT marked, telling the operating system that the file space is available for use. MS-DOS doesn't write over this space immediately. However, UNIX and Linux returns the space (actually, the inodes) formerly used by the deleted program back to the free pool. When the space is moved to the free pool, the file can never be recovered!

From Here...

Managing files and utilities in Linux is a relatively simple chore. Organizing files into directories is easy. Finding, moving, copying, renaming, and deleting files and directories are simple with the commands `find`, `mv`, `cp`, and `rm`. For more information, see the following:

- Chapter 14, "Managing File Systems," which discusses practices for keeping your file system under control

- The man pages for the various commands discussed in this chapter: `ls`, `mkdir`, `mv`, `cp`, `rm`, `mkdir`, `rmdir`, `cat`, `less`, `more`, `find`, `touch`, `gzip`, `compress`, `tar`, `zip`, and `unzip`

Working with Linux

## CHAPTER 17

Understanding Linux Shells

Although graphical interfaces have been added to the UNIX system in recent years, most of the utilities for using and administering Linux (and other UNIX-like systems) are run by typing commands. In Linux, the command-line interpreter is called the *shell*. This chapter describes how to use the features of the various shells to work with Linux utilities and file systems. ■

Logging in

Before issuing any commands to Linux, you must announce yourself to the system by logging in to your account.

Understanding the various shells included with Linux

Command shells allow you to issue commands to the underlying operating system. Linux provides various command shells with different capabilities.

Understanding shell command parsing

Various shells *parse*, or break up, command lines in different ways. Depending on the position and options used, shell commands can be made to do various actions.

Editing and aliasing shell commands

The various shells allow you to recall a command and to edit that command's parameters to work on different files or to perform different operations. You also can create a new name, or *alias*, for a command.

Writing shell scripts

Shell *scripts* are groups of shell commands in a text file that the shell executes. Shell scripts are analogous to DOS batch files.

Logging In

As a new user and novice system administrator on your Linux system, you've chosen a login ID and password. Because Linux is a multiuser operating system, it must be able to distinguish between users and classes of users. Linux uses your login ID to establish a session in your name and determine the privileges you have. Linux uses your password to verify who you are.

Because any user can log in to any terminal in theory (there is an exception), the UNIX operating system begins by displaying a login prompt on every terminal. Because it's unlikely you'll have multiple terminals connected to your initial Linux system (although connecting multiple terminals is certainly possible), you'll have the alternate, or virtual, terminals available to you.

To switch to the various virtual terminals, press the <Alt> key and any of the first six function keys to switch between the various virtual terminals. For example, to log in to virtual terminal one as root, press <Alt-F1>, which displays the following prompt:

```
Red Hat Linux release 4.0 (Colgate)
Kernel 2.0.18 on an i486

web Login:
```

N O T E   The prompt line in the code line declares this example session to be running under the 2.0.18 version of the Linux kernel. As newer kernels are released, this number is incremented, so you may see a different version on the accompanying CD-ROMs. The stable released kernels are given even numbers for the middle number and the odd numbers indicate the latest (and beta) releases. ▓

Enter your user ID (root) and password.

When you log in to any terminal, you own the session on that terminal until you log out. When you log out, Linux displays the login prompt for the next user. Between logging in and logging out, Linux makes sure that all the programs you run and any files you might create are owned by you. Conversely, Linux doesn't allow you to read or alter a file owned by another user unless that user or the system administrator has given you permission to do so. Your login ID and password allow Linux to maintain the security of your files and those of others.

As the system administrator for your Linux system, you assign every user a user ID, temporary password, group ID, home directory, and shell. This information is kept in a file named /etc/passwd, which is owned and controlled by the system administrator, also known as root or the superuser. After you successfully log in, you can change your password, which is then encrypted in a form that no one else can read. If you forget your password, you (the system administrator) have to log in as the root user to create a new password. You can change your own password with the passwd command (although you have to type in the old password).

N O T E   For more information on basic system administration duties, such as adding users and fixing forgotten passwords, see the chapters in Part II, "Systems Administration," particularly Chapter 10, "Managing User Accounts." ▓

Understanding Shells

After you log in, Linux places you in your home directory and runs a program called a *shell*. A shell is really nothing more than a program designed to accept commands from you and execute them. Many kinds of programs can be used as shells, but several standard shells are available with almost all versions of Linux.

N O T E Linux shells are equivalent to COMMAND.COM used by MS-DOS. Both accept and execute commands, run batch files, and execute programs. ◼

Looking at Different Shells

Red Hat Linux provides the following shells: sh, bash (Bourne Again SHell), tcsh, csh, pdksh (Public Domain Korn SHell), zsh, ash, and mc. Try each shell and pick one you like. This chapter concentrates on the sh and bash shells, because most Linux distributions install bash as the default shell. Also, sh is available on most UNIX systems, and you'll find many shell scripts written with sh commands.

Because the shell serves as the primary interface between the operating system and the user, many users identify the shell with Linux. They expect the shell to be programmable, but the shell isn't part of the kernel of the operating system. With enough background in systems programming and knowledge of the Linux operating system, you can write a program that can become a shell.

Although many different shells have been created, there are several prevalent shells: the Bourne, C, T, and Korn shells. The Bourne shell is the oldest, and the others have some features not in the Bourne shell. In fact, Linux uses a variation of the Bourne shell, the bash shell, as its default shell. (To the novice user, the Bourne and Korn shells look identical; indeed, the Korn shell grew out of the Bourne shell.)

N O T E The Slackware 96 distribution doesn't provide a copy of the Korn shell. The Red Hat distribution provides a version of the Korn shell called pdksh, for Public Domain Korn Shell. ◼

The C shell was developed at the University of California at Berkeley as a shell more suitable for programmers than the Bourne shell. The T shell is a derivative of the C shell. The Korn shell has all the features of the C shell but uses the syntax of the Bourne shell. If all of this sounds confusing at the moment, don't worry. You can do a lot without knowing or worrying about the shell you're using.

In their simplest forms, the Bourne and Korn shells use the dollar sign ($) as the standard prompt; the C shell uses the percent sign (%) as the prompt. Fortunately (or not, depending on your disposition), these prompts can be changed so that you may or may not see either the dollar or the percent sign when you first log in.

The Bourne shell, known as sh, is the original UNIX shell. It was written by Steve Bourne with some help and ideas from John Mashey, both of AT&T Bell Laboratories. It's available on all Linux systems. The executable program for this shell is in the file /bin/sh. That the Bourne shell is available on all Linux systems and that it has all the properties described in the preceding sections—as well as its powerful programming capabilities—make this a widely used shell.

N O T E   Many of the shell script examples in this chapter are written so that they can be used with the Bourne shell. *Shell scripts* are sequences of shell commands, normally written with an ASCII editor such as vi. You can think of shell scripts as similar to DOS batch files.

▶ **See** "Introducing *vi*," **p. 390** ◼

The C shell, known as csh, was developed by Bill Joy at the University of California at Berkeley. The students and faculty at Berkeley have had a great deal of influence on UNIX and hence Linux. Two results of that influence are the C shell and the vi text editor. The Bourne shell has superior shell programming capabilities, but the C shell was developed to reflect the fact that computing was becoming more interactive. The executable program for the C shell is in the file /bin/csh.

The syntax of the C shell closely resembles the C programming language. This is one reason that shell scripts written for the C shell often can't run under the Bourne or Korn shell. But the C shell has some desirable features not available in the Bourne shell: command editing, history, and aliasing.

The default Linux shell is the bash shell. bash is located in /bin/bash and provides several enhanced features detailed in the next few paragraphs, such as command editing, command history, and command completion.

All Linux systems have the bash shell. You also might have installed several other shells during installation—for example, the C shell or the T shell. To determine which shell you're using, enter

```
echo $SHELL
```

The echo command prints whatever follows the word echo to the terminal screen. SHELL is a variable, maintained by the shell, that holds the name of your current shell; $SHELL is the value of that variable.

To see whether the C shell is available, enter

```
csh
```

If you see the percent sign (%) as the prompt, the C shell is available and running (enter exit to return to your previous shell). If you're logged in as root, the prompt for the C shell is #. If you get an error message, the C shell isn't available to you.

The shell you use as a login shell is specified in the password file. Each login ID is represented by a record or line in the password file; the last field in the record specifies your login shell. To change your login shell, you must change that field. The act of changing to another shell is relatively easy. Before you change shells, however, decide whether learning a new syntax and operating method are worth the change. See the man pages for detailed information on your shell's syntax.

> **CAUTION**
>
> Never directly edit the password file (/etc/passwd) in Linux. Because of the security features added to these releases, the password file should be manipulated only with the appropriate commands. For example, with Slackware Linux, to change to the C shell by using usermod, enter **usermod -s /bin/csh** *user*, where *user* is replaced by the user ID of the user for whom you're changing the shell.

A variety of other shells is available; some are proprietary and others are available on the Internet or through other sources. To determine which shell you want to use, simply read the man pages for the various shells and give each a try. Because shells are programs, you can run them just like any other application.

Configuring Your Login Environment

Before you see the shell prompt, Linux sets up your default environment. The Linux environment contains settings and data that control your session while you're logged in. Of course, as with all things in Linux, you're completely free to change any of these settings to suit your needs.

Your session environment is divided into two components:

- The first component, called the *terminal environment*, controls your terminal (more properly, the behavior of the computer's port to which you connect the cable from your terminal).

N O T E Because Linux runs on a PC, the "terminal" is actually your monitor and keyboard. You may or may not have other terminals connected to your Linux system. Of course, you do have six virtual terminals that you can log in from. ▨

- The second component, called the *shell environment*, controls various aspects of the shell and any programs you run.

You should first know about your terminal environment.

Setting the Terminal Environment Your login session actually consists of two separate programs that run side by side to give you the appearance of having the machine to yourself. Although the shell is the program that receives your instructions and executes them, before the shell ever sees your commands, everything you type must first pass through the relatively transparent program called the *device driver*.

The device driver controls your terminal. It receives the characters you type and determines what to do with them—if anything—before passing them on to the shell for interpretation. Likewise, every character generated by the shell must pass through the device driver before being delivered to the terminal. This section is first concerned with how to control the behavior of your device driver.

Linux is unique in that every device connected to the system looks, to a program, just like every other device, and all devices look like files. It's the task of the different device drivers in your system to accomplish this transformation. A hard disk in the system behaves very differently from your terminal, yet it's the job of their respective device drivers to make them look identical to a program.

For example, a disk has blocks, sectors, and cylinders, all of which must be properly addressed when reading and writing data. Your terminal, on the other hand, accepts a continuous stream of characters, but those characters must be delivered to the terminal in an ordered and relatively slow manner. The device driver orders this data and sends it to you at 1200, 2400, 9600, or higher bits per second (bps) and inserts stop, start, and parity bits in the data stream.

Because your terminal is always connected to the system, the device driver allows you to define special characters, called *control characters*, that serve as end-of-file and end-of-line markers for your shell. The device driver also allows you to define control characters that send signals to a running process (such as the interrupt signal, which can, in most cases, stop a running process and return you to the shell). Figure 17.1 shows one way that the Linux kernel, shell, and device driver behave.

FIG. 17.1

You can understand how Linux interacts with the user through the command shell.

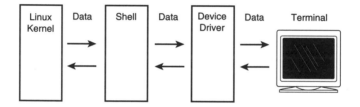

You can set dozens of parameters for your terminal, but most of them are handled automatically. However, you should know about a few parameters and modes.

The device driver has two modes of operation, called *cooked* and *raw*. In raw mode, all the characters you type pass directly to the shell or to a program run by the shell. Programs such as editors and spreadsheets require raw mode and set it up automatically. When such programs end, they normally reset your terminal to cooked mode—but not always. When your terminal is in raw mode, it doesn't respond to control keys such as the interrupt key.

When your terminal is in cooked mode, every key you type is interpreted by the device driver. Normal keys are stored in a buffer until the end-of-line key is pressed. In most cases, the end-of-line key is the <Enter> or <Return> key (however, this key can be changed). When the device driver receives the end-of-line character, it interprets the entire line before passing the interpreted or parsed line on to the shell or application program. Table 17.1 lists the most important control keys.

Table 17.1   Control Keys

Key Name	Description
Interrupt	Interrupts the execution of a running program. When you give Linux a command and press the end-of-line key, a program normally runs until normal completion. If you press the interrupt key, you send a signal to the running program, telling it to stop. Some programs ignore this signal; if your terminal is in raw mode, the interrupt key passes directly to the program and may not have the desired effect. The UNIX convention is to use the <Del> key as the interrupt key, but Linux changes this key to <Ctrl-c> for the convenience of people familiar with MS-DOS and other systems that use this key combination.
Erase	Deletes the last character in the buffer. This key is defined as the <Backspace> key. The erase key works just like the Backspace key on a typewriter. On some terminals and systems, there's confusion between the <Delete> and <Backspace> keys.
Kill	Deletes everything in the buffer before it passes to the shell or application program. This key is normally defined as the @ character. Unlike pressing the interrupt key, you don't see a new shell prompt when you press the kill key—the device driver simply waits for you to type more text.
End-of-line	Tells the device driver that you've finished entering text and want the text interpreted and passed on to the shell or application program. Linux uses the <Enter> or <Return> key.
End-of-file	Tells the shell to exit and display the login prompt. The end-of-file character is the <Ctrl-d> character. Linux treats all devices as though they were files; because your terminal is a source of virtually unlimited characters, Linux uses the end-of-file key as a way for you to signal that you're done with your login session.

Part
IV

Ch

17

The command used to set and display these control-key parameters is `stty`, which stands for *set teletype*. In the "old days," a teletype terminal was the only terminal available; a lot of UNIX terminology is left over from this era. For example, your terminal is defined as a tty device with a name such as tty14. To display all your present settings, enter **stty -a** from the command line. If you use this command, you see something like

```
speed 38400 baud; rows 25; columns 80; line = 0;
intr = ^C; quit = ^\; erase = ^?; kill = ^U; eof = ^D; eol = <undef>;
eol2 = <undef>; start = ^Q; stop = ^S; susp = ^Z; rprnt = ^R; werase = ^W;
lnext = ^V; flush = ^O; min = 1; time = 0;
-parenb -parodd cs8 hupcl -cstopb cread -clocal -crtscts
-ignbrk -brkint -ignpar -parmrk -inpck -istrip -inlcr -igncr icrnl ixon ixoff
-iuclc -ixany -imaxbel
opost -olcuc -ocrnl onlcr -onocr -onlret -ofill -ofdel nl0 cr0 tab0 bs0 vt0 ff0
isig icanon iexten echo echoe echok -echonl -noflsh -xcase -tostop -echoprt
echoctl echoke
```

Notice that on this system, the interrupt key (`intr`) is defined as <Ctrl-c> (shown as ^C), and the kill key is <Ctrl-u>. Although you can set all the settings listed here, as a matter of practicality, users usually only reset the interrupt and kill keys. For example, if you want to change the kill key from ^U to ^C, enter

```
stty kill '^C'
```

N O T E   If your terminal is behaving strangely, reset it to a "most reasonable" setting by giving the command `stty sane`. ▓

 T I P   If you want a certain setting to take effect every time you log in, place the command in your .profile file (located in your home directory) if you're running the `bash` or Bourne shell. For the C shell, place the command in your .login file.

Setting the Shell Environment   Part of the process of logging in—that is, of creating a Linux session—is the creation of your environment. All Linux *processes* (as running programs are called) have their own environment separate and distinct from the program itself. It could be said that a program runs from within an environment. The Linux environment, called the *shell environment*, consists of a number of variables and their values. These variables and values allow a running program, such as a shell, to determine what the environment looks like.

Environment refers to things such as the shell that you use, your home directory, and what type of terminal you're using. Many of these variables are defined during the login process and either can't or shouldn't be changed. You can add or change as many variables as you like as long as a variable hasn't been marked "read-only."

Variables are set in the environment in the form *VARIABLE=value*. The meaning of *VARIABLE* can be set to anything you like. However, many variables have predefined meanings to many standard Linux programs. For example, the TERM variable is defined as being the name of your terminal type, as specified in one of the standard Linux terminal databases. Digital Equipment Corporation for years made a popular terminal named the VT-100. The characteristics of this terminal have been copied by many other manufacturers and often emulated in software for personal computers. The name of such a terminal type is vt100; it's represented in the environment as TERM=vt100.

Many other predefined variables exist in your environment. If you use the C shell, you can list these variables with the `printenv` command; with the Bourne or Korn shell, use the `set` command. Table 17.2 lists the most common environment variables and their uses. The Variable column shows what you type at the command line.

N O T E   Some of these variables can be changed and some can't be changed. ▓

Table 17.2 Common Bourne Shell Environment Variables

Variable	Description
HOME=/home/*login*	HOME sets your home directory, which is the location that you start out from. Replace *login* with your login ID. For example, if your login ID is jack, HOME is defined as /home/jack.
LOGNAME=*login*	LOGNAME is automatically set the same as your login ID.
PATH=*path*	The *path* option represents the list of directories that the shell looks through for commands. For example, you can set the path like this: PATH=/usr:/bin:/usr/local/bin.
PS1=*prompt*	PS1 is the primary shell prompt that defines what your prompt looks like. If you don't set it to anything specific, your prompt is the dollar sign ($). If you prefer, you can set it to something more creative. For example, PS1="Enter Command >" displays Enter Command > as your command-line prompt.
PWD=*directory*	PWD is automatically set for you. It defines where you are in the file system. For example, if you checked PWD (by entering **echo $PWD** at the command line) and Linux displays /usr/bin, you're in the /usr/bin directory. The pwd command also displays the current directory.
SHELL=*shell*	SHELL identifies the location of the program that serves as your shell. For example, you can set SHELL in your .profile or .login file as SHELL=/bin/ksh to make the Korn shell your login shell.
TERM=*termtype*	Sets the name of your terminal type, as specified by the terminal database. For example, you can set TERM in your .profile or .login file as TERM=vt100.

Part
IV

Ch

17

> **N O T E** If you want an environment variable defined every time you log in, place the definition in your .profile file (located in your home directory) if you're running the bash or Bourne shell. For the C shell, place the definition in your .login file. ▪

Perhaps the single most important variable in your environment is the PATH variable.

> **N O T E** DOS users should be familiar with the PATH variable. It performs the same function under both DOS and Linux. ▪

The PATH variable contains a colon-delimited string that points to all the directories containing the programs you use. The order in which these directories are listed determines which directories are searched first. The list order is important on systems that support several different forms of the same command. Your system may also have locally created commands you may want to access. For example, your PATH variable may contain the following values:

```
/usr/ucb:/bin:/usr/bin:/usr/local/bin
```

This statement tells your shell to explore the /usr/ucb directory first. If the shell finds the command in the first directory it searches, it stops searching and executes that command. The /bin and /usr/bin directories contain all the standard Linux commands. The /usr/local/bin directory often contains the local commands added by you and other users of your system. This task of adding local commands is usually the responsibility of the system administrator.

If you intend to create your own commands, you can modify the PATH variable to include directories that contain your own commands. How you do this depends on which shell you use. For example, if you use the Bourne or Korn shell, you can add a directory to your PATH variable by typing the following at the command prompt:

```
$ PATH=$PATH:newpath
```

When you place a $ in front of the name of a variable, its current value is substituted. In this command, the $PATH variable represents whatever the current path is; the colon and the *newpath* parameters add to the current path.

The following section describes several other ways of manipulating variables in your environment. For now, it's sufficient to say that the shell environment contains variables and functions and that these objects can be manipulated by both shells and application programs. Application programs can access and modify the environment, but they generally manipulate variables within the program. Shells, on the other hand, can only manipulate variables in the environment.

Using Special Shell Variables   The shell keeps track of a number of special variables. You can see what they are with the env command, which lists the variables available to you within your working environment. Following is an abbreviated list of what you might see when you enter **env**:

```
HOME=/usr/wrev
SHELL=/bin/sh
MAIL=/usr/mail/wrev
LOGNAME=wrev
PATH=/bin:/usr/bin:.
TZ=PST8PDT
PS1=$
TERM=vt100
```

Any of these special variables can be used in the same way you use any other shell variable. Table 17.3 defines the special variables.

Table 17.3   Special Environment Variables

Variable Name	Meaning
HOME	Full path name of your home directory
SHELL	Name of your current shell
MAIL	Full path name of your mailbox
LOGNAME	Your login name

Variable Name	Meaning
PATH	Directories the shell searches for commands
TZ	Time zone for the date command
SECONDS	Number of seconds since invoking shell
PS1	System prompt
TERM	The type of terminal you're using

The HOME Variable   The HOME variable always specifies your home directory. When you log in, you're in your home directory. Occasionally, you use the cd command to move to other directories. To change to the directory /usr/local/games, for example, enter **cd /usr/local/games**. To get back to your home directory, all you have to do is enter cd. You can use the HOME variable when you're writing shell scripts that specify files in your home directory. Rather than write a command such as grep $number /usr/wrev/sales/data.01, it's better to enter the command as **grep $number $HOME/sales/data.01** for these reasons:

- The command line is easier to read.
- If your home directory is moved, the command still works.
- $HOME always represents the home directory of whoever is using the command. If you enter the command by using $HOME, others can use the command as well.

The PATH Variable   The PATH variable lists the directories in which the shell searches for commands. The shell searches those directories in the order they're listed. If PATH=/bin:/usr/bin/:., whenever the shell interprets a command, it first looks in the directory /bin. If it can't find the command there, the shell looks in the directory /usr/bin. Finally, the shell searches the . directory (remember that the dot represents your current directory). When you enter **cal** to print this month's calendar, the shell first looks in /bin. Because the command isn't there, the shell then looks in /usr/bin and finds it.

TIP   If you have a personalized command named cal, the shell never finds it; the shell executes the cal command in /usr/bin first whenever you give the command. Give your commands names that aren't the same as system commands.

You may want to put all your shell scripts in one directory and change the PATH variable to include that directory. This arrangement allows you to execute your shell scripts from whatever directory you happen to be in. To do this, follow these steps:

1. Create a directory to hold the scripts. Use the mkdir $HOME/bin command to create the bin subdirectory in your home directory.
2. Move each shell script to that subdirectory. For example, to move a shell script named stamp to your bin subdirectory, use the mv stamp $HOME/bin command.
3. Add the script subdirectory to your PATH variable with the PATH=$PATH:$HOME/bin command. Do this in your .profile file so that the change takes effect every time you log in to your system.

You need to create that new bin directory and modify the PATH variable only once. Under Linux, the directory called /usr/local/bin is created to hold "local" commands and scripts that aren't part of the standard Linux package but that you've added locally and have made available to all users. In this case, you should expect that /usr/local/bin is also part of PATH.

The MAIL Variable   The MAIL variable contains the name of the file that holds your e-mail. Whenever mail comes into the system for you, it's put into the file specified by the MAIL variable. If you have a program that notifies you when new mail has arrived, it checks the file associated with the MAIL variable.

The PS1 Variable   The PS1 variable holds the string of characters you see as your primary prompt. The prompt is the string of characters the shell displays whenever it's ready to receive a command. You see how you can change this variable—and any of the others—in the section "Customizing Linux Shells" near the end of this chapter.

The TERM Variable   The TERM variable is used to identify your terminal type. Programs that operate in full-screen mode, such as the vi text editor, need this information.

The TZ Variable   The TZ variable holds a string that identifies your time zone. The date program and some other programs require this information.

Your computer system keeps track of time according to Greenwich Mean Time (GMT). If the TZ variable is set to PST8PDT, the time and date are determined as Pacific Standard Time (PST), eight hours west of GMT, with support for Pacific Daylight Savings Time (PDT). Your computer system automatically changes between daylight savings time and standard time.

The LOGNAME Variable   The LOGNAME variable holds your login name, the name or string of characters that the system associates you with. Among the things the LOGNAME variable is used for is to identify you as the owner of your files, as the originator of any processes or programs you may be running, and as the author of mail or messages sent by the write command.

The following example is an extension of safrm, a shell script created for the safe removal of files. The LOGNAME variable is used to remove all the files you own from the directory /tmp. To do that, the shell script uses the find command. The find command has a number of options; the shell script uses this find command line:

```
find /tmp -user $LOGNAME -exec rm {} \;
```

The first parameter, /tmp, is the directory to search. The option -user indicates that you want to search for all files that belong to a specified user. Before the command is executed, the shell replaces $LOGNAME with the current user's login name. The option -exec indicates that the following command is to be applied to every file found by the find program. In this case, the rm program is used to remove the found files. The braces ({}) represent the position of each file name passed to the rm command. The last two characters, \;, are required by the find command (an example of using the backslash to pass a character on to a program without being interpreted by the shell). Add this command line to the shell script in Listing 17.1 to obtain a program that removes files safely and also cleans up anything a user has in the /tmp directory over 10 days old.

Listing 17.1 The *safrm* Shell Script

```
# Name:     safrm
# Purpose:  copy files to directory /tmp, remove them
#           from the current directory, clean up /tmp,
#           and finally send mail to user
# first copy all parameters to /tmp
cp $* /tmp
# remove the files
rm $*
# create a file to hold the mail message
#   The file's name is set to msg
#   followed by process ID number of this process
#   For example, msg1208
msgfile=/tmp/msg$$
# construct mail message
date > $msgfile
echo "These files were deleted from /tmp" >>$msgfile
# get list of files to be deleted from tmp
# -mtime +10 gets all files that haven't been
# modified in 10 or more days, -print displays the names.
find /tmp -user $LOGNAME -mtime +10 -print >> $msgfile
# remove the appropriate files from /tmp
find /tmp -user $LOGNAME -mtime +10 -exec rm {} \;
# mail off the message
mail $LOGNAME < $msgfile
# clean up
rm $msgfile
```

Understanding Processes

A running program in Linux is called a *process*. Because Linux is a multitasking system, many processes can run at the same time. To distinguish between processes, Linux assigns each new process a unique ID called a *process ID*.

The process ID is simply a number that uniquely identifies each running process. To see what process IDs are now associated with your process, use the ps command. To look at most of the process IDs now running on your system, issue the command with the flags -guax, and you see something like the following:

```
USER   PID %CPU %MEM SIZE  RSS TTY STAT START  TIME COMMAND
jack    53  3.2  7.0  352  468 p 1 S    02:01  0:01 -bash
jack    65  0.0  3.5   80  240 p 1 R    02:01  0:00 ps -guax
root     1  0.8  3.1   44  208 con S    02:00  0:00 init
root     6  0.0  1.8   24  124 con S    02:00  0:00 bdflush (daemon)
root     7  0.0  1.9   24  128 con S    02:01  0:00 update (bdflush)
root    40  1.0  3.5   65  240 con S    02:01  0:00 /usr/sbin/syslogd
root    42  0.2  2.9   36  200 con S    02:01  0:00 /usr/sbin/klogd
root    44  0.5  3.2   68  216 con S    02:01  0:00 /usr/sbin/inetd
root    46  0.2  3.0   64  204 con S    02:01  0:00 /usr/sbin/lpd
root    52  0.1  2.0   32  140 con S    02:01  0:00 selection -t ms
root    58  0.2  2.4   37  164 p 6 S    02:01  0:00 /sbin/agetty 38400 tt
```

Part
IV

Ch
17

The process ID is identified by the column titled PID. Also note the boldfaced line, which indicates the first process started by the system—init. The init process is also described later in this chapter.

When Linux is told to run a program (that is, to create a process), it does so by making an exact copy of the program making the request. In the simplest case, you request that a program be run by telling your shell; the shell makes a fork request to the Linux kernel.

Fork, *init*, and the *exec* Process   A *fork* is the process of cloning an existing process. Linux creates all new processes through the mechanism of forking. When a process is forked, an almost exact duplicate of an existing process (including its environment and any open files) is created; what keeps the duplicate from being exactly the same as its parent application is a flag that tells the forked process which is the parent and which is the child.

Because all processes are created in this fashion, all processes have a parent process and a parent-process ID. Every process running on a Linux system can trace its lineage back to init, the mother of all processes. init itself, process ID 1, is the only process run directly by the Linux kernel that you as a user have any contact with. Every process you create during a session has your login shell as an ancestor, and your login shell has init as its parent.

After a process successfully forks, the child process calls the exec routine to transform itself into the process you requested. The only thing that changes after an exec function is the identity of the running process; the environment of the new process is an exact copy of the environment of its parent.

Standard Input and Output   Every new process is created with three open "files." Because Linux treats files and devices exactly the same, an open "file" can be a real file on a disk or a device such as your terminal. The three open files are defined as standard input (stdin), standard output (stdout), and standard error output (stderr). All Linux commands, as well as application programs, accept input from the standard input and place any output on the standard output. Any diagnostic messages are automatically placed on the standard error output.

When you first log in, the standard input, output, and error files are attached to your terminal; any programs you run (processes you create) inherit your terminal as the three open files.

Understanding Shell Command Parsing

Parsing is the act of splitting the command line, or what you type, into its component parts for processing. In Linux, parsing constitutes a lot more than simply splitting the command line. The command string is first split into its component parts: the file names expanded if you used any wild cards, shell variables expanded, I/O redirection set up, any command groupings or subshells set up, and command substitution performed. Only then can the command line, as you typed it, be executed.

If terms such as *wild cards* and *I/O redirection* are new to you, you can find explanations of them, in the order they're performed, later in this chapter. You must first start, however, with the basic command syntax.

Using Commands, Flags, and Parameters

To execute a Linux command, you merely type the name of the file. The command to list files is ls; you can find a file by that name in the /bin directory. If /bin is listed in your PATH variable (and it should be), your shell finds and executes /bin/ls.

Some Linux commands aren't independent files. These commands are built into the shells themselves. For example, the cd (change directory) command is built into most shells and executed directly by the shell without looking up a file. Read the man pages for the shell you're using to determine what commands are executed internally or externally. Some shells have a command file that contains commands executed directly by the shell.

Flags If a command is to execute properly, you must present it to your shell in the proper fashion. The command name itself must be the first item on the line; it's followed by any flags and parameters. Flags (sometimes called *options*) are single letters preceded by a hyphen (-) that modify the behavior of a command. For example, the list command, ls, simply lists the names of the files in the current directory in alphabetical order. By adding various flags, you can list the contents of a directory in many different ways. You can list files and all their attributes with the "long" flag, -l. This command takes the following form:

```
ls -l
```

▶ **See** "Listing Files," **p. 302**

-l is the flag. When you want to use more than one flag, simply string the flags together, as in ls -lF. The -F flag displays an asterisk (*) if the file is executable, an @ sign if the file is a symbolic link, and a slash (/) if the file is a subdirectory. The man page for every command usually lists all the modifying flags and their meanings before describing any parameters. Flags can also be listed separately; the shell parses them before passing them on to the program. For example, you can write the ls -lF command as ls -l -F.

> **N O T E** Linux provides a popular feature—color highlighting. When you issue the ls command, Slackware Linux displays files in different colors depending on the file's type. This allows you to quickly identify files that are executable, directories, or linked to other files located in other directories. Also, if you redirect the output from ls to a file, this file contains the control codes used to indicate color. The control codes' information may cause problems with other programs, such as less, when used with this file.
>
> For Red Hat Linux, you must provide the --color flag to ls to get the same effect:
> ```
> ls --color ▨
> ```

One type of flag signals that the next parameter has some special meaning. For example, the -t flag in the sort command is used to indicate that the next character is a field separator. If you want to sort the /etc/passwd file, whose fields are separated by a colon (:), you can enter

```
sort -t: /etc/passwd
```

In the case of the sort command, the -t flag is needed only if the file uses a field separator other than the default. The default field separator is defined in the IFS (Inter Field Separator) environment variable. The shell uses the IFS variable to parse the command line so that the shell knows to use the standard field separator unless the -t flag indicates otherwise.

Part
IV

Ch
17

Parameters　Flags must be presented to the command before any other parameters. *Parameters* are strings separated by any of the characters defined in the IFS environment variable. The default string in IFS is a space, a tab, and a newline character. You can place any number of field-separator characters between parameters; when the shell parses the command line, it reduces these characters to one character before proceeding. For example, if a command is followed by three spaces, a tab character, and then the first parameter, the shell automatically reduces the three spaces and a tab to one tab character. Thus,

```
command<space bar><space bar><space bar><Tab>parameter
```

becomes

```
command<Tab>parameter
```

Parameters are usually file names or strings that tell the command to perform some function. If a parameter contains an embedded space, the string must be placed in quotation marks to prevent the shell from expanding it. The following command line contains two parameters; the shell attempts to find the word New in a file named York:

```
grep New York
```

If the intent is to find the string *New York* in the standard input, the command must be entered as

```
grep "New York"
```

In this case, the string *New York* is passed to the grep command as one parameter.

Performing File-Name Matching

Most modern operating systems (including all versions of Linux and DOS) support the use of wild cards for file and string searches. Table 17.4 summarizes the file-name completion characters, otherwise known as *wild cards*.

Table 17.4　File-Name Completion Characters

Character	Meaning
*	Represents any collection of characters except a period when it's the first character in a file name. The example combines into a file named allsales all files whose names begin with sales: `cat sales* > allsales`
?	Represents a single character. The example prints a collection of files with names in the form sales.*yy*, where *yy* represents a year in the nineties (sales.90, sales.91, and so on): `lp sales.9?`
[ ]	Represents a single character in a range. The example removes the collection of files with the names sales.90, sales.91, sales.92, and sales.93: `rm sales.9[0-3]`

N O T E   If you place a file-name wild card or expression inside quotation marks, the file-name expansion is suppressed during command-line parsing. For example, if you type **ls ***, you get all files in the current directory. On the other hand, if you type **ls "*"**, you probably get the error message `file not found` because you're instructing `ls` to search for a file named *. ▨

The * Wild Card   The asterisk (*) is the most universal wild card used. It simply means any and all characters. For example, the string `a*` means all files beginning with a. You can use as many asterisks in a single expression as you need to define a set of files. For example, the expression `*xx*.gif` means any file name with the .gif extension that has xx anywhere in the rest of the name. Matches include the file names abxx.gif, xxyyzz.gif, and xx.gif.

Use the asterisk character (*) to represent any sequence of characters. For example, to print all files in your current directory with names that end with .txt, enter

lp *.txt

Pay attention when using the asterisk wild card. If you enter the following command, you print all files whose names end with txt:

lp *txt

The file named reportxt is included with the files printed with the second command but not with the first. If you enter the following command, the shell passes the name of every file in your directory, as well as the single file named txt, to the command `lp` (the file named txt in your directory is passed twice to `lp`):

lp * txt

In the last example, the `lp` command first prints the files represented by the *; that is, it prints all files. The `lp` command then moves to the second item in the list of files it is to print (Linux interprets the space character between the * and txt as a delimiter—in effect, as a comma in an English command). The `lp` command processes txt as the name of the next file it is to print.

The * symbol can be used anywhere in a string of characters. For example, if you want to use the `ls` command to list the names of all files in your current directory whose names contain the characters *rep*, enter

ls *rep*

Linux lists files with names such as frep.data, report, and janrep. There's one exception: Files with names starting with a period aren't listed. To list files with names starting with a period (often called *hidden files*), you must specify the leading period. For example, if you have a file named .reportrc and want to see it listed, enter the following variation of the preceding command:

ls .*rep*

CAUTION

Be careful of using the asterisk wild card when you're deleting or removing files. The command rm * removes *all* files in your directory. An all-too-common mistake is to accidentally delete all files when you mean to delete a collection of files with a common suffix or prefix. If rather than enter **rm *txt** (which would remove all files with names ending in txt) you enter **rm * txt**, Linux first deletes all files and then attempts to delete a file named txt. But at that point no files are left.

To be safe, use the –i option with rm if you use the asterisk for file-name completion. The rm –i *txt command prompts you for confirmation before each file is deleted.

The ? Wild Card   Use the question mark (?) wild card to represent a single character. Suppose that you have the files report1, reportb, report10, reportb3, report.dft, and report.fin in your current directory. You know that the lp rep* command prints all the files, but to print just the first two (report1 and reportb), enter

```
lp report?
```

To list the names of all files whose names are three characters long and end with the character x, enter

```
ls ??x
```

This command lists a file with the name tax but not trax.

Because the question mark represents a single occurrence of any character, the string ??? represents all files consisting of just three letters. You can generate a list of files with three-letter extensions with the string *.???. For example, if you're searching a directory containing graphic images as well as other data, the following command lists all files with extensions such as .tif, .jpg, and .gif, as well as any other files with three-letter extensions:

```
ls *.???
```

N O T E   Remember that Linux isn't MS-DOS; file names aren't limited to eight characters with a three-character extension. Also remember that file names are case-sensitive under Linux.

The [] Expression   Sometimes you must be more selective than either of the more general-purpose wild cards allow. Suppose that you want to select the files job1, job2, and job3, but not jobx. You can't select the right files with the ? wild card because it represents one occurrence of any character. You can, however, use job[123] as the file descriptor.

You can also represent a single character by enclosing a range of characters within a pair of square brackets. To list the names of all files that begin with an uppercase letter, enter

```
ls [A-Z]*
```

Suppose that you have files named sales.90, sales.91, sales.92, and sales.93 and want to copy the first three to a subdirectory named oldstuff. Assuming that the subdirectory oldstuff exists, enter

```
cp sales.9[0-2] oldstuff
```

Like the question mark, items inside square brackets ([ ]) represent exactly one character. You can describe a discrete series of permissible values, such as [123], which permits only the characters 1, 2, or 3; you can also describe a range of characters, as in [A-Z], which represent any character between uppercase A and uppercase Z, inclusive.

You can also specify a set of ranges, which incorporates more than one range. For example, if you want to specify only alphabetic characters, you can use [A-Z,a-z]. In the ASCII character set, there are special characters between ASCII Z and ASCII a; if you specified [A-z], you include those special characters in your request.

Connecting Processes with Pipes

Frequently, you need to use the output of one program or command as the input of another. Rather than enter each command separately and save results in intermediate files, you can connect a sequence of commands by using a pipe (¦).

For example, to sort a file named allsales and then print it, enter

```
sort allsales ¦ lp
```

The name *pipe* is appropriate. The output of the program on the left of the pipe (the vertical bar) is sent through the pipe and used as the input of the program on the right. You can connect several processes with pipes. For example, to print a sorted list of the data in all files with names that begin with sales, enter

```
cat sales* ¦ sort ¦ lp
```

Redirecting Input and Output

Many programs expect input from the terminal or keyboard; many programs send their output to the terminal screen. Linux associates keyboard input with a file named stdin; it associates terminal output with a file named stdout. You can redirect input and output so that rather than come from or go to the terminal, it comes from a file or is sent to a file.

Use the < (less than) symbol to redirect input into a command or program so that it comes from a file instead of the terminal. Suppose that you want to send a file named info by e-mail to someone whose address is sarah. Rather than retype the contents of the file to the mail command, give this command to use the info file as the input (stdin) to the mail command:

```
mail sarah < info
```

Use the > (greater than) symbol to redirect the output of a program to a file. Rather than go to the terminal screen, the output is put into a file. The command date displays the current time and date on the terminal screen. If you want to store the current time and date in a file named now, enter

```
date > now
```

> **CAUTION**
>
> If the file name on the right side of the > already exists, it's overwritten. Be careful not to destroy useful information this way.

If you want to append, or concatenate, information to an existing file, use the two-character >> symbol. To append the current date to a file named report, enter

```
date >> report
```

For a slightly more lengthy example, suppose that the file named sales consists of sales data; the first field of each line contains a customer ID code. The first command line puts the output of the date command into a file named sales_report. The second command line uses the sales file as input to the sort command and appends the output to the sales_report file. The last line sends the sales_report file to users sarah and brad by e-mail:

```
date > sales_report
sort < sales >> sales_report
mail sarah brad < sales_report
```

> **CAUTION**
>
> Be careful not to redirect the same file as both input and output to a command. Most likely, you'll destroy the contents of the file.

Table 17.5 summarizes the redirection symbols used in Linux.

Table 17.5   Linux's Redirection Symbols

Symbol	Meaning	Example
<	Take input from a file	`mail sarah < report`
>	Send output to a file	`date > now`
>>	Append to a file	`date >> report`

Substituting Shell Variables

You learned about shell variable expansion earlier in this chapter when you set your PATH variable to PATH=$PATH:*newpath*. The shell replaced $PATH with the current values of the PATH variable. Shells are really interpreted languages, almost like BASIC; the shell variable is the primary object manipulated. Because shell variables are frequently manipulated, each shell provides methods of testing and defining the shell variables.

Shell variables are stored as strings. When two variables are placed together, their respective strings are concatenated. For example, if you have two variables, X=hello and Y=world, the expression XY results in the string helloworld. If you give the following command, the shell parses the two parameters and the values of X and Y (the two strings `hello` and `world`) are substituted before being passed to the `echo` command:

```
echo $X $Y
```

The `echo` command then prints `hello world`.

> **N O T E** If you place a dozen tab characters between $X and $Y, the output results are still the same. ■

If the substitution can be ambiguous, the shell picks the most obvious substitution—often with unpredictable results. For example, if you type **echo $XY**, the shell substitutes `helloY`. If you also had a variable XY, its value is substituted instead. To get around these ambiguities, the shell has a simple mechanism to allow you to define exactly what you mean. If you type **${X}Y**, the shell substitutes the value of X before appending the character Y to the string.

The Bourne and Korn shells have a rich collection of shell-variable expansion techniques that perform various tests on the variable before making the substitution. See the man pages for `sh` and `ksh` for more details.

Substituting Command Results

After the shell performs its substitution of variables, it scans the line again for commands to be run before the command line is finally ready. *Command substitution* means that Linux substitutes the results of a command for a positional parameter. This is specified in the following way:

```
command-1 parameter `command-2`
```

Be careful in the use of apostrophes, or single quotes (`'`), and backquotes (`` ` ``, also known as grave accents). Table 17.6 lists what each mark does.

Table 17.6 Quotation Marks and Apostrophes

Symbol	Meaning
"	Quotation marks disable file-name generation and suppress parameter expansion; however, shell-variable and command substitution still take place.
'	The apostrophe disables all parsing. Whatever is enclosed within the apostrophes is passed on as a single parameter.
`	The backquote, or grave accent, implies command substitution. Whatever is enclosed within backquotes is executed as though the command was performed on a line by itself. Any output placed on the standard output then replaces the command. The command line is then parsed again for parameters.

Part

IV

Ch

17

Consider the following command line:

```
echo Today\'s date and time are `date`
```

It produces this output:

```
Today's date and time are Mon May 18 14:35:09 EST 1994
```

To make the echo command behave properly, the 's in *Today's* in the preceding command was preceded by a backslash (\), also called the *escape character* (Today\'s). Virtually every non-alphanumeric character on your keyboard has some special meaning to the shell. To use any of the special characters in a string and to prevent the shell from interpreting the character, you must "escape" the character—that is, you must precede it with the backslash. If you want to pass the backslash character itself, use \\. To pass a dollar sign to a command, use \$.

Understanding Command Groups, Subshells, and Other Commands

You terminate a simple command with a carriage return. If you want to place more than one command on the command line before pressing <Return>, you can delimit individual commands with a semicolon (;), thus forming a group of commands. When the shell parses the command line, it treats the semicolon as an end-of-line character. If you type the following string, the shell executes each command sequentially as though you had typed each on a line by itself:

```
command-1;command-2;command-3
```

For example, you can enter **clear;ls** to clear your screen and display a directory listing.

Command Groups   If you want to redirect input or output to all the commands as a group, you can do so by making the command line a command group. A *command group* is defined as any number of commands enclosed in braces ({}). For example, the following command string directs the output of both commands to the file named output-file:

```
{command-1;command-2} > output-file
```

Any form of redirection can also be used. The output of a command group can be piped, as in the following example:

```
{command-1;command-2} ¦ command-3
```

In this case, the output of command-1 is fed into the pipe, the output of command-2 is then fed into the same pipe, and command-3 sees just one stream of data.

N O T E   Commands executed in a command group run in the current shell. That means that they may modify the environment or change directories. ▇

Subshells   When you run a series of commands as a command group, those commands run in the current shell. If one of the commands modifies the environment or changes directory, the changes are in effect when the command group finishes running. To avoid this problem, run a command group in a *subshell*.

A subshell is a clone of the present shell, but because child processes can't modify the environment of their parent process, all commands run in a subshell have no effect on the environment when the command group finishes. To run a command group in a subshell, replace the braces with parentheses. The command-group example in the preceding section then becomes the following:

```
(command-1;command-2) ¦ command-3
```

Only *command-3* runs in the current shell, but the output of the subshell is piped into the standard input of *command-3*.

Doing Background Processing

Because Linux is a multitasking operating system, you can run commands in the background in several ways. The simplest form of background processing allows you to run a command concurrently with a command in the foreground. Other methods place commands deeper and deeper in the background.

Part

IV

Ch

17

Arranging for Processes to Run in the Background

The shell allows you to start one process and, before the first one completes, start another. When you do this, you put the first process in the background. You put a process in the background by using the ampersand (&) character as the last character on the line containing the command you want to run in the background. Consider the following command:

```
sort sales > sales.sorted &
```

If you enter this command, you see a number on-screen. This number is the process ID (PID) number for the process you put in the background. The PID is the operating system's way of identifying that process.

Normally when you run a command, the shell suspends operation until the command is complete. If you append the ampersand to the end of a command string, the command string runs concurrently with the shell. By placing the ampersand *after* a command string, the shell resumes operation as soon as the background command is launched. Unless you use I/O redirection with the background command, the background command and the present shell expect input from and produce output to your terminal. Unless your background command takes care of I/O itself, the proper syntax for background processing is as follows:

```
command-string [input-file] output-file &
```

For example, to copy a collection of files whose names end with the characters .txt to a subdirectory named oldstuff and, without waiting for that process to finish, print a sorted list of the data in all files with names that begin with sales, use the following two commands:

```
cp *.txt oldstuff &
cat sales* ¦ sort ¦ lp
```

Put jobs in the background when you don't want to wait for one program to finish before starting another. You can also put jobs in the background when you have a collection of tasks in which at least one can run on its own. Start that one and put it in the background.

You can also use the virtual terminals offered by Linux to execute a command and then log in to another terminal.

Because the background process is a child of your shell, it's automatically killed when you log out. All child processes are killed when their parent dies.

Using the *nohup* Command

To place a command deeper in the background than the & operator allows, use the nohup command (which stands for *no hang up*). The nohup command takes as its arguments a command string. However, nohup must be used with the & operator if you want the command to actually be placed in the background. If a command is run with nohup in the foreground, the command is immune to being killed when you disconnect your terminal or hang up a modem (its original purpose). The syntax for the nohup command is

```
nohup command-string [input-file] output-file &
```

Using the *cron* Daemon

If you run a command with the nohup command, the command executes immediately. If you want to run the command at a later time or on a "time-available" basis, you must invoke the services of the cron daemon.

The cron daemon is a command run in the background by Linux—or, more specifically, by init, the master program. cron provides scheduling services to all Linux processes. You can ask cron to run a program at a specific time, periodically, at a particular time every day, or whenever the load on cron permits.

▶ **See** "Scheduling Commands with *cron* and *crontab*," **p. 374**

The *at* Command   The at command expects a time or date as a parameter and takes any number of command strings from its standard input. When the at command detects an end-of-file marker, it creates a Bourne shell script for execution at the time you specified.

The at command is flexible about the types of dates and times it accepts. For example, if you enter the command **at now + 1 day**, the next commands, taken from the standard input, are executed tomorrow at this time. One way to use the at command is from within a shell script.

A *shell script* is nothing more than a file containing all the commands necessary to perform a series of commands. The name of the file then becomes your own addition to the Linux command language. One way of using the at command is

```
at now + 1 day
command-1
command-2
```

When placed in a shell script, these lines let you conveniently run one or more commands the next day. To run any number of different commands, simply enter new commands after the at command line. You can run any number of commands from this script.

The *batch* Command   The batch command is the logical equivalent of at now. If you attempt to use the at now command, you see an error message that says something along the lines of now has passed. The batch command works exactly as at now works if it were logically possible, with one minor exception: The cron daemon maintains a separate queue for commands generated by at, batch, and cron. Suppose that you entered the following commands into the file named backup:

```
tar -cvf tackettbkup /usr/home/tackett
```

Then you can tell the system to back up the directory /usr/home/tackett by using the command

```
batch backup
```

▶ **See** "Creating Your First *vi* File," **p. 394**

The *crontab* Command   One of the best uses of the cron daemon is in automating the maintenance of a system. With cron, you as the system administrator can set up automatic backups of your system every morning at 4 a.m., Monday through Saturday. You install, delete, and list commands you want run in this fashion with the crontab command.

To run commands periodically, you must create a file in the crontab format. The crontab file consists of six fields separated by spaces or tabs. The first five fields are integers specifying minute (00-59), hour (00-23), day of the month (01-31), month of the year (01-12), and day of the week (0-6, with 0 referring to Sunday). The sixth field is a command string. Each numeric field can contain an inclusive range of numbers (such as 1-5 to indicate Monday through Friday), or discrete sets of numbers (such as 0,20,40 to indicate that an instruction should be run every 20 minutes). A field can also contain an asterisk to indicate all legal values.

The following example runs the calendar command every 20 minutes, starting at midnight Monday and ending at 11:40 p.m. Friday:

```
0,20,40 * * * 1-5 calendar -
```

If you name this file cronfile, you can install it in the cron system by issuing the command crontab cronfile.

The cron daemon has a time granularity of one minute—meaning, the shortest time duration you can work with is one minute. You, as system administrator, can place limits on the number of commands allowed to be run at any one time. Just because you ask cron to run an at, batch, or crontab file doesn't mean that it runs at precisely the time you've indicated.

Part

IV

Ch

17

Understanding Command Feedback

Linux provides instant feedback for commands that abort for one reason or another. In most cases, errors are limited to misspellings of the command name or badly formed file names. If you attempt to run a nonexistent command, Linux replies with

```
command: command not found
```

If you try to use a nonexistent file name, Linux responds with

```
command: file: No such file or directory
```

If the error is caused by something other than a command-line error, the command itself usually reports what happened—although not always in an easily decipherable form.

If you try to run a command with nohup and haven't redirected the standard error, Linux automatically places any error messages in a file named nohup.out in the directory from which the command was run.

Because commands run by cron have less urgency, any errors—indeed, any output placed on the standard output and not redirected—is sent to you through e-mail.

Editing and Aliasing Shell Commands

Different shells include features that provide shortcuts for running commands. *Command editing* lets you modify commands that have already been typed in. By using Linux's *command history* feature, you can recall commands you've previously entered. *Aliasing* lets you create commands that represent other commands. *Command completion* lets you fill in the rest of a file name after you type part of it.

Editing Commands

Command editing means that after you type a command—and before you press <Return>—you can edit or change parts of the command without having to retype most of it. To edit a command, press <Esc> to get into editing mode and then use any of the line-movement commands from the vi editor to modify the command. You can use <Backspace> to return to the portion of the command you want to change, and use other vi commands such as x to delete a character, r to replace a character, and so on.

Viewing Command History

The command history feature allows you to look back at previously entered commands and recall them. This feature saves you the time and trouble of retyping commands. When you combine this feature with command editing, you can easily correct mistakes in complicated commands and deal effectively with some repetitive tasks.

In both shells, the history command displays the list of past commands the shell has saved. The commands are numbered. To execute command 10, for example, enter ! 10. The bash shell also takes advantage of your PC's arrow keys; you can recall previous commands by pressing the <↑> key.

Aliasing Commands

Command aliasing allows you to define a name for a command. Consider this example: The man command displays Linux documentation, or *man pages*. To make the word help an alias, or alternative, for man, enter

```
alias help=man
```

Now you can enter **help cp** or **man cp** to display Linux man pages about the cp command.

You also can use aliases with commands that have options or arguments. For example, if you want to list the names of all the files in the current directory sorted in descending order by the time they were last modified (so that the most recent files are at the bottom of the list), you can use this command:

```
ls -art
```

The ls command is the command to list files; the -a option specifies all files, the -r option arranges the files in reverse, descending order, and the -t option sorts by time last modified. That's a lot to remember. You can assign the alias timedir to this complex command with the following command:

```
alias timedir="ls -art"
```

The quotation marks (" ") are necessary because the shell expects the alias for timedir to be terminated by a space or <Return>. Now, if you enter **timedir**, you get the directory listing you want.

> **N O T E** Setting an alias from the command line keeps that alias in effect only for the current session. To have the alias active whenever you log in, include the alias definition in the .profile file if you use the Bourne shell; keep it in the .login file if you use the C shell. ▪

Completing Commands

Command completion allows you to type the beginning of a file name and then press the <Tab> key to expand the file name. This can save time and spelling mistakes when entering a command. If two files share a common prefix, Linux expands the command to the last common character, stops expanding the file name, and then beeps. You need to provide the unique file name.

Adding Text with Cut and Paste

Red Hat Linux and Slackware Linux both offer a program that can be started at boot time that allows you to use the mouse to select text from anywhere on-screen and then paste the text onto the command line for the shell to interpret. To get a mouse cursor, you simply press one of the mouse buttons. You then select the desired text from anywhere on-screen by first clicking with the left mouse button on the beginning of the text and, while holding down the button, dragging the cursor to the desired end point of the text. After you select the text, click with the right mouse button to copy the text to the command line.

Working with Shell Scripts

The shell accepts commands, interprets them, and arranges for the operating system to execute the commands in the manner you specify. In the previous sections, you saw how the shell interprets special characters to complete file names, redirects input and output, connects processes through pipes, and puts jobs or processes in the background.

You can type commands at the terminal, or they can come from a file. A *shell script* is a collection of one or more shell commands in a file. To execute the commands, you type the name of the file. The advantages to this approach are as follows:

- You don't have to retype a sequence of commands.
- You determine the steps to accomplish a goal once.
- You simplify operations for yourself and others.

By using variables and keywords, you can write programs that the shell can interpret. This is useful because it allows you to create general shell scripts you or others can use in various situations.

Suppose that after you log in, you regularly like to see who's logged in to your system, run a program named `calendar` that displays your appointments for today and tomorrow, and print the current date and time to the screen. To do all that, you enter the following commands:

```
who
calendar
date
```

If you put these three commands into a file named whatsup and make that file executable, you have a shell script that you can execute just like any other command. The file whatsup must be a text file. You can use the `vi` or `emacs` text editor to put the commands in the whatsup file. To make the file executable, enter

chmod +x whatsup

The `chmod` command modifies or sets the permissions for a file. The +x option makes the file executable—that is, it makes the file work just like a standard Linux command. Putting commands into the file and making the file executable are both one-time operations. From that point on, you can enter **whatsup** to execute your shell script. You can use the shell script just like any other command. For example, to print the results of the `whatsup` command, enter

whatsup ¦ lp

To put the results of the `whatsup` command into a file named info for future reference, enter

whatsup > info

As a review, follow these steps to create a shell script that you can use whenever you want:

1. Use a text editor, such as `vi` or `emacs`, to put the shell commands into a text or ASCII file. In the preceding example, the commands were put in the file named whatsup.

2. Make it so that you have execute permission on the file. Use chmod +x *filename* (for example, chmod +x whatsup).

3. Test the command by typing the name of the command and pressing <Return>.

After using this process a few times, you'll see how easy it is to create useful scripts. Of course, the hardest part is figuring out which shell commands to use and how to use the shell's programming capabilities to express the steps you need to carry out.

You can test a shell script and see all the steps it goes through by entering

```
sh -x script-name
```

In this syntax, *script-name* is the name of the file that holds the script you're considering. The sh -x command displays all the steps the script goes through and is useful when you're trying to debug a script.

Writing Programs with the Shell

To write programs that use the shells, you must know about *variables* and *control structures*. Don't let either term scare you. A variable is an object that, at any one time, has one of possibly many different values assigned to it. Control structures specify the way you can control the flow of execution of a script. There are two basic types of control structures: decision structures (such as if...then...else structures or case structures), and iterative structures or loops (such as a for or while loop). With a decision structure, you choose a course of action from one or more alternatives, usually depending on the value of a variable or the outcome of a command. With an iterative structure, you repeat a sequence of commands. The earlier section "Setting the Shell Environment" discusses shell variables; the later section "Programming with Control Structures" provides more information on control structures.

Using *echo*   You can use the echo command to display informative messages about what's happening in a shell script. The echo command displays its arguments—that is, whatever follows the word echo—on-screen. Putting a string of characters in quotation marks ensures that all the characters are displayed. You also can redirect the results of echo to a file.

The command

```
echo "Please stand by ..."
```

displays the following line on the terminal screen:

```
Please stand by ...
```

The following command puts Please stand by ... in the file named messg:

```
echo "Please stand by ..." > messg
```

 TIP   Using the echo command can make users feel as though something is happening when they enter a command—a particularly good idea if the command doesn't give any output for several seconds or longer.

The echo command is also useful when you want to trace a shell script. Using the echo command at key points tells you what's happening in a script. Here is the file whatsup with an echo command or two added:

```
echo " Let's see who is on the system."
who
echo " Any appointments? "
calendar
date
echo " All done"
```

When you run the whatsup file, you see the following:

```
$ whatsup
 Let's see who is on the system.
sarah      tty01     Dec 20 08:51
brad       tty03     Dec 20 08:12
ernie      tty07     Dec 20 08:45
 Any appointments?
12/20      Sales meeting at 1:45
12/21      party after work!
Mon Dec 20 09:02 EST 1993
 All done
$
```

Using Comments   It's always possible that after you write a shell script and don't use it for a while, you'll forget what the shell script does or how it accomplishes its task. Put comments in your shell scripts to explain the purpose of the task and how the task is achieved. A *comment* is a note to yourself or whoever is reading the script. The shell ignores comments; they're important to and for human beings.

The pound sign (#) signals the beginning of a comment to the shell. Every character from the pound sign to the end of the line is part of that comment. Here's how you might comment the shell script whatsup:

```
# Name:      whatsup
# Written:   1/19/97, Patty Stygian
# Purpose:   Display who's logged in, appointments, date
    echo "Let's see who is on the system."
    who             # See who is logged in
    echo " Any appointments? "
    calendar        # Check appointments
    date            # Display date
    echo " All done"
```

Run the shell script again, and you see the same results as before. The comments don't change the behavior of the shell script in any way.

Using Variables in Shell Programs   To use variables, you must know how to give a variable a value and how to access the value stored in a variable. Using the value of a variable is straightforward, but there are four ways of giving a variable a value:

- Using direct assignment
- Using the read command

- Using command-line parameters
- Substituting the output of a command

Using Direct Assignments   The most direct way to give a variable a value is to write an expression such as

```
myemail=edsgar@crty.com
```

This expression gives the variable `myemail` the value `edsgar@crty.com`. Don't include spaces on either side of the equal sign (=). The direct-assignment method of assigning a value to a variable is of the following form:

```
variable-name=variable-value
```

If `variable-value` contains blanks, enclose the value in quotation marks. To assign an office address of Room 21, Suite C to the variable `myoffice`, for example, use the following command:

```
myoffice="Room 21, Suite C"
```

The shell retrieves the value of the variable whenever it sees a dollar sign ($) followed by the name of a variable. You can see that when the following two statements are executed:

```
echo " My e-mail address is $myemail"
echo " My office is $myoffice"
```

Suppose that you frequently copy files to a directory named /corporate/info/public/sales. To copy a file named current to that directory, enter

```
cp current /corporate/info/public/sales
```

To make this easier, you can assign the long directory name to the variable `corpsales` with the following expression:

```
corpsales=/corporate/info/public/sales
```

Now, to copy the current file to that directory, you enter

```
cp current $corpsales
```

The shell replaces `$corpsales` with the value of the variable `corpsales` and then issues the copy command.

Using the read Command   The `read` command takes the next line of input and assigns it to a variable. The following shell script extends the preceding `corpsales` example to ask the user to specify the name of the file to be copied:

```
# Name: copycorp
# Purpose: copy specified file to
#          /corporate/info/public/sales
    corpsales=/corporate/infor/public/sales
    echo "Enter name of file to copy"     # prompt user
    read filename                         # get file name
    cp $filename $corpsales               # do the copy
```

The `read` command pauses the script and waits for input from the keyboard. When <Return> is pressed, the script continues. If <Ctrl-d> (sometimes represented as ^D) is pressed while the `read` command is waiting for input, the script is terminated.

Using Command-Line Parameters When the shell interprets a command, it attaches variable names to each item on the command line. The items on the command line are the sequences of characters separated by blanks or tab characters. (Use quotation marks to signal that a collection of characters separated by spaces represents one item.) The variables attached to the items in the command line are $0, $1, $2, and so on through $9. These 10 variables correspond to the positions of the items on the line. The command name is $0, the first argument or parameter for the command is $1, and so on. To demonstrate this concept, consider the following sample shell script named shovars:

```
# Name:       shovars
# Purpose:    demonstrate command-line variables
    echo $0
    echo $2 $4!
    echo $3
```

Now suppose that you enter

```
shovars -s hello "look at me" bart
```

The output of the shell script is

```
shovars
hello bart!
look at me
```

In this output, the first line is the command's name (variable $0), the second line is the second and fourth arguments (variables $2 and $4), and the last line is the third argument (variable $3).

Following is a more serious example. This shell script deletes a file but first copies it to the directory /tmp so that you can retrieve it if necessary:

```
# Name:     safrm
# Purpose:  copy file to directory /tmp and then remove it
#           from the current directory
# first copy $1 to /tmp
    cp $1 /tmp
# now remove the file
    rm $1
```

If you enter **safrm abc def**, only the file abc is removed from the current directory because the safrm shell script deletes only variable $1. You can, however, represent all the parameters on the command line with $*. Make safrm more general by replacing each occurrence of $1 with $*. If you then enter **safrm abc def xx guio**, all four files (abc, def, xx, and guio) are removed from the current directory.

Substituting the Output of a Command You can assign to a variable the result of an executed command. To store the name of the current working directory in a variable named cwd, for example, enter

```
cwd= `pwd`
```

Notice that pwd, the print working directory command, is surrounded by backquotes rather than single quotation marks.

The following shell script changes the name of a file by appending the current month, day, and year to the file name:

```
# Name:       stamp
# Purpose:    rename file: append today's date to its name
# set td to current date in form of mmddyy
    td='+%m%d%y'
# rename file
    mv $1 $1.$td
```

In this example, the variable td is set to the current date. In the final line, this information is appended to variable $1. If today is February 24, 1997, and you use this script on a file called myfile, the file is renamed (moved) to myfile.022497.

Using Special Characters in Shell Programs You've seen how the shell gives special treatment to certain characters, such as >, *, ?, $, and others. What do you do if you don't want those characters to get special treatment? This section provides a few answers.

You can use the single quote to make the shell ignore special characters. Enclose the character string with a pair of single quotes, as in this example:

```
grep '^Mary Tuttle' customers
```

The result of this grep command is that the lines in the file customers that begin with Mary Tuttle are displayed. The caret (^) tells grep to search from the beginning of the line. If the text Mary Tuttle wasn't enclosed in single quotes, it might be interpreted literally (or as a pipe symbol on some systems). Also, the space between Mary and Tuttle isn't interpreted by the shell when it occurs within the single quotes.

You can also use quotation marks to make the shell ignore most special characters, with the exception of the dollar sign and backquote. In the following example, the asterisks, spaces, and the greater-than sign are treated as regular characters because the string is surrounded by quotation marks:

```
echo " ** Please enter your response -->"
```

In this next example, however, $LOGNAME evaluates correctly, but there's no value for $5:

```
echo " >>>Thanks for the $5, $LOGNAME"
```

Use the backslash (\) to make the shell ignore a single character. For example, to make the shell ignore the dollar sign in front of the 5, issue this command:

```
echo " >>>Thanks for the \$5, $LOGNAME"
```

The result is what you expect:

```
>>>Thanks for the $5, wrev
```

Programming with Control Structures

There are two primary control structures in shell programming: decision structures and iterative structures. In *decision structures*, such as if...then...else and case, you can have the shell script decide which commands to execute based on the value of an expression (such as a variable, the properties associated with a file, the number of parameters in a script, or the result of executing a command). In *iterative structures*, such as `for` and `while` loops, you can execute a sequence of commands over a collection of files or while some condition holds.

The following sections use examples that aren't too complicated, yet demonstrate the essentials of programming with some control.

Using *case*   The `case` structure is a decision structure that lets you select one of several courses of action, based on the value of a variable. Listing 17.2 shows a short menu program.

Listing 17.2   Implementing a Menu Shell Script with *case*

```
# Name:      ShrtMenu
# Purpose:   Allow user to print a file, delete a file,
#            or quit the program
# Display menu
     echo "Please choose either P, D, or Q to "
     echo " [P]rint a file"
     echo " [D]elete a file"
     echo " [Q]uit"
# Get response from user
     read response
# Use case to match response to action
     case $response in
        P¦p) echo "Name of file to print?"
             read filename
             lp $filename;;
        D¦d) echo "Name of file to delete?"
             read filename
             rm $filename;;
          *) echo "leaving now";;
     esac
```

The syntax of the `case` statement is

```
case word in
   pattern) statement(s);;
   pattern) statement(s);;
   ...
esac
```

The *word* parameter is matched against each *pattern* parameter, starting with the pattern at the top of the list. The statements that execute if *word* matches a pattern are terminated by two semicolons (`;;`). The end of the `case` statement is marked by the word `esac` (that's *case* spelled backward).

In Listing 17.2, the pipe character was used to give a choice for a match. For example, `P¦p` means that an uppercase or lowercase letter P is considered a match.

The pattern `*` is used to represent all other patterns not explicitly stated. If users press any key besides <P>, <p>, <D>, or <d>, they exit from the menu.

Listing 17.3 uses a case statement that makes a selection based on the number of parameters that the shell represents as $#.

Listing 17.3 Command-Line Parsing with *case*

```
# Name:     recent
# Purpose:  list the most recent files in a directory
# If user types recent <Return> then the names of
#   the 10 most recently modified files are displayed
# If the user types recent n <Return> then the names of
#   the n most recently modified files are displayed
# Otherwise, user is notified of incorrect usage
#
# Case based on number of parameters
    case $# in
        0) ls -lt ¦ head ;;
           # ls -lt lists names of file in order of
           # most recently modified
           # head displays the first 10 lines of a file
        1) case $1 in
           [0-9]*) ls -lt ¦ head -$1 ;;
           *)echo "Usage: recent number-of-files";;
           esac;;
        *) echo "Usage: recent number-of-files";;
    esac
```

Finding the Exit Status   When a shell command executes, it's either successful or not. If you use the command grep "American Terms" customers to see whether the string *American Terms* is in the file customers, and the file exits, you have read permission to the file, and *American Terms* is in the file, the shell command has executed successfully. If any of those conditions isn't true, the shell command executes unsuccessfully.

The shell always reports back about the status of the termination of a command, program, or shell script. The value reported back is called the *exit status* of a command and is represented by the variable #?. If you enter the following commands, you see the value of $?.

```
grep "American Terms" customers
echo $?
```

N O T E   If $? has a value of 0, this command was successful; otherwise, the command was unsuccessful. ▪

The following is an example in which the exit status of the command who ¦ grep $1 is used in the case statement:

```
# Name:     just.checking
# Purpose:  Determine if person is logged in
# Usage:    just.checking login_name
#
    case 'who ¦ grep $1 > /dev/null` in
```

```
            0) echo "$1 is logged in.";;
            *) echo "$1 is not here. Try again later.";;
        esac
        echo "Have a great day!"
```

If you enter **just.checking rflame** and rflame is logged in, you see

```
rflame is logged in.
Have a great day!
```

If rflame isn't logged in, you see

```
rflame is not here. Try again later.
Have a great day!
```

Using *if* Structures   The if...then...else...fi structure is a decision structure that allows you to select one of two courses of action based on the result of a command. The else portion of the structure is optional. One or more commands go in place of the ellipsis (. . .). Provided that the exit status of the last command following the if is zero (that is, the command executed successfully), the commands following the then and preceding the else (if there is one) are executed. Otherwise, the commands following the else are executed.

In other words, one or more commands are executed. If the last command was successful, the commands in the then portion of the statement are performed and then the commands following the fi (the end of the structure) are executed. If the last commands aren't successful, the commands after the else are performed.

Here's a familiar example that behaves exactly the same as when it was written using the case statement:

```
# Name:    just.checking
# Purpose: Determine if person is logged in
# Usage:   just.checking login_name
#
if
    who ¦ grep $1 > /dev/null
then
    echo "$1 is logged in."
else
    echo "$1 is not here. Try again later."
fi
echo " Have a great day!"
```

Using the *test* Command   Many of the shell scripts used in this chapter expect users to behave nicely. The scripts have no check to see whether users have permission to copy or move files or whether what the users were dealing with was an ordinary file rather than a directory. The test command can deal with these issues as well as some others. For example, test -f abc is successful if abc exists and is a regular file.

You can reverse the meaning of a test by using an exclamation point in front of the option. For example, to test that you don't have read permission for file abc, use test ! -r abc. Table 17.7 lists several options for the test command.

Table 17.7 Options for Using the *test* Command with Files

Option	Meaning
-f	Successful if file exists and is a regular file
-d	Successful if file is a directory
-r	Successful if file exists and is readable
-s	Successful if file exists and isn't empty
-w	Successful if file exists and can be written to
-x	Successful if file exists and is executable

Listing 17.4 is an example of the use of the test command.

Listing 17.4 A Sample Script That Uses the *test* Command

```
# Name:    safcopy
# Purpose: Copy file1 to file2
#          Check to see we have read permission on file1
#          If file2 exists then
#               if file2 is a file we can write to
#               then warn user, and get permission to proceed
#               else exit
#          else
#               copy file
#
# Check for proper number of arguments
  case $# in
    2) if test ! -r $1      # cannot read first file;;
       then;;
               exit (1)     # exit with non-zero exit status;;
       fi;;
       if test -f $2        # does second file exist?;;
       then;;
         if test -w $2      # can we write to it?;;
         then;;
               echo " $2 exists, copy over it ? (Y/N)";;
               read    resp             # get permission from user;;
               case $resp in;;
                   Y¦y)     cp $1 $2;;   # go ahead;;
                     *) exit(1);;        # good bye!;;
               esac;;
         else;;
               exit (1)     # Second file exists but can't write;;
         fi
       else    # Second file doesn't exist; go ahead and copy!;
         cp $1 $2;;
       fi;;
    *) echo "Usage: safcopy source destination";;
       exit (1);;
  esac
```

You can also use the `test` command to test numbers. To determine whether a value in the variable `hour` is greater than 12, use `test $hour -gt 12`. Table 17.8 lists some options you can use with `test` when you're comparing numbers.

Table 17.8 Options for Using *test* When Comparing Numbers

Option	Meaning
-eq	Equal
-ne	Not equal
-ge	Greater than or equal
-gt	Greater than
-le	Less than or equal
-lt	Less than

Listing 17.5 shows these options used to display a timely greeting.

Listing 17.5 Displaying a Greeting with the *test* Command

```
# Name:      greeting
# Purpose:   Display Good Morning if hour is less than 12
#                    Good Afternoon if hour less than 5PM
#                    Good Evening if hour is greater than 4PM
# Get hour
    hour='date +%H'
# Check for time of day
    if test $hour -lt 12
    then
        echo "Good Morning, $LOGNAME"
    else
        if test $hour -lt 17
        then
            echo "Good Afternoon, $LOGNAME"
        else
            echo "Good Evening, $LOGNAME"
        fi
    fi
```

Using Iterative Structures Iterative control structures allow you to write shell scripts that contain loops. The two basic types of loops are `for` and `while` loops.

With `for` loops, you specify a collection of files or values to use with some commands. To copy all the files whose names end with the characters .txt to the directory textdir, for example, use the following `for` loop:

```
for i in *.txt
do
      cp $i textdir/$i
done
```

The shell interprets the statement for i in *.txt and allows the variable i to take on the name of any file in the current directory whose name ends with .txt. You can then use the variable $i with any statements between the do and the done keywords.

The script in Listing 17.6 prints a collection of files, each with its own banner page. It also sends mail to the user concerning the status of the print requests. The characters $* represent all the parameters given to the shell command.

Listing 17.6 Processing Files with the *for* Command

```
# Name:        Prntel
# Purpose:     Print one or more files
#              each with own title page
#              Notify user which files were sent to the printer
#              and which were not.
#              Do this for all parameters to the command
for i in $*
do
      if lp -t $i -dlasers $i > /dev/null
      then
            echo $i >> printed
      else
            echo $i >> notprinted
      fi
done
# end of loop
if test -s printed
then
      echo "These files were sent to the printer " > mes
      cat printed >> mes
      mail $LOGNAME < mes
      rm mes printed
fi
if test -s notprinted
then
      echo "These files were not sent to the printer " >mes
      cat notprinted >> mes
      mail $LOGNAME < mes
      rm mes notprinted
fi
```

Part
IV

Ch
17

A while loop looks at the exit status of a command in the same way the if statement looks at the status. The script in Listing 17.7 notifies users when they've received new mail. The script makes the assumption that if a mailbox changes, a user has new mail. The script uses the command diff to compare two files and then reports on the differences. If the files are the same, the exit status is zero (the command is successful).

Listing 17.7   Repeating Commands with *while*

```
# Name:        checkmail
# Purpose:     Notify user if their mail box has changed
# Suggestion:  Run this in the background
# get a size of mail box for comparison
    cp $MAIL omail         # Get set for first time through
# MAIL is a "special" variable indicating the user's mailbox
# while omail and $MAIL are the same, keep looping
    while diff omail $MAIL > /dev/null
    do
        cp $MAIL omail
        sleep 30           # sleep, pause for 30 seconds
    done
# There must be a change in the files
    echo "New mail!!" ¦ write $LOGNAME
```

You can see that some of the commands and concepts used with if...then...else statements can be transferred to while loops. The difference, of course, is that with while loops, you're dealing with an iterative, repetitive process.

Customizing Linux Shells

The shell starts when you log in. Tables 17.2 and 17.3 show you that special variables are given values by the shell to help define your shell environment. The shell sets some of these variables. You can change these settings and give other variables values by editing the file .profile if you're using the Bourne or bash shell. If you're using the C shell, you set the variables by editing the file .login. You can also use command aliasing to define aliases for commands.

Whenever you issue a command, a new shell starts; it inherits many of the characteristics—or much of the environment—of the existing shell. Note these two things about the new shell:

- The new shell runs in your current directory. The pwd command returns the same value within a shell as it gives before the shell was started.

- The new shell receives many of its variables from the existing shell. There are ways to make sure that variables set in the existing shell are exported to the new shell.

Exporting Variables to the New Shell

When you create shell variables or give existing variables values, they exist in the running shell. A variable set in the login shell is available to all command-line arguments. A variable set within a shell has that value only within that shell. The value disappears or is reset when you exit that shell.

For example, enter these two commands from the command line:

```
today=Thursday
echo $today
```

Suppose that the echo command displays Thursday. Now suppose that you write and execute the following shell script named whatday:

```
# Name: whatday
# display the current value of the variable today
    echo "Today is $today."
# set the value of today
    today=Friday
# display the current value of the variable today
    echo "Today is $today."
```

Now enter the following four commands from the command line:

```
chmod +x whatday
today=Thursday
whatday
echo $today
```

The following lines appear on-screen:

```
Today is .
Today is Friday.
Thursday
```

The value of the variable today in the login shell is Thursday. When you execute the shell script whatday, you see that initially the variable today isn't defined (as shown by the display Today is .). Then the today variable has the value Friday in the shell. When the whatday script terminates, you return to the login shell and today has its original value, Thursday.

To give the variable today the same value that it has in the login shell when the shell script whatday starts, use the command export. This command "exports," or passes on, the variables from one shell to subsequent shells:

```
export today
```

Now any shell started from the login shell inherits the value of the variable today. Add the export command to the preceding sequence of commands:

```
today=Thursday
export today
whatday
echo $today
```

You see the following output:

```
Today is Thursday.
Today is Friday.
Thursday
```

Notice that the value the variable receives in the shell started by the whatday script isn't carried back to the login shell. Exportation or inheritance of variable values goes in only one direction—from a running shell down to the new shell, never back up. That's why when you change your current directory inside one shell, you're back to where you started when that shell terminates.

Part
IV

Ch
17

You can export any variable from one shell down to another shell by using the following syntax:

```
export variable-name
```

In this syntax, *variable-name* is the name of the variable you want to export. To change your terminal type from its current setting to a vt100, for example, enter the following commands to make the new value of TERM available to all subsequent shells or programs:

```
TERM=vt100
export TERM
```

When you change or set bash shell variables in the .profile file, be sure to export them. For example, if you want the PATH variable to be PATH=/bin:/usr/bin:/usr/local/bin:., set it in the .profile file and follow it with this export command:

```
export PATH
```

To change the shell prompt, you must set a value for PS1 in the file .profile. To change it from $ to Ready $, for example, use a text editor to put these lines in the file .profile:

```
PS1="Ready $"
export PS1
```

N O T E   Changes you make to .profile or .login don't take effect until you log out and log in again. ▧

Defining Command Aliases

Command aliases are useful for defining commands you use regularly but for which you don't want to bother remembering the details. Command aliases are also useful for enhancing your working environment with a set of useful tools. This command assigns the alias recent to a command that lists the 10 most recently modified files in the current directory:

```
alias recent="ls -lat¦head"
```

To avoid typing your command aliases each time you log in, put them in the .login file if you're using the C shell or the .profile file if you're using bash or a similar shell. The command aliases are now available to you when you're in your shell.

From Here...

The shell is the primary interface between you and the Linux operating system. Although a shell can be almost any executable program, several standard shells are supplied with Linux or are freely available in source code (written in C) or already compiled for your machine. All Linux shells can be viewed as highly sophisticated, special-purpose programming languages containing all the usual constructs found in a programming language. The special purpose of

Linux shell languages is to tie together the many small commands and utilities found in the Linux environment. By making use of I/O redirection and background processing, the shell languages allow you to write complex programs with minimal effort. For more information, see

■ Chapter 5, "Running Linux Applications," for basic information on navigating through Linux.

■ Chapter 19, "Using the *vi* Editor," for information on editing text files.

## CHAPTER 18

Managing Multiple Processes

Linux is a multiuser and multitasking operating system. *Multiuser* means that several people can use the computer system simultaneously (unlike a single-user operating system, such as MS-DOS). *Multitasking* means that Linux, like Windows NT, can work on several tasks concurrently; it can begin work on one task and take up another before the first task is finished.

Taking care of several user requests and multitasking are the jobs of the operating system. Most systems have only one CPU and one collection of chips that make up main memory, or RAM. A system may have more than one disk or tape drive for secondary memory and several input/output devices. All these resources must be managed and shared between several users. The operating system creates the illusion that each user has a dedicated computer system. ∎

Start multiple processes

Linux gives you a way to start multiple programs running at the same time and then interact with each individually.

Schedule multiple processes by using *at*, *batch*, *cron*, and *crontab*

Linux also provides a way to start programs at different times of the day without human interaction.

Monitor the state of the system by using who and ps

By using the who and ps commands on any UNIX system, you can quickly determine who's logged in and what they're doing.

Manage processes by changing their relative priority with *nice* and *renice*

There are only so many CPU cycles to go around, so sometimes one process may need more cycles than another. With nice and renice, Linux lets you control the priority at which a process gets CPU cycles.

Terminate processes with the *kill* command

Sometimes a program can stop functioning, or maybe you've issued a command that scans the entire drive. In either case, Linux lets you get rid of a running (or dead) process with the kill command.

Understanding Multitasking

As mentioned earlier, it's Linux's job to create the illusion that when you make a request, you have the system's undivided attention. In reality, hundreds of requests may be handled between the time you press <Return> and the time the system responds to your command.

Imagine having to keep track of dozens of tasks simultaneously. You have to share the processing power, storage capabilities, and input and output devices among several users or several processes belonging to a single user. Linux monitors a list—also known as a *queue*—of tasks waiting to be done. These tasks can include user jobs, operating system tasks, mail, and background jobs such as printing. Linux schedules slices of system time for each task. By human standards, each time slice is extremely short—a fraction of a second. In computer time, a time slice is adequate for a program to process hundreds or thousands of instructions. The length of the time slice for each task may depend on the relative priority of each task.

Linux works on one task from the queue for a while, puts the task aside to begin work on another task, and so on. It then returns to the first task and works on it again. Linux continues these cycles until it finishes a task and takes the task out of the queue, or until the task is terminated. In this arrangement, sometimes called *time-sharing*, the resources of the system are shared among all the tasks. Naturally, time-sharing must be done in a reliable and efficient manner. The UNIX term for a task is *process*. Table 18.1 shows several types of processes.

Table 18.1 Types of Processes

Process Type	Description
interactive	Initiated by a shell and running in the foreground or background
batch	Typically a series of processes scheduled for execution at a specified point in time
daemon	Typically initiated at boot time to perform operating system functions on demand, such as LPD, NFS, and DNS

You've already seen that you can put or run a program in the background. While the program runs in the background, you can continue entering commands and working with other material. This is a feature of multitasking: Linux uses the time-sharing method to balance your immediate commands and the ones running in the background. This chapter shows other ways to schedule processes so that they can run without your attention (*batch process*).

▶ **See** "Doing Background Processing," **p. 345**

The Linux operating system has the primary responsibility of handling the details of working with several users and several processes. As a user, you have the power to specify which programs you want to run. Some Linux commands let you specify when you want a process to start. You also can monitor your processes as well as see what other processes are running. In some cases, you can change their relative priority. And you can always terminate your processes if the need arises. If you're the system administrator, you have all these capabilities, plus the responsibility and power to initiate, monitor, and manage processes that belong to the operating system or any user.

Table 18.2 lists the commands that make it possible to control the multiuser and multitasking capabilities of Linux.

Table 18.2   Multiuser and Multitasking Commands

Command	Action
at	Executes commands at a given time
batch	Executes commands when system load allows
cron	Executes scheduled commands
crontab	Maintains crontab files for individual users
kill	Stops processes
nice	Adjusts the priority of a process before it starts
nohup	Allows a process to continue after you log out
ps	Displays process information
renice	Adjusts the priority of a running process
w	Shows you who is logged in and what they're doing
who	Displays the system's logged-in users

N O T E For more information on the commands in Table 18.2, you can consult the man page :

man *command*

You also can use the `--help` option:

command `--help` ▧

Initiating Multiple Processes

You can start a program running by entering its name. You can also start programs from files that contain shell commands. Running programs can interact with many different parts of the system. A program can read from or write to files, manage its information in RAM, or send information to printers, modems, or other devices. The operating system also attaches information to a process so that the system can keep track of and manage it.

A process is a running program, yet different from a program. In one sense, a process is more than a program because a program is only a set of instructions; a process is dynamic because it uses the resources of a running system. On the other hand, a single Linux program can start several processes.

Linux identifies and keeps track of processes by assigning a process ID number (PID) to each process.

Starting Multiple Processes

You've already seen that your login shell is always running. Whenever you enter a command, you start at least one new process while the login shell continues to run. If you enter the following command, for example, the file named report.txt is sent to the lp program:

```
lp report.txt
```

▶ **See** "Understanding Shells," **p. 325**

When the lp program completes its task, the shell prompt reappears. Before the shell prompt reappeared, the login shell and the lp command were running; you initiated multiple processes in that case. The shell waited until the lp command finished before putting the shell prompt back on-screen.

Starting a Background Process

You can run a process as a background job by giving the command to start a process and placing an ampersand (&) after the command. For example, if you enter the command **lp report.txt &**, the shell responds immediately with a number—the PID for that process. The shell prompt reappears without waiting for the process to complete. The following is a sample of what you would see:

```
$ lp report.txt &
3146
$
```

In this example, 3146 is the PID of the process started by the lp command.

Regardless of whether you run the lp command in the background, the process associated with lp is started from the current shell. The lp process is a child process of the current shell. This example points to a common relationship between processes—that of parent and child. Your current shell is the parent process, and the running lp process is a child process. Usually, a parent process waits for one or more of its child processes to complete before it continues. If you want the parent to continue without waiting for the child to finish, attach the ampersand (&) to the command that *spawns*, or initiates, the child process. You can continue with other work or commands while the child runs.

N O T E If you're working from a character terminal or a remote login, your current shell is usually your login shell. However, if you're using a virtual terminal or a terminal window from a GUI, a separate shell is associated with each session. ▪

Using Pipes to Start Multiple Processes

Another way to start multiple processes is to use one or more pipes on a command line. To print a long listing of the 10 most recently modified files in your current directory, enter

```
ls -lt ¦ head ¦ lp
```

This command starts three processes simultaneously, and they're all children of the current shell. A pipe works this way: Commands on either side of the vertical bar (¦) begin at the same time. Neither is the parent of the other; they're both children of the process that was running when they were created. In this sense, you can think of commands on either side of the pipe symbol as sibling processes.

Some programs are written so that they themselves spawn several processes. One example is the `ispell` command, which lists the words in a document that Linux can't find in a system dictionary. The `ispell` command spawns some child processes. Suppose that you enter

```
ispell final.rept > final.errs &
```

You see the following results displayed:

```
1286
$
```

Here, 1286 is the PID of the `ispell` process; the `$` prompt indicates that the shell is ready to handle another command from you. Even though `ispell` may spawn some children and wait for them to complete, you don't have to wait. In this example, the current shell is the parent of `ispell`, and `ispell`'s children can be thought of as grandchildren of the login shell. Although a parent can wait for its children, a grandparent doesn't.

All these examples show how it's possible for users to start multiple processes. You can wait until child processes are finished before continuing or not. If you continue without waiting for the child process to complete, you've made the children background processes. The following section looks at some Linux commands you can use to schedule processes to run at specified times or at a lower relative priority.

Using the Scheduling Commands

The Linux environment provides many ways to handle command execution. Linux lets you create lists of commands and specify when they're to be run. The `at` command, for example, takes a list of commands typed at the keyboard or from a file and runs them at the time specified by the command. The `batch` command is similar to the `at` command, except that `batch` runs commands when the system finds time for them rather than allow the user to specify a particular time. The `cron` command allows for commands to be run periodically, and the `crontab` command allows users to edit the files used by `cron`.

All scheduling commands are useful for running tasks at times when the system isn't too busy. They're also good for executing scripts to external services—such as database queries—at times when it's least expensive to do so.

Running Commands at Specified Times with *at*

To schedule one or more commands for a specified time, use the `at` command. With this command, you can specify a time, a date, or both. The command expects two or more arguments.

At a minimum, you specify the time you want the command(s) executed and the command(s) you want to execute.

The following example performs its job at 1:23 a.m. If you're working in the wee hours of the morning before 1:23 a.m. (that is, between midnight and 1:23 a.m.), the command is done today, at 1:23 a.m. Otherwise, it's done at 1:23 a.m. the following day. The job prints all files in the directory /usr/sales/reports and sends a user named boss some mail announcing that the print job was done at 1:23 a.m. Type the following commands on the terminal, pressing <Return> at the end of each line. After you enter each line, press <Ctrl-d> to finish the command.

```
at 1:23
lp /usr/sales/reports/*
echo "Files printed, Boss!" ¦ mail -s"Job done" boss
```

▶ **See** "Setting the Terminal Environment," **p. 327**

Commands to be scheduled by at are entered as a list of commands on the line following the at command.

After you terminate the at command, you see a display similar to the following:

```
job 756603300.a at Tues Jan 21 01:23:00 1997
```

This response indicates that the job will execute at 1:23 as specified. The job number, 756603300.a, identifies the job. If you decide you want to cancel the job, do so by using the job number associated with it, like so:

```
at -d 756603300.a
```

If you have several commands you want to schedule by using at, it's best to put them in a file. If the file name is getdone, for example, and you want to schedule the commands for 10 a.m., enter

```
at 10:00 < getdone
```

or

```
at 10:00 -f getdone
```

Remember that the less-than symbol (<) means to use the contents of the getdone file as input to the at command. The -f option allows you to specify the command file without using redirection.

You can also specify a date for an at job. For example, to schedule a job at 5 p.m. on January 24, enter these commands:

```
at 17:00 Jan 24
lp /usr/sales/reports/*
echo "Files printed, Boss!" ¦ mail -s"Job done" boss
```

The jobs you schedule with at are put into a queue that the operating system checks periodically. You don't have to be logged in for the job to be executed. The at command always runs in the background, freeing resources but still accomplishing the job. Any output produced by the commands in your at job is automatically mailed to you.

To see which jobs you scheduled with at, enter **at -l**. Working with the preceding examples, you see the following results:

```
job 756603300.a at Sat Dec 21 01:23:00 1996
job 756604200.a at Fri Jan 24 17:00:00 1997
```

Only your at jobs are listed.

To remove a scheduled at job, enter **at -d** followed by the job number. To remove the second job just listed, for example, enter

at -d 756604200.a

Table 18.3 summarizes the different ways to use the at command.

Table 18.3 Summary of *at* Commands

Format	Action
at *hh:mm*	Schedules job at the hour (*hh*) and minute (*mm*) specified by using a 24-hour clock
at *hh:mm month day year*	Schedules job at the hour (*hh*), minute (*mm*), month, day, and year specified
at -l	Lists scheduled jobs; an alias for the atq command
at now *+count time-units*	Schedules the job right now plus the count number of time units; time units can be minutes, hours, days, or weeks
at -d *job_id*	Cancels the job with the job number matching *job_id*; an alias for the atrm command

As the root user, you can use any of these commands; for other users, the files /etc/at.allow and /etc/at.deny determine the permission to use the commands. If /etc/at.allow exists, only the user names listed in the file are allowed to use the at command. If the /etc/at.allow file doesn't exist, the system checks the /etc/at.deny, and every user name *not* mentioned in /etc/at.deny is allowed to use at (in other words, any user listed in /etc/at.deny isn't allowed to use at). If neither file exists, only the superuser (root) can use at. If /etc/at.deny is empty, every user can use at.

Running Long Tasks with *batch*

Linux has more than one command for scheduling tasks. The preceding section describes the at command, which gives you the power to dictate when a task will run. However, it's always possible that the system can be loaded down with more jobs scheduled at one time than it can comfortably handle. The batch command lets the operating system decide an appropriate time

Part
IV

Ch
18

to run a process. When you schedule a job with batch, Linux starts and works on the process whenever the system load isn't too great. Jobs run under batch execute in the background, just as those run with at. In fact, batch is an alias for at -b in Red Hat Linux.

TIP It's useful to put commands you want to run with at or batch in a file so that you don't have to retype the commands each time you want to run the jobs. To use batch to schedule the commands in the file getdone, enter the **batch < getdone** command.

The format for batch commands is to enter the list of commands on the lines following the batch command; you terminate the list of commands with <Ctrl-d>. You can put the list of commands in a file and then redirect the input of the file to batch. To sort a collection of files, print the results, and notify user boss that the job is done, enter the following commands:

```
batch
sort /usr/sales/reports/* ¦ lp
echo "Files printed, Boss!" ¦ mailx -s"Job done" boss
```

The system returns the following response:

```
job 7789001234.b at Fri Feb 21 11:43:09 1997
```

The date and time listed are the date and time you pressed <Ctrl-d> to complete the batch command. When the job is complete, check your mail; anything that the commands normally display is mailed to you.

Scheduling Commands with *cron* and *crontab*

Both at and batch schedule commands on a one-time basis. To schedule commands or processes on a regular basis, you use the cron program. You specify the times and dates you want to run a command in crontab files. Times can be specified in terms of minutes, hours, days of the month, months of the year, or days of the week.

The cron program is started only once, when the system is booted. Individual users shouldn't have permission to run cron directly. Also, as the system administrator, you shouldn't start cron by typing the name of the command; cron should be listed in a shell script as one of the commands to run during a system boot-up sequence.

When started, cron (short for *chronograph*) checks queues for at jobs to run and also checks to see whether users or the root have scheduled jobs by using crontab files. If there's nothing to do, cron "goes to sleep" and becomes inactive; it "wakes up" every minute to check whether there are commands to run. You can see how important and useful this facility is; also, cron uses very few system resources.

Use crontab to install a list of commands that will be executed on a regular schedule. The commands are scheduled to run at a specified time (such as once a month, once an hour, once a day, and so on). The list of commands to be performed on the specified schedule must be included in the crontab file, which is installed with the crontab command. After you install the crontab file, cron reads and executes the listed commands at the specified times. Also with the crontab command, you can view the list of commands included in the file and cancel the list if you want.

Before you install your crontab file with the crontab command, create the file containing the list of commands you want to schedule by using a text editor such as vi or emacs. The crontab command handles the placement of the file. Each user has only one crontab file, created when the crontab command is issued. This file is placed in a directory that's read by the cron command.

Linux stores the user's crontab file in the /usr/spool/cron/crontabs directory and gives that file the user's name. If your user name is mcn and you use a text editor to create a file called mycron and install it by typing **crontab mycron**, the file /usr/spool/cron/crontabs/mcn is created. (In this example, the mcn file is created, or overwritten, with the contents of mycron, which may contain entries that launch one or more commands.)

N O T E For users to use the crontab command, they must be listed in the /etc/cron.d/cron.allow file. If you add a user to the system from the command line (by using the useradd command), he or she isn't added automatically to the /etc/cron.d/cron.allow file. As the root user, you must add the new user to the cron.allow file with a text editor.

Although you can initially create your crontab file with a text editor, after you create your crontab file, modify it by using only the crontab command. Don't try to replace or modify the file that cron examines (that is, the /usr/spool/cron/crontabs/user file) by any other means than by using the crontab command. ■

Each line in the crontab file contains a time pattern and a command. The command is executed at the specified time pattern. The time pattern is divided into five fields separated by spaces or tabs. Any output that usually appears—that is, information that isn't redirected to stdout or stderr—is mailed to the user.

Following is the syntax for the commands you enter in a file to be used by crontab:

minute hour day-of-month month-of-year day-of-week command

The first five fields are time option fields. You must specify all five of these fields. Use an asterisk (*) in a field if you want to ignore that field.

N O T E Technically, an asterisk in a crontab field means "any valid value" rather than "ignore the value"—that is, match anything. The crontab entry 02 00 01 * * date, for example, says to run the date command at two minutes after midnight (zero hour) on the first day of the month. Because the month and day of the week fields are both asterisks, this entry runs on the first day of every month and any day of the week that the first of the month happens to land on. ■

Table 18.4 lists the time-field options available with crontab.

Part

IV

Ch

18

Table 18.4   Time-Field Options for the *crontab* Command

Field	Range
minute	00 through 59
hour	00 through 23 (midnight is 00)
day-of-month	01 through 31
month-of-year	01 through 12
day-of-week	01 through 07 (Monday is 01, Sunday is 07)

You can have as many entries as you want in a crontab file and designate them to run at any time. This means that you can run as many commands as you want in a single crontab file.

To sort a file named /usr/wwr/sales/weekly and mail the output to a user named twool at 7:30 a.m. each Monday, use the following entry in a file:

```
30 07 * * 01 sort /usr/wwr/sales/weekly ¦mail –s"Weekly Sales" twool
```

This command specifies the minute as 30, the hour as 07, any day of the month with the asterisk, any month of the year with another asterisk, and the day-of-week as 01 (which represents Monday).

Notice the pipe between the `sort` and `mail` commands in the preceding example. The command field can contain pipes, semicolons, arrows, or anything else you can enter on a shell command line. At the specified date and time, `cron` runs the entire command field with a standard shell (`bash`).

To specify a sequence of values for one of the first four fields, use commas to separate the values. Suppose that you have a program, `chkquotes`, that accesses a service that provides stock quotes and puts the quotes in a file. To get those quotes at 9 a.m., 11 a.m., 2 p.m., and 4 p.m. on Monday, Tuesday, and Thursday of every week—and definitely on the 10th of March and September—use the following entry:

```
* 09,11,14,16 10 03,09 01,02,04 chkquotes
```

Put the command lines into a file by using `vi` or some other editor that allows you to save files as text files. Assume that you put your commands in a file named cronjobs. To use `crontab` to put the file where `cron` can find it, enter

```
crontab cronjobs
```

Each time you use `crontab` this way, it overwrites any crontab file you may have already launched.

The `crontab` command has three options:

- ■ The `-e` option edits the contents of the current crontab file. (The `-e` option opens your file by using the `ed` editor or whatever editor is assigned to the EDITOR variable in your shell.)

- The -r option removes the current crontab file from the crontabs directory.
- The -l option lists the contents of the current crontab file.

 ▶ **See** "Setting the Shell Environment," **p. 330**

In all these cases, crontab works with the crontab file that has your login name. If your login name is mcn, your crontab file is /usr/spool/cron/crontabs/mcn. The crontab command does this automatically.

The system administrator and users share responsibility for making sure that the system is used appropriately. When you schedule a process, be aware of the impact it may have on the total system. Linux allows you, as the system administrator, to grant access to the at, batch, and cron commands to all users, specific users, or no users (or to deny access to individual users).

TROUBLESHOOTING

The commands I put in my crontab file don't work. The cron command runs your crontab entries by using the Bourne Again shell (bash). Your entries fail if you use shell features not supported by bash. For example, the Public Domain Korn shell (pdksh) allows you to use a tilde (~) to represent a home directory or the alias command to designate aliases for certain commands.

When I try to use the at command, I'm told I don't have permission to use it. You haven't added your login ID to the /etc/cron.d/at.allow file.

I tried to use the at now command to run a command immediately. No matter how fast you type, at now always responds with the message ERROR: Too late. The best alternative is to use the batch command to run the command for you. You can, however, use at now +5 min to run the command in five minutes. After you press <Return>, type quickly to enter your command before the five minutes expire.

Reporting On and Monitoring the Multitasking Environment

You know that Linux is a multiuser, multitasking operating system. Because so many people can do so many things with the system at the same time, users find it useful to determine who's using the system and what processes are running, as well as to monitor processes.

Knowing that others can keep track of the commands you enter is important. Most users can't access your files without your permission, but they can see the names of commands you enter. Also, you (as the system administrator) or someone else who has the root password can peruse all the files on the system.

Although you don't have to be paranoid about privacy on a Linux system, you should know that the system can be monitored by anyone who wants to take the time to do it. The information you can gain about what's going on in the system is more useful than just satisfying curiosity: By seeing what jobs are running, you can appropriately schedule your tasks. You can also see whether a process of yours is still active and whether it's behaving properly.

Finding Out Who's on the System with *who*

The purpose of the who command is to find out who's logged in to the system. The who command lists the login names, terminal lines, and login times of users now logged in.

The who command is useful in many situations. If you want to communicate with someone on the computer by using the write command, for example, you can find out whether that person is on the system by using who. You can also use who to see when certain users are logged in to the computer to keep track of their time spent on the system.

Using *who* to List Users Logged In to the System   To see everyone who's now logged in to the system, enter **who**. You see a display similar to the following:

```
$ who
root        console    Dec 13 08:00
ernie       tty02      Dec 13 10:37
bkraft      tty03      Dec 13 11:02
jdurum      tty05      Dec 13 09:21
ernie       ttys7      Dec 11 18:49
$
```

This listing shows that root, ernie, bkraft, and jdurum are now logged in. It shows that root logged in at 8 a.m., bkraft at 11:02, and jdurum at 9:21. You can also see that ernie is logged in to two terminals and that one login occurred at 6:49 p.m. (18:49) two days earlier (which may be some reason for concern, or it may just be ernie's usual work habits).

Using Headers in User Listings   Several options are available with who, but this chapter describes how to use only two to monitor processes on the system:

-u   Lists only users who are now logged in

-H   Displays headers above each column

With these two options, you can get more information about the users now logged in. The headers displayed with the -H option are NAME, LINE, TIME, IDLE, PID, and COMMENTS. Table 18.5 explains the terms appearing in the heading.

Table 18.5   Output Format for the *who* Command

Field	Description
NAME	Lists the user's login name.
LINE	Lists the line or terminal being used.
TIME	Lists the time the user logged in.

Field	Description
IDLE	Lists the hours and minutes since the last activity on that line. A period is displayed if activity occurred within the last minute of system time. If more than 24 hours elapsed since the line was used, the word old is displayed.
PID	Lists the process ID number of the user's login shell.
COMMENT	Lists the contents of the comment field if comments have been included in /etc/inittab or if there are network connections.

N O T E You probably won't see the COMMENT field filled in very often in any recent Linux systems. In the old days, processes that let you log in to UNIX (getty or uugetty) were started directly from entries in the /etc/inittab file and usually listened for login requests from a particular terminal. The COMMENT field might identify the location of that terminal and could tell you who was logged in and at what terminal they were sitting. Today, processes that listen for login requests are typically handled by the Service Access Facility and are no longer listed in /etc/inittab. ■

The following example uses the –u and –H options and shows the response Linux returns:

Part

IV

Ch

18

```
$ who -uH
NAME      LINE       TIME        IDLE    PID    COMMENT
root      console  Dec 13 08:00    .      10340
ernie     tty02    Dec 13 10:37    .      11929  Tech-89.2
bkraft    tty03    Dec 13 11:02   0:04     4761  Sales-23.4
jdurum    tty05    Dec 13 09:21   1:07    10426
ernie     ttys7    Dec 11 18:49   old     10770  oreo.coolt.com
$
```

You can infer from this listing that the last session associated with ernie is from a network site named oreo.coolt.com and that there hasn't been any activity in that session in more than 24 hours (which might signal a problem). The session for root and the first one for ernie have both been accessed within the last minute. The last activity on the session for bkraft was four minutes ago; it has been one hour and seven minutes since any activity was reported on the session for jdurum.

Also note that this listing includes the PID (process ID number) for the login shell of each user's session. The next section shows how you can use the PID to further monitor the system.

Reporting on the Status of Processes with *ps*

The ps command reports on the status of processes. You can use it to determine which processes are running, whether a process has completed, whether a process is hung or having some difficulty, how long a process has run, the resources a process is using, the relative priority of a process, and the PID (process ID number) needed before you can kill a process. All this information is useful to a user and very useful to a system administrator. Without any options, ps lists the PID of each process associated with your current shell. It's also possible to see a detailed listing of all the processes running on a system.

Monitoring Processes with *ps*   A common use of the ps command is to monitor background jobs and other processes on the system. Because background processes don't communicate with your screen and keyboard in most cases, you use ps to track their progress.

The ps listing displays four default headings as indicators of the information in the fields below each heading: PID, TTY, TIME, and COMMAND. Table 18.6 explains these headings.

Table 18.6   Headings in the Output of *ps*

Field	Explanation
PID	The process identification number
TTY	The terminal that the process originated on
TIME	The cumulative execution time for the process, in minutes and seconds
COMMAND	The name of the command being executed

Suppose that you want to sort a file named sales.dat, save a copy of the sorted file in a file named sales.srt, and mail the sorted file to the user sarah. If you also want to put this job in the background, enter

```
sort sales.dat ¦ tee sales.srt ¦ mailx -s"Sorted Sales Data" sarah &
```

To monitor this process, enter **ps** and see a display such as this one:

```
PID    TTY     TIME COMMAND
16490 tty02    0:15 sort
16489 tty02    0:00 mailx
16492 tty02    0:00 ps
16478 tty02    0:00 bash
16491 tty02    0:06 tee
16480 tty02   96:45 cruncher
```

You see the accumulated time and PID for each process started with the command. You also see information for your login shell (bash) and for ps itself. Notice that all the commands in the pipe are running at once, just as you would expect (this is the way the piping process works). The last entry is for a command that has been running for more than an hour and a half. If that's a problem, you may want to terminate the process by using the kill command (described later in this chapter). If you enter **ps** and see only the following listing, you know the previous job you put into the background is complete:

```
PID    TTY     TIME COMMAND
16492 tty02    0:00 ps
16478 tty02    0:00 bash
16480 tty02   99:45 cruncher
```

N O T E Use ps occasionally to check the status of a command. If, however, you use ps every
second while waiting to see whether the background job is complete, putting the job in the
background doesn't make much sense in the first place. ■

Obtaining More Information About Processes with _ps_   Sometimes, you need to know more
about your processes than what the default ps listing provides. To generate additional information, you can invoke some of the flags listed in Table 18.7.

Table 18.7   Commonly Used Flags for the _ps_ Command

Option	Action
-a	Shows processes of other users also.
-c	Command name from `task_struct` environment.
-e	Shows environment after command line and ` and '.
-f	Shows "forest" family tree format (processes and subprocesses).
-h	No header.
-j	Jobs format.
-l	Long format.
-m	Displays memory info.
-n	Numeric output for USER and WCHAN. WCHAN is the name of the kernel function where the process is sleeping, with the `sys_` stripped from the function name. If /etc/psdatabase doesn't exist, the number is hexadecimal instead.
-r	Running processes only.
-s	Signal format.
-S	Adds child CPU time and page faults.
-t_xx_	Processes associated with tty_xx_ only.
-u	User format; gives user name and start time.
-v	vm (virtual memory) format.
-w	Wide output; doesn't truncate command lines to fit on one line.
-x	Shows processes without controlling terminal.

Part
IV

Ch
18

The ps command gives only an approximate picture of process status because things can and
do change while the ps command is running. The ps command gives a snapshot of the process
status at the instant ps executed. The snapshot includes the ps command itself.

In the following examples, three commands are shown. The first command is the login shell (bash). The second command is `sort`, used to sort the file named inventory. The third command is the `ps` command you're now running.

To find out what processes you're now running, use the following command:

```
$ ps
PID    TTY     TIME      COMMAND
65     tty01   0:07      -bash
71     tty01   0:14      sort inventory
231    tty01   0:09      ps
```

To obtain a full listing, use the following command:

```
$ ps -uax
UID      PID    PPID   C    STIME      TTY     TIME    COMD
amanda   65     1      0    11:40:11   tty01   0:06    -bash
amanda   71     65     61   11:42:01   tty01   0:14    sort inventory
amanda   231    65     80   11:46:02   tty01   0:00    ps -f
```

Notice a few things about this full listing. In addition to the PID, the PPID is listed. The PPID is the process ID number of that process's parent process. In this example, the first process listed, PID 65, is the parent of the following two. The entry in the fourth column (the column headed C) gives the amount of CPU time a process has used recently. In selecting the next process to work with, the operating system chooses a process with a low C value over one with a higher value. The entry in the STIME column is the time at which the process started.

To monitor every process on the system and get a full listing, enter **ps -uax**. By piping the command through the `grep $LOGNAME` command, the processes belonging to your login name are displayed while all others are filtered out. To see a full listing of all your processes, enter

ps -uax ¦ grep $LOGNAME

To list processes for two terminals (for example, tty1 and tty2), use the following command:

```
$ ps -t "1 2"
PID    TTY     TIME      COMMAND
32     tty01   0:05      bash
36     tty02   0:09      bash
235    tty02   0:16      vi calendar
```

In this example, the `-t` option is used to restrict the listing to the processes associated with terminals tty01 and tty02. Terminal tty2 is running the shell command (PID 32) and using `vi` to edit the calendar (PID 235). The cumulative time for each process is also listed. If you're using shells from a graphical interface (the `xterm` command), use device names pts001, pts002, and so on with the `-t` option to see the processes from those sessions.

Sometimes a process is marked as `<defunct>`, which means that the process has terminated and its parent process has been notified, but the parent hasn't acknowledged that the process is "dead." A process like that is called a *zombie process*. It's possible that the parent is busy with something else and the zombie will soon disappear. If you see a number of defunct processes or ones that linger for some time, this is a sign of some difficulty with the operating system.

N O T E Because a zombie process has no parent, you can't kill the zombie. The only way to get rid of a zombie process is to reboot your machine. ▣

Controlling Multiple Processes

Linux gives you the power to run several processes concurrently. It also allows a user or an administrator to have control over running processes. This control is advantageous when you need to do the following:

- ▣ Initiate a process that continues after its parent quits running (use the `nohup` command)
- ▣ Schedule a process with a priority different than other processes (use the `nice` command)
- ▣ Terminate or stop a process (use the `kill` command)

Using *nohup* with Background Processes

Normally, the children of a process terminate when the parent dies or terminates. This means that when you start a background process, it terminates when you log out. To have a process continue after you log out, use the `nohup` command. Put `nohup` at the beginning of a command line:

```
nohup sort sales.dat &
```

This sample command tells the `sort` command to ignore the fact that you log out of the system; it should run until the process completes. In this way, you can initiate a process that can run for days or even weeks. What's more, you don't have to be logged in as it runs. Naturally, you want to make sure that the job you initiate behaves nicely—that is, it eventually terminates and doesn't create an excessive amount of output.

When you use `nohup`, the command sends all the output and error messages of a command that normally appear on-screen to a file named nohup.out. Consider the following example:

```
$ nohup sort sales.dat &
1252
Sending output to nohup.out
$
```

The sorted file and any error messages are placed in the file nohup.out. Now consider this example:

```
$ nohup sort sales.dat > sales.srt &
1257
Sending output to nohup.out
$
```

Any error messages are placed in the nohup.out file, but the sorted sales.dat file is placed in sales.srt.

Part

IV

Ch

18

NOTE When you use nohup with a pipeline, you must use nohup with each command in the pipeline:

```
nohup sort sales.dat ¦ nohup mailx -s"Sorted Sales Data" boss & ■
```

Scheduling the Priority of Commands with *nice*

Use the nice command to run a command at a specific scheduling priority. The nice command gives you some control over the priority of one job over another. If you don't use nice, processes run at a set priority. You can lower the priority of a process with the nice command so that other processes can be scheduled to use the CPU more frequently than the nice job. The superuser (the person who can log in as the root user) can also raise the priority of a process.

NOTE nice --help and nice --version don't work in the GNU implementation of nice. ■

The general form of the nice command is as follows:

```
nice -number command
```

The priority level is determined by the *number* argument (a higher number means a lower priority). The default is set to 10, and *number* is an offset to the default. If the *number* argument is present, the priority is incremented by that amount up to a limit of 20. If you enter the following command, the sort process starts with a priority of 10:

```
sort sales.dat > sales.srt &
```

If you want to start another process—say, with the lp command—but give preference to the sort command, you can enter

```
nice -5 lp mail_list &
```

To give the lp command the lowest possible priority, enter

```
nice -10 lp mail_list &
```

NOTE The number flag above is preceded by the flag specifier -, which you shouldn't confuse with the negative number sign. ■

Only superusers can increase the priority of a process. To do that, they use a negative number as the argument to nice. Remember—the lower the nice value, the higher the priority (up to a maximum priority of 20). To give a job "top priority," a super user initiates the job as follows:

```
nice --10 job &
```

The ampersand (&) is optional; if job is interactive, you wouldn't use the ampersand to place the process in the background.

Scheduling the Priority of Running Processes with *renice*

The renice command, available on some systems, allows you to modify the priority of a running process. Berkeley UNIX systems have the renice command; it's also available in the

/usr/ucb directory in Linux System V systems for compatibility with Berkeley systems. With renice, you can adjust priorities on commands as they execute. The format of renice is similar to that of nice:

renice *-number PID*

To change the priority on a running process, you must know its PID. To find the PID of all your processes, enter

ps -e ¦ grep *name*

In this command, *name* is replaced by the name of the running process. The grep command filters out all processes that don't contain the name of the process you're looking for. If several processes of that name are running, you have to determine the one you want by looking at the time it started. If you want to affect all processes belonging to a certain group or a certain user, you can specify the GID or UID of the running processes to the renice command.

The entry in the second column of the ps listing is the PID of the process. In the following example, three processes are running for the current user (in addition to the shell). The current user's name is pcoco.

```
$ ps -ef ¦ grep $LOGNAME
 pcoco 11805 11804  0  Dec 22   ttysb     0:01 sort sales.dat>sales.srt
 pcoco 19955 19938  4  16:13:02 ttyp0    0:00 grep pcoco
 pcoco 19938     1  0  16:11:04 ttyp0    0:00 bash
 pcoco 19940 19938 142 16:11:04 ttyp0    0:33 find . -name core -exec rm {};
$
```

To lower the priority on the process with PID 19940 (the find process), enter

renice -5 19940

As you would expect, the following are true about renice:

- You can use renice only with processes you own.
- The superuser can use renice on any process.
- Only the superuser can increase the priority of a process.

Terminating Processes with *kill*

Sometimes, you want or need to terminate a process. The following are some reasons for stopping a process:

- It's using too much CPU time.
- It's running too long without producing the expected output.
- It's producing too much output to the screen or to a disk file.
- It appears to have locked a terminal or some other session.
- It's using the wrong files for input or output because of an operator or programming error.
- It's no longer useful.

Part IV
Ch 18

Most likely, you'll come across a number of other reasons to kill a process as well. If the process to be stopped is a background process, use the `kill` command to get out of these situations.

To stop a command that isn't in the background, press <Ctrl-c>. When a command is in the background, however, pressing an interrupt key doesn't stop it. Because a background process isn't under terminal control, keyboard input of any interrupt key is ignored. The only way you can stop background commands is to use the `kill` command.

Normal Termination of Background Processes   The `kill` command sends signals to the program to demand that a process be terminated or killed. To use `kill`, use either of these two forms:

```
kill PID(s)
```

```
kill -signal PID(s)
```

To kill a process whose PID is 123, enter **kill 123**. To kill several processes whose PIDs are 123, 342, and 73, enter **kill 123 342 73**.

By using the `-signal` option, you can do more than simply kill a process. Other signals can cause a running process to reread configuration files or stop a process without killing it. Valid signals are listed by the command `kill -l`. An average user, however, will probably use `kill` with no signal or, at most, with the `-9` signal (the I-mean-it-so-don't-ignore-me signal, described in the next section).

> **CAUTION**
>
> Use the correct PID with the `kill` command. Using the wrong PID can stop a process you want to keep running. Remember that killing the wrong process or a system process can have disastrous effects. Also remember that if you're logged in as the system administrator, you can kill *any* process.

If you successfully kill the process, you get no notice from the shell; the shell prompt simply reappears. You see an error message if you try to kill a process you don't have permission to kill or if you try to kill a process that doesn't exist.

Suppose that your login name is chris and that you're now logged in to tty01. To see the processes you have running, enter **ps -f** and see the following response:

```
UID     PID   PPID  C   STIME     TTY     TIME    COMMAND
chris   65    1     0   11:40:11  tty01   0:06    -bash
chris   71    65    61  11:42:01  tty01   0:14    total_updt
chris   231   65    80  11:46:02  tty01   0:00    ps -f
chris   187   53    60  15:32:01  tty02   123:45  crunch stats
chris   53    1     0   15:31:34  tty02   1:06    -bash
```

Notice that the program `total_updt` is running at your current terminal. Another program, `crunch`, is running on another terminal, and you think it has used an unusually large amount of

CPU time. To kill that process, it may be sufficient to enter **kill 187**. To kill the parent of that process, enter **kill 53**.

You may want to kill a parent and its child if you logged in as the system administrator and see that someone left their terminal unattended (if you've set up Linux with remote terminals). You can kill a clock process that the user has running (the child process) and the login shell (the parent process) so that the unattended terminal is no longer logged in.

Stopping the parent of a process sometimes terminates the child process as well. To be sure, stop the parent and its children to halt all activity associated with a parent process. In the preceding example, enter **kill 187 53** to terminate both processes.

 T I P If your terminal locks up, log in to another virtual terminal with <Alt-*function-key*> (F1-F6), enter **ps -ef ¦ grep $LOGNAME**, and kill the login shell for the locked terminal.

Unconditional Termination of Background Processes   Issuing the kill command sends a signal to a process. Linux programs can send or receive more than 20 signals, each of which is represented by a number. For example, when you log out, Linux sends the hang-up signal (signal number 1) to all the background processes started from your login shell. This signal kills or stops those processes unless they were started with nohup (as described earlier in this chapter).

Using nohup to start a background process lets the process ignore the signal that tries to stop it. You may be using programs or shell scripts written to ignore some signals. If you don't specify a signal when you use kill, signal 15 is sent to the process. The command kill 1234 sends signal 15 to the process whose PID is 1234. If that process is set to ignore signal 15, however, the process doesn't terminate when you use this command. You can use kill in a way that a process "can't refuse," however.

The signal 9 is an unconditional kill signal; it always kills a process. To unconditionally kill a process, use the following format:

```
kill -9 PID
```

Suppose that you enter **ps -f** and see the following response:

```
UID     PID   PPID  C   STIME      TTY     TIME    COMMAND
chris   65    1     0   11:40:11   tty01   0:06    -bash
chris   71    65    61  11:42:01   tty01   0:14    total_updt inventory
chris   231   65    80  11:46:02   tty01   0:00    ps -f
chris   187   53    60  15:32:01   tty02   123:45  crunch stats
chris   53    1     0   15:31:34   tty02   1:06    -bash
```

To kill process 187, normally you enter **kill 187**. If you then enter **ps -f** again and see that the process is still there, you know the process is set up to ignore the kill command. Kill it unconditionally with kill -9 187. When you enter **ps -f** again, you see that the process is no longer around.

Part
IV

Ch
18

> **CAUTION**
>
> A disadvantage to using this unconditional version of the `kill` command is that `kill -9` doesn't allow a process to finish what it's doing before it terminates the process. If you use `kill -9` with a program that's updating a file, you could lose the updated material or the entire file.
>
> Use the powerful `kill -9` command responsibly. In most cases, you don't need the `-9` option; the `kill` command issued without arguments stops most processes.

Termination of All Background Processes   To kill all background jobs, enter `kill 0`. Commands that run in the background sometimes initiate more than one process; tracking down all the PID numbers associated with the process you want to kill can be tedious. Because `kill 0` terminates all processes started by the current shell, it's a faster and less tedious way to terminate processes. Enter the `jobs` command to see what commands are running in the background for the current shell.

From Here...

This chapter presented the commands you need to manage multiple processes. You saw that you run multiple processes whenever you put jobs in the background with the ampersand (&) or when you use pipes. You can schedule jobs at a specific time with the `at` command, at a time the system feels is appropriate with the `batch` command, and at regularly scheduled times with `cron` and `crontab`. For more information, see

■ The chapters in Part II, "Systems Administration," discuss how to monitor and maintain your Linux system. Systems administration isn't an easy topic to learn, and in fact requires a hands-on learning approach. This part of the book provides you with a basic understanding of the concepts and the tasks required of a systems administrator (often called a *sys admin*).

■ Chapter 17, "Understanding Linux Shells," provides the shell-specific information to program scripts to start, stop, and monitor processes on your Linux system.

See also the man pages for the various commands discussed in this chapter.

## CHAPTER 19

Using the *vi* Editor

Earlier chapters have shown you how convenient and advantageous it is to have sequences of commands or shell programs stored in a file. You probably have to create data, e-mail, lists, memos, notes, reports, and so on; you use some type of text editor to do these tasks. You may have several editors or word processors available on your Linux system to help you with those tasks. To put commands or shell programs in a file, however, you need an editor that can save your work in a text file—a file in ASCII format. Linux comes with a standard text editor called vi, which you can use for all but the most complex writing and editing projects.

Your Linux system also has other text editors: a graphical editor for use under the XFree86 system and two standard, non-graphical text editors called ed and ex. They're both line-oriented editors—that is, you work with only one line at a time. Another editor, called emacs, is also supplied with most Linux distributions. vi and emacs are full-screen editors; when you use them, you see a screen's worth of information, so you can make changes or additions in context. This chapter doesn't discuss ed or ex very much because you'll find vi easier to use and available on every UNIX machine, including Linux.

The basic *vi* commands

To use an editor, you must know how to position the cursor, insert and remove characters, and save your work.

How to create new files and modify existing files

Creating and modifying files is the bread and butter of all editors.

Understand *vi*'s two modes

Unlike other editors you may encounter, vi has two distinct modes: command mode, which allows you to enter commands to the editor, and input mode, which lets you enter text.

How to perform basic word processing functions

Simply entering text does not an editor make. This chapter shows you how to use vi as a general-purpose word processor. You learn how to search and replace text throughout a document, cut and paste, and edit multiple documents at once.

How to set the *vi* environment

Everyone has different preferences for how they want their editor to behave. vi lets you customize its behavior to suit your needs.

▶ **See** "Using *emacs*," **p. 417**

N O T E The vi, ex, and ed editors that ship with the Slackware distribution are actually other names for an editor called elvis. The names vi, ex, and ed are symbolically linked to elvis, so when you type **vi**, you're actually running elvis. The Red Hat distribution of vi is actually a program called vim (for VI iMproved). ■

Introducing *vi*

To understand vi (pronounced *vee eye*), you need to understand some of vi's history within the UNIX world. And although today's systems (including Linux) have much more user-friendly and robust editors, you should learn how to use vi because every UNIX (and, thus, Linux) system has a copy of vi available. Sometimes vi is the only editor available at a crucial moment; as a result, you need to know some of its basic operations.

UNIX was developed in an environment in which the user's terminal was a teletype or some other slow, hard-copy terminal; video display monitors generally weren't used. A natural editor for that environment was a line-oriented editor—one that the user sees and works on one line of text at a time. Two line-oriented editors are on UNIX systems today: ed and ex.

In its early days, UNIX was made available to universities essentially free of charge. Students and faculty at several universities made many contributions to the UNIX working environment. Several notable improvements came out of the University of California at Berkeley, including a full-screen editor—one that lets you work with a screen of information at once rather than a single line of text. That full-screen editor is called vi, which stands for *visual*. The time was right for the transition to screen-oriented work. Users were working with video terminals rather than hard-copy devices.

T I P You don't have to become an expert to use vi. Simply type **man vi** at the command prompt for help. If you're using Red Hat's version of Linux, you also can ask for help by pressing <Esc> and then entering **:help**.

N O T E This chapter doesn't cover all of vi's features; that requires more space than is available. (In fact, entire books are written just on vi.) Instead, you learn the commands to do the most necessary editing tasks. If you want to know about the more advanced features of vi and advanced text-editing operations, consult the man pages supplied with Linux. ■

What Is *vi*?

Because it's part of the standard UNIX environment, vi has been learned and used (to one degree or another) by millions of UNIX users. You find that it starts quickly and can be used for simple and complex tasks. As you would expect, you use it to enter, modify, or delete text; search or replace text; and copy, cut, and paste blocks of text. You also see that it can be customized to match your needs. You can move the cursor to any position on-screen and move through the file you're editing. You use the same methods with any text file, regardless of its contents.

The *vi* editor isn't a word processor or desktop publishing system. There are no menus and virtually no help facilities.

N O T E The original version of *vi* doesn't have a help facility. However, newer versions of *vi*, such as elvis for Slackware 96 distributions and vim for the Red Rat distribution, provide some online help. ■

Word-processing systems usually offer screen and hard-copy formatting and printing such as representing text as **bold**, *italic*, or underlined, but *vi* doesn't. Other Linux commands can perform some of these functions—for example, lp can print and nroff can format text. Some text-processing programs, such as TeX (pronounced tek) and LaTeX, can process embedded commands into text, such as bold and underlined attributes.

The *vi* editor operates in two modes:

- In command mode, your keystrokes are interpreted as commands to *vi*. Some of the commands allow you to save a file, exit *vi*, move the cursor to different positions in a file, and modify, rearrange, delete, substitute, and search for text.
- In input or text-entry mode, your keystrokes are accepted as the text of the file you're editing. When *vi* is in input or text-entry mode, the editor acts as a typewriter.

In an editing session, you can freely switch between modes. You have to remember the mode you're using and know to change modes. Some people find this uncomfortable at first; there's a learning curve you must deal with. Later in this chapter, you learn about the showmode option, which tells you *vi*'s current mode. With a little practice, however, you'll find *vi* extremely convenient for editing Linux ASCII files, especially configuration files and shell scripts.

Understanding the Editing Process

You edit text by creating new text or by modifying existing text. When you create new text, you place the text in a file with an ordinary Linux file name. When you modify existing text, you use the existing file name to call a copy of the file into the editing session. In either case, as you use the editor, the text is held in the system's memory in a storage area called a *buffer*. Using a buffer prevents you from directly changing the contents of a file until you decide to save the buffer. This is to your benefit if you decide you want to forget the changes you've made and start over.

As you make changes and additions to the text, these edits affect the text in the buffer not in the file stored on disk. When you're satisfied with your edits, you issue a command to save the text. This command writes the changes to the file on the disk. Only then are the changes made permanent. You can save changes to disk as often as you like (it's usually a good idea to save any file you're editing frequently in case of lockups or power loss). You don't have to exit the editor when you save changes. This chapter shows you several ways to exit the editor; some of those ways write the buffer to the text file on the disk.

The *vi* editor is said to be *interactive* because it interacts with you during the editing session. The editor communicates with you by displaying status messages, error messages, or sometimes nothing on-screen (in typical Linux fashion). The last line on-screen, called the *status line*, holds the messages from Linux. You see the changes you make in the text on-screen.

You use the editor to modify, rearrange, delete, substitute, and search for text. You conduct these editing operations while using the editor in command mode. In several instances, a command is a single letter that corresponds to the first letter of an action's name. For example, i corresponds to the insert action, and r is used when replacing a character.

Most commands operate on a single line or range of lines of text. The lines are numbered from 1 (the top line) to the last line in the buffer. When you add or delete lines, the line numbers adjust automatically. A line's number is its address in the buffer. An address range is simply two addresses or line numbers separated by a comma. If you want to specify the range consisting of the third through the eighth line of the buffer, you use 3,8.

The position of the cursor always indicates your current location in the editing buffer. Some of the commands you issue in command mode affect the character at the cursor position. Unless you move the cursor, changes take place at that position. Naturally, vi has several commands for moving the cursor through the edit buffer.

You know now that vi is a full-screen editor. You give vi commands to move the cursor to different positions in a file, and you see the changes you make as you make them. So vi has to be able to move to and modify the text on your terminal as well as on a host of other terminal types. It knows what terminal you're using and what its video capabilities are by checking the shell variable TERM. Linux uses the TERM variable to determine your terminal's capabilities, such as underlining, reverse video, the screen-clearing method, function-key assignment, and color capability.

TROUBLESHOOTING

My vi editor doesn't appear to be working correctly with my terminal or screen; I see "strange" characters. The TERM variable may not be set correctly. Another symptom of an improper terminal setup is that blocks of characters overwrite legible text. The $TERM expression gives the value of your current terminal setting. To check the value of TERM, enter **echo $TERM**. If you work at a terminal that is—or emulates—a vt100, this command displays the following result (type the command on the terminal, not while in the vi editor):

vt100

If the proper terminal type isn't echoed back, set the value of TERM by entering the following command, if you're using the bash shell:

TERM=vt100

export TERM

If you're using the C shell, enter the following (the spaces around the = sign are important):

setenv TERM = vt100

export TERM

Your specific terminal type may be different from vt100; set TERM accordingly.

▶ **See** "Setting the Shell Environment," **p. 330**

I start vi but don't get the expected responses. Check to see whether your terminal is properly set up. Your terminal type isn't the same as the name of your terminal; your terminal type must match one of the terminal types contained in the directory /usr/lib/terminfo.

Using *vi*

To start vi, simply type its name at the shell prompt (command line). If you know the name of the file you want to create or edit, you can issue the vi command with the file name as an argument. For example, to create the file myfile with vi, enter **vi myfile**.

When vi becomes active, the terminal screen clears and a tilde character (~) appears on the left side of every screen line, except for the first. The ~ is the empty-buffer line flag. The following is a shortened version of what you should see on your screen (only five lines are listed to save space):

```
~
~
~
~
```

The cursor is at the leftmost position of the first line (represented here as an underscore character). You'll probably see 20 to 22 of the tilde characters at the left of the screen. If that's not the case, check the value of TERM (as described in the preceding troubleshooting section) and perhaps talk with your system administrator.

When you see this display, you've successfully started vi; vi is in command mode, waiting for your first command.

N O T E Unlike most word processors, vi starts in command mode. Before you start entering text, you must switch to input mode with the <a> or <i> keys, both of which are described in the next section. ■

Looking at *vi*'s Two Modes

As mentioned earlier, the vi editor operates in two modes: command mode and input mode. In command mode, vi interprets your keystrokes as commands; there are many vi commands. You can use commands to save a file, exit vi, move the cursor to various positions in a file, or modify, rearrange, delete, substitute, or search for text. You can even pass a command to the shell. If you enter a character as a command but the character isn't a command, vi beeps. Don't worry; the beep is an audible indication for you to check what you're doing and correct any errors.

You can enter text in input mode (also called *text-entry mode*) by appending characters after the cursor or inserting before the cursor. At the beginning of the line, this doesn't make much difference. To go from command mode to input mode, press one of the following keys:

<a>   To append text after the cursor

<i>   To insert text in front of the cursor

Use input mode only for entering text. Most word processors start in input mode, but vi doesn't. When you use a word processing program, you can type away, entering text; to issue a command, you have to use function keys or keys different than those you use when typing normal text. vi doesn't work that way: You must go into input mode by pressing <a> or <i> before you start entering text, and then explicitly press <Esc> to return to command mode.

Creating Your First *vi* File

The best way to learn about vi is to use it. This section gives a step-by-step example of how to create a file by using vi. In each step, you see an action to perform and then the necessary keystrokes. Don't be concerned with complete accuracy here. The example takes you through the motions and concepts of using vi to create a file, moving between command and input modes, and saving your results. If you run into difficulties, you can quit and start over by pressing <Esc>; then enter :q!.

1. Start vi by entering **vi**. You see the screen full of flush-left tildes.

2. Go into input mode to place characters on the first line. Press the <a> key; don't press <Return>. Now you can append characters to the first line. You shouldn't see the character a on-screen.

3. Add lines of text to the buffer by typing

   ```
   Things to do today.
   a. Practice vi.
   b. Sort sales data and print the results.
   ```

   You can use the <Backspace> key to correct mistakes on the line you're typing. Don't worry about being precise here: this example is for practice. You learn other ways to make changes in some of the later sections of this chapter.

4. Go from input mode to command mode by pressing <Esc>. You hear a beep from your system if you press <Esc> when you're already in command mode.

5. Save your buffer in a file called vipract.1 by entering **:w vipract.1**. The characters :w vipract.1 appear on the bottom line of the screen (the status line). The characters shouldn't appear in the text. The :w command writes the buffer to the specified file. This command saves or writes the buffer to the file vipract.1.

6. Look at your action confirmed on the status line. You should see the following on the status line:

   ```
   "vipract.1" [New File] 3 lines, 78 characters
   ```

   This statement confirms that the file vipract.1 has been created, is a new file, and contains 3 lines and 78 characters. Your display may be different if you didn't type the information exactly as specified.

7. Exit vi by entering **:q**.

When you type **:q**, you're still in command mode and see these characters on the status line. When you press <Return>, however, vi terminates and you return to the login shell prompt.

You use these steps, or variations of them, for all your editing tasks. Make sure that you can work through them before continuing.

Things to Remember about *vi*

- vi starts in command mode.
- To move from command mode to input mode, press <a> (to append text) or <i> (to insert text), respectively.
- You add text when you're in input mode.
- You give commands to vi only when you're in command mode.
- You give commands to vi to save a file and can quit only when you're in command mode.
- To move from input mode to command mode, press <Esc>.

Starting *vi* by Using an Existing File

To edit or look at a file that already exists in your current directory, type **vi** followed by the file name. Try this with the file you created in the preceding section by entering

```
vi vipract.1
```

You see the following display (the number of lines shown here are fewer than you see on-screen):

```
Things to do today.
a. Practice vi.
b. Sort sales data and print the results.
~
~
~
"vipract.1" 3 lines, 78 characters
```

As before, tilde characters appear on the far left of empty lines in the buffer. Look at the status line: It contains the name of the file you're editing and the number of lines and characters.

TROUBLESHOOTING

I type a file name that I know exists, but vi acts as though I'm creating a new file. No one is a perfect typist; you may have typed the name of a file that doesn't exist in your current directory. Suppose that you type **vi vipract.1**, but there's no file named vipract.1 in your current directory. You still start vi, but vi acts as though you were creating a new file.

continues

Part
IV

Ch
19

continued

I try to edit a file, but `vi` displays a message about read permission denied and I see the shell prompt again. You've tried to edit a file you aren't permitted to read. Also, you can't edit a directory—that is, if you type `vi directory_name`, where *directory_name* is the name of a directory, `vi` informs you that you opened a directory and doesn't let you edit it. If you try to use `vi` with a file that's an executable program in binary, as opposed to ASCII, you'll see a screen full of strange (control) characters. It won't be something you can read and edit. `vi` expects files to be stored as lines.

I open a file in `vi`, but I see a message that the line is too long. You're trying to use `vi` on a data file that's just one long string of bytes. You can modify this file, but doing so will probably corrupt the data file.

I open a file in `vi`, but I'm seeing some very strange characters on-screen. You may be using `vi` with a file produced by a word processor.

In all these cases, exit `vi` to return to your login shell prompt by pressing <Esc> to go to command mode and then typing `:q!`. Using `:q!` ensures that you quit `vi` and make no changes to the existing file.

Exiting *vi*

You can exit or quit `vi` in several ways. Table 19.1 lists the commands you can use to exit `vi`.

N O T E   Remember that you must be in command mode to quit `vi`. To change to command mode, press <Esc>. (If you're already in command mode when you press <Esc>, you hear a harmless beep from the terminal.) ■

Table 19.1   Ways to Quit or Exit *vi*

Command	Action
`:q`	Exits after making no changes to the buffer, or exits after the buffer is modified and saved to a file
`:q!`	Exits and abandons all changes to the buffer since it was last saved to a file
`:wq`, `:x`, or ZZ	Writes the buffer to the working file and then exits

As shown in Table 19.1, several keystrokes accomplish the same end. To practice, use `vi` to edit the file vipract.1 created earlier in this chapter. To edit the file, enter **vi vipract.1**. You see a display similar to

```
Things to do today.
a. Practice vi.
b. Sort sales data and print the results.
```

```
~
~
~
"vipract.1" 3 lines, 78 characters
```

The cursor is indicated by an underscore character; when you first open the file, it's under the first character of the file, the T in Things. Because you haven't made any changes to the file since you opened it, you can exit by entering **:q**. You see the shell prompt. You can also type **:wq** to exit the file; if you do so, you see the following message before the shell prompt appears:

```
"vipract.1" 3 lines, 78 characters
```

This message appears because *vi* first writes the buffer to the file vipract.1 and then exits.

Start *vi* again with the same file (type **vi vipract.1**). You see a display similar to

```
Things to do today.
a. Practice vi.
b. Sort sales data and print the results.
~
~
~
"vipract.1" 3 lines, 78 characters
```

Although *vi* starts in command mode, just to be sure, press <Esc>. Now press the space bar enough times so that the cursor moves under the period following today in the first line. To replace that character with an exclamation mark, press <r> (for replace) and type **!**. The first line now looks like

```
Things to do today!
```

Because you've changed the buffer, *vi* won't let you exit unless you save the changes or explicitly give a command to quit without saving the changes. If you try to exit *vi* by typing **:q**, *vi* displays the following message to remind you that you haven't written the file to disk since you changed it:

```
No write since last change (:quit! overrides)
```

To abandon the changes you've made to the file, quit by typing **:q!**. To save the changes, quit by typing **:wq** or any other equivalent form (**ZZ** or **:x**).

Part

IV

Ch

19

> **N O T E**   *vi* doesn't keep backup copies of files. After you enter **:wq**, the original file is modified and can't be restored to its original state. You must make your own backup copies of *vi* files. ∎

▶ **See** "Performing Backups and Restoring Files," **p. 230**

CAUTION

Use the **:q!** command sparingly. When you enter **:q!**, all the changes you've made to the file are lost.

Rather than issue a **:q!** command, it's often safer to save the file to a different file name. That subject is covered later in the section "Saving as a New File."

Undoing a Command

In vi, you can "undo" your most recent action or change to the buffer as long as you haven't saved that change to the disk file. You do this in command mode. Suppose that you've inadvertently deleted a line of text, changed something you shouldn't have, or added some text incorrectly. Press <Esc> to change to command mode and then press <u>; things are back the way they were before the buffer was changed.

N O T E The undo command can undo only the latest action. Also, you can't use the undo command to undo changes that have been written to a file. ■

The following is an example of using the undo command. Start vi again with the file vipract.1 (enter **vi vipract.1**). You see a display similar to

```
Things to do today!
a. Practice vi.
b. Sort sales data and print the results.
~
~
~

"vipract.1" 3 lines, 78 characters
```

To add the phrase *for 60 minutes* between vi and the period on the second line, move to the second line by pressing <Return>. The cursor now appears under the first character of the second line. Now move the cursor to the period after vi by pressing the space bar until the cursor moves to that location. Insert the phrase *for 60 minutes* by pressing <i> to give the input command and then typing the characters of the phrase. Press <Esc> to return to command mode. Your screen now looks like

```
Things to do today!
a. Practice vi for 60 minutes.
b. Sort sales data and print the results.
~
~
~
```

Is 60 minutes a good idea? Maybe not. To undo the change to the second line, make sure that you're in command mode (press <Esc>) and then press <u>. The second line of the file now looks like

```
a. Practice vi.
```

Then again, maybe it was a good idea to practice for 60 minutes. Press <u> again (you're already in command mode) and you see the phrase *for 60 minutes* reappear. Will you or won't you practice for that long? You decide. Use the undo command to undo the change (and undo the undo) as many times as you want. Even if you decide to leave the buffer in its original form, vi assumes that the buffer has changed and you must exit with :q! (abandon changes) or :wq (save the changes).

If you decide to save the file with the changes, save it to another file by entering **:w vipract.2**.

TIP You can use the <Backspace> key to correct mistakes you make while typing a single line. Unfortunately, as you backspace, you erase all the characters you go back over. The left-arrow key (<←>) doesn't erase characters. The arrow keys are covered later in this chapter.

Writing Files and Saving the Buffer

You've seen how to write the buffer to a file and quit *vi*. Sometimes, however, you want to save the buffer to a file without quitting *vi*. You should save your file regularly during an editing session. If the system goes down because of a crash or a power failure, you may lose your work if you haven't saved it recently. To save the buffer, issue the :w (write) command from command mode.

N O T E Before you issue the write command, first press <Esc> to make sure that you're in command mode, if you aren't already there. If you're already in command mode, you hear a harmless beep. ∎

There are some variations to the steps you follow to save a file. The form of the write command you use depends on the case, of which there are four distinct ones. The following sections describe these cases; Table 19.2 lists the variations of the write command.

Table 19.2   Commands to Save or Write a File

Command	Action
:w	Writes buffer to the file *vi* is editing
:w *filename*	Writes buffer to the named file
:w! *filename*	Forces *vi* to overwrite an existing file

Saving a New File   If you started *vi* without specifying a file name, you must provide a file name if you want to save the file to disk. The write command you issue in this case has this format:

```
:w filename
```

This command writes the buffer to the file *filename*. If the command is successful, you see the name of the file and the number of lines and characters in the file. If you specify the name of an existing file, an appropriate message appears on the status line:

```
File exits - use "w! filename" to overwrite.
```

This condition is described in later in the section "Overwriting an Existing File."

Saving to the Current File   You may want to save the buffer to the file you're now editing. For example, if you started *vi* with an existing file, made some changes to the file, and want to save the changes to the original file, you can simply enter :**w**, a form of the write command.

The :w command saves the buffer to the file you're now working with (your working file). The status line tells you the name of the file and the number of lines and characters written to the file.

Saving as a New File   You may want to save the buffer to a new file, a different file name from the one you originally started with. For example, if you started vi with the file vipract.1, made some changes to the file, and want to save the changes to a new file without losing the original vipract.1 file, you can save the file as a new file. Type this form of the write command to save the file with a new file name:

:w *filename2*

This form of the write command is essentially the same as the original form described earlier in the section "Saving a New File." The buffer is written to the file named *filename2*. If the command is successful, you see the name of the file and the number of lines and characters in the file. If you specify the name of an existing file, an appropriate message appears on the status line:

File exists – use ! to overwrite.

The following section explains this scenario.

Overwriting an Existing File   If you try to save the buffer to an existing file different from the one you started with, you must explicitly tell vi that you want to overwrite or replace the existing file. If you specify an existing file name when you try to save the buffer, vi displays the following message:

File exists – use ! to overwrite.

If you really want to save the buffer over the existing file, use this form of the write command:

:w! *existing_file*

In this syntax, *existing_file* is the name of the file you want to replace. Be careful; after you overwrite a file, you can't bring it back to its original form.

Positioning the Cursor

When you edit text, you need to position the cursor where you want to insert additional text, delete text, correct mistakes, change words, or append text to the end of existing text. The commands you enter in command mode to select the spot you want are called *cursor-positioning commands*.

The Arrow Keys   You can use the arrow keys on many, but not all, systems to position the cursor. It's easy to see whether the arrow keys work: Start vi with an existing file and see what effects the arrow keys have. You should also be able to use the <Page Up> and <Page Down> keys on the Linux keyboard, providing you have the correct terminal type indicated in your TERMCAP environment variable.

To create a new file called vipract.3 that contains a list of the files and directories in the directory usr, enter

```
ls /usr > vipract.3
```

You can use this file to experiment with cursor-positioning commands.

After the file is created, start `vi` with the vipract.3 file (enter `vi vipract.3`). Now try using the arrow keys and the <Page Up> and <Page Down> keys to move around the editing buffer.

It may be the case that, although it appears as though the cursor-positioning keys work, they're introducing strange characters into the file. To check whether the keys are entering characters instead of just moving the cursor, press <Esc> to make sure that you're in command mode and then enter `:q`. If `vi` allows you to quit and doesn't complain that the file was modified, everything is fine.

TIP In `vi`, you can clear the screen of spurious or unusual characters by pressing <Ctrl-l>.

Other Cursor-Movement Keys   You can position the cursor in `vi` without using the arrow keys in other ways. You should become familiar with these methods in case you can't or don't want to use the arrow keys. This section also shows you some ways to position the cursor more efficiently than using the arrow keys.

When `vi` was developed, many terminals didn't have arrow keys. Other keys were and still are used to position the cursor. `vi` uses the <h>, <j>, <k>, and <l> keys to position the cursor, because they're in a convenient position for touch-typists. It takes a little practice to get comfortable with these keys, but some experienced `vi` users prefer these keys over the arrow keys.

The following are some other keys that move the cursor:

- Press the space bar or <l> to move the cursor one position to the right .
- Press <Return> or <+> to move to the beginning of the next line. Note that using the <j> key to go down one line preserves your position in the line.
- Press the minus sign (<–>) to move to the beginning of the previous line. Note that using the <k> key to go up one line preserves your position in the line.
- Press <h> to move one character to the left.
- Press <0> (zero) to move to the beginning of a line.
- Press <$> (the dollar sign) to move to the end of a line.

Some `vi` commands allow you to position the cursor relative to words on a line. A *word* is defined as a sequence of characters separated from other characters by spaces or usual punctuation symbols such as

```
. ? , -
```

These commands are as follows:

Keystroke	Action
\<w\>	Moves forward one word
\<b\>	Moves to the beginning of the current word
\<e\>	Moves to the end of the current word

The following example demonstrates some of these actions. Start vi and open the vipract.1 file by entering **vi vipract.1**. Now use any of the cursor-positioning commands just described to move the cursor (indicated by an underscore) to the t in the word data on the third line of the file. The third line looks like

```
b. Sort sales data and print the results.
```

To move to the beginning of the next word, press \<w\>; the cursor is positioned under the a of the word and. To move to the end of that word, press \<e\>; the cursor is positioned under the d in and. To move to the beginning of that word, press \<b\>; the cursor is positioned under the a in and again.

You can move forward several words to the beginning of another word by pressing a number key before pressing \<w\>. For example, to move the cursor from its current position (under the a of the word and) to the beginning of the word three words forward (under the r of the word results), press \<3\>\<w\>. Likewise, you can move backward four words by pressing \<4\>\<b\>; you can move forward to the end of the second word by pressing \<2\>\<e\>.

You can also use this whole-number technique with the keys \<h\>, \<j\>, \<k\>, \<l\>, \<+\>, and \<-\>. For example, press \<1\>\<5\>\<j\> to position the cursor down 15 lines. If 15 lines aren't left in the buffer, you hear a beep, and the cursor stays where it is.

Big-Movement Keys   You can quickly position the cursor to the top, middle, or bottom of the screen. In each case, the cursor appears at the beginning of the line. The following commands allow you to position the cursor on-screen:

- Press \<Shift-h\> to move to the first line of the screen. This is sometimes called the *home position*.
- Press \<Shift-m\> to move to the line in the middle of the lines now displayed.
- Press \<Shift-l\> to move to the last line on-screen.

If you want to move through a file one screen at a time (which is more efficient than pressing \<Return\> or \<j\> 23 times), use commands that scroll through a file. Pressing \<Ctrl-f\> moves you forward one screen. Pressing \<Ctrl-b\> moves you backward one screen.

To move quickly to the last line of the file or buffer, press \<Shift-g\>. To move to the first line of the file, press \<1\>\<Shift-g\>. In fact, to move to a specific line in the buffer, type the line number before you press \<Shift-g\>. To move to line 35 of the file (if there is a line 35), press \<3\>\<5\>\<Shift-g\>.

N O T E   Take a little time to practice positioning the cursor by using the commands described in these last few sections. Remember that you must be in command mode for the cursor-positioning commands to work. Press \<Esc\> before you issue a cursor-positioning command. ■

Adding Text

To add text to the editing buffer, you must go from command mode to input mode. Any usual text characters you type are then added to the buffer. If you press <Return> while you're in input mode, vi "opens," or adds, a line to the buffer. Before you start adding text, first position the cursor at the location you want to add text. Press <a> to go to input mode and append text after the cursor position. Press <i> to go to input mode and insert text in front of the cursor position. When you're done adding text, press <Esc> to return to command mode.

The following are two examples of typing in input mode. The position of the cursor is represented by an underscore character. For each case, a before-and-after view is shown.

■ Example showing the use of <i> (the insert command) to add text

Before:

```
This report is important.
```

Press <i> to insert text in front of the word important, type **very**, press the space bar, and press <Esc>.

After:

```
This report is very_important.
```

Note that the cursor is positioned under the last character you added (in this case, the space).

■ Example showing the use of <a> (the append command) to add text

Before:

```
This report is important.
```

Press <a> to append text after the word is, press the space bar, type **very**, and press <Esc>.

After:

```
This report is very important.
```

Note again that the cursor is positioned under the last character you added (in this case, the y in very).

When you want to append text at the end of a line, you can position the cursor at the end of a line and press <a>; alternatively, you can position the cursor anywhere in the line and press <Shift-a> to position the cursor at the end of the line, put you in input mode, and allow you to append text—all with one command. Likewise, you can move to the beginning of the current line and insert text at the beginning of a line by pressing <Shift-i>.

To add a line of text below or above the current line, you press <o> or <Shift-o>, respectively. Each keystroke "opens" a line in the buffer and allows you to add text. In the following two examples, you add a line to some existing text.

■ Example showing the use of <o> to insert lines below the current line

Before:

```
All jobs complete
please call
if you have any questions.
```

Part

IV

Ch

19

The cursor is on the second line. Press <o> to add a line or lines below that line. Now type the following lines:

```
Jack Tackett, Jr.
555-1837
```

Press <Esc>.

After:

```
All jobs complete
please call
Jack Tackett, Jr.
555-1837
if you have any questions.
```

■ Example showing the use of <Shift-o> to insert lines above the current line

Before:

```
All jobs complete
please call
if you have any questions.
```

The cursor is on the third line. Press <Shift-o> to add a line or lines above that line. Now type the following lines:

```
Jack Tackett, Jr.
555-1837
```

Press <Esc>.

After:

```
All jobs complete
please call
Jack Tackett, Jr.
555-1837
if you have any questions.
```

In both cases, when you press <Esc>, the cursor is positioned under the last character you typed (the 7 in the phone number). Although you added only two lines, you could have added more lines by pressing <Return> at the end of each line. Naturally, you could have added only one line by not pressing <Return> at all.

Table 19.3 summarizes the commands for adding text. Press <Esc> to make sure that you're in command mode before using these commands.

Table 19.3 Commands to Add Text

Keystroke	Action
<a>	Appends text after the cursor position
<Shift-a>	Puts you in input mode and appends text to the end of the current line

Keystroke	Action
\<i\>	Inserts text in front of the cursor position
\<Shift-i\>	Puts you in input mode and inserts text at the beginning of the current line
\<o\>	Opens a line below the current line to add text
\<Shift-o\>	Opens a line above the current line to add text

Deleting Text

Making corrections or changes to a file may involve deleting text. You must be in command mode to delete characters. If you're in input mode when you type the delete-character commands, the letters of the commands appear as characters in the buffer file. If that should happen, press \<Esc\> to go to command mode and press \<u\> to "undo" the mistake.

With *vi*, you can delete a character, a word, a number of consecutive words, all the text to the end of a line, or an entire line. Because *vi* is a visual editor, the characters, words, or lines are removed from the screen as you delete them. Table 19.4 describes the delete commands.

Table 19.4   Commands to Delete Text

Keystroke	Action
\<x\>	Deletes character at the cursor position
\<d\>\<w\>	Deletes from the cursor position in the current word to the beginning of the next word
\<d\>\<$\>	Deletes from the cursor position to the end of the line
\<Shift-d\>	Same as \<d\>\<$\>: deletes the remainder of the current line
\<d\>\<d\>	Deletes the entire current line, regardless of cursor position in the line

All these commands take effect from the current cursor position. Move the cursor to the character, word, or line you want to change, and then issue the desired delete command. Practice using them to see their effect. You'll find they're helpful in making corrections to files.

These commands can be applied to several objects—characters, words, or lines—by typing a whole number before the command. (This whole-number technique was introduced earlier in this chapter in the section on positioning the cursor.) Some examples are as follows:

- Press \<4\>\<x\> to delete four characters.
- Press \<3\>\<d\>\<w\> to delete three words.
- Press \<8\>\<d\>\<d\> to delete eight lines.

 TIP To have *vi* display line numbers, press \<Esc\> to make sure that you're in command mode, and then enter **:se number**. To turn off the line numbers, enter **:se nonumber**.

Part **IV**

Ch **19**

You can also specify a range of lines to delete. You do that by pressing the colon (<Shift-;>), typing the two line numbers you want to delete (inclusive) separated by a comma, pressing <d>, and pressing <Return>. For example, to delete lines 12 through 36 (inclusive), type `:12,36d` and press <Return>.

When you delete two or more lines, the status line states how many lines were deleted. Remember that you can press <u> to undo the deletion.

Changing and Replacing Text

Another often-faced editing task is changing text or replacing one text string with another (there isn't too much difference between the two operations). The change commands in *vi* allow you to change a word or the remainder of a line. In effect, you're replacing one word or the remainder of a line with another. You use the replace commands to replace or change a single character or sequence of characters. Table 19.5 summarizes the change and replace commands. After you enter the command, simply type the new material as appropriate.

Table 19.5   The Change and Replace Commands

Keystroke	Action
<r>	Replaces a single character
<Shift-r>	Replaces a sequence of characters
<c><w>	Changes the current word, from the cursor position to the end of the word
<c><e>	Changes the current word, from the cursor position to the end of the word (same as <c><w>)
<c><b>	Changes the current word, from the beginning of the word to the character before the cursor position
<c><$>	Changes a line, from the cursor position to the end of the line
<Shift-c>	Changes a line, from the cursor position to the end of the line (same as <c><$>)
<c><c>	Changes the entire line

The changes take place relative to the position of the cursor. You must be in command mode before you can use these commands. Position the cursor at the location in the buffer file you want to correct and press <Esc> before using these commands. Because *vi* is visual, the changes are made to the buffer as you execute the commands.

Each of these commands puts you into input mode. Except for when you use <r> to replace a single character, you must press <Esc> to finish making changes and return to command mode.

> **TIP** To change several words, use a whole number (representing the number of words to change) before pressing <c><w>.

Here are three examples of how to use the change and replace commands:

- Example showing the use of <c><e> to change to the end of the word

  Before:

  ```
  The report demonstraits thw,strengths of are apporach.
  ```

  The cursor is located at the point in the incorrectly spelled word where corrections are to begin. To change the spelling, press <c><e>, type **tes**, and press Esc.

  After:

  ```
  The report demonstrates thw,strengths of are apporach.
  ```

- Example showing the use of <Shift-r> to replace a sequence of characters

  Before:

  ```
  The report demonstrates thw,strengths of are apporach.
  ```

  The cursor is located at the point in the incorrectly spelled word where you want to start replacing characters. To correct thw, to the and a space, press <Shift-r>, type **e**, press the space bar, and press <Esc>.

  After:

  ```
  The report demonstrates the_strengths of are apporach.
  ```

- Example showing the use of <c><w> to change text, beginning with the current word and continuing for two words

  Before:

  ```
  The report demonstrates the strengths of are apporach.
  ```

  The cursor is positioned under the letter of the word where you want to begin changes. To fix the last two words on the line, press <2><c><w>, type **our approach**, and press <Esc>.

  After:

  ```
  The report demonstrates the strengths of our approach.
  ```

Remember to press <Esc> after you make changes to the lines and return to command mode.

Searching

Finding a word, phrase, or number in a file can be difficult if you have to read through each line yourself. Like most editors and word processors, vi has a command that allows you to search for a string of characters. You can search forward or backward from your current position in the buffer. You also can continue searching. vi starts searching from the beginning of the buffer file when it reaches the end, and vice versa. Table 19.6 summarizes the commands for searching. In each case, vi searches for the string you specify, in the direction you specify, and positions the cursor at the beginning of the string.

Table 19.6 The Search Commands

Command	Action
/string	Searches forward through the buffer for *string*
?string	Searches backward through the buffer for *string*
\<n>	Searches again in the current direction
\<Shift-n>	Searches again in the opposite direction

When you type the search command, it appears on the status line. To search forward for the string `sales > 100K` in a file, first make sure that you're in command mode and then enter

/sales > 100K

The typed command appears on the status line. If the string is in the buffer, `vi` positions the cursor under the first `s` in the word `sales`. If the string isn't in the buffer, `vi` displays the message `Pattern not found` on the status line. To search for another occurrence of the string, press \<n>; `vi` positions the cursor under the next occurrence of the string or, if there's no "next occurrence," the cursor doesn't move.

TROUBLESHOOTING

I typed a string I know exists in the file, but `vi` doesn't find it. The most common cause for this error is that you typed the string incorrectly. `vi` (and computers in general) doesn't do a good job of thinking; `vi` has a terrible time figuring out what you really mean when you type something. If you're looking for the string *vegi-burger* but you type **vigi-burger**, `vi` can't find what you want (unless you happened to misspell *vegi-burger* in the buffer and it matches the search string). Check the search string carefully before you press \<Return>.

I searched for a phrase that incorporates a punctuation mark, but `vi` returned some odd results. Searching in `vi` may not give you the results you want if you're looking for characters that are "special" to `vi`. For example, if you want to find a word you know is located at the end of a sentence (for example, the string *end.*), you must "escape" the period; to `vi`, the period means "any character," not "end of sentence." If you enter **/end.** and press \<Return>, `vi` locates *ending*, the word *end* followed by a space, as well as *end* followed by a period. To find only *end* followed by a period, enter **/end\..**.

Searching in `vi` is also case-sensitive. If you're looking for the word *Tiger* in your buffer, enter **/Tiger**, not **/tiger**.

Copying, Cutting, and Pasting

When you delete or cut characters, words, lines, or a portion of a line, the deleted object is saved in what's called the *general-purpose buffer*. The name isn't too important; what's important is that you can put or paste the contents of that buffer anywhere in the text you're editing. You do that with the \<p> or \<Shift-p> command. The \<p> command pastes the object to the right of or after the cursor position; the <Shift-p> command pastes the object to the left of or before the cursor.

Here are some examples of cutting and pasting text:

- Example showing the use of <p> to paste the contents of the general-purpose buffer after the cursor

    Before:

    `Carefully carry these` ̲o̲ut instructions.

    Delete the characters out and a space by pressing <d><w>. Now move the cursor to the space after the y in carry and press <p>.

    After:

    `Carefully carry out`_`these instructions.`

- Example showing the use of <Shift-p> to paste the contents of the general-purpose buffer in front of the cursor

    Before:

    `Carefully carry` ̲these `out instructions.`

    Delete the characters these and a space by pressing <d><w>. Now move the cursor to the first i in instructions and press <Shift-p>.

    After:

    `Carefully carry ou`t̲ `these instructions.`

 TIP To change the order of two characters, position the cursor under the first character and press <x><p>. Try it to change the word *tow* to the word *two*.

The preceding examples showed you how to paste after deleting text. But you don't have to delete before you can paste. You can use an operation called *yank*, which is the same as the copy operation in some word processors. The forms of the yank command are similar to the forms of the delete command. The idea is that you yank, or copy, a portion of text and then paste it somewhere else by pressing <p> or <Shift-p>. The following table lists some of the yank commands (notice that most of the yank commands use the lowercase letter y):

Keystroke	Action
<y><w>	Yanks from the cursor position in the current word to the beginning of the next word
<y><$>	Yanks from the cursor position to the end of the line
<Shift-y>	Same as <y><$>: yanks the remainder of current line
<y><y>	Yanks the entire current line

All these commands can be applied to several objects—characters, words, or lines—by typing a whole number before the command.

To copy a sequence of four lines to another portion of the text, follow these steps:

1. Position the cursor at the beginning of the first of the four lines.
2. Press <4><y><y> to yank from the cursor to the end of the line four times. The buffer (what you see on-screen) is unchanged.
3. Position the cursor elsewhere in the text.
4. Press <p> to paste the yanked lines below the line holding the cursor.

Repeating Commands

Not only does *vi* keep the text just deleted or yanked for future use, it also stores the last command you used for future use. You can repeat the last command that changed the buffer by pressing <.>.

Suppose that you've completed a report but think it would be a good idea to put two lines containing this text at key points in the report:

```
*************** Please comment ******
*************** On this section ******
```

To do so, follow these steps:

1. Position the cursor in the buffer file where you want to place these lines the first time.
2. Insert the lines by pressing <o> to open a line and typing the two lines of asterisks and text.
3. Press <Esc> to make sure that you're in command mode.
4. As often as necessary, position the cursor to another section of the report and press <.> to insert these same two lines again and again.

Setting the *vi* Environment

The *vi* editor has several options you may or may not choose to use. Some of these options can be set on a system-wide basis by the system administrator. You can customize your environment with a number of options that are in effect whenever you start *vi*. Table 19.7 summarizes all the environment options you can set for *vi*. When setting environment options (as described in the next section), you can use the abbreviation shown in the first column of the table or the full name used in the second column.

Table 19.7 Environment Options for *vi*

Abbreviated Option	Function
ai	autoindent indents each line to the same level as the line above (useful for writing programs). The default is autoindent off.
ap	autoprint prints the current line to the screen when the line is changed. The default is autoprint on.

Abbreviated Option	Function
eb	errorbells causes the computer to beep when you introduce a command error. The default is errorbells off.
nu	number displays line numbers when editing a file. The default is number off.
redraw	redraw keeps the screen up-to-date as changes occur. The default is redraw on.
report	report sets the size of an editing change that results in a message on the status line. For example, report=3 triggers a message when you delete three lines but not when fewer than three lines are deleted. The default is report=5.
sm	showmatch shows a matching open parenthesis when the closing parenthesis is entered. This option is useful mainly for programmers writing program code. The default is showmatch off.
smd	showmode displays INPUT, REPLACE, or CHANGE on the right side of the status line when the associated command is given. The default is showmode off.
warn	warn displays a warning message when an attempt is made to exit vi if the buffer has been changed and not saved to the disk file. The default is warn on.
wm=*n*	wrapmargin defines the right margin. In the syntax of this command, *n* is a whole number. If *n* is greater than 0, the command forces a carriage return so that no word is *n* or less characters from the right margin. For example, wm=5 tells vi to wrap the line when a character occurs within five characters of the end of the line. Turn this option off by specifying wm=0, which is the default.
ws	word search (called wrapscan on some systems) wraps from the <eof> (end-of-file) character to the <bof> (beginning-of-file) character during a search. Default is word search on.

Part
IV

Ch
19

Using *set* to See and Set Options

To see the options now set for your system, enter **:set** while in command mode in vi. The options now set for this session of vi are displayed on the status line. The options displayed with the set command vary depending on the default options and on your particular implementation of vi. Here is an example of what you might see when you issue the set command:

```
autoprint errorbells redraw report=1 showmatch showmode term=vt100 wrap margin=5
```

> **N O T E**   Issuing the `set` command with no arguments results in a display of only the user-set
> options. You can abbreviate the `set` command as `se`. To set a number of options on the
> same line, use the `se` command and separate the options with a space, as in the following example:
>
> `:se ap eb redraw report=1 sm smd warn wm=5 ws`
>
> Notice that the first character is the colon character, which indicates to `vi` that a command is to be
> entered. ▓

To see the list of all possible options and their settings, enter `:set all`. The options and their settings from Table 19.7 are displayed.

Setting the *showmode* Option

One of the most used options is `showmode`. To learn about the `showmode` option, start `vi` again with the vipract.1 file (enter `vi vipract.1`).

When `vi` executes, you see the text from your first `vi` session on-screen. In your first session, you may have noticed that there was no way to determine whether you were in input mode when you entered the text for this file. You can tell `vi` to inform you when you're in input mode by using the `showmode` option. The `showmode` option identifies the mode you're in on the status line.

When you set the `showmode` option, `vi` displays whatever type of input mode it's in: regular INPUT MODE, APPEND MODE, REPLACE 1 CHAR mode, and so on. To set `showmode` in `vi`, press <Esc> to make sure that you're in command mode and then enter `:set showmode`. Now go to input mode (press <i>). You should see the message INPUT MODE on the status line. Press <Esc> to return to command mode. You may want to see what happens when you give the commands to replace or change text.

Setting Toggle Options

Any option that doesn't take a number argument is like a toggle switch: You can turn it on or off. For example, as you learned in the preceding section, you set the `showmode` option by entering

`:se showmode`

To turn the `showmode` option off, you simply add `no` in front of the option:

`:se noshowmode`

Changing Options for Every *vi* Session

Setting an option during a `vi` session sets that option only for the current session. You can customize your `vi` sessions by putting the `set` commands in a file named .exrc in your home directory. To see whether such a file exists, type the following commands:

```
cd
vi .exrc
```

The first command takes you to your home directory. The second starts vi by using the .exrc file. If the file exists, it appears on the vi screen. If the file doesn't exist, vi lets you know it's a new file.

The set commands in the .exrc file start with the word set but no colon. For example, the following line sets the options number and showmode:

```
set number showmode
```

N O T E The .exrc file is read when you start vi. If you create it while you're in vi, you must restart vi to have the settings take effect. ■

The options you set and the values you give to some options depend on your preferences and the type of editing you'll be doing. Experiment with some options or talk with more experienced users.

From Here...

Although this chapter can't discuss all the options or features of vi, you know where to start and how to use the basic features of vi. vi is a very important editor for you to learn because it's available on every Linux/UNIX box. The editor is also quick to load and doesn't require many system resources, so you can use it when other editors may not be able to load. System administrators use vi for many quick-and-dirty editing tasks. For more information, see the following chapters:

- Chapter 11, "Backing Up Data," discusses how to protect your text files from accidental erasure. This chapter shows you how to back up those important files you create with vi.
- Chapter 15, "Understanding the File and Directory System," shows you how to deal with files and how those files are treated under Linux. You should have a basic understanding of the file system when using vi or any other editor.
- Chapter 20, "Using the *emacs* Editor," discusses one of the other editors available with Linux. emacs provides many enhancements over vi. emacs also provides you with an environment from which you can do many tasks you would normally do with other programs, such as read mail and read news.
- Chapter 21, "Printing," shows you how to print your text files after you create them with vi.

Using the *emacs* Editor

The name emacs stands for Editor MACroS, which began its life as a replacement for an early text editor named teco. emacs is one of the most used, most widely ported editors available in the UNIX/Linux world today. In fact, versions of emacs are available on almost every computing platform known to the industry, from Linux to Microsoft Windows.

A full version of emacs is very large, taking up several megabytes of disk space. It's a full-featured editor, very powerful, and has been extended for functions beyond text editing. In some installations, you can use it to edit files, keep a calendar, work with e-mail, manage files, read Usenet or network news, create outlines, use it as a calculator, and even browse the World Wide Web. In some ways, emacs is a working environment that contains a text editor. A popular version of emacs is distributed via the GNU license. This is the version of emacs Linux installed during installation. ■

How to use basic *emacs* commands

You can begin editing files fairly easily after learning just a few commands.

How to create new files and modify existing files by using *emacs*

The bread and butter of all editors is creating and modifying files.

How to perform basic word processing functions

Simply entering text does not an editor make. This chapter teaches you how to use emacs as a general-purpose word processor. You learn how to search and replace text throughout a document, cut and paste, and edit multiple documents at once.

Starting *emacs*

GNU patriarch Richard Stallman created the emacs editor. The source code for emacs is essentially available for free under the GNU licenses. Stallman is the founder and proponent of the Free Software Foundation and the GNU (GNU's Not UNIX) project. The fact that emacs is freely available matches Stallman's philosophy that all software should be free and that computer systems should be open for use by anyone. Users are also encouraged to make modifications but must then share those changes with others.

▶ **See** "The GNU License," **p. 724**

The emacs editor doesn't have the two basic modes that vi does, which means that anything you type is put into the file buffer. To give the editor commands to save files, search for text, delete text, and so on, you must use other keys. In emacs, you use the <Ctrl> key in combination with various characters (usually <Ctrl-x> and <Ctrl-c>) and the <Esc> key to accomplish the various commands. A variety of common commands are described later in this chapter.

▶ **See** "Looking at *vi*'s Two Modes," **p. 393**

These emacs commands are actually shortcuts for the full text commands. For example, <Ctrl-x><Ctrl-s>, which saves the current buffer to a file, is actually a shortcut freeing the user from pressing <Esc> and then typing the actual emacs command: **-x save-buffer**. As you can see, using the <Ctrl-x><Ctrl-s> key sequence is a lot more simple and much easier to remember than the full emacs command. A brief list of the basic commands are presented at the end of this chapter.

emacs also allows you to edit multiple *buffers*, or files, in the same session. That is, you can edit more than one file at a time with emacs. This chapter also covers some of the buffer-manipulation commands. emacs also uses buffers to hold deleted text and also to prompt for commands.

To start emacs, type **emacs** and press <Return>. A blank screen with a status line at the bottom appears.

This chapter doesn't discuss all the keystrokes and commands used in emacs, but you can get help by pressing <Ctrl-h><h>. After that, you can use <Ctrl-x><Ctrl-c> to exit completely, or <Ctrl-x><1> to return to your editing session. Thus, unlike vi, emacs has online help facilities and even a tutorial.

After you ask for online help, emacs presents another buffer and is ready to provide help. If you press <t>, emacs starts an excellent tutorial. If you press <k>, emacs provides help on the next command/key you enter. Thus, if you pressed <Ctrl-h><k><Ctrl-w>, emacs presents information on deleting a marked region.

To return to your editing session, press <Ctrl-x><1> to return emacs to editing only one buffer.

The complete GNU emacs system is large but can be customized to match your local environment. Some smaller versions of emacs that are readily available are Freemacs by Russell Nelson and `MicroEmacs`, originally by Dave Conroy. Remember too that the Linux distribution provides for a few other emacs-like editors—namely `JED` and `JOVE`, which are much smaller in size than the full `emacs` installation.

> **N O T E** This chapter doesn't cover all the features of `emacs`—that would take more space than is available. In fact, there are entire books written just on `emacs`. Instead, you learn the commands to do most necessary editing tasks. If you want to know about the more advanced features of `emacs` and advanced text-editing operations, consult the reference manual supplied with your system. You don't have to become an `emacs` expert to use it. `emacs` also has a very detailed tutorial as part of the system. More information on running the tutorial is presented later in this chapter, but you can start the tutorial by pressing <Ctrl-h><t>. ■

Using *emacs*

You edit text by creating new text or by modifying existing text. When creating new text, you place the text in a file with an ordinary Linux file name. When you modify existing text, you use the existing file name to call a copy of the file into the editing session. In either case, as you use the editor, the text is held in the system's memory in a storage area called a buffer.

Using a buffer prevents you from directly changing the contents of a file until you decide to save the buffer. This is to your benefit if you decide you want to forget the changes you've made and start over.

emacs allows you to edit multiple buffers at once. This way, you can cut and paste text from one buffer to another, compare text from different files, or merge one file into another file. emacs even uses a special buffer to accept commands and report information to the user. This buffer, the *mini-buffer*, appears at the bottom of the screen.

emacs also lets you display the contents of various buffers in their own windows; thus, you can see several files at once, even if you aren't using a graphical user interface.

Looking Over the *emacs* Screen

Figure 20.1 shows a typical emacs screen. The top portion displays the contents of various buffers, sometimes in multiple windows. Then a mode line is displayed at the bottom of the screen. This line, usually displayed in reverse video, provides users with information about the buffer, such as the buffer's name, the major and minor mode, and the amount of text displayed in the buffer. Under the mode line is the one-line mini-buffer, where you enter emacs commands and where emacs reports the outcome of various commands.

The current position in the buffer is shown by a cursor. emacs refers to the cursor as the *point*, especially in the online help system, so it's important to remember this term for the cursor.

FIG. 20.1

A typical emacs screen shows the buffer and mini-buffer areas.

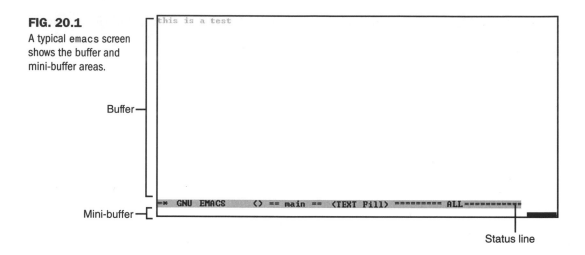

Buffer —

this is a test

=* GNU EMACS   () == main == <TEXT Fill> ========= ALL==========

Mini-buffer —

Status line

Creating Your First *emacs* File

The following instructions show how to edit your first emacs file. If you run into difficulties, you can quit and start over by pressing <Ctrl-x><Ctrl-c>. Follow these steps:

1. Start emacs (type **emacs** and press <Return>). You see the screen shown in Figure 20.1.

2. Add lines of text to the buffer. Type

   ```
   Things to do today.
   a. Practice emacs.
   b. Sort sales data and print the results.
   ```

   N O T E   Notice the mini-buffer at the bottom of the screen. Your keystrokes are appearing there because you're typing commands to the emacs editor. ■

   You can use the <Backspace> key to correct mistakes on the line you're typing. Don't worry about being precise here: this example is for practice. You learn other ways to make changes in some of the later sections of this chapter.

3. Save your buffer in a file called emacs-pract.1. First press <Ctrl-x><Ctrl-s> and type **emacs-pract.1**. Notice at the bottom of the screen that emacs-pract.1 appears. Press <Return>. This command saves or writes the buffer to the file emacs-pract.1 because it was the specified file.

   N O T E   Notice the number of characters in the file name. Unlike MS-DOS and Windows, Linux allows you to enter more than eight characters and a three-character extension for a file name. ■

You should see the following confirmation on the status line:

```
Wrote /root/emacs-pract.1
```

This statement confirms that the file emacs-pract.1 has been created and saved to disk. Your display may be different if you didn't type the information exactly as specified.

4. Exit emacs by pressing <Ctrl-x><Ctrl-c> and then <Return>. If you have unsaved material, emacs might prompt you to save an unsaved buffer/file. If emacs does prompt you, simply press <y> to save the information, or <n> if you don't want to save the information. emacs then terminates, and you return to the login shell prompt.

TROUBLESHOOTING

emacs is placing the characters I type into the mini-buffer and attempting to do strange actions with the characters. If you press the <Esc> key twice, emacs enters a LISP programming environment. LISP is the original language that Stallman used to program emacs, and it's through LISP that programmers can extend and customize emacs. If you press <Esc><Esc>, emacs enters the eval-expression mode and expects the user to enter a LISP command; simply press <Return> to exit this mode.

Starting *emacs* by Using an Existing File

To edit or look at a file that already exists in your current directory, enter **emacs** followed by the file name. Try this with the file you created in the preceding section by entering

```
emacs emacs-pract.1
```

You see the following:

```
Things to do today.
a. Practice emacs.
b. Sort sales data and print the results.
```

Look at the mini-buffer: It contains the name of the file you're editing.

TROUBLESHOOTING

I typed a file name I know exists, but emacs acts as though I'm creating a new file. You may have typed the name of a file incorrectly or one that doesn't exist in your current directory. Suppose that you type **emacs pract1.** and press Return, but there's no file named pract1. in your current directory. You still start emacs, but emacs acts as though you were creating a new file.

I try to edit a file, but emacs displays a message about read permission denied. Also, the shell prompt appears. You've tried to edit a file you aren't permitted to read. Also, you can't edit a directory—that is, if you type **emacs *directory_name***, where *directory_name* is the name of a directory, emacs informs you that you opened a directory and doesn't let you edit it. If you try to use

continues

continued

emacs with a binary file, as opposed to an ASCII file, you'll see a screen full of strange (control) characters. It won't be something you can read and edit. emacs expects files to be stored as plain text.

I opened a file in emacs, but a message about the line being too long appeared. You're trying to use emacs on a data file or a binary file that's just one long string of bytes.

I tried to save a file with the <Ctrl-x><Ctrl-s> keys, but the terminal then hangs, not responding to the keyboard. Your terminal is probably responding to the flow-control characters <Ctrl-s> and <Ctrl-q>. Press <Ctrl-q> to restart your session.

I opened a file in emacs, but there are some strange characters on-screen. You may be using emacs with a file produced by a word processor.

In all these cases, exit emacs to return to your login shell prompt by pressing <Ctrl-x><Ctrl-c>, and then answer **n** to the prompt asking if you want to save the file. Using those keystrokes ensures that you quit emacs and make no changes to the existing file.

Exiting *emacs*

As already stated, to exit emacs, press <Ctrl-x><Ctrl-c>. If you haven't saved any changes to the file, emacs prompts you to save the buffer. If you type **y**, emacs saves the file and returns you to the Linux shell. If you haven't provided a file name, emacs prompts for a file name and then exits. If you respond **n** to the request to save the buffer, emacs prompts again to make sure that you want to exit without saving the buffer. This time you must completely type out the response to the prompt—**yes** or **no**. If you answer yes, emacs returns you to Linux without saving any of the modifications you made to the buffer. Also, if you have multiple buffers open, emacs prompts you for each buffer.

> **CAUTION**
>
> The default installation of emacs performs periodic saves while you're editing a buffer. emacs does not, per se, make backup copies of files, although the first time you save the file, a snapshot of the file is save in *#filename#*. After you press <Ctrl-x><Ctrl-s>, the original file is modified and can't be restored to its original state. Thus, you should make your own backup copies of emacs files before starting the editing session to make sure that the automatic updates don't inadvertently overwrite an important file to the point where you can't recover a previous version of the file.

> **CAUTION**
>
> Answer **n** to the exit-without-saving prompt sparingly. When you answer **n**, all the changes you've made to the file since it was last saved are lost. It's better to be safe and save the file to a different file name if you're not sure about losing all your changes to the file.

Perhaps you aren't quite finished with your emacs session but do need to perform other activities with Linux. In that case, you have several options:

- You can suspend emacs and return to the Linux shell.
- You can switch to another virtual terminal.
- You can issue a shell command from within emacs.

Suspending *emacs*   You can suspend emacs—in fact, you can suspend almost any Linux application—by pressing Ctrl-z. This keystroke combination places the current application into the background and provides you with another shell prompt. The command to reactivate emacs depends on which shell you're executing. You can type the command **fg**, which means to bring the background task to the foreground. If the shell you're using doesn't understand this command, type **exit**, which reactivates your emacs session with all your files and buffers still intact.

Switching Between *emacs* and Other Virtual Terminals   Linux provides the user with six virtual terminals—hence, you have six different sessions. While in emacs you can press <Ctrl-Alt-F*x*>, where F*x* is one of the keyboard function keys F1 through F6, to activate another terminal. If you haven't already logged in to a session on that terminal, then you must do so, just like when you're first booting Linux. You then have a completely active Linux session. To switch back to emacs, simply repeat the process of pressing <Ctrl-Alt-F*x*>. If you forget which session is running emacs, you can cycle through each of the virtual terminals by pressing <Ctrl-Alt> with each function key one by one.

▶ **See** "Managing Users," **p. 119**

You can also use the ps command to display all active processes, as shown in Listing 20.1. The output of the ps -guax command indicates which terminal each process is now executing.

Listing 20.1   Output from the *ps* Command

USER	PID	%CPU	%MEM	SIZE	RSS	TTY	STAT	START	TIME	COMMAND
root	1	0.5	3.1	44	208	?	S	20:48	0:00	init
root	6	0.0	1.8	24	124	?	S	20:48	0:00	bdflush (daemon)
root	7	0.0	1.9	24	128	?	S	20:48	0:00	update (bdflush)
root	23	0.0	2.9	56	200	?	S	20:48	0:00	/usr/sbin/crond -l10
root	36	0.6	3.5	65	240	?	S	20:48	0:00	/usr/sbin/syslogd
root	38	0.1	2.9	36	200	?	S	20:48	0:00	/usr/sbin/klogd
root	40	0.3	3.2	68	216	?	S	20:48	0:00	/usr/sbin/inetd
root	42	0.1	3.0	64	204	?	S	20:48	0:00	/usr/sbin/lpd
root	47	0.1	6.0	259	404	?	S	20:48	0:00	sendmail:accepting c
root	51	0.1	2.0	32	140	?	S	20:48	0:00	selection -t ms
root	52	1.5	7.2	376	484	v01	S	20:48	0:01	-bash
root	53	0.3	3.4	88	232	v02	S	20:48	0:00	/sbin/getty tty2 3840
root	54	0.3	3.4	88	232	v03	S	20:48	0:00	/sbin/getty tty3 3840
root	55	0.2	3.4	88	232	v04	S	20:48	0:00	/sbin/getty tty4 3840
root	56	0.3	3.4	88	232	v05	S	20:48	0:00	/sbin/getty tty5 3840
root	57	0.3	3.4	88	232	v06	S	20:48	0:00	/sbin/getty tty6 3840
root	67	0.0	3.5	80	240	v01	R	20:49	0:00	ps -guax

Part

IV

Ch

20

You can then use that TTY value, in the range of v01 to v06, to pick the correct virtual terminal. For example, if the ps command indicates that emacs is now operating on tty v01 and tty v02, pressing <Alt-F1> or <Alt-F2> brings you back to the appropriate emacs session.

Accessing Linux Commands from Within *emacs*   Sometimes all you need to do is a quick check to see whether a file exists or to perform some other quick Linux command; you don't need a full shell session to perform the action. In that case, you can execute shell commands from within emacs. To execute a shell within emacs, press <Ctrl-u><Esc><!>. You're prompted to enter a shell command; enter the command and press <Return>. emacs passes the command to the Linux shell, which executes the command.

If you don't press <Ctrl-u>, emacs places the output into a buffer/window called *Shell Command Output*. You learn more about windows later in this chapter, but basically windows allow you to see multiple buffers at once. emacs provides various commands to move around between windows and to delete windows (without deleting their corresponding buffers). To delete the output window, press <Ctrl-x><1>.

Undoing a Command

In emacs, you can "undo" your most recent action or change to the buffer, as long as you have not saved that change to the disk file. You can undo by pressing <Ctrl-x><u>. By repeatedly using this command, you can undo the changes made to the buffer.

> **N O T E**   emacs keeps track of the "undone" material first in memory buffers and then in a file, so theoretically you could undo every change you've made to a buffer up to the limits of your disk space. Practically, though, you'll find the undo command useful for only the last few commands or edits you've done. ■

Unfortunately, you can't use the undo command to undo writing something to a file as opposed to writing to the buffer.

If you want to reread a file from disk (thus overwriting your current buffer changes), you can press <Ctrl-x><Ctrl-r>. This command reads the specified file into the current buffer, erasing its previous contents. Thus, if you specify the same file name, emacs replaces the current buffer with the contents of the file on disk. This is a quick way to undo many changes without exiting and restarting emacs.

But what if the emacs has autosaved the file or you've saved the file with unwanted changes? Well, emacs creates a backup file the first time you save a file, but not until you save the file. The name of this backup file is the same as the file name, except with a # character at the beginning and end of the name. Thus, if your file was named emacs-prtc.1, the backup file name is #emacs-prtc.1#. If you accidentally overwrite your current file with unwanted changes, you may be able to use the backup file to start over.

Writing Files and Saving the Buffer

You've seen how to write the buffer to a file and quit emacs. Sometimes, however, you want to save the buffer to a file without quitting emacs. You should save the file regularly during an editing session. If the system goes down because of a crash or a power failure, you may lose your work if you haven't saved it recently. To save the buffer, press <Ctrl-x><Ctrl-s>.

If you started emacs without specifying a file name, you must provide a file name if you want to save the file to disk. In this case, you press <Ctrl-x><Ctrl-s>, type the file name, and press <Return>.

You may want to save the buffer to a new file name different from the one you originally started with. For example, you start emacs with the file emacs-pract.1, make some changes to the file, and want to save the changes to a new file without losing the original emacs-pract.1 file. To save the file with a new file name, press <Ctrl-x><Ctrl-w>. emacs prompts you for the file name. The buffer is then written to the named file. If the command is successful, you see the name of the file.

If you specify the name of an existing file, a message appears in the mini-buffer, asking whether you want to overwrite the file. Simply answer the question appropriately.

Using Files

If you want to load another file to edit, emacs can let you load a new file into the current buffer, or load a file into a new buffer, leaving the current buffer alone. emacs also lets you insert the contents of a file into the current buffer.

To replace the current buffer with the contents of another file, press <Ctrl-x><Ctrl-v>. emacs prompts for a file name in the mini-buffer. If you don't remember the entire file name or if the name is rather long, you can use the completion option of emacs. When emacs prompts for a file name, you can enter just the first few letters in the name and then press <Tab>. emacs then expands the file name to match any files with those first few letters. If more than one file matches, emacs displays a window containing all the files matching the characters you entered and allows you to choose one.

To retrieve a file into a new buffer, press <Ctrl-x><Ctrl-f>. Enter the file name at the mini-buffer prompt. emacs normally names the buffer after the file name, but you can change the name of the buffer by pressing <Esc><x>, entering the new name for the buffer, and pressing <Return>. emacs prompts for the new name. Enter the new buffer name and press <Return>. The mode line displays the new name.

To insert a file into the current buffer, simply move the cursor to the desired position in the file and press <Ctrl-x><i>.

Part
IV
Ch
20

Positioning the Cursor

When you edit text, you need to position the cursor where you want to insert additional text, delete text, correct mistakes, change words, or append text to the end of existing text. The commands you enter are called *cursor-positioning commands*.

The Arrow Keys   You can use the arrow keys on many—but not all—systems to position the cursor. It's easy to see whether the arrow keys work: Start emacs with an existing file and see what effects the arrow keys have. You may also be able to use the <Page Up> and <Page Down> keys.

Enter the following command to create a new file called emacs-pract.3 that contains a list of the files and directories in the directory /usr. You can use this file to experiment with cursor-positioning commands.

```
ls /usr > emacs-pract.3
```

If you create the file with the <Ctrl-u><Esc><!> command sequence, you see the message

```
(Shell command completed with no output)
```

N O T E   Don't worry about the message; it doesn't mean there's a problem. Standard output was redirected to the file and, thus, emacs had no output to capture to a buffer. ■

When the file is created, start emacs with the emacs-pract.3 file (type **emacs emacs-pract.3** and press <Return>). Now try using the arrow keys and the <Page Up> and <Page Down> keys (if they're on your keyboard) to move around the editing buffer. If the keys work, you may want to use those keys for cursor positioning.

It may be that, although it appears that the cursor-positioning keys work, they're introducing strange characters into the file. These characters are the codes the computer uses to represent the various keys instead of the characters themselves. If you see such characters, you have to use the various keyboard commands to position the cursor rather than the keyboard keys.

TIP   To clear the screen of spurious or unusual characters in emacs, press <Ctrl-l>.

Other Cursor-Movement Keys   You can position the cursor in emacs in other ways without using the arrow keys. You should become familiar with these methods in case you can't or don't want to use the arrow keys. This section also shows you some ways to position the cursor more efficiently than using the arrow keys.

When emacs was developed in 1975, many terminals didn't have arrow keys; other keys were and still are used to position the cursor. It takes a little practice to get comfortable with these keys, but some experienced emacs users prefer these keys over the arrow keys. Here are some other keys that move the cursor:

- ■ Press <Ctrl-f> to move the cursor to the right ("forward") one position.
- ■ Press <Ctrl-b> to move the cursor to the left ("back") one position.

- Press <Ctrl-n> to move to the beginning of the next line, preserving your position in the line.
- Press <Ctrl-p> to move to the previous line, preserving your position in the line.
- Press <Ctrl-a> to move to the beginning of a line.
- Press <Ctrl-e> to move to the end of a line.

Some emacs commands allow you to position the cursor relative to words on a line. A *word* is defined as a sequence of characters separated from other characters by spaces or usual punctuation symbols, such as periods, question marks, commas, and hyphens. These commands are as follows:

- Press <Esc><f> to move forward one word.
- Press <Esc><b> to move backward one word.

The following example demonstrates some of these actions. Start emacs and open the emacs-pract.1 file by typing **emacs emacs-pract.1** and pressing <Return>. Now use any of the cursor-positioning commands just described to move the cursor, indicated by an underline character, to the t in the word data on the third line of the file. The third line looks like

```
b. Sort sales data and print the results.
```

To move to the beginning of the next word, press <Esc><f>; the cursor is positioned under the a of the word and in the previous sentence. Press <Esc><f> to move to the p in print. To move to the beginning of the word and, press <Esc><b>; the cursor is positioned under the a in and again.

Big-Movement Keys   If you want to move through a file a screen at a time, which is more efficient than pressing <Page Down>, use commands that scroll through a file. The command <Ctrl-x><]> moves you forward one page. The scrolling keystrokes are as follows:

- Press <Ctrl-v> to move forward one screen.
- Press <Esc><v> to move backward one screen.
- Press <Ctrl-x><]> to move forward one page.
- Press <Ctrl-x><[> to move backward one page.

To move quickly to the last line of the file or buffer, press <Esc><Shift-.>. To move to the first line of the file, press <Esc><Shift-,>. In fact, to move to a specific line in the buffer, type the command **goto-line** *n*, where *n* is the line number you want to move to. To move to line 35 of the file (if there is a line 35), press <Esc>, enter **goto-line 35**, and press <Return>.

You can repeat any command you want by pressing <Esc-*n*>, where *n* is the number of times you want to repeat the command, and then entering the command you want to repeat.

Take a little time to practice positioning the cursor by using the commands described in these last few sections. Remember that you must be in command mode for the cursor-positioning commands to work.

Part

IV

Ch

20

Adding Text

To add text to the editing buffer, you must position the cursor at the position you want to start entering text. Any usual text characters you type are then added to the buffer. If you press <Return>, emacs "opens," or adds, a line to the buffer. Before you start adding text, first position the cursor at the location you want to add text. You then simply type the text.

To add a line of text below the current line, you use the command <Ctrl-o>. This "opens" a line in the buffer and allows you to add text. In the following example, you add a line to some existing text.

> *Before:*
> ```
> All jobs complete
> please call
> if you have any questions.
> ```

The cursor is on the second line. Press <Ctrl-o> to add a line or lines below that line. Type

```
Lee Nashua
555-1837
```

> *After:*
> ```
> All jobs complete
> please call
> Lee Nashua
> 555-1837
> if you have any questions.
> ```

Although you added only two lines, you could have added more lines by pressing <Return> at the end of each line. Naturally, you could have added only one line by not pressing <Return> at all.

Deleting Text

Making corrections or modifications to a file may involve deleting text. With emacs, you can delete a character, a word, a number of consecutive words, all the text to the end of a line, or an entire line. Because emacs is a visual editor like vi, the characters, words, or lines are removed from the screen as you delete them.

Table 20.1 lists the delete commands and describes their actions. They all take effect from the current cursor position. Move the cursor to the character, word, or line you want to change and then issue the desired delete command. Practice using them to see their effect. You'll find they are helpful in making corrections to files.

Table 20.1 Commands to Delete Text

Keystroke	Action
<Ctrl-d>	Deletes character at the cursor position
<Esc><d>	Deletes the word the cursor is on
<Ctrl-k>	Deletes from the cursor position to the end of the line
<Esc><k>	Deletes the sentence the cursor is on
<Ctrl-w>	Deletes a marked region (see *Marked Text* later in Table 20.4 for commands to mark a region)

If you use the <Ctrl-k> command, the information just doesn't disappear into the bit bucket. The characters deleted are added to a *kill buffer*, which you can yank back at any time with the <Ctrl-y> command.

Searching and Replacing Text

Finding a word, a phrase, or a number in a file can be difficult if you have to read through each line yourself. Like most editors and word processors, emacs has a command that allows you to search for a string of characters and, if you want, replace those characters with others. You can search forward or backward from your current position in the buffer. You also can continue searching. emacs starts searching from the beginning of the buffer file when it reaches the end, and vice versa. Table 20.2 summarizes the commands for searching. In each case, emacs searches for the string you specify, in the direction you specify, and positions the cursor at the beginning of the string.

Table 20.2 The Search and Replace Commands

Command	Action
<Ctrl-s>	Search forward from current position
<Ctrl-r>	Reverse search from current position
<Ctrl-x><s>	Repeat search forward
<Ctrl-x><r>	Repeat search in reverse
<Esc><r>	Replace all instances of first typed string in mini-buffer with second typed string, ending each string with <Esc>
<Esc><Ctrl-r *query*>	Before performing the replacement, answer inthe mini-buffer with • <Ctrl-g>: Cancel operation • <!>: Replace the rest • <?>: Get a list of options

continues

Table 20.2   Continued

Command	Action
	• <.>: Replace and exit to where command was initiated
	• <,>: Replace the rest without asking
	• <y> or space bar: Replace and continue with replace operation
	• <n>: Don't replace but continue with operation

Searching   When you type the search command, it appears in the mini-buffer. To search forward for the string `sales > 100K` in a file, use

`<Ctrl-s>sales > 100K`

This command starts an incremental search through the buffer. Notice that as you type the characters for the search string, emacs positions the cursor on the sequence of characters. If emacs can't find the text, the `search failed` message appears. If the string is in the buffer, emacs positions the cursor under the first s in the word `sales`. When you find the first occurrence of the string, you must press <Esc> to stop the search; otherwise, emacs continues looking for a match as you enter other text. emacs refers to these types of searches as *incremental searches*; emacs searches as you enter the search string.

emacs can also perform non-incremental searches if you preface the search string with the <Esc> key and press the <Return> key at the end, as shown here:

`<Ctrl-s><Esc>sales > 100K`

If you're searching a large file and realize that you've entered the wrong search string, emacs searches the entire file. To stop the search, press <Ctrl-g>.

TROUBLESHOOTING

I typed a string I know exists in the file, but `emacs` can't find it. The most common cause for this error is that you typed the string incorrectly. emacs—and computers in general—don't do a good job of thinking; emacs has a terrible time figuring out what you really mean. If you're looking for the string *vegi-burger* but you type `vigi-burger`, emacs can't find what you want (unless you happened to misspell *vegi-burger* in the buffer and it matches the search string). Check the search string carefully before you press <Return>.

Replacing   Although searching for text can help you locate a particular word or section of text, many times you want to replace the found text. An example is if you find a spelling error and want to correct the entire buffer rather than one mistake at a time. For example, to replace every occurrence of the word *misstake* with *mistake*, press <Esc><r>. The mini-buffer prompts for the string to search for; enter **misstake**. emacs then prompts for the replacement string; enter **mistake**. emacs proceeds through the file, looking for the string `misstake` and replacing it with `mistake`. emacs also tries to match capitalization as best as possible. Thus, if `misstake` appeared as `Misstake`, emacs replaces it with `Mistake`.

Maybe you don't want to replace every occurrence of a search string with the replacement string, in which case you can instruct emacs to query before replacing the string. To have emacs query and replace, press <Esc><Ctrl-r>.

For example, if you want to selectively replace the name of your operating system, Linux, with its ancestor UNIX, press <Esc><Ctrl-r>. emacs responds in the mini-buffer with Query replace:. Now enter the search string **Linux**. The Query replace Linux with: prompt appears. Enter the replacement string **UNIX**. emacs begins the search and states, Query replacing Linux with UNIX. If you want to terminate the search-and-replace operation, press <Ctrl-g>.

When emacs finds an occurrence of Linux, it stops and prompts for an action. The possible responses are as follows:

Keystroke	Action
<Ctrl-g>	Cancels operation
<!>	Replaces the rest without prompting
<?>	Gets a list of options
<.>	Replaces the current instance and quits
<,>	Replaces current instance but doesn't move on to next instance
<y> or space bar	Replaces and continues with replace operation
<n>	Doesn't replace but continues with replace operation

Changing Text   Another editing task you're often faced with is changing text or replacing one text string with another (there isn't too much difference between the two operations). You use the replace commands to replace a single character or sequence of characters. You can also use the change commands to fix one of the most common typing mistakes made—transposing two letters. Table 20.3 summarizes the change commands.

Table 20.3   Change Commands

Keystroke	Action
<Ctrl-t>	Transposes two adjacent letters
<Esc><t>	Transposes two words
<Ctrl-x><Ctrl-t>	Transposes two lines
<Esc><c>	Properly capitalizes the word (initial capitalization)
<Esc><l>	Lowercases the entire word
<Esc><u>	Uppercases the entire word

The changes take place relative to the position of the cursor. Position the cursor at the location in the buffer file you want to correct before using these commands.

Copying, Cutting, and Pasting

When you delete or cut characters, words, lines, or a portion of a line, the deleted object is saved in what's called the *kill buffer*. The name isn't too important; what's important is that you can put or paste the contents of the kill buffer anywhere in the text you're editing. You do that with <Ctrl-y>, the yank command. <Ctrl-y> pastes the object to the right of or after the cursor position.

Here is an example showing the use of <Ctrl-y> to paste the contents of the kill buffer after the cursor:

> *Before:*
> ```
> Carefully carry these out instructions.
> ```

Delete the word out and a space by pressing <Esc-d>. Now move the cursor to the space after the y in carry and press <Ctrl-y>.

> *After:*
> ```
> Carefully carry out these instructions.
> ```

To copy a sequence of four lines to another portion of the text, you must first mark the four lines of text, delete them to the kill buffer, and then yank them back at the appropriate places. Follow these steps:

1. Position the cursor at the beginning of the first of the four lines.
2. Press <Ctrl-space bar> to set the mark.
3. Move the cursor to the end of the fourth line. This creates what emacs refers to as a *region*.
4. Delete the text by pressing <Ctrl-w>.
5. Because you want to copy the lines, you must replace the deleted text. Do this with the <Ctrl-y> command.
6. Move the cursor to the point in the buffer where you want to copy the text.
7. Press <Ctrl-y> to paste the yanked lines below the line holding the cursor.

TROUBLESHOOTING

I deleted the marked region, but the region I marked wasn't deleted. Unfortunately, GNU emacs supplied with Linux doesn't display any type of marker to indicate the mark, so it's very easy to forget to set the mark or to place it in an inappropriate position. To check the position of the mark, use the command <Ctrl-x><Ctrl-x>. This command swaps the position of the cursor and the mark. If the cursor moves to the position you thought the mark was located, you know the mark is properly set. To move the cursor back to the proper position, simply reissue <Ctrl-x><Ctrl-x> to swap them back.

Basic Command Summary

Table 20.4 gives a brief listing of the major commands provided by emacs. <Esc><c> means to press and release the *meta key*—usually the <Esc> key on a PC keyboard, although on some keyboards you can use the <Alt> key and then press the following <c> key. <Ctrl-c> means to press the <Ctrl> key and the <c> key at the same time. Remember, pressing <Ctrl-g> at any time stops the currently executing command.

Table 20.4 Basic *emacs* Commands

Key Sequence	Description
Saving to Disk	
<Ctrl-x><Ctrl-s>	Saves current buffer to disk
<Ctrl-x><Ctrl-w>	Writes current buffer to disk, asking for a new file name
<Ctrl-x><n>	Changes file name of current buffer
<Esc><z>	Writes all changed buffers to disk and exits emacs
Reading from Disk	
<Ctrl-x><Ctrl-f>	Finds file, reads into a new buffer created from file name
<Ctrl-x><Ctrl-r>	Reads file into current buffer, erasing previous contents
<Ctrl-x><Ctrl-i>	Inserts file into the current buffer at the cursor's location
Moving the Cursor	
<Ctrl-f>	Moves forward one character
<Ctrl-b>	Moves backward one character
<Ctrl-a>	Moves to front of current line
<Ctrl-e>	Moves to end of current line
<Ctrl-n>	Moves to next line
<Ctrl-p>	Moves to previous line
<Esc><f>	Moves forward a word
<Esc><b>	Moves backward a word
<Esc><a>	Goes to a line
<Esc><Shift-.>	Moves to beginning of buffer
<Esc><Shift-,>	Moves to end of buffer

Part
IV

Ch
20

continues

Table 20.4   Continued

Deleting and Inserting

\<Ctrl-d>	Deletes next character
\<Ctrl-c>	Inserts a space
\<Esc>\<d>	Deletes next word
\<Ctrl-k>	Deletes to end of current line
\<Return>	Inserts a new line
\<Ctrl-j>	Inserts a new line and indent
\<Ctrl-o>	Opens a new line
\<Ctrl-w>	Deletes region between mark and cursor
\<Esc>\<w>	Copies region to kill buffer
\<Ctrl-x>\<Ctrl-o>	Deletes lines around cursor

Searching and Replacing

\<Ctrl-s>	Searches forward from current position
\<Ctrl-r>	Reverses search from current position
\<Ctrl-x>\<s>	Repeats search forward
\<Ctrl-x>\<r>	Repeats search in reverse
\<Esc>\<r>	Replaces all instances of first typed string in mini-buffer with second typed string, ending each string with \<Esc>
\<Esc>\<Ctrl-r>	Queries before performing the replacement. Answer in the mini-buffer with • \<Ctrl-g>: Cancels operation • \<!>: Replaces the rest • \<?>: Gets a list of options • \<.>: Exits to where command was initiated • \<y> or space bar: Replaces and continues with replace operation • \<n>: Doesn't replace but continues with replace operation

Marked Text

\<Ctrl>\<space bar>	Sets mark at current cursor position
\<Ctrl-x>\<Ctrl-x>	Exchanges mark and cursor
\<Ctrl-w>	Deletes the marked region

\<Esc-w>	Copies marked region to kill buffer
\<Ctrl-y>	Inserts the kill buffer at the current cursor position

Buffers

\<Ctrl-x>\<b>	Switches to another buffer
\<Ctrl-x>\<x>	Switches to next buffer in buffer list
\<Esc>\<Ctrl-n>	Changes name of current buffer
\<Ctrl-x>\<k>	Deletes a non-displayed buffer

Customizing *emacs*

You can customize your version of emacs by placing custom functions within a file called .emacs. This file must reside in your home directory. This file contains functions written in emacs LISP, with which you can personalize emacs to your liking. An example LISP function follows:

```
(keyboard-translate ?\C-h ?\C-?)
```

This function is helpful if your terminal translates the \<Backspace> key into the \<Ctrl-h> characters. These characters are, by default, the sequence used to summon help from within emacs. By specifying a new function and binding this function to a key, you can customize how emacs responds to these key sequences.

In the preceding example, ?\C-h represents the \<Ctrl-h> keypress. ?\C-? represents the \<Delete> key. On nearly all ASCII keyboards, both keys represent the same ASCII value, namely 8. After you enter this function line into your .emacs file and save it, the next time you invoke emacs, you'll be able to delete characters by using the \<Backspace> key.

Of course, this also means you'll no longer have access to help from the keyboard. To alleviate this problem, you can bind the help function to a new key sequence, just as you did with the delete function. Simply place the following line into your .emacs file, specifying your chosen key for *key*:

```
(keyboard-translate ?\C-key ?\C-h)
```

From Here...

You can find more information on another editor and about Linux's files system in the following chapters:

- Chapter 11, "Backing Up Data," shows you how to properly back up your text files from accidental erasure.

Part

IV

Ch

20

■ Chapter 15, "Understanding the File and Directory System," discusses the basics of files and directories. You should have a basic understanding of the file system when using emacs or any other editor. Whereas the editor creates and modifies files, it's up to you to name them and place them in the appropriate directories.

■ Chapter 19, "Using the *vi* Editor," discusses the basics of using this popular editor. vi is important because it's found on all Linux/UNIX systems. If you know how to use vi, you should be able to edit a file on any system. Systems administrators also use vi for many systems admin tasks.

■ Chapter 21, "Printing," provides information on printing your text files under Linux. Printing files under Linux can be tricky; this chapter helps you prepare your system for printing.

Printing

Although everyone thought the computer revolution would bring the paperless office, it hasn't. More paper is used today than was used 20 years ago. When the UNIX operating system was in its infancy, Bell Labs used it to produce—and print—technical documentation. As a result, UNIX, and thus Linux, has a great many utilities designed around printing (or at least formatting data to be printed). This chapter concentrates on the mechanics of actually printing a file.

The printing systems common to UNIX/Linux are called the *lpr systems*. ■

Configuring your printer

Linux requires a bit more configuration than operating systems such as Windows 95 and OS/2. Linux relies on a series of directories and configuration files in order to print files correctly. The printing daemon, lp, uses these configuration files and directories to print your file.

Sending a file to a printer

The command to print a file is deceptively simple, but behind the simple command lies a powerful printing system available to every Linux user.

Checking printer status

Because Linux spools files to be printed, you may need to check the status of your print job, especially if something goes wrong.

Canceling a print job

Sometimes users get in a hurry and print a file before realizing just how many pages the file contains. If you print a file by mistake, you need to know how to cancel the print job.

Troubleshooting problems

Many different items must work together to print files under Linux. If any item isn't correct—for example, a configuration file isn't in the correct directory or has the incorrect file permissions—you'll have problems.

Selecting a Printer to Work with Linux

If you can access the printer from MS-DOS, you should be able to print ASCII characters to the printer from Linux. The only downside is that you may not be able to access certain features of your printer from Linux. One of the main reasons is that under Linux, the system first sends the file to be printed to another file. Linux sends the files to a temporary area because printers are relatively slow peripherals, and the system doesn't want to slow down your session just to print a file. This process is called *spooling*, and printers are thus called *spooled devices*. When you print a file in Linux, the file doesn't go directly to a printer; instead, it goes to a queue to wait its turn to be printed. If your file is the first in the queue, it prints almost immediately.

> **N O T E** *Spool* is an acronym for Simultaneous Peripheral Operation Off Line. The term was coined in the early days of the big IBM mainframes, when smaller computers were used to print reports offline from the mainframe. This technique allowed expensive mainframes to continue their tasks without wasting time on such trivial matters as printing. ▓

Because Linux inherits a great deal of UNIX functionality, Linux supports many types of printers, as shown in Table 21.1. The printers listed aren't the only printers supported, so if you can access your printer from DOS (as mentioned earlier), you should be able to access the printer from Linux.

Table 21.1   Supported Printers Under Linux

Linux Device Name	Description
appledmp	Apple dot-matrix printer (ImageWriter)
bj10e	Canon BubbleJet BJ10e
bj200	Canon BubbleJet BJ200
cdeskjet	Hewlett-Packard DeskJet 500C with 1-bit/pixel color
cdjcolor	Hewlett-Packard DeskJet 500C with 24-bit/pixel color and high-quality color (Floyd-Steinberg) dithering
cdjmono	Hewlett-Packard DeskJet 500C printing black only
cdj500	Hewlett-Packard DeskJet 500C (same as cdjcolor)
cdj550	Hewlett-Packard DeskJet 550C
declj250	Alternate DEC LJ250 driver
deskjet	Hewlett-Packard DeskJet and DeskJet Plus
dfaxhigh	DigiBoard, Inc.'s DigiFAX software format
dfaxlow	DigiFAX low (normal) resolution
djet500	Hewlett-Packard DeskJet 500

Linux Device Name	Description
djet500c	Hewlett-Packard DeskJet 500C (same as cdjcolor)
epson	Epson-compatible dot-matrix printers (9- or 24-pin)
eps9high	Epson-compatible 9-pin, interleaved lines
epsonc	Epson LQ-2550 and Fujitsu 3400/2400/1200 color printers
escp2	Epson ESC/P 2 language printers, including Stylus 800
ibmpro	IBM 9-pin Proprinter
jetp3852	IBM Jetprinter inkjet color printer (Model #3852)
laserjet	Hewlett-Packard LaserJet
la50	DEC LA50 printer
la75	DEC LA75 printer
lbp8	Canon LBP-8II laser printer
ln03	DEC LN03 printer
lj250	DEC LJ250 Companion color printer
ljet2p	Hewlett-Packard LaserJet IId/IIp/III with TIFF compression
ljet3	Hewlett-Packard LaserJet III with Delta Row compression
ljet4	Hewlett-Packard LaserJet 4 (defaults to 600 dpi)
ljetplus	Hewlett-Packard LaserJet Plus
m8510	C.Itoh M8510 printer
necp6	NEC P6/P6+/P60 printers at 360×360 DPI resolution
nwp533	Sony Microsystems NWP533 laser printer (Sony only)
oki182	Okidata MicroLine 182
paintjet	Hewlett-Packard PaintJet color printer
pj	Alternate PaintJet XL driver
pjxl	Hewlett-Packard PaintJet XL color printer
pjxl300	Hewlett-Packard PaintJet XL300 color printer
r4081	Ricoh 4081 laser printer
sparc	SPARC printer
t4693d2	Tektronix 4693d color printer, 2 bits per R/G/B component
t4693d4	Tektronix 4693d color printer, 4 bits per R/G/B component

Part

IV

Ch

21

continues

Table 21.1   Continued

Linux Device Name	Description
t4693d8	Tektronix 4693d color printer, 8 bits per R/G/B component
tek4696	Tektronix 4695/4696 inkjet plotter

N O T E   Table 21.1 and the following sections are adapted from "The Linux Printing-HOWTO,"
© 1994-1996 by Grant Taylor and Brian McCauley.

▶ **See** "Linux HOWTOs," **p. 680**
▶ **See** "HOWTO Index," **p. 687** ■

Knowing What You Need to Configure Printers

This chapter assumes that you know how to edit a text file under Linux and that you have a basic understanding of file ownership and permissions. It also assumes that you have your Linux system set up and running correctly. In particular, if you're going to use remote printing, your networking subsystems must be installed and operating correctly. Check out the man pages on the commands chmod and chown for more information. Also review Chapters 19 and 20 for using the vi and emacs editors, because you need to edit several files when configuring your printers.

Knowing How Printing Works Under Linux

The simplest way to print under UNIX (and thus under Linux) is to send the print data directly to the printer device. The following command sends a directory listing to the first parallel printer (LPT1 in DOS terms):

```
ls > /dev/lp0
```

This method doesn't take advantage of Linux's multitasking capabilities because the time taken for this command to finish is however long it takes the printer to actually physically print the data. On a slow printer or a printer that's deselected or disconnected, this could be a long time. A better method is to *spool* the data—that is, to collect the print data into a file and then start a background process to send the data to the printer.

Spooling files to be printed later is essentially how Linux works. For each printer, a spool area is defined. Data for the printer is collected in the spool area, one file per print job. A background process (called the *printer daemon*) constantly scans the spool areas for new files to print. When one appears, the data is sent to the appropriate printer, or *despooled*. When more than one file is waiting to be printed, the files are printed in the order they're completed—first in, first out. Thus, the spool area is effectively a queue, and the waiting jobs are often referred to as being *in the print queue* or *queued*. In the case of remote printing, the data is first spooled locally as for any other print job, but the background process is told to send the data to a particular printer on a particular remote machine.

The necessary information that the printer daemon needs to do its job—the physical device to use, the spool area to look in, the remote machine and printer for remote printing, and so on—is all stored in a file called /etc/printcap. The details of this file are discussed later in the section "Understanding the /etc/printcap File."

The term *printer* is used to mean a printer as specified in /etc/printcap. The term *physical printer* is used to mean the thing that actually puts characters on paper. It's possible to have multiple entries in /etc/printcap that all describe one physical printer but do so in different ways. If this isn't clear to you, read the section on /etc/printcap.

Part
IV

Ch
21

Understanding the Important Programs for Printing

Five programs comprise the UNIX print system. They should be in the locations shown in Table 21.2, owned by root, belong to the group daemon, and have the permissions shown in Table 21.2.

Table 21.2   The Important Printing Programs

File Permissions	File Locations
-rwsr-sr-x	/usr/bin/lpr
-rwsr-sr-x	/usr/bin/lpq
-rwsr-sr-x	/usr/bin/lpc
-rwsr-sr-x	/usr/bin/lprm
-rwxr-s---	/usr/sbin/lpd

The first four file permissions in Table 21.2 are used to submit, cancel, and inspect print jobs. /usr/sbin/lpd is the printer daemon.

N O T E The locations, ownerships, and permissions in Table 21.2 are a simplification and may be wrong for your system, so note the lpd files and permissions. ■

All these commands have man pages, which you should consult for more information. The important points are that by default, lpr, lprm, lpc, and lpq operate on a printer called lp. If you define an environment variable called PRINTER, the name defined is used instead. You can override lp and the PRINTER environment variable by specifying the printer name to use on the command line. For example,

```
lpc -PMYPRINTER
```

The *lpd* Daemon

Linux handles all print jobs via the lpd daemon. If this process isn't running, no printing can take place and print files will remain in their spool directories until the lpd process is started (more information about spool directories appears later in the section "Understanding the Important Directories"). If your system doesn't load lpd at startup, or if for some reason you must kill and then restart the lpd daemon, the following command starts the printer daemon:

```
lpd [options]
```

The man page on lpd gives a list of options, but one important option when configuring your Linux printers is -l, which creates a logfile that logs each print request to the system. This logfile can be useful when you're debugging your printing system.

The *lpr* Command

The lpr command submits a job to the printer, or queues a print job. What actually happens is that the file you specify is copied to the spool directory. Each printer specified for your Linux system must have its own spool directory. The size of this spool directory is specified in the minfree file located in each directory. The minfree file specifies the number of disk blocks to reserve for spooling files to the printer. This is done to keep the lpd daemon from using up the entire hard drive when spooling a print request.

lpd finds the file, which then takes care of moving the data to the physical printer. If you don't specify a file, lpr uses standard input.

The *lpq* Command

The lpq command shows you the contents of the spool directory for a given printer. One important piece of information displayed by lpq is the job ID, which identifies a particular job. This number must be specified if you want to cancel a pending job.

lpq also indicates with a number a rank for each job in the queue (meaning, where the job is in the queue). active means the file is actually printing—or at least that lpd is trying to print it.

The *lprm* Command

The lprm command removes a job from the queue—that is, it removes unprinted files from the spool directory. You can specify a job ID (obtained by using the lpq command) or specify – as the job ID, in which case all jobs belonging to you are canceled.

If you issue lpq– as root, all jobs for the printer are canceled. If you are root and want to remove all the jobs belonging to a specific user, specify the user's name.

The *lpc* Command

The lpc command lets you check the status of printers and control some aspects of their use. In particular, lpc lets you start and stop despooling on printers, enable or disable printers, and rearrange the order of jobs in a print queue. The following commands disable printing on myprinter, enable the spool queue on yourprinter, and moves job number 37 to the top of the queue:

```
lpc down myprinter
lpc enable yourprinter
lpc topq 37
```

If you invoke lpc without any command arguments, lpc is interactive, prompting you for actions to take. Some of the more important commands are shown in Table 21.3; read the man page for complete instructions. Most lpc commands take the name of the printer, as specified in /etc/printcap, as the parameter.

Table 21.3 Some Common *lpc* Commands

Command	Parameter	Description
stop	*printer*	Stops the printer, but print requests are still spooled.
start	*printer*	Allows the printer to start printing previously spooled files and any new files spooled to this printer.
exit, quit	(None)	exit or quit leaves lpc interactive mode.
status	*printer*	Displays the current status of the printer. status provides such information as whether the queue is enabled, whether the printer is enabled, and the number (if any) of jobs now in the queue waiting to be printed.

N O T E Bear in mind that some lpc commands are restricted to root—that is, the superuser. ▪

CAUTION

lpc is very unstable in its current implementation under Linux. Some users have reported that lpc can display incorrect status messages and sometimes even hang the system outright.

Understanding the Important Directories

There's only one important directory in printing—the spool area where data to be printed is accumulated before /etc/lpd prints it. However, a system is typically set up with multiple spool directories, one for each printer, to make printer management easier. For example, my system is set up to use /usr/spool/lpd as the main spool area, with each separate printer having a directory under that with the same name as the printer. Thus, a printer named ps_nff has /usr/spool/lpd/ps_nff as its spool directory.

The spool directories should belong to the daemon group and be user and group read/writable and world readable—that is, after you create the directory, make sure that it has the permissions −rwxrwxr-x (0775) with the chmod command. For the directory myprinter, the appropriate command is

```
chmod ug=rwx,o=rx myprinter
chgrp daemon myprinter
```

▶ **See** "File Permissions," **p. 293**

N O T E The locations, ownerships, and permissions given here are a simplification and may be incorrect for your system, so you should take notes on the lpd files and permissions. ▪

Understanding the Important Files

Apart from the programs discussed so far, each spool directory contains files that have the permissions −rw-rw-r-:

- ▪ */etc/printcap*   This file contains the printer specifications for each named printer in your system.
- ▪ *.seq*   This file contains the job number counter for lpr to assign.
- ▪ *status*   This file contains the message to be reported by lpc stat.
- ▪ *lock*   lpd uses this file to prevent itself from trying to print two jobs to the same printer at once.
- ▪ *errs*   This file logs printer failures.

The errs file isn't required by Linux in order to print, but the file must exist for lpd to be able to log printer failures. The errs file can be called whatever you like as long as the name is specified in /etc/printcap. The errs file is usually created manually when you set up the spool area. Later, the section "Putting It All Together" has more on this.

One very important file is /etc/printcap, which the following section describes in detail.

Understanding the /etc/printcap File

The /etc/printcap file is a text file that you can edit with your favorite editor. /etc/printcap should be owned by root and have the permissions -rw-r--r--.

The contents of /etc/printcap typically look very cryptic, but when you know how the file works, the contents are much easier to understand. To compound the problem, in some distributions there's no man page for printcap, and most printcap files are created either by programs or by people with no thought for readability. For your own sanity, make the layout of your printcap file as logical and readable as possible with lots of comments. And get the man page from the lpd sources if you don't already have it.

One printcap entry describes one printer. Essentially, a printcap entry provides a logical name for a physical device and then describes how data sent to that device should be handled. For example, a printcap entry defines what physical device is to be used, what spool directory any data for that device should be stored in, what preprocessing should be performed on the data, where errors on the physical device should be logged, and so forth. You can limit the amount of data that may be sent in a single job, or limit access to a printer to certain classes of users. The following shows how a printer is defined in the printcap file:

```
# Sample printcap entry with two aliases
myprinter¦laserwriter:\
# lp is the device to print to - here the first parallel printer.
:lp=/dev/lp0: \
# sd means spool directory - where print data is collected
:sd=/usr/spool/lpd/myprinter:
```

It's okay to have multiple printcap entries defining several different ways to handle data destined for the same physical printer. For example, a physical printer may support PostScript and HP LaserJet data formats, depending on some setup sequence being sent to the physical printer before each job. It makes sense to define two printers: one that preprocesses the data by preappending the HP LaserJet sequence, and the other that preappends the PostScript sequence. Programs that generate HP data send it to the HP printer, whereas programs generating PostScript print to the PostScript printer.

N O T E   If you don't designate a default printer via an environment variable or don't specify a printer on the lpr command line, Linux will route the print job to the lp printer. Thus, you should specify one of the printers in the printcap file as the lp printer. ▪

Programs that change the data before it's sent to the physical printer are called *filters*. It's possible for a filter to send no data at all to a physical printer—that is, the filter filters out everything.

Understanding the Fields in /etc/printcap

The printcap file has too many fields to describe fully in this chapter, so only the most important ones are described. All fields in /etc/printcap (except for the names of the printer) are enclosed between colons and denoted by a two-letter code. The two-letter code is followed by a value that depends on the type of field. There are three types of fields: string, Boolean, and numeric. Table 21.4 describes the most common and most important fields; the following sections go into more detail.

Table 21.4   The /etc/printcap Fields

Field	Type	Description
lp	String	Specify the device to print to—for example, /dev/lp0
sd	String	Specify the name of the spool directory for this printer
lf	String	Specify the file that errors on this printer are to be logged to

continues

Table 21.4 Continued

Field	Type	Description
if	String	Specify the input filter name
rm	String	Specify the name of a remote printing host
rp	String	Specify the name of a remote printer
sh	Boolean	Specify this to suppress headers (banner pages)
sf	Boolean	Specify this to suppress end-of-job form feeds
mx	Numeric	Specify the maximum allowable print job size (in blocks)

The *lp* Field   If you specify /dev/null as the print device, all other processing is performed correctly, but the final data goes to the *bit bucket*—that is, to nowhere. Printing to nowhere is rarely useful except for test printer configurations or with weird printers. When you're setting up a remote printer (that is, you've specified rm and rp fields), specify :lp=:.

Don't leave the field empty unless you're using a remote printer. The printer daemon complains if you don't specify a print device.

The *lf* Field   Whatever file you specify should already exist, or logging doesn't occur.

The *if* Field   *Input filters* are programs that take print data on their standard input and generate output on their standard output. A typical use of an input filter is to detect plain ASCII text and convert it into PostScript—that is, raw text is its input and PostScript is its output.

When you specify an input filter, the printer daemon doesn't send the spooled print data to the specified device. Instead, it runs the input filter with the spooled data as standard input and the print device as standard output.

The *rm* and *rp* Fields   Sending your print data to a printer attached to another machine is as simple as specifying the remote machine rm and the remote printer rp and making sure that the print device field lp is empty.

N O T E   Data is still spooled locally before it's transferred to the remote machine. Any input filters you specify are also run. ■

The *sh* and *sf* Fields   Unless you have a lot of different people using your printer, you're most likely not interested in banner pages, so specify sh.

Suppressing form feeds, by specifying sf, is most useful if your printer is typically used for output from word-processing packages. Most word-processing packages create complete pages of data, so if the printer daemon is adding a form feed to the end of each job, you get a blank page after each job. If the printer is usually used for program or directory listings, however, having that form feed ensures that the final page is completely ejected, so each listing starts at the top of a new page.

The *mx* Field   The mx field allows you to limit the size of the print data to be spooled. The number you specify is in BUFSIZE blocks (1K under Linux). If you specify zero, the limit is removed, allowing print jobs to be limited only by available disk space.

N O T E   The limit is on the size of the spooled data, not the amount of data sent to the physical printer. ▨

If a user tries to exceed this limit, the file is truncated. The user sees a message saying

```
(lpr: file-name: copy file is too large)
```

For non-PostScript printers, this limit is useful if you have users or programs that may deliberately or accidentally create excessively large output. For PostScript printers, the limit isn't useful at all because a very small amount of spooled PostScript data can generate a large number of output pages.

Setting the *PRINTER* Environment Variable

You may want to add a line to your login script—or even to the default user login script—that sets up a PRINTER environment variable. Under the bash shell, a suitable line is export PRINTER=myprinter. This prevents people having to specify -Pmyprinter every time they submit a print job.

To add more printers, just repeat this process with different printer names. Remember that you can have multiple printcap entries, all using the same physical device. This way, you can treat the same device differently, depending on what you call it when you submit a print job to it.

Creating a Test printcap Entry

The following shell script is a very simple input filter—it simply concatenates its input onto the end of a file in /tmp after an appropriate banner. Specify this filter in the printcap entry and specify /dev/null as the print device. The print device is never actually used, but you have to set it to something; otherwise, the printer daemon complains.

```
#!/bin/sh
# This file should be placed in the printer's spool directory and
# named input_filter. It should be owned by root, group daemon, and
# be world executable (-rwxr-xr-x).
echo -------------------------------------------- >> /tmp/
date                                               >> /tmp/
echo -------------------------------------------- >> /tmp/
cat                                                >> /tmp/
```

In the following printcap entry, notice the reasonably readable format and the use of the continuation character (\) on all but the last line:

```
myprinter¦myprinter: \
:lp=/dev/null: \
:sd=/usr/spool/lpd/myprinter: \
:lf=/usr/spool/lpd/myprinter/errs: \
```

Part
IV

Ch
21

```
:if=/usr/spool/lpd/myprinter/input_filter: \
:mx#0: \
:sh: \
:sf:
```

Putting It All Together

To put all the preceding bits together, the following steps guide you through setting up a single printer on /dev/lp0. You can then extend this to other printers. (You have to be root to do all this, by the way.)

1. Check the permissions and locations of lpr, lprm, lpc, lpq, and lpd. Earlier in this chapter, Table 21.2 lists the correct settings and directories.

2. Create the spool directory for your printer (named myprinter for now). Make sure that both the directory and printer are owned by root, group daemon, and are user and group writable, and read-only for others (-rwxrwxr-x). Use the following commands:

```
mkdir /usr/spool/lpd
mkdir /usr/spool/lpd/myprinter
chown root.daemon /usr/spool/lpd /usr/spool/lpd/myprinter
chmod ug=rwx,o=rx /usr/spool/lpd /usr/spool/lpd/myprinter
```

3. In the /usr/spool/lpd/myprinter directory, create the necessary files and give them the correct permissions and owner. Use the following commands:

```
cd /usr/spool/lpd/myprinter
touch .seq errs status lock
chown root.daemon .seq errs status lock
chmod ug=rw,o=r .seq errs status lock
```

4. Create the shell script input_filter in the /usr/spool/lpd/myprinter directory. Use the input filter given earlier in the "Creating a Test printcap Entry" section for your filter. Make sure that the file is owned by root, group daemon, and is executable by anyone. Use the following commands:

```
cd /usr/spool/lpd/myprinter
chmod ug=rwx,o=rx input_filter
```

5. Create the /etc/printcap file if it doesn't already exist. Remove all entries in it and add the test printcap entry given earlier in the "Creating a Test printcap Entry" section. Make sure that the file is owned by root and is read-only to everyone else. You can use the chmod command to set the proper file permissions: -rw-r--r-- or 644 (in octal).

6. Edit the rc.local file (you can use any ASCII editor, such as vi or emacs). Add the line /etc/lpd to the end, which runs the printer daemon each time the system boots. It's not necessary to boot now, however; just run it by hand with the lpd command.

   ▶ **See** "Starting *vi* by Using an Existing File," **p. 395**

7. Do a test print by entering

```
ls -l ¦ lpr -Pmyprinter
```

8. Look in /tmp, by using the ls command, for a file named testlp.out. It should contain your directory listing, which you can check with the more, less, or cat command. See Chapter 16, "Managing Files and Directories," for more information on these commands.

▶ **See** "Viewing the Contents of a File," **p. 309**

9. Edit /etc/printcap by using an ASCII editor such as vi:

- In the first printer entry, change both occurrences of myprinter to testlp only in the first line.
- In the second entry, change /dev/null to your real print device—for example, /dev/lp0.
- In the second entry, remove the if line completely.

Now, copy the myprinter entry so that you have two identical entries in the file.

10. Either reboot the system, or kill the printer daemon and restart it. You do this because the printer daemon looks only at the /etc/printcap file when it first starts up.

11. Do a test print again. This one should come out on your physical printer. You can use the following command:

```
ls -l ¦ -lpr  Pmyprinter
```

TROUBLESHOOTING

I get a message saying `lpd: connect: No such file or directory.` The printer daemon /etc/lpd isn't running. You may have forgotten to add it to your /etc/rc.local file. Alternatively, you did add it but haven't booted since. Add it and reboot, or just run /etc/lpd. Remember that you have to be root to do this.

I get a message saying `Job queued, but cannot start daemon.` This often appears right after the lpd: connect message—same problem as the preceding.

I get a message saying `lpd: cannot create spooldir/.seq.` You haven't created the spool directory specified in the printcap entry, or you've misnamed it. An alternative (though much less likely) answer is that you have too little disk space left.

I get a message saying `lpr: Printer queue is disabled.` As root, use lpc enable *printer-name* to enable the printer. Note that as root, you can submit jobs even to a disabled printer.

I submit a print job and there are no error messages, but nothing comes out on the physical printer. There could be many reasons:

- Make sure that the physical printer is switched on, selected, and physically connected to the device specified in the /etc/printcap file.
- Use the lpq command to see whether the entry is in the queue. If it is, the device may be busy, the printer may be down, or there may be an error on the printer. If there are errors, check the error log specified in the printcap entry for clues.

continues

continued

- You can use the `lpc status` command to check whether the printer is down and `lpc up` *printer-name*, or `lpc restart` *printer-name*, to bring it back up if it is (you need to be root to do this).

If, after checking, your print jobs still don't come out, make sure that any input filter you've specified is present in the correct directory and has the correct permissions. If you're running `syslogd`, you can look in your logs for messages from `lpd`. If you see log entries saying `cannot execv name of input filter`, this is almost certainly the problem.

Another possibility is that your printer is a PostScript printer and you're not sending PostScript to it. Most PostScript printers ignore non-PostScript data. You may need to install an appropriate text-to-PostScript input filter.

Last (and you'll feel silly if this is the cause), check that your input filter actually generates output and that the output device isn't `/dev/null`.

My printer seems to have locked up. None of the preceding techniques seems to solve the problem. When all else fails in the case of a non-printing printer, the next-to-last resort is to kill the `lpd` daemon and restart it. If that doesn't work, the last resort is to reboot your Linux system with the `shutdown -r now` command. Make sure that no one else is logged in and that you've saved any files before using the now option; otherwise, specify a time and also give a message to your other users before shutting down the system. You also can test the printer on a DOS/Windows machine to make sure that the physical device itself is working.

Configuring Red Hat Printers

If you've installed XFree86 under Red Hat, you can use the printer configuration tool shown in Figure 21.1 to add and delete printers as well as maintain the /etc/printcap and spooler files and directories. You can find this tool in the control panel.

FIG. 21.1

Managing printers is easy with Red Hat's graphical utilities.

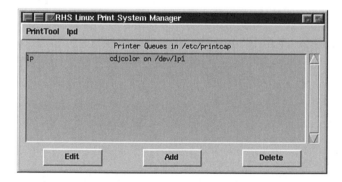

To add a new printer, click the Add button. To edit an existing printer configuration, select the entry and click the Edit button. Both actions bring up the dialog box shown in Figure 21.2.

FIG. 21.2

To print properly from Linux, you must specify certain options, such as printer name and physical port location.

If you're adding a printer, you must first specify whether it's a local or remote printer. A *local printer* is one connected to your parallel or serial port; a *remote printer* is one connected to your network. You must enter a value for each field in the dialog box. Table 21.5 describes each field.

Table 21.5   Field Items for Each Printer

Field Name	Description
Names	The name of the printer and its queue. You can specify multiple names by using the ¦ character to separate names.
Spool Directory	The directory for spooling documents for this printer, such as /usr/spool/lpd/myprinter.
File Limit	The maximum document size (in kilobytes). A 0 value indicates no limit.
Printer Device	The physical connection for you printer, such as lp0.
Input Filter	Enter the full path and file name of your custom filter. If your printer requires an EOF character to be sent at the end of the job (many DOS printers require this), click the Select button and check the EOF check box.
Suppress Headers	Check this box if you don't want a header page printed with each document.
Remote Host	This field in the Remote Host dialog box specifies the name of the remote host to which the printer is connected.
Remote Queue	This field in the Remote Host dialog box specifies the printer queue on the remote machine. Enter the full path.

After you add or change a printer entry, you may find that you need to restart the lpd daemon. To do this, simply select the lpd menu item on the RHS Linux Print System Manager and click the Restart lpd item.

From Here...

The lpr command is the standard Linux interface for printing files. From the command line, you can use lpr to print to many different types of printers and to request many different options. Later, you can check the status of your print jobs with the lpq command. If you change your mind and want to cancel a print job, you may do so with the lprm command. No matter what, you should read the latest edition of the printing HOWTO for more information.

For information on related topics, see the following:

- Chapter 3, "Installing Red Hat," discusses how to install the Red Hat distribution of Linux.

- The chapters in Part II, "Systems Administration," discuss all the details about what a systems administrator is and does.

- Appendix A, "Sources of Information," tells you how to locate the Linux Printing HOWTO.

P A R T

V

Network Administration

## CHAPTER 22

Understanding the TCP/IP Protocol Suite

The suite of widely used protocols known as Transmission Control Protocol/Internet Protocol (TCP/IP) has become extremely important as networks of all sizes, including the Internet, depend on it for their communications.

TCP/IP sprouted from initial development as a government-sponsored project to widespread use today, connecting networks of all sizes. Recognized for its capability to enable communication among dissimilar machines, it's found on virtually all workstations, minicomputers, and mainframes. This chapter describes the origins and language of TCP/IP, its addressing and naming conventions, and concepts fundamental to the creation of the Internet. ■

The history of TCP/IP

Learn how TCP/IP has grown from its roots as a U.S. Department of Defense project into the preferred set of protocol suites used to connect to the Internet.

Basic TCP/IP components

Learn about the components that make up the TCP/IP protocols and how they compare to the other major computer networking architecture model, Open Systems Interconnection.

Network addressing

This chapter explains how the addresses used by TCP/IP to identify systems on the Internet are assigned and used.

Logical networks

Learn how the parts of a computer network—servers, routers, and other devices—can be put together to form a TCP/IP network that connects to the Internet

The History of TCP/IP

In the mid-1970s, the U.S. Department of Defense (DOD) recognized an electronic communication problem developing within the department. Communicating the ever-increasing volume of electronic information among DOD staff, research labs, universities, and contractors had hit a major obstacle. The various entities had computer systems from different computer manufacturers, running different operating systems, and using different networking topologies and protocols. How could information be shared?

The Advanced Research Projects Agency (ARPA) was assigned to resolve the problem of dealing with different networking equipment and topologies. ARPA formed an alliance with universities and computer manufacturers to develop communication standards. This alliance specified and built a four-node network that's the foundation of today's Internet. During the 1970s, this network migrated to a new, core protocol design that became the basis for TCP/IP.

The mention of TCP/IP requires a brief introduction to the Internet. The Internet is a huge network of networks that allows computers all over the world to communicate. It's growing at a phenomenal rate. If I were to give an estimate of the number of computers and users on the Internet, it would be far out of date by the time this book went to print! Nodes include universities, major corporations, research labs in the United States and abroad, schools, businesses large and small, and individually owned computers. It's the backbone for the World Wide Web, a repository for millions of shareware programs, news on any topic, public forums and information exchanges, and e-mail. Another feature is remote login to any computer system on the network by using the Telnet protocol. Because of the number of systems that are interconnected, massive computer resources can be shared, enabling large programs to be executed on remote systems.

Internet Terminology

The Internet protocol suite is composed of many related protocols based on the foundation formed by TCP and IP. To clarify the relationship of these components, Table 22.1 provides some definitions and notations.

Table 22.1   Networking Terms

Term	Definition
datagram	Used interchangeably with the words *data packet* and *network message* to identify a unit of information that's exchanged.
DNS	Domain Name Service, a service provided by one or more computers in a network to help locate a path to a desired node. This saves every system on a network from having to keep a list of every system it wants to talk to. Used by mail gateways.
GOSIP	Government Open System Interconnection Profile, a collection of OSI protocols used in U.S. government computer networks and projects.

Term	Definition
Internet	A computer network based on TCP/IP and related protocols. A public network of networks interconnecting businesses, universities, government facilities, and research centers.
FTAM	File Transfer, Access, and Management, a file transfer and management protocol as specified by OSI.
FTP	File Transfer Protocol, which enables file transfer between systems.
IP	Internet Protocol, a protocol responsible for transporting datagrams across the Internet.
NFS	Network File System, a network virtual disk system that enables a client computer to mount remote file systems and directories. Originally developed by Sun Microsystems.
NIC	Network Information Center, responsible for administering Internet, TCP/IP addresses, and network names.
node	A computer on a network.
OSI	Open System Interconnection, the ISO standard model for defining data communication.
RFC	Request For Comments, the documentation maintained by the NIC relating to Internet protocols, addressing, routing, configuration, and other related Internet topics.
RIP	Routing Information Protocol, which is used to exchange information between routers.
RMON	Remote MONitor, a remote network monitor that enables the collection of information about network traffic.
RPC	Remote Procedure Call, which enables procedures to be executed on a server.
SMTP	Simple Mail Transfer Protocol, which is used to transfer electronic mail between systems.
SNMP	Simple Network Management Protocol, a protocol used to manage remote network devices and to collect information from remote devices related to configuration, errors, and alarms.
TCP	Transmission Control Protocol, the protocol between a pair of applications responsible for reliable, connection-oriented data transmission.
Telnet	The protocol used to establish remote terminal connections.
UDP	User Datagram Protocol, a connectionless protocol used to transfer data between agents.
VT	Virtual terminal, a method for using Telnet to log in to remote systems through the network.

The Open Systems Interconnection Model

Many different types of computers are used today, varying in operating systems, CPUs, network interfaces, and many other variables. These differences make the problem of communication between diverse computer systems important. In 1977, the International Organization for Standardization (ISO) created a subcommittee to develop data communication standards to promote multivendor interoperability. The result is the Open Systems Interconnection (OSI) model.

The OSI model doesn't specify any communication standards or protocols; instead, it provides guidelines that communication tasks follow.

N O T E It's important to understand that the OSI model is simply a model—a framework—that specifies the functions to be performed. It doesn't detail *how* these functions are performed. ISO, however, does certify specific protocols that meet OSI standards for parts of the OSI model. For example, the CCITT X.25 protocol is accepted by ISO as an implementation that provides most of the services of the Network layer of the OSI model.

To simplify matters, the ISO subcommittees took the divide-and-conquer approach. By dividing the complex communication process into smaller subtasks, the problem becomes more manageable, and each subtask can be optimized individually. The OSI model is divided into seven layers:

- Application
- Presentation
- Session
- Transport
- Network
- Data Link
- Physical

 T I P One easy way to remember the order of the layers (from the top down) is by making a sentence from the first letters of the layer names: All People Seem To Need Data Processing.

Each layer is assigned a specific set of functions. Each layer uses the services of the layer beneath it and provides services to the layer above it. For example, the Network layer uses services from the Data Link layer and provides network-related services to the Transport layer. Table 22.2 explains the services offered at each layer.

N O T E The concept of a layer making use of services and providing services to its adjacent layers is simple. Consider how a company operates: the secretary provides secretarial services to the president (the next layer up) to write a memo. The secretary uses the services of a messenger (the next layer down) to deliver the message. By separating these services, the secretary (application) doesn't have to know how the message is actually carried to its recipient. The secretary merely has to ask the messenger (network) to deliver it. Just as many secretaries can send memos in this way by using a standard messenger service, a layered network can send packets by handing them to the network layer for delivery. ▪

Table 22.2 Services Provided at Each OSI Layer

Layer	Description
Physical (Layer 1)	This layer provides the physical connection between a computer system and the network. It specifies connector and pin assignments, voltage levels, and so on.
Data Link (Layer 2)	This layer "packages" and "unpackages" data for transmission. It forms the information into frames. A *frame* represents the exact structure of the data physically transmitted across the wire or other medium.
Network (Layer 3)	This layer provides routing of data through the network.
Transport (Layer 4)	This layer provides sequencing and acknowledgment of transmission.
Session (Layer 5)	This layer establishes and terminates communication links.
Presentation (Layer 6)	This layer does data conversion and ensures that data is exchanged in a universal format.
Application (Layer 7)	This layer provides an interface to the application that a user executes: a "gateway" between user applications and the network communication process.

N O T E Don't confuse the Application layer with application programs you execute on the computer. Remember that the Application layer is part of the OSI model that doesn't specify *how* the interface between a user and the communication pathway happens; an application program is a specific implementation of this interface. A real application typically does Application, Session, and Presentation layer services, and leaves Transport, Network, Data Link, and Physical layer services to the network operating system. ▪

Each layer communicates with its peer in other computers. For example, Layer 3 in one system communicates with Layer 3 in another computer system.

When information is passed from one layer down to the next, a header is added to the data to indicate where the information is coming from and going to. The header-plus-data block of information from one layer becomes the data for the next. For example, when Layer 4 passes data to Layer 3, it adds its own header. When Layer 3 passes the information to Layer 2, it considers the header-plus-data from Layer 4 as data and adds its own header before passing that combination down.

In each layer, the information units are given different names (see Table 22.3). Therefore, by knowing the terms used to reference the data, you know which layer of the model is being discussed.

Table 22.3 Terms Used by OSI Layers to Refer to Information Units

OSI Layer	Information Unit Name
Application	Message
Transport	Segment
Network	Datagram
Data Link	Frame (also called *packet*)
Physical	Bit

Before the advent of the OSI model, the U.S. Department of Defense defined its own networking model, known as the *DOD model*. The DOD model is closely related to the TCP/IP suite of protocols, as explained in the following section.

The TCP/IP Protocol Stack

The TCP/IP protocol stack represents a network architecture that's similar to the ISO OSI networking model. Figure 22.1 shows the mapping of TCP/IP layers onto the ISO protocol stack.

TCP/IP doesn't make as fine distinctions between the top layers of the protocol stack as does OSI. The top three OSI layers are roughly equivalent to the Internet process protocols. Some examples of process protocols are Telnet, FTP, SMTP, NFS, SNMP, and DNS.

The Transport layer of the OSI model is responsible for reliable data delivery. In the Internet protocol stack, this corresponds to the host-to-host protocols. Examples of these are TCP and UDP. TCP is used to translate variable-length messages from upper-layer protocols and provides the necessary acknowledgment and connection-oriented flow control between remote systems.

UDP is similar to TCP, except that it's not connection-oriented and doesn't acknowledge data receipt. UDP only receives messages and passes them along to the upper-level protocols. Because UDP doesn't have any of the overhead related to TCP, it provides a much more efficient interface for such actions as remote disk services.

FIG. 22.1
OSI and TCP/IP
compared.

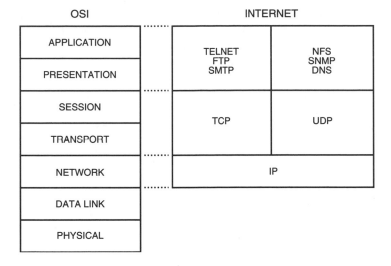

The Internet Protocol (IP) is responsible for connectionless communications between systems. It maps onto the OSI model as part of the Network layer, which is responsible for moving information around the network. This communication is accomplished by examining the Network layer address, which determines the systems and the path to send the message.

IP provides the same functionality as the Network layer and helps get the messages between systems, but it doesn't guarantee the delivery of these messages. IP may also fragment the messages into chunks and then reassemble them at the destination. Each fragment may take a different network path between systems. If the fragments arrive out of order, IP reassembles the packets into the correct sequence at the destination.

IP Addresses

The Internet Protocol requires that an address be assigned to every device on the network. This address, known as the *IP address*, is organized as a series of four octets. These octets each define a unique address, with part of the address representing a network (and optionally a subnetwork) and another part representing a particular node on the network.

Several addresses have special meanings on the Internet:

- An address starting with a zero references the local node within its current network. For example, 0.0.0.23 references workstation 23 on the current network. Address 0.0.0.0 references the current workstation.
- The loopback address, 127, is important in troubleshooting and network diagnoses. The network address 127.0.0.0 is the local loopback inside a workstation.

■ The ALL address is represented by turning on all bits, giving a value of 255. Therefore, 192.18.255.255 sends a message to all nodes on network 192.18; similarly, 255.255.255.255 sends a message to every node on the Internet. These addresses are important to use for multicast messages and service announcements.

> **CAUTION**
>
> It's important that when you assign node numbers to your workstations, you don't use 0, 127, or 255, because these are reserved numbers and have special meanings.

IP Address Classes

The IP addresses are assigned in ranges referred to as *classes*, depending on the application and the size of an organization. The three most common classes are A, B, and C. These three classes represent the number of locally assignable bits available for the local network. Table 22.4 shows the relationships among the different address classes, the available number of nodes, and the initial address settings.

Table 22.4   IP Address Classes

Class	Available Nodes	Initial Bits	Starting Address
A	2^{24}=167,772	0xxx	0-127
B	2^{16}=65,536	10xx	128-191
C	2^{8}=256	110x	192-223
D		1110	224-239
E		1111	240-255

Class A addresses are used for very large networks or collections of related networks. Class B addresses are used for large networks having more than 256 nodes (but less than 65,536 nodes). Class C addresses are used by most organizations. It's a better idea for an organization to get several class C addresses because the number of class B addresses is limited. Class D is reserved for multicast messages on the network, and class E is reserved for experimentation and development.

Obtaining IP Addresses   The administration of Internet addresses is through the Network Information Center (NIC):

Network Solutions
ATTN: InterNIC Registration Services
505 Huntmar Park Drive
Herndon, VA   22070
(703) 742-4777

ON THE WEB

You also can reach the InterNIC on the Web at **http://www.internic.net**.

When you connect a computer or a network to the Internet, in most cases your Internet service provider will be able to arrange for your network IP address registration.

Obtaining RFCs   In addition to assigning addresses, the NIC can provide other information of value. It's a repository for all technical documentation related to the Internet. It has a collection of documents that describe all the associated protocols, routing methodologies, network management guidelines, and methods for using different networking technologies.

As mentioned in Table 22.1, RFC stands for Request For Comments. You can obtain RFCs from the Internet by using the FTP protocol to connect to several different repositories. The RFC series is available on the Internet via anonymous FTP from various sites, such as **ftp.internic.net** in the /rfc directory.

Table 22.5 lists the pertinent RFCs for establishing a network. Some of these documents go into great detail about how the different protocols function and the underlying specifications and theory. Others are more general and provide key information that can be useful to a network manager. At a minimum, an Internet network manager should know where these documents are located and how to obtain them. They provide information that can help in planning and growing an organization's network.

Table 22.5   RFCs of Interest

RFC Name	Description
RFC791.txt	Internet Protocol DARPA Internet Program Protocol Specification
RFC792.txt	Internet Control Message Protocol
RFC793.txt	Transmission Control Protocol DARPA Internet Program Protocol Specification
RFC950.txt	Internet Standard Subnetting Procedure
RFC1058.txt	Routing Information Protocol
RFC1178.txt	Choosing a Name for Your Computer
RFC1180.txt	A TCP/IP Tutorial
RFC1208.txt	A Glossary of Networking Terms
RFC1219.txt	On the Assignment of Subnet Numbers
RFC1234.txt	Tunneling IPX Traffic through IP Networks

Network Naming

The naming of network nodes requires some planning. When you select names, keep network management and user acceptance in mind. Many organizations have network naming standards. If your organization has such standards in place, it's best to follow them to prevent confusion. If not, there's plenty of room for imagination. Computer and network names can be as simple as naming the workstations after the users, such as Diane, Beth, or John.

If you have many similar computers, numbering them (for example, PC1, PC2, and PC128) may be appropriate. Naming must be done in a way that gives unique names to computer systems. Don't name a computer "thecomputerinthenorthoffice" and expect users not to complain. After all, even the system administrator must type the names of computers from time to time. Also avoid names like "oiiomfw932kk." Although such a name may prevent network intruders from connecting to your computer, it may also prevent you from connecting to your workstation.

Names that are distinctive and follow a theme work well, helping the coordination of future expansion and giving the users a sense of connection with their machines. After all, it's a lot easier to have a good relationship with a machine called "sparky" than a machine called "OF1284."

Remember the following points when selecting a naming scheme:

- Keep names simple and short—six to eight characters at most. Although the Internet Protocol allows names up to 255 characters long, you should avoid this, as some systems can't handle long names. (Each label can be up to 63 characters long. Each part of a period-separated full domain name for a node is a label.)

- Consider using a theme such as stars, flowers, or colors, unless other naming standards are required at your site.

- Don't begin the name with numbers.

- Don't use special characters in the name.

- Don't duplicate names.

- Be consistent in your naming policy.

If you follow these guidelines, you can establish a successful naming methodology.

Internet names represent the organizations and the functionality of the systems within the network. Following are examples of names that you can use:

```
spanky.engineering.mycompany.com
nic.ddn.mil
```

The following are examples of names that are difficult to use or remember:

```
thisismyworkstation.thelongwindeddepartment.longcompnam.com
34556nx.m3422.mycompany.com
```

The last listed name could be encoded information about a workstation in room 345 on network 56 with network executive functions, but this type of naming scheme is usually considered poor practice because it can lead to confusion and misdirected messages.

Internet names enable you to reference a user on a particular node—for example,

Eddie@PC28.Programming.mycompany.com

NIC Naming Tree

The NIC maintains a network naming tree. This tree is used to group similar organizations under similar branches of the tree. Figure 22.2 shows the naming tree. Major organizations are grouped under similar branches. This is the source for Internet labels, such as **com**, **edu**, and **gov**, that are seen in Internet names.

FIG. 22.2
The NIC naming tree.

Table 22.6 shows some of the common leaf names and definitions for the NIC tree. Many other leaves are under the tree, but these are the most common.

Table 22.6 Common NIC Names

Name	Types of Organizations
edu	Educational facilities (such as universities and colleges)
com	Commercial (most corporations)
gov	United States non-military government bodies (White House, Department of Agriculture)
mil	Military (military users and their contractors)
net	Internet network management and administration
org	Other types of organizations (usually non-profit)

Subnetworks and Subnet Masks

Subnetting is the process of dividing a large logical network into smaller physical networks. Reasons for dividing a network may include electrical limitations of the networking technology, a desire to segment for simplicity by putting a separate network on each floor of a building (or in each department or for each application), or a need for remote locations connected with a high-speed line.

The resulting networks are smaller chunks of the whole and are easier to manage. Smaller subnets communicate among one another through gateways and routers. Also, an organization may have several subnetworks that are physically on the same network, so as to logically divide the network functions into workgroups.

The individual subnets are a division of the whole. Suppose that a class B network is divided into 64 separate subnets. To accomplish this subnetting, the IP address is viewed in two parts: network and host (see Figure 22.3). The network part becomes the assigned IP address and the subnet information bits. These bits are, in essence, removed from the host's part of the address. The assigned number of bits for a class B network is 16. The subnet part adds 6 bits, for a total of 22 bits to distinguish the subnetwork. This division results in 64 networks with 1,024 nodes in each. The network part can be larger or smaller, depending on the number of networks desired or the number of nodes per network.

FIG. 22.3

An example of Class B subnetwork masking.

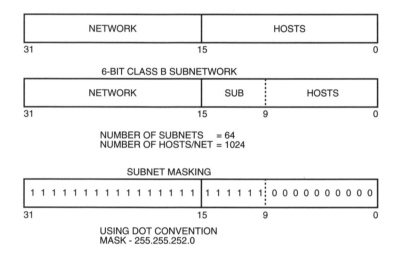

Setting a subnet mask is a matter of determining where the network address ends and the host address begins. The subnet mask contains all 1's in the network field and 0's in the host field.

Suppose that a class C network is composed of the following:

```
N = network
H = Host
NNNNNNNN.NNNNNNNN.NNNNNNNN.HHHHHHHH
```

Each position represents a single bit out of the 32-bit address space. If this class C network is to be divided into four class C networks, the pattern resembles the following:

```
NNNNNNNN.NNNNNNNN.NNNNNNNN.NNHHHHHH
```

The subnet mask looks like the following:

```
11111111.11111111.11111111.11000000
```

If this address is written in base-10 dot notation, the subnet mask is 255.255.255.192. This mask is used to communicate among nodes on all subnetworks within this particular network.

If three bits are taken from the host field, eight networks can be formed, and the resulting network mask is as follows:

`11111111.11111111.11111111.11100000`

The subnet mask is 255.255.255.224. Each of the eight networks would have 29 nodes because five address bits are available. (It would be 32 except that all 1's, all 0's, and 127 aren't legal addresses.)

This concept can be extended to class B and class A networks. The only difference is that the remaining fields are 0 (zero).

Consider a class B network. The address space is divided as follows:

`NNNNNNNN.NNNNNNNN.HHHHHHHH.HHHHHHHH`

If two bits are taken from the host field and added to the network part, the following subnet mask is used:

`11111111.11111111.11000000.00000000`

The mask is written as 255.255.192.0.

The bits needed for the subnet mask can be taken from any of the bit positions within the host field, but this leads to complex subnet masks and address exclusions. You should avoid this if at all possible.

Routing

Routing is a method of transferring information between networks. A router works at the Network layer of network protocols. Data may be routed by several different means. The routing method implemented for an Internet network is the Routing Information Protocol (RIP).

Routing Information Protocol (RIP)

RIP is designed to be used in small to medium-sized networks and is based on Xerox Network Systems (XNS) routing protocols. RIP determines a message route by using a distance-vector routing algorithm. This algorithm assumes that each path is assigned a cost. This cost can be representative of network throughput, type of line, or desirability of the path. The protocol then determines the lowest cost path over which to transmit the message. (You can obtain information about routing from several RFCs.)

How a Routing Protocol Works

To maintain a list of hops to adjacent nodes, a RIP router keeps a routing table in the router or computer memory. This table is updated at 30-second intervals with information from neighboring routers. The information is used to recalculate the lowest cost path between systems. Each router on a network sends out, or advertises, and receives routing information.

continues

continued

The routing protocol is limited in the distance a message can be routed. Each router can route a message only to a cost of 16. If the message sent out on a wire costs more than 16, the host is deemed unreachable. *Cost* is a method of assigning values to different paths through the network and is a way of ensuring an efficient route to a destination when there's more than one way to get there.

When a network break occurs, the routers must relearn least-cost paths. This takes time and can result in messages being transmitted at a higher cost for a period of time. When a node goes down, all routers must readjust their respective routing tables. During this time, messages can be lost in the network. After a period of time, the routers are again synchronized and routing continues.

Router crashes are also a concern. In the event of a crash, adjacent routers update their adjacency to a crashed router in 180 seconds. After that period of time, if no routing information is received from the crashed router, that path is removed from the local router's database.

RIP doesn't manage routing distances, just cost. As a result, RIP may not use the shortest physical path between two points. Work and modifications have been made to the protocols to help correct this problem. A newer routing protocol being developed and tested is Open Shortest Path First (OSPF), which is beginning to gain acceptance and use.

Network Segmentation

Internet networks are divided into segments for various reasons. Some of these reasons are related to the underlying networking technologies; others are related to geographical locations. Some of the best reasons to isolate network segments are based on network usage. If a lot of traffic in a network is between a few nodes, it's best to isolate those nodes. This isolation drops the usage and provides a more responsive network for the other network users.

Other reasons to segment are to change networking technologies or to communicate between different networking technologies. For example, an office area may be running Token Ring and the shop floor area may be running Ethernet. Each has a distinct function. The office may require Token Ring to communicate with an AS/400. The shop floor may have Ethernet to enable shop floor controllers and computers to communicate. The shop floor information then may be uploaded to the office network for order tracking. The connection between the technologies is usually through routers. The routers forward only information that must be exchanged from one network to the other. This information can then be shared between nodes on the respective networks.

Excessive use of routers in a network can become a burden to the network, thus outweighing their benefits. The use of a router is of little benefit if all the nodes on one network must get to all the nodes on another network, and vice versa. In this instance, the advantages of routing would be diminished because of the overhead in the routing protocols. In that kind of situation, a bridge is a better alternative.

A bridge enables all information from two networks to be shared. The access is at the Physical layer and not at the Network layer, so address translation and routing overhead aren't incurred.

A bridge enables all information, including system broadcast messages, to be transmitted. If two networks rarely share information, a router is a better choice; otherwise, a bridge is the proper choice.

Internet Network Setup

The design and configuration of an Internet network is similar to the design of any computer network. It encompasses many types of nodes, including workstations, servers, printers, mainframes, routers, bridges, gateways, print servers, and terminals. The Internet requires that each device have a unique IP address. A device can have more than one address, depending on its function, but at least one address is required for communication with the other devices.

Understanding the Types of Connections

A TCP/IP network can consist of several systems connected to a local area network or hundreds of systems with connections to thousands of systems on the Internet. Each organization can create the type of network appropriate for its needs.

Figure 22.4 shows a simple network that consists of several workstations and a file server. Each station on the network is assigned the network address of 194.62.23. Each device is assigned an individual node address. This network is typical of most departments within a company or even a small office. There's room to connect printers and more workstations to the network. The network has no provisions for connections to other local or wide area networks.

FIG. 22.4
A simple network.

The network in Figure 22.5 is more complex. It includes three separate networks interconnected through a combination of routers and servers. Each workstation and computer on each segment may or may not be isolated from using information on one of the other two networks. This is a characteristic of the subnet mask and security enabled on the servers and routers.

Information from one network is routed to one of the other networks on an as-needed basis. This type of configuration is typical of most large corporate networks. It may be chosen based on physical-length limitations of the underlying network technology or individual network loading. One or more of the networks may experience high traffic that must be distributed across several networks.

FIG. 22.5

A more complex network.

Router 1 between networks 1 and 2 provides for routing information between the two networks. If server 1 connecting networks 2 and 3 has routing enabled, information from network 3 to network 2 is routed. Also, information can be routed from network 3 to network 2 by means of server 1 and from network 2 to network 1 by means of router 1. Server 1, connecting networks 2 and 3, has two IP addresses: one IP address on network 2 and another address on network 3. The same is true for router 1, with addresses on network 2 and network 1.

Consider a situation in which there's a lot of Internet network traffic between network 3 and network 1. In this case, it may be worthwhile to place an additional router between network 1 and network 3. The additional router can eliminate some of the routing overhead on server 1 and enable information to be passed between networks when server 1 is down.

The additional router can add a level of fault tolerance to the network. This fault tolerance is based on the fact that information can still be routed to network 2 from network 3, even when server 1 is down. The path between network 3 and network 2 would be through network 1 and router 1. Figure 22.6 shows the addition of router 2.

The fault tolerance of a network improves its integrity and can be of particular importance in certain applications. If time-critical information must be shared between two networks, an alternative path should be provided between the networks. This could be provided through the use of additional routers. Because these paths may be indirect (through a third network), a configuration parameter should be used.

This parameter is usually referred to as *network cost*. The cost of a hop can be increased by increasing the value a packet takes across a network path. The default preferred path is the low-cost path; the alternative path is the high-cost path. This arrangement prevents information from being routed over the high-cost path on a regular basis.

FIG. 22.6
The network after adding a second router for fault tolerance.

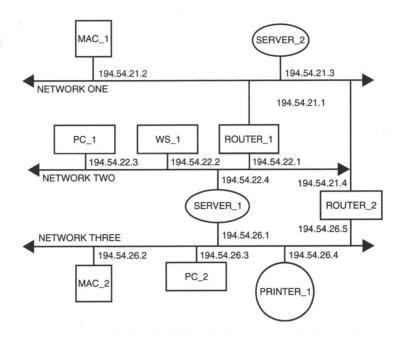

Figure 22.6 shows an additional router added between networks 1 and 3. The desired path for information from network 3 to network 2 is through server 1. Because router 2 connects network 3 and network 1, information can be routed between those two networks. Also, because router 2 is between network 1 and network 2, information is routed through that path. Information from network 3 that's bound for network 2 can go over one of the two paths: either through server 1, or through router 2 and router 1. The latter isn't the preferred path, because information can be routed directly over server 1. Therefore, a higher cost is assigned to the path of router 2 and router 1 from network 2. This type of path analysis must be performed in a multiple-segment network.

Choosing a Networking Configuration

The physical media used by an Internet network can be almost any network technology in current use. Internet network traffic isn't limited to Ethernet, ARCnet, or Token Ring. It can travel over asynchronous RS-232, T1 lines, and through frame relay. Whatever networking topology is selected for the network, the configuration, installation, and operation rules associated with that networking technology must be followed.

Keep in mind the bandwidth that an application requires. Many applications require megabytes of data to be transferred, so bandwidth becomes a prime consideration. You can usually save bandwidth by compressing files before sending them over the network.

▶ **See** "Compressing Files," **p. 315**

Another consideration is the physical location of the network. If all nodes are in the same building, a single LAN can be used. However, if the networks are located across town, a T1 connection may be needed. If the nodes are located in different geographic locations, a frame relay or a packet-switched network can be used.

In laying out a network, you must consider the type of information to be carried over the network, the physical location, and network loading. To help determine the capacity of the network, examine the type of workstations, servers, and applications.

If diskless workstations are used in a network, a higher network load is placed on the network for each node. The reason for this is that each remote diskless workstation requires all operating system code to be downloaded through the network. Because all applications, utilities, and data files are stored remotely, every action on that workstation requires network access.

Also of concern is the amount of NFS traffic that will occur on the network. NFS provides remote virtual disk services, so information retrieved and stored on these remote disks is constantly used on the network.

Other considerations are large graphical images, swapping and page files used for virtual memory, distributed database applications, printer traffic, and terminal traffic. These are all considerations in any network, but the designers and users of PC-based LANs don't usually have to contend with them. When a network is connected into a general user community, all aspects of the networking environment come into play.

Other items to be examined are the need for dial-up and remote access. If this access is related to terminal and screen traffic, a serial port from an existing system may suffice. If a Point-to-Point Protocol (PPP) connection is made, you must consider how much overhead it will impose on the network when users are loading software utilities, programs, and databases over the phone lines. This is of concern because IP isn't limited to a high-speed link such as Novell IPX and other networking protocols.

Understanding Network Configuration Guidelines

A network must be designed based on guidelines and rules. Some questions to consider when planning a network include the following:

- How will the network be used today?
- How will the network be used for the next several years?
- What applications are going to be used on the network?
- Will workgroups within the organization require networking resources in the future?
- What types and numbers of workstations will be on the network?
- How many servers, minicomputers, and other hosts will be on the network?
- What other network devices, such as printers and plotters, will be on the network?
- Will shared disk arrays and optical jukeboxes be necessary?
- Will management of the network be centralized?
- Will the network be connected to the Internet or other corporate networks, or will it be the basis for a wide area network?

- What other protocols will use the networking technology (IPX, DECNET, LAT, OSI protocols, and TCP/IP)?
- Where will critical data be interchanged (determine several different paths)?
- How will the network grow and change?

After you address all these questions, the network can be defined. The number of nodes indicates how many class C address spaces are needed or whether a class B is needed.

Connection to remote facilities should also be addressed. The load can be distributed across multiple network segments. Try to minimize the traffic that has to go across networks. For example, if you have two systems that exchange a lot of information and hops across three networks are required for them to communicate, consider moving the systems to the same network.

Determine the best networking topology to meet the requirements specified in the network analysis. To allow for growth in the network, the best approach is to determine the maximum load and to develop a network in which that load is at a minimum.

Using Routers and Bridges

Special-purpose devices are used to provide connections between networks and systems. Sometimes the terms *gateway* and *router* are used interchangeably. Strictly speaking, *gateway* describes a system that sends messages between different types of networks; a *router* sends messages between networks of the same type.

In this text, *router* is routinely used to describe any device that takes messages from one network and passes them through to another network. The router contains enough intelligence to know whether the message received must be forwarded to another network or a router.

Routers operate at the Network layer and are usually associated with a protocol, such as IP or IPX. Most routers that route IPX traffic can route IP traffic as well. The router is used to connect multiple local and wide area networks. It provides a method of sharing data between networks. Also, because a router works at the Network layer, it can help reduce broadcast traffic.

If one network uses a lot of different protocols and another network uses only IP, a router that routes only IP messages is needed if those two networks are to communicate. The router prevents messages from being placed on a network that can't manage them.

Bridges, on the other hand, can be used to interconnect local and wide area networks; they share information regardless of protocol. A bridge allows two interconnected networks to have many different protocols on them at the same time. The messages forwarded by a bridge usually don't contain any further routing information. The messages are usually left undisturbed.

One drawback of bridges is that all network broadcast and multicast messages from all interconnected networks are seen on all legs connected by a bridge. This results in a lot of overhead related to network update messages. Also, a bridge forwards messages only to network addresses on the other side of the bridge, but it can forward all network protocols and broadcast messages.

Routers and bridges are used to share information between networks. The appropriateness of each is determined by networking requirements, the protocols involved, network capacity, and user demands. The proper selection of components can help a network operate efficiently, allow for future growth, and help ensure continued reliability.

N O T E Use bridges only if multiple protocol packets are to be shared. Otherwise, a router is a better choice because it helps reduce network overhead. ■

From Here...

You can find more information about TCP/IP in the following chapters:

- Chapter 23, "Configuring a TCP/IP Network," shows how to set up and configure your networking system for Linux.

- Chapter 24, "Configuring Domain Name Service," explains the Internet name resolution system.

- Chapter 25, "Using SLIP and PPP," shows how to configure asynchronous TCP/IP over serial lines.

Configuring a TCP/IP Network

Configuring a TCP/IP network is one of the more common tasks you'll face when administering Linux machines. In the most basic cases, it's not very complex, but it does require a bit of thought on the design of your network and knowledge of a small number of programs and configuration files. ■

Configuring TCP/IP

Configuring TCP/IP involves a set of configuration files in the /etc directory. These files tell Linux what its IP address, host name, and domain name are; they also control the network interfaces.

Configuring the interface

To configure your Ethernet interfaces, you use the ifconfig program. ifconfig sets up network interfaces such as the software loopback and Ethernet cards so Linux can use them.

Routing

Routing determines the path a packet takes from its source through the network to its destination. You use the route program to specify routes and other networking information.

Monitoring your network

The netstat program displays the kernel routing table, the status of active network connections, and useful statistics about each network interface. Use the netstat program to monitor and troubleshoot networking problems.

Understanding the TCP/IP Configuration Files

TCP/IP networking in Linux is controlled by a set of configuration files in the /etc directory. These files tell Linux what its IP address, host name, and domain name are and also control the network interfaces. Table 23.1 shows you what each file does; the following sections discuss these files in detail.

Table 23.1 Linux TCP/IP Networking Configuration Files

File	Description
/etc/hosts	Maps host names to IP addresses
/etc/networks	Maps domain names to network addresses
/etc/rc.d/rc3.d/S10network	Configures and activates your Ethernet interfaces at boot time

The /etc/hosts File

Every computer on a TCP/IP network has an IP address, canonical host name, and zero or more host name aliases. The /etc/hosts file is the original method for mapping host names to IP addresses.

N O T E All host names, domain names, and IP addresses used in this chapter are fictional and don't reflect *any* true network on the Internet. ■

For illustrative purposes, look at the network that Tristar, Inc. has built. This network consists of the single class B network address assigned to Tristar by InterNIC (the organization that controls Internet addresses); this network has been split into two class C subnetworks. The format for the hosts file is as follows:

```
# /etc/hosts for unix1.tristar.com
#
# For loopbacking.
127.0.0.1      localhost

# This machine
166.82.1.21      unix1.tristar.com unix1      # the local machine

# Other hosts on our network
166.82.1.20      server.tristar.com server       # the server
166.82.1.22      wk1.tristar.com                 # workstation 1
166.82.1.10      netpr1.tristar.com netpr1       # networked printer
166.82.1.1       gateway.tristar.com gateway      # the router
166.82.1.1       gate-if1                 # 1st interface on gateway
166.82.2.1       gate-if2                 # 2nd interface on gateway
166.82.1.30      unixlt.tristar.com unixlt      # Laptop via PLIP

# end of hosts file
```

Notice that the preceding gateway has two host names for the IP address 166.82.1.1. Giving a unique name to each network interface on a machine is a good idea. Doing so makes it easier to see what's going on when you use the `ifconfig` and `route` commands.

The format of the hosts file consists of one IP address per line beginning in the first column, the canonical host name associated with that address, and then zero or more aliases. The fields are separated by spaces or tabs. Empty lines and text following a # character are treated as comments and are ignored.

The IP address 127.0.0.1 is known as the *local loopback address* and is reserved for this purpose. It's normally assigned the name localhost. If you're going to use your machine only as a stand-alone system or use SLIP or PPP to connect to the outside world, you need only the localhost address in your hosts file.

N O T E The function of the /etc/hosts file has been mostly taken over by Domain Name Service (DNS) on machines connected to the Internet or large internal networks. DNS isn't available during boot-up or when you're running in single-user mode, however, so it's a good idea to place the information for essential machines such as servers and gateways in /etc/hosts.

On a network with only a few machines that aren't connected to the Internet, it's easier to keep a complete listing of all hosts in /etc/hosts rather than configure and maintain DNS. ■

 Naming your networks makes it convenient to do things such as static routing that take a host name or network name. You don't have to remember the subnets by their IP addresses, just their names.

The /etc/networks File

Just as hosts have names and IP addresses, networks and subnets can be named. This naming is handled by the /etc/networks file. The IP addresses in the networks file include only the network address portion plus the subnetwork byte. The following is an example file for tristar.com:

```
# /etc/networks for tristar.com

localnet      127.0.0.0      # software loopback network
tristar-c1    166.82.1       # Development Group Network, Class C
tristar-c2    166.82.2       # MIS Network, Class C

# end of networks file
```

First is the localnet name and IP address, 127.0.0.0. If you aren't connecting your Linux machine to a TCP/IP network or are using only SLIP or PPP, all you need to put in this file is the localnet name and IP address.

The next lines identify the two class C subnetworks that Tristar has made from its class B network.

Initializing Ethernet Interfaces

The ifconfig program makes network interfaces such as the software loopback and Ethernet cards known to the Linux kernel, so that Linux can use them. The ifconfig program is also used to monitor and change the state of network interfaces. A simple invocation of ifconfig is

ifconfig *interface address*

which activates the specified network interface and assigns an IP address to it. This is called *bringing up an interface*. The generalized calling syntax for ifconfig is

ifconfig *interface* [*aftype*] [*options*] ¦ *address*

Table 23.2 lists the command-line arguments for ifconfig.

Table 23.2 Command-Line Arguments for *ifconfig*

Argument	Description
interface	The name of the network interface, usually the name of the device driver followed by an identification number. This argument is required.
aftype	The address family that should be used for decoding and displaying all protocol addresses. Now, the inet (TCP/IP), ddp (Appletalk Phase 2), ipx (Novell), and AX.25 and netrom (both amateur packet radio) address families are supported. The inet family is the default.
up	Activates the specified interface.
down	Deactivates the specified interface.
[-]arp	Turns on or off the use of the ARP protocol on the specified interface. The minus sign is used to turn off the flag.
[-]trailers	Turns on or off trailers on Ethernet frames. This isn't currently implemented in the Linux networking system.
[-]allmulti	Turns on or off the promiscuous mode of the interface. Turning this mode on tells the interface to send all traffic on the network to the kernel, not just traffic addressed to your machine.
metric *N*	Sets the interface metric to the integer value N. The metric value represents the "cost" of sending a packet on this route. Route costing isn't currently used by the Linux kernel but is to be implemented at a future date.
mtu *N*	Sets the maximum number of bytes the interface can handle in one transfer to the integer value N. The current networking code in the kernel doesn't handle IP fragmentation, so make sure that the MTU (Maximum Transmission Unit) value is set large enough.

Argument	Description
dstaddr *addr*	Sets the IP address of the other end of a point-to-point link. It has been made obsolete by the pointopoint keyword.
netmask *addr*	Sets the IP network mask for the specified interface.
[-]broadcast [*addr*]	Sets the broadcast address for the interface when an address is included. If no address is given, the IFF_BROADCAST flag for the specified interface is turned on. A leading minus sign turns off the flag.
[-]pointopoint [*addr*]	Turns on point-to-point mode on the specified interface. This tells the kernel that this interface is a direct link to another machine. The address, when included, is assigned to the machine on the other end of the list. If no address is given, the IFF_POINTOPOINT flag for the interface is turned on. A leading minus sign turns off the flag.
hw	Sets the hardware address for the specified interface. The name of the hardware class and the ASCII equivalent of the hardware address must follow this keyword. Ethernet (ether), AMPR AX.25 (ax25), and PPP (ppp) are now supported.
address	The host name or IP address to be assigned to the specified interface. Host names used here are resolved to their IP address equivalents. This parameter is required.

You normally don't need to use all the options. ifconfig can set everything needed from just the interface name, netmask, and IP address assigned. You only need to explicitly set most parameters when ifconfig misses or you have a complex network.

> **CAUTION**
>
> If your Linux machine is on a network, the ifconfig program must be kept secure from unauthorized use. Setting a network interface to promiscuous mode allows a person to snoop in your network and get sensitive data such as passwords. This is a serious breach of security.
>
> ▶ **See** "Handling Physical Security," **p. 238**

Using *ifconfig* to Inspect a Network Interface

Running ifconfig with no arguments causes it to output the status of all network interfaces the kernel knows about. Running ifconfig with just an interface name on the command line prints the status of the interface:

```
$ ifconfig lo
lo        Link encap Local Loopback
          inet addr 127.0.0.1 Bcast 127.255.255.255 Mask 255.0.0.0
          UP LOOPBACK RUNNING MTU 2000 Metric 1
          RX packets 0 errors 0 dropped 0 overruns 0
          TX packets 1658 errors 10 dropped 0 overruns 0
```

Part
V

Ch
23

This example uses lo, the software loopback interface. You can see the assigned IP address (inet addr), broadcast address (Bcast), and netmask (Mask). The interface is UP with an MTU of 2000 and a Metric of 1. The last two lines give statistics on the number of packets received (RX) and transmitted (TX), along with packet error, dropped, and overrun counts.

Configuring the Software Loopback Interface

All Linux machines with the networking layer installed in the kernel have a software loopback interface. This interface is used to test networking applications and to provide a network for local TCP/IP services when the machine isn't connected to a real network.

The network interface name for the loopback system is lo. Enter the following to run ifconfig:

ifconfig lo 127.0.0.1

This activates the loopback interface and assigns the address 127.0.0.1 to it. This is the address traditionally used for the loopback because the class A network, 127.0.0.0, will never be assigned to anyone by InterNIC.

To make the loopback system fully operational, you need to add a route for it with the route command, which is discussed later in the section "Understanding TCP/IP Routing."

Configuring a Network Interface

Configuring an Ethernet network interface takes a little bit more work, especially if you're using subnetworks. The basic call to ifconfig looks like this for unix1.tristar.com:

```
ifconfig eth0 unix1
```

This causes ifconfig to activate Ethernet interface 0, look up the IP address for unix1 in the /etc/hosts file, and assign it to this interface. Examining the eth0 interface at this point reveals the following code:

```
$ ifconfig eth0
eth0      Link encap 10Mbps Ethernet HWaddr 00:00:E1:54:3B:82
          inet addr 166.82.1.21Bcast166.82.1.255 Mask 255.255.255.0
          UP BROADCAST RUNNING MTU 1500 Metric 0
          RX packets 3136 errors 217 dropped 7 overrun 26
          TX packets 1752 errors 25 dropped 0 overrun 0
          Interrupt:10 Base address:0x300
```

Note that the broadcast address and netmask were set automatically by ifconfig based on the IP address it found in /etc/hosts. If you're using subnetworks, you need to specify the broadcast address and netmask explicitly. For example, if you have a class C network and are using the first bit in the host portion of the address to make two subnetworks, you must specify the broadcast address and netmask when running ifconfig:

```
ifconfig eth0 unix1 broadcast 166.82.1.127 netmask 255.255.255.128
```

Configuring Parallel IP Interfaces

The Parallel IP (PLIP), Serial Line IP (SLIP), and Point-to-Point Protocol (PPP) interfaces are managed by `ifconfig` somewhat differently. To bring up a PLIP interface, you add the `pointopoint` option to the `ifconfig` command line. Assume that the Tristar laptop unixlt is attached to the first parallel port on unix1. You call `ifconfig` as follows to activate the PLIP link:

```
ifconfig plip0 unix1 pointopoint unixlt
```

This activates the `plip0` interface with the IP address for unix1, sets the `pointopoint` flag, and tells the interface that the IP address for the other end of the link is unixlt. `ifconfig` looks up the IP addresses for unix1 and unixlt in /etc/hosts and assigns the addresses appropriately. On a laptop, you use the analogous call

```
ifconfig plip0 unixlt pointopoint unix1
```

▶ **See** "Understanding the Requirements for SLIP and PPP," **p. 506**

See "Understanding the Requirements for SLIP and PPP," p. 506

Understanding TCP/IP Routing

Routing determines the path a packet takes from its source through the network to its destination. This path is determined by matching the destination IP address against the kernel routing tables and transmitting the packet to the indicated machine, which may or may not be the destination of the packet. The kernel routing table contains information in the form "To get to network X from machine Y, send the packet to machine Z with a cost of 1," along with time-to-live and reliability values for that route.

Deciding on a Routing Policy

The first step in setting up routing on your network is deciding on a routing policy. For small, unconnected networks, using the `route` command to set up static routes on each machine at boot time is sufficient. Large networks with many subnets or networks connected to the Internet need to use dynamic routing. The routing program provides dynamic routing by communicating with routing programs on other machines and installing routes based on what it learns about the topology of the network.

A very common strategy combines static and dynamic routing. Machines on each subnet use static routing to reach their immediate neighbors. The default route—the route used for packets that match no other route in the routing table—is set to a gateway machine that's doing dynamic routing and knows about the rest of the world. Large networks can be constructed this way, minimizing the hassle of configuration files and the amount of bandwidth used by the dynamic routing programs.

Using the /sbin/route Program

The /sbin/route program manipulates the kernel routing table and is used to set static routes to other computers or networks via interfaces that have been configured and activated by `ifconfig`. This is normally done at boot time by the /etc/rc.d/rc3.d/S10network script. Table 23.3 describes the command-line arguments for /sbin/route.

Part
V

Ch
23

Table 23.3 Command-Line Arguments for /sbin/route

Argument	Description
(None)	Giving no option to /sbin/route causes it to output the current routing table.
-n	This argument causes the same output as giving no option, but replaces host names with their numerical IP addresses.
del	This argument deletes the route for the specified destination address from the routing table.
add	This argument adds to the routing table a route to the specified address or network.

Examining the Kernel Routing Table   Running /sbin/route without any command-line arguments or just -n outputs the routing table:

```
/sbin/route
Kernel routing table
Destination Gateway Genmask    Flags Metric Ref UseIface
127.0.0.0   *       255.0.0.0 U     0      0   100 lo
```

This is from a machine with just the loopback interface activated. Table 23.4 describes the fields in the routing table report.

Table 23.4 The Fields in the Routing Table Report

Field	Description
Destination	The destination IP address of the route.
Gateway	The host name or IP address of the gateway the route uses. If there's no gateway, an asterisk is output.
Genmask	The netmask for the route. The kernel uses this to set the generality of a route by bitwise ANDing the Genmask against a packet's IP address before comparing it to the destination IP address of the route.
Flags	The flags for the route (U means up, H means host, G means gateway, D means dynamic route, and M means modified).
Metric	The metric cost for the route. This isn't currently supported in the kernel networking layer.
Ref	The number of other routes that rely on the presence of this route.
Use	The number of times the routing table entry has been used.
Iface	The network interface to which this route delivers packets.

Returning to the Tristar network, the following is an example from the laptop unixlt, with a
SLIP link up and running:

```
$ /sbin/route
Kernel routing table
Destination     Gateway         Genmask          Flags Metric Ref Use Iface
slip.tristar.c  *               255.255.255.255  UH    0      0   0   sl0
127.0.0.0       *               255.0.0.0        U     0      0   100 lo
default         slip.tristar.c  *                UG    0      0   1   sl0
```

The table entry for the loopback is the same as before, and there are two new entries. The first
specifies a route to slip.tristar.com. The other new entry specifies a default route by using
slip.tristar.com as a gateway.

> **N O T E** Every machine connected to a network must have a default route in its routing table. The
> default route is used when no other routing table entry matches the destination for a
> packet. ▪

Adding Static Routes   You add routes to the routing table by running the route program
with the add argument. The command-line argument syntax for the route add command is

```
route add [ -net ¦ -host ] addr [gw gateway] [metric cost]
➥[netmask mask] [dev device]
```

Table 23.5 describes the command-line arguments that the route add command uses.

Table 23.5   Command-Line Arguments Used by *route add*

Argument	Description
-net ¦ -host	Forces the specified address to be treated as a network or host address.
addr	The destination address for the new route. This can be an IP address, host name, or network name.
gw gateway	Specifies that any packets for this address be routed through the specified gateway.
metric cost	Sets the metric field in the routing table.
netmask mask	Specifies the netmask of the route being added. The route program will guess what this is, so you don't need to specify it under normal circumstances.
dev device	Forces route to associate the new route with the specified network interface device. Again, route usually guesses correctly what device to use for the new route, so you don't have to use this often.

Part V Ch 23

CAUTION

When adding a gateway route to the routing table, you must make sure that the specified gateway is reachable. You usually have to add a static route for the gateway before adding the route by using the gateway.

Looking at Routing Examples   Now for some examples, starting with the loopback interface. After configuring the loopback interface with `ifconfig`, you need to add a route to it, as in the following:

```
# route add 127.0.0.1
```

Nothing else is needed because `route` compares the address given to it with the addresses for the known interfaces and assigns the loopback interface to the new route. The following example shows how to set the routing for the SLIP link on the Tristar unixlt machine after the SLIP link is established and `ifconfig` is used to activate the interface:

```
# route add slip.tristar.com
# route add default gw slip.tristar.com
```

The first command adds a static route for the host slip.tristar.com; the second one tells the kernel to use slip.tristar.com as a gateway for all packets with unknown destinations.

CAUTION

Make sure that any host names you use with the `route` command are in the /etc/hosts file so that `route` can find the IP addresses for them; otherwise, `route` fails.

If you're subnetting your network by splitting the IP address in the middle of an octet, you'll have to specify the required netmask when running `route`. For example, if you have a class C network and have four subnets using the first two bits of the last octet, you need to run `route` like this:

```
# route add hostname netmask 255.255.255.192
```

This ensures that `route` puts the right netmask in the routing table entry.

For Ethernet and other broadcast network interfaces, you need to add routes that tell the kernel what network can be reached via each configured interface. After using `ifconfig` to bring up the eth0 network interface on unix1.tristar.com as you did previously, you need to run `route` to install the route to the network on that interface:

```
# route add -net 166.82.1.0
```

That may not look like enough to set the routing table entry correctly, because no interface is indicated; however, `route` manages to find the interface by comparing the IP address on the command line to the IP address of each network interface. It assigns the route to the interface that matches it. In this case, eth0 has been assigned the address 166.82.1.21 with a netmask of 255.255.255.0. This matches the network address given in the `route` command, so `route` installs a route to the network 166.82.1.0 by using interface eth0, as follows:

```
$ route
Kernel routing table
Destination     Gateway       Genmask          Flags Metric Ref  UseIface
166.82.1.0      *             255.255.255.0    UN    0      0    0 eth0
127.0.0.0       *             255.0.0.0        U     0      0    100 lo
```

To tell unix1 how to reach the other subnet, you need two more routing table entries to be safe:

```
# route add gateway.tristar.com
# route add -net 166.82.2.0 gw gateway.tristar.com
```

This adds a static route to gateway.tristar.com and then adds a network route for 166.82.2.0 by using gateway.tristar.com as the gateway for that network, as shown in the following:

```
$ route
Kernel routing table
Destination     Gateway          Genmask          Flags Metric Ref UseIface
gateway.tristar *                255.255.255.0    UH    0      0   0 eth0
166.82.1.0      *                255.255.255.0    UN    0      0   0 eth0
166.82.2.0      gateway.tristar  255.255.255.0    UN    0      0   0 eth0
127.0.0.0       *                255.0.0.0        U     0      0   100 lo
```

This shows the static route you added for gateway.tristar.com and the gatewayed route to the 166.82.2.0 network.

Deleting Routes with the *route* Command   You delete routes by calling route with the del option and specifying the destination address of the route you want to delete. For example,

```
# route del -net 166.82.2.0
```

deletes the network route for network 166.82.2.0.

Monitoring a TCP/IP Network with *netstat*

The netstat program is an invaluable tool in monitoring your TCP/IP network. It can display the kernel routing table, the status of active network connections, and useful statistics about each network interface. Table 23.6 describes the common command-line arguments for netstat; a few additional arguments are targeted for advanced users. Refer to the man page for more information.

Table 23.6   Common Command-Line Arguments for the *netstat* Program

Argument	Description
-a	Shows information about all Internet connections, including those that are just listening.
-i	Shows statistics for all network devices.
-c	Shows continually updating network status. This makes netstat output a network status listing once per second until it's interrupted.

continues

Part
V

Ch
23

Table 23.6   Continued

Argument	Description
-n	Shows remote and local addresses and port information in numeric/raw form rather than resolve host names and service names.
-o	Shows the timer state expiration time and backoff state of each network connection.
-r	Shows the kernel routing table.
-t	Shows only TCP socket information, including those that are just listening.
-u	Shows only UDP socket information.
-v	Shows the version information for netstat.
-w	Shows raw socket information.
-x	Shows UNIX domain socket information.

Displaying Active Network Connections

Running netstat with no command-line arguments generates a listing of the active network connections on your machine. The following demonstrates the default output from netstat:

```
$ netstat
Active Internet connections
Proto Recv-Q Send-Q Local Address          Foreign Address        (State)
tcp        0      0 unix1.tristar.com:1266 server.tristar.:telnet ESTABLISHED
Active UNIX domain sockets
Proto RefCnt Flags     Type         State      Path
unix 1       [ ACC ]   SOCK_STREAM  LISTENING  /dev/printer
unix 2       [ ]       SOCK_STREAM  CONNECTED  /dev/log
unix 2       [ ]       SOCK_STREAM  CONNECTED
unix 1       [ ACC ]   SOCK_STREAM  LISTENING  /dev/log
```

The first section shows an active TCP protocol connection from port 1266 on unix1.tristar.com to the telnet port on server.tristar.com by user lance. Table 23.7 describes the fields in the Active Internet Connections listing.

Table 23.7   Active Internet Connection Fields

Field	Description
Proto	The protocol used by this connection, TCP, or UDP.
Recv-Q	The number of bytes received on this socket but not yet copied by the user program.

Field	Description
Send-Q	The number of bytes sent to the remote host that haven't been acknowledged.
Local Address	Local host name and port number assigned to this connection. The socket IP address is resolved to the canonical host name for that address, and the port number is translated into the service name unless the -n flag is used.
Foreign Address	The foreign host name and port number assigned to this connection. The -n flag affects this field as it does the Local Address field.
State	The current state of the socket. It can be in one of the following states:

	ESTABLISHED	The connection is fully established. The
	SYN_SENT	socket is now trying to make a connection to a remote host.
	SYN_RECV	The connection is being initialized. The
	FIN_WAIT1	socket has been closed and is waiting for the connection to shut down.
	FIN_WAIT2	The connection has been closed. The socket is waiting for a shutdown from the remote host.
	TIME_WAIT	The socket is closed and is waiting for a remote host shutdown retransmission.
	CLOSED	The socket isn't in use.
	CLOSE_WAIT	The remote host has shut down its connection. The local host is waiting for the socket to close.
	LAST_ACK	The remote connection is shut down and the socket is closed. The local host is waiting for an acknowledgment.
	LISTEN	The socket is listening for the incoming connection attempt.
	UNKNOWN	The state of the socket isn't known.
	User	The login ID of the user who owns the socket.

The second section displays active UNIX domain sockets. UNIX domain sockets are an IPC (interprocess communication) mechanism that uses the UNIX file system as the rendezvous system. Processes create special files in the file system that are then opened by other processes on the machine that wants to communicate. The preceding netstat listing show two sockets listening: one on /dev/printer and the other on /dev/log. There are also two currently connected sockets: one to /dev/log and one which has no specified path associated with it. Table 23.8 describes the fields in the Active UNIX Domain Sockets listing.

Table 23.8   Fields in the Active UNIX Domain Sockets Listing

Field	Description
Proto	The protocol in use on this socket. This will usually be `unix`.
RefCnt	The number of processes attached to this socket.
Flags	The flags for this socket. Now, the only known flag is SO_ACCEPTON (ACC), which indicates that the socket is unconnected and the process that made the socket is waiting for a connection request.
Type	The mode in which the socket is accessed. This field will contain one of the following keywords:

	OCK_DGRAM	Datagram, connectionless mode
	OCK_STREAM	Connection-oriented stream mode
	OCK_RAW	Raw mode
	OCK_RDM	Reliably delivered message mode
	OCK_SEQPACKET	Sequential packet mode
	NKNOWN	Mode not known to `netstat` program

Field	Description
State	The current state of the socket. The following keywords are used:

	FREE	The socket isn't allocated.
	LISTENING	The socket is waiting for a connection request.
	UNCONNECTED	There's no current connection on the socket.
	CONNECTING	The socket is attempting to make a connection.
	CONNECTED	The socket has a current connection.
	DISCONNECTING	The socket is attempting to shut down a connection.
	UNKNOWN	The state of the socket is unknown. You won't see this under normal operating conditions.

Field	Description
Path	This is the path name used by other processes to connect to the socket.

 TIP

Network interfaces that drop many packets or are getting many overrun errors can be a symptom of an overloaded machine or network. Checking the network interface statistics is a quick way of diagnosing this problem.

Invoking `netstat` with the -o option adds the internal state information to the Active Internet Connections listing. The following is an example of this:

```
$ netstat -o
Active Internet connections
Proto Recv-Q Send-Q Local Address       Foreign Address       (State)
tcp        0      0 localhost:1121      localhost:telnet      ESTABLISHED
➥off (0.00/0)
tcp        0      0 localhost:telnet    localhost:1121        ESTABLISHED
➥on  (673.69/0)
```

The added data is at the end of each line and includes receiver retransmission byte count, transmitter retransmission byte count, timer state (on/off), and time/backoff values (in parentheses). The time displayed is the time left before the timer expires. The backoff is the retry count for the current data transmission. This data is useful in diagnosing network problems by making it easy to see which connection is having problems.

N O T E Because the –o option outputs the state of internal TCP/IP data, the format of this data may change or this option may be removed in a later release of the networking software. ▨

Examining the Kernel Routing Table

Invoking netstat with the -r option prints out the kernel routing table. The format is the same as for the route command.

Displaying Network Interface Statistics

Invoking netstat with the -i option prints out usage statistics for each active network interface—another excellent tool for debugging network problems. With this command, it's very easy to see when packets are being dropped, overrun, and so on.

The following is an example of using the -i option, and Table 23.9 explains each field in the listing.

```
$ netstat -i
Kernel Interface table
Iface  MTU Met  RX-OK RX-ERR RX-DRP RX-OVR TX-OK TX-ERR TX-DRP TX-OVR Flags
lo     2000 0      0      0      0      0  1558      1      0      0 LRU
```

Table 23.9   Fields in the Kernel Interface Table

Field	Description
Iface	The name of the network interface.
MTU	The largest number of bytes that can be sent in one transmission by this interface.
Met	The metric value for this interface.
RX-OK	The number of packets received with no errors.
RX-ERR	The number of packets received with errors.
RX-DRP	The number of packets dropped.
RX-OVR	The number of packet overrun errors.
TX-OK	The number of packets transmitted with no errors.
TX-ERR	The number of packets transmitted with errors.

continues

Table 23.9 Continued	
Field	**Description**
TX-DRP	The number of packets dropped during transmission.
TX-OVR	The number of packets dropped due to overrun errors.
Flags	The following flags can be shown in this field:

A	The interface receives packets for multicast addresses.
B	The interface receives broadcast packets.
D	The interface debugging feature is now activated.
L	This is the loopback interface.
M	The interface is in promiscuous mode.
N	The interface doesn't process trailers on packets.
O	The Address Resolution Protocol is turned off on this interface.
P	This interface is being used as a point-to-point connection.
R	The interface is running.
U	The interface has been activated.

From Here...

This chapter covers the basics of configuring a Linux machine for use on a network. More information can be found in the man pages for the discussed commands. For more information on TCP/IP networking and configuration, see the following chapters:

- Chapter 17, "Understanding Linux Shells," gives more details on writing shell scripts.

- Chapter 22, "Understanding the TCP/IP Protocol Suite," explains the details of the TCP/IP protocols.

- Chapter 24, "Configuring Domain Name Service," shows you how to set up Linux as a DNS client and server.

Configuring Domain Name Service

Originally, when the Internet was first formed, the number of hosts on the Net was very small. It was fairly easy to maintain the name/address mapping. Each host simply had a complete list of all host names and addresses in a local file. As the growth of the Internet accelerated, this system quickly became unwieldy. When a new host was added, it was necessary to update every host file on every computer. Also, because each new computer resulted in a new line in every host file, the size of the host files began to grow to quite a large size. Clearly, a new solution was needed.

Mapping Internet system names to IP addresses is a task that requires a good degree of consideration. With the explosive growth of the Internet over the past few years, the original system of maintaining host name to IP address mappings in a local flat ASCII file quickly proved impractical. With thousands of computers on the Net and more being added daily, a new system was needed. That new system was a network-wide distributed database known as BIND, the Berkeley Internet Domain server. Also referred to variously as the Domain Name Service, the Domain Name System, or DNS, this system provides an effective, relatively transparent host name to the IP address mapping mechanism.

Understanding DNS

The Domain Name System (DNS) provides an effective, relatively transparent host name to the IP address mapping mechanism.

Configuring the resolver

You must configure your local resolver library if you intend to use DNS name resolution.

Setting up the server with *named*

The DNS name server under Linux is provided by the named daemon, which reads its configuration information from a set of configuration files. In this chapter, you learn to set up named and get full DNS running on your Linux system.

Troubleshooting DNS

Because DNS is a very complex system, you can do many things wrong. Most of the problems result from syntax errors in your configuration files.

DNS is notoriously hard to configure, but when you're successful, it's fairly easy to maintain. This chapter provides a basic overview of how to set up and configure a DNS system. It is, by no means, a complete reference; whole books are available on the subject. ■

Introducing DNS

DNS provides a mechanism for converting IP addresses into mnemonic names that represent hosts, networks, and mail aliases. It does this by dividing the entire Internet IP and name space into different logical groups. Each group has authority for its own computers and other information.

Because DNS is a complicated topic, it has its own specialized set of terms. Table 24.1 lists the definitions of some commonly used DNS terms.

Table 24.1 Commonly Used DNS Terms

Term	Definition
Domain	The logical entity or organization that represents a part of a network. For example, **unc.edu** is the name of the primary domain for the University of North Carolina at Chapel Hill.
Domain name	The name portion of a host name that represents the domain that contains the host. For example, in the address **sunsite.unc.edu**, the domain name is **unc.edu**. Also used interchangeably with *domain*.
Host	A computer on a network.
Node	A computer on a network.
Name server	A computer that provides DNS services to map DNS names to IP addresses.
Resolve	The act of translating a DNS name into its corresponding IP address.
Resolver	A program or library routine that extracts DNS information from a name server.
Reverse resolution	Matching a given IP address to its DNS name.
Spoof	The act of appearing to the network as having a different IP address or domain name.

DNS can be conceptually divided into the following three parts:

■ *Domain name space.* This is a specification for a tree structure that identifies a set of hosts and provides information about them. Conceptually, each node in the tree has a database of information about the hosts under its authority. Queries attempt to extract the appropriate information from this database. In simple terms, this is just the listing of all different types of information, names, IP addresses, mail aliases, and such that are available for lookup in the DNS system.

■ *Name servers.* These are programs that hold and maintain the data located in the domain name space. Each name server has complete information about a subset of the domain name space and cached information about other portions.

A name server has complete information for its area of authority. This authoritative information is divided into areas known as *zones*, which can be divided among different name servers to provide redundant service for a zone. Each name server knows about other name servers that are responsible for different zones. If a request comes in for information from the zone that a given name server is responsible for, the name server simply returns the information. However, if a request comes in for information from a different zone, the name server contacts the appropriate server with authority for that zone.

■ *Resolvers.* These are simply programs or library routines that extract information from the name servers in response to a query about a host in the domain name space.

Configuring the Resolver

The first step in using DNS is to configure the resolver library on your computer. You must configure your local resolver if you intend to use DNS name resolution, even if you're not going to run a local domain name server.

The /etc/host.conf File

The local resolver libraries are configured via a file named host.conf that's located in the /etc directory. This file tells the resolver what services to use and in what order. This file is a plain ASCII file that lists resolver options, one per line. Fields in this file may be separated by spaces or tabs. The # character indicates the start of a comment.

Several options may be specified in the host.conf file, as shown in Table 24.2.

Table 24.2   Configuration Options for the /etc/host.conf File

Option	Description
order	Specifies in what order different name resolution mechanisms are tried. The specified resolving services are tried in the order listed. The following name resolution mechanisms are supported: hosts Attempts to resolve the name by looking in the local /etc/ host file bind Queries a DNS name server to resolve the name nis Uses the Network Information Service (NIS) protocol to try to resolve the host name

continues

Table 24.2   Continued

Option	Description
alert	Takes off or on as arguments. If turned on, any attempt to spoof an IP address is logged via the syslog facility.
nospoof	If reverse resolution is used to match a host name to a specified address, resolves the host name that's returned to verify that it does match the address that you queried. Prevents "spoofing" of IP addresses. Enabled by specifying nospoof on.
trim	Takes a domain name as an argument. trim removes the domain name before performing an /etc/hosts lookup on the name. This allows you to put just the base host name in /etc/hosts without specifying the domain name.
multi	Takes off or on as arguments. Used only with host queries to determine whether a host is allowed to have more than one IP address specified in /etc/hosts. This option has no effect on NIS or DNS queries.

The following is an example of an /etc/host.conf configuration file that uses these options:

```
# Sample /etc/host.conf file
#
# Lookup names via DNS first then fall back to /etc/hosts
order bind hosts
# We don't have machines with multiple addresses
multi off
# check for IP address spoofing
nospoof on
# and warn us if someone attempts to spoof
alert on
# Trim the tristar.com domain name for host lookups
trim tristar.com
```

This example shows a general resolver configuration for the domain tristar.com. The resolver looks up the host names by using DNS first and then tries the local /etc/hosts file.

N O T E   Specifying the local /etc/hosts file in the resolution search is a good idea. If for some reason your name servers should be unavailable, you can still resolve the names for hosts listed in your local hosts file. You should also keep a list of all your local hosts in your /etc/hosts files on each of your local computers. ▮

Multiple IP addresses for a single machine are disabled. This host checks for IP address spoofing by re-resolving the host name that a reverse IP address lookup returns. This is a bit of a performance hit, but it helps make sure that no one is pretending to be a different host than they really are. Also, you've set up the resolver to warn you if an attempt to spoof is detected. Finally, the resolver trims the domain tristar.com from any host names that are looked up in the local /etc/hosts file.

The /etc/resolv.conf File

Now that you've configured the basic behavior of the resolver library, you need to set up some information for the DNS portion of the resolver. You need to do this only if you're using DNS for host name resolution—that is, by specifying bind in the order statement of the /etc/host.conf file. But then you wouldn't be reading this chapter if you weren't going to use DNS, would you?

The /etc/resolv.conf controls the way the resolver uses DNS to resolve host names. It specifies the DNS name servers to contact when resolving a host name and in what order to contact them. It also provides the local domain name and some clues as to how to guess at the domain name of hosts that are specified without a domain name.

Table 24.3 lists the valid options for the /etc/resolv.conf file.

Table 24.3   Configuration Options for the /etc/resolv.conf File

Option	Description
domain	Specifies the local domain name of this host. If it's not given, the resolver tries to get the local domain name from the getdomainname() system call.
nameserver	Specifies the IP address of a DNS name server to contact for name resolution. You can list up to three name servers by using the nameserver option multiple times. The name servers are tried in the order listed. You should put your most reliable name server first so that queries don't time out on a server that's likely to be down.
search	Lists domains to try if no domain name is specified as part of a query host name. If no search option is given, the list of domains is created by using the local domain plus each parent domain of the local domain.

The following is a sample /etc/resolv.conf file for tristar.com:

```
# /etc/resolv.conf for tristar.com
#
# Set our local domain name
domain tristar.com
# Specify our primary name server
nameserver 166.82.1.3
```

In this example, you specify the local domain via the domain option and list one name server to use for resolving host names.

N O T E You need to specify the IP address of the DNS name server as an argument to the nameserver option—not the host name. If you specify the host name, DNS doesn't know what host to contact to look up the host name of the name server. ▪

You didn't use the search option to specify the search order. This means that if you try to query the address of a machine—for example, skippy—the resolver tries to look up skippy first. If this fails, it looks up skippy.tristar.com, and then skippy.com.

DNS servers can and do go down unexpectedly. If you rely solely on a DNS server for name resolution, you may find yourself unable to work if it crashes. Make sure that you specify multiple servers and keep a good list of hosts in your local /etc/hosts file, just in case.

Using the *named* Daemon to Set Up the Server

Here is where the real magic starts. You've seen how to set up the basics of resolver configuration and how to tell your resolver which name servers to contact. In the following sections, you learn the mechanics of setting up a name server.

The DNS name server under Linux is provided by the named (pronounced *name-dee´*) daemon. This daemon is typically started at boot time and reads its configuration information from a set of configuration files. named typically runs until the machine is shut down. After named starts and is initialized with its configuration information, it writes its process ID to the /etc/named.pid ASCII file. It then starts listening for DNS requests on the default network port specified in /etc/services.

The named.boot File

The first file that named reads when it starts is typically /etc/named.boot. This very small file is the key to all the other configuration files used by named—it contains pointers to the various configuration files and to other name servers. In the named.boot file, comments start with a semicolon and continue to the end of the line. Several options can be listed in the named.boot file; Table 24.4 lists these options.

Table 24.4   Configuration Options for the named.boot File

Option	Description
directory	Specifies the directory where the DNS zone files are located. You can specify several different directories by using the directory option repeatedly. You can give file path names as being relative to these directories.
primary	Takes a domain name and file name as arguments. The primary option declares named to be authoritative for the specified domain and causes named to load the zone information from the specified file.
secondary	Tells named to act as a secondary server for the specified domain. It takes a domain name, a list of addresses, and a file name as arguments. named tries to transfer the zone information from the hosts specified in the address list and then stores the zone information in the file specified on the option line. If named can't contact any of the hosts, it tries to retrieve the information from the secondary zone file.

Option	Description
cache	Sets up caching information for named. Takes a domain name and a file name as arguments. The domain name is typically specified as . (dot). The file contains a set of records, known as *server hints*, which list information about the root name servers.
forwarders	Takes a list of name servers as arguments. Tells the local name server to try to contact the servers in this list if it can't resolve an address from its local information.
slave	Turns the local name server into a slave server. If the slave option is given, the local server tries to resolve DNS names via recursive queries. It simply forwards the request to one of the servers listed in the forwarders option line.

In addition to these options, a few additional options aren't commonly used. Refer to the named man page for more information on these options.

N O T E Because tristar.com isn't attached to the Internet, many of the IP host and network addresses in these examples are fake. When setting up your own name server, make sure that you use the correct addresses assigned to you. ■

The following is a sample named.boot file:

```
; named.boot file
; A sample named.boot for tristar.com
;
directory /var/named
;
cache . named.ca
primary tristar.com named.hosts
primary 197.198.199.in-addr.arpa named.rev
```

This example sets up the primary name server for tristar.com. As you can see, comments start with the ; character. The directory statement in the file tells named that all its working files are located in the /var/named directory. Because none of the other files listed in the named.boot file have directory paths associated with them, they're located in /var/named.

The next line sets up the caching information for this name server. This option should be present on almost every machine running as a name server. It tells named to enable caching and load the root server information from the file named.ca.

N O T E The cache entry is very important. Without it, no caching is enabled on the local name server. This can cause severe performance problems for name lookups. Also, the local server can't contact any root name servers and, as a result, can't resolve any non-local host names, unless it's set up as a forwarding name server. ■

Part
V

Ch
24

The next line in the named.boot file tells named that this server has primary authority for the domain tristar.com. The zone and host information records are in the file named.hosts. You learn about these zone authority records in detail in the following section.

A second primary line in the named.hosts file shows that you also have primary zone authority for the zone 197.198.199.in-addr.arpa with zone information in the named.rev file. This strange syntax is named's way of getting information to match IP addresses to DNS names. Because DNS was originally set up to match DNS names to IP addresses, a different primary line is needed to do reverse resolution.

N O T E The in-addr.arpa domain is used to specify reverse, or IP address, to DNS name resolution. ■

Database Files and Resource Records

All information in the various named database files is stored in a format known as a *resource record*. Each resource record has a type associated with it, which tells the record's function. A resource record is the smallest piece of information that named uses.

Most people find the syntax for resource records and master database files in general to be a bit arcane and obscure. It doesn't help matters that some resource records have to appear in certain places in certain files. Most DNS configuration problems can be traced to errors in these master configuration files. All this said, it's time to dive in and look at the resource record syntax and the various master files.

N O T E Within the master configuration files, you have the option of specifying absolute host names or host names relative to this domain. Host names are considered absolute if they end in a . character, as in foo,tristar,com.. Host names that don't end with a dot are considered relative to the local domain, also known as the *origin*. You can refer to the origin itself by using the @ character. ■

Resource records use a general syntax that's consistent across all types of resource records. To add to the confusion, however, several parts of the record are optional depending on the record type, and may assume a default value if not specified. The basic format of a resource record is

```
[owner] [ttl] [class] type data
```

Fields are separated by white space such as spaces or tabs. Table 24.5 discusses what the various fields mean.

Table 24.5   Fields in the Resource Record Data Format

Field	Description
owner	The domain or host name that the record applies to. If no name is given, the domain name of the previous resource record is assumed.
ttl	The time-to-live field, which tells how long, in seconds, the information in this record is valid after it's retrieved from a DNS server. If no ttl value is given, the minimum ttl of the last Start of Authority (SOA) record is used.

Field	Description
class	Specifies a networking address class. For TCP/IP networks, use the value IN. If the class isn't given, the class of the previous resource record is used.
type	Lists the type of the resource record. This value is required. The various resource record types are listed in the next section.
data	Specifies the data associated with this resource record. This value is required. The format of the data field depends on the content of the type field.

As you can see, the format of a resource record can get quite confusing. There are several optional fields, and the data field depends on the type of the resource record. To make matters worse, there are several different types of resource records. Table 24.6 lists the most common resource record types; a few additional types are rarely used. If you're interested in the additional types, refer to the appropriate RFCs and the man pages for named.

Table 24.6   Commonly Used Resource Record Types

Type	Description
A	An address record that associates a host name with an address. The data field holds the address in dotted decimal format. There can be only one A record for any given host, as this record is considered authoritative information. Any additional host name or address mappings for this host must be given by using the CNAME type.
CNAME	Associates an alias for a host with its canonical name, the name specified in the A record for this host.
HINFO	Provides information about a host. The data field holds the hardware and software information for a particular host. It's just a free-format text string, so you can put in whatever makes sense for your hardware.
MX	Sets up a mail exchanger record. The data field holds an integer preference value followed by a host name. MX records tell a mail transport to send mail to another system that knows how to deliver it to its final destination.
NS	Points to a name server for another zone. The data field of the NS resource record contains the DNS name of the name server. You need to specify an A record as well to match the host name with the address of the name server.
PTR	Maps addresses to names, as in the in-addr.arpa domain. The host name must be the canonical host name.

continues

Part

V

Ch

24

Table 24.6 Continued

Type	Description
SOA	Tells the name server that all the resource records following it are authoritative for this domain. (SOA stands for *start of authority*.) The data field is enclosed by () and is typically a multiline field. The data field of the SOA record contains the followingentries: origin The canonical name of the primary name server for this domain. It's usually given as an absolute domain name ending with a . (dot), so it's not modified by the named daemon. contact The e-mail contact of the person who's responsible for maintaining this domain. Because the @ character has special meaning in resource records, it's replaced by a . (dot). If the responsible person for maintaining zone information about tristar.com is Dave, the contact address is dave.tristar.com. serial The version number of the zone information file, which is given as an integer. It's used by secondary name servers to determine when the zone information file has changed. You should increment this number by 1 every time you change the information file. refresh The length of time in seconds that a secondary server should wait before trying to check the SOA record of the primary name server. The SOA records don't change very often, so you can usually set this value to be on the order of one day or so. retry The time in seconds that a secondary server waits to retry a request to a primary server if the primary server wasn't available. Typically, it should be on the order of a few minutes. expire The time in seconds that the secondary server should wait before throwing away the zone information if it has been unable to contact the primary server. This number should typically be very large, on the order of 30 days or so. minimum The default ttl value for resource records that don't specify a ttl. If your network doesn't change very much, this number can be set to a fairly large value, such as a couple of weeks. You can always override it by specifying a ttl value in your resource records.

As you can see, the format of the resource records gets complicated in a hurry. Things should get clearer as you look at a few of the master configuration files used by named.

The named.hosts File

In your named.boot file, you listed named.hosts as being the file that contains information about your local domain, tristar.com. You could have named the file anything you wanted by listing the name on the primary line of named.boot. The named.hosts file contains authoritative information about the hosts in the zone of authority—tristar.com. Listing 24.1 shows a sample named.hosts file that uses several of the resource record types.

Listing 24.1 An Example named.hosts File

```
; named.hosts file for tristar.com
;
@          IN       SOA     ns.tristar.com. dave.tristar.com. (
6 ; serial number
86400 ;refresh 24 hrs
300 ; retry 5 minutes
2592000 ; expire 30 days
86400 ; minimum 24 hrs
)
IN      NS       ns.tristar.com.
;
; your domain itself tristar.com
;
@          IN       A       199.198.197.1
IN       MX      100      mailhost.tristar.com
IN       HINFO    PC-486     Linux
;
; your primary nameserver
;
ns         IN       A       199.198.197.1
nameserver      IN      CNAME     ns.tristar.com.
;
; other hosts
;
mailhost      IN       A       199.198.197.2
opus           IN      A        199.198.197.3
IN      MX       100      mailhost.tristar.com
skippy         IN       A       199.198.197.4
IN      MX       100      mailhost.tristar.com
;
; the localhost
;
localhost      IN       A       127.0.0.1
```

Part

V

Ch

24

N O T E Host names in resource records that end with a . (dot) aren't translated any further. If the dot isn't the last character in the host name, named assumes that the host name you gave is relative to the origin domain name referred to by @ and appends the domain name to the host name. ■

Look at the named.hosts file in Listing 24.1 in detail. The first record that you come to in this file is the SOA (start of authority) record for the example domain. The first line of this record starts with the @ character, which indicates the current origin or domain (tristar.com). The definition of the origin comes from the domain listed on the corresponding primary line in named.boot. After that, you see the codes IN SOA, which tells named that this resource record uses Internet (TCP/IP) addressing and is a start-of-authority record.

The next two entries on the line are the canonical name of the primary name server for this domain (ns.tristar.com), and the e-mail contact with the @ replaced by a dot (dave.tristar.com). You then list the various fields of the data required by an SOA record, one per line. (Refer to Table 24.6 for a complete explanation of each of these entries.)

After the SOA record, the next line is a name-server resource record, which lists ns.tristar.com as being a name server for the domain. Because no domain is listed in the domain field, it's assumed to be the last domain specified, which was @, listed in the SOA record. And, of course, the @ character really expands to be the local domain, tristar.com. What could possibly be easier to understand?

The next three lines set up some information about the tristar.com domain itself. Although you've listed the domain name as @ for clarity because it was the last domain name listed in the file, these resource records still apply to it by default if you had left the domain field blank. The line

```
@         IN      A       199.198.197.1
```

allows users to refer to tristar.com as though it were a real machine. It has been assigned the IP address of 199.198.197.1, which, as you'll see, is really the IP address of ns.tristar.com. The next line sets up a mail exchanger MX record for tristar.com so that all mail going to it gets forwarded to mailhost.tristar.com instead. The last line in this group sets up a host information HINFO record for tristar.com, which tells the world that it's a PC-486 running Linux.

A few lines earlier in the file, you listed ns.tristar.com as being your name server via an NS resource record. For named to work correctly, you must provide an address or A record that gives the address of ns.tristar.com. The next line in your file does just that. Following the "glue record" that gives the address of the name server, you have a CNAME resource record. This record tells you that nameserver.tristar.com is an alias for ns.tristar.com.

You then proceed to set up address records for three other hosts in your domain: mailhost, opus, and skippy. Notice that after the A records for opus and skippy are MX records that route any mail received by opus or skippy to mailhost.tristar.com. Because no name was specified in the first field of these MX records, they apply to the previous name—opus or skippy.

N O T E Because the owner field of a resource record defaults to the last one specified if it's left blank, it's easy to group records that apply to one host. However, you must be careful if you add new records for new hosts to a file. If you add them to the middle of a file, you may cause the default host to change for some of the existing resource records. Look carefully before you add resource records to an existing file. ■

Finally, the last host in this named.hosts file is the localhost, which is mapped to address 127.0.0.1. As you can see, the syntax for these files gets quite complicated and gives you lots of room for errors.

The named.rev File

The named.rev file is very similar to the named.hosts file, except that it essentially works in reverse—it maps addresses to host names. Listing 24.2 shows a sample named.rev file for tristar.com.

Listing 24.2 An Example named.rev File

```
; named.rev file for tristar.com
;
@         IN      SOA      ns.tristar.com. dave.tristar.com. (
6 ; serial number
86400 ;refresh 24 hrs
300  ; retry 5 minutes
2592000 ; expire 30 days
86400 ; minimum 24 hrs
)
IN      NS      ns.tristar.com.
;
; reverse map your IP addresses
;
1         IN      PTR      ns.tristar.com.
2         IN      PTR      mailhost.tristar.com.
3         IN      PTR      opus.tristar.com.
4         IN      PTR      skippy.tristar.com.
```

Part
V

Ch
24

In this example, you have the same SOA record that you saw in the named.hosts file. This just sets up the authority information for the domain. In this case, @, the value of the origin, is set to 197.198.199.in-addr.arpa from the primary line in the named.boot file. Recall that the in-addr.arpa domain refers to reverse mapping of addresses to names.

N O T E The addresses listed as part of your in-addr.arpa line is your network address backward. Your example network for this chapter has the address 199.198.197.0. When you list it in the reverse mapping data files, you list it as

```
197.198.199.in-addr.arpa
```

You have the NS record that lists the name server for your domain. Following that are the records that make up the reverse address resolution records. These are PTR records and give the host number (the part of the IP address not listed in the in-addr.arpa value) and the canonical host name that matches it. You must use the canonical host name here instead of a relative host name. For example, the line

```
2           IN      PTR      mailhost.tristar.com.
```

tells named to map the host address 199.198.197.2 to the host name mailhost.tristar.com.

The named.ca File

As stated earlier in this chapter, the caching operation of named is very important. Fortunately, the named.ca file that sets up caching is also usually the simplest of the named configuration files. It just lists the root name servers for the various domains with their IP addresses. It contains a couple of special field indicators that tell named that these are root servers.

You can probably just copy the format of the sample named.ca file in Listing 24.3. To get a complete current list of the root name servers, use the nslookup utility.

Listing 24.3   An Example named.ca File

```
; named.ca file
;
.       99999999        IN      NS      NS.NIC.DDN.MIL.
99999999        IN      NS      NS.NASA.GOV.
99999999        IN      NS      KAVA.NISC.SRI.COM.
99999999        IN      NS      TERP.UMD.EDU.
99999999        IN      NS      C.NYSER.NET.
99999999        IN      NS      NS.INTERNIC.NET.
;
NS.NIC.DDN.MIL.         99999999        IN      A       192.112.36.4
NS.NASA.GOV.            99999999        IN      A       128.102.16.10
KAVA.NISC.SRI.COM.      99999999        IN      A       192.33.33.24
TERP.UMD.EDU.           99999999        IN      A       128.8.10.90
C.NYSER.NET.            99999999        IN      A       192.33.4.12
NS.INTERNIC.NET.        99999999        IN      A       198.41.0.4
```

As you can see, the named.ca file simply maps NS name server records to the appropriate addresses for them.

Troubleshooting

DNS is a very complex system. You can do many things wrong that will cause your system to not behave properly. Many of the problems that occur with a DNS setup will appear to be identical but come from different causes. However, most of the problems result from syntax errors in your configuration files.

Make sure that you specify the host names correctly in your DNS configuration files. If it's an absolute host name, be sure to end it with a dot.

Be especially careful with the names used in SOA and CNAME records. If you make errors here, these resource records can redirect host name queries to computers that don't exist.

Be sure to increment the serial number in your configuration files when making changes. If you forget, DNS will not reread the file.

Be sure to enter the correct IP address for A records, and check to see that it matches your /etc/hosts file (if you have one). Also, make sure that the DNS name and IP address match the corresponding reverse resolution information in named.rev.

Your best tool for figuring out errors is the nslookup command. Use nslookup to test your DNS server thoroughly. Do regular and reverse resolution for every address in your DNS database to make sure that all the names and addresses are correct.

From Here...

This chapter shows the various components of the DNS system and explores the various configuration files necessary to get a DNS name server running on your Linux system. Because the syntax for the resource records is fairly arcane, you need to pay close attention to your configuration files as you write them.

You can find more information about networking in the following chapters:

- Chapter 23, "Configuring a TCP/IP Network," shows how to set up and configure TCP/IP networking.
- Chapter 25, "Using SLIP and PPP," shows how to configure SLIP and PPP for dial-up Internet access.
- Chapter 26, "Understanding the Internet," gives an overview of the Internet and DNS.

Part
V

Ch
24

Using SLIP and PPP

The Linux kernel supports two serial-line protocols for transmitting Internet Protocol (IP) traffic: SLIP (Serial Line Internet Protocol) and PPP (Point-to-Point Protocol). These protocols were developed as a poor man's alternative to expensive leased-line setups for getting Internet connectivity. Anyone with a reasonably high-speed modem and a service provider that supports these protocols can get their Linux machine IP-connected for a very low cost compared to leased-line systems. SLIP drivers for Linux were available soon after Linux was first released, with PPP support added shortly thereafter. ■

Setting up SLIP and PPP

You need to make sure that a few things are set up in your Linux kernel or configuration files for SLIP and PPP to work on your server.

Automating connections

dip, the Dial-up IP Protocol driver, provides a scripting language for automating control of the modem and setting up the SLIP network interface and kernel routing tables.

Setting up security

PPP provides a direct IP connection, effectively putting the machines on both ends of the link on the same network. Two authentication protocols have been developed to make PPP more secure—Password Authentication Protocol (PAP) and the Challenge Handshake Authentication Protocol (CHAP).

Understanding the Requirements for SLIP and PPP

You need to make sure that a few things are set up in your Linux kernel or configuration files. TCP/IP networking must be enabled and the loopback interface should be configured.

▶ **See** "Configuring the Software Loopback Interface," **p. 478**

You'll want to have the IP address of your Domain Name Service (DNS) server included in your /etc/resolv.conf file to make accessing other machines besides your dial-up host convenient. If your dial-up link is slow or error-prone, you might want to run a name server on your Linux box, to cache any DNS lookups and decrease the amount of DNS IP traffic on your dial-up link.

▶ **See** "The /etc/resolv.conf File," **p. 491**

▶ **See** "Using the *named* Daemon to Set Up the Server," **p. 494**

Using *dip* to Automate SLIP Operations

Linux offers a number of programs to manage your SLIP operations. dip, the Dial-up IP Protocol driver, is one of the most versatile tools. It provides a scripting language for automating control of the modem and automatically sets up the SLIP network interface and kernel routing tables. You can use dip to initiate SLIP connections or provide dial-up SLIP service to other machines. The syntax for dip is

```
dip [-tvi] [-m mtu] [scriptfile]
```

Table 25.1 describes dip's most common command-line arguments.

Table 25.1 *dip* **Common Command-Line Arguments**

Argument	Description
-a	Prompts users for their user name and password.
-t	Runs dip in command mode. Command mode gives you full access to everything dip can do, allowing you to initiate a SLIP connection manually.
-v	Used with -t to display the current error level.
-i	Tells dip to operate in input mode. This flag is used when dip provides SLIP service for others dialing into your machine.
-m mtu	Forces dip to use the specified MTU value.
scriptfile	Name of the dip script to run.

Using *dip* in Command Mode

Invoking dip with the -t option places it in command mode. This mode lets you control dip directly and is an excellent tool for developing and debugging dip scripts. The following shows you what dip's command mode looks like:

```
$ /sbin/dip -t
DIP: Dialup IP Protocol Driver version 3.3.7i-uri (17 Apr 95)
Written by Fred N. van Kempen, MicroWalt Corporation.

DIP>
```

From the DIP> prompt, you can run any dip command by typing it and pressing <Return>. The help command displays a list of the available commands. Invoking a command with incorrect arguments displays a brief usage statement for that command. Table 25.2 describes the commands available at the command-mode prompt or in dip scripts.

Table 25.2 Commands Available in *dip*

Command	Description
chatkey *keyword* [*code*]	Adds a keyword and error-level code to the set of error codes returned by the dial command. The chatkey command can be used to detect when your modem returns BUSY, VOICE, or other specific messages.
config [*arguments*]	Allows you to directly manipulate the SLIP interface dip provides. This command normally is disabled because it's a severe security risk. The source code file command.c must be modified slightly to enable this command.
databits *bits*	Sets the number of bits that can be used as data in each byte. This accommodates 6- and 7-bit dial-up connections.
default	Causes dip to set a default route in the kernel routing table pointed at the remote host.
dial *num*	Dials the specified telephone number.
echo on¦off	Turns echo on or off. Echo on makes dip display what it's sending to and receiving from the modem.
flush	Throws away any responses from the modem that haven't been read yet.
get $var	Sets the variable $var to either the constant ask or remote constant specified, prompts the user for a value, or takes the next word from the serial line and assigns it to $var.
goto *label*	Jumps to the specified label in the dip script.
help	Displays a listing of available commands in command mode.
if $var op *number*	Performs a conditional branch in a goto label script. $var must be one of $errlvl, $locip, or $rmtip. The number must be an integer andthe following operators are available and have their traditional C language meanings: ==, !=, <, >, <=, and >=.

continues

Part

V

Ch

25

Table 25.2 Continued

Command	Description
init *initstring*	Sets the initialization string sent to the modem by the reset command to *initstring*.
mode SLIP¦CSLIP	Sets the protocol mode for the connection and makes dip go into daemon mode. This command normally causes dip to go into daemon mode and not return control to the script or the DIP> command line.
modem HAYES	Sets the modem type. Only the HAYES modem type is now supported. (HAYES must be capitalized.)
netmask *mask*	Sets the netmask for the routes dip installs to *mask*.
parity E¦O¦N	Sets the parity of the serial line: even, odd, or none.
password	Prompts the user for a password and retrieves it in a secure manner. This command doesn't echo the password as you type it.
print	Echoes text to the console dip started on. Variables included in the text are replaced with their values.
port *dev*	Sets the device dip uses.
quit	Exits the dip program.
reset	Sends the init string to the serial line.
send *text*	Sends the specified text to the serial line. The traditional C-style backslash sequences are properly handled.
sleep *num*	Delays processing for the specified number of seconds.
speed *num*	Sets the serial line speed.
stopbits *bits*	Sets the number of stop bits used by the serial port.
timeout *num*	Sets the default timeout to the integer value *num*. This is measured in seconds.
term	Makes dip go into terminal emulation mode. This allows you to interface directly with the serial link. Pressing <Ctrl-]> returns you to the DIP> prompt.
wait *word num*	Makes dip wait for the specified word to arrive on the serial line with a timeout of *num* seconds.

dip also provides a number of variables for your use. Some, such as the local and remote IP addresses, can be set by you; others are read-only and are used for diagnostic and informational purposes. Each variable begins with a dollar sign and must be typed in lowercase letters. Table 25.3 lists these variables and their uses.

Table 25.3 Variables Provided by *dip*

Variable	Description
$local	The host name of the local machine.
$locip	The IP address assigned to the local machine.
$remote	The host name of the remote machine.
$rmtip	The IP address of the remote machine.
$mtu	The MTU value for the connection.
$modem	The modem type being used (read-only).
$port	The name of the serial device *dip* is using (read-only).
$speed	The speed setting of the serial device (read-only).
$errlvl	The result code of the last command (read-only) executed. Zero indicates success; any other value is an error.

TIP Setting the $local or $remote variable to a host name causes *dip* to resolve the host name to its IP address and store that in the respective IP address variable. This saves a step in the scripts you write.

N O T E You can't set the read-only variables directly by using the get command. ■

Using *dip* with Static IP Addresses

Assigning individual IP addresses to each machine that uses a SLIP provider is very common. When your machine initiates a SLIP link to the remote host, *dip* configures the SLIP interface with this known address. Listing 25.1 is a *dip* script using static IP addresses for initiating a SLIP link from unixlt.tristar.com to unix1.tristar.com.

Listing 25.1   A Sample *dip* Script for Using Static IP Addresses over SLIP

```
# Connect unixlt to unix1 using static IP Addresses
# Configure Communication Parameters
port /dev/cua1 # use modem on /dev/cua1 serial line
speed 38400
```

continues

Listing 25.1   Continued

```
modem HAYES
reset                            # Send initialization string to modem
flush                            # Throw away modem response

get $local unixlt                # Set local IP address
get $remote unix1                # Set remote IP address

# Dial number for unix1 modem
dial 555-1234
if $errlvl != 0 goto error       # If the dial command fails, error out
wait CONNECT 75
if $errlvl != 0 goto error       # If we don't get a CONNECT string
# from the modem, error out

send \r\n                        # Wake up login program
wait ogin: 30                    # Wait 30 seconds for login prompt
if $errlvl != 0 goto error       # Error out if we don't get login prompt
send Sunixlt\n                   # Send SLIP login name for unixlt
wait ssword: 5                   # Wait 5 seconds for password prompt
if $errlvl != 0 goto error       # Error out if we don't get password
send be4me\n                     # Send password
wait running 30                  # Wait for indication that SLIP is up
if $errlvl != 0 goto error       # Otherwise error out

# We're in, print out useful information
print Connected to $remote with address $rmtip
default                          # Make this link our default route
mode SLIP                        # Turn on SLIP mode on our end

# Error routine in case things don't work
error:
print SLIP to $remote failed.
```

TIP Tracking SLIP accounts can be difficult. Traditionally, UNIX user accounts are assigned login names with all lowercase letters. Using the client machine name with a capital S added to the front as the login name for that machine's SLIP account makes tracking it easier and avoids login name collisions with normal user accounts.

The script in Listing 25.1 initializes the modem and sets the local and remote IP addresses for the SLIP link. If you use host names here, dip resolves them to their IP address equivalents. The script then dials the modem and works its way through the login sequence. When logged in and sure that the SLIP link is up on the remote host, the script has dip configure the routing table and then switch the serial line into SLIP mode.

If an error occurs, the error routine at the end of the script prints a warning message and aborts the script. dip is excellent about leaving the serial line in a reasonable state when it's done with it.

Using *dip* with Dynamic IP Addresses

As SLIP became more popular, the task of managing IP addressees for SLIP clients got more and more difficult. This problem got worse when terminal servers supporting SLIP came into use. Now, you might be assigned any one of a range of IP addresses, depending on which port the terminal server received your call. This led to changes in dip that captured IP address information from the incoming data on the serial line. Listing 25.2 is a dip script that captures the local and remote IP addresses from the serial line.

Listing 25.2 A Sample *dip* Script for Dynamic IP Addresses

```
# Connection script for SLIP to server with dynamic IP address
# assignment. The terminal server prints out:
#
# remote address is XXX.XXX.XXX.XXX the local address is YYY.YYY.YYY.YYY

# Set the desired serial port and speed.
port /dev/cua1
speed 38400

# Reset the modem and terminal line.
Reset
flush

# Prepare for dialing.
dial 555-1234
if $errlvl != 0 goto error
wait CONNECT 60
if $errlvl != 0 goto error

# We are connected. Login to the system.
login:
wait name: 10                          # Log in to system
if $errlvl != 0 goto error
send Sunixlt\n                         # Send user ID
wait ord: 10
if $errlvl != 0 goto error
send be4me\n                           # Send password
if $errlvl != 0 goto error
get $remote remote 10                  # Get remote IP address
if $errlvl != 0 goto error
get $local remote 10                   # Get local IP address
if $errlvl != 0 goto error
done:
print CONNECTED to $remote with address $rmtip we are $local
default                                # Set routing
mode SLIP                              # Go to SLIP mode
goto exit
error:
print SLIP to $host failed.
exit:
```

The script in Listing 25.2 uses `get $remote remote 10` to watch the serial line and to capture the first thing that looks like an IP address in the `$remote` variable. The command times out in 10 seconds with an error if it doesn't see an IP address.

Using *diplogin* to Provide SLIP Service

The `dip` program automates starting SLIP links from the client machine. Linux also supports incoming dial-up SLIP links. A few packages are available for doing this as well. You use the `diplogin` program here, which is really just another name for `dip`.

Providing SLIP service to others requires that you create a specific account for each person on your Linux box and configure that account correctly. You also need to write an /etc/diphosts file with appropriate information for each host that you're providing SLIP service for.

Creating SLIP Accounts

You can manually create the SLIP account or use the `adduser` script with appropriate responses to each question. Here's an example /etc/passwd entry for unixlt.tristar.com in the passwd file on unix1.tristar.com:

```
Sunixlt:IdR4gDZ7K7D82:505:100:unixlt SLIP Account:/tmp:/sbin/diplogin
```

It's recommended that /tmp be used as the home directory for SLIP accounts to minimize security risks by preventing SLIP users from writing files into sensitive areas of your file system by default. Make sure that you use the correct path to the `diplogin` program.

Using the /etc/diphosts File

The /etc/diphosts file controls access to SLIP on your machine and contains the connection parameters for each account allowed to use SLIP. It contains lines that look similar to the following:

```
Sunixlt::unixlt.tristar.com:unixlt SLIP:SLIP,296
```

The fields in this file are the user ID, secondary password, host name or IP address of the calling machine, an informational field not currently used, and the connection parameters for this account. The connection parameters field contains the protocol (SLIP or CSLIP) and the Maximum Transmission Unit (MTU) value for this account.

If the second field isn't empty, `diplogin` prompts for an external security password when the specified account logs in to your machine. If the response from the remote host doesn't match the string in this field, the login attempt is aborted.

> **CAUTION**
>
> The `diplogin` program requires superuser privileges to modify the kernel routing table. If you aren't running `dip setuid root`, you can't use a link between `dip` and `diplogin`. You must make a separate copy of `dip` called `diplogin` and have its suid root.

That's all it takes. Setting up SLIP accounts and the /etc/diphosts file completely configures your system to support incoming SLIP links.

Using PPP

Point-to-Point Protocol (PPP) is another protocol for sending datagrams across a serial link. Developed after SLIP, PPP contains a number of features SLIP lacks. It can automatically negotiate options such as IP addresses, datagram sizes, and client authorization. It can also transport packets from protocols other than IP.

Automating PPP Links with *pppd* and *chat*

PPP operates in two parts: the PPP driver in the Linux kernel and a program called pppd that the user must run. The most basic means of using PPP is to log in manually to the remote host by using a communications program, and then manually start pppd on the remote and local hosts. It's much more convenient to use a chat script with pppd that handles the modem, logging in to the remote host, and starting the remote pppd. Before diving into pppd, take a short look at chat.

Using the *chat* Program   chat is a program for automating the interaction between your computer and a modem. It's used mainly to establish the modem connection between the local and remote pppd daemon processes. The syntax for chat is

```
chat [options] script
```

Table 25.4 lists the command-line options for the chat program.

Table 25.4   *chat* Command-Line Options

Option	Description
-f filename	Uses the chat script in the specified file
-l lockfile	Makes a UUCP style lock file by using the specified lock file
-t num	Uses the specified number as the timeout in seconds for each expected string
-v	Makes a chat log of everything it sends and receives to syslog
script	The chat script to use

You can't use the -f option and specify a chat script at the same time—they're mutually exclusive. If you use the -l option for chat, don't use the lock option with pppd because the lock file created by chat causes pppd to fail, thinking that the modem device is already in use.

 T I P   When debugging chat scripts, run tail -f /var/adm/messages on one virtual console and use the -v option when you run chat in another. You can then watch the conversation chat is having as it comes up on the first virtual console.

Part
V

Ch
25

Creating *chat* Scripts   chat scripts consist of one or more expect-reply pairs of strings separated by spaces. The chat program waits for the expected text and sends the reply text when it receives it. Optional subexpect-subreply pairs can be included in the expect portion, separated by hyphens.

Here is a typical chat script for logging in to a Linux machine:

```
ogin:-\r\n-ogin: abbet1 word: costello
```

This script says that chat should wait for the string ogin: to appear. If chat times out before receiving it, chat should send a carriage return and line feed and wait for the string ogin: again. When chat sees the ogin: string, it sends abbet1 and then waits for the word: and sends costello in response.

> **TIP**
>
> Include only the text necessary in expect strings to positively identify what you're looking for, to minimize the chance of a mismatch or having your script blow up because of garbled text. For example, use ogin: instead of login:, and word: instead of password:.

chat normally sends a carriage return after each reply string unless a \c character sequence ends the string. Carriage returns aren't looked for in expect strings unless explicitly requested with the \r character sequence in the expect string.

Most modems can report why a call failed when it gets a busy signal or can't detect a carrier. You can use the abort expect string to tell chat to fail if it receives the specified strings. Multiple abort pairs are cumulative. The following script is an example of using the abort expect string:

```
abort 'NO CARRIER' abort 'BUSY' ogin:--ogin: ppp word: be4me
```

This chat script makes chat fail if it receives NO CARRIER or BUSY at any point during the script.

chat recognizes a number of character and escape sequences (see Table 25.5).

Table 25.5   Character and Escape Sequences Recognized by *chat*

Sequence	Description
BREAK	Used as a reply string, this makes chat send a break to the modem. This special signal normally causes the remote host to change its transmission speed.
' '	Sends a null string with a single carriage return.
\b	The backspace character.
\c	Suppresses the newline sent after a reply string and must be at the end of the reply string.
\d	Makes chat wait for one second.
\K	Another means of specifying a break signal.

Sequence	Description
\n	Sends a newline character.
\N	Sends a null character.
\p	Pauses for 1/10th of one second.
\q	Prevents the string it's included in from showing in the syslog file.
\r	Sends or expects a carriage return.
\s	Sends or expects a space character.
\t	Sends or expects a tab character.
\\	Sends or expects a backslash character.
\ddd	Specifies an ASCII character in octal.
^C	Specifies the control character represented by C.

 T I P   You can use the abort string to prevent low-speed calls on your high-speed modem. Configure your modem to return a CARRIER 14400 string when it makes a connection and add abort CARRIER 2400 to your chat script. This way, chat fails if your modem connects at 2400 bps instead of 14400 bps.

Using PPP with *chat*   The pppd program has command-line options that control all aspects of the PPP link. The syntax for the pppd command is

pppd [*options*] [*tty_name*] [*speed*]

Table 25.6 describes the most commonly used options.

Table 25.6   Frequently Used *pppd* Command-Line Options

Option	Description
device	Uses the specified device. pppd adds /dev/ to the string if needed. When no device is given, pppd uses the controlling terminal.
speed	Sets the modem speed.
asyncmap *map*	Sets the async character map. This map specifies which control characters can't be sent through the connection and need to be escaped. The map is a 32-bit hex number where each bit represents a character. The 0th bit (00000001) represents character 0×00.

continues

Table 25.6 Continued	
Option	**Description**
`auth`	Requires the remote host to authenticate itself.
`connect program`	Uses the program or shell command to set up the connection. This is where `chat` is used.
`crtscts`	Uses hardware flow control.
`xonxoff`	Uses software flow control.
`defaultroute`	Makes `pppd` set a default route to the remote host in your kernel routing table.
`disconnect program`	Runs the specified program after `pppd` terminates its link.
`escape c1,c2,...`	Causes the specified characters to be escaped when transmitted. The characters are specified by using the ASCII hex equivalent.
`file filename`	Reads `pppd` options from the specified file.
`lock`	Uses UUCP-style locking on the serial device.
`mru num`	Sets the maximum receive unit to the specified number.
`netmask mask`	Sets the PPP network interface netmask.
`passive`	Makes `pppd` wait for a valid connection rather than fail when it can't initiate a connection immediately.
`silent`	Keeps `pppd` from initiating a connection. `pppd` waits for a connection attempt from the remote host instead.

More than 40 other command-line arguments control all aspects of PPP at all levels. Refer to the man page for information about them.

N O T E   The pppd program demands that the file /etc/ppp/options exist, even if it's empty. This file is read by pppd and is an excellent place to put options you want pppd to use every time it runs. ■

You can combine `pppd` and `chat` in a number of ways. You can specify all the command-line arguments for both programs on the command line, put the `pppd` options in a file, or put the `chat` script in a file. Following is a simple example with everything on the command line:

```
$ pppd connect 'chat "" ATDT5551234 ogin: unixlt word: be4me' \
/dev/cua1 38400 mru 296 lock debug crtscts modem defaultroute
```

This runs `pppd` with a simple `chat` script that dials a phone number and logs the user unixlt in to the remote host. The device, speed, MRU, and a number of other options are included.

At the other extreme, you can place most of the options for pppd in a file and have chat read a script file. The following is the call to pppd:

```
pppd /dev/cua1 38400 connect 'chat -f unix1.chat'
```

The following lines display the contents of the reference file:

```
# Global PPP Options File
mru 296                          # Set MRU value
lock                             # Use UUCP locking
crtscts                          # Use hardware handshaking
modem                            # Use modem control lines
defaultroute                     # Make PPP set up default route
```

pppd reads this file and processes the options it finds within. Any text following a # character is treated as a comment and ignored.

The following chat script sets a number of abort strings, dials the phone number, waits for a login prompt, and logs the ppp user in to the remote host with password ppp-word:

```
abort 'NO CARRIER'
abort 'BUSY'
abort 'VOICE'
abort 'CARRIER 2400'
"" ATDT555-1234
CONNECT '\c'
ogin:-BREAK-ogin: ppp
word: ppp-word
```

Providing PPP Service

Configuring your Linux machine to be a PPP server is even easier than setting up a SLIP server. It requires only one new account and a shell script that properly runs the pppd program.

Create an account called ppp with an /etc/passwd entry that looks like

```
$ ppp:*:501:300:PPP Account:/tmp:/etc/ppp/ppplogin
```

and set the passwd appropriately. The uid (501) and gid (300) numbers need not be the same. You can also assign one account to each PPP client you have, if you want. The /etc/ppp/ppplogin file should be an executable script such as the following:

```
#!/bin/sh
# PPP Server Login Script
# Turn off messages to this terminal
mesg n
# Turn off echoing
stty -echo
# Run pppd on top of this sh process
exec pppd -detach silent modem crtscts
```

This script executes pppd with the -detach argument, to keep pppd from detaching itself from the tty it's on. If pppd detaches, the script exits, causing the dial-up connection to close. The `silent` option makes `pppd` wait for the remote `pppd` daemon to initiate the link. The `modem` options make `pppd` monitor the modem control lines, and `crtscts` makes `pppd` use hardware flow control.

That's all there is to it. When users log in to your machine with the proper user ID and password, the PPP link is established automatically on your box.

Keeping Your PPP Link Secure

Keeping your PPP link secure is very important. Allowing anyone to connect your machine to a PPP server or allowing anyone to connect to your PPP server is as bad as letting anyone put their machine directly on your network. PPP provides a direct IP connection, effectively putting the machines on both ends of the link on the same network.

Two authentication protocols have been developed to make PPP more secure—Password Authentication Protocol (PAP) and the Challenge Handshake Authentication Protocol (CHAP). While a PPP connection is being established, each machine can request the other to authenticate itself. This allows complete control of who can use your PPP service. CHAP is the more secure protocol and is discussed here.

CHAP uses a set of *secret keys*, which are text strings that are kept secret by the owners of the machines using CHAP, and an encrypted challenge system to authenticate each other. A useful feature of CHAP is that it periodically issues challenge requests as long as the PPP link is up. This, for example, can detect intruders who have replaced the legitimate user by switching phone lines.

The secret keys for CHAP are stored in /etc/ppp/chap-secrets. To use authentication on your PPP link, you add the `auth` option to the call to `pppd` and add the appropriate information for the host being authenticated into the chap-secrets file. The following is a sample chap-secrets file for unixlt.tristar.com:

```
# unixlt.tristar.com CHAP secrets file
# client/server/secret/IP addr
unixlt.tristar.com unix1.tristar.com "It's Full of Stars"
➥unixlt.tristar.com
unix1.tristar.com unixlt.tristar.com "three stars" unix1.tristar.com
* unixlt.tristar.com "three stars" tristar.com
```

Each line contains up to four fields: the client host name, server host name, secret key, and an optional list of IP addresses that this client can request be assigned to it. The client and server designations in this file are determined by the host that makes the authentication request (the server). The client has to respond to the request.

This file defines three different CHAP secrets. The first line is used when unix1.tristar.com requests CHAP authentication from unixlt.tristar.com; the second is used for the reverse situation. The last line defines a wild-card situation for the client. This allows any machine that knows the proper secret key to make a PPP link to unixlt.tristar.com. The wild-card designator (*) can be used in the client or server field.

Careful management of the chap-secrets file allows you complete control over the machines that can access your PPP server and the machines that you can access with PPP.

From Here...

SLIP and PPP are low-cost alternatives to a leased-line IP connectivity solution. You've looked at the requirements for running SLIP and PPP and at how to automate SLIP and PPP links by using the dip and chat commands. You've learned how to configure Linux as a SLIP or PPP server and how to enhance the security of PPP using the CHAP protocol. You can find complete documentation for dip, chat, and pppd in the man pages.

- Chapter 10, "Managing User Accounts," shows you how to add and delete user accounts.
- Chapter 22, "Understanding the TCP/IP Protocol Suite," explains what TCP/IP is and how the protocols work.
- Chapter 23, "Configuring a TCP/IP Network," shows you how to set up a Linux machine for use on a network.
- Chapter 24, "Configuring Domain Name Service," shows you how to make Linux use DNS.

Part
V

Ch
25

Using the Internet

## CHAPTER 26

Understanding the Internet

Everywhere you turn, you hear about the Internet and the World Wide Web. Hundreds of books on the market are aimed at getting novice and experienced computer users on the Internet. Lots of companies also provide you with a connection—for a small fee, of course. But what is the Internet? How does it work and why is it useful? This chapter addresses these and other questions about this rapidly growing information network. ■

Background information on the Internet
Learn about the history and size of the Internet.

The basics of Internet names
Understand the meanings of different parts of Internet computer names.

The DNS name system
Get an introduction the Domain Name Service, and see how it resolves computer names.

Finding hosts on the Internet
Learn to use `nslookup` to search for hosts on the Net.

Many computer users refer to the Internet simply as *the Net.*

The Structure of the Internet

The Internet is really a network of computer networks that exchange information with each other. In fact, the word *Internet* comes from the term *internetwork*, which means "to communicate between networks." An easy way to visualize the Internet is to think of a large cloud with computers attached to it (see Figure 26.1). This cloud is constantly changing and growing as new computers and networks are added and existing networks are changed.

FIG. 26.1

The logical cloud structure of the Internet includes many interconnected networks.

Within this Internet cloud are many computer networks that are connected to each other. These systems use the TCP/IP protocol suite for data communication.

A Brief History

The Internet grew out of a research program of the U.S. Defense Advanced Research Projects Agency (DARPA), which focused on ways to link various computer networks. The result was the ARPANET, initiated in 1969. By 1971, approximately 40 computers, or hosts, were connected to the ARPANET, and researchers were developing the capability to send e-mail across networks. The ARPANET continued to grow throughout the '70s, and other computer networks began to connect to it as well.

Internetworking research led to the development of the TCP/IP network protocols, which replaced an older protocol suite known as the Network Control Protocol (NCP) and became the standard for the ARPANET. As more and more networks connected to the ARPANET and each other, this large complex of networks came to be known as the Internet. The original ARPANET was shut down in 1990, leaving the Internet as its thriving successor.

Size

The Internet has experienced incredible growth over the last 10 years. In 1984, approximately 1,000 hosts were on the Internet. By 1989, this total had grown to more than 100,000. Three years later, in 1992, the total was more than 1 million computers on the Internet. As of July 1994, more than 3.2 million host computers were on the Net, with an estimated 20 million users. The number is far larger than that today. With the development of easy-to-use information-retrieval provided by the World Wide Web, many non-technical users are discovering that the Internet has vast information resources that they can access.

As to the geographic size of the Internet, it essentially spans the entire world. Almost every industrialized nation has some form of Internet connectivity.

N O T E Basically, there are two different levels of Internet connectivity:

- At the most interactive level, a site has some sort of physical connection to an Internet member network. This site runs the TCP/IP protocol suite as its networking protocol and can make direct network connections in real time to other computers. This is referred to as being *IP connected*.

- The other connection type typically uses the UUCP protocol to transfer e-mail, and Usenet news to and from an IP-connected site. Users with this type of connection can't access other computers interactively on the Net. ■

Internet Names

With millions of computers on the Internet, how do you specify the one that you want to interact with? You must know the name of the computer, just as you must know the name of someone you want to send a letter to. These names are specified by a convention called the Domain Name Service (DNS), which is specified in Internet Request For Comments (RFC) numbers 1032, 1033, 1034, and 1035. (See Chapter 24, "Configuring Domain Name Service," for more information.)

Part VI
Ch 26

N O T E *Requests For Comments* provide the official documentation, policies, and procedures of the Internet community. These documents are typically referred to by the abbreviation RFC and a number. ■

A DNS name has the following format:

```
[subdomain].[subdomain].[...].domain
```

Sometimes a domain name won't refer to a specific computer; instead, it might refer to an alias of some sort.

N O T E Brackets ([ ]) indicate optional items. Hence, don't type the brackets as part of the name. ■

Domains

A domain name typically gives a hierarchical structure for a computer or group within an organization. The portion of the name to the far right, the *domain field*, provides the most general category. The United States has nine domain fields, listed in Table 26.1.

Table 26.1 Listing of U.S. Domains	
Domain	**Description**
arpa	ARPANET members (obsolete)
com	Commercial and industrial organizations
edu	Universities and educational institutions
gov	Non-military government organizations
int	International organizations
mil	Military
net	Network operation organizations
org	Other organizations
us	United States ISO domain

T I P   Refer to RFC 1480 for more information on the us domain.

Outside the United States, each nation has a two-letter domain assigned to it based on its country code as defined in the International Standards Organization (ISO) document 3166. (Because the Internet basically started in the United States, the us domain wasn't widely used initially.) Table 26.2 lists the domains for other nations.

Table 26.2 International DNS Domains			
Country	**Domain**	**Country**	**Domain**
Afghanistan	**af**	Antarctica	**aq**
Albania	**al**	Antigua and Barbuda	**ag**
Algeria	**dz**	Argentina	**ar**
American Samoa	**as**	Armenia	**am**
Andorra	**ad**	Aruba	**aw**
Angola	**ao**	Australia	**au**
Anguilla	**ai**	Austria	**at**

Country	Domain	Country	Domain
Azerbaijan	az	China	cn
Bahamas	bs	Christmas Island	cx
Bahrain	bh	Cocos (Keeling) Islands	cc
Bangladesh	bd	Colombia	co
Barbados	bb	Comoros	km
Belarus	by	Congo	cg
Belgium	be	Cook Island	ck
Belize	bz	Costa Rica	cr
Benin	bj	Cote d'Ivoire (Ivory Coast)	ci
Bermuda	bm	Croatia	hr
Bhutan	bt	Cuba	cu
Bolivia	bo	Cyprus	cy
Bosnia-Hercegovina	ba	Czech Republic	cz
Botswana	bw	Denmark	dk
Bouvet Island	bv	Djibouti	dj
Brazil	br	Dominica	dm
British Indian Ocean Territory	io	Dominican Republic	do
Brunei Darussalam	bn	East Timor	tp
Bulgaria	bg	Ecuador	ec
Burkina Faso	bf	Egypt	eg
Burundi	bi	El Salvador	sv
Cambodia	kh	Equatorial Guinea	gq
Cameroon	cm	Estonia	ee
Canada	ca	Ethiopia	et
Cape Verde	cv	Falkland Islands	fk
Cayman Islands	ky	Faroe Islands	fo
Central African Republic	cf	Fiji	fj
Chad	td	Finland	fi
Chile	cl	France	fr

continues

Table 26.2 Continued

Country	Domain	Country	Domain
French Guiana	gf	Ireland	ie
French Polynesia	pf	Israel	il
French Southern Territories	tf	Italy	it
		Jamaica	jm
Gabon	ga	Japan	jp
Gambia	gm	Jordan	jo
Georgia	ge	Kazakhstan	kz
Germany	de	Kenya	ke
Ghana	gh	Kiribati	ki
Gibraltar	gi	Korea, Democratic People's Republic of (North)	kp
Greece	gr		
Greenland	gl		
Grenada	gd	Korea, Republic of (South)	kr
Guadeloupe	gp	Kuwait	kw
Guam	gu	Kyrgyzstan	kg
Guatemala	gt	Lao People's Democratic Republic	la
Guinea	gn		
Guinea-Bissau	gw	Latvia	lv
Guyana	gy	Lebanon	lb
Haiti	ht	Lesotho	ls
Heard and McDonald Islands	hm	Liberia	lr
Honduras	hn	Libyan Arab Jamahiriya (Libya)	ly
Hong Kong	hk	Liechtenstein	li
Hungary	hu	Lithuania	lt
Iceland	is	Luxembourg	lu
India	in	Macau (Macao)	mo
Indonesia	id	Madagascar	mg
Iran	ir	Malawi	mw
Iraq	iq	Malaysia	my

Country	Domain	Country	Domain
Maldives	mv	Norway	no
Mali	ml	Oman	om
Malta	mt	Pakistan	pk
Marshall Islands	mh	Palau	pw
Martinique	mq	Panama	pa
Mauritania	mr	Papua New Guinea	pg
Mauritius	mu	Paraguay	py
Mexico	mx	Peru	pe
Micronesia	fm	Philippines	ph
Moldovia	md	Pitcairn Island	pn
Monaco	mc	Poland	pl
Mongolia	mn	Portugal	pt
Montserrat	ms	Puerto Rico	pr
Morocco	ma	Qatar	qa
Mozambique	mz	Reunion Island	re
Myanmar (Burma)	mm	Romania	ro
Namibia	na	Russian Federation	ru
Nauru	nr	Rwanda	rw
Nepal	np	St. Helena	sh
Netherlands	nl	St. Kitts and Nevis	kn
Netherlands Antilles (Dutch West Indies)	an	St. Lucia	lc
Neutral Zone	nt	St. Pierre and Miquelon	pm
New Caledonia	nc	St. Vincent and the Grenadines	vc
New Zealand	nz		
Nicaragua	ni	Samoa	ws
Niger	ne	San Marino	sm
Nigeria	ng	Sao Tome and Principe	st
Niue	nu		
Norfolk Island	nf	Saudi Arabia	sa
Northern Mariana Islands	mp	Senegal	sn
		Seychelles	sc

continues

Part
VI

Ch
26

Table 26.2   Continued

Country	Domain	Country	Domain
Sierra Leone	**sl**	Turkmenistan	**tm**
Singapore	**sg**	Turks and Caicos Islands	**tc**
Slovak Republic	**sk**		
Slovenia	**si**	Tuvalu	**tv**
Solomon Islands	**sb**	Uganda	**ug**
Somalia	**so**	Ukraine	**ua**
South Africa	**za**	United Arab Emirates	**ae**
Spain	**es**	United Kingdom	**uk**
Sri Lanka	**lk**	United States	**us**
Sudan	**sd**	Uruguay	**uy**
Suriname	**sr**	Uzbekistan	**uz**
Svalbard and Jan Mayen Islands	**sj**	Vanuatu	**vu**
		Vatican City	**va**
Swaziland	**sz**	Venezuela	**ve**
Sweden	**se**	Vietnam	**vn**
Switzerland	**ch**	Virgin Islands (British)	**vg**
Syrian Arab Republic	**sy**		
Taiwan	**tw**	Virgin Islands (U.S.)	**vi**
Tajikistan	**tj**	Wallis and Fortuna Islands	**wf**
Tanzania	**tz**		
Thailand	**th**	Western Sahara	**eh**
Togo	**tg**	Yemen	**ye**
Tokelau	**tk**	Yugoslavia (former)	**yu**
Tonga	**to**	Zaire	**zr**
Trinidad and Tobago	**tt**	Zambia	**zm**
Tunisia	**tn**	Zimbabwe	**zw**
Turkey	**tr**		

Subdomains

The subdomain fields of a DNS name serve to identify a specific computer or address within a domain. The subdomains become more specific from right to left in the domain name. The rightmost subdomain field, the one next to the domain field, usually serves to indicate a particular organization within a given domain. The name ncsu.edu, for example, refers to the North Carolina State University (ncsu) subdomain in the edu domain. Secondary subdomain fields specify a department, group, or computer within an organization. These subdomain groupings produce a logical tree structure within the domain. Chapter 29, "Using Electronic Mail," discusses this subject in more detail.

To specify a user at a certain location, a special delimiter, @, is used to specify a user, alias, or mailbox in a site's DNS name. For example, Joe Smith in Sales has the user account smith at the machine linux1.somewhere.com. The full address for Joe is

smith@linux1.sales.somewhere.com

The @ symbol is used to separate the destination mailbox from the computer destination.

> **N O T E**   It's not uncommon for the DNS name portion of an e-mail address to specify a department or organization instead of a machine. In the preceding example, to avoid having to use a specific computer's name in an e-mail address, the system administrator can set up the receiving mailer with an address of smith@sales.somewhere.com or even smith@somewhere.com. ■

Basics of Domain Name Service

You've learned how host names are represented by using the DNS convention, but exactly how does Linux know how to communicate with a computer when you send mail to smith@linux1.somewhere.com? This simple question really opens up the whole can of worms about networking. However, understanding how DNS translates names is useful for the average user and is absolutely critical for the systems administrator.

Part
VI

Ch
26

Names and Numbers

As you recall, this chapter has briefly discussed sites being IP connected to the Internet and using the TCP/IP protocol suite to facilitate communication. TCP/IP identifies each host with a unique 32-bit number value known as an *IP address*. Like the DNS name, the address is divided into four 8-bit fields, each separated by a period.

> **N O T E**   In networking terminology, an 8-bit field is referred to as an *octet* instead of a *byte*. This avoids confusion, as a few types of computers use a byte size of other than 8 bits. ■

Each computer has exactly one IP address for each physical interface that it has connected to a network.

The IP address of a computer is divided into two parts: a network section, which specifies a particular network, and a host portion, which identifies a particular machine on the network. There now are five categories of IP addresses, based on the type of network address—*class A* through *class E.*

In a class A address, the first octet has a value between 1 and 126, and the network portion consists of the first octet. This obviously limits the number of class A networks to 126; however, each network can have more than 16 million computers. Class A networks are limited to major corporations and network providers.

Class B networks use the first two octets to specify the network portion and have the first octet in the range of 128 to 191. This leaves the last two octets free for the host ID. The Class B network space provides for 16,384 network ID numbers, each with 65,534 host IDs. Large companies and organizations such as universities are typically assigned class B addresses.

Class C addresses use three octets to specify the network portion, with the first octet in the range from 192 to 223. This provides for more than 2 million different class C networks, but with only 254 hosts per network. Class C networks are usually assigned to small businesses or organizations.

In class D addresses, the first octet is in the range from 224 to 239 and is used for multicast transmissions.

Class E addresses, with the first octet in the range of 240 to 247, are reserved for future use.

N O T E   The values 0, 127, and 255 have special meaning in an IP address. A 0 in an octet indicates that the host doesn't know that part of its address; a 127 refers to a *loopback* (local host) address; and a 255 refers to a broadcast address. When 4.2BSD UNIX was released, the broadcast address was specified by using a 0 in the host portion of the IP address. This was later changed to 255 and is standardized in an RFC. A few old systems might still be around that use the 0 for their broadcast—this is referred to as *Berkeley broadcast.* ■

When computers communicate by using TCP/IP, they use the numeric IP address just described. DNS is simply a device that helps us poor humans remember which host is which and what network it's connected to. Originally, when the Internet was first formed, the number of hosts on the Net was very small. As a result, each host had a complete list of all host names and addresses in a local file. For obvious reasons, this system quickly became unwieldy. When a new host was added, it was necessary to update every host file on every computer.

With the explosive growth of the Internet, the host files also grew quite large. The mapping of DNS names to IP addresses is now accomplished via a distributed database and specific software that performs the lookup. The distributed database and software that make up the DNS name resolution system is composed of the following basic parts:

- Domain name space
- Name servers
- Resolvers

Domain Name Space   The *domain name space* is a specification for a tree structure that identifies a set of hosts and provides information about them. Conceptually, each node in the tree has a database of information about the hosts under its authority. Queries try to extract the appropriate information from this database. In simple terms, the domain name space is just the listing of all different types of information—names, IP address, mail aliases, and such—that's available for lookup in the DNS system.

Name Servers   Programs that hold and maintain the data located in the domain name space are known as *name servers*. Each name server has complete information about a subset of the domain name space and cached information about other portions. Also, a name server has complete information for its area of authority. This authoritative information is divided into areas known as *zones*, which can be divided among different name servers to provide redundant service for a zone. Each name server knows about other name servers that are responsible for different zones. If a request comes in for information from the zone that a given name server is responsible for, the name server simply returns the information. If a request comes in for information from a different zone, however, the name server contacts the appropriate server with authority for that zone.

Resolvers   *Resolvers* are simply programs that extract information from the name servers in response to a query about a host in the domain name space.

Finding Host Information

To find information about a host or domain, you can use two basic sources of information: the whois information system and the nslookup program.

Using *whois*   whois queries the DNS system and returns information on network address numbers, administrative and technical contact information, telephone numbers, and postal and e-mail addresses. The syntax for this command is

whois [*name*]

name is a network or domain name, or a registered user. The whois utility is a local client program that connects to a server and returns the information to your computer.

In addition to using the whois utility, you can connect directly to an information server and get this information. You can telnet to **rs.internic.net** and type **whois** at the first prompt. The Whois: prompt appears, where you can make your queries. Here are a few sample whois sessions:

```
Whois: ncsu.edu
North Carolina State University NCSU-DOM
   Computing Center
   Box 7109
   Raleigh, NC 27695-7109

   Domain Name: NCSU.EDU
```

```
Administrative Contact:
    Malstrom, Carl W.  CWM10  Carl_Malstrom@ncsu.EDU
    (919) 515-5455
Technical Contact, Zone Contact:
    Fatmi, Mohammad  MF210  Mohammad_Fatmi@NCSU.EDU
    (919) 515-5492

Record last updated on 10-Apr-95.
Record created on 16-Apr-87.

Domain servers in listed order:

FBI.CC.NCSU.EDU                152.1.1.22
CC00NS.UNITY.NCSU.EDU          152.1.1.161
EOS01A.EOS.NCSU.EDU            152.1.9.5
```

Whois: **interpath.net**
```
Interpath INTERPATH-DOM
    PO Box 12800
    Raleigh, NC 27605

    Domain Name: INTERPATH.NET

    Administrative Contact, Technical Contact, Zone Contact:
        Interpath Hostmaster  INTP-HM  hostmaster@interpath.net
        (919) 890-6300 (919) 890-6305 fax (919) 890-6319

    Record last updated on 23-Apr-96.
    Record created on 18-Nov-93.

    Domain servers in listed order:

    DNS1.INTERPATH.NET          199.72.1.1
    DNS3.INTERPATH.NET          199.72.1.5
```

Whois: **ibm.com**
```
International Business Machines IBM-DOM

    Domain Name: IBM.COM

    Administrative Contact, Technical Contact, Zone Contact:
        Trio, Nicholas R.  NRT1  nrt@WATSON.IBM.COM
        914) 945-1850

    Record last updated on 07-Nov-96.
    Record created on 19-Mar-86.

    Domain servers in listed order:

    NS.WATSON.IBM.COM           129.34.139.2
    NS.AUSTIN.IBM.COM           192.35.232.34
    NS.ALMADEN.IBM.COM          198.4.83.35
    NS.EUROPE.IBM.COM           193.129.186.200
```

Using *nslookup* The nslookup utility queries the DNS system to return information about specific hosts and networks. Although nslookup returns several different types of information, the default behavior is to resolve a DNS name and return its corresponding IP address.

The nslookup command has two basic forms: interactive and non-interactive. The non-interactive form has the following syntax:

```
nslookup [hostname]
```

This form of nslookup tries to resolve the DNS name *hostname* and return its IP address.

You can select interactive mode either when you give no arguments, or when the first argument starts with a hyphen and the second argument is the name or IP address of a name server. In interactive mode, you can customize the behavior of nslookup by specifying the name server to query, changing the type of information to search for, changing the default domain name, enabling debugging, and so forth. Although many different options are available in interactive mode, it's used mostly to search for information other than the IP address. Refer to the nslookup man page for all the gory details on the other features.

You can change the search type in nslookup interactive mode with the set type= command. Table 26.3 lists the types of information that you can specify and the appropriate type code for the set type= command.

Table 26.3   Search Information Available in *nslookup*

Information	Type Code
Host's IP address (default)	A
Canonical alias name	CNAME
CPU and operating system info	HINFO
Mail destination	MD
Mail group records	MG
Mail exchanger records	MX
Mail rename domain name	MR
Mailbox or mail list information	MINFO
Name server for zone	NS
Any information found	ANY

Part
VI

Ch
26

Additional type codes that can be used with nslookup are specified in RFC 1035.

From Here...

You can find more information about the Internet in the following chapters:

- Chapter 24, "Configuring Domain Name Service," discusses configuring the Domain Name Service in detail.
- Chapter 27, "Accessing the Network with *telnet*, *ftp*, and the *r-* Commands," discusses the different methods for working with the Internet.
- Chapter 28, "Surfing the Internet with the World Wide Web," describes the different types of information available on the Internet.

Accessing the Network with *telnet*, *ftp*, and the *r–* Commands

Executing remot commands

Learn how to log in to remote computers, transfer files, and execute commands.

The *telnet* command

This chapter discusses how to use telnet to log in to remote computers.

The *ftp* command

Learn how to transfer files with the ftp command.

The *r–* commands

Learn about the various remote commands that are available under Linux.

The major advantage that you gain from computer networking is the capability to share resources and information, and to access that information from remote locations. Linux provides a robust set of tools for doing just that. Whereas the World Wide Web lets you access lots of information in a hypertext format, additional tools allow you to log in to remote computers, transfer files, and execute remote commands. ■

Using *telnet* to Access Remote Computers

The telnet command is the basic tool for remote login under Linux. telnet gives you a terminal session on the remote computer that allows you to execute commands as though you were logged in locally.

To log in to a computer via telnet, you must know a valid user name and password on the remote machine. Although some systems do provide guest login capabilities, such capabilities are fairly rare due to security concerns. When guest logins are allowed, they almost always place users in a restricted shell or in a menu system. The idea behind these two guest environments is to provide computer security and protect the system from malicious or careless unknown users. A restricted shell prevents the user from executing specific commands; a menu system only allows choices from a predefined set of menus, blocking out shell access entirely.

telnet also allows users to log in to their own computer from a remote location by entering their user name and password. This way, users can check e-mail, edit files, and run programs on their normal computer as though they were logged in locally. However, you have to make do with a terminal-based environment instead of the X Windows system. telnet provides only terminal emulation for common terminals such as the DEC VT-100, which doesn't support graphical environments such as X Windows.

telnet Command Summary

The basic syntax for telnet is

telnet [hostname]

hostname is the name of a remote computer. If you don't specify a remote host, telnet starts in its interactive command mode. If you give a remote host name, telnet tries to initiate a session immediately.

telnet accepts several command-line arguments in addition to the *hostname* argument, as listed in Table 27.1.

Table 27.1   Command-Line Arguments for the *telnet* Command

Argument	Description
–d	Turns on debugging.
–a	Attempts automatic login.
–n *tracefile*	Turns on tracing and saves trace data in *tracefile*.
–e *escape_char*	Sets the escape character for the session to be *escape_char*. If the *escape_char* character is omitted from the argument, there is no escape character for this telnet session.
–l *user*	Sends the user name *user* to the remote system for automatic login. This argument automatically includes the –a argument.

Argument	Description
port	Indicates the port number to connect to on the remote system. This argument is used for specifying different network programs. If it's not specified, telnet connects to the default telnet port.

Sample *telnet* Session

It's time to take a walk through a sample telnet session. You start the telnet session by typing **telnet**, followed by the host name of the computer you want to connect to. telnet then returns with the message Trying *some IP address* (*some IP address* is the address of the computer you specified). If telnet successfully connects to the computer (that is, the computer is up and running and the network isn't down), Linux reports Connected to *computer name* and then tells you that the escape character is some specific character sequence, almost always <Ctrl-]>. The escape character specifies the character sequence that you type to drop from your terminal session into the telnet command interpreter. You do this if you want to send commands directly to the telnet program and not to your remote computer session.

After telnet successfully connects to the remote system, the login information is displayed and the system prompts you for your login ID and password. Assuming that you have a valid user name and password, you successfully log in and can now work interactively on the remote system.

The following is an example of a telnet session from a Linux computer that connects to a Linux computer:

```
$ telnet server.somewhere.com
Trying 127.0.0.1...
Connected to server.somewhere.com.
Escape character is '^]'.
"Red Hat Linux release 4.0 (Colgate)

kernel 2.0.18 on an I486

login:bubba
Password: password
Last login: Mon Nov 11 20:50:43 from localhost
Linux 2.0.6. (Posix).
server:~$
server:~$ logout
Connection closed by foreign host.
$
```

When you're finished with the remote session, be sure to log out. telnet then reports that the remote session is closed, and you return to your local shell prompt.

Part
VI

Ch
27

Using FTP for Remote File Transfer

File Transfer Protocol (FTP) is a simple and effective means of transferring files between computers that are connected on a TCP/IP network. FTP allows users to transfer ASCII and binary files.

During an FTP session, you connect to another computer by using the `ftp` client program. From this point, you can move up and down through the directory tree, list directory contents, copy files from the remote computer to your computer, and transfer files from your computer to the remote system. Normal file protections apply; you can't get or put a file on the remote system if you don't have the proper permissions for that file.

To use `ftp` to transfer files, you must know a valid user name and password on the remote computer. This user name/password combination is used to validate your FTP session and to determine what access you have to files for transfer. Also, you obviously need to know the name of the computer with which you want to conduct an FTP session.

You should be aware that FTP clients have different command sets, depending on the operating system in question. This chapter covers the Linux `ftp` client; however, when you start an FTP session with a remote computer, the commands that the remote system expects might be different. It's rare for FTP systems to be completely incompatible with each other. Typically, the commands that you normally use are slightly different or unavailable.

Anonymous FTP

Due to the explosive growth of the Internet, many organizations have made huge repositories of information available via FTP. These FTP sites have everything from text files to software of every conceivable type available. But how do you access this enormous storehouse of data if you don't have an account on the remote computer? Do you need to get an account on every FTP site in order to access these files?

In short, the answer is no. A common convention on the Internet allows guest FTP access to file repositories so that users can transfer files. This guest access is referred to as *anonymous FTP*. To use anonymous FTP, you start an FTP session to the remote system, and use the user name of anonymous and your e-mail address as the password. For example, the user smith on linux.somewhere.com wants to initiate an FTP session with a common FTP site:

```
$ ftp ftp.uu.net
ftp.uu.net (login:smith): anonymous
Password: smith@linux.somewhere.com
```

N O T E Many sites don't allow anonymous FTP. Allowing guest users to connect to your computer does involve some risk. In cases where anonymous FTP isn't allowed, the `ftp` command fails with a message similar to `Login failed – User "anonymous" unknown`. Sites that do permit anonymous FTP typically place the user in a restricted directory tree with read-only access. If you're allowed to place files on the remote computer, you usually can put them in only one directory. ■

ftp Command Summary

The Linux ftp command provides a verbose set of command options in interactive mode. As mentioned earlier, some remote hosts might not support all these commands. Also, you probably won't need to use many of them. Table 27.2 lists the commands available while in FTP.

Table 27.2 *ftp* Commands Available in Interactive Mode

Command	Description
!	Escapes to the shell
$	Executes a macro
account	Sends the account command to remote server
append	Appends to a file
ascii	Sets the file-transfer type to ASCII mode
bell	Beeps when a command is completed
binary	Sets the file-transfer type to binary mode
bye	Terminates the FTP session and exits
case	Toggles mget upper- or lowercase file name mapping
cd	Changes the working directory on the remote computer
cdup	Changes the remote working directory to the parent directory
chmod	Changes file permissions of the remote file
close	Terminates the FTP session
cr	Toggles carriage return stripping when receiving an ASCII file
delete	Deletes the remote file
debug	Toggles debugging mode
dir	Lists the contents of the remote directory (gives size and permissions)
disconnect	Terminates the FTP session (same as close)
exit	Terminates the FTP session and exits
form	Sets the file-transfer format
get	Gets a file from the remote computer
glob	Toggles wild-card expansion of local file names
hash	Toggles printing the # character for each buffer transferred

continues

Part
VI

Ch
27

Table 27.2   Continued

Command	Description
help	Prints local help information
idle	Gets or sets the idle timer on the remote computer
image	Sets the file transfer type to binary mode (same as `binary`)
lcd	Changes the local working directory
ls	Lists the contents of the remote directory (gives size and permissions)
macdef	Defines a macro
mdelete	Deletes multiple files on the remote computer
mdir	Lists the contents of multiple remote directories
mget	Gets multiple files from the remote computer
mkdir	Makes a directory on the remote machine
mls	Lists the contents of multiple remote directories
mode	Sets the file-transfer mode
modtime	Shows the last modification time of the remote file
mput	Sends multiple files to the remote computer
newer	Gets a remote file if the remote file is newer than the corresponding local file
nmap	Sets templates for default file name mapping
nlist	Lists the contents of the remote directory
ntrans	Sets the translation table for default file name mapping
open	Connects to the remote FTP site
passive	Enters passive transfer mode
prompt	Forces interactive prompting on multiple commands
proxy	Issues command on alternate connection
put	Sends one file to the remote computer
pwd	Prints the working directory on the remote machine
quit	Terminates the FTP session and exits
quote	Sends an arbitrary `ftp` command
recv	Receives a file
reget	Gets file restarting at end of the local file

Command	Description
rstatus	Shows the status of the remote machine
rhelp	Gets help from the remote server
rename	Renames a file
reset	Clears queued command replies
restart	Restarts the file transfer at the specified byte count
rmdir	Removes a directory on the remote machine
runique	Assigns a unique file name to each file received when retrieving multiple files with the same file name to the same directory
send	Sends one file to the remote computer
site	Sends a site-specific command to the remote server, one of umask, idle, chmod, help, group, gpass, newer, or minfo
size	Shows the size of the remote file
status	Shows the current status
struct	Sets the file-transfer structure
system	Shows the remote system type
sunique	When sending multiple files with the same file name to the same directory, assigns a unique file name to each file sent
tenex	Sets the tenex file-transfer type
tick	Toggles printing byte size counter during transfers
trace	Toggles packet tracing
type	Sets the file-transfer type
user	Sends new user information
umask	Gets or sets the umask on the remote computer
verbose	Toggles verbose mode
?	Prints local help information

Part
VI
Ch
27

As you can see, ftp has quite a few commands. However, you really need to look at only the ones that you use most frequently.

Starting an FTP Session   The open command is used to open an FTP session with a remote host. Its syntax is

open *hostname*

You usually need this command only if you're going to connect to more than one site during an

FTP session. If you want to connect to only one computer during the session, just specify the remote *hostname* on the command line as an argument to the ftp command.

Ending an FTP Session   The close, disconnect, quit, and bye commands are used to end an FTP session with a remote computer. The identical close and disconnect commands close your connection to the remote computer but leave you in the ftp program on your local computer. The quit, exit, and bye commands close your connection to the remote computer if one is active; then they exit the ftp program on your computer.

Changing Directories   The cd *[directory]* command is used to change directories on the remote computer during your FTP session. The cdup command takes you to the parent directory of the current directory. The lcd command changes your local directory so that you can specify where to find or put local files.

Remote Directory Listing   The ls command lists the contents of a remote directory, just like ls from an interactive shell. The syntax for ls is

```
ls [directory] [local_file]
```

If a directory is specified as an argument, ls lists the contents of that directory. If a local file name is given, the directory listing is put into the file you specified on your local computer.

The dir and ls commands provide a long listing, giving protections, size, owner, and date. The syntax of the dir command is

```
dir [directory] [local_file]
```

The following is an example of a dir directory listing:

```
-rw-r--r--    1 root   archive   2928  May   17   1993    README
-rw-r--r--    1 root   archive   1723  Jun   29   1993    README.NFS
dr-xr-xr-x    2 root   wheel     8192  Jun    6   12:16   bind
-rwxr-xr-x    5 root   wheel     8192  Aug    2   06:11   decus
drwxr-xr-x   19 root   archive   8192  Feb    7   1994    doc
drwxr-xr-x    6 root   wheel     8192  Jun   15   15:45   edu
dr-xr-xr-x    7 root   wheel     8192  Sep   28   09:33   etc
```

Getting Files from a Remote System   The get and mget commands are used to retrieve files from a remote computer. The get command retrieves the file that you specify as an argument (*filename*); the get command's syntax is

```
get filename [remote_filename]
```

You can also give a local file name, which is the name of the file when it's created on your local computer. If you don't give a local file name, *remote_filename* is used.

The mget command retrieves multiple files at once. mget's syntax is

```
mget filename_list
```

You specify these files by giving a list of file names separated by spaces or by using a wild-card pattern to mget. You're prompted for each file. To turn prompting off, use the prompt command before using mget. In both cases, the files are transferred as ASCII files, unless you've set the transfer mode to something else.

Sending Files to a Remote System   The `put` and `mput` commands are used to send files to a remote computer. The `put` command sends the local file that you specify as an argument. The syntax is

`put filename`

The `mput` command sends a series of local files. The syntax for `mput` is

`mput filename_list`

You specify these files by giving a list of file names separated by spaces or by using a wild-card pattern to `mput`. When using `mput`, you're prompted for each file. To turn prompting off, use the `prompt` command. In both cases, the files are transferred as ASCII files, unless you've set the transfer mode to something else.

Changing the File Transfer Mode   `ftp` transfers files as ASCII files unless you specify something else. This is fine for plain text but renders any binary data useless. The `ascii` and `binary` commands set the transfer mode so that you can prevent damage to your binary files.

N O T E   Many files that you'll want to transfer are in binary format. Files ending with .tar are archives created with the `tar` command. Files ending in .Z and .gz are compressed with either the `compress` command or the GNU `gzip` command, respectively. Files ending in .zip are compressed archives created with PKZIP. When in doubt, use binary transfer mode. Using ASCII mode corrupts binary data files. ▪

Checking Transfer Status   When transferring a large file, you may find it useful to have `ftp` give you feedback on how far along the transfer is. The `hash` command causes `ftp` to print a # character on-screen each time the transmission of a data buffer has been completed. This command works for sending and receiving files.

Local Commands While in FTP   The `!` character is used to pass a command to the command shell on your local computer while you're in FTP. This can be very useful if you need to do something while you're in the midst of an FTP session. Suppose that you need to create a directory to hold received files. If you enter `!mkdir new_dir`, Linux makes a directory named new_dir in your current local directory.

A Sample FTP Session

Listing 27.1 shows a short FTP session.

Listing 27.1   Making an FTP Connection and Doing a Directory Listing

```
$ ftp opus
Connected to opus.
220 opus FTP server (Linux opus 2.0.6 #4 Mon Nov 11 16:01:33 CDT 1996) ready.
Name (opus:smith): smith
Password (opus:smith): password
```

continues

Listing 27.1 Continued

```
331 Password required for smith.
230 User smith logged in.
Remote system type is UNIX.
Using ASCII mode to transfer files.
ftp> dir
200 PORT command successful.
150 Opening ASCII mode data connection for /bin/ls.
total 8
-rw-r--r--  1 root      daemon      1525 Sep 29 15:37 README
dr-xr-xr-x  2 root      wheel        512 Jun 24 11:35 bin
dr--r--r--  2 root      wheel        512 Jun 24 11:18 dev
dr--r--r--  2 root      wheel        512 Jun 24 11:24 etc
dr-xr-xr-x  4 root      wheel        512 Sep 29 15:37 pub
dr-xr-xr-x  3 root      wheel        512 Jun 24 11:15 usr
-r--r--r--  1 root      daemon       461 Jun 24 13:46 welcome.msg
226 Transfer complete.
433 bytes received in 0.027 seconds (16 Kbytes/s)
ftp> get README
200 PORT command successful.
150 Opening ASCII mode data connection for README (1525 bytes).
226 Transfer complete.
local: README remote: README
1561 bytes received in 0.0038 seconds (4e+02 Kbytes/s)
ftp> quit
221 Goodbye.
$
```

In the preceding example, a user opens an FTP session to the host opus and logs in as smith. The remote FTP server prompts for the password, which the user types (the password doesn't appear on-screen). ftp then logs smith in to the remote system and displays the ftp> prompt for interactive mode commands. The user tells ftp to list the remote directory with the dir command and then transfers the file README with the get command. When finished with the FTP session, the intrepid user then logs out with the quit command and is returned to the local Linux shell prompt.

A Sample Anonymous FTP Session

In the previous section, you saw a user initiate an FTP session with a system and look at some directories. The user had a valid user name and password on the remote system. Now look at an anonymous FTP session to a major software archive site on the Internet. Listing 27.2 is very similar to Listing 27.1, but it has some interesting differences.

Listing 27.2 Performing an Anonymous FTP Connection

```
$ ftp ftp.uu.net
Connected to ftp.uu.net.
220 ftp.UU.NET FTP server (Version wu-2.4(1) Wed Nov 13 15:45:10 EST 1996) ready.
Name (ftp.uu.net:bubba): anonymous
331 Guest login ok, send your complete e-mail address as password.
```

```
Password: your_e-mail_address
230-
230-                  Welcome to the UUNET archive.
230-    A service of UUNET Technologies Inc, Falls Church, Virginia
230-    For information about UUNET, call +1 703 204 8000,
230-    or see the files in /uunet-info
230-
230-    Access is allowed all day.
230-    Local time is Wed Nov 13 15:53:02 1996.
230-
230-    All transfers are logged with your host name and email address.
230-    If you don't like this policy, disconnect now!
230-
230-    If your FTP client crashes or hangs shortly
230-    after login, try using a
230-    dash (-) as the first character of your password.
230-    This will turn off the informational messages which may
230-     be confusing your ftp client.
230-
230-Please read the file /info/README.ftp
230-  it was last modified on Mon Nov 11 17:39:53 1996 - 2 days ago
230 Guest login ok, access restrictions apply.
ftp>
ftp> dir
200 PORT command successful.
150 Opening ASCII mode data connection for /bin/ls.
total 4149
drwxr-sr-x   2 34    0          512 Jul 26  1992 .forward
-rw-r--r--   1 34    uucp         0 Jul 26  1992 .hushlogin
-rw-r--r--   1 34    archive     59 Jul 31  1992 .kermrc
-rw-r--r--   1 34    archive      0 Jul 26  1992 .notar
drwx--s--x   5 34    archive    512 Jul 23 19:00 admin
lrwxrwxrwx   1 34    archive      1 Jul 26  1992 archive -> .
drwxrws--x   4 0     archive    512 Apr 20 16:29 bin
lrwxrwxrwx   1 34    archive     23 Sep 14  1993 by-name.gz ->
                                     index/master/by-name.gz
lrwxrwxrwx   1 34    archive     23 Sep 14  1993 by-time.gz ->
                                     index/master/by-time.gz
-rw-r--r--   1 34    archive  90112 Apr 26  1991 compress.tar
lrwxrwxrwx   1 0     archive      9 Jul 23 18:50 core -> /dev/null
drwxrws--x   2 0     archive    512 Jul 26  1992 dev
drwxrwsr-x  21 34    archive   1024 Sep 29 15:18 doc
drwxrws--x   6 0     archive    512 Apr 14 16:42 etc
lrwxrwxrwx   1 34    archive     31 Dec  8  1993 faces ->
                                     /archive/published/usenix/faces
drwxrwsr-x   2 34    archive    512 Jul 26  1992 ftp
drwxrwsr-x   4 34    archive    512 Sep 29 10:34 government
drwxrwsr-x  18 34    archive   1024 Sep 29 10:28 graphics
-rw-rw-r--   1 27    archive 798720 Jul 11 20:54 gzip.tar
lrwxrwxrwx   1 34    archive     17 Jul 26  1992 help -> info/archive-help
drwxrwsr-x  20 34    archive   1024 Dec  2  1993 index
drwxrwsr-x  19 34    archive    512 Sep 29 10:30 inet
drwxrwsr-x   4 34    archive    512 Sep 29 15:36 info
drwxrwsr-x  25 34    archive    512 Sep 29 10:29 languages
```

continues

Part

VI

Ch

27

Listing 27.2   Continued

```
drwxrwsr-x   4 34    archive     512 Sep 29 10:28 library
drwx--s--x   2 0     0          8192 Jul 26  1992 lost+found
lrwxrwxrwx   1 34    archive      20 Aug  2  1992 ls-lR.Z ->
                                                  index/master/ls-1R.Z
lrwxrwxrwx   1 34    archive      21 Sep 14  1993 ls-1R.gz ->
                                                  index/master/ls-1R.gz
lrwxrwxrwx   1 34    archive      21 Aug  2  1992 ls-1tR.Z ->
                                                  index/master/ls-1tR.Z
lrwxrwxrwx   1 34    archive      22 Sep 14  1993 ls-1tR.gz ->
                                                  index/master/ls-1tR.gz
drwxrwsr-x  24 34    archive    1024 Sep 29 15:10 networking
drwxrwsr-x   2 34    archive     512 Aug 10 09:26 packages
d--xrws--x  17 34    archive     512 Sep 26 12:29 private
drwxrwsr-x  25 34    archive    1536 Sep 29 15:30 pub
drwxrwsr-x  17 34    archive    1024 Sep 29 15:38 published
lrwxrwxrwx   1 34    archive      10 Jul 26  1992 sco-archive -> vendor/sco
drwxrwsr-x  20 34    archive     512 Sep 29 04:18 systems
drwxrwxrwx  14 34    archive    1536 Sep 29 15:36 tmp
lrwxrwxrwx   1 34    archive      17 Jul 26  1992 unix-today ->
                                                  vendor/unix-today
lrwxrwxrwx   1 34    archive      17 Jul 26  1992 unix-world ->
                                                  vendor/unix-world
drwxrwsr-x  36 34    archive    1024 Sep 29 15:29 usenet
drwxrws--x   6 0     archive     512 Oct 22  1992 usr
lrwxrwxrwx   1 34    archive      16 Aug  2  1992 uumap -> networking/uumap
-rw-rw-r--   1 34    archive 3279895 Sep 28 21:05 uumap.tar.Z
drwxrwsr-x   3 210   archive    2560 Sep 29 15:36 uunet-info
drwxrwsr-x  64 34    archive    1536 Sep 29 10:29 vendor
226 Transfer complete.
3257 bytes received in 0.76 seconds (4.2 Kbytes/s)
ftp>
ftp> cd systems/unix/linux
250-Files within this subtree are automatically mirrored from
250-tsx-11.mit.edu:/pub/linux
250-
250 CWD command successful.
ftp>
ftp> binary
200 Type set to I.
ftp> get sum.Z
200 PORT command successful.
150 Opening BINARY mode data connection for sum.Z (80959 bytes).
226 Transfer complete.
local: sum.Z remote: sum.Z
80959 bytes received in 5.6 seconds (14 Kbytes/s)
ftp> quit
221 Goodbye.
$
```

Here, an FTP session is initiated with **ftp.uu.net**, which is a major FTP archive site on the Internet. The user name given at the login prompt is anonymous because this is anonymous FTP. For the password, the full e-mail address is used. **ftp.uu.net** then displays a welcome banner that gives some information about the archive. In this example, you can see that the user changes directories, sets the file mode to binary, gets a compressed binary file, and exits.

TROUBLESHOOTING

I transferred a binary file, but it doesn't work properly. I can't unzip it, untar it, uncompress it, or anything. Make sure that you set the transfer mode to binary. You can do this with the `binary` command at the `ftp>` prompt.

I'm in the process of transferring a large file and want to check the progress. Use the `hash` command. `ftp` prints the # character on-screen after every data buffer that's processed. The data buffer may vary depending on your version of Linux, but it's typically 1,024, 4,096, or 8,192 bytes.

I was trying to do an anonymous FTP, but the site told me that the user *anonymous* was unknown and that the login failed. You either misspelled `anonymous`, or the site doesn't allow anonymous FTP. In the latter case, you must have a valid user name and password on the remote computer.

I want to transfer several files, but I don't want FTP to prompt me for each one. Use the `prompt` command, which toggles prompting on and off.

I tried to use anonymous FTP, but the site told me that I didn't enter a valid e-mail address as the password. In the past, the convention during an anonymous FTP connection was to enter **guest** as the password. Now, the convention is to enter your e-mail address. Many FTP sites run special FTP server software that checks the password and makes sure that it's in the form *user@host.somewhere.domain*. Try again and make sure that you enter your full e-mail address correctly.

Using the *r*– Commands

In addition to `ftp` and `telnet`, several other commands allow you to access remote computers and exchange files over a network. These commands are known collectively as the `r`– commands.

The `r`– commands deserve special notice because one of their features can cause a severe security loophole if you aren't careful. When you issue an `r`– command, the remote system checks a file named /etc/hosts.equiv to see whether your local host is listed. If it doesn't find your local host, it checks for a file named .rhosts in your home directory on the remote machine. The `r`– command then checks to see whether your local host name is in the .rhosts file. If your local host is listed in either place, the command is executed without checking for a password.

Although it can be very convenient not to type your password every time you need to access a remote computer, it can obviously cause severe security problems. It's recommended that you carefully consider the security implications of the `r`– commands before setting up /etc/hosts.equiv and .rhosts files on your local system.

rlogin

The `rlogin` command is very similar to the `telnet` command because it allows you to start an interactive command session on a remote system. The syntax of `rlogin` is

`rlogin [-8EKLdx] [-e char] [-k realm] [-l user-name] hostname`

although the most common usage is simply

`rlogin hostname`

Table 27.3 explains the various options for `rlogin`.

Table 27.3   Command-Line Options for the *rlogin* Command

Option	Description
–8	Allows an 8-bit input data path at all times, which allows for formatted ANSI characters and other special codes to be sent. If this option isn't used, parity bits are stripped except when the remote stop and start characters are other than <Ctrl-s> and <Ctrl-q>.
–E	Stops any character from being recognized as an escape character. When used with the –8 option, this provides a completely transparent connection.
–K	Turns off all Kerberos authentication. It's used only when connecting to a host that uses the Kerberos authentication protocol.
–L	Allows the `rlogin` session to be run in `litout` mode. Refer to the `tty` man page for more information.
–d	Turns on socket debugging on the TCP sockets used for communication with the remote host. Refer to the `setsockopt` man page for more information.
–e	Used to set the escape character for the `rlogin` session. The escape character is ~ by default. You can specify a literal character or an octal value in the form `\nnn`.
–k	Requests `rlogin` to obtain Kerberos tickets for the remote host in the specified realm instead of the remote host's realm as determined by `krb_realmofhost(3)`.
–l	Allows the remote name to be specified. If available, Kerberos authentication is used.
–x	Turns on DES encryption for all data passed via the `rlogin` session. This can affect response time and CPU usage, but provides increased security.

rsh

The rsh command, an abbreviation for *remote shell*, starts a shell on the specified remote host and executes the command, if any, that you specify on the rsh command line. If you don't give a command to execute, you're logged in to the remote machine by using rlogin.

The syntax of the rsh command is

```
rsh [-Kdnx] [-k realm] [-l user-name] hostname [command]
```

although the most common usage is just

```
rsh hostname [command]
```

The command argument can be virtually any Linux command that can be entered from the shell prompt. Table 27.4 explains the command-line options for rsh.

Table 27.4 Command-Line Options for the *rsh* Command

Option	Description
–K	Turns off all Kerberos authentication. It's used only when connecting to a host that uses Kerberos.
–d	Turns on socket debugging on the TCP sockets used for communication with the remote host. See the setsockopt man page for more information.
–k	Requests rsh to obtain Kerberos tickets for the remote host in the specified realm instead of the remote host's realm as determined by krb_realmofhost(3).
–l	Allows the remote name to be specified. If available, Kerberos authentication is used, and authorization is determined as in the rlogin command.
–n	Redirects input from the special device /dev/null.
–x	Turns on DES encryption for all data passed. This can affect response time and CPU usage, but provides increased security.

Linux takes the standard input to the rsh command and copies it to the standard input of the remotely executed command. It copies the standard output of the remote command to standard output for rsh. It also copies the remote standard error to the local standard error file descriptor. Any quit, terminate, and interrupt signals are sent to the remote command. Also, any special shell characters that aren't enclosed with quotation marks, as in "`>>`", are handled locally. If enclosed with quotation marks, these characters are handled by the remote command.

Part
VI
Ch
27

rcp

The rcp command, which stands for *remote copy*, is the last of the r– commands that you need to look at. It's used to copy files between computers. You can use rcp to copy files from one remote computer to another, without either the source or destination being on the local machine.

The rcp command has two forms. The first form is used to copy a file to a file. The second form is used when copying files or a directory to a directory. The syntax for the rcp command is

```
rcp [-px] [-k realm] filename1 filename2
rcp [-px] [-r] [-k realm] file(s) directory
```

Each file or directory argument is either a remote file name or a local file name. Remote file names have the form *rname@rhost:path*, where *rname* is the remote user name, *rhost* is the remote computer, and *path* is the path to the file. The file name must contain a colon.

Table 27.5 explains the arguments for rcp.

Table 27.5 Command-Line Arguments for the *rcp* Command

Option	Description
-r	Recursively copies the source directory tree into the destination directory. To use this option, the destination must be a directory.
-p	Tries to preserve the modification times and modes of the source files, ignoring the umask.
-k	Requests rcp to obtain Kerberos tickets for the remote host in the specified realm instead of the remote host's realm, as determined by krb_realmofhost(3).
-x	Turns on DES encryption for all data passed by rcp. This can affect response time and CPU usage but provides increased security.

If the path specified in the file name isn't a full path name, it's interpreted as being relative to the login directory of the specified user on the remote computer. If no remote user name is given, your current user name is used. If a path on a remote host contains special shell characters, it can be quoted by using \, ", or ' as appropriate. This causes all the shell metacharacters to be interpreted remotely.

N O T E rcp doesn't prompt for passwords. It performs its copies via the rsh command. ■

From Here...

You can find more information about the Internet in the following chapters:

- Chapter 26, "Understanding the Internet," gives an overview and introduction to the Internet.
- Chapter 28, "Surfing the Internet with the World Wide Web," describes the various types of information available on the Internet and the tools for accessing this information.
- Chapter 29, "Using Electronic Mail," shows how to send and receive e-mail over the Internet.

Surfing the Internet with the World Wide Web

You've heard that all kinds of information are available on the Internet. And there is. You'll find everything from the latest weather satellite photo software to statistics, and online shopping.

This chapter discusses the services you can use to get to information on the Internet. You might use the World Wide Web, FTP, gopher, telnet, WAIS, or archie. Most likely you'll use some combination. This chapter goes through each major service and shows you some basic information on how to use that service. Because the Web provides such an easy way to access information on the Internet, and because many of the other services can be used from your Web browser, this chapter concentrates on how to use these services from a Web browser. ■

The Web

The World Wide Web—also known as *the Web* or *WWW*—is one of the fastest-growing areas of the Internet. In this chapter, you're introduced to the Web.

All about URLs

URLs (uniform resource locators) are the means through which you access Web pages.

Searching the Web

In this chapter, you learn to use Linux to search for information on the Web.

Other network tools

The Web is just a part of the Internet. You also can use FTP, telnet, archie, gopher, and WAIS to access information.

Other information sources

This chapter also introduces you to Usenet news and mailing lists.

Introducing the World Wide Web

The Internet is a completely distributed network, which means that your computer is connected directly not only with the computer down the hallway, but with thousands of others all over the world. Your computer connects to another computer, which is connected to a couple of other computers, and so on.

To make matters more complex, the Internet is international in scope. Virtually every country in the world has some form of access to the Internet. For years, there were many services to get to information (FTP, gopher, and so on), but none were easy to use. You had to have all the appropriate software. Then you had to know what service to use, and when. And so on. Something like the World Wide Web was needed as a form of "information navigator," to make it easier for users to get to information on the Internet. (For more details on the Internet, see Chapter 26, "Understanding the Internet.")

The Web began as a network and hypertext project at CERN, a European physics research lab, in 1989. Researchers saw a need for people from any location to be able to share and exchange information and documents in real time from any type of computer. They also wanted a simple and consistent way to handle this information. From this, the Web was born.

The Web uses a set of hypertext links that allow users to easily navigate between documents, graphics, files, audio clips, and so on from sites anywhere on the Internet. When you select a hypertext link in a document, whatever item the link points to is automatically retrieved. One link at a time, Internet users quickly find their way to the various bits of information they want.

Understanding the Web's Structure

The Web is based on a client/server model. The client software package (Web browser software on your computer) contacts a server computer (Web server software) and exchanges messages with that computer through a set of rules that both client and server understand. This set of rules is known as a *protocol*. Web servers and clients communicate through a protocol known as the Hypertext Transfer Protocol (HTTP). When a Web client program retrieves a document from a Web server, the programs are probably communicating by using HTTP. As you'll see later in this chapter, other Internet protocols also may be supported by the Web server.

Of Clients and Servers

The client/server relationship is an important concept in networking, and especially in navigation of the Web. A *server* is a computer that offers services for other computers to use. *Services* can be any kind of program, routine, or data provided by the server. For example, a server might return information from a database to which you don't have direct access.

A *client* is a computer that uses services from a server. The client contacts the server and requests some sort of service. Many times, a client computer uses special software designed to interact with a specially designed server program on the server computer.

Under this client/server model, people with different computers in different locations can access information on the same server. You can set up different server computers with different types of data. Because people are using a client software program to communicate with the server, you can develop a different client program for each computer platform that they use. That way, people using Windows or a Macintosh can use client software to access information on a UNIX or Linux server just as easily as UNIX or Linux users can.

To access the Web, you need client software known as a *Web browser*. A Web browser is a program that understands how to communicate to a Web server via the HTTP protocol, displays information, and provides a way to represent hypertext links. Many browsers are available. Now, the most commonly used browsers are Netscape's Navigator and Microsoft's Internet Explorer. You can get a browser in any number of ways: from your Internet Service Provider (ISP), by buying it in store, by downloading it off the Internet, and so on. After you install the browser and configure the software with your Internet access information, you're ready to go.

Understanding URLs

You get information on the Web by using a descriptive address known as a *uniform resource locator* (URL, pronounced "earl"). Think of an URL as a pointer to an object on the Internet that tells you not only where the object is located, but also what it's named and how to access it. Everything you access through the Web has an URL.

The syntax of URLs may look intimidating but is really quite straightforward. Here's an example:

http://www.ncsa.uiuc.edu/SDG/Software/Mosaic/Docs/whats-new.html

Scary? It's really not that bad. The part to the left of the colon (:) specifies the access method to get to the data. This access method defines the protocol used to communicate with the server, and also gives a good clue as to the type of interaction that will take place. Table 28.1 lists several valid access methods.

Table 28.1   Valid Access Methods for URLs

Method	Description
http	Protocol for accessing most Web pages. Provides interactive hypermedia links to pages written in Hypertext Markup Language (HTML)
wais	Used for accessing a Wide Area Information Service (WAIS) site
gopher	Used for accessing a gopher server
ftp	Provides an anonymous FTP connection
telnet	Opens a telnet connection to a site
news	Used for reading Usenet news

Part

VI

Ch

28

Before the Web, There Was...

Many services and sources of information existed before the Web. These services use protocols other than HTTP. However, many Web clients such as Netscape Navigator allow you to access these services from within the browser. For example, you can transfer files to your computer by using the FTP protocol, retrieve documents from gopher servers, do text searches with WAIS (Wide Area Information Service), and read Usenet news.

Following the :// in the URL is the host name of the server computer you want to contact. After the server name is the directory path to the document you want to view or retrieve. This path depends totally on where the file is located on the remote server. (You might not have a path in some cases, if the file is in a default directory.) Finally, the file name of the document is given. This document can be text, a hypermedia document, a sound file, a graphic, or some other type of file.

So, look again at the example. The URL

http://www.ncsa.uiuc.edu/SDG/Software/Mosaic/Docs/whats-new.html

uses the HTTP protocol to contact the server computer **www.ncsa.uiuc.edu**, and says that you're interested in the document named whats-new.html located in the directory /SDG/Software/Mosaic/Docs.

The html extension on the document name tells your Web client (for example, Netscape Navigator) that this document is written in Hypertext Markup Language (HTML). HTML is a special syntax used to write hypertext pages for the Web. For more details on HTML, see Chapter 31, "Creating Web Documents with HTML."

Searching the Web

The Web is huge, and getting bigger every day. Rather than click through thousands of pages, you can use search engines to help you find information faster. A *search engine* is a program that looks through its database for information that matches your request. Some search engines, such as AltaVista and Infoseek, search the entire Web and store their information in huge databases. Other search engines are only for a specific Web site.

When you see a Search button at a typical Web site, it's usually only for that Web site. When you want to search the entire Web, you need a more general search tool. The following list shows some of the many search engines that scan Web sites across the Internet. Some even let you search other Internet information sources, like those on Usenet or FTP sites.

- *AltaVista* (**http://www.altavista.com**), for Web and Usenet. You can find anything, anywhere on the Web or Usenet. But you'll want to narrow your search as much as possible; you may get too much information back!
- *Yahoo!* (**http://www.yahoo.com**), for Web, Usenet, e-mail addresses, current news, people search, city maps, and stocks. Yahoo! isn't really a search engine. It's basically a huge list of Web sites, sorted into categories, that have been submitted by users. It's useful for common information and for getting an idea of just how much—and varied—the information on the Web is. Yahoo! also provides links to search engines.

- *Infoseek* (**http://www.infoseek.com**) for Web, Usenet, FAQs, current news, e-mail addresses, maps, stocks, and company listings. Infoseek contains a search engine and listing service and is good when you want to search more than the Web or Usenet. Infoseek has a different search language than many of the other search engines.

- *Open Text Index* (**http://index.opentext.net**) for Web, Usenet, current news, and e-mail addresses. This is an easy-to-use alternative to AltaVista and is good to use when you need to search for obscure topics. You can also search in other languages, such as Japanese and Spanish.

- *Excite* (**http://www.excite.com**) for Web, Usenet, and Excite Web site reviews. Excite does conceptual searching of the Web and is good when you're not sure of the exact term you need to search for. Because Excite uses a single-site search engine on many Web sites, it's free.

- *Lycos* (**http://www.lycos.com/**) for Web, FTP sites, and gopher sites. Lycos has Yahoo!-like features. It's good for simple searches on common topics. You can search for sounds, graphics, or subject.

- *Search.Com* (**http://www.search.com/**) for Web and Usenet. This search engine also lets you search other search engines such as AltaVista, HotBot, or Infoseek. Search.Com provides an A-to-Z listing of other search engines and has a handy utility to suggest what search engines will find what you need.

- *Inference Find!* (**http://www.inference.com/**) for Web only. Not a search engine itself, Inference Find! groups the results of other search engines and eliminates repeats. As of this writing, it calls WebCrawler, Yahoo, Lycos, AltaVista, InfoSeek, and Excite.

- *HotBot* (**http://www.hotbot.com**) for Web and Usenet. HotBot is good for finding sites that use a particular technology, such JavaScript or VRML. You can also narrow your search to a specific geographic location (such as Europe), class of domains (such as **edu**), or a single Web site (such as **www.apple.com**).

Good keywords make your search more effective. Come up with words that are unique to what you really want to find. Try to avoid heavily used terms, such as *www, Internet, computer*, and so on. If you do need them, combine them with other more specific terms and Boolean operators to help narrow your search—for example,

> WWW and "Search Engines"

N O T E Most search engines also allow you to use quotes ("") to search for phrases. Check your search engine's help for specific details. ■

You'll probably find that even a search engine lists too many sites to look through. You can reduce the number of sites you find by narrowing your search. Correctly using some simple terms—AND, OR, and NOT—can help narrow thousands of sites down to just a few.

These aren't your everyday AND, OR, and NOT. They come from the symbolic logic system developed by a 19th-century mathematician named George Boole. Boolean searches use a basic syntax made up of operators and search terms. Because the terms don't work quite the same as in English grammar, make sure that you get them straight. Table 28.2 shows examples of how to use AND, OR, and NOT.

Table 28.2   Useful Boolean Expressions

Expression	Description
AND or +	Returns pages that contain all your search terms. If all words aren't on the page, the page isn't displayed. Use AND or + when you have dissimilar terms and want to narrow the results to a few precise hits. For example, BMW AND roadster or BMW + roadster will display only pages that contain both *BMW* and *roadster* on the page.
OR	Returns pages that contain any of your search terms. Use OR to return pages with any of the terms listed in your search. For example, BMW OR roadster will display all pages that contain either *BMW*, *roadster*, or both.
NOT	Returns pages that don't contain words specified in your search (not supported by all search engines).

Don't be afraid to experiment. Try several different searches with the same goal in mind so that you can get a better feel for the results that some of these expressions and your search words or phrases return. You'll find that some experimentation with search terms will help you become more adept at narrowing your selections to a manageable size.

Now that I've gone over URLs and searching on the Web, let's go over some of the other access methods listed earlier in Table 28.1 in more detail. Each section provides a description of the service, how to access it with and without a browser, and a sampling of what information the service returns.

Using FTP with a Web Browser

FTP, or File Transfer Protocol, is the method that the Internet uses to exchange files between computers. No matter what you're searching for—software, documentation, FAQ lists, programs, or just about anything else—you probably can get a copy through anonymous FTP.

Anonymous FTP is a service that lets you retrieve data from around the Internet without having an account on that machine. By using anonymous FTP, you can access any files that the systems administrators on the remote system have made publicly available.

▶ **See** "Using FTP for Remote File Transfer," **p. 540**

FTP supports ASCII-mode transfers for text files, and binary-mode transfers for other types of files. Fortunately, most Web clients automatically determine the file type for you, so you don't have to worry about it. You usually can determine the type of archive or compression program that was used on the file by looking at the file extension. Table 28.3 lists the most common file extensions you'll encounter.

Table 28.3   Common File Extensions on Binary Files Available Through FTP

Extension	Description
.Z	Compressed with the UNIX `compress` program
.z	Probably compressed with the GNU `gzip` program or the UNIX `compress` program
.gz	Compressed with the GNU `gzip` program
.tar	An archive of several files created by the UNIX `tar` program
.zip	An archive of several files created by `pkzip`

Sometimes you'll find files that have been created by more than one of these methods. For example, the file programs.tar.Z is an archive of several files created by the `tar` utility, and then compressed with the `compress` utility.

To use a Web client such as Netscape (which has built-in FTP support) to perform anonymous FTP transfers, replace the protocol portion of the URL with **ftp**. For example, to start an anonymous FTP session to **sunsite.unc.edu**, use the following URL:

> **ftp://sunsite.unc.edu**

This URL causes your Web client to try to make an FTP connection to **sunsite.unc.edu** and log you in as an anonymous FTP session. After your FTP session is established, you can navigate through directories and transfer files by clicking the hyperlinks displayed.

N O T E   Most anonymous FTP servers request that you use your e-mail address as your password. If you have problems, check that your e-mail preferences are set in your browser. ▪

To specify non-anonymous FTP session in Netscape, enter

`ftp://username@ftp.startup.com`

where *username* is your user name, and `ftp.startup.com` is where you want to go. You'll then be prompted to enter your password.

N O T E   When you select a text file to transfer from a remote server in an FTP session, most Web clients display the file on-screen. You need to save the file to disk via a menu selection. Some Web browsers allow you to specify loading a file to disk rather than to the screen. ▪

ON THE WEB

For a listing of FTP sites via the Web, see **http://www.yahoo.com/Computers_and_Internet/ Internet/FTP_Sites/**.

Using *archie* with a Web Browser

Just like with the Web, one major problem with anonymous FTP is figuring out where the files that you're interested in are located on the Internet. To help users locate files, the archie system was created. archie is basically a search engine for anonymous FTP sites.

archie is a database query program that contacts anonymous FTP sites around the world and asks each site for a complete list of all its files. archie then indexes this information in its own internal database. You can search this database for the location of files on the Internet. Because updating archie databases is obviously a time-consuming process, the databases are updated usually only about once a month. Thus, it's possible—although unlikely—that the location archie gives you is incorrect.

archie is a popular service. The various archie servers around the world can get very heavily loaded, and requests can take a while to complete. Some sites place limits on the number of simultaneous connections, to keep the servers from becoming too slow to use. If you try an archie server and find that it's fully loaded, you can try a different server, or wait a few minutes and try again.

ON THE WEB

Many archie servers now support inquires via Web forms. To conduct archie searches, see **http://www.nexor.co.uk/public/archie/servers.html** for a list of archie gateways to the Web. From this page, you can link to many of the mirror sites of the archie database. It's usually quickest to link to the site closest to you.

Table 28.4 lists some of the archie servers available worldwide.

Table 28.4   Active archie Servers

Server	IP Address	Location
archie.unl.edu	129.93.1.14	USA (NE)
archie.internic.net	198.49.45.10	USA (NJ)
archie.rutgers.edu	128.6.18.15	USA (NJ)
archie.ans.net	147.225.1.10	USA (NY)
archie.sura.net	128.167.254.179	USA (MD)
archie.au	139.130.4.6	Australia
archie.uni-linz.ac.at	140.78.3.8	Austria
archie.univie.ac.at	131.130.1.23	Austria

Server	IP Address	Location
archie.cs.mcgill.ca	132.206.51.250	Canada
archie.uqam.ca	132.208.250.10	Canada
archie.funet.fi	128.214.6.102	Finland
archie.univ-rennes1.fr	129.20.128.38	France
archie.th-darmstadt.de	130.83.128.118	Germany
archie.ac.il	132.65.16.18	Israel
archie.unipi.it	131.114.21.10	Italy
archie.wide.ad.jp	133.4.3.6	Japan
archie.hana.nm.kr	128.134.1.1	Korea
archie.sogang.ac.kr	163.239.1.11	Korea
archie.uninett.no	128.39.2.20	Norway
archie.rediris.es	130.206.1.2	Spain
archie.luth.se	130.240.12.30	Sweden
archie.switch.ch	130.59.1.40	Switzerland
archie.twnic.net	192.83.166.10	Taiwan
archie.ncu.edu.tw	192.83.166.12	Taiwan
archie.doc.ic.ac.uk	146.169.11.3	United Kingdom
archie.hensa.ac.uk	129.12.21.25	United Kingdom

To connect to one of these servers, telnet to it and log in as archie. Each server is slightly different, but most are basically the same. After you log in to a server, you get a prompt such as

```
archie>
```

where you can enter your search commands. Different servers have different default search values. To determine what the default setup is for the server that you connect to, use the show search command. The show search command returns one of the following values:

regex	archie interprets your search string as a UNIX regular expression.
exact	Your search string must exactly match a file name.
sub	Your search string matches if a file name contains it as a substring. This is a case-insensitive search.
subcase	Similar to the sub search type, except that the case of the letters in the string must match.

You can set the desired search type by using the set search command. For example,

```
archie> set search search-type
```

Part

VI

Ch

28

When you have your search set up the way you want it, you use the `prog` command to search by file name. For example,

```
archie> set search sub
```

```
archie> prog linux
```

performs a case-insensitive search of the archie database for all files that contain the substring `linux`. For each match that `archie` finds, it reports the host computer that has the file, along with the full path name of the file on that host.

If you get confused or just need some assistance when you're using `archie`, just type **help** at the `archie>` prompt. This will give you information on how to get help in `archie`. From the `help>` prompt, typing a **?** will give you a list of subtopics that you can get help on.

After you find the information you're looking for, you need to exit `archie` by typing **exit** or **quit** at the `archie>` prompt.

Using *telnet* with a Web Browser

`telnet` has been around almost as long as the Internet. By using `telnet`, you can connect to databases, library catalogs, and other information resources around the world. Want to see what the weather's like in Vermont? Check on crop conditions in Azerbaijan? Get more information about somebody whose name you've seen online? `telnet` lets you do this, and more. When you telnet to another computer, you're going across the Internet and logging in to that machine. You won't find graphics as you do on the Web; `telnet` is text only.

> **N O T E**   gopher is another early Internet tool, and many telnet sites are most easily found through gopher menus. See the following section on gopher. ■

To start `telnet` from your browser, enter the URL of the telnet site you want to go to. For example,

telnet://pac.carl.org

will start a `telnet` program and will take you the location you entered. From there, you're out of the browser and have entered "menu land."

▶ **See** "Using *telnet* to Access Remote Computers," **p. 538**

Configuring Netscape to Work with *telnet*

`telnet` probably isn't built into your browser. You'll need to get a `telnet` program, install it on your computer, and then configure the browser to use it. Here's an example set of instructions for configuring `telnet` for Netscape:

1. From the Netscape Navigator Options menu, choose Preferences.
2. Select Applications and Directories from the available tabs.
3. Select Browse next to the Telnet Application window.

4. Find and select the telnet executable.

5. Press <Return>. Netscape is now configured.

Windows 95 and Windows NT include `telnet` applications in the Windows system folder. For Macs and older versions of Windows, NCSA Telnet is a popular choice.

Most telnet sites are fairly easy to use and have online help systems. Most also work best—and, in some cases, only—with VT100 emulation. You may also find that many of the resources are now also available on the Web.

Using *gopher* with a Web Browser

`gopher` is an Internet service that allows you to access information by making selections from a series of menus. `gopher` was one of the first Internet services that made a serious attempt at having a user-friendly interface.

When you connect to a site that offers `gopher` services, you get a menu of available choices. Each menu is either a file or another menu. You can select your choice from the menu without having to know the name or IP address of the destination site, or the directory and file names of the particular information you're asking for. `gopher` handles the details for you.

N O T E No information resources on the Internet are actually "gopher-specific." Anything you can get through gopher could be made available by other means, such as an HTML Web page, FTP, or `telnet`. In some cases, sites may have chosen to make resources available only via gopher for security reasons. ▨

To access a gopher server with a Web browser, change the protocol part of the URL so that it says **gopher** instead of **http**. For example, the URL for the gopher server at **sunsite.unc.edu** is

gopher://sunsite.unc.edu

`gopher` provides an easy means to navigate the Internet. Unfortunately, the information that `gopher` can retrieve isn't well organized, so finding what you want can be a bit of an adventure. Because the items in Gopherspace are presented as a set of menus, you sometimes have to wade through many different menus to get to the file you're searching for. This problem aside, however, a lot of good information is available through `gopher`.

One disadvantage of `gopher` is the lack of a standard subject list for the various gopher servers. The administrators for each gopher server have organized their information in their own manner. This means that each gopher server you access has different subjects. If gopher servers do happen to have some of the same subjects, chances are they aren't named the same way.

Part
VI

Ch
28

TIP Because Gopherspace has been around longer than the World Wide Web, it's too large to search randomly. `veronica` is like `archie`, except that it searches gopher servers. See **gopher:// gopher.scs.unr.edu/00/veronica/veronica-faq** for more information on `veronica`.

ON THE WEB

For a listing of gopher sites, see **http://www.yahoo.com/Computers_and_Internet/Internet/Gopher/**.

Accessing Usenet News with a Web Browser

In the simplest definition, Usenet news (also called *netnews* or simply *news*) is a forum for online discussion. Many computers around the world exchange chunks of information, called *articles*, on almost every subject imaginable. These computers aren't physically connected to the same network; they're logically connected in their capability to exchange data. See Chapter 30, "Surviving Usenet News," for a complete discussion of Usenet news.

News articles on Usenet are divided into newsgroups by subject. These groups are then divided into hierarchies based on very general subject distinctions.

▶ **See** "How Usenet Is Structured," **p. 597**

Usenet news has conversation and discussion on almost any topic that you can think of. It's a great way to find and exchange information.

Getting on Mailing Lists

Another avenue for discussion on the Internet comes from e-mail mailing lists. Mailing lists vary from Usenet news in that the various messages and discussion articles are sent via e-mail rather than via the Usenet news medium.

Why use a mailing list instead of a Usenet newsgroup? Usually, mailing lists are targeted at a smaller group of people. It's fairly difficult to set up a new newsgroup on Usenet as there are proposal, discussion, and voting periods required. Any systems administrator can set up a mailing list. Also, because each mailing list is maintained on one computer, the systems administrator has more control over who can be on the list and can deal with problem users more effectively. Some mailing lists, such as those that discuss computer security issues, are restricted to certain people. If you need to be on one of these lists, you have to apply with the list manager to be allowed to subscribe.

Finding Mailing Lists

As with Usenet news, there are mailing lists on a wide variety of subjects. A complete list of publicly available mailing lists is posted regularly to the Usenet newsgroup **news.answers**.

ON THE WEB

You can search for mailing lists via the Web at **http://www.liszt.com/**.

Using Mailing Lists

Mailing lists are typically set up by using a mail reflector. A *mail reflector* is a special e-mail address that's set up to reflect any mail sent to it back out to a group of people. Usually, two e-mail addresses are associated with a mailing list: that of the list maintainer and that of the list itself.

Suppose that there's an e-mail address for the users of widgets. The e-mail address for the list might be something like widgets@somewhere.com. If you send an e-mail message to this list address, it's reflected to all the people that subscribe to the list.

By convention, Internet mailing lists use a special e-mail address for administrative requests, such as subscribing to the list. This address is constructed by adding `-request` to the name of the list. So for the imaginary widgets mailing list, the administrative e-mail address would be widgets-request@somewhere.com. All mail that addresses administrative topics should be sent to the administrative address.

Each mailing list (and Usenet newsgroup) has its own rules and culture. You should become familiar with the local customs before sending mail out onto the list. Usually, you get an introduction message and possibly a list of frequently asked questions (FAQ) when you subscribe to a list. The introduction message contains any special rules that apply to the list. Make sure that you read the FAQ first so that you don't ask the same questions as hundreds of other people.

▶ **See** "Netiquette Etiquette on Usenet," **p. 603**

Using Wide Area Information Servers (WAIS)

WAIS (Wide Area Information Servers) is a system for searching a large set of databases for information. The term *wide area* implies being able to use a large network, such as the Internet, to conduct searches by using client/server software.

By using WAIS, you can retrieve text or multimedia documents that are stored on databases throughout the Internet. You can think of WAIS as being similar to `gopher`, except that WAIS does the searching for you.

Like `gopher`, to use WAIS, you need client software or have to use `telnet` to connect to a site that provides public access to a WAIS client. There's an interactive UNIX WAIS client known as *swais*. To use this system, you can telnet to **sunsite.unc.edu** and log in as swais. You then get a menu of databases that you can search.

From Here...

The World Wide Web is a wonderful way to explore the Internet and tap its vast resources. Various Web browsers are available as free software or as commercial products. Using a Web browser makes it easy to surf the Net and find the information you need. You can learn more about the Web and the Internet in the following chapters:

- Chapter 26, "Understanding the Internet," provides an overview of the Internet and its basic services.

- Chapter 31, "Creating Web Documents with HTML," gives an introduction to the Hypertext Markup Language that's used to create pages for the Web.

## CHAPTER 29

Using Electronic Mail

Electronic mail, or e-mail, seems to have taken the world by storm. Millions of computer users worldwide have access to electronic mail. A large number of commercial networks or Internet service providers (ISPs) can give you or your organization access to electronic mail around the world. ∎

Understanding e-mail basics

In this chapter, you learn how to send, read, and reply to e-mail by using the mail and elm e-mail programs.

Working with e-mail messages

You also learn how to print messages, save them to files, and delete them.

Routing e-mail

This chapter also explains how to route e-mail by forwarding it, creating mailing lists, and sending copies to others.

Understanding E-Mail

E-mail is any program that users on a single computer system or a network of systems use to send and receive electronic messages. At a minimum, you provide the program with the address of the recipient and the message you want to send. The address includes the login name of the person who is to receive the mail. If that user is on another system in a network, the address also includes a means of identifying the target computer system. You either prepare the message while you're using your e-mail program, or you prepare it beforehand by using a text editor such as vi.

▶ **See** "Using *vi*," **p. 393**

Using electronic mail has several advantages:

- You can send reports, data, and documents that can reach their destination in a matter of seconds or minutes.

- You don't have to worry about interrupting someone when you send them a message, nor are you necessarily interrupted when you receive messages—that's handled by the computer system.

- You don't need to play phone tag or make an appointment to communicate with someone.

- You can send and receive at a convenient time.

When you send e-mail, it's up to the computer system to make the delivery, which can involve putting your message out on a network to be delivered at some other site. At this point, you say that the mail has been sent. Soon after that, the message arrives at the recipient's machine.

If the sender and the receiver are on the same computer system, the sending and receiving all takes place on one machine. The e-mail system on the target computer verifies that the addressee exists, and the message is added to a file that holds all the e-mail for that user (if no network is involved, the local computer system verifies the addressee). The mail-storage file is called the user's *system mailbox* and usually has the same name as the user who's receiving the mail. For example, if your login name is george, your system mailbox is the file named george in the directory /var/spool/mail. When the message has been "delivered" to the mailbox, you say that the mail has been received.

N O T E   There's a common kind of e-mail, called Post Office Protocol (POP) mail, where e-mail is stored on a remote system and is then retrieved as you read mail. This chapter assumes that you're running a full mail system on your Linux computer, complete with the sendmail program, which handles the background jobs of sending and receiving e-mail. ■

Figure 29.1 shows the relationship between sending and receiving e-mail.

FIG. 29.1
Sending and receiving
e-mail.

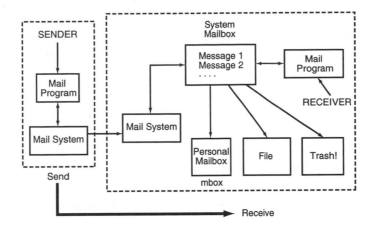

Does the Mail Always Get Through?

When you send e-mail, you may see a message on-screen that says Mail Sent! This means that the mail has been sent—not that it has been received or delivered. Usually, your e-mail system will notify you if your message can't be delivered.

E-mail messages may not go through for several reasons. If mail is going out to a network, the network address may be correct but the name of the user on that network may not be correct. Or perhaps the complete address is correct, but because of problems with permissions or quotas, the message couldn't be placed in the user's system mailbox. In both cases, the mail was sent but was undeliverable. Another scenario is that the e-mail was delivered but the user's mailbox was corrupted or destroyed. A final possibility is that the recipient ignores e-mail or doesn't log in for several days, weeks, or more.

Your computer system notifies you when you have mail. When you read your e-mail, you can treat it on a message-by-message basis. Some of the things you can do with your mail are the following:

- Delete individual messages after you read them—or without bothering to read them (using e-mail doesn't mean that you won't get junk mail)
- Keep some messages in the system mailbox
- Keep some messages in a personal mailbox
- Keep other messages in individual files or folders
- Reply directly to the sender of a message
- Do a "group reply" to a group of users who all received the same message
- Forward mail to others
- Print your mail

It's up to you to manage your mail so that it doesn't take up any more disk space than necessary. You really don't have to save every piece of e-mail you get. You'll also see that it's easier to read your incoming mail if you regularly delete or remove messages from your system mailbox.

Several different e-mail programs are available for Linux, including e-mail programs that are integrated with Web browsers such as Netscape. The most common e-mail interface, available on virtually every UNIX environment, is `mail`. With the `mail` program, you can do the following:

- Manage and view your e-mail
- Include a subject header on e-mail you send
- Include a cc header for sending copies of e-mail to others
- Forward e-mail to others
- Set up mailing lists

This chapter shows examples of `mail`. Later, you're introduced to another mail program for Linux—the `elm` mailer.

Sending E-Mail with *mail*

You can send e-mail to an individual, a group of individuals, or a mailing list. Just as when you want to send a paper letter, you must specify the address of the recipients with e-mail. Sometimes, you'll compose or write a message while you're sending e-mail; at other times, you'll send a prepared message; you may even send the output of a command or program with e-mail. When using `mail` or `elm`, the message you send has to be a text file—that is, an ASCII file.

N O T E   The Simple Mail Transport Protocol (SMTP) is used to transfer mail between computers. It now supports only ASCII files. To send a binary file via e-mail, you have to convert the file to ASCII by using the `uuencode` utility. ▄

Regardless of how the message is prepared, you send mail by using a command of the following form:

`mail *address*`

This command starts the `mail` system. You can then compose the mail message and send it to the specified address. In this syntax, `*address*` is the e-mail address of the person who is to receive the message. An address can have several different forms. To send e-mail to someone who has a login ID on the machine you're using, use the login ID of that person. For example, to send e-mail to someone on your system whose login name is george, enter the following command:

`mail george`

If george is on another system that you can access through some network or collection of networks, you must include the name by which that system is known on the network. Suppose that george is the name of a user on a computer system whose network name is apples.startup.com. You can send e-mail by entering this command:

```
mail george@apples.startup.com
```

The exact form of the address depends on the type of network being used and any local conventions or rules. Ask a local expert or your system administrator about the form of addresses on a network in your company.

To send the same message to several users, include each of their addresses on the line with the `mail` command, as in this example:

```
mail fred bill george@apples.startup.com
```

Writing a Message While Sending E-Mail

Many users compose or write messages while they're in the e-mail program, rather than compose a message beforehand. This is usually the quickest—but not the neatest—way to send mail. It's not neat because you have limited editing capabilities while composing your message. Generally, you can deal with only one line at a time. First, you type the command to send e-mail, specify the address(es), and then press <Return>. Then you type the message, indicating that you're done by typing a period on a line by itself. You can also use <Ctrl-d> to end the message. For an example of how to send e-mail to a user named lynn, enter this command to start the mail system and specify lynn's address on your system:

```
mail lynn
Subject: Congratulations! Lunch Thursday?
```

Now type the message, pressing <Return> when you want to end a line. Here's a sample message that you may want to send to lynn (press <Return> at the end of each line to space the paragraphs of the message):

```
Lynn,

Just wanted to tell you that I thought you did a great
job at the meeting yesterday! It seems as if we're
finally turning this problem around.

Want to get together for lunch Thursday?
Give me a call.
joe
.
```

You can also end the message with <Ctrl-d> instead of a period. The computer responds by displaying EOT, which means *end of transmission*.

Canceling a Message

You can cancel a message while you're writing it, but you can't cancel it after it's sent. To cancel a message while you're writing it, press whatever key is configured on your system as the interrupt key (usually <Ctrl-c> or <Del>). When a message is canceled, it's saved in a file named dead.letter. You can delete this file or edit it later for another message. When using mail, you must press <Ctrl-c> twice to cancel (in case you press <Ctrl-c> or <Del> by mistake). After canceling your mail message, you see the command-line prompt. The following example shows how the cancel function works:

```
mail lynn
Subject: Congratulations! Lunch Thursday?
Lynn,

Just wanted to tell that I thought you did a great
job<Ctrl-c>
 (Interrupt -- one more to kill letter)
```

You now must decide whether you want to continue the letter or kill it. If you decide to continue, you just keep typing the text of the letter as follows:

```
at the meeting yesterday! It seems as if we're finally
turning this problem around.
```

At this point, you decide to cancel the letter again, so you press <Ctrl-c> or <Del>. The system responds with (Interrupt -- one more to kill letter). Because you want to kill the message, press <Ctrl-c> or <Del> a second time; mail quits and you see the shell prompt.

Sending a Prepared Message

You may want to use a text editor such as vi to compose a message to be sent by e-mail. If you use a text editor, you have the tools to do things such as format the text and check your spelling. It doesn't matter what program you use to create the text, as long as you end up with a text or ASCII file.

Suppose that the file you want to send is named report.txt and that the recipient's address is bigshot@turn.green.com. There are essentially three ways to send the file, as shown in the following list. In the following examples, the mail command uses the option -s, and the string that serves as the subject heading is surrounded by quotation marks:

- *Use a pipe.* To send report.txt with the mail command, enter

  ```
  cat report.txt ¦ mail -s" Sales Report" bigshot@turn.green.com
  ```

- *Redirect input.* To send report.txt with the mail command and the -s option, enter

  ```
  mail -s" Sales Report" bigshot@turn.green.com < report.txt
  ```

- *Use ~r to include a file in a message.* To use mail to send the file (by using the default Subject prompt), enter these commands:

  ```
  mail bigshot@turn.green.com
  Subject: Sales Report
  ~r report.txt
  ~ .
  EOT
  ```

You see the system prompt after you complete any of these three methods; the result is the same in any case.

NOTE In the third example, you use ˜r to *read*, or include, the file report.txt in the e-mail message. This is an example of a *tilde command*. To use such commands, you precede a command with the tilde character (˜) while you're reading or sending mail. You may find several other tilde commands useful; they're discussed at appropriate points throughout the chapter. ■

Sending the Result of a Command or Program by E-Mail

▶ **See** "Understanding Shells," **p. 325**

If you run a command or program that produces results to the screen (known as stdout), you can pipe that output to a `mail` command. Suppose that you have some information in a file called contrib.lst, use the `sort` command to sort the file, and then send the results to yourself (login name imgood) and bigshot (who you met earlier in this chapter). To do all that, enter

```
sort contrib.lst ¦ mail -s "Sorted Contrib Info" imgood bigshot@turn.green.com
```

Reading Your Mail

Most Linux systems notify you when you log in that you have e-mail. It's up to you to read and act on it. You can use `mail` or another e-mail program to read any mail you have. As you read your mail, the e-mail program marks a message as read. Depending on what commands you use and how you quit the e-mail program, the messages you've read are kept either in your system mailbox, /var/spool/mail/$LOGNAME, or in your login directory in the file named mbox.

Using *mail* to Read Mail

To read your mail with `mail`, enter **mail**. If your login name is imgood, you'll see a display similar to this (what you type is in bold):

```
mail
mail     Type ? for help.
"/var/spool/mail/imgood": 5 messages 2 new 1 unread
     1 sarah Wed Jan  8 09:17  15/363
     2 bigshot@turn.green.com Thu Jan  9 10:18  26/657   Meeting on Friday
U    3 fred Fri Jan  10 08:09  32/900   New Orders
> N  4 jones Fri Jan  10 13:22  35/1277  Draft Report
N    5 smith@somewhere.com Sat Jan  11 13:21  76/3103  Excerpt from book
?
```

Here are some things to note about the display:

- ■ The first line identifies the program and says to type a question mark for help.
- ■ The second line indicates that `mail` is reading your system mailbox, /var/spool/mail/imgood, and that you have five messages. Two have arrived since you last checked your mail, one appeared previously but you haven't yet read it, and two messages have already been read.

- The next five lines give information about your mail. Ignore the first few characters for now. Each line holds a message number, the address of the sender, the date the message was sent, the number of lines and characters in the message, and the subject (if one was given). Consider the following line:

```
2 bigshot@turn.green.com    Thu Jan  9 10:18  26/657   Meeting on Friday
```

  This line indicates that message number 2 is from bigshot@turn.green.com—an address that indicates the message came to your machine from a network (mail from a local user is marked with just the user's login ID). The message was sent on Thursday, January 9, at 10:18; it consists of 26 lines and 657 characters. The subject is *Meeting on Friday*.

- A message line starting with N indicates new mail—mail received since you last checked your e-mail. A message line starting with U indicates unread mail. A message line without N or U indicates mail you've read and saved in your system mailbox.

- The greater-than character (>) on a message line marks the current message—the message you'll act on next.

- The question mark (?) on the last line is the command prompt from mail.

Reading the Current Message   The current message is the message marked by the greater-than character (>). To read that message, just press <Return>. When you open it, you see the following:

```
Message 4:
From jones Fri, Jan 10 13:22 EST 1997
Received: by your.system.com
Date: Fri, 10 Jan 1997 13:22:01 -0500
From: Carol Jones <jones>
Return-Path: <jones>
To: aborat, lynn, oackerm, imgood
Subject: Draft Report
Here is a draft of the report I intend to submit next week.
Please take a look at it and let me know your comments.
Thanks.
----------------Report Starts Here----------------
Opportunities for Expansion
Prepared by Carol Jones
Over the past 6 months, we've seen an indication of an increase in the
demand for our services. Current market trends indicate that the demand
will continue for at least 18 months and possibly longer. The manager of
our service staff states "We're up to our necks in new customers and
:
```

The message is displayed one screen at a time. Any time you see a colon, you can press <Return> to see the next screen or <q> to quit viewing the message. Press <Return> to see the next screen of the message.

When you see the last screen, you see EOF: (for *end of file*). Press <q> or <Return> to get back to the ? prompt. Notice that the greater-than character still points to the message you've just read. The message that was the current message is still the current message.

Some lines were displayed before the message itself began. This is the header information—and it can be useful. Typically, header information includes the following:

- The message number
- Who sent the message
- When it was sent
- The name of the system that received the message
- The date the message was received
- The "real name" of the sender, as well as his or her login ID
- The return path
- To whom the message was sent
- The subject

All this information is passed on with each e-mail message. The sender is always identified, making forgeries difficult. The real name that appears in the From line is taken from a field from the sender's entry in the password file. The mail system uses the Return-Path or Reply-To information if you generate a reply (as discussed later in this chapter). The To line contains the address or list of addresses of the recipients of this message. (This sample message was a group message.) The sender provided the Subject line.

Reading the Next Message   There are two ways to read the next message (the message following the current message in your mailbox). You can press <Return> or <n> to display the next message. It becomes the current message after you read it. You read the next message in the same way you read the current message. After you read the last message in the list, you see the message 'At EOF'.

Reading Any Message   All the messages in your mailbox are numbered. You can read messages in any order by entering the message number when you see the ? prompt. For example, to read message number 2, type **2** and press <Return>. Message number 2 then becomes the current message.

Reading E-Mail from Other Files

When you start mail, you read messages kept in your system mailbox, /var/spool/mail/$LOGNAME. Recall from Chapter 17, "Understanding Linux Shells," that LOGNAME is the shell variable that holds your login name. If you log in as imgood, your mail is held in /var/spool/mail/imgood. You can read mail from other files that hold complete e-mail messages—that is, messages with the headers and text of the messages. Naturally, you must have read permission for those files.

To read messages from a file, type the command to start the e-mail program followed by **-f** *filename*, and press <Return>. For example, to read the e-mail in the file mbox, enter

```
mail -f mbox
```

You can read the mail in that file in the same way you read e-mail from your system mailbox.

NOTE The mbox file is located in your home directory and automatically contains messages you've already read but haven't deleted. These messages are saved to mbox when you exit mail. ■

Sending Mail While Reading

You can send e-mail while you're using the `mail` program to read your messages. To do so, enter **m** *address* at the ? prompt. Follow these steps:

1. Start the `mail` program (type **mail** and press <Return>).

2. Read some messages or do other things, but at the ? prompt, enter the following to send e-mail to a user whose login name is ernie:

   m ernie

3. At the prompt for a subject, type a subject heading:

   Subject: **Game Time**

4. Type the message and end it with a period on the last line, as in the following example:

   Don't forget we're playing V-ball at 6:30
   .

   The computer responds with the following lines:

   EOT
   ?

5. Continue using `mail`.

Printing Mail Messages

By using `mail`, you can print the current message to a printer connected to your system. First, make the message you want to print the current message. Then enter ¦ **lpr** at the ? prompt. You are, in effect, piping the current message to the `lpr` program.

To print a collection of messages, save them in a file and then print the file. See "Saving E-Mail to Files with *mail*" later in this chapter for information on effective ways to save messages.

Getting Help with *mail*

When you type the command to start your e-mail program, you see a ? prompt. The `mail` program tells you to type **?** for help. To get a list of commands and some information about each command, type **?** and press <Return>.

After you type **?** and press <Return>, you see a display similar to the following:

```
Mail    Commands
t <message list>     type messages
n                goto and type next message
e <message list>     edit messages
```

```
f <message list>      give head lines of messages
d <message list>      delete messages
s <message list>       file append messages to file
u <message list>      undelete messages
R <message list>      reply to message senders
r <message list>      reply to message senders and all recipients
pre <message list>      make messages go back to /usr/spool/mail
p <message list>      print message
m <user list>           mail to specific users
q                quit, saving unresolved messages in mbox
x                quit, do not remove system mailbox
h                print out active message headers
!                shell escape
cd [directory]    chdir to directory or home if none given
A <message list> consists of integers, ranges of same, or user names
separated by spaces. If omitted, Mail uses the last message typed.
A <user list> consists of user names or aliases separated by spaces.
Aliases are defined in .mailrc in your home directory.
&
```

This listing shows you the commands you can use from the ? prompt. Although some of these commands are explained later in this chapter, here are some things to note right now:

■ In each case, you can use the first letter of the command or type the entire command.

■ Items in [ ] and <> are optional; you don't type the brackets as part of the command.

■ You can make the term message list refer to all messages by using *. To save all messages in a file named allmail, for example, type **s * allmail** and press <Return>.

■ You can make the term message list refer to a single message number. To save message number 2 to a file named meeting, for example, type **s 2 meeting** and press <Return>.

■ You can make the term message list refer to a range of message numbers by separating the two message numbers with a hyphen. For example, 2-4 refers to messages numbered 2, 3, and 4. To save messages 2, 3, and 4 in a file named memos, type **s 2-4 memos** and press <Return>.

■ The term print in the line print message doesn't mean to print messages on a printer. It means to display the messages.

■ The edit command is useful for modifying messages before forwarding them to someone else or saving them in a file.

Saving E-Mail to Files with *mail*

You'll want to save some of the e-mail you receive. It's not practical to keep all your mail in your system mailbox for these reasons:

■ You'll have too many messages to wade through whenever you want to read your mail.

■ System administrators often limit the size of your system mailbox. This size limit depends on how your system administrator set it up. If you reach that limit, you may be prevented from receiving any new mail.

■ Your mail won't be organized, and it can be difficult to find important messages or all messages relating to a specific project or topic.

Earlier in this chapter, you learned that the messages you've read are saved (unless you say otherwise) in the file mbox. You also know that you can read these messages by typing **mail -f mbox** and pressing <Return>. You can also read messages from other files by using mail's –f option.

There are two primary ways (with and without a header) to save the current message in a file when you use mail. With both methods, you can specify a file to hold the message, and the message is added to that file. If you don't specify a file, the message is added to the file mbox (your personal mailbox) in your home directory. If you use q to quit the mail program, the messages are removed from your system mailbox.

When you see the ? prompt, you can use any of the following methods to save a message:

■ Type **s** to add the current message to mbox in your home directory.

■ Type **s *filename*** to add the text of the current message to the named file with the headers intact (useful if you want to use your e-mail program to read the messages later).

■ Type **w *filename*** to add the text of the current message to the named file without the header information (useful when you want to use only the text of the messages in a file that may be processed by some other program).

TIP To keep messages in your system mailbox rather than the mbox file after you read them, use the preserve command, pre. You can use this command with a message list.

You know that messages you've already read are automatically saved to mbox, unless you use the preserve command.

It's a good idea to get in the habit of specifying a file name when you use the save command, s. If you don't specify a file name, the current message is added to the file mbox. If you include a message list but don't specify a file, mail uses the message list as the name of the file to which it saves the current message. If you use q to quit the e-mail program, the saved messages are removed from your system mailbox.

Deleting and Undeleting Messages with *mail*

To delete a message from a file of messages you're reading, you use the d command. If you quit the mail program by using q, any messages you deleted with the d command are removed from the file.

You use the d or delete command to mark messages for deletion when you use mail to read your e-mail. If you then quit the program with q, the marked messages are removed from your mailbox. Unless you've saved them, they're gone for good. For some messages, deleting without saving them is a very good idea.

To delete the current message, type **d** and press <Return>. You can also specify a message list.

If you mark a message or a group of messages to be deleted, you can change your mind and undelete the message or messages by using the u command. You must use the u command before you enter **q** to quit; when you enter q, the messages are gone for good. Use the u or `undelete` command in the same way you use d or `delete`.

 T I P To undelete all the messages you marked for deletion, enter **u** * at the ? prompt.

Replying to E-Mail with *mail*

To reply to e-mail, use the address specified in the `Reply-To` header field. If that field isn't present, use the information in the `Return-Path` header field. Following are partial headers of two messages; one has both header fields, and the other has only the `Return-Path` header field. The pertinent fields are in bold in each example.

Message 1:

```
From server@malte.abc.com Mon Nov  8 18:31 EST 1993
Received: from MALTE.ABC.COM by s850.mwc.edu with SMTP
Return-Path: <server@matle.ams.com>
Date: Mon, 8 Nov 93 18:17:15 -0500
Comment: From the DuJour List
Originator: dujour@mathe.abc.com
Errors-To: asap@can.org
Reply-To: <dujour@mathe.abc.com>
Sender: dujour@mathe.abc.com
```

Message 2:

```
From jones Fri, Jan 7 13:22 EST 1994
Received: by your.system.com
Date: Fri, 7 Jan 1994 13:22:01 -0500
From: Carol Jones <jones>
Return-Path: <jones>
To: aborat, lynn, oackerm, imgood
Subject: Draft Report
```

To reply to the first message, use the `Reply-To` address dujour@mathe.abc.com. Note that the `Reply-To` and `Return-Path` fields are different. In the second example, use jones to respond to the sender of the message.

N O T E Always use the `Reply-To` address if it's included in the header because it represents the specific address of the sender. When the `Reply-To` address isn't available, the `Return-Path` address usually provides an adequate address back to the sender. ■

You can let the `mail` program determine the address to use to reply to an electronic mail message. To do this, use either of the following commands:

R Addresses a reply to the sender of the message

r Addresses a reply to the sender and all recipients of an e-mail message

With either command, you can specify a message list, as explained earlier in this chapter. Otherwise, the R or r command applies to the current message.

The following partial header shows how to use these two commands. This header is excerpted from a message from Carol Jones, in which she asks a group to comment on a draft of a report she has prepared:

```
From jonesFri, Jan 7 13:22 EST 1994
Received: by your.system.com
Date: Fri, 7 Jan 1994 13:22:01 -0500
From: Carol Jones <jones>
Return-Path: <jones>
To: aborat, lynn, oackerm, imgood
Subject: Draft Report
```

To respond to only jones, enter **R** at the ? prompt. You see the following response:

```
To: jones
Subject: Re: Draft Report
```

The To line tells you that the reply is going to one person. The Subject header indicates that the message is a reply to the one originally sent.

To make comments for everyone on the distribution list to see, enter **r** at the ? prompt. You see the following response lines:

```
To: jones, aborat, lynn, oackerm, imgood
Subject: Re: Draft Report
```

The To line tells you that the reply is going to everyone on the original distribution list, as well as the author. The Subject header indicates that the message is a reply to the one originally sent.

From here on, you enter your message in the manner described earlier in the section "Sending E-Mail with *mail.*"

CAUTION

Be careful about using r to reply to a message. Whatever you send is sent to everyone who got a copy of the original message. Because Linux is case-sensitive, most people aren't used to typing capital letters as commands. It's a very common mistake and can sometimes be embarrassing.

N O T E Think about what you write and who will read your message before you send a reply. Being sarcastic or scathing doesn't work very well with e-mail—you usually end up sounding like a bully. Using e-mail isn't the same as talking with someone: You don't get a chance to see or hear their reactions, and they don't get a chance to see or hear you, either. When you use e-mail, it's a lot easier and more effective to be polite and direct.

You can see how easy it is to forward mail; as soon as you send something to one person, you can never tell where the message will end up or how many people will see it. Think, and be considerate.

▶ **See** "Lack of Visual Reference," **p. 600** ▉

Routing Mail to Others

E-mail is distributed by addresses. Tasks such as forwarding a message, sending copies (cc:) of a message, creating aliases or simpler forms of addresses, and creating mailing lists all involve manipulating addresses. You don't have to do the manipulation directly—the mail program has these capabilities built in.

Forwarding Messages

To forward a message (actually, you're including the message with a message you compose), you must first start mail in the same way that you start it to read your messages. Then you use the m, r, or R command to send a message. As you compose your message, you use a tilde command, ~f, to forward one or several messages. The general form of the ~f command is ~f *msglist*. Here is a step-by-step example of how to forward a message:

1. Start mail (type **mail** and press <Return>). The system responds with something similar to the following:

```
mail      Type ? for help.
"/var/spool/mail/imgood": 5 messages 2 new 1 unread
      1 sarah Wed Jan  8 09:17  15/363
      2 bigshot@turn.green.com Thu Jan  9 10:18  26/657    Meeting on Friday
U     3 fred Fri Jan  10 08:09  32/900    New Orders
> N   4 jones Fri Jan  10 13:22  35/1277  Draft Report
N     5 smith@somewhere.com Sat Jan  11 13:21  76/3103  Excerpt from book
?
```

2. Read message 5 by typing **5** and pressing <Return>. (The text of that message isn't shown here.) Suppose that you want to forward it to your friends with addresses sarah, anglee@hb.com, and lynn@netcong.com.

3. Use the m command to send mail to the addresses listed in step 2, type a subject, and type a beginning for your message, as follows:

```
? m sarah anglee@hb.com lynn@netcong.com
Subject: Forwarding an excerpt from new Que Linux book
Hi!
I'm forwarding an excerpt I came across from a new book by Que.
It's Special Edition Using Linux, Third Edition. I'll be
getting my own copy tomorrow.
Do you want me to pick up a copy for you, too?
```

4. Use the ~f command to forward message number 5 (type ~f **5** and press <Return>). mail responds with the following message:

```
Interpolating: 5
(continue)
```

5. The cursor is now under the word `continue`. You can continue adding text to your mail message or end it by typing `~.` and then pressing <Return>. The `?` prompt appears.

Sending a Copy with *mail*

You can send a copy of an e-mail message to one or more addresses by putting those addresses on what's known as the *cc: list*. The cc: list works as you expect it to: The mail is sent to the primary address or addresses (those in the `To` header) and also to the address or addresses in the `Cc` header. To include addresses in the cc: list, use the tilde command `~c address` while you're sending the message.

The following example shows how to send a brief memo to a primary address (wjones) and a copy of it to yourself and another address (your address is imgood and the other user's address is ecarlst). You send one to yourself so that you have a copy of the memo. Follow these steps to add a cc: list to the list of recipients:

1. Start `mail` to send e-mail to the primary address, wjones, and give a subject header. Enter the following commands to achieve this:

   ```
   $ mail fred
   Subject: Memo - Sales Agreement with Framistan
   ```

2. Enter the text of the memo you want to send. For example, type the following:

   ```
   TO:          Fred Jones
   Date:        Oct 31, 1996
   From:        Henry Charleston
   RE:          Sales Agreement With Framistan Motors
   On October 29,1996, I held a meeting with the CEO of Framistan Motors.
   We concluded and initialed a sales agreement by which Framistan would
   purchase 10,000 units of our thermo-embryonic carthurators. The agreement
   has been forwarded to the appropriate parties in our organization and
   we intend to formally complete the agreement within two weeks.
   ```

3. Give the `~c address` command to add addresses to the cc: list. For example, type the following to send copies to yourself (imgood) and to ecarlst:

   ```
   ~c ecarlst imgood
   ```

4. To send the message, enter a tilde and period (`~.`). The `EOT` message appears, followed by the shell prompt.

 TIP To review and possibly modify the headers on an outgoing message, enter `~h` while you're composing the message. You're shown the headers one at a time and you can modify them.

When a message is sent this way, all the recipients can see the headers `To` and `Cc`. Anyone who replies to the message with the `r` command will send the reply to every address in the `To` and `Cc` lists, as well as the author.

You can customize `mail` so that it always prompts you for a `Cc` header in the same way that it prompts you for the `Subject` header (this is discussed later in the section "Customizing Your *mail* Environment"). Of course, you can keep from entering anything in the `Cc` list by pressing <Return>.

Using Aliases and Mailing Lists

The mail program, like most e-mail programs, allows you to create an alias for an address and a group alias for a list of addresses. You can treat the group alias as a mailing list. Using an alias for an individual address is easier than using the regular address because the alias is typically shorter and easier to remember.

To set an individual or group alias for one mail session, you use the alias command at the ? prompt while you're reading your e-mail. To make the aliases more useful, put the aliases in a file named .mailrc in your home directory (as described in the following section).

The following is an example of setting and using aliases with the mail program:

1. Start mail by entering **mail** at the prompt. After the headers are presented, you see the ? prompt:

```
mail    Type ? for help.
"/var/spool/mail/imgood": 5 messages 2 new 1 unread
      1 sarah Wed Jan  5 09:17  15/363
      2 croster@turn.green.com Thu Jan  6 10:18  26/657   Meeting on Friday
U     3 wjones Fri Jan  7 08:09  32/900   Framistan Order
> N   4 chendric Fri Jan  7 13:22  35/1277  Draft Report
N     5 kackerma@ps.com Sat Jan  8 13:21  76/3103 Excerpt from GREAT new
Linux
?
```

2. To set up an individual alias, use the alias command followed by the alias for the address. The following example creates the alias ros for the address croster@turn.green.com:

```
alias ros croster@turn.green.com
```

3. Use the ros alias in an address; mail expands it to its complete form. For example, you can enter the command **m ros** to start a message you want to mail to croster@turn.green.com.

To set up a group alias, use the alias command followed by the alias for the addresses. The following creates an alias called friends and then forwards some mail to the group:

```
alias friends chendric karlack abc.com!homebase!fran eca@xy.srt.edu
m friends
Subject: Excerpts from new Linux book - get a copy!
~f 5
Interpolating: 5
~.
EOT
?
```

Customizing Your *mail* Environment

You can customize your mail environment by putting commands or set-environment variables in the .mailrc file in your home directory. The mail program checks that file whenever you use the program. You can set quite a few environment variables and commands in .mailrc, and different mail programs will use different commands. Check your man page for your mail program for a list of all the .mailrc options. Some of the commands `mail` recognizes are given earlier in the section "Getting Help with *mail*"; this section describes a subset of the commands and variables that can be used in the .mailrc file. Table 29.1 lists these commands; Table 29.2 lists the environment variables.

Table 29.1 *mail* Commands

Command	Definition
#	Denotes a comment. No action is taken.
alias	Sets an individual or group alias. Used as `alias alias-name address-list`.
set	Sets an environment variable. Used as `set variable-name` or `set variable-name=string`.

TIP You can issue any of the commands in Table 29.1 from the ? prompt any time you use `mail`; they'll be active only for that session.

Table 29.2 *mail* Environment Variables

Variable	Definition
askcc	Prompts for the cc: list after the message is entered. Default is `noaskcc`.
asksub	Prompts for the `Subject` list before the message is entered. Enabled by default.
noheader	Doesn't print header information on available messages when you start `mail`. Disabled by default.
ignore	Ignores interrupt characters when you enter messages. Useful if you have a "noisy" connection over some telephone or other communication lines. Default is `noignore`.
metoo	When you have your name in a group alias, a message normally isn't sent to you. Setting this variable allows you to receive messages sent to a group alias that contains your address. Default is `nometoo`.

TIP You can set a system-wide environment by putting the commands or set variables in the /etc/mail.rc file.

The following example sets up the .mailrc file so that you use the commands and environment variables listed in Tables 29.1 and 29.2. The pound sign (#) is used to document the work. You can create this file by using `vi` or any other editor that can produce a text or ASCII file.

```
# .mailrc file for D. Gunter
# make sure interrupts are NOT ignored
```

```
set noignore
# set variables so that prompts for Subject and Cc always appear
set asksub
set askcc
# individual aliases
alias billy wbracksto
alias ham jhron@cucumber.abc.com
alias me gunter
# group aliases, mailing list
alias pirates jroger@blackflag.net bbow
alias research jones jreynold eackerma
alias framistan wjones imgood cornlo@framistan.org imgood
```

Place these statements in the .mailrc file. Now whenever you start mail, these command statements are processed.

Quitting the *mail* Program

As you read e-mail in a mailbox, you can read, skip, or delete messages. These actions don't take place in the mailbox itself, but in a temporary copy of the mailbox. You can quit the e-mail program so that your mailbox is changed by your actions (the modified temporary copy replaces the original mailbox), or you can quit so that your mailbox is unchanged regardless of what you did during your e-mail session.

Quitting and Saving Changes

To quit the mail program and save the changes that occur, press <q><Return> at the ? prompt. You see the shell prompt again. When you quit mail this way, messages you read but didn't delete are saved in a file named mbox in your home directory.

Suppose that you use mail to read your mail. Your login name is imgood, and your home directory is /home/imgood. When you enter **mail** to start the mail program, you see the following screen of information:

```
mail    Type ? for help.
"/var/spool/mail/imgood": 5 messages 2 new 1 unread
     1 sarah Wed Jan  8 09:17  15/363
     2 bigshot@turn.green.com Thu Jan  9 10:18  26/657    Meeting on Friday
U    3 fred Fri Jan  10 08:09  32/900    New Order
> N  4 jones Fri Jan  10 13:22  35/1277  Draft Report
N    5 smith@somewhere.com Sat Jan  11 13:21  76/3103  Excerpt from book
?
```

Now suppose that you read the current message by pressing <Return>, and then you read message 1 by typing **1** and pressing <Return> at the ? prompt. If you then press <q><Return> to quit, you see the following information:

```
Saved 2 messages in /home/imgood/mbox
Held 3 messages in /var/spool/mail/imgood
```

The two messages you read are saved in the file mbox in your home directory; the other three messages are saved in your system mailbox, /var/spool/mail/imgood.

If you save read messages like this often, mbox can become quite large. You may want to print that file occasionally and delete it. You can also read the mail from that file as though it were your system mailbox, as described later in this chapter.

N O T E   You can read mail and indicate that the current message is to be kept in your system mailbox, /var/spool/mail/imgood, and not in the file mbox. To do this after you read a message, enter **pre** (for preserve) at the ? prompt. ■

Quitting and Not Saving Changes

The other way to quit the mail program is to press <x><Return> at the ? prompt. When you do that, you exit the program with no changes to your system mailbox or any other file—as if you didn't read your mail at all. You then see the shell prompt. You may want to exit the mail program in this way when you want to leave the program but save the mail in your system mailbox.

Using the *elm* Mailer

As stated earlier in this chapter, several different mail programs are available for Linux. Each has its own advantages and disadvantages.

One mail reader that comes with the Slackware distribution of Linux is the elm mailer. This mail program is a screen-oriented mailer rather than a line-oriented one. It provides a set of interactive menu prompts and is extremely easy to use. Virtually everything that you can do with mail can be done under elm, and usually much more easily!

Because elm is so easy to use, the following sections just touch on the highlights of using it. You can find more in-depth information by using elm's online help or by reading its man page.

Starting *elm*

To start a mail session with elm, just type **elm** at the command prompt. If this is the first time you've used elm, it will prompt you for permission to set up a configuration directory in your account and create an mbox mail file if one doesn't exist. Here's what you see as you start elm for the first time:

```
$ elm
Notice:
This version of ELM requires the use of a .elm directory in your home
directory to store your elmrc and alias files. Shall I create the
directory .elm for you and set it up (y/n/q)? y
Great! I'll do it now.

Notice:
ELM requires the use of a folders directory to store your mail folders in.
```

Part
VI

Ch
29

```
Shall I create the directory /home/gunter/Mail for you (y/n/q)? y
Great! I'll do it now.
```

After `elm` creates its directory and mbox file, it runs the main mail program. This is a full-screen-oriented mailer. Your screen clears and you'll see a display similar to the following:

```
Mailbox is '/var/spool/mail/gunter' with 2 messages [ELM 2.4 PL25]
N  1   Nov 11 Jack Tackett   Linux book
N  2   Nov 11 Jack Tackett   more ideas

You can use any of the following commands
by pressing the first character;
d)elete or u)ndelete mail,  m)ail a message,
r)eply or f)orward mail,  q)uit
To read a message, press <return>. j = move down, k = move up, ? = help

Command:
```

At the top of the screen, `elm` tells you where your system mailbox is located, how many messages are in it, and what version of `elm` you're running. `elm` then lists one line for each message in your mailbox. It places the letter N before each new message, just like the `mail` program. The summary line for each message tells you whether the message is new, the message date, the sender, and the subject. (As always, your display may vary slightly depending on your version of `elm`.) The current message is highlighted in the list (in the preceding listing, the current message is in boldface).

Using *elm* Commands

At the bottom of the screen is a command summary that tells you what commands you have available for the current screen. As you can see in the preceding example, you can delete or undelete mail, mail a message, reply to a message, forward mail, or quit. Pressing the <j> key moves the message selection to the previous message; the <k> key moves it to the next message. Help is available by pressing the <?> key. The Command: prompt at the bottom of the screen tells you to press a command key for `elm` to do something.

As you can see, `elm` is very easy to use due to the large number of prompts and on-screen help that's available. Table 29.3 lists all the commands that can be executed from within `elm`.

Table 29.3   Command Summary for *elm*

Command/Keystroke	Description
<Return>, space bar	Displays current message
¦	Pipes current message or tagged messages to a system command
!	Shell escape
$	Resynchronizes folder
?	Displays online help

continues

Table 29.3   Continued

Command/Keystroke	Description
+, <—>>	Displays next index page
-, <←—>	Displays previous index page
=	Sets current message to first message
*	Sets current message to last message
<number><Return>	Sets current message to *number*
/	Searches subject lines for pattern
/ /	Searches entire message texts for pattern
>	Saves current message or tagged messages to a folder
<	Scans current message for calendar entries
a	Changes to "alias" mode
b	Bounces (remails) current message
C	Copies current message or tagged messages to a folder
c	Changes to another folder
d	Deletes current message
<Ctrl-d>	Deletes messages with a specified pattern
e	Edits current folder
f	Forwards current message
g	Groups (all recipients) reply to current message
h	Displays header with message
J	Increments current message by one
j, <↓>	Advances to next undeleted message
K	Decrements current message by one
k, <↑>	Advances to previous undeleted message
l	Limits messages by specified criteria
<Ctrl-l>	Redraws screen
m	Mails a message
n	Next message, displaying current, then increment
o	Changes elm options
p	Prints current message or tagged messages

Command/Keystroke	Description
q	Quits, maybe prompting for deleting, storing, and keeping messages
Q	Quick quit—no prompting
r	Replies to current message
s	Saves current message or tagged messages to a folder
t	Tags current message for further operations
T	Tags current message and goes to next message
<Ctrl-t>	Tags messages with a specified pattern
u	Undeletes current message
<Ctrl-u>	Undeletes messages with a specified pattern
x, <Ctrl-q>	Exits leaving folder untouched; asks if you want to exit if you have changed the folder
X	Exits leaving folder untouched, unconditionally

From Here...

You can find more information about exchanging information over the Internet in the following chapters:

- Chapter 28, "Surfing the Internet with the World Wide Web," describes the various types of information available on the Internet.
- Chapter 30, "Surviving Usenet News," describes the Usenet news system that's used to exchange public messages.

Surviving Usenet News

With the explosive growth of the Internet, Usenet news has attracted lots of attention. Many online services now offer access to Usenet. But what's Usenet? Usenet—short for *User Network*—is a proto-network of machines that exchange information grouped into subject hierarchies. The term *proto-network* is used because Usenet isn't a physical network in the normal sense. It's made up of all the computers that exchange Usenet news. ■

What is Usenet news?

This chapter provides an introduction to the huge selection of discussion groups available on the Net.

The history of Usenet

You get a brief history explaining where Usenet came from and why. This chapter also presents a brief glossary of Usenet terms.

The newsgroup structure of the Usenet news system

Learn how newsgroups work and how they're organized.

The culture of Usenet

To survive in the Usenet world, you need to know how to get along with your fellow Usenet denizens.

A look at the *rn* news reader

Learn how to use the most widely available news reader.

What's Usenet News?

In the simplest definition, *Usenet news*, *netnews*, or simply *news* is a forum for online discussion. Many computers around the world exchange chunks of information, called *articles*, on almost every subject imaginable. These computers aren't physically connected to the same network; they're logically connected in their capability to exchange data. Thus, they form the logical network referred to as Usenet. In this chapter, the terms *Usenet*, *news*, and *netnews* are used interchangeably.

N O T E The software that drives Usenet is divided into two parts: news readers (the software that users use to read and post news articles) and the software that processes articles and transfers them between systems.

Many people initially think of a PC bulletin board system (BBS) when trying to understand Usenet. Although Usenet news does bear some similarity to a BBS at first glance, there are very substantial and important differences:

- The various news articles on different subjects don't reside on one computer, as with a BBS. They're sent from computer to computer via a store-and-forward mechanism. Each site that receives news exchanges articles with one or more neighbors in transactions that are known as *news feeds*. As a result, news articles take time to propagate from place to place.

- No one is in charge. Yes, you read that right. Usenet has no overall manager, such as a BBS sysop (system operator). Each site has a good deal of autonomy. Usenet news has been described, very accurately, as "organized anarchy."

In general, Usenet news is divided into two logical parts: the programs and protocols that make up the mechanism for posting articles and transferring news articles between computers, and the user programs for reading and posting news articles. This chapter deals primarily with the user portion.

A Usenet Glossary

Usenet news has its own structure and culture, which are discussed later in the section "Usenet Culture." Usenet also has a terminology all its own. These "buzzwords" tend to confuse new users, especially those who use BBS systems. Table 30.1 is a brief glossary of common terms found on Usenet.

Table 30.1   Common Terms Encountered in Usenet

Term	Definition
article	A single message posted to a newsgroup.
bandwidth	An engineering term referring to the amount of data a given transmission medium can hold. Commonly used as in the phrase *waste of bandwidth* for articles that contain little useful information.

Term	Definition
BTW	Acronym for *By the Way*.
FAQ	An acronym for the *Frequently Asked Questions* list. Most newsgroups have a FAQ that they post on a regular basis. It's usually considered impolite to post a question whose answer is in the FAQ for a group.
flame	An article that's full of rude, angry, insulting statements directed at another person.
FYI	Acronym for *For Your Information*.
hierarchy	Usenet's system of grouping newsgroups into a tree structure based on subject.
IMHO	Stands for *In My Humble Opinion*.
newsgroup	A logical group of articles that are about one general subject.
news reader	A user program, such as rn, that's used to read and post articles to Usenet.
net.personality	Someone who's famous within the Usenet or Internet community.
net.police	A mythical organization responsible for enforcing the rules on Usenet. Typically used as sarcasm.
netiquette	The etiquette of Usenet.
newbie	Someone who's new to using Usenet news.
quoting	Including parts of a message to which you're responding. Most news readers allow you to quote articles. You should quote only relevant portions of an article to save bandwidth. Sometimes also referred to as *quotebacks*.
ROFL	Acronym for *Rolling On the Floor, Laughing*.
RTFM	An acronym for *Read The Fripping Manual*. Typically used as in "Here's a short answer to your question. RTFM for more info."
post	To submit an article to a newsgroup.
signal-to-noise	Engineering term referring to the ratio of the amount of data to the amount of background noise. On Usenet, it refers to how much useful information is in a newsgroup versus the amount of off-topic background chatter. A high signal-to-noise ratio refers to a newsgroup that has lots of useful information and very little off-topic chatter.
signature	A short file that's included at the end of all your posts. Typically includes your name, e-mail address, and possibly a witty quote of some sort.

Part
VI

Ch
30

continues

Table 30.1   Continued

Term	Definition
sig file	See *signature*.
smileys	Common symbols for denoting emotion in a post or e-mail message. For example, :-) and :-(are a happy face and a sad face. (Tilt your head toward your left shoulder and look at them sideways.)

A Brief History

In late 1979, two graduate students at Duke University began considering how to connect UNIX computers so that they could exchange text messages. Another grad student at the University of North Carolina became involved in this effort and wrote the first news transfer system, which consisted of a collection of shell scripts. This software was installed on the first two Usenet sites, unc and duke. In early 1980, another computer at Duke, phs, was added. The news software was eventually rewritten in C for public distribution. This became known as the *A News* software.

As the news software grew in popularity, it quickly became obvious that the current news transport software couldn't handle the increasing flow of news. Programmers at the University of California at Berkeley began to rewrite the current A News software to increase its capabilities. This new version, known as *B News*, was released in 1982.

Throughout this time, news articles were being transferred by using the UNIX-to-UNIX Copy Program (UUCP) protocol. As more sites joined the news network, the network load grew to unmanageable levels. Soon realizing that UUCP no longer worked as the main transport protocol for news, people began looking to the Internet and the TCP/IP protocols for help. In 1986, a software package was released that implemented the Network News Transport Protocol (NNTP). This protocol is defined in RFC 977. NNTP allowed news articles to be exchanged by using TCP/IP instead of the slower UUCP protocol. It also allowed users to read and post news from remote machines so that the main news processing software didn't have to be installed on every computer.

Now that NNTP was available on the Net, the already rapid growth of the Usenet news system exploded. The current news-processing software, B News, quickly became too slow to handle the increasing news flow. In 1987, Henry Spencer and Geoff Collyer of the University of Toronto developed a new news-processing software, *C News*. Then, Rich Salz developed a news transport system known as *INN,* one of the most widely used news servers on the Internet.

The Usenet news system continues to grow at a rapid pace. Other commercial information service providers are now carrying Usenet news as part of their online services. Several BBS networks, such as FidoNet, also carry Usenet news.

N O T E An excellent reference for the history of Usenet news is the news article "Usenet Software: History and Sources," by Dr. Gene Spafford. This article is regularly posted to the newsgroup **news.announce.newusers**.

How Usenet Is Structured

Part
VI

Ch
30

There are literally many thousands of newsgroups. How many, exactly? Well, nobody knows for sure—well over 20,000. There are thousands of groups on virtually every topic, and that number is growing every day.

Group Hierarchies

With so many different newsgroups, it would be a nightmare trying to find information on the subjects that you were interested in if the newsgroups weren't organized in some way. Usenet newsgroups are organized in a hierarchy based on subject. The names of the newsgroups are made up of subnames, each separated by a period. These names go from a general category to a specific category as you read the name from left to right. At the top of the hierarchy are several standard group categories, plus lots of specialized categories. These standard categories are well established. Table 30.2 lists the top-level groups standard categories in the Usenet news system.

Table 30.2 Top-Level Group Standard Categories in the Usenet Hierarchy

Class	Description
comp	Many different computer-related topics
misc	Miscellaneous topics that don't easily fit into another category
news	Various topics that relate to the Usenet news system itself
rec	Recreational and hobby subjects
soc	Social issues
sci	Various scientific topics
talk	Subjects designed for ongoing conversations

As with everything else on the Internet, there are exceptions to the rules in Table 30.2. Many other top-level hierarchies exist; most are devoted to different regions of the world. For example, the **ba** and **triangle** group hierarchies are concerned with topics of interest to the San Francisco Bay area and the North Carolina Research Triangle Park area, respectively.

One of these additional group hierarchies deserves special discussion. The **alt** hierarchy has very relaxed rules for newsgroup creation. Virtually anyone can create a group under the **alt** hierarchy; however, creating a newsgroup under any other top-level group is extremely difficult. The **alt** hierarchy carries many newsgroups that discuss topics that are out of the mainstream of society. In fact, many people find some of the topics in the **alt** hierarchy to be objectionable. Many Net debates on censorship have started because sites decided to ban part or all of the newsgroups in the **alt** hierarchy.

News Distributions

In addition to grouping articles in hierarchies, Usenet also provides a feature for limiting the spread of an article within the news system. New distributions provide a mechanism for limiting articles to a particular geographic area. If a distribution is set to a particular area, only sites within that distribution area receive the article. The systems administrator at each site decides what distributions apply to their site.

Why limit the distribution of an article? Suppose that you live in North Carolina and you're posting a meeting announcement for a local user group meeting. It's unlikely that Usenet readers in Australia are interested in your meeting. By limiting the distribution of your article to the appropriate geographical area, you can save network bandwidth, reduce the cost of sending your message, and reduce the aggravation of users around the world who have to read your message.

You can limit the distribution of your article by including a `Distribution:` line in the header of your article as you post it. Most news readers ask you for the distribution when you post an article. After the colon in the `Distribution:` line, enter the appropriate geographical distribution. Table 30.3 lists some commonly used news distribution areas.

Table 30.3   Commonly Used News Distribution Values

Value	Explanation
local	Typically, articles with a local distribution are limited to a group of local news servers within your organization. This distribution is often used for local organizational newsgroups.
nc	Every state has a statewide distribution that's the same as the postal abbreviation for the state. The nc used in this example limits the article to machines within the state of North Carolina.
us	Sends the article to all Usenet sites in the United States.
na	Sends the article to all Usenet sites in North America.
world	Sends the article to every reachable Usenet site in the world. Typically, this is the default distribution if no other distribution value is specified.

Your site may have some additional distributions that apply. There may be organization-wide or regional distributions that you can use to determine the scope of your article. In general, you should try to pick a distribution that sends your article only to the areas where it will be of interest.

No Central Authority

That Usenet has no central authority mystifies many people. Your local systems administrator really has authority over only the local system. No central group or organization dictates policy or takes complaints. Despite this glaring lack of regulated structure, Usenet works remarkably well. In fact, many people argue that it works better than if there were some central authority.

How do things keep working in an orderly manner? Usenet is run by cooperation between sites and by customs that have evolved over its life.

Usenet tends to be very good at policing itself. If a user starts to abuse the network, you can rest assured that the user and his or her systems administrator will get thousands of e-mail messages and several phone calls about the problem. This usually results in quick problem resolution.

Usenet Culture

Usenet has a particular culture all its own. You should take some time to try to become familiar with the facets of this culture before just diving in. Life on Usenet will be much easier if you do.

In the past couple of years, several online communication services have added Usenet news as a feature. As a result, thousands of people who are new to Usenet have started reading and posting Usenet news. Many of these users have complained about Usenet participants being rude or generally unlike the users of their online service. Well, the culture of Usenet is different from almost any other information service that you'll find. It's not better or worse—just different. If you try to make allowances for differences in Net culture, you'll probably find that your experiences on Usenet are a bit easier to handle.

Well over 1 million people—probably several million, though no one knows for sure—read and post Usenet news articles daily. These people are from all occupations, all walks of life, and many different countries around the world. Because Usenet news is carried on computers all over the world, it truly forms an international community. Many of the people that you encounter on Usenet don't speak English as a primary language. You can't assume that the people reading your articles share your cultural background, ethnic group, religion, or social values. The most that you can assume is that whoever reads your article is probably very different from you in several ways.

One aspect of Usenet culture, the *flame*, is usually an unpleasant experience for new users. A flame is a rude message, usually degrading and filled with insults that someone posts in response to one of your articles. Unfortunately, as you'll see, you can do very little about flames other than ignore them. Usenet is far too large a place for you to try to make everyone happy, and some people really seem to like flaming other people just for the fun of it. Perhaps they find it cheaper than psychotherapy...

Lack of Visual Reference

One problem with electronic communications is that you lack any kind of visual input during the conversation. When people talk to each other in person, you constantly receive information on a conscious and subconscious level from the other person's body language. Because you can't see the other people that read and post on Usenet, these visual cues are missing. Because you typically use body language and visual cues to represent emotion and feeling, it can be easy to misunderstand someone's post without them.

Fortunately, you can use several conventions on Usenet to replace part of the missing visual cues. You can place added emphasis on a particular phrase by surrounding it in asterisks, as in `"I *really* mean it!"` Also, the use of all capital letters is considered shouting. If you accidentally post an article with your <Caps Lock> key on, several people will probably tell you about it.

You can also express emotions by writing them into your message. For example, if you make a sarcastic statement, you can make sure that it's understood as such by adding `<sarcasm>` at the end of the line. *Smileys*, also known as *emoticons*, also work to add emotion to your post. A smiley is an ASCII representation of a face, which you look at sideways to see clearly. `:-)` is a happy, smiling face; `:-(` is a sad face.

ON THE WEB

A canonical list of smileys is available at **http://www.eff.org/papers/eggtti/eeg_286.html**. Have a look at it if you're really interested; some of them are quite funny and original, but the happy and sad faces are the most commonly used.

Newsgroup Culture

Just as people are different, each newsgroup on Usenet has a different culture. Each newsgroup has a different subject focus and attracts different types of people. In some groups, you may find large numbers of college students, whereas in others, you may primarily find research scientists.

Some of the more technical hierarchies, such as **comp** and **sci**, tend to be more oriented toward factual discussion, although heated debates do take place. Members of these groups are usually interested in discussing facts and issues related to some technical subject. When you post here, make sure that you take time to carefully compose your article and have references for the various points that you make.

The less technical hierarchies, such as **rec**, tend to be somewhat more opinion-oriented. Remember, you'll probably get replies to your articles that reflect other people's opinions that are quite different from your own. Groups in the **talk** hierarchy, along with some of the **misc** groups, get into some very heated discussions. Many of these groups discuss very sensitive topics such as abortion and gun control. Be careful in these groups if you're new to Usenet. Make sure that you take time to get familiar with the group before posting. Be prepared to receive strongly worded replies and e-mail about your articles. Many of the people here hold very strong beliefs.

N O T E When you first start reading a newsgroup, you should take some time to familiarize yourself with the culture of the particular group before posting. Read the group for a few days and try to get a feel for the tone of the articles and the things that appear to be acceptable and unacceptable behavior.

In a few newsgroups, posting articles is restricted. These are known as *moderated newsgroups*. Moderated newsgroups are managed by a person known as a *moderator*. All articles posted to the group must be approved by the moderator before posting. The moderator decides if the content of the article is appropriate to the group and, if so, posts the article to the group. Most news software automatically detects if a newsgroup is moderated and e-mails your article to the moderator rather than posts it directly.

Part

VI

Ch

30

Reading and Posting News

Now that you're familiar with Usenet, look at the basic process for reading and posting news articles. This section discusses reading and posting news in general terms; the exact details depend on the news-reading software that you're using. Many different software packages are available for interacting with news, and each of them is different. Many people use a Web browser with an integrated news reader, such as Netscape. Others prefer to use a line-oriented tool, such as rn. These general concepts should apply across all news reading software.

Subscribing to Newsgroups

The first thing you want to do when you start reading news is to decide which newsgroups you want to read. The process of selecting the newsgroups is known as *subscribing*.

Most news readers offer you a list of available newsgroups so that you can select the ones in which you're interested. The actual process of subscribing varies between news-reading software packages, but it usually involves selecting a series of newsgroups from a list. From then on, only the groups that you've subscribed to are visible when you read news. You can always subscribe to additional groups any time you want, or unsubscribe from a group in which you're no longer interested.

Reading News

After you subscribe to your newsgroups, you can begin reading news. You select a newsgroup from a list of your subscribed groups. Your news reader displays a list of article subjects for the various articles in the newsgroup. These subjects may be sorted in some order or they may be unsorted, depending on your news reader. Some news readers can sort articles based on subject, showing which articles are replies to other articles. This is known as *threading*.

When you select an article to read, you see several lines of information at the top of the article. These lines make up the *article header*. The header contains lots of information about the article, including the author, the date it was written, the subject, the newsgroups that the article was posted to, and the path the article took to get to your site. You also might see additional information, such as the organization the author is affiliated with and a set of keywords that identify the content of an article.

Under most news readers, an article is marked as read when you look at it. Usually, only new articles are displayed when you select a newsgroup. This means that after you look at an article, it probably won't show up in your article list again. If you want to keep the article, you can save it to disk or print it. You can also usually mark the article as unread so that your news reader displays it again the next time you go into the newsgroup. Many news readers also allow you to list old articles; this way, you have a list of old news articles in a newsgroup that are marked as having been read but haven't yet been deleted by the news system.

Replying via E-Mail

After you read an article, you may decide that you want to comment on the topic under discussion. If your information isn't of general interest to everyone in the newsgroup, you may want to reply to the article via e-mail, which most news readers allow you the option of doing.

If you choose to reply through e-mail, the news reader software uses the information in the article header to figure out the e-mail address of the author and then invokes an e-mail editor for you to edit your message. You usually also have the option of including the original article in your reply. If you do include the original article, make sure that you edit the original message to include only the relevant portions. After you finish editing your reply, you can send your e-mail message to the article's author.

Posting an Article

The act of creating a news article and sending it out through the Usenet system is known as *posting an article*. When you decide to post an article, you can either post a follow-up article to another article or create a new article on a new subject. Your news reader typically has different commands for the different types of posts that it can perform.

Posting a Follow-Up   A *follow-up article* is a reply to another article. This article stays in the same subject thread as the original article and is shown as a reply by threaded news readers.

When you post a follow-up, you can choose to include the original post. Including parts of the original post is a good way to provide a frame of reference for your reply. Remember that several days may pass between the time some sites see the original article and your reply. If you do choose to include the original article, try to include, or *quote*, only the parts of the article that are relevant to your reply. It gets tedious trying to wade through several levels of included files and quotes looking for the new information.

You should check the `Subject` line to make sure that the subject still accurately reflects the content of your post. Also, take a look at the `Newsgroup` line to make sure that your follow-up is going to the appropriate newsgroups.

Posting a New Article   If you decide to start a thread of discussion on a new subject, you want to post a new article instead of a follow-up. The mechanics of posting the article are very similar to those of posting a follow-up—you give the appropriate command to your news reader; your news reader asks for some information, such as the destination newsgroups, subject, and distribution; and you're placed into an editor. The major difference is that you're creating a subject thread instead of replying to one.

T I P A complete document on Usenet writing style is posted regularly to the newsgroup **news.announce.newusers**.

You should think about several things as you write your article. You can think of them as "Usenet Style Tips," if you want. These tips cover the format of your article and its content.

You should keep your lines less than 80 characters long. Many terminals can't display lines that are more than 80 characters. Similarly, you should try to keep the length of your article under 1,000 lines or so. Some sites are still running old versions of the news transport software, and long articles can cause them problems.

You probably want to create a signature file that's automatically included at the end of every post. Most news readers support signature files, although the exact mechanism varies depending on your software. Most people put their name and e-mail address in their signature file, along with their geographical location. Some people add a witty quote or a small ASCII picture. Try to avoid having a large signature file. Some news software limits your signature to four lines or so.

You need to give a subject to your article when you post it. Try to pick a subject line that's short, yet descriptive. Thousands of people scan the subjects in any particular newsgroup, and you want them to be able to pick out your article if it's of interest to them. Also, carefully consider which newsgroups you're going to post your article to. Most news readers allow you to post an article to more than one newsgroup. You should post to only the smallest number of groups that you need. Remember that thousands of people are reading each newsgroup.

Netiquette Etiquette on Usenet

Throughout this chapter, the importance of being aware of how the tone and content of your message are interpreted has been stressed. This general consideration of behavior on Usenet, and the Internet in general, has its own term—*netiquette*. Netiquette applies to all areas of the Internet, including electronic mail.

The term *netiquette* simply refers to "proper and polite" behavior as it applies to Usenet news. Most of the time, you should have no real problems on Usenet as long as you remember that it's a very big and diverse place. Not everyone on Usenet shares your background, beliefs, or values, and you should try to remember this as you post articles.

Make sure that you clearly communicate your ideas in your posts. With the lack of body language and the delay between posts and replies, it's surprisingly easy to interpret someone's meaning incorrectly. Also, remember that many participants don't speak English as a native language and may be unaware of local idioms and sarcasm.

Blatant commercial advertising is frowned on in Usenet news. There are appropriate newsgroups for advertising products and services. Similarly, don't post chain articles, such as the infamous MAKE.MONEY.FAST or Craig Shergold get-well card article. These articles have been circulating around Usenet for years, and you (and your systems administrator) will incur the wrath of thousands of people instantly if you post one of them.

Resist the urge to post flames, especially spelling and grammar flames. Even though flames seem to be a permanent part of the Usenet "landscape," these personal attacks and raving messages accomplish little. If someone should flame you for one of your posts, take time to calm down and carefully consider how to respond; the best solution might be not to respond at all. Sometimes you may receive a flame, but a calm response from you may elicit an apology from the person who flamed you. If you just zip off another flame in anger, you only escalate the problem. Remember that the person on the other end is really a person, not a computer.

N O T E   If a user is causing a real problem, you can add them to your *kill file*, a configuration file for your news reader that contains a list of users or subjects. Anything that appears in your kill file is automatically not displayed when you read news. Most news readers support some version of a kill file. This is a fairly painless way to cut down the noise from really annoying users.

In general, a little common sense and courtesy go a long way to avoiding any problems on Usenet. However, remember that Usenet is a huge place. There are simply too many people for you to try to make everyone happy. Eventually, someone will get angry over one of your posts and you'll probably be flamed.

Using the *rn* News Reader

Many different types of news-reading software are available—far too many to describe in this chapter. The rn news reader is a very common news-reading program that can be found on almost every UNIX variant. It was developed by Larry Wall and is widely available. Although rn isn't the easiest news reader to use, nor does it have some of the fanciest features, it's still one of the most popular news readers in existence. rn allows you to read news via an ASCII interface that's suitable for local work on a terminal or from a remote network session.

N O T E   Another news reader, trn, is quite popular and is distributed with many distributions of Linux. The trn news reader is almost identical to rn except for the threading support. For compatibility with a wide variety of UNIX systems, only the rn news reader is discussed in this chapter. For more information on the threading capabilities of trn, refer to its Linux man page.

When you start rn for the first time, you see a message welcoming you to the program, followed by a list of newsgroups. You have the opportunity to subscribe to different groups at this point. If your site carries a large number of groups, it can be quite time-consuming to set up your initial subscription information. rn saves your subscription information in your home directory in a file named .newsrc.

After you complete your subscriptions, rn places you in a newsgroup selection mode. The name of each of your subscribed newsgroups is displayed one at a time. You can enter the newsgroup and start reading articles by pressing <y>, skip to the next group by pressing <n>, or go to the previous newsgroup by pressing <q>. You can also get a list of subjects in the newsgroup by pressing <=> at the newsgroup prompt. Most of the commands in rn and trn are one-character commands, and help is available at every command prompt by pressing <h>.

After you select a newsgroup to read, you enter article-selection mode. In this mode, several commands can help you navigate the articles in the newsgroup. Table 30.4 lists some of the commands available in article-selection mode.

Table 30.4   Some Commands Available in Article-Selection Mode

Command	Description
<n><space bar>	Scans forward for the next unread article. The space bar does this only at the end of the article, at the article-selection prompt.
<space bar>	Shows the next page of the current article if not at the article-selection prompt.
<Shift-n>	Goes to the next article.
<Ctrl-Shift-n>	Goes to the next article with the same subject as the current article.
<p>	Scans backward for the previous unread article; stays at current article if none is found.
<Shift-p>	Goes to the previous article.
<Ctrl-Shift-r>	Goes to the last previous article with the subject that's the same as the current article.
<h>	Displays help for article selection mode.
<r>	Replies to the article author via e-mail.
<Shift-r>	Replies to the article author via e-mail, including the current article.
<f>	Posts a follow-up article.
<Shift-f>	Posts a follow-up article, including the original article in the new article.
<s>*filename*	Saves the current article to a file named *filename*.
<q>	Quits the current group and returns to newsgroup selection mode.

These are only some of the options available within rn and trn. These are feature-rich programs that allow lots of user customization. Refer to the man pages and the online help for more information.

From Here...

In this chapter, you explored the structure of Usenet, the basics of reading and posting articles, the hierarchy of newsgroups, and Usenet's general culture. With a little patience, you'll find Usenet news to be an indispensable source of information. You can find more information about electronic communication and the Internet in the following chapters:

- Chapter 26, "Understanding the Internet," introduces the Internet and the various services it provides.

- Chapter 28, "Surfing the Internet with the World Wide Web," describes the various types of information you can find on the Internet.

- Chapter 29, "Using Electronic Mail," shows how to communicate with other people by using the e-mail system.

## PART VI

Setting Up a Web Site

Creating Web Documents with HTML

In Chapter 28, "Surfing the Internet with the World Wide Web," you learned how to access the World Wide Web and were introduced to the various types of information available. You can click hypertext links and jump from place to place as fast as your connection allows. You can see Web pages with snazzy graphics and sound, lists, forms, and all sorts of neat stuff. But how do you actually create a Web page that other Web users can get to? It's not really as difficult as you might think. All you need is access to a Web server that uses HyperText Transport Protocol (HTTP) and a set of documents written in HyperText Markup Language (HTML).

This chapter looks at HTML to see what's involved in writing Web pages using HTML. ■

Understanding HTML

Before you can start creating Web pages, you need to get a basic understanding of HTML, the language used to develop Web pages.

Working with HTML

This chapter shows where to look for HTML software for editing and conversion software. You also learn basic HTML coding.

Using tags

The basic building blocks of HTML, *tags* are the part of HTML that tells a Web browser how to display text and graphics, along with other format information. This chapter describes the main HTML tags and their attributes, as well as how they're used.

Incorporating anchors and hypertext links

For a more dynamic Web page, you can provide anchors and links so that users can move to other Web pages for related information.

Using graphics

One of the Web's most popular features is its use of graphics. This chapter shows how to include graphics in your HTML documents.

Understanding HTML

The HyperText Markup Language (HTML) is the language used to develop Web pages and documents. HTML isn't a programming language like C++, Java, Pascal, or Perl; instead, it's basically a cross-platform markup language that's designed to be flexible enough to display text and other elements (such as graphics) on a variety of viewers.

An HTML document consists of special tags that are embedded in an ASCII document. These tags are interpreted by Web browser programs, which format and display documents.

N O T E   HTML is a subset of Standard Generalized Markup Language (SGML), which is an international standard (ISO 88791) for electronic document exchange. SGML is a meta-language for defining and standardizing the structure of documents. SGML also describes a grammar you can use to design other markup languages. Any valid HTML document is also valid SGML. Like any SGML derived language, HTML's grammar is described by a Document Type Definition (DTD) file. ▪

HTML tells Web browsers how to display Web documents; however, the format information HTML provides is pretty general. Many different Web browsers are available for the Internet, such as Netscape Navigator, Microsoft Internet Explorer, or NCSA Mosaic. Many run under graphical interfaces such as the X Windows system or MS Windows. Some, such as Lynx, are ANSI browsers and are limited in terms of which graphical characteristics they can display.

As you write HTML documents, remember that they will look different depending on which browser the reader is using. All available Web browsers try to format HTML documents as properly as possible; however, what you see may not be what someone else using a different browser or even the same browser running under a different operating system sees.

Working with HTML

As tools for the Web continue to evolve, creating HTML documents keeps getting easier. Many of the new tools hide much of the actual HTML coding from you. All you have to do is write the words, format your document, and save it to an appropriate location. Some browsers, such as Netscape Navigator Gold, include an editor that lets you point and click to create HTML pages. Other point-and-click tools include Microsoft FrontPage, Adobe PageMill, and Macromedia Backstage.

If you don't want to use an HTML editor or already have documents you want to put on the Web, there is lots of software you can use to convert word processing, desktop publishing, spreadsheet, or other documents into HTML. Newer software packages are beginning to include HTML as an option when you save a file.

ON THE WEB

http://www.yahoo.com/Computers_and_Internet/Software/Internet/World_Wide_Web/
HTML_Converters/ has lots of conversion software available.

At some point, you'll want to try your hand at creating your own HTML. Although many tools are available to help make writing HTML less tedious, you'll probably find that they won't let you do everything you want.

You'll also find that HTML is relatively easy to work with. Because HTML is an ASCII-based markup language, all you need is an editor that will let you save files in ASCII format, and a Web browser that you can use to view your Web pages as you develop them. You don't need a network connection to develop Web documents. Any Web browser should let you open a local HTML file and view it as though you had retrieved it from the Internet.

N O T E You may find that using an HTML editor is useful. Some editors allow you to select the text you want to format, and then apply HTML tags from a menu rather than type the tags in yourself. Other editors look more like word processors—you select the text and select the type of formatting you want from a tool bar. In either case, you'll probably need to edit the HTML directly to get the exact look and feel you want. ▪

ON THE WEB

You can check out some editors from AOLpress at **http://homepage.interaccess.com/~cdavis/ editrev/index.html**; Sausage Software HotDog/HotDog Pro at **http://www.sausage.com.au**; and Bradbury Software Homesite at **http://homepage.interaccess.com/~cdavis/editrev/index.html**. You can find a listing of HTML editors at **http://www.yahoo.com/Computers_and_Internet/ Software/Internet/World_Wide_Web/HTML_Editors/**.

Before you go any further into the syntax of HTML, look at a Web page and its HTML source code. Figure 31.1 shows a simple Web page.

Listing 31.1 shows the HTML source for this Web page. Here you'll see the basic elements of an HTML page.

Listing 31.1 Source Code for a Simple HTML Page

```
<HTML>

<HEAD>
   <TITLE>Hello Web!</TITLE>
</HEAD>

<BODY>
<H1>Hello!</H1>
This is the body section of a simple HTML page.
<P>
<IMG src="example.gif">

</BODY>

</HTML>
```

Part
VII

Ch
31

FIG. 31.1

A simple HTML page.

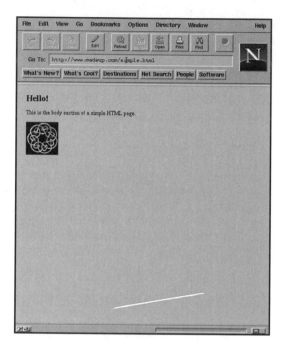

You'll find that HTML is pretty straightforward:

- All HTML tags are enclosed by angle brackets (the < and > characters). The <HTML> tag at the beginning of Listing 31.1 is an example.

- Most HTML tags require you to use a starting tag (<tag_name>) and an ending tag (</tag_name>). You start and stop formatting by the placement of these tags. If you leave out a required ending tag, you won't see any formatting; you may not even see the text.

- Many HTML tags have attributes that you can customize. An *attribute* allows you change the default behavior of a tag. If you want a table without a border, for example, you change it by setting an attribute (BORDER=*some_number*) within the <TABLE> tag.

- All HTML files require an <HTML> tag at the beginning of the file and the closing </HTML> tag at the end. These tags tell a Web browser that the document it's processing is written in HTML.

An HTML document typically consists of two logical sections: the head and the body. The *head* contains information about the document; the *body* contains the document information itself. As you may have guessed, the header section is enclosed with the <HEAD> and </HEAD> tags, whereas the body is enclosed with the <BODY> and </BODY> tags.

The head section of an HTML page contains information related to the document itself. You can place several tags in the header section, but the <TITLE> tag is the most widely used. The document title—whatever is enclosed with the <TITLE> and </TITLE> tags—appears in the title bar of a Web browser.

The body section of an HTML page contains most of the elements you see when viewing the page with a Web browser. This is where you enter all the elements you want people to see, such as text, graphics, links (URLs), lists, and tables.

N O T E The <TITLE> element identifies the name of your page, When someone makes a book-mark to the page, this is name that is used. Although HTML doesn't limit the length of the <TITLE> element, you should consider giving the page a short, descriptive title that can easily be displayed. A good rule of thumb for the length of a title is no more than a single phrase and no longer than 60 characters.

Because the document title is displayed in a separate window and isn't part of the document itself, the title text itself must be plain text and not have any hyperlinks or text formatting. ■

T I P One really nice thing about HTML source code is that you can look at it. Find an interesting page and want to know how it was done? Take a look! You can learn a lot by looking at other people's source code.

Viewing the source code is usually done through a menu choice in your Web browser. For example, to see HTML source code for a page under Netscape, choose Document Source from the View menu.

Part
VII

Ch
31

Now that you've seen the basics of HTML (yes, that's really it!), it's time to learn about tags and how they're used. Although there are many different tags, you'll find that by mastering just a handful (and combining them in different ways), you can create excellent Web pages.

Using Basic HTML Elements

Basic HTML syntax consists of three components: tags, attributes, and URLs. These components, respectively, give the details of how items are to be formatted and displayed, the specifics of certain actions, and the locations of other files and documents.

Tags

The basic building blocks of HTML, *tags* are the part of HTML that tells a Web browser how to display text and graphics, along with other format information. As you may recall, tags are written between angle brackets (<*tag_name*>) and most tags also require an ending tag (</*tag_name*>) as well. As you may recall from Figure 31.1, you saw the <TITLE> tag used:

```
<TITLE>Hello Web!</TITLE>
```

This line tells your browser to format the text string Hello Web! as a <TITLE>. See the starting (<TITLE>) and ending tags (</TITLE>)? All of the elements within these tags—text, in this case—are displayed in the title bar of your Web browser window. Similarly, other tags only affect the elements they enclose.

Attributes

Sometimes, tags need to specify exact information, such as where a file is located. *Attributes* are used with tags to provide more detail about how the tag is to be implemented. For example, consider the following tag:

```
<IMG SRC="example.gif">
```

This tag is an `<IMG>` (image) tag that tells your Web browser to display a graphic image. But which image? That's where the attribute comes in. In this example, the attribute field is `SRC="example.gif"`, which gives detailed information about how the `<IMG>` tag is to be interpreted. In this case, the example.gif file is to be displayed as the image.

 TIP Using the height and width attributes with the `<IMG>` tag helps your browser display the graphic more quickly. In Netscape, if the image is GIF or JPG format, you can open the image by itself. Then, from the View menu choose View Document Info to see the size of the image.

URLs

Web resources are accessed by a descriptive address known as a *uniform resource locator* (URL). Everything that you access on the Web has an URL. HTML uses URLs to specify the location of needed files or of other Web pages that are connected by hypertext links.

Understanding HTML Syntax

As you've seen, HTML breaks down into three basic components: tags, attributes, and URLs. Of these, the basic building block is the tag. Tags are used to give commands to a Web browser, whereas attributes and URLs are used to provide details about the commands.

Tags can be grouped into several categories, depending on their function. Some tags give information about the document as a whole, some are used for formatting text, and some are used for graphics and hypertext links to other documents.

 ON THE WEB
For a listing of HTML tags and their attributes, look at the online version of Que's *HTML Quick Reference* at **http://www.mcp.com/que/developer_expert/htmlqr/toc.htm** and Que's *Special Edition Using HTML* at **http://www.mcp.com/que/et/se_html2/toc.htm**.

Using Document Tags

The `<HTML>` and `</HTML>` tags are used to tell a Web browser that the document it's processing is written in HTML. The `<HTML>` tag should be the first tag in your document, and the `</HTML>` tag should be the last.

HTML documents are divided into a header and a body section. The header contains information about the document, and the body contains the document information itself. As you may have guessed, the header section is surrounded by the <HEAD> and </HEAD> tags, whereas the body is surrounded by the <BODY> and </BODY> tags. Several tags can be placed in the header section, but now only the <TITLE> tag is widely used. The document title—whatever is enclosed with the <TITLE> and </TITLE> tags—appears in the title bar of a Web browser.

Formatting Text

HTML provides several different ways to format text for display. Remember that the actual formatting of the text in your Web page is controlled by the Web browser used to view the page.

Headings   HTML supports six levels of headings that you can display in a document by using the <H1> through <H6> tags. Figure 31.2 shows how these headings may appear in a Web browser (Netscape in this case). Remember that these headings are displayed differently on different browsers—the font and size may not appear the same with your Web browser. Listing 31.2 shows the source.

Part
VII

Ch
31

FIG. 31.2

Heading levels as displayed in Netscape.

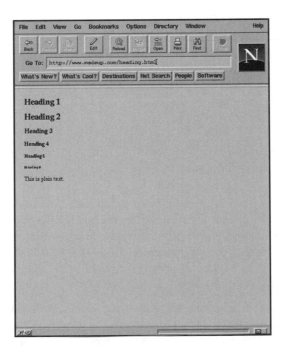

Listing 31.2 Example Heading Style Source

```
<HTML>

<HEAD>
    <TITLE>Heading example</TITLE>
</HEAD>

<BODY>
    <H1>Heading 1</H1>
    <H2>Heading 2
    </H2>

    <H3>Heading 3

    </H3>
    <H4>Heading 4</H4>
    <H5>Heading 5</H5>
    <H6>Heading 6</H6>
This is plain text.
</BODY>

</HTML>
```

Look at the location of the level 2 and level 3 heading tags in Listing 31.2. HTML doesn't care whether the tags are at the end of the line, or where they occur. These tags just tell the browser that all the text between them is in the particular heading level that they define. Also, notice that the line This is plain text has no tags around it. This line will be displayed as generic text by a browser.

 TIP It's usually a good idea to use only three levels of headings in a Web document. If you need more than three levels of headings, consider using additional pages.

Regular Text HTML gives you several ways to format normal text in your documents. For one thing, Web browsers completely ignore where the text lines end in your HTML file. Carriage returns also are ignored, so you have to use special tags to indicate where line breaks and paragraphs are to begin. The <BR> tag causes the browser that's displaying your document to insert a line break. Think of this as inserting a carriage return at that point in the line. Subsequent text is moved down to the next line.

If you want to create a new paragraph, use the <P> tag instead. <P> has the same effect as <BR>, except that most browsers insert a blank line as part of a paragraph break, to visually separate one block of text from another. Because browsers control the text display, the actual behavior of the <P> tag can vary. With the <P> tag, you usually don't need a </P> ending tag. However, it is required if you use any of the <P> attributes.

Sometimes you'll want to visually separate different sections of the same page. To do so, HTML provides a way to draw a horizontal line across the document display. The <HR> tag, which stands for *horizontal rule*, is used to draw a horizontal line. It inserts a paragraph break before the line so you don't need the <P> tag. As with the <P> tag, no ending tag is needed for <HR>.

You've seen several ways to control the format of text on an HTML page. Now look at another short HTML sample to see the effect of line breaks, paragraph marks, and horizontal rules on the text display. Listing 31.3 shows an HTML sample that uses these formatting tags.

Listing 31.3   An HTML Sample Showing Basic Text Formatting

```
<HTML>
<HEAD>
<TITLE>A Sample Text Formatting Page</TITLE>
</HEAD>
<BODY>
<H2>Text Sample 1</H2>
Here is some sample text that is written on separate lines without using line
breaks. <P>
<H2>Text Sample 2</H2>
This sample text has a<BR>
line break in the middle.<P>
<H2>Text Sample 3</H2>
Text before a paragraph mark.<P>
Text after a paragraph mark.<HR>
Text after a horizontal rule mark.
</BODY>
</HTML>
```

Part
VII

Ch
31

Figure 31.3 shows this sample displayed in Mosaic.

FIG. 31.3

Text formatting as displayed Mosaic.

Suppose that you want to display some text, such as a table, and that you want the carriage returns and spacing to be kept exactly as you entered them. You can use the <PRE> and </PRE>

tags to define preformatted text. Any text that you surround with these tags is displayed in a monospace font, and all returns and spaces are used exactly as entered.

To some degree, you can define the way text is displayed. HTML provides tags that tell browsers to display text in boldface, underline, or italic. These tags are known as *physical styles*. The tags for boldfaced text are <B> and </B>, the tags for underline are <U> and </U>, and the tags for italic are <I> and </I>. Enclose the text that you want to format with the starting and ending tag of the style that you want.

HTML also provides some *logical styles* for formatting text. The <EM> and </EM> tags are used to mark emphasized text, which is usually shown in italic. The <STRONG> and </STRONG> tags are used to indicate stronger emphasis, which is usually shown in boldface.

Figure 31.4 shows how different text formats may appear.

FIG. 31.4
Examples of text formatting as displayed in Netscape.

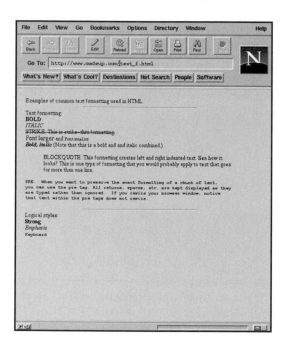

Table 31.1 provides a quick listing of some of the most common HTML tags for text formatting.

Table 31.1   Selected HTML Text-Formatting Tags

Tag	Action
<B>...</B>	Makes text **bold**.
<BLOCKQUOTE>...</BLOCKQUOTE>	Formats text with left and right indents.

Tag	Action
`<FONT>...</FONT>`	Controls various aspects of text with attributes—for example, text color (`COLOR=rgb_value`) and size (`SIZE=number`).
`<I>...</I>`	Makes text *italic*.
`<PRE>...</PRE>`	Leaves text formatting exactly as it appears.
`<STRIKE>...</STRIKE>`	Formats text as ~~strikethrough~~.
`<U>...</U>`	<u>Underlines</u> text.
`<EM>...</EM>`	Logical style; emphasizes text (typically displayed as *italic*).
`<KBD>...</KBD>`	Logical style; shows text as a keyboard style (usually displayed in a `monospaced` font).
`<STRONG>...</STRONG>`	Logical style; emphasizes text (typically displayed as **bold**).

Miscellaneous Text   Two formatting tags that don't fit in with other tag categories are the `<ADDRESS>` and `</ADDRESS>` tags. These tags are used to mark addresses, signatures, and so on within a document. Typically, text with this format is placed at the end of a document, following a horizontal rule mark. The exact formatting of `<ADDRESS>` text is determined by the individual Web browser.

Organizing Information with Lists

Sometimes you need to deliver information that's logically grouped in some fashion. For example, you might have a list of graphic images to display, or you might want to show a numbered top 10 list. HTML provides several different ways to format and display lists of information. Using lists in HTML is a powerful way to deliver information, because the user's Web browser formats all the text in the list in a consistent manner. All you have to do is decide how the information fits together.

Displaying Unordered Lists   An *unordered list* is text displayed separately with a bullet or other formatting character. Each text entry in an unordered list can be several lines long.

Two sets of tags are used to create an unordered list. The `<UL>` and `</UL>` tags define the beginning and end of the list, and the `<LI>` tag is used to mark each list item. Listing 31.4 shows the HTML source for a simple unordered list. Figure 31.5 shows how Mosaic displays this list.

Listing 31.4   An Unordered List

```
<HTML>
<HEAD>
<TITLE>An Unordered List</TITLE>
</HEAD>
<BODY>
```

continues

Listing 31.4 Continued

```
<LI>This is list item 1.
<LI>This is list item 2.
<LI>This is list item 3.
</UL>
</BODY>
</HTML>
```

FIG. 31.5
An unordered list viewed in Mosaic.

Presenting Ordered Lists An *ordered list* presents list information in numerical order. Each time a new list item is identified, the number of the list item is incremented. Ordered lists are defined by the <OL> and </OL> tags, and the same <LI> tag used in unordered lists is also used in ordered lists to mark each list item.

Listing 31.5 shows the HTML source for a simple ordered list. Figure 31.6 shows how this list is displayed in Mosaic.

Listing 31.5 An Ordered List

```
<HTML>
<HEAD>
<TITLE>An Ordered List</TITLE>
</HEAD>
<BODY>
<OL>
<LI>This is list item 1.
<LI>This is list item 2.
<LI>This is list item 3.
</OL>
</BODY>
</HTML>
```

Using Definition Lists Think of how a glossary in a book looks: You typically have each word or term offset by itself, and then a paragraph giving its definition. HTML definition (or glossary) lists provide a way to do this with Web pages. A definition list consists of a term—this can be one word or a series of words—followed by a definition. The definition is usually explanatory text.

FIG. 31.6

An ordered list viewed in Mosaic.

Although definition lists are particularly useful for glossaries, you can use them to present any kind of information where you need a title and an explanation. One common use is to make the glossary term a hypertext link to another document, and make the definition a description of the linked document. (Creating hypertext links is discussed later in this chapter, so keep this application of a definition list in mind.)

Definition lists require the <DL> and </DL> tags to mark the start and end of the list. Rather than use a simple list item tag, definition lists use dual tags: <DT> to mark the glossary item, and <DD> to mark the definition. Listing 31.6 shows the HTML source for a simple definition list. Figure 31.7 shows how this list is displayed in Mosaic.

Part
VII

Ch
31

Listing 31.6   A Simple Definition List

```
<HTML>
<HEAD>
<TITLE>A Simple Glossary List</TITLE>
</HEAD>
<BODY>
<DL>
<DT>Item 1
<DD>This is the definition field for list item 1.
<DT>Item 2
<DD>This is the definition field for list item 2.
<DT>Item 3
<DD>This is the definition field for list item 3.
</DL>
</BODY>
</HTML>
```

FIG. 31.7

A simple definition list viewed in Mosaic.

Combining Lists As you can see, the various lists in HTML give you several ways to present information to a user. In fact, HTML allows you to combine list types to gain even more control over how your information is presented. You can nest one list type within another easily.

Suppose that you want to create a section of your home page to tell users your favorite movies and music. You can nest two glossary lists within an unordered list to create a detailed outline. Listing 31.7 shows an example HTML source that uses nested lists.

Listing 31.7   Creating a Custom List by Nesting Different List Types

```
<HTML>
<HEAD>
<TITLE>A Custom List</TITLE>
</HEAD>
<BODY>
This list shows some of my favorite musicians and movies.
It uses two definition lists nested in an unordered list.
It also uses some text formatting tags.<P>
I hope that you enjoy it.<HR>

<LI>Here are some of my favorite movies<P>
 <DL>
 <DT>Hopscotch
 <DD>This is a wonderful film about an ex-CIA agent traveling the world
 writing his memoirs
 <DT>Highlander
 <DD>An action adventure about a battle between immortals.
 "There can be only one!"
 </DL>
<P>
<LI>Here are some of my musical groups<P>
 <DL>
 <DT>Tannahill Weavers
 <DD>One of the best Scottish folk bands around.
 <DT>Altan
 <DD>A high-energy Irish folk band.

 <DT>Jimmy Buffet
 <DD>Folk hero of parrot-heads everywhere.
 </DL>
 </UL>
</BODY>
</HTML>
```

This combination list example is a bit more complicated than the others you've seen, but it still uses only techniques covered so far in this chapter. Notice that the glossary lists are indented in the HTML source code. The indent is only to make the source code easier to read (recall that Web browsers ignore line breaks and extra spaces when they display the page). Figure 31.8 shows how this page is displayed in Netscape.

FIG. 31.8
A custom list viewed in Netscape.

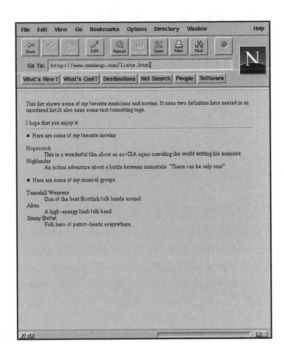

As a quick review, Table 31.2 shows the HTML tags for creating lists we've gone over.

Table 31.2   HTML List Tags

Tag	Action
`<UL>...</UL>`	Create an unordered (bulleted) list; list items begin with the `<LI>` tag
`<OL>...</OL>`	Create an ordered (numbered) list; list items begin with the `<LI>` tag
`<DL>...</DL>`	Create a definition list; list items begin with a `<DT>` tag for a definition term or a `<DD>` tag for a definition

Linking Pages with Anchors

Now comes the neat stuff. In this section, you learn how to hook multiple Web pages together and create hypertext links that jump from place to place.

Hypertext links in HTML are known as *anchors*, and the `<A>` and `</A>` tags are used to define an anchor. These tags are placed around the words you want to use for the hypertext link. Web browsers typically underline hypertext links automatically and show them in a different color.

To tell the Web browser which document to retrieve when the hypertext link is clicked, you use the HREF attribute and an URL with the anchor tag. Suppose that you want to create a hypertext link to the NCSA Mosaic home page. If you want to include the sentence Click here to go to the NCSA Mosaic home page., where the word here is the hypertext link, you need the following HTML lines:

```
Click <A HREF="http://www.ncsa.uiuc.edu/SDG/Software/Mosaic/index.html">
here</A> to go to the NCSA Mosaic home page.
```

The anchor tags surround the hypertext link—in this case, the word here. The HREF attribute is inserted inside the opening anchor tag. That's all there is to it.

> **N O T E** You can place any URL in the HREF attribute. You can link to a Web page, an FTP site, a
> Gopher server, or any other location.

In addition to just creating hypertext links, you can also give names to links by using the NAME attribute. Named links are very useful for jumping to specific locations in a document. You can list a table of contents at the beginning of a long document, and have each entry in the table of contents be a hypertext link to the appropriate place in the document. By combining them with an HREF, you can send users to a specific location in another document.

Assume that you have a long document—maybe a Frequently Asked Questions (FAQ) list that discusses widgets. You can create a hypertext link from the table of contents to the "How to Use Widgets" section. The first thing you need to do is to create a named anchor in the "How to Use Widgets" section, so that you can jump to it from the table of contents. The HTML to do this looks like the following:

```
<A NAME="howtouse">How to Use Widgets</A>
Widgets are a very powerful tool if used properly.
Unfortunately, no one knows enough about them to use
them properly. Since they have no relevance to HTML, you
don't need to discuss them further in this chapter.
```

Now, all you need to do is to put a hypertext link from the table of contents to this spot. To do that, you use the HREF attribute to link to this anchor, and give the anchor's name preceded by a # character. The table of contents entry looks like this:

```
<A HREF="#howtouse">How to Use Widgets</A>
```

When someone clicks the entry How to Use Widgets in the table of contents, the browser jumps to the anchor named howtouse later in the document.

> **N O T E** You can name an anchor that's a hypertext link to another location. Just use the NAME and
> HREF attributes in the same anchor. For example,
>
> ```
> <A HREF="http://www.doesnotexist.com/index.html#end">Go to the end</A>
> ```
>
> would take you to another document. It also would display the file starting from wherever the <#end>
> anchor is located in that file.

Using Graphics

One feature that has made the Web so popular is its capability to incorporate graphics and text in a simple format. HTML makes it easy to insert graphics into your documents. Before you start putting all sorts of graphic images into documents, though, remember that many people access the Web via low-speed telephone lines, and that graphics can take a long time to transfer at these rates. Also, some people use text-based browsers, such as Lynx, which can't display graphics at all. You should make sure that someone can navigate your Web documents easily, even if they have graphics turned off or if their browser doesn't support graphics. In a moment, you'll learn a technique for checking for graphics support.

You can use graphics in your HTML documents in two ways: by using hypertext links or by using inline images.

- You can make hypertext links to the graphics files themselves. This method requires the user to have a helper program that can display the graphics file properly. The exact type of graphic that can be displayed depends on the helper application used. Links for this method are hypertext links that name the graphics image as the destination document.
- You can insert the graphics directly into your HTML document. Graphics inserted this way are known as *inline images*. Many browsers support graphics in the JPG, GIF, or X Bitmap formats as inline images.

  HTML uses the <IMG> tag to indicate an inline image. This tag is combined with the SRC="*filename*" attribute to define which image file is displayed. HTML also provides the ALIGN= attribute to tell Web browsers how they should line up the graphic image with any text that's near it. The valid values for ALIGN are TOP, MIDDLE, and BOTTOM.

As mentioned earlier, you need to make your Web pages usable by browsers that don't support graphics. To do this, you should provide some text reference any time you use a graphic image. HTML provides a way for you to define some text to be displayed if a browser can't display a graphic image. The ALT="text about the graphic" attribute defines some alternate text that will be displayed when the graphic can't be displayed.

An example might help pull this all together. Listing 31.8 is a section of HTML that displays an inline GIF image. If a browser can't display the image, a description of the image is shown instead.

Part VII

Ch 31

Listing 31.8 Inserting a Graphic into Your Script

```
<HTML>

<HEAD>
   <TITLE>Image example</TITLE>
</HEAD>
<BODY>

<H2>Images</H2>
```

continues

Listing 31.8 Continued

```
<P>
<P>
<IMG src="venus.jpg"
     align="right"
     height="160" width="82"
     alt="Statue of Aphrodite">

<UL>
<LI>Statue of Aphrodite, known as the "Venus de Milo".
<LI>Carved out of marble in Greece, circa 100 B.C.
<LI>Currently in the Louvre in Paris
<LI>Part of the Louvre's Greek, Etruscan and Roman Antiquities Collection
</UL>

<HR>
To go to the Louvre's web site click <A HREF="http://mistral.culture.fr/louvre/
louvrea.htm">HERE</A>

</BODY>

</HTML>
```

Figure 31.9 shows how this page is displayed in Netscape. You can see how different elements (heading, a list, horizontal line, graphic and a link) combine to make up a page.

FIG. 31.9

An inline graphic
displayed in Netscape.

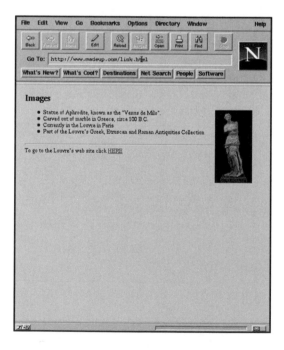

You can combine graphic images and anchors to create graphic hypertext links as well. Simply surround the `<IMG>` tag with anchor tags that define which document to load. A picture serves as a hypertext link to another HTML document in the following example:

```
Click the picture to find out more about this statue.
<A HREF="statue.html"><IMG SRC="statue.gif"
ALIGN=BOTTOM ALT="[Photo of statue]">
</A>
```

From Here...

This chapter introduces you to basic HTML and how to create a Web page. You learned how to use tags, which provide commands to a Web browser, and how to use attributes and URLs, which provide details for the commands. Many HTML guides are available on the Internet that cover everything from syntax to design. Use one of the many search engines to look up HTML topics that interest you.

ON THE WEB

A good starting point for ideas is Yahoo!'s listings for HTML at **http://www.yahoo.com/ Computers_and_Internet/Information_and_Documentation/Data_Formats/HTML/**.

You can find out more about the World Wide Web and the Internet in the following chapters:

- Chapter 26, "Understanding the Internet," provides a basic overview of the Internet.

- Chapter 28, "Surfing the Internet with the World Wide Web," introduces you to the Web and how to search it.

Part

VII

Ch

31

## CHAPTER 32

Getting Started with Apache

To use a Linux system as a Web server, you must install special server software on your system. Two of the most popular UNIX Web server packages are Apache and NCSA. In fact, a November 1996 survey showed that Apache accounted for more than 40 percent of all installed Web servers. Although this chapter, like several others, is specific to the Apache server, the vocabulary is certainly applicable to other Web servers. The NCSA family of servers has much in common with Apache with respect to configuration files, because Apache was derived originally from the NCSA 1.3 server, and maintaining backward compatibility with existing NCSA servers was a mandate with the development team.

This chapter deals with all the essential steps needed to install the software and bring up a running, breathing, living server. If you've installed an Apache or NCSA server before, you can probably safely skip this chapter, although you should skim it to look for essential differences. ■

How to compile the Apache source code

Learn how to go through the compilation process of the source code for the server.

How to configure the server

This chapter covers the elemental parts of the configuration files.

Debugging information

In this chapter, you get some basic "Why didn't the Web server come up?" debugging help.

What about Apache-SSL?

You also get information concerning how to obtain, install, and launch Apache-SSL.

Compiling Apache

Apache is known to compile on just about every UNIX variant: Solaris 2.X, SunOS 4.1.X, Irix 5.X and 6.X, Linux, FreeBSD/NetBSD/BSDI, HP-UX, AIX, Ultrix, OSF1, NeXT, Sequent, A/UX, SCO, UTS, Apollo Domain/OS, QNX, and probably a few you've never even tried yet. A port to OS/2 has been done, and a Windows NT port is rumored to be in the works. Portability has been a high priority for the development team.

The CD-ROMs contain a recent binary release of Apache in both a.out and ELF formats. The complete source code for Apache is also provided. Because there are Apache binaries on the CD-ROMs, you can skip the compilation process and move on to the next section, if you're in a hurry to get Apache up and running. However, if you ever want to add new modules or tweak the functionality provided by Apache, you need to know how to compile it.

Copy the source code package to a part of your file system. You need several spare megabytes of disk to compile the server. Unpack it and go to the /src subdirectory. A sequence of commands to do this might look like the following:

```
cd /CDROM
cp apache_1.1.1.tar.gz /usr/local/etc/httpd/
cd /usr/local/etc/httpd/
tar -zxvf apache_1.1.1.tar
cd src
```

Step 1: Edit the Configuration File

The Configuration file is used by the Configure program to create a Makefile specifically targeted to your platform, with any runtime defines set, if necessary, and with the modules you've chosen compiled together. It also creates a modules.c, which contains information about which modules to link together at compilation time.

You must declare which C compiler you're using (most likely gcc), and you must uncomment the appropriate setting for AUX_CFLAGS. Just look down through the Makefile for the Linux entry for AUX_CFLAGS. For example,

```
CC=gcc
AUX_CFLAGS = -DLINUX
```

N O T E   For the CFLAGS definition, if you want every file with the execute bit set to be parsed for server-side includes, set -DXBITHACK. If you want to eliminate the overhead of performing the reverse-DNS lookup when an entry is written to the logfile, set -DMINIMAL_DNS.

▶ **See** "Server-Side Includes," **p. 650**

If, on the other hand, you want to have an even greater sense of confidence in the host name, you can set -DMAXIMAL_DNS. You would set this if you were protecting parts of your site based on host name. Doing this is optional and is provided mostly for backward compatibility with NCSA 1.3. ▪

At the bottom of the file is a list of packaged modules that come with the Apache distribution. Notice that not all of them are compiled in to the final program by default. To include a module in the build, uncomment the entry for it. Notice that some modules are mutually exclusive. For example, it wouldn't be wise to compile the configurable logging module and the common logging module at the same time.

Also, some modules, such as mod_auth_dbm, might require linking to an external library and need an entry added to the EXTRA_LIBS line. You learn more about modules in a little bit; for the purposes of getting up and running, I recommend simply using the defaults as provided.

Step 2: Run the Configure Script

The configure script is a simple Bourne shell script that takes the configuration file and creates a Makefile out of it, as well as modules.c.

Step 3: Run *make*

The make command compiles the server. You might see some warnings about data types, particularly if you compiled with -Wall set, but none of the errors should be fatal.

If all went well, you should now have an executable program in your src/ directory called httpd.

Establishing the File Hierarchy

The next step in the process of setting up a server is to make some fundamental decisions regarding where on the file system different parts of the server will reside. Write down your decisions for each of these; you will need them in the next section, "Performing a Basic Configuration."

The first thing you need to decide is where the *server root* will be. This is the subdirectory in which the server will reside, and from which the conf/ directory, the logs/ and cgi-bin/ subdirectories, and other server-related directories lead. The default suggestion is to have this as /usr/local/etc/httpd. You can have your configuration files and logfiles in other locations. The server root was designed to be a convenient place to keep everything server-related together. Also, if the server crashes and leaves a core file, it will be found in the server root directory.

The second decision is where the *document root*, the directory in which all your HTML and other media reside, will be located. A file called myfile.html in the document root would be referenced as http://host.com/myfile.html. This directory can be a subdirectory of the server root, or it can be outside the server root and in its own directory. It's commonly located as a subdirectory of the server root and named htdocs. If, for more disk space or other reasons, you choose to move the document root out of the server root directory, you should give it a pretty short name—for example, /home/www or /www/htdocs. If you're implementing a Web server on top of an FTP server, for example, you might want to point the document root at /home/ftp/pub.

Finally, you need to decide where on your server you'll keep your logfiles. This space should have a fairly large working area, depending on how busy you estimate your server will be. For a point of reference, a site with 100K hits per day (which would fall under moderate traffic, relatively speaking) can expect to generate 15M per day of logfile information. For performance reasons, it's usually best to have the log directory on a separate disk partition or even a separate disk drive altogether, because on even a moderately busy server the access log can be written to several times per second.

Performing a Basic Configuration

This section covers the minimal set of changes you need to make to the configuration files in order to launch a basic Web site.

Apache has three separate configuration files. This model goes back to NCSA, and the reasoning is sound: there are largely three main areas of administrative configuration, so setting them up as separate files allows Webmasters to give different write permissions to each if they so desire.

You'll find the configuration files for Apache in the conf/ subdirectory of the server root directory. Each has been provided with a -dist file-name suffix; it's recommended that you make a copy without the -dist and edit those new files, keeping the -dist versions as backups and reference.

The basic format of the configuration files are a combination of a shell-like interface and pseudo-HTML. The elemental unit is the directive, which can take a number of arguments—essentially,

```
Directive argument argument....
```

that is,

```
Port 80
```

or

```
AddIcon /icons/back.gif ..
```

You can also group directives together inside certain pseudo-HTML tags. Unlike HTML, these tags should be on their own line—for example,

```
<Virtualhost www.myhost.com>
DocumentRoot /www/htdocs/myhost.com
ServerName www.myhost.com
</Virtualhost>
```

httpd.conf

The first configuration file to look at is httpd.conf. This is the file that sets the basic system-level information about the server, such as what port it binds to, which users it runs under, and so on. If you aren't the systems administrator of the site at which you're installing the server, you might want to ask the administrator to help you with these questions.

The essential items to cover in this file are as follows:

■ `Port` *number*

For example,

`Port 80`

This is the TCP/IP port number to which the Web server binds. Port 80 is the default port in http: URLs; in other words, http://www.myhost.com/ is equivalent to http://www.myhost.com:80/.

For a number of reasons, however, you might want to run your server on a different port; for example, there's already a server running on port 80, or this is a server you want to keep secret. (If there's sensitive information, however, you should at least do host-based access control, if not password protection.)

■ `User` *#number_or_uid*
`Group` *#number_or_uid*

as in

`User nobody`
`Group nogroup`

Apache needs to be launched as root to bind to a port lower than 1024. Immediately after grabbing the port, Apache changes its effective user ID to something else, typically as user nobody. This is very important for security reasons. Running your Web servers as root means that any hole in the server (be it through the server itself, or through a CGI script, which is much more likely) could be exploited by an outside user to run a command on your machine. Thus, setting the user to nobody, www, or some other reasonably innocuous user ID is the safest bet. This user ID needs to be able to read files in the document root, as well as have read permission on the configuration files. The argument should be the actual user name; however, if you want to give a numeric user ID, prepend the number with a pound sign (#). The Group directive is the same issue; decide which group ID you want the server to run with.

■ `ServerAdmin` *email_address*

Set the e-mail address of a user who can receive mail related to the actions of the server. In the case of a server error, the message given to the browser visiting your site will include a message to the effect of "please report this problem to user@myhost.com." In the future, Apache might send warning e-mail to the ServerAdmin user if it encounters a major systems-related problem.

■ `ServerRoot` *directory*

For example,

`ServerRoot /usr/local/etc/httpd`

Set the server root decided on earlier. Give the full path, and don't end it with a slash.

■ `ErrorLog` *directory*/*filename*
`TransferLog` *directory*/*filename*

Specify exactly where to log errors and Web accesses. If the file name given doesn't start with a slash, it's presumed to be relative to the server root directory. I suggested earlier that the logfiles be sent to a separate directory outside the server root; this is where you specify the logging directory and the name of the logfiles within that directory.

▪ ServerName *DNS_hostname*

At times, the Web server will have to know the host name it's being referred to as, which can be different from its real host name. For example, the name www.myhost.com might actually be a DNS alias for gateway.myhost.com. In this case, you don't want the URLs generated by the server to be http://gateway.myhost.com/. ServerName allows you to set that precisely.

srm.conf

The second configuration file to cover before launch is srm.conf. The important things to set in that file are as follows:

▪ DocumentRoot *directory*

As described before, this is the root level of your tree of documents, be that /usr/local/etc/httpd/htdocs or /www/htdocs. This directory must exist and be readable by the user (usually nobody) the Web server runs as.

▪ ScriptAlias *request_path_alias directory*

ScriptAlias lets you specify that a particular directory *outside* the document root can be aliased to a path in the request, *and* that objects in that directory are executed rather than simply read from the file system. For example, the default offering

ScriptAlias /cgi-bin/ /usr/local/etc/httpd/cgi-bin/

means that a request for http://www.myhost.com/cgi-bin/fortune will execute the program /usr/local/etc/httpd/cgi-bin/fortune. Apache comes bundled with a number of useful beginner CGI scripts, simple shell scripts that illustrate CGI programming.

Finally, the directory containing the CGI scripts should *not* be under the document root. Bizarre interactions between the code that handles ScriptAlias and the code that handles request/path name resolution could cause problems.

access.conf

access.conf is structured more rigidly than the other configuration files; the content is contained within <Directory></Directory> pseudo-HTML tags that define the scope of the directives listed within.

▶ **See** "Configuration Basics," **p. 642**

So for example, the directives between

<Directory /www/htdocs>

and

```
</Directory>
```

affect everything located under the /www/htdocs directory. Furthermore, wild cards can be used; for example,

```
<Directory /www/htdocs/*/archives/>
....
</Directory>
```

applies to /www/htdocs/list1/archives/, /www/htdocs/list2/archives/, and so on.

Starting Up Apache

To start Apache, simply run the binary you compiled earlier (or your precompiled binary) with the `-f` flag pointing to the httpd.conf file also created earlier; for example,

```
/usr/local/etc/httpd/src/httpd -f /usr/local/etc/httpd/conf/httpd.conf
```

It's probably a good idea at this point to use the `ps` command to see if httpd is running. Typically, something like

```
ps -aux ¦ grep
```

will suffice. To your surprise, you'll see a number of simultaneous httpd processes running. What's going on?

The first Web servers, such as CERN and NCSA, used the model of one main Web server cloning itself with every single request that came in. The clone would respond to the request, while the original server returned to listening to the port for another request. Although certainly a simple and robust design, the act of *cloning* (or, in UNIX terms, *forking*) was an expensive operation under UNIX, so loads above a couple hits per second were quite punishing even on the nicest hardware. It was also difficult to implement any sort of *throttling*, which reduced the amount of cloning that took place. When the number of clones was very high, it was hard for the original server to know how many clones were still around. Thus, servers had no easy way to refuse or delay connections based on a lack of resources.

Apache—like NCSA 1.4+, Netscape's Web servers, and a couple of other UNIX-based Web servers—instead uses the model of a group of persistent children running in parallel. The children are coordinated by a parent process, which can tell how many children are alive, spawn new children (if necessary), and even terminate old children if there are many idle ones, depending on the situation. (*Parent* and *child* are the actual UNIX terms.)

Back to the server. Fire up your Web browser and point it to your local server. (Use the usual http:// format and append the `ServerName` parameter you defined in the httpd.conf file.) Did it work? If all went well, you should be able to see a directory index listing of everything in the document root directory, or if an index.html is in that directory, you would see the contents of that file.

Table 32.1 shows other command-line options.

Table 32.1   Command-Line Options for httpd

Option	Result
-d *serverroot*	Sets the initial value for ServerRoot
-X	Runs the server in single-process mode; useful for debugging purposes, but don't run the server in this mode for serving content to the outside world
-v	Prints the version of the server, and then exits
-?	Prints the list of available command-line arguments to Apache

After you check to make sure that Apache starts up correctly, you'll probably want to add the startup command to your system boot scripts so that Apache will start automatically when the system boots. A typical location for the startup command would be in the file /etc/rc.d/ rc.local.

Debugging the Server Startup Process

Apache is usually pretty good about giving meaningful error messages, but some are explained in more detail in the following sections.

Open File Error Messages

```
httpd: could not open document config file .....
fopen: No such file or directory
```

These open file error messages are usually the result of giving just a relative path to the -f argument, so Apache looks for the file(s) relative to the compiled-in server root (what's set in src/httpd.h) instead of relative to the directory you're in. You must give the full path or the path relative to the compiled-in server root.

Port and Bind Error Messages

```
httpd: could not bind to port [X]
bind: Operation not permitted
```

The port and bind error messages are most likely caused by attempting to run the server on a port below 1024 without launching it as "root." Most UNIX operating systems, including Linux, prevent people without root access from trying to launch any type of server on a port less than 1024. If you launch the server as root, the error message should disappear.

```
httpd: could not bind to port
bind: Address already in use
```

These port and bind error messages mean that something is already running on your machine at the port you've specified. Do you have another Web server running? No standard UNIX mechanism is available for determining what's running on what ports; on most systems, the file /etc/services can tell you what the most common daemons are, but it's not a complete list. You could also try using the `netstat` command, with various options such as -a.

Bad User or Group Name Messages

```
httpd: bad user name ....
httpd: bad group name ....
```

Bad user or group name error messages mean that the user or the group you had set in httpd.conf doesn't actually exist on your system. You might see errors telling you that particular files or directories don't exist. If it looks as though the files are there, make sure that they're readable by the user IDs that the server runs as (that is, both `root` and `nobody`).

Initial Server Startup Error Messages

Suppose that Apache has started up and, according to `ps`, it's actually running. But when you go to the site, you experience the following problems or error messages:

- *No connection at all.* Make sure that no firewalls are between you or the server that would filter out packets to the server. Secondly, try using `telnet` to the port you launched the Web server on—for example, `telnet myhost.com 80`. If you don't get a `Connected to myhost.com` message back, your connection isn't even making it to the server in the first place.

- `403 Access Forbidden`. Your document root directory may be unreadable, or you might have something in your access.conf file that prevents access to your site from the machine where your Web browser is.

- `500 Server Error`. Is your front page a CGI script? The script might be failing.

These are the most common errors made in initial server startups. If you can establish that contact with the server is actually being made, the next best place to look for error information is in the `ErrorLog`.

Setting Up Apache-SSL

At this point, we'll take a slight detour and discuss setting up a variant of the Apache Web server, Apache-SSL, which can conduct secure transactions over the Secure Sockets Layer protocol. SSL is an RSA public-key-based encryption protocol developed by Netscape Communications for use in the Netscape Navigator browser and Netscape Web servers.

Until recently, the only options for doing SSL transactions on the World Wide Web has been to use a proprietary server, such as the Netscape Commerce server or the OpenMarket Secure server. Strongly encrypting versions of these servers haven't been available outside the United States due to export restrictions in the states.

Eric Young, author of the widely used `libdes` package, with Tim Hudson wrote a library that implements SSL, eponymously named `SSLeay`. The `SSLeay` package has since expanded to become an all-purpose cryptography and certificate-handling library, while retaining the same name, `SSLeay`.

Ben Laurie, a member of the Apache Group, then took the `SSLeay` library and interfaced it with the Apache server, making his patches available to people on the Net. Sameer Parekh of Community ConneXion, Inc. (hereafter referred to as C2) then took Ben Laurie's patches and built a package legal for use within the United States.

Because the RSA technology used by SSL in the United States is covered by patents owned by RSA Data Security, Inc. (RSADSI) (**www.rsa.com**), it isn't legal to use the `SSLeay` package "out-of-the-box" within the United States. C2 licensed the RSA technology to make use of the package legal within the United States by using the "RSAREF" package, produced by RSADSI and Consensus Development Corporation (**www.consensus.com**).

Due to export restrictions, it isn't legal for someone outside the United States to download and install the C2 Apache-SSL package. In fact, we couldn't even put the SSL patches on the CD-ROM included with this book because the book would suddenly have earned the label "munition," and clearance from the U.S. government to export the book would have been required!

The installation process for Apache-SSL differs for those within the United States from those who live outside the country. People within the states can simply download and install the package from C2 at **http://stronghold.c2.net/**. Outside the United States, people must separately install `SSLeay`, and then patch Apache with Ben Laurie's patches from his site.

Installation Within the U.S.

Within the United States, it's legal to use the version of Apache-SSL available for download from C2 for non-commercial purposes only. To use Apache-SSL commercially, you must purchase an Apache-SSL Commerce license from C2. After downloading the package from C2, the installation of the server is rather straightforward.

Before you can begin using SSL, however, you need to generate your key/certificate pair for use with SSL. The C2 Apache-SSL distribution comes with the program `genkey`, which you can use to generate your key and certificate. Run /usr/local/ssl/bin/genkey httpd to generate a public/private RSA key pair for use with the server. It also generates a PKCS #10 Certificate Signing Request, which you send to the certificate authority of your choice (for example, Verisign) along with the proper documentation. The script also generates a test certificate so that you can start using the server immediately, without waiting for your certificate authority to reply with a signed certificate.

After the key/certificate pair is generated and installed in the proper location, you're ready to start using the server. First, however, familiarize yourself with the configuration directives specific to Apache-SSL:

  ■ `SSLCertificateFile` *filename*

    The `SSLCertificateFile` file name is the location where your server's certificate is stored. The `SSLCertificateFile` directive is required.

- `SSLCertificateKeyFile` *filename*

  The `SSLCertificateKeyFile` directive is required unless the file listed in `SSLCertificateFile` also contains the key.

- `SSLLogFile` *filename*

  The `SSLLogFile` is where Apache-SSL logs specific information regarding SSL for each connection, such as the cipher used, and client-authentication information.

- `SSLVerifyClient 0 ¦ 1 ¦ 2`

  `SSLVerifyClient` determines whether the server should use X509 client authentication. 0 means no, 1 means it's optional, and 2 means that a client certificate is required.

- `SSLVerifyDepth` *depth*

  `SSLVerifyDepth` is how far along a certificate chain the server should look for a root certificate authority when verifying a given client certificate. If you're not using X509 client certificates, a good default value is probably 1.

- `SSLFakeBasicAuth`

  The `SSLFakeBasicAuth` directive allows you to use X509 client certificates to provide for Basic HTTP/1.0 authentication for accessing various realms of your Web server's document tree.

N O T E `SSLFakeBasicAuth` must be used with `SSLVerifyClient` 2. If used with any other `SSLVerifyClient` setting, it's subject to subversion. ▓

Part
VII

Ch

32

After installing the certificate and key, you can start the server by merely running /usr/local/ etc/httpd/start, which starts up the server with some default configuration files located in conf/httpd.conf and conf/httpsd.conf.

Installation Outside the U.S.

For people outside the United States, the installation process is more involved. You must obtain the `SSLeay` package (**ftp://ftp.psy.uq.oz.au/pub/Crypto/SSL/**) and then install it according to the directions in the package.

Second, you must obtain Ben's patches to Apache from his site, at **http://www.algroup. co.uk/ApacheSSL/**. The patches must then be installed to your Apache source tree, according to the directions included with the package.

It should be noted that, at publication time, Verisign (**www.verisign.com**, a spin-off from RSA, which was the first certificate authority for SSL) had just started signing keys generated for Apache-SSL. Other CAs are expected to crop up. Netscape 3.0 comes with half a dozen others defined and waiting to be recognized. In fact, Netscape 3.0 (and hopefully by the time you read this, other browsers) allow for arbitrary CAs to be used, warning the user that a new CA is being used, but still allowing the encrypted conversation to take place.

From Here...

You can learn more details about setting up, configuring, and running the Apache Web server in the following chapters:

- Chapter 33, "Configuring Apache," discusses the configuration options for Apache in greater detail.
- In Chapter 34, "Managing an Internet Web Server," you learn how to make your server robust, efficient, automated, and secure.

Configuring Apache

By now you should have a running Web server, although it will be minimally configured. In this chapter, you learn about most of the functionality that comes bundled with the server. This chapter is organized as a series of tutorials so that if you're new to Apache, you can get up to speed quickly. Toward the end of the chapter, you dive into some experimental Apache modules as well.

Because of its rapid pace of development, it's possible that Apache will have some significantly new functionality by the time you read this chapter. However, the existing functionality isn't likely to change much. The Apache Group has had a strong ethic toward backward compatibility. ■

Configuring MIME types

You can configure the MIME types of objects on the server and use those MIME types to trigger special actions.

Managing requests

You can redirect and alias requests for different parts of your site and configure directory indexing.

Using server-side includes

In this chapter, you learn how to set up and implement server-side includes in your HTML files.

Using cookies

HTTP *cookies* are a method for maintaining statefulness in a stateless protocol. In this chapter, you learn not only what this means, but also how to implement cookies to track user sessions.

Configuration Basics

The srm.conf and access.conf files are where most of the configuration related to the actual objects on the server takes place. The srm.conf file is also known as the `ResourceConfig` file, which is a directive that can be set in httpd.conf; the access.conf file is also known as the `AccessConfig` file, which also is a directive in httpd.conf.

The names *srm.conf* and *access.conf* are mostly historical. At one point, when the server was still NCSA, the only thing access.conf was used for was setting permissions, restrictions, authentication, and so forth. Then, when directory indexing was added, the cry went out for the capability to control certain characteristics on a directory-by-directory basis. The access.conf file was the only configuration file that had any kind of structure for tight access control: the pseudo-HTML `<Directory>` container.

▶ **See** "access.conf," **p. 634**

With Apache's revamped configuration file-parsing routines, most directives can literally appear anywhere—for example, within `<Directory>` containers in access.conf, within `<VirtualHost>` containers in httpd.conf, and so on. However, for sanity's sake, you should keep some structure to the configuration files. You should put server-processing-level configuration options (such as `Port` and `<VirtualHost>` containers) in httpd.conf, generic server resource information (such as `Redirect`, `AddType`, and directory indexing information) in srm.conf, and per-directory configurations in access.conf.

In addition to the `<Directory>` container is the `<Limit>` container, which is used within `<Directory>` containers to specify certain HTTP methods to which particular directives apply. Examples are given later in this chapter.

Per-Directory Configuration Files

Before you get too deep into the different configuration options, look at a mechanism that controls configuration on a directory-by-directory basis. This is a accomplished by using a configuration file that's local to the directory that you want to configure. You can already control subdirectory options in access.conf, as outlined in Chapter 32, "Getting Started with Apache." However, for several reasons, you may want to allow these configurations to be maintained by users other than those with the power to restart the server (such as users maintaining their home pages). For that purpose the `AccessFileName` directive was invented.

▶ **See** "Performing a Basic Configuration," **p. 632**

The default `AccessFileName` is .htaccess. If you want to use something else—for example, .acc—you would say the following in the srm.conf file:

```
AccessFileName .acc
```

If looking for the `AccessFileName` file is enabled and a request comes in that translates to the file /www/htdocs/path/path2/file, the server will look for /.acc, /www/.acc, /www/htdocs/.acc, /www/htdocs/path/.acc, and /www/htdocs/path/path2/.acc, in that order. Also, if it finds the file, the server will parse the file to see what configuration options apply. (Remember that this parsing has to happen with each hit, separately, so this can be a big performance hit.)

You can turn off the `AccessFileName` directive by setting the following options in your access config file:

```
<Directory />
AllowOverride None
</Directory>
```

For the sake of brevity and clarity, assume that the `AccessFileName` option has set the name of these files to be .htaccess. What options can these files affect? The `AllowOverride` directive controls the range of available options within the `<Directory>` container in the `AccessConfig` file, as mentioned previously. Table 33.1 lists the exact arguments for `AllowOverride`.

Table 33.1 The *AllowOverride* Arguments

Argument	Result
AuthConfig	When listed, .htaccess files can specify their own authentication directives, such as `AuthUserFile`, `AuthName`, `AuthType`, and `require`.
FileInfo	When listed, .htaccess can override any settings for meta-information about files by using directives such as `AddType`, `AddEncoding`, and `AddLanguage`.
Indexes	When listed, .htaccess files can locally set directives that control the rendering of the directory indexing, as implemented in the mod_dir.c module—for example, `FancyIndexing`, `AddIcon`, and `AddDescription`.
Limit	This argument allows the use of the directives that limit access based on host name or host IP number (`allow`, `deny`, and `order`).
Options	This argument allows the use of the `Options` directive.
All	This argument allows all of the preceding arguments to be true.

`AllowOverride` options aren't merged, meaning that if the configuration for /path/ is different than the configuration for /, the /path/ one will take precedence because it's deeper.

MIME Types: *AddType* and *AddEncoding*

A fundamental element of the HTTP protocol, and the reason why the Web was so natural as a home for multiple media formats, is that every data object transferred through HTTP had an associated MIME type.

> **N O T E** The origins of MIME (*Multipurpose Internet Mail Extensions*) lie in an effort to standardize the transmission of documents of multiple media through e-mail. Part of the MIME specification was that e-mail messages could contain meta-information in the headers identifying the data being sent. One type of MIME header is `Content-Type`, which states the format or data type the object is in. For example, HTML is given the label `"text/html"`, and JPEG images are given the label `"image/jpeg"`.

ON THE WEB

A registry of MIME types is maintained by the Internet Assigned Numbers Authority at **http://www.isi.edu/div7/iana/**.

When a browser asks a server for an object, the server gives that object to the browser and states what its `Content-Type` is. That way, the browser can make an intelligent decision about how to render the document. For example, it can send it to an image program, to a PostScript viewer, or to a VRML viewer.

What this means to the server maintainer is that every object being served out must have the right MIME type associated with it. Fortunately, there has been a convention of expressing data type through two-, three-, or four-letter suffixes to the file name—for example, foobar.gif is most likely to be a GIF image.

What the server needs is a file to map the suffix to the MIME content type. Fortunately, Apache comes with such a file in its configuration directory—a file named mime.types. The simple format of this file consists of one record per line, where a record is a MIME type and a list of acceptable suffixes. Although more than one suffix may map to a particular MIME type, you can't have more than one MIME type per suffix. You can use the `TypesConfig` directive to specify an alternative location for the file.

The Internet is evolving so quickly that it would be hard to keep the mime.types file completely up-to-date. To overcome this difficulty, you can use a special directive, `AddType`, which can be put in the srm.conf file as follows:

```
AddType x-world/x-vrml wrl
```

Now, whenever the server is asked to serve a file that ends with .wrl, it knows to also send a header like the following:

```
Content-type: x-world/x-vrml
```

Thus, you don't have to worry about reconciling future distributions of the mime.types file with your private installations and configuration.

As you'll see in later pages, `AddType` is also used to specify "special" files that get magically handled by certain features within the server.

A sister to `AddType` is `AddEncoding`. Just as the MIME header `Content-Type` can specify the data format of the object, the `Content-Encoding` header specifies the *encoding* of the object. An encoding is an attribute of the object as it's being transferred or stored; semantically, the browser should know that it has to "decode" whatever it gets, based on the listed encoding. The most common use is with compressed files. For example, if you have

```
AddEncoding x-gzip gz
```

and if you then access a file named myworld.wrl.gz, the MIME headers sent in response will look like the following:

```
Content-Type: x-world/x-vrml
Content-Encoding: x-gzip
```

And any browser worth its 2 cents will know, "Oh, I have to decompress the file before handing it off to the VRML viewer."

Alias, ScriptAlias, and *Redirect*

The `Alias`, `ScriptAlias`, and `Redirect` directives—all denizens of srm.conf and all implemented by the mod_alias.c module—allow you to have some flexibility with the mapping between URL-Space on your server and the actual layout of your file system.

If that last statement sounded cryptic, don't worry. What it basically means is that any URL that looks like http://myhost.com/x/y/z doesn't have to necessarily map to a file named x/y/z under the document root of the server:

```
Alias /path/ /some/other/path/
```

The preceding directive takes a request for an object from the mythical subdirectory */path* under the document root and maps it to another directory somewhere else entirely. For example, a request for

```
http://myhost.com/statistics/
```

might normally go to document root /statistics, except that for whatever reason you wanted it to point somewhere outside the document root (for example, /usr/local/statistics). For that you'd have the following:

```
Alias /statistics/ /usr/local/statistics/
```

To the outside user, this would be completely transparent. If you use `Alias`, it's wise not to alias to somewhere else inside the document root. Furthermore, a request like

```
http://myhost.com/statistics/graph.gif
```

would get translated into a request for the file

```
/usr/local/statistics/graph.gif
```

`ScriptAlias` is just like `Alias`, with the side effect of making everything in the subdirectory by default a CGI script. This might sound a bit bizarre, but the early model for building Web sites had all the CGI functionality separated into a directory by itself, and referenced through the Web server as shown in the following:

```
http://myhost.com/cgi-bin/script
```

If you have in your srm.conf file

```
ScriptAlias /cgi-bin/ /usr/local/etc/httpd/cgi-bin/
```

then the preceding URL points to the script at /usr/local/etc/httpd/cgi-bin/script. As you'll see in a page or two, there's a more elegant way to specify that a file is a CGI script to be executed.

`Redirect` does just that—redirects the request to another resource. That resource could be on the same machine or somewhere else on the Net. Also, the match will be a substring match, starting from the beginning. For example, if you did

```
Redirect /newyork http://myhost.com/maps/states/newyork
```

Part
VII

Ch
33

then a request for

```
http://myhost.com/newyork/index.html
```

will get redirected to

```
http://myhost.com/maps/states/newyork/index.html
```

Of course, the second argument to `Redirect` can be an URL at some other site. Just make sure that you know what you're doing.

> **CAUTION**
>
> Be wary of creating loops accidentally. For example,
>
> `Redirect /newyork http://myhost.com/newyork/newyork`
>
> can have particularly deleterious effects on the server.

A Better Way to Activate CGI Scripts

You read earlier that there's a more elegant way of activating CGI scripts than by using `ScriptAlias`. You can use the `AddType` directive and create a custom MIME type, like so:

```
AddType application/x-httpd-cgi cgi
```

When the server gets a request for a CGI file, the server maps to that MIME type, and then catches itself and says, "I need to execute this rather than just dish it out like regular files." Thus, you can have CGI files in the same directories as HTML, GIF, and all your other files.

Directory Indexing

When Apache is given an URL to a directory, instead of to a particular file—for example,

```
http://myhost.com/statistics/
```

Apache first looks for a file specified by the `DirectoryIndex` directive in srm.conf. In the default configs, this file is index.html. You can set a list of files to search for, or even an absolute path to a page or CGI script:

```
DirectoryIndex index.cgi index.html /cgi-bin/go-away
```

The preceding directive says to look for an index.cgi file in the directory first. If that can't be found, look for an index.html file in the directory. If neither can be found, redirect the request to /cgi-bin/go-away.

If the Apache server fails to find a match, Apache will create—completely on the fly—an HTML listing of all the files available in the directory.

There are quite a few ways to customize the output of the directory indexing functionality. First, you need to ask yourself if you care about seeing things such as icons and last-modified times in the reports. If you do, then you want to turn to

```
FancyIndexing On
```

Otherwise, you'll just get a simple menu of the available files, which you may want for security or performance reasons.

If you choose to use the `FancyIndexing` option, you must ask whether you need to customize it further and, if so, how. The default settings for the directory indexing functionality are already pretty elaborate.

The `AddIcon`, `AddIconByEncoding`, and `AddIconByType` directives customize the selection of icons next to files. `AddIcon` matches icons at the file name level by using the pattern

```
AddIcon iconfile filename [filename] [filename]...
```

Thus, for example,

```
AddIcon /icons/binary.gif .bin .exe
```

means that any file that ends in .bin or .exe should get the binary.gif icon attached. The file names can also be a wild-card expression, a complete file name, or even one of two "special" names: `^^DIRECTORY^^` for directories and `^^BLANKICON^^` for blank lines. Thus, you can see lines like

```
AddIcon /icons/dir.gif ^^DIRECTORY^^
AddIcon /icons/old.gif *~
```

Finally, the `iconfile` can be a string containing the icon file's name and the alternate text to put into the `ALT` attribute. So, your examples should really be

```
AddIcon (BIN,/icons/binary.gif) .bin .exe
AddIcon (DIR,/icons/dir.gif) ^^DIRECTORY^^
```

The `AddIconByType` directive is a little bit more flexible and probably comes more highly recommended in terms of actual use. Rather than tie icons to file-name patterns, it ties icons to the MIME type associated with the files. The syntax is very roughly the same:

```
AddIconByType iconfile mime-type [mime-type]...
```

`mime-type` can be either the exact MIME type matching what you've assigned a file, or it can be a pattern match. Thus, you see entries in the default configuration files like the following:

```
AddIconByType (SND,/icons/sound2,gif) audio/*
```

Using pattern matching is more robust than trying to match only against file-name suffixes.

`AddIconByEncoding` is used mostly to distinguish compressed files from other types of files. This makes sense only if used with `AddEncoding` directives in your srm.conf file. The default srm.conf has these entries:

```
AddEncoding x-gzip gz
AddEncoding x-compress Z
AddIconByEncoding (CMP,/icons/compressed.gif) x-compress x-gzip
```

The `AddIconByEncoding` option sets the icon next to compressed files appropriately.

The `DefaultIcon` directive specifies the icon to use when none of the patterns match a given file when the directory index is generated:

```
DefaultIcon /icons/unknown.gif
```

It's possible to add text to the top and the bottom of the directory index listing. This capability is very useful as it turns the directory indexing capabilities from just a UNIX-like interface into a dynamic document interface. There are two directives to control this—HeaderName and ReadmeName, which specify the file names for the content at the top and bottom of the listing, respectively. These directives are shown as follows in the default srm.conf file:

```
HeaderName HEADER
ReadmeName README
```

When the directory index is being built, Apache will look for HEADER.html. If it finds it, it'll throw the content into the top of the directory index. If it fails to find that file, it'll look for just HEADER. If it finds HEADER, it will presume that the file is plain text and do things such as translate < characters to the < character sequence, and then insert it into the top of the directory index. The same process happens for the file README, except that the resulting text goes into the bottom of the generated directory index.

In many cases, be it for consistency or just plain old security reasons, you'll want to have the directory indexing engine just ignore certain types of files, such as emacs backup files or files beginning with a . (hidden files). The IndexIgnore directive allows you to specify the types of files to ignore when creating a directory index. The default setting is

```
IndexIgnore */.??* *~ *# */HEADER* */README* */RCS
```

This line might look cryptic, but it's basically a space-separated list of patterns. The first pattern matches against any . file that's longer than three characters. This way, the link to the higher-up directory (..) can still work. The second (*~) and third (*#) patterns are common for matching old emacs backup files. The next patterns are to avoid listing the same files used for HeaderName and ReadmeName. The last (*/RCS) is given because many sites use RCS, a software package for revision control maintenance, which stores its extra (rather sensitive) information in RCS directories.

Finally, you get to two very interesting directives for controlling the last set of options regarding directory indexing. The first is AddDescription, which works similarly to AddIcon:

```
AddDescription description filename [filename]...
```

For example,

```
AddDescription "My cat" /private/cat.gif
```

As elsewhere, *filename* can actually be a pattern, so you can have

```
AddDescription "An MPEG Movie Just For You!" *.mpg
```

Finally, you have the granddaddy of all options-setting directives, the smorgasbord of functionality control—IndexOptions. The syntax is simple:

```
IndexOptions option [option]...
```

Table 33.2 lists the available options.

Table 33.2 Available Options for *IndexOptions*

Option	Explanation
FancyIndexing	This option is the same as the separate FancyIndexing directive. (Sorry to confuse everyone, but backward compatibility demands bizarre things sometimes!)
IconsAreLinks	If this option is set, the icon will be clickable as a link to whatever resource the entry it's associated with links to. In other words, the icon becomes part of the hyperlink.
ScanHTMLTitles	When given a listing for an HTML file, the server will open the HTML file and parse it to obtain the value of the <TITLE> field in the HTML document, if it exists. This can put a pretty heavy load on the server, because it's a lot of disk accessing and some amount of CPU to extract the title from the HTML. Thus, it's not recommended unless you know you have the capacity.
SuppressDescription, SuppressLastModified, SuppressSize	These will suppress their respective fields (Description, Last Modified, and Size). Normally, each of those is a field in the output listings.

By default, none of these IndexOptions are turned on. The options don't *merge*, which means that when you're setting these on a per-directory basis by using access.conf or .htaccess files, setting the options for a more specific directory requires resetting the complete options listing. For example, envision the following in your access configuration file:

```
<Directory /pub/docs/>
IndexOptions ScanHTMLTitles
</Directory>
<Directory /pub/docs/others/>
IndexOptions IconsAreLinks
</Directory>
```

Directory listings done in or below the second directory, /pub/docs/others/, wouldn't have ScanHTMLTitles set. Why? Well, you figured administrators would need to be able to disable an option they had set globally in a specific directory. This was simpler than writing NOT logic into the options listings.

If you run into problems getting directory indexing to work, make sure that the settings you have for the Options directive in the access config files allow for directory indexing in that directory. Specifically, the Options directive must include Indexing. What's more, if you're using .htaccess files to set things such as AddDescription or AddIcon, the AllowOverride directive must include FileInfo in its list of options.

User Directories

Sites with many users sometimes prefer to be able to give their users access to managing their own parts of the Web tree in their own directories, using the URL semantics of

```
http://myhost.com/~user/
```

Part VII

Ch

33

where ˜user is actually an alias to a directory in the user's home directory. This is different from the Alias directive, which could map only a particular pseudo-directory into an actual directory. In this case, you want ˜user to map to something like /home/user/public_html. Because the number of "users" can be very high, some sort of macro is useful here. That macro is the UserDir directive.

With UserDir, you specify the subdirectory within the users' home directory where they can put content, which is mapped to the ˜user URL. So in other words, the default

```
UserDir public_html
```

will cause a request for

```
http://myhost.com/~dave/index.html
```

to cause a lookup for the UNIX file

```
/home/dave/public_html/index.html
```

presuming that /home/dave is Dave's home directory.

Special Modules

Most of the functionality that distinguishes Apache from the competition has been implemented as modules to the Apache API. This has been extremely useful in allowing functionality to evolve separately from the rest of the server, and for allowing for performance tuning. The following sections cover that extra functionality in detail.

Server-Side Includes

Server-side includes are best described as a preprocessing language for HTML. The "processing" takes place on the server side. As such, visitors to your site never need to know that you use server-side includes, and thus requires no special client software. The format of these includes looks something like the following:

```
<!--#directive attribute="value" -->
```

Sometimes a given "directive" can have more than one attribute at the same time. The funky syntax is due to the desire to hide this functionality within an SGML comment—that way, your regular HTML validation tools will work without having to learn new tags or anything. The syntax is important; leaving off the final --, for example, will result in errors.

#include   The #include directive is probably the most commonly used. You use it to insert another file into the HTML document. The allowed attributes for #include are virtual and file. The functionality of the file attribute is a subset of that provided by the virtual attribute, and it exists mostly for backward compatibility, so its use isn't recommended.

The virtual attribute tells the server to treat the value of the attribute as a request for a relative link—meaning that you can use ../ to locate objects above the directory and that other transformations, such as Alias, will apply. For example,

```
<!--#include virtual="quote.txt" -->
<!--#include virtual="/toolbar/footer.html" -->
<!--#include virtual="../footer.html" -->
```

#exec The #exec directive is used to run a script on the server side and insert its output into the SSI (server-side includes) document being processed. There are two choices: executing a CGI script by using the cgi attribute, or executing a shell command by using the cmd attribute. For example,

```
<!--#exec cgi="counter.cgi" -->
```

takes the output of the CGI program counter.cgi and inserts it into the document.

> **N O T E** The CGI output still has to include the "text/html" content-type header; otherwise, an error will occur. ▉

Likewise,

```
<!--#exec cmd="ls -l" -->
```

takes the output of a call to ls -l in the document's directory and inserts it into the output page as a replacement for the #exec command. Like the file attribute for the #include directive, this type of #exec command is mostly for backward compatibility, because it's something of a security hole in an untrusted environment.

> **N O T E** There are definitely security concerns with allowing users access to CGI functionality and even greater concerns with #exec cmd, such as
>
> cmd="cat /etc/passwd"
>
> If a site administrator wants to let users use server-side includes but not use the #exec directive, he or she can set IncludesNOEXEC as an option for the directory in the access configurations. ▉

#echo The #echo directive has one attribute—var—whose value is any CGI environment variable as well as a small list of other variables, as shown in Table 33.3.

Table 33.3 Values for the *var* Attribute

Attribute	Definition
DATE_GMT	The current date in Greenwich Mean Time.
DATE_LOCAL	The current date in the local time zone.
DOCUMENT_NAME	The file system name of the SSI document, not including the directories below it.
DOCUMENT_URI	URI stands for *Uniform Resource Identifier*. In a Uniform Resource Locator (URL) of the format http://*host/path/file*, the URI is the /*path/file* part.
LAST_MODIFIED	The date the SSI document was modified.

Part

VII

Ch

33

For example,

```
<!--#echo var="DATE_LOCAL" -->
```

inserts something along the lines of Wednesday, 05-Mar-97 10:44:54 GMT into the document.

#fsize, #flastmod   The #fsize and #flastmod directives print out the size and the last-modified date, respectively, of any object given by the URI listed in the file or virtual attribute, as in the #include directive. For example,

```
<!--#fsize file="index.html" -->
```

returns the size of the index.html file in that directory.

#config   You can modify the rendering of certain SSI directives by using the #config directive. The sizefmt attribute controls the rendering of the #fsize directive with values of bytes or abbrev. The exact number of bytes is printed when bytes is given, whereas an abbreviated version of the size (in K for kilobytes or M for megabytes) is given when abbrev (the default) is set. For example, a snippet of SSI HTML like

```
<!--#config sizefmt="bytes" -->
The index.html file is <!--#fsize virtual="index.html" --> bytes
```

returns The index.html file is 4,522 bytes. Meanwhile,

```
<!--#config sizefmt="abbrev" -->
```

returns The index.html file is 4K bytes.

The timefmt directive controls the rendering of the date in the DATE_LOCAL, DATE_GMT, and LAST_MODIFIED values for the #echo directive. It uses the same format as the strftime call. (In fact, the server does call strftime, a system call that formats the time in a string of specified length.) The string format consists of variables that begin with %. For example, %H is the hour of the day, in 24-hour format. For directions on how to construct a strftime-format date string, consult strftime's man page for a list of variables.

An example might be

```
<!--#config timefmt="%Y/%m/%d-%H:%M:%S" -->
```

with the resulting date string for Jan. 2, 1997, at 12:30 in the afternoon as

```
1997/01/02-12:30:00
```

Finally, the last attribute the #config directive can take is errmsg, which is simply the error to print out if there are any problems parsing the document. For example, the right default is

```
<!--#config errmsg="An error occurred while processing this directive" -->
```

Internal Imagemap Capabilities

The default imagemap module supplied with Apache allows you to reference imagemaps without using or needing any CGI programs. (An *imagemap* is a graphical image with defined selectable regions.) This functionality is contained in the mod_imap module. First, you add to your srm.conf file yet another `AddType` directive:

```
AddType application/x-httpd-imap map
```

This now means that any file ending with .map will be recognized as an imagemap file. After restarting the server to pick up the change, you can make reference to a .map file directly.

For example, the following document, index.html, has an imagemap on it, where the image is usa.jpg and the mapfile is usa-map.map. The HTML to build that imagemap would look like this:

```
<A HREF="usa-map.map"><IMG SRC="usa.jpg" ISMAP></A>
```

Cookies

HTTP *cookies* are a method for maintaining statefulness in a stateless protocol. What does this mean? In HTTP, a session between a client and a server typically spans many separate actual TCP connections, thus making it difficult to tie together accesses into an application that requires state, such as a shopping-cart application. Cookies are a solution to that problem. As implemented by Netscape in its browser and subsequently by many others, servers can assign clients a cookie, meaning some sort of opaque string whose meaning is significant only to the server itself, and then the client can give that cookie back to the server on subsequent requests.

The mod_cookies module nicely handles the details of assigning unique cookies to every visitor, based on the visitor's host name and a random number. This cookie can be accessed from the CGI environment as the `HTTP_COOKIE` environment variable, for the same reason that all HTTP headers are accessible to CGI applications. The CGI scripts can use this as a key in a session-tracking database, or it can be logged and tallied up to get a good, if undercounted, estimate of the total number of users that visited a site, not just the number of hits or even number of unique domains.

Happily, there are no configuration issues here. Simply compile with mod_cookies and away you go. It couldn't be easier.

Configurable Logging

For most folks, the default logfile format (also known as *Common Logfile Format*, or CLF) doesn't provide enough information when it comes to doing a serious analysis of the efficacy of your Web site. It provides basic numbers in terms of raw hits, pages accessed, hosts accessing, timestamps, and so forth, but it fails to capture the "referring" URL, the browser being used, and any cookies being used. So there are two ways to get more data for your logfiles: by using the NCSA-compatibility directives for logging certain bits of information to separate browsers, or by using Apache's own totally configurable logfile format.

NCSA Compatibility   For compatibility with the NCSA 1.4 Web server, two modules were added. These modules log the `User-Agent` and `Referer` headers from the HTTP request stream.

User-Agent is the header most browsers send that identifies what software the browser is using. Logging of this header can be activated by an AgentLog directive in the srm.conf file, or in a virtual-host-specific section. This directive takes one argument, the name of the file to which the user-agents are logged—for example,

```
AgentLog logs/agent_log
```

To use the AgentLog directive, you need to ensure that the mod_log_agent module has been compiled and linked to the server.

Similarly, the Referer header is sent by the browser to indicate the tail end of a link. In other words, when you're on a page with an URL of "A," and there's a link on that page with an URL of "B," and you follow that link, the request for page "B" includes a Referer header with the URL of "A." This is very useful for finding what sites link to your site, and what proportion of traffic they account for.

The logging of the Referer header is activated by a RefererLog directive, which points to the file to which the referers get logged:

```
RefererLog logs/referer_log
```

One other option the Referer logging module provides is RefererIgnore, a directive that allows you to ignore Referer headers. RefererIgnore is useful for weeding out the referers from your own site, if all you're interested in is links to you from other sites. For example, if your site is www.myhost.com, you might want to use the following:

```
RefererIgnore www.myhost.com
```

Remember that logging of the Referer header requires compiling and linking in mod_log_referer.

Totally Configurable Logging The previous modules were provided, like many Apache features, for backward compatibility. They have some problems, though. Because they don't contain any other information about the request they're logging from, it's nearly impossible to tell which Referer fields went to which specific objects on your site. Ideally, all the information about a transaction with the server can be logged into one file, extending the common logfile format or replacing it altogether. Well, such a beast exists in the mod_log_config module.

The mod_log_config module implements the LogFormat directive, which takes as its argument a string, with variables beginning with % to indicate different pieces of data from the request. Table 33.4 lists the variables.

Table 33.4 Variables for the *LogFormat* Directive

Variable	Definition
%h	Remote host.
%l	Remote identification via identd.
%u	Remote user, as determined by any user authentication that may take place. If the user wasn't authenticated and the status of the request is a 401 (authorization error), this field may be bogus.

Variable	Definition
%t	Common logfile format for time.
%r	First line of request.
%s	Status. For requests that are internally redirected, this is the status of the original request; %>s will give the last.
%b	Bytes sent.
%{Foobar}i	Contents of Foobar: header line(s) in the request from the client to the server.
%{Foobar}o	Contents of Foobar: header line(s) in the response from the server to the client.

For example, if you want to capture in your log just the remote host name, the object requested, and the timestamp, you would use the following:

```
LogFormat "%h \"%r\" %t"
```

And that would log things that looked like

```
host.outsider.com "GET / HTTP/1.0" [06/Mar/1996:10:15:17]
```

You Can Quote Me on This

You really have to use quotation marks around the request variable. The configurable logging module will automatically interpret the values of the variables, rather than just read the variable name. Use a slash-quote, \", to indicate that you want an actual quote character rather than the end of the string. For example, if you want to add logging of the User-Agent string, your log format would become

```
LogFormat "%h \"%r\" %t \"%{User-Agent}i\""
```

Because the User-Agent field typically has spaces in it, it too should be quoted. Suppose that you want to capture the Referer field:

```
LogFormat "%h \"%r\" %t %{Referer}i"
```

You don't need the escaping quotation marks because Referer headers, as URLs, don't have spaces in them. However, if you're building a mission-critical application, you may as well quote it also, because the Referer header is supplied by the client and, thus, there are no guarantees about its format.

The default logfile format is the Common Logfile Format (CLF), which is expressed as

```
LogFormat "%h %l %u %t \"%r\" %s %b"
```

In fact, most existing logfile analysis tools for CLF will ignore extra fields tacked onto the end. To capture the most important extra information and yet still be parsable by those tools, you might want to use this format:

```
LogFormat "%h %l %u %t \"%r\" %s %b %{Referer}i \"%{User-Agent}i\""
```

T I P If you want even more control over what gets logged, you can use the configurable logging module to implement a simple conditional test for variables. This way, you can configure it to log variables only when a particular status code is—or isn't—returned. The format for trapping a status code is to insert a comma-separate list of those codes between the % and the letter of the variable:

`%404,403{Referer}i`

This example means that the Referer header will be logged only if the status returned by the server is a `404 Not Found` or a `403 Access Denied`. All other times just a – is logged. Having only 403 or 404 errors logged would be useful if all you cared about using `Referer` for was to find old links that point to resources no longer available.

The negation of the `Referer` status code is to put a ! at the beginning of the list of status codes. For example,

`%!401u`

logs the user in any user authentication transaction, unless the authentication failed, in which case you probably don't want to see the name of the bogus user anyway.

Remember that, like many functions, logging functions can be configured per virtual host. Thus, if you want all logs from all virtual hosts on the same server to go to the same log, you might want to do something like

`LogFormat "hosta ...."`

in the `<VirtualHost>` sections for hosta and

`LogFormat "hostb ...."`

in the `<VirtualHost>` sections for hostb. More details about virtual hosts appear later in the section "Virtual Hosts."

N O T E You have to compile in mod_log_config in order to configure logging on a "per-virtual-host" basis. You must also make sure that the default logging module, mod_log_common, isn't compiled in; otherwise, the server will get confused. ■

Content Negotiation

Content negotiation is the mechanism by which a Web client can express to the server what data types it knows how to render and, based on that information, the server can give the client the "optimal" version of the resource requested. Content negotiation can happen on a number of different characteristics—the content type of the data (also called the *media type*), the human language the data is in (such as English or French), the character set of the document, and its encodings.

Content-Type Negotiation   If you want to use JPEG images inline on your pages but don't want to alienate users with browsers that can't handle inline JPEG images, you also can make a GIF version of that image. Although the GIF file might be larger or only 8-bit, that's still better than giving the browser something it can't handle, causing a broken link. So, the browser and the server *negotiate* for which data format the server sends to the client.

The specifications for content negotiation have been a part of HTTP since the beginning. Unfortunately, it can't be relied on as extensively as you'd like. For example, current browsers that implement plug-ins by and large don't express in the connection headers which media types they have plug-ins for. Thus, content negotiation currently can't be used to decide whether to send someone a ShockWave file or its Java equivalent. The only safe place to use content negotiation now is to distinguish between inline JPEG or GIF images on a page. Enough browsers in use today implement content negotiation closely enough to get this functionality.

The mod_negotiation.c file in Apache 1.0 implements the content-negotiation specifications in an older version of the HTTP/1.0 IETF draft, which at this writing is on its way to RFC status. Content negotiation was removed because the specification wasn't entirely complete. Content negotiation is getting significantly enhanced for HTTP/1.1. However, this doesn't mean it can't be safely used now for inline image selection.

To activate content negotiation, you must include the mod_negotiation.c module into the server. There are actually two ways to configure content negotiation:

- Using a type-map file describing all the variants of a negotiable resource with specific preference values and content characteristics
- Setting an `Options` value called `MultiViews`

Because your focus is pragmatic, you'll go only into the `MultiViews` functionality. If you're interested in the type-map functionality, the Apache Web site has documentation on it.

In your access.conf file, find the line that sets the options for the part of the site for which you want to enable content negotiation. (You can also set content negotiation for the whole site.) If `MultiViews` isn't present in that line, it must be. Ironically enough, the `All` value doesn't include `MultiViews`. This is again for backward compatibility. So, you might have a line that looks like

```
Options Indexes Includes Multiviews
```

or

```
Options All MultiViews
```

When the `MultiViews` parameter is changed, you need to restart your server to implement the new configuration.

With `MultiViews` turned on, you can do the following: place a JPEG image in a directory, such as /path/, and call it image.jpg. Now, make an equivalent GIF format image and place it in the same /path/ directory as image.gif. The URLs for these two objects are

```
http://host/path/image.jpg
```

and

```
http://host/path/image.gif
```

respectively. Now, if you ask your Web browser to fetch

```
http://host/path/image
```

the server will go into the /path/ directory, see the two image files, and then determine which image format to send based on what the client says it can support. In the case where the client says it can accept JPEG or GIF images equally, the server will choose the version of the image that's smaller, and send that to the client. Usually, JPEG images are much smaller than GIF images.

So if you made your HTML look something like the following,

```
<HTML><HEAD>
<TITLE>Welcome to the Gizmo Home Page!</TITLE>
</HEAD><BODY>
<IMG SRC="/header" ALT="GIZMO Logo">
Welcome to Gizmo!
<IMG SRC="/products" ALT="Products">
<IMG SRC="/services" ALT="Services">
```

you can have separate GIF and JPEG files for header, products, and services. The clients will, for the most part, get what they claim they can support.

N O T E   If you have a file named image and a file named image.gif, the file named image will be requested if a request is made for image. Likewise, a request specifically for image.gif would never return image.jpg, even if the client knew how to render JPEG images. ▤

Human-Language Negotiation   If MultiViews is enabled, you can also distinguish resources by the language they're in, such as French, English, and Japanese. This is done by adding more entries to the file suffix name space, which map to the languages the server wants to use, and then by giving them a ranking in which ties can be broken. Specifically, in the srm.conf file, add two new directives—AddLanguage and LanguagePriority. The formats are as follows:

```
AddLanguage en .en
AddLanguage it .it
AddLanguage fr .fr
AddLanguage jp .jp
LanguagePriority en fr jp it
```

Suppose that you want to negotiate the language on the file index.html, which you have available in English, French, Italian, and Japanese. You would create index.html.en, index.html.fr, index.html.it, and index.html.jp, respectively, and then reference the document as index.html. When a multilingual client connects, it should indicate in one of the request headers (specifically, Accept-Language) which languages it prefers, and the browser expresses that in standard two-letter notation. The server sees what the clients can accept and gives them "the best one." LanguagePriority is what organizes that decision of "the best one." If English is unacceptable to the client, try French; otherwise, try Japanese; otherwise, try Italian. LanguagePriority also states which one should be served if there's no Accept-Language header.

Because the language-mapping suffixes and the content-type suffixes share the same name space, you can mix them around. index.fr.html is the same as index.html.fr. Just make sure that you reference it with the correct negotiable resource.

As-Is Files

Often, you want to use headers in your documents, such as Expires:, but don't want to make the page a CGI script. The easiest way is to add the httpd/send-as-is MIME type to the srm.conf file.

```
AddType httpd/send-as-is asis
```

This means that any file that ends in .asis can include its own MIME headers. However, it must include two carriage returns before the actual body of the content. Actually, it should include two carriage-return/line-feed combinations, but Apache is forgiving and will insert the line feed for you. So if you want to send a document with a special custom MIME type that you don't want registered with the server, you can send

```
Content-type: text/foobar

This is text in a very special "foobar" MIME type.
```

The most significant application I've run across for this is as an extremely efficient mechanism for doing *server-push* (inline graphic animation) objects without CGI scripts. The reason a CGI script is needed to create a server-push usually is that the content type usually includes the multipart separator (because a server-push is actually a MIME multipart message). In the following examples, XXXXXXX indicates the boundary between the parts of the multipart message:

```
Content-type: multipart/x-mixed-replace;boundary=XXXXXXXX

--XXXXXXXX
Content-type: image/gif

....(GIF data)....
--XXXXXXXX
Content-type: image/gif

....(GIF data)....
--XXXXXXXX
....
```

By making a stream of data a simple file with the .asis parameter in the AddType directive instead of with a CGI script, you potentially save yourself a lot of overhead. Just about the only thing you lose is the capability to do timed pushes. For many people, slow Internet connection acts as a sufficient time valve.

If you have MultiViews turned on, you can add .asis to the end of a file name, and none of your links need to be renamed. For example, foobar.html can easily become foobar.html.asis, yet you can still call it foobar.html.

One last compelling application of "asis" is being able to do HTTP redirection without needing access to server config files. For example, the following .asis file will redirect people to another location:

```
Status 302 Moved
Location: http://some.other.place.com/path/
Content-type: text/html

<HTML>
<HEAD><TITLE>We've Moved!</TITLE></HEAD>
<BODY>
<H1>We used to be here, but now we're
<A HREF="http://some.other.place.com/path/">over there. </A>
</H1>
</BODY></HTML>
```

The HTML body is there simply for clients who don't understand the 302 response.

Advanced Functionality

You may want to exert even more control over your server or customize the operating environment in very specific ways. You can configure the Apache server to support advanced functionality, such as access control and user authentication.

Host-Based Access Control

You can control access to the server, or even a subdirectory of the server, based on the host name, domain, or IP number of the client's machine. This is done by using the directives `allow` and `deny`, which can be used together with `order`. `allow` and `deny` can take multiple hosts:

```
deny from badguys.com otherbadguys.com
```

Typically, you want to do one of two things: you want to deny access to your server from everyone but a few other machines, or you want to grant access to everyone except a few hosts. Denying access from all but a few machines is handled as follows:

```
order deny,allow
allow from mydomain.com
deny from all
```

This directive means, "Only grant access to hosts in the domain mydomain.com." This domain could include host1.mydomain.com, ppp.mydomain.com, and the-boss.mydomain.com.

The preceding directive tells the server to evaluate the `deny` conditions before the `allow` conditions when determining whether to grant access. Likewise, the "only exclude a couple of sites" case described earlier can be handled by using

```
order allow,deny
allow from all
deny from badguys.com
```

`order` is needed because—again—the server needs to know which rule to apply first. The default for `order` is `deny,allow`.

In a third argument to order, called mutual-failure, a condition has to pass the allow and deny rules to succeed. In other words, it has to appear in the allow list, and it must not appear in the deny list. For example,

```
order mutual-failure
allow from mydomain.com
deny from the-boss.mydomain.com
```

In this example, the-boss.mydomain.com is prevented from accessing this resource, but every other machine at mydomain.com can access it.

CAUTION

Protecting resources by host name is dangerous. It's relatively easy for a determined person who controls the reverse-DNS mapping for his IP number to spoof any host name he wants. Thus, it's strongly recommended that you use IP numbers to protect anything sensitive. In the same way, you can simply list the domain name to refer to any machine in that domain. You also can give fragments of IP numbers:

```
allow from 204.62.129
```

This will allow only hosts whose IP numbers match, such as 204.62.129.1 or 204.62.129.130.

Typically, these directives are used within a <Limit> container, and even that within a <Directory> container, usually in an access.conf configuration file. The following example is a good template for most protections; it protects the /www/htdocs/private directory from any host except those in the 204.62.129 IP space:

```
<Directory /www/htdocs/private>
Options Includes
AllowOverride None
<Limit GET POST>
order allow,deny
deny from all
allow from 204.62.129
</Limit>
</Directory>
```

User Authentication

When you place a resource under *user authentication*, you restrict access to it by requiring a name and password. This name and password is kept in a database on the server. This database can take many forms; Apache modules have been written to access flat-file databases, database management (DBM) file databases, mSQL databases (a freeware database), Oracle and Sybase databases, and more. This chapter covers only flat-file and DBM-format databases.

First, some basic configuration directives. The AuthName directive sets the authentication "realm" for the password-protected pages. The realm is what gets presented to clients when prompted for authentication, as in Please enter your name and password for the realm.

The `AuthType` directive sets the authentication type for the area. In HTTP/1.0, there's only one authentication type—Basic. HTTP/1.1 will have a few more, such as MD5.

The `AuthUserFile` directive specifies the file that contains a list of names and passwords, one pair per line. The passwords are encrypted by simple UNIX `crypt()` routines. For example,

```
joe:D.W2yvlfjaJoo
mark:21slfoUYGksIe
```

The `AuthGroupFile` directive specifies the file that contains a list of groups and members of those groups, separated by spaces. For example,

```
managers: joe mark
production: mark shelley paul
```

Finally, the `require` directive specifies what conditions need to be met for access to be granted. It can list only specified users who may connect, specify a group or list of groups of users who may connect, or say any valid user in the database is automatically granted access. For example,

```
require user mark paul
  (Only mark and paul may access.)

require group managers
  (Only people in group managers may access.)

require valid-user
  (Anyone in the AuthUserFile database may access.)
```

The configuration file ends up looking something like this:

```
<Directory /www/htdocs/protected/>
AuthName Protected
AuthType basic
AuthUserFile /usr/local/etc/httpd/conf/users
<Limit GET POST>
require valid-user
</Limit>
</Directory>
```

If you want to protect a directory to a particular group, the configuration file looks something like the following:

```
<Directory /www/htdocs/protected/>
AuthName Protected
AuthType basic
AuthUserFile /usr/local/etc/httpd/conf/users
AuthGroupFile /usr/local/etc/httpd/conf/group
<Limit GET POST>
require group managers
</Limit>
</Directory>
```

Database Management File Authentication

You also can configure Apache to use DBM files for faster password and group-membership lookups. To use a DBM file, you must have the mod_auth_dbm module compiled into the server.

DBM files are UNIX file types that implement a fast hash table lookup, making them ideal for handling large user/password databases. The flat-file systems require parsing the password file for every access until a match is found, potentially going through the entire file before returning a "can't find that user" error. Hash tables, on the other hand, know instantly whether a "key" exists in the database, and what its value is.

Some systems use the ndbm libraries; some use the berkeley db libraries. However, the interface through Apache is exactly the same.

To use a DBM file for the database rather than a regular flat file, you use a different directive—AuthDBMUserFile—instead of AuthUserFile. Likewise, for the group file, AuthDBMGroupFile is used instead of AuthGroupFile.

Part
VII

Ch
33

Virtual Hosts

Apache implements a very clean way of handling *virtual hosts*, which is the mechanism for being able to serve more than one host on a particular machine. Due to a limitation in HTTP, serving multiple hosts is now accomplished by assigning more than one IP number to a machine, and then having Apache bind differently to those different IP numbers. For example, a UNIX box might have 204.122.133.1, 204.122.133.2, and 204.122.133.3 pointing to it, with www.host1.com bound to the first, www.host2.com bound to the second, and www.host3.com bound to the third.

T I P Apache 1.2, via the HTTP 1.1 protocol specification, supports non-IP based virtual hosts as well. With this new feature, you no longer have to provide an IP address for each virtual host.

Virtual hosts are configured by using a container in httpd.conf. They look something like this:

```
<VirtualHost www.host1.com>
DocumentRoot /www/htdocs/host1/
TransferLog logs/access.host1
ErrorLog logs/error.host1
</VirtualHost>
```

The attribute in the VirtualHost tag is the host name, which the server looks up to get an IP address.

N O T E If there's any chance that www.host1.com can return more than one number, or that the Web server might have trouble resolving the host name to an IP number at any point, you might want to use the IP number instead. ■

Any directives put within the `VirtualHost` container pertain only to requests made to that host name. `DocumentRoot` points to a directory that presumably contains content specifically for www.host1.com.

Each virtual host can have its own access log, its own error log, its own derivative of the other logs out there, its own `Redirect` and `Alias` directives, its own `ServerName` and `ServerAdmin` directives, and more. In fact, the only things a virtual host server can't support out of the core set of directives are

ServerType	MaxRequestsPerChild
UserId	BindAddress
GroupId	PidFile
StartServers	TypesConfig
MaxSpareServers	ServerRoot
MinSpareServers	

If you plan to run Apache with a large number of virtual hosts, you need to be careful to watch the process limits. For example, some UNIX platforms allow processes to open only 64 file descriptors at once. Because an Apache child will consume one file descriptor per logfile per virtual host, 32 virtual hosts—each with its own transfer and error log—would quickly cross that process limit. You'll notice when you're running into problems of this kind if your error logs start reporting such errors as `unable to fork()`, or your access logs aren't getting written to at all. Apache does try to call `setrlimit()` (a system function call to try to limit processes) to handle this problem on its own, but the system sometimes prevents it from making the system call successfully.

Customized Error Messages

Apache can give customized responses in the event of an error. This is controlled by using the `ErrorDocument` directive. The syntax is

`ErrorDocument HTTP_response_code action`

`HTTP_response_code` is the event that triggers the `action`. The `action` can be

- A local URI to which the server is internally redirected
- An external URL to which the client is redirected
- A text string that starts with a `"` character, and where the `%s` variable contains any extra information, if available

For example,

```
ErrorDocument 500 "Ack! We have a problem here: %s.
ErrorDocument 500 /errors/500.cgi
ErrorDocument 500 http://backup.myhost.com/
ErrorDocument 401 /subscribe.html
ErrorDocument 404 /debug/record-broken-links.cgi
```

Two extra CGI variables are passed to any redirected resource: REDIRECT_URL contains the original URL requested, and REDIRECT_STATUS gives the original status that caused the redirection. This will help the script if its job is to try to figure out what caused the error response.

Assorted httpd.conf Settings

A few additional configuration options just don't fit in anywhere else, because their functionality is a bit unique or different. These options include BindAddress, PidFile, and Timeout.

BindAddress   At startup, Apache binds to the port that it's specified to bind to for all IP numbers that the box has available. The BindAddress directive can be used to specify only a specific IP address to bind to. By using this specific address, you can run multiple copies of Apache, each serving different virtual hosts, rather than have one daemon handle all virtual hosts. This is useful if you want to run two Web servers with different system user IDs, for security and access control reasons.

Suppose that you have three IP addresses: 1.1.1.1, 1.1.1.2, and 1.1.1.3, with 1.1.1.1 being the primary address for the machine. You want to run three Web servers, but want one of them to run as a different user ID than the other two. You'd have two sets of configuration files; the first configuration file would say something like

```
User web3
BindAddress 1.1.1.3
ServerName www.company3.com
DocumentRoot /www/company3/
```

The other configuration file would have

```
User web1
ServerName www.company1.com
DocumentRoot /www/company1/
<VirtualHost 1.1.1.2>
ServerName www.company2.com
DocumenbtRoot /www/company2/
</VirtualHost>
```

If you launch the first, it will bind only to IP address 1.1.1.3. The second one, because it has no BindAddress directive, will bind to the port on all IP addresses. So you want to launch a server with the first set of configuration files, and then launch another copy of the server with the second set of configuration files. Two servers essentially would be running on the same machine.

PidFile   PidFile is the location of the file containing the process ID for Apache. This file is useful for being able to automate the shutdown or restart of the Web server. By default, this parameter is logs/httpd.pid. For example, you could shut down the server by saying

```
cat /usr/local/etc/httpd/logs/httpd.pid ¦ xargs kill -15
```

You might want to move this out of the logs directory and into a directory such as /var, but it's not necessary.

Timeout   The `Timeout` directive specifies the amount of time that the server will wait between packets sent before considering the connection "lost." For example, 1200 (the default) means that the server will wait for 20 minutes after sending a packet before it considers the connection dead if no response comes back. Busy servers may want to shorten the time, at the cost of reduced service to low-bandwidth customers.

From Here...

You can learn more about running the Apache Web server in the following chapters:

■ Chapter 32, "Getting Started with Apache," discusses the basics of installing and configuring the Apache Web server.

■ Chapter 34, "Managing an Internet Web Server," shows you how to make your server robust, efficient, automated, and secure.

Managing an Internet Web Server

One of the biggest strengths of the Apache Web server is that it's highly tunable. Just about every feature that imposes any sort of extra server load is an option, which means you can sacrifice features for speed if you need to do so. That said, Apache is designed for speed and efficiency. Even with all of Apache's features, you'll probably swamp a full T1 worth of bandwidth before exhausting the resources of a well-constructed Linux/ Pentium box.

Apache has also been designed to give site administrators control over where to draw the line between security and functionality. For some sites with many internal users, such as an Internet service provider, being able to control the policies toward what functionality can be used where is important. Meanwhile, a Web design shop might want complete flexibility, even if it means that an errant Common Gateway Interface (CGI) script could expose a security hole or do damage. In fact, many people feel that CGI in general is one big security risk, but I'll get to that in a bit. ■

Server child process control

See how you can have Apache effectively manage child processes.

Increasing efficiency

This chapter explains techniques for configuring Apache so that it performs more efficiently.

Logfile rotation

Learn how to configure your system to rotate logfiles for long-term logging.

Security issues

You'll learn about the security aspects of Apache, including how to limit access to specific directories and control CGI scripts.

Controlling Server Child Processes

As described in Chapter 32, "Getting Started with Apache," Apache uses the concept of a *swarm* of semi-persistent daemons, sometimes called *children*, running and answering queries simultaneously. Although the size of that swarm varies, there are limits to how large it can get and how quickly or slowly it can grow. This is critical; one of the main performance problems with older servers that executed a `fork()` system call at every request was that there was no way to control the total number of simultaneous daemons, so when the main memory of a machine would get consumed and start swapping, the machine would just become unusable. This was colloquially called *daemon-spamming*.

▶ **See** "Starting Up Apache," **p. 635**

Other server software lets you specify a fixed number of processes, with the "fork for every request" behavior kicking in if all the children are busy when a new request comes in. This is also not the best model—not only do many people set that fixed number too high (having 30 children running when only five need to be, which can hinder performance), but this model also removed the protection against daemon-spamming.

So, the Apache model is to start out with a certain number of persistent processes, and make sure that you always keep some number (actually, a range somewhere between a minimum and a maximum) of "spare" processes to handle a wave of simultaneous requests. If you have to launch a few more processes to maintain the minimum number of spares, no problem. If you find yourself with more idle servers than your maximum number of spares, the excess idle ones can be killed. There's a maximum number of processes, beyond which no more will be launched, to protect the machine against daemon-spamming.

The algorithm to protect against too many processes bogging down or killing a server is configured by using the following configuration directives:

```
StartServers   10
MinSpareServers 5
MaxSpareServers 10
MaxClients    150
```

These numbers are the defaults. This says that when Apache launches, 10 children (`StartServers`) are automatically launched, regardless of the request load at start. If all 10 children are swamped, more are forked until all requests can be answered as fast as they're received. This requires at least five (`MinSpareServers`) but not more than 10 (`MaxSpareServers`) free servers to deal with *spikes* in requests (that is, when a sudden burst of requests comes in well within half a second of each other). Incidentally, these spikes are often caused by browsers that open a separate TCP connection for each inline image in a page in an attempt to improve perceived performance to the user, often at the expense of the server and network.

Usually a stable number of simultaneous child processes is reached, but if the requests are just pouring in (you've installed the Pamela Anderson Fan Club page on your site, for example), you might reach the `MaxClients` limit. At that point, requests will queue into your kernel's "listen" queue, waiting to get served. If still more pour in, your visitors will eventually see a "connections refused" message. However, this is still preferable to leaving the number of simultaneous processes unlimited, because the server would just launch children with wild abandon and start daemon-spamming, resulting in nobody getting any response from the server at all.

It's recommended that you don't adjust MaxClients, because 150 is a good number for most systems. However, you might be itching to see how many requests you can handle with that multiprocessor Sun Netra j 2/1200 with a gigabyte of RAM; in that case, setting MaxClients much higher makes sense. On the opposite end of the spectrum, you might be running the Web server on a machine with limited memory or CPU resources, and you might want to make sure that Apache doesn't consume all resources at the cost of possibly not being able to serve all requests that come to your site. In that context, setting MaxClients lower makes sense.

Using the Scoreboard File

Because the multiprocess model described in the preceding section required some decent communication between the parent and child processes, the most cross-platform method of performing that communication was chosen. This is a *scoreboard file*, where each child had a chunk of space in the file to which it was authorized to write. The parent httpd process watched that file to get a status report and make decisions about whether to launch more child processes or kill idle processes.

At first, this file was located in the /tmp directory. However, because of problems with Linux setups that regularly clear out /tmp directories (causing the server to go haywire), the scoreboard file has since been moved into the /var/log/ directory. You can configure where the scoreboard file goes exactly with a ScoreBoardFile directive.

A program called httpd_monitor, in the support/ subdirectory in the Apache distribution, can be run against the scoreboard file to give a picture of the state of all the child processes and whether they're just starting, active, sleeping, or dead. It can give you a good idea of whether your settings for MaxSpareServers and MinSpareServers are decent. Consider it a close equivalent to the system command iostat.

Increasing Efficiency in the Server Software

You can increase performance over the standard setup in many ways, including smarter ways to configure your resources, features that can be turned off for better performance, and even things at the operating system and hardware level that can be addressed. All these factors make a difference between a regular Web server and a high-performance Web server.

Most non-hardware improvements fall into three categories: those that reduce the load on the CPU, those that reduce the amount of I/O to the disk, and those that reduce the memory requirements.

Part
VII

Ch
34

Using Server-Side Includes

Server-side includes (SSI) are preprocessing HTML statements that can cause an increased disk access load and an increased CPU load. The CPU penalty comes from having to parse the HTML file looking for the includes; parsing a file is more intensive than just reading the file and spitting it out to the socket.

The disk access penalty comes from having to make two, three, four, or more separate disk accesses to pull together the page to get served. For example, a typical SSI document might need a header and footer pulled into memory to get served. That's three disk accesses to pull the document together, instead of one. If the inline HTML files were large, the difference wouldn't be as great. Because the HTML files are usually small, the disk access penalty is relatively large. The problem is compounded by any CGI script that might be included as well; if you had an SSI page with two CGI scripts included, you'd probably get at least twice the performance hit than if you had one CGI script that just rendered the whole page in the first place.

Using .htaccess Files

Apache uses special files, known as .htaccess files, for controlling access to directories. Searching directories for .htaccess files is fairly painful. Because .htaccess files work hierarchically, when a request is made for /path/path2/dir1/dir2/foo, Apache will look for an .htaccess file in *every* subdirectory. In the example of /path/path2/dir1/dir2/foo, that's at least five—a significant disk access load that's best to avoid if possible.

To solve the problem of too many disk hits, you should put anything controlled via your .htaccess files into the access.conf configuration file or even the srm.conf file. If you have to look for .htaccess files in subdirectories and can narrow it down to a specific subdirectory, it's possible to have the server look only for .htaccess files in that subdirectory by the use of `AllowOverride`.

Suppose that your document root is in /www/htdocs, and you want to turn off the searching for all .htaccess files except those in /www/htdocs/dir1/dir2 and everywhere below. You would put something like the following into your access.conf configuration file:

```
<Directory /www/htdocs>
Options All
AllowOverride None
</Directory>
<Directory /www/htdocs/dir1/dir2>
Options All
AllowOverride All
</Directory>
```

It's important that the directories are listed in that order so that the second `<Directory>` doesn't take precedence over the first.

Using .asis Files for Server-Push Animations

.asis files, are distinguished by having their HTTP headers directly embedded in the file itself. They are a useful optimization for certain types of files, such as server-push animations, which demand the capability to set their own headers and are usually dished out by CGI scripts. The usual server-push CGI script has the additional overhead of assembling the images on the fly, whereas with an .asis file, the whole stream can be linked into one file, reducing the I/O hit and the memory and CPU performance situation.

▶ **See** "As-Is Files," **p. 659**

The only thing you lose by using the .asis parameter is the ability to do *timed pushes*, where there's a lapse of time between frames implemented as a `sleep()` (a system call where a program is paused for a defined number of seconds). But because server-push is also bandwidth-limited, many consider the ability to do timed pushes to be a dubious feature.

Automating Logfile Rotation

Certainly one goal for the site administrator should be to automate the rotation of access and error logs. Even a lightly loaded server will generate a couple of megabytes of log activity per day. Left unchecked, your disk space could dry up fast.

The most basic element of logfile rotation is to get the Web server to stop writing to the old log and start writing to another without disrupting service to the outside users. The most straight-forward way to accomplish logfile rotation is by renaming the log just slightly and sending a `SIGHUP` signal to the parent process. *Just slightly* means renaming it to access_log.0 or something similar on the same hard disk, on the same partition. Why? Each child has a file descriptor open to the logfile. When you rename the file, the file descriptor will still point to the same actual log right up until the time the child receives an "echo" of the `SIGHUP` from the parent process. When the `SIGHUP` echo happens, the file descriptor is closed, a new one is obtained, and the new access_log gets created. This is pretty much the only way to guarantee not losing traffic reports while rotating logs.

Here is an example script that performs a logfile rotation:

```
#!/bin/sh
logdir="/usr/local/etc/httpd/logs"    # name of the log directory
acclog="access_log"                   # name of the access log
errlog="error_log"                    # name of the error log
pidfile="$logdir/httpd.pid"           # file that stores the parent's
                                      # process ID

mv $logdir/$acclog $logdir/$acclog.0
mv $logdir/$errlog $logdir/$errlog.0
kill -HUP 'cat $pidfile'
```

The logfile rotation script needs to be run as the same user that launched the HTTP daemon originally—for example, "root." You may want to write additional scripts to place these .0 files into an archive of some sort; my favorite one is to use the year and month as subdirectories,

Part
VII

Ch
34

such that the logs for January 1, 1997, go into a file named 1997/01/01 somewhere off a directory with a lot of room. That way, the log files are easy to archive somewhere else (to DAT tape, to CD-ROM, or even to remove it) by moving a directory.

Understanding Security Issues

The security of your server is, no doubt, one of your biggest concerns as a Web site administrator. Running a Web server is, by nature, a security risk. For that matter, so is plugging your machine into a network at all. However, a lot can be done to make your Web server more secure from external forces (people trying to break into your site) and internal forces (your own Web site users mistakenly or willingly opening up holes).

CGI Issues

The biggest cause for concern about protecting your site from external threats are CGI scripts. Most CGI scripts are shell-based, using Perl or C-shell interpreted programs rather than compiled programs. Thus, many attacks have occurred by exploiting "features" in those shells. This section won't go into too much detail about how to make CGI scripts themselves safe. You should know a couple of important things, however, as an administrator.

A CGI script runs with the user ID of the server child process. In the default case, this is "nobody." To adequately protect yourself, you may want to consider the "nobody" user an untrustworthy user on your site, making sure that this user doesn't have read permission to files you want to keep private and doesn't have write permission anywhere sensitive. Certain CGI scripts—for example, a guestbook application that allows users to record comments about your Web site—will demand write access to certain files. So if you want to enable those types of applications, it's best to specify a directory to which CGI scripts can write without worrying about a malicious or misdirected script overwriting data that it shouldn't.

Furthermore, site administrators can limit the use of CGI to specific directories by using the ScriptAlias directive. Alternatively, if you have turned on .cgi as a file extension for CGI scripts, you can use the Options ExecCGI directive in access.conf to further control the use of CGI files.

As an example of controlling access with ExecCGI, if you want to allow for CGI to be used everywhere on the site (with a document root of /home/htdocs) except for the "users" subdirectory because you don't trust your users with CGI scripts, your access.conf should look something like Listing 34.1.

Listing 34.1   A Sample access.conf File Showing Directory Configuration Information

```
<Directory /home/htdocs/>
Options Indexes FollowSymLinks Includes Multiviews ExecCGI
AllowOverride None
</Directory>
```

```
<Directory /home/htdocs/users/>
Options Indexes SymLinksIfOwnerMatch IncludesNOEXEC Multiviews
AllowOverride None
</Directory>
```

Because `ExecCGI` isn't in the `Options` list for the second directory, no one can use CGI scripts there.

Unfortunately, there really is no middle ground between allowing CGI scripts and disallowing them. Now, most languages used for CGI programs don't have security concepts built into them, so applying rules such as "don't touch the hard disk" or "don't send the /etc/passwd file in e-mail to an outside user" need to be dealt with in the same manner as though you had actual Linux users who needed the same restrictions applied to them. Maybe this will change when Sun's Java language gets more use on the server side, or when people use raw interpreted languages less and higher-level programming tools more often.

Server-Side Includes

As you can see from Listing 34.1, there was another change between the *trusted* part of the server and the *untrusted* part: the `Includes` argument to `Options` was changed to `IncludesNOEXEC`. `IncludesNOEXEC` allows your untrusted users to use server-side includes without allowing the `#include` of CGI scripts or the `#exec` command to be run. The `#exec` command is particularly troublesome in an untrusted environment because it basically gives shell-level access to an HTML author.

Symbolic Links

In an untrusted environment, UNIX *symbolic links* (which enable linking across file-system boundaries) also are a concern for Web site administrators. Malicious users could very easily create symbolic links from directories where they have write permission to an object or resource, even outside the document root, to which all they need is read permission. For example, a user could create a link to the /etc/passwd file and then release that onto the Web, exposing your site to potential crack attempts—particularly if your operating system doesn't use shadow passwords.

> **N O T E** In a recent incident involving the Alta Vista search engine (**www.altavista.digital.com**), a search for words common to password files (*bin*, *root*, *ftp*, and so on) turned up references to actual password files that had, intentionally or not, been left public. These password files included a few with encrypted passwords, which were easy enough to break with a few hours of CPU time on most workstations. ▓

To protect against symbolic link security breaches, the site administrator has two options: to allow only symbolic linking if the owner of the link and the owner of the linked-to resource are the same by using `SymLinksIfOwnerMatch`, or to disallow symbolic links altogether by not specifying `FollowSymLinks` or `SymLinksIfOwnerMatch`.

Part
VII

Ch
34

Also note that both `<Directory>` segments in Listing 34.1 included `AllowOverride None`. Not allowing symbolic links is the most conservative setting; if you want to allow certain things to be tunable in those directories by using .htaccess files, you can specify them with the `AllowOverride` directive. However, stating `None` is the safest policy.

Publicly Writable Spaces

The last security threat that's specific to Web servers is that of allowing publicly writable spaces to be served up via HTTP. For example, many sites allow their FTP "incoming" directory to be accessed via the Web directly. This can be a security hole if someone were to place there a malicious CGI script or a server-side include file that calls `#exec` to do some damage. If you decide you need to take the risk of providing public writable spaces, you can do some things to protect yourself:

■ The most conservative setting you should set for the `Options` directive is

    `Options Indexes`

You could use `None`, but `Indexes` really doesn't introduce any additional security problems, as long as you're comfortable with others being able to download anything that has been submitted. In the light of recent legislation by the U.S. government regarding "indecent" materials, you may not want to take this risk either.

■ Make sure that you set `AllowOverride None` so that people can't upload an .htaccess file into your directory and modify all your settings and security policies.

■ Make sure that the FTP daemon you're using doesn't allow the execute bit to be set. By preventing the execute bit to be set, you prevent the execution of uploaded CGI scripts. If you're using `XBitHack` to activate your server-side includes, you can prevent those includes from being run as well. This is mainly a backup for setting the `Options` as in Listing 34.1, which should protect you against these threats anyway.

These same rules apply if you have CGI scripts that generate their own uniquely addressable HTML or CGI files. For example, if the guestbook.cgi program constantly appends the submitted personal information to a guestbook.html file, all the same rules apply; the contents of that HTML file must be considered unsafe. This possible security breach can be plugged if the CGI script double-checks what's getting written and removes "dangerous" code, such as server-side includes.

From Here...

You can learn more details about setting up, configuring, and running the Apache Web server in the following chapter:

■ Chapter 32, "Getting Started with Apache," provides an introduction to the Apache Web server.

Appendixes

Sources of Information

Because Linux is based on UNIX, almost any UNIX-based
book provides some information on Linux. The best
source for information, however, is the Linux community
itself, which offers everything from updated versions of
Linux to extremely active Usenet newsgroups. Linux also
provides online documents through the Linux Documentation Project (LDP), which is writing a complete set of
manuals for Linux. The most recent editions of this project
are available via the Internet. The entire project is spear-
headed by Matt Welsh, and most of the information is
provided in the /usr/doc/faq directory on your local
drive.

The following listings provide Internet FTP sites, magazines, and newsgroups from which you can gather more
information about Linux. ■

Usenet Newsgroups

If you have access to Usenet newsgroups, you'll enjoy the following newsgroups that provide a variety of information about Linux. Only two, **comp.os.linux.announce** and **comp.os.linux.answers**, are moderated.

▶ **See** "Usenet Culture," **p. 599**

N O T E The original Linux-related newsgroup, **comp.os.linux**, no longer exists, because more specific newsgroups have been created. ▩

- **comp.os.linux.announce** This moderated newsgroup is used for important announcements, such as bug fixes.

- **comp.os.linux.answers** This moderated newsgroup provides answers to any of your Linux questions, especially about setting up Linux. Please read the appropriate Linux documentation and FAQs before posting a question to this group.

- **comp.os.linux.development.system** This newsgroup is devoted to the many programmers around the world who are developing the Linux system.

- **comp.os.linux.development.apps** This newsgroup is devoted to the many programmers around the world who are developing applications for Linux.

- **comp.os.linux.hardware** This newsgroup provides answers to hardware compatibility questions.

- **comp.os.linux.setup** This newsgroup provides help with Linux setup and installation problems.

- **comp.os.linux.advocacy** This newsgroup provides a medium to discuss why Linux is the greatest OS.

- **comp.os.linux.networking** This newsgroup provides answers to networking Linux with the rest of the world.

- **comp.os.linux.x** This newsgroup provides answers to installing and running X under Linux.

- **comp.os.linux.m68k** The purpose of this newsgroup is to promote interest and development of the port of Linux to Motorola's 680x0 architecture.

A newsgroup named **comp.os.linux.misc** serves as a catch-all for any Linux topic not suited to the other newsgroups. Also, more than 170 other Usenet newsgroups contain the word *Linux*. A sample of the more common Linux newsgroups are listed as follows. Go exploring!

alt.linux.sux	**dc.org.linux-users**
alt.os.linux	**de.comp.os.linux.hardware**
alt.uu.comp.os.linux.questions	**de.comp.os.linux.misc**
alt.os.linux.slackware	**de.comp.os.linux.networking**
aus.computers.linux	**de.comp.os.linux.x**

de.alt.sources.linux.patches
uk.comp.os.linux
fj.os.linux
fr.comp.os.linux
han.sys.linux
linux.apps.bbsdev
linux.apps.linux-bbs
linux.apps.seyon
linux.apps.seyon.development
linux.apps.flexfax
linux.debian
linux.debian.announce
linux.debian.user
linux.dev.gcc
linux.dev.680x0
linux.dev.admin
linux.dev.apps
linux.dev.bbs
linux.dev.c-programming
linux.dev.config
linux.dev.debian
linux.dev.doc
linux.dev.fido
linux.dev.fsf
linux.dev.fsstnd
linux.dev.ftp
linux.dev.hams
linux.dev.ibcs2
linux.dev.interviews
linux.dev.japanese
linux.dev.laptop
linux.dev.linuxbsd
linux.dev.linuxnews
linux.dev.linuxss
linux.dev.localbus

linux.dev.lugnuts
linux.dev.mca
linux.dev.mgr
linux.dev.msdos
linux.dev.net
linux.dev.new-lists
linux.dev.newbie
linux.dev.normal
linux.dev.nys
linux.dev.oasg
linux.dev.oi
linux.dev.pkg
linux.dev.ppp
linux.dev.qag
linux.dev.scsi
linux.dev.serial
linux.dev.seyon
linux.dev.sound
linux.dev.standards
linux.dev.svgalib
linux.dev.tape
linux.dev.term
linux.dev.uucp
linux.dev.wabi
linux.dev.word
linux.dev.kernel
linux.dev.x11
linux.fido.ifmail
linux.free-widgets.
announce
linux.free-widgets.bugs
linux.free-widgets.
development
linux.local.chicago
linux.local.nova-scotia

linux.local.silicon-valley	**linux.samba**
linux.motif.clone	**linux.samba.announce**
linux.new-tty	**linux.sdk**
linux.news.groups	**linux.wine.users**
linux.ports.alpha	**linux.test**

Online Documents

Matt Welsh spearheads a dedicated group of Linux enthusiasts who are systematically writing a complete set of Linux manuals that are made available on the Internet. The latest versions of the documentation can be found at **sunsite.unc.edu** in the /pub/Linux/docs directory. You can also find earlier versions of these documents in your version of Linux's /docs directory. Available documents include the following:

- "Linux Installation and Getting Started," by Matt Welsh
- "The Linux System Administrators' Guide," by Lars Wirzenius
- "The Linux Network Administrators' Guide," by Olaf Kirch
- "The Linux Kernel Hackers' Guide," by Michael K. Johnson
- "The Linux Frequently Asked Questions (FAQ) List," maintained by Ian Jackson; it's composed of questions and answers on myriad Linux topics
- "The Linux META-FAQ," maintained by Michael K. Johnson
- "The Linux INFO-SHEET," maintained by Michael K. Johnson
- "The Linux Software Map," maintained by Aaron Schab; information about each of the software packages available for Linux via FTP

Linux HOWTOs

The Linux HOWTO Index provides an index to all the available HOWTO documents. These HOWTO documents provide a detailed explanation of their topic. Some of the titles include

- The Linux Installation HOWTO
- The Linux Hardware HOWTO and The Linux Printing HOWTO

See Appendix B, "The Linux HOWTO Index," for a complete list of Linux HOWTO and mini HOWTO site addresses. These files are located in the /usr/doc/faq/howto directory on your local drive. Most are archived with gzip to save disk space. To read these or other compressed files, use the zless command.

Many FAQs about Linux topics and GNU programs are shipped with Linux and can be found in the /usr/info directory.

man Pages

The Linux operating system itself provides plenty of online help via the man command. To access online help, enter **man** followed by the topic for which you want information.

▶ **See** "Getting Help for Commands with *man*" **p. 126**

Magazines

Linux Journal is currently the only periodical devoted explicitly to Linux. You can request more information about this publication from the following address:

> *Linux Journal*
> P.O. Box 85867
> Seattle, WA 98145
> (206) 527-3385
> **http://www.ssc.com/lj/**

Linux FTP Sites

Linux is a child of the Internet, so naturally the Internet is where you find the greatest amount of up-to-date information regarding Linux. Table A.1 lists the FTP sites that maintain Linux archives. The main archive site, located at the University of North Carolina-Chapel Hill, is named **sunsite.unc.edu**.

Table A.1   FTP Sites with Linux Archives

Site Name	Directory
tsx-11.mit.edu	/pub/linux
sunsite.unc.edu	/pub/Linux
nic.funet.fi	/pub/Linux
ftp.mcc.ac.uk	/pub/linux
ftp.dfv.rwth-aachen.de	/pub/linux
ftp.informatik.rwth-aachen.de	/pub/Linux
ftp.ibp.fr	/pub/linux
kirk.bond.edu.au	/pub/OS/Linux
ftp.uu.net	/systems/unix/linux
wuarchive.wustl.edu	/systems/linux
ftp.win.tue.nl	/pub/linux

continues

Table A.1 Continued	
Site Name	**Directory**
ftp.stack.nl	/pub/Linux
ftp.ibr.cs.tu-bs.de	/pub/os/linux
ftp.denet.dk	/pub/OS/Linux

▶ **See** "Using *ftp* for Remote File Transfer," **p. 540**

Linux Web Sites

Because Linux is a child of the Internet, you find not only FTP sites but also Web sites related to Linux. In fact, Linux is a pretty popular subject on the Web. The URLs in Table A.2 access the major Linux information sites on the Web.

Table A.2 Major Linux Web Sites	
URL	**Description**
http://sunsite.unc.edu/mdw	*The* site for Linux information; the home of the Linux Documentation Project
http://www.Linux.org.uk	The Web site for European Linux users
http://www.li.org	The Linux International Web site
http://www.linux.org	The Linux Organization Web site
http://sunsite.unc.edu/linux-source	The Linux Source Navigator, which allows you to view Linux source code in hypertext
http://www.yahoo.com/Computers_and_Internet/Operating_Systems/Unix/Linux	The Yahoo! site pointing to many current sites

Contacting InfoMagic

InfoMagic produces the CD-ROMs enclosed with this book, and the company is gracious enough to help support the product. If your disc is damaged, please contact Que Publishing at **http://www.quecorp.com**. If you've exhausted the resources above, contact InfoMagic's support at **support@infomagic.com**.

For Linux Developers

So you think that Linux is the greatest thing to come along in quite some time, and you want to help develop future releases. Well, you're in luck. An active set of mailing lists on the Internet is devoted to various topics and issues surrounding Linux development. This is a multichannel mailing list, meaning that messages on different topics are sent to different groups of people. You must subscribe to each channel that you're interested in. If you think you want to get involved in a Linux development project, you can get more information by sending an e-mail message to

App

A

      majordomo@vger.rutgers.edu

with `lists` in the body to get a list of the lists there. Add a line with `help` in the body to get the standard Majordomo help file, which has instructions for subscribing and unsubscribing.

The Linux HOWTO Index

by Greg Hankins, gregh@sunsite.unc.edu
v2.10.7, 13 November 1996.

This document contains an index to the Linux HOWTOs and mini-HOWTOs, as well as other information about the HOWTO project. ■

What Are Linux HOWTOs?

Linux HOWTOs are documents which describe in detail a certain aspect of configuring or using Linux. For example, there is the Installation HOWTO, which gives instructions on installing Linux, and the Mail HOWTO, which describes how to set up and configure mail under Linux. Other HOWTO examples include the NET2 HOWTO and the Printing HOWTO.

HOWTOs are comprehensive documents—much like a FAQ (Frequently Asked Questions) document but generally not in question-and-answer format. However, many HOWTOs contain a FAQ section at the end. There are several HOWTO formats available: plain text, PostScript, DVI, and HTML.

In addition to the HOWTOs, there are a multitude of mini-HOWTOs. These are short, specific HOWTOs, such as the Colour-ls mini-HOWTO. They are only available in plain text format.

Where Do I Get Linux HOWTOs?

HOWTOs can be retrieved via anonymous FTP from the following sites:

- **ftp://sunsite.unc.edu/pub/Linux/docs/HOWTO**
- **ftp://tsx-11.mit.edu/pub/linux/docs/HOWTO**

as well as many mirror sites:

<ftp://sunsite.unc.edu/pub/Linux/MIRRORS.html>

You can also browse HOWTOs in HTML format

<http://sunsite.unc.edu/LDP/HOWTO/>

on the World Wide Web. Many mirror sites **<http://sunsite.unc.edu/LDP/hmirrors.html>** also mirror the HOWTO WWW files. **sunsite.unc.edu** is heavily used, so please use a mirror site if possible.

HOWTOs are also posted monthly to the Usenet newsgroup

comp.os.linux.answers

HOWTO Translations

French translations of the HOWTO documents can be found at

ftp://ftp.ibp.fr/pub/linux/french/docs/HOWTO

Japanese translations can be found at the following locations:

- **http://jf.gee.kyoto-u.ac.jp/JF/index.html** (English)
- **http://jf.gee.kyoto-u.ac.jp/JF/JF.html** (Japanese)
- **ftp://ftp.kuis.kyoto-u.ac.jp/Linux/JF/**
- **ftp://wcarchive.cdrom.com/pub/linux/jf/**

Italian translations are available at:

- **ftp://ftp.unipd.it/pub/Linux/pluto/docs/HOWTO**
- **http://www.psico.unipd.it/ildp/docs/HOWTO/INDEX.html**

Spanish translations are available at:

- **http://lml.ls.fi.upm.es/~jjamor/**
- **ftp://luna.gui.uva.es/pub/docs-esp/**
- **ftp://volcan.us.es**

German translations are available at **http://www.tu-harburg.de/~semb2204/dlhp/**.

If you know of any other translation projects, please let me know and I will add them to this list.

HOWTO Index

The following Linux HOWTOs are currently available: (The JE HOWTO is only available in plain text format. This is because it has still not been converted to the SGML source format.)

- *Linux AX25 HOWTO*, by Terry Dawson <**terry@perf.no.itg.telecom.com.au**>. How to configure AX25 networking for Linux. Updated 14 June 1996.

- *Linux Access HOWTO*, by Michael De La Rue <**access-howto@ed.ac.uk**>. How to use adaptive technology with Linux. Updated 1 August 1996.

- *Linux BootPrompt HOWTO*, by Paul Gortmaker <**Paul.Gortmaker@anu.edu.au**>. List of boot time arguments and overview of booting software. Updated 1 July 1996.

- *Linux Bootdisk HOWTO*, by Graham Chapman <**grahamc@zeta.org.au**>. How to create a boot/root maintenance disk for Linux. Updated 18 August 1996.

- *Linux Busmouse HOWTO*, by Mike Battersby <**mib@deakin.edu.au**>. Information on bus mouse compatibility with Linux. Updated 2 August 1994.

- *Linux CDROM HOWTO*, by Jeff Tranter <**tranter@software.mitel.com**>. Information on CD-ROM drive compatibility for Linux. Updated 8 September 1996.

- *Linux Commercial HOWTO*, by Martin Michlmayr <**tbm@sypher.com**>. Listing of commercial software products for Linux. Updated 9 November, 1996.

- *Linux Consultants HOWTO*, by Martin Michlmayr <**tbm@sypher.com**>. Listing of Linux consultants. Updated 9 November, 1996.

- *Linux Cyrillic HOWTO*, by Alexander L. Belikoff <**abel@wisdom.weizmann.ac.il**>. How to configure Linux for use with the Cyrillic character set. Updated 17 September 1995.

- *Linux DNS HOWTO*, by Nicolai Langfeldt <**janl@math.uio.no**>. How to set up DNS. Updated 30 June 1996.

- *Linux DOSEMU HOWTO*, by Mike Deisher <**deisher@dspsun.eas.asu.edu**>. HOWTO about the Linux MS-DOS Emulator, DOSEMU. Updated 11 August 1995.

- *Linux Danish HOWTO*, by Thomas Petersen <**petersen@post1.tele.dk**>. How to configure Linux for use with the Danish character set. Updated 2 June 1996.

- *Linux Distribution HOWTO*, by Eric S. Raymond <**esr@snark.thyrsus.com**>. A list of Linux distributions. Updated 10 November 1996.

- *Linux ELF HOWTO*, by Daniel Barlow <**daniel.barlow@linux.org**>. How to install and migrate to the ELF binary file format. Updated 14 July 1996.

- *Linux Emacspeak HOWTO*, by Jim Van Zandt <**jrv@vanzandt.mv.com**>. How to use "emacspeak" with Linux. Updated 16 Aug 1996.

- *Linux Ethernet HOWTO*, by Paul Gortmaker <**Paul.Gortmaker@anu.edu.au**>. Information on Ethernet hardware compatibility for Linux. Updated 4 October 1996.

- *Linux Finnish HOWTO*, by Pekka Taipale <**pjt@iki.fi**>. How to configure Linux for use with the Finnish character set. Updated 14 February 1996.

App

B

- *Linux Firewall HOWTO*, by Mark Grennan, <**markg@netplus.net**>. How to set up a firewall using Linux. Updated 8 November 1996.
- *Linux Ftape HOWTO*, by Kevin Johnson <**kjj@primenet.com**>. Information on ftape drive compatibility with Linux. Updated 20 September 1996 for ftape-2.08.
- *Linux GCC HOWTO*, by Daniel Barlow <**daniel.barlow@linux.org**>. How to set up the GNU C compiler and development libraries. Updated 28 February 1996.
- *Linux German HOWTO*, by Winfried Trümper <**winni@xpilot.org**>. Information on using Linux with German-specific features. Updated 20 January 1996.
- *Linux HAM HOWTO*, by Terry Dawson <**terry@perf.no.itg.telecom.com.au**>. HOWTO configure amateur radio software for Linux. Updated 10 October 1996.
- *Linux HOWTO Index*, by Greg Hankins <**gregh@sunsite.unc.edu**>. Index of HOWTO documents about Linux. Updated 13 November 1996.
- *Linux Hardware Compatibility HOWTO*, by Tawei Wan <**frac@pobox.com**>. A list of hardware known to work with Linux. Updated 14 November 1995.
- *Linux Hebrew HOWTO*, by Yair G. Rajwan <**yair@hobbes.jct.ac.il**>. How to configure Linux for use with the Hebrew characterset. Updated 12 September 1995.
- *Linux INFO-SHEET*, by Michael K. Johnson <**johnsonm@redhat.com**>. Generic introduction to the Linux operating system. Updated 31 October 1996.
- *Linux IPX HOWTO*, by Terry Dawson <**terry@perf.no.itg.telecom.com.au**>. How to install and configure IPX networking. Updated 10 October 1996.
- *Linux ISP Hookup HOWTO*, by Egil Kvaleberg <**egilk@sn.no**>. Basic introduction to hooking up to an ISP. Updated 9 March 1996.
- *Linux Installation HOWTO*, by Eric S. Raymond <**esr@snark.thyrsus.com**>. How to obtain and install Linux. Updated 10 November 1996.
- *Linux Italian HOWTO*, by Marco "Gaio" Gaiarin <**gaio@dei.unipd.it**>. How to configure Linux for use with the Italian character set. Updated 0.6 Beta, 2 Agosto 1996.
- *Linux JE HOWTO*, by Hiroo Yamagata <**hiyori13@interramp.com**>. Information on JE, a set of Japanese language extensions for Linux.
- *Linux Java HOWTO*, by Eric S. Raymond <**esr@snark.thyrsus.com**>. How to get started with Java and HotJava.
- *Linux Kernel HOWTO*, by Brian Ward <**ward@blah.tu-graz.ac.at**>. Upgrading and compiling the Linux kernel. Updated 1 August 1996.
- *Linux Keyboard HOWTO*, by Andries Brouwer <**aeb@cwi.nl**>. Information about the Linux keyboard, console and non-ASCII characters. Updated 8 November 1995.
- *Linux META-FAQ*, by Michael K. Johnson <**johnsonm@redhat.com**>. A listing of Linux sources of information. Updated 16 July 1996.
- *Linux MGR HOWTO*, by Vincent Broman <**broman@nosc.mil**>. Information on the MGR graphics interface for Linux. Updated 30 May 1996.

- *Linux Electronic Mail HOWTO*, by Vince Skahan <**vince@halcyon.com**>. Information on Linux-based mail servers and clients. Updated 29 November 1995.

- *Linux Module HOWTO*, by Lauri Tischler <**ltischler@efore.fi**>. How to load modules and a listing of parameters. Updated 20 October 1996.

- *Linux NET-2 HOWTO*, by Terry Dawson <**terry@perf.no.itg.telecom.com.au**>. HOWTO configure TCP/IP networking, SLIP, PLIP, and PPP under Linux. Updated 16 January 1996.

- *Linux NIS HOWTO*, by Erwin Embsen <**erwin@nioz.nl**>. Information on using NIS/YP on Linux systems. Updated 24 January 1995.

- *Linux News HOWTO*, by Vince Skahan <**vince@halcyon.com**>. Information on USENET news server and client software for Linux. Updated 29 November 1995.

- *Linux PCI HOWTO*, by Michael Will <**Michael.Will@student.uni-tuebingen.de**>. Information on PCI-architecture compatibility with Linux. Updated July 1996.

- *Linux PCMCIA HOWTO*, by Dave Hinds <**dhinds@allegro.stanford.edu**>. How to install and use PCMCIA Card Services. Updated 29 September 1996 .

- *Linux PPP HOWTO*, by Robert Hart <**iweft@ipax.com.au**>. Information on using PPP networking with Linux. Updated 25 August 1996.

- *Linux Polish HOWTO*, by Sergiusz Pawlowicz <**ser@arch.pwr.wroc.pl**>. Information on using Linux with Polish-specific features. Updated 24 June 1996.

- *Linux Portuguese HOWTO*, by Joao Carlos Rodrigues Pereira <**jcrp@caravela.di.fc.ul.pt**>. How to configure Linux for use with the Portuguese character set. Updated 14 September 1995.

- *Linux Printing HOWTO*, by Grant Taylor <**gtaylor+pht@picante.com**>. HOWTO on printing software for Linux. Updated 10 September 1996.

- *Linux Printing Usage HOWTO*, by Mark Komarinski <**markk@auratek.com**>. How to use the printing system for a variety of file types and options. Updated 10 September 1996.

- *Linux SCSI HOWTO*, by Drew Eckhardt <**drew@PoohSticks.ORG**>. Information on SCSI driver compatibility with Linux. Updated 30 August 1996.

- *Linux SCSI Programming HOWTO*, by Heiko Eissfeldt <**heiko@colossus.escape.de**>. Information on programming the generic Linux SCSI interface. Updated 7 May 1996.

- *Linux SMB HOWTO*, by David Wood <**dwood@plugged.net.au**>. How to use the Session Message Block (SMB) protocol with Linux. Updated 10 August 1996.

- *Linux Serial HOWTO*, by Greg Hankins <**greg.hankins@cc.gatech.edu**>. Information on use of serial devices and communications software. Updated 9 October 1995.

- *Linux Shadow Password HOWTO*, by Michael H. Jackson <**mhjack@tscnet.com**>. How to obtain, install, and configure shadow passwords. Updated 3 April 1996.

- *Linux Slovenian HOWTO*, by Primoz Peterlin <**primoz.peterlin@biofiz.mf.uni-lj.si**>. Information on using Linux with Slovenian-specific features. Updated 30 October 1996.

■ *Linux Sound HOWTO*, by Jeff Tranter <**Jeff_Tranter@Mitel.COM**>. Sound hardware and software for the Linux operating system. Updated 8 September 1996.

■ *Linux Sound Playing HOWTO*, by Yoo C. Chung <**wacko@power1.snu.ac.kr**>. How to play various sound formats under Linux. Updated 12 November 1996.

■ *Linux Spanish HOWTO*, by Gonzalo Garcia Agullo <**Gonzalo.Garcia-Agullo@jrc.es**>. Information on using Linux with Spanish-specific features. Updated 20 August 1996.

■ *Linux Term HOWTO*, by Patrick Reijnen <**patrickr@bart.nl**>. HOWTO use the "term" communications package on Linux systems. Updated 15 July 1995.

■ *Linux Tips HOWTO*, by Paul Anderson <**paul@geeky1.ebtech.net**>. Miscellaneous tips and tricks for Linux. Updated 12 October 1996.

■ *Linux UMSDOS HOWTO*, by Jacques Gelinas <**jacques@solucorp.qc.ca**>. How to install and use the UMSDOS file system. Updated 13 November 1995.

■ *Linux UPS HOWTO*, by Harvey J. Stein <**hjstein@math.huji.ac.il**>. Information on using a UPS power supply with Linux. Updated 16 April 1995.

■ *Linux UUCP HOWTO*, by Vince Skahan <**vince@halcyon.com**>. Information on UUCP software for Linux. Updated 29 November 1995.

■ *Linux WWW HOWTO*, by Peter Dreuw <**pdreuw@wing.gun.de**>. How to set up WWW clients and servers. Updated 6 October 1996.

■ *Linux XFree86 HOWTO*, by Eric S. Raymond <**esr@snark.thyrsus.com**>. How to obtain, install, and configure XFree86 3.2 (X11R6). Updated 10 November 1996.

Mini-HOWTOs Index

The following mini-HOWTOs are available (plain text only):

■ *Linux 3 Button Mouse mini-HOWTO*, by Geoff Short <**geoff@kipper.york.ac.uk**>. How to configure your mouse to use 3 buttons. Updated 25 October 1996.

■ *Linux ADSM Backup mini-HOWTO*, by Thomas Koenig <**Thomas.Koenig@ciw.uni-karlsruhe.de**>. How to install and use the ADSM backup program. Updated 3 January 1996.

■ *Linux AI-Alife mini-HOWTO*, by John A. Eikenberry <**jae@ai.uga.edu**>. Information about AI software for Linux. Updated 13 November 1996.

■ *Linux Assembly mini-HOWTO*, by Francois-Rene Rideau <**rideau@ens.fr**>. How to program x86 assembly language. Updated 15 June 1996.

■ *Linux Backup with MSDOS mini-HOWTO*, by Christopher Neufeld <**neufeld@physics.utoronto.ca**>. How to backup Linux machines with MSDOS. Updated 6 February 1996.

■ *Linux Boca mini-HOWTO*, by David H Dennis <**david@amazing.cinenet.net**>. How to install a Boca 16-port serial card (Boca 2016). Updated 16 February 1995.

- *Linux BogoMips mini-HOWTO*, by Wim C.A. van Dorst <**baron@clifton.hobby.nl**>. Information about BogoMips. Updated 7 November 1996.

- *Linux Bridge mini-HOWTO*, by Chris Cole **chris@polymer.uakron.edu**>. How to setup an Ethernet bridge. Updated 23 August 1996.

- *Linux CD Writer mini-HOWTO*, by Winfried Trümper <**winni@xpilot.org**>. How to write CDs. Updated 8 November 1996.

- *Linux Colour ls mini-HOWTO*, by Thorbjoern Ravn Andersen <**ravn@dit.ou.dk**>. How to set up the colours with `ls`. Updated 27 April 1996.

- *Linux Consoles mini-HOWTO*, by R. Mark Salathiel <**RSalathi@nyx.cs.du.edu**>. How to set up multiple virtual consoles. Updated 25 December 1994.

- *Linux Consoles-Many mini-HOWTO*, by Winfried Trümper <**winni@xpilot.org**>. How to set up many virtual consoles. Updated 17 September 1996.

- *Linux DOS2Linux mini-HOWTO*, by Guido Gonzato <**Guido@ibogfs.cineca.it**>. A short guide on getting started with Linux. Updated 26 April 1996.

- *Linux Diald mini-HOWTO*, by Harish Pillay <**h.pillay@ieee.org**>. How to use `diald` to dial an ISP. Updated 3 June 1996.

- *Linux Dip+SLiRP+CSLIP mini-HOWTO*, by Zenon Fortuna <**zenon@netcom.com**>. How to use Dip+SLiRP+CSLIP together. Updated 15 October 1995.

- *Linux Diskless mini-HOWTO*, by Robert Nemkin <**buci@math.klte.hu**>. How to set up a diskless Linux box. Updated 31 May 1996.

- *Linux Dynamic IP Hacks mini-HOWTO*, by Michael Driscoll <**fenris@lightspeed.net**>. Tips and tricks for people with dynamic IP addresses. Updated 26 October 1996.

- *Linux GUI Development mini-HOWTO*, by Philip Markwalder <**pgmarkwa@stud.ee. ethz.ch**>. Information about GUI Development Software and Books. Updated 6 June 1995.

- *Linux Graphics Tools mini-HOWTO*, by Michael J. Hammel <**mjhammel@csn.net**>. Introduction to graphics tools available for Linux. Updated 15 May 1996.

- *Linux Gravis-UltraSound mini-HOWTO*, by J-F Mammet <**mammet@diva.univ-mlv.fr**>. How to install the Gravis UltraSound PnP card. Updated 27 March 1996.

- *Linux HTML Validation mini-HOWTO*, by Keith M. Corbett <**kmc@specialform.com**>. How to validate HTML 2.0 documents with `nsgmls`. Updated 29 October 1995.

- *Linux HTTP+Netware mini-HOWTO*, by Pramod Karnad <**karnadp@mozart. inet.co.th**>. How to setup a Linux HTTP server on a NetWare LAN. Updated 14 March 1996.

- *Linux IO Port Programming mini-HOWTO*, by Riku Saikkonen <**rjs@spider. compart.fi**>. How to use I/O ports in C Programs. Updated 26 August 1996.

- *Linux IP Alias mini-HOWTO*, by Harish Pillay <**h.pillay@ieee.org**>. How to use IP aliasing. Updated 12 November 1996.

- *Linux IP Masquerade mini-HOWTO,* by Ambrose Au **<achau@wwonline.com>**. How to use IP masquerading. Updated 17 August 1996.

- *Linux Java WorkShop mini-HOWTO,* by Mike Gaertner **<mg@genyosha.in-chemnitz.de>**. How to use Java WorkShop (JWS) for Solaris/Intel with Linux. Updated 8 September 1996.

- *Linux Jaz Drive mini-HOWTO,* by Bob Willmot **<bwillmot@cnct.com>**. How to use an Iomega Jaz drive with Linux. Updated 5 August 1996.

- *Linux Kerneld mini-HOWTO,* by Henrik Storner **<storner@osiris.ping.dk>**. How to use "kerneld" (dynamic module loading). Updated 3 June 1996.

- *Linux Key Setup mini-HOWTO,* by Stephen Lee **<sl14@cornell.edu>**. How to set up cursor control keys. Updated 16 September 1995.

- *Linux Keystroke mini-HOWTO,* by Zenon Fortuna **<zenon@netcom.com>**. How to assign special action to keys. Updated 4 April 1995.

- *Linux LBX mini-HOWTO,* by Paul D. Smith **<psmith@BayNetworks.com>**. How to use Low-Bandwidth X (LBX). Updated 23 October 1995.

- *Linux LF1000 mini-HOWTO,* by Skip Rye **<root@brspc_0064.msd.ray.com>**. How to use the Panasonic LF1000 optical disk drive. Updated 29 March 1996.

- *Linux LILO mini-HOWTO,* by Cameron Spitzer **<cls@truffula.sj.ca.us>**. Examples of typical LILO installations. Updated 4 June 1995.

- *Linux Linux+DOS+Win95 mini-HOWTO,* by Alan L. Wendt **<alan@ez0.ezlink.com>**. How to use Linux, DOS, and Windows 95 together. Updated 10 September 1996.

- *Linux Linux+OS2+DOS mini-HOWTO,* by Hamish Moffatt **<moffatt@yallara.cs.rmit.edu.au>**. How to use Linux, OS/2, and DOS together. Updated 20 May 1996.

- *Linux Linux+DOS+Win95+OS2 mini-HOWTO,* by Mike Harlan **<r3mdh@dax.cc.uakron.edu>**. How to use Linux, DOS, OS/2, and Windows 95 together. Updated 6 March 1996.

- *Linux Linux+Win95 mini-HOWTO,* by Jonathan Katz **<jkatz@in.net>**. How to use Linux and Windows 95 together. Updated 25 June 1996.

- *Linux Linux+WinNT mini-HOWTO,* by Bill Wohler **<wohler@uluru.worldtalk.com>**. How to use Linux and Windows NT together. Updated 27 August 1996.

- *Linux Large Disk mini-HOWTO,* Andries Brouwer **<aeb@cwi.nl>**. How to use disks with > 1024 cylinders. Updated 26 July 1996.

- *Linux Locales mini-HOWTO,* by Peeter Joot **<joot@ecf.toronto.edu>**. How to configure Linux to use locales. Updated 6 June 1996.

- *Linux MIDI+SB mini-HOWTO,* by Hideki Saito **<hideki@eskimo.com>**. How to use a MIDI keyboard with a Sound Blaster. Updated 13 October 1996.

- *Linux Mail Queue mini-HOWTO,* by Leif Erlingsson **<Leif.Erlingsson@mailbox.swipnet.se>**. How to queue remote mail and deliver local mail. Updated 19 September 1995.

App

B

■ *Linux Sendmail+UUCP mini-HOWTO*, by Jamal Hadi Salim <**jamal@glcom.com**>. How to use sendmail and UUCP together. Updated 25 October 1996.

■ *Linux Swap Space mini-HOWTO*, by H. Peter Anvin <**hpa@yggdrasil.com**>. How to share swap space between Linux and Windows. Updated 19 June 1995.

■ *Linux TIA mini-HOWTO*, by Irish <**irish@eskimo.com**>. How to use "TIA" with Linux. Updated 16 December 1995.

■ *Linux Term Firewall mini-HOWTO*, by Barak Pearlmutter <**barak.pearlmutter@alumni.cs.cmu.edu**>. How to use "term" over a firewall. Updated 22 May 1996.

■ *Linux Tiny News mini-HOWTO*, by Kent Lewis <**kent@fiona.umsmed.edu**>. How to use "INN" to make a small news spool. Updated 25 May 1995.

■ *Linux Token Ring mini-HOWTO*, by Mike Eckhoff <**meckhoff@zaphod.wayne.esu1.k12.ne.us**>. How to use token ring cards. Updated 5 July 1995.

■ *Linux Upgrade mini-HOWTO*, by Greg Louis <**glouis@dynamicro.on.ca**>. How to upgrade your Linux distribution. Updated 6 June 1996.

■ *Linux Virtual Web mini-HOWTO*, by Dan Pancamo <**pancamo@infocom.net**>. How to set up a virtual WWW site. Updated 24 November 1995.

■ *Linux Virtual wu-ftpd mini-HOWTO*, by Winfried Trümper <**winni@xpilot.org**>. How to set up wu-ftpd with virtual domains. Updated 22 October 1996.

■ *Linux Visual Bell mini-HOWTO*, by Alessandro Rubini <**rubini@ipvvis.unipv.it**>. How to disable audible bells and enable visual bells. Updated August 1996.

■ *Linux Win95+Win+Linux mini-HOWTO*, by Robert Goodwin <**Robert.Goodwin@mcc.ac.uk**>. How to get Windows 95, Windows 3.x, and Linux to work together. Updated 4 August 1996.

■ *Linux WordPerfect mini-HOWTO*, by Wade Hampton <**tasi029@tmn.com**>. How to set up SCO WordPerfect for Linux. Updated 17 May 1995.

■ *Linux X Big Cursor mini-HOWTO*, by Joerg Schneider <**schneid@ira.uka.de**>. How to use enlarged cursors with X Windows. Updated 12 September 1996.

■ *Linux X Notebook mini-HOWTO*, by Darin Ernst <**darin@castle.net**>. How to set up X on notebooks with WD90C24 video chips. Updated 10 August 1995.

■ *Linux XFree86-XInside mini-HOWTO*, by Marco Melgazzi <**s64912@athena.polito.it**>. How to convert XFree86 to Inside modelines. Updated July 1996.

■ *Linux xterm Title mini-HOWTO*, by Winfried Trümper <**winni@xpilot.org**>. How to put strings into the title bar of an X terminal. Updated 22 October 1996.

■ *Linux Xterminal mini-HOWTO*, by Scot W. Stevenson <**scot@catzen.gun.de**>. How to connect X terminals to Linux boxes. Updated July 1995.

■ *Linux ZIP Drive mini-HOWTO*, by Grant Guenther <**grant@torque.net**>. How to use an Iomega ZIP drives with Linux. Updated 15 April 1996.

Writing and Submitting a HOWTO

If you are interested in writing a HOWTO or mini-HOWTO, please get in touch with me FIRST at **gregh@sunsite.unc.edu**.

Here are a few guidelines that you should follow when writing a HOWTO or mini-HOWTO:

- Try to use meaningful structure and organization, and write clearly. Remember that many of the people reading HOWTOs do not speak English as their first language.

- If you are writing a HOWTO, you must use the Linuxdoc-SGML package, available from **sunsite.unc.edu:/pub/Linux/utils/text/**, to format the HOWTO. This package allows us to produce LaTeX (for DVI and PostScript), plain text, and HTML from a single source document, and was designed by Matt Welsh specifically for the HOWTOs. This also gives all of the HOWTOs a uniform look.

- If you are writing a mini-HOWTO, you can use any form you wish. Mini-HOWTOs are meant to be short, free-form HOWTOs on very specific subjects. In general, these should be quick to write and maintain, so it's not worth bothering with the Linuxdoc-SGML package. This does not mean that the mini-HOWTOs are any less important! Only plain text versions of mini-HOWTOs are distributed.

- Make sure that all of the information is correct. I can't stress this enough. When in doubt, speculate, but make it clear that you're only guessing.

- Make sure that you are covering the most recent version of the available software. Also, be sure to include full instructions on where software can be downloaded from (FTP site name, full path name), and the current version number and release date of the software.

- Include a FAQ section at the end, if appropriate. Many HOWTO documents need a FAQ or Common Problems section to cover information which can't be covered in the regular text.

- Use other HOWTOs as a model. The SGML source to the HOWTOs is available on Linux FTP sites.

- Make sure that your name, e-mail address, the date, and a version number is near the beginning of the document. You can also include WWW addresses and a snail mail address if you want.

- Lastly, be prepared to receive questions and comments about your writing. There are several hundreds of accesses to the HOWTO collection every day from around the world!

After you have written the HOWTO, e-mail it to me. If you used Linuxdoc-SGML, simply e-mail me the SGML source; I take care of formatting the documents. I'll also take care of archiving the HOWTOs on **sunsite.unc.edu** and posting them to the various newsgroups.

It is important that you go through me when submitting a HOWTO, as I maintain the archives and need to keep track of what HOWTOs are being written and who is doing what.

Then, all you have to do is send me periodic updates whenever appropriate.

App
B

Copyright

Unless otherwise stated, Linux HOWTO documents are copyrighted by their respective authors. Linux HOWTO documents may be reproduced and distributed in whole or in part, in any medium physical or electronic, as long as this copyright notice is retained on all copies. Commercial redistribution is allowed and encouraged; however, the author would like to be notified of any such distributions.

All translations, derivative works, or aggregate works incorporating any Linux HOWTO documents must be covered under this copyright notice. That is, you may not produce a derivative work from a HOWTO and impose additional restrictions on its distribution. Exceptions to these rules may be granted under certain conditions; please contact the Linux HOWTO coordinator at the address given below.

In short, we wish to promote dissemination of Linux information through as many channels as possible. However, we do wish to retain copyright on the HOWTO documents, and would like to be notified of any plans to redistribute the HOWTOs.

If you have questions, please contact Greg Hankins, the Linux HOWTO coordinator, at **gregh@sunsite.unc.edu** via email.

The Linux Hardware Compatibility HOWTO

This HOWTO is the most current available as of January 1997. Although somewhat out-of-date, the information on what does and doesn't work with Linux is of value. Most enhancements and upgrades to the listed hardware will work with the current versions of Linux. You can find all the HOWTOs mentioned in this HOWTO in the /usr/doc/HOWTO or usr/doc/HOWTO/mini directories on your local drive.

Use the following command to read the HOWTO files with the .gz extension:

```
zcat filename ¦ more
```

Introduction

FRiC, <frac@pobox.com> v6969, 14 November 1995

This document lists most of the hardware supported by Linux and helps you locate any necessary drivers.

Welcome to the Linux Hardware Compatibility HOWTO. This document lists most of the hardware supported by Linux; now if only people would read this first before posting their questions on USENET!

Subsections titled "Others" list hardware with alpha or beta drivers in varying degrees of usability, or list drivers that aren't included in standard kernels. Also note that some drivers only exist in alpha kernels, so if you see something listed as supported that isn't in your version of the Linux kernel, you should upgrade.

The latest version of this document can be found on the Net at the usual sites where the Linux HOWTOs are kept. (See Appendix B of this book for a list of HOWTO sites.)

If you know of any Linux hardware (in)compatibilities not listed here, please let me know—send e-mail or find me on Internet Relay Chat (IRC). Thanks.

Standard Linux Documentation Project (LDP) copyrights apply. If you use this or any other Linux HOWTO's in a commercial distribution, it would be nice to send the authors a complimentary copy of your product.

System Architectures

This document only deals with Linux for Intel platforms; for other platforms, check the following:

Platform	Site
Linux/ARM	http://whirligig.ecs.soton.ac.uk/~rmk92/armlinux.html
Linux/68k	http://www-users.informatik.rwth-aachen.de/~hn/linux68k.html
Linux/MIPS	http://www.waldorf-gmbh.de/linux-mips-faq.html
Linux/PowerPC	http://liber.stanford.edu/linuxppc/
Linux/8086	http://www.linux.org.uk/Linux8086.html
Linux/Alpha	http://www.azstarnet.com/~axplinux/
Linux for Acorn	http://www.ph.kcl.ac.uk/~amb/linux.html
MacLinux	http://www.ibg.uu.se/maclinux/

Computers/Motherboards/BIOS

Industry Standard Architecture (ISA), VESA Local Bus (VLB), Extended ISA (EISA), and Peripheral Component Interconnect (PCI) buses all are supported.

PS/2 and Microchannel (MCA) buses are not supported in the standard kernel. Alpha test PS/2 MCA kernels are available but not yet recommended for beginners or serious users.

Specific Systems

- Compaq Deskpro XL—**http://www-c724.uibk.ac.at/XL/**
- IBM PS/2 MCA systems—**ftp://invaders.dcrl.nd.edu/pub/misc/**

Laptops

Some laptops have unusual video adapters or power management and it is not uncommon to be unable to use the power management features under Linux.

See the Linux Laptop Homepage at

http://www.cs.utexas.edu/users/kharker/linux-laptop/

Controller	Site
APM	**ftp://tsx-11.mit.edu/pub/linux/packages/laptops/apm/**
PCMCIA	**ftp://cb-iris.stanford.edu/pub/pcmcia/**
Non-blinking cursor	**ftp://sunsite.unc.edu/pub/Linux/kernel/ patches/console/noblink-1.5.tar.gz**
Power savings (WD7600 chipset)	**ftp://sunsite.unc.edu/pub/Linux/ system/Misc/low-level/pwrm-1.0.tar.Z**
Other general info	**ftp://tsx-11.mit.edu/pub/linux/packages/ laptops/**

Specific Laptops

Laptop Make and Model	Site
Compaq Contura Aero	**http://domen.uninett.no/~hta/linux/ aero-faq.html**
IBM ThinkPad	**http://peipa.essex.ac.uk/tp-linux/tp-linux.html**
NEC Versa M and P	**http://www.santafe.edu:80/~nelson/ versa-linux/**
Tadpole P1000	**http://peipa.essex.ac.uk/tadpole-linux/tadpole-linux.html**

App

C

PCMCIA

See **http://hyper.stanford.edu/~dhinds/pcmcia/**.

PCMCIA drivers currently support all common PCMCIA controllers, including Databook TCIC/2, Intel i82365SL, Cirrus PD67xx, and Vadem VG-468 chipsets. The Motorola 6AHC05GA controller used in some Hyundai laptops is not supported. And see a list of supported PCMCIA cards at the end of this appendix.

CPU/FPU

Intel/AMD/Cyrix 386SX/DX/SL/DXL/SLC, 486SX/DX/SL/SX2/DX2/DX4, Pentium: Basically all 386 or better processors will work. Linux has built-in FPU emulation if you don't have a math coprocessor.

Experimental SMP (multiple CPU) support is included in kernel 1.3.31 and newer. Check the Linux/SMP Project page for details and updates.

Controller	Site
Linux/SMP Project	**http://www.linux.org.uk/SMP/title.html**

A few very early AMD 486DXs might hang in some special situations. All current chips should be okay, and getting a chip swap for old CPUs should not be a problem.

ULSI Math*Co series has a bug in the FSAVE and FRSTOR instructions that causes problems with all protected mode operating systems. Some older IIT and Cyrix chips might also have this problem.

There are problems with TLB flushing in UMC U5S chips in very old kernels (1.1.x).

Processor	Site
Enable cache on Cyrix processors	**ftp://sunsite.unc.edu/pub/Linux/ kernel/patches/CxPatch030.tar.z**
Cyrix software cache control	**ftp://sunsite.unc.edu/pub/Linux/ kernel/patches/linux.cxpatch**

Video Cards

Linux works with all video cards in text mode. VGA cards not listed below probably will still work with mono VGA and/or standard VGA drivers.

If you're looking into buying a cheap video card to run X, keep in mind that accelerated cards (such as ATI Mach, ET4000/W32p, and S3) are much faster than unaccelerated or partially accelerated cards (for example, Cirrus and WD). S3 Trio64-based cards with 2 MB DRAM go for around US$160, and S3 868-based cards with 2 MB DRAM are around US$200.

"32 bpp" is actually 24-bit color aligned on 32-bit boundaries. It does NOT mean the cards are capable of 32-bit color; it's still 24-bit color (16,777,216 colors). 24-bit packed-pixel modes are not supported in XFree86, so cards that can do 24-bit color modes in other OSes may not be able to do 24-bit color in X using Xfree86. These cards include Mach32, Cirrus 542x, S3 801/805/868/968, ET4000, and others.

Diamond Video Cards

Most currently available Diamond cards are supported by the current release of XFree86. Early Diamond cards may not be officially supported by XFree86, but there are ways of getting them to work. Diamond is now actively supporting the XFree86 Project. The supported cards are shown in the following table:

Video Card	Site
Diamond support for Xfree86	**http://www.diamondmm.com/linux.html**
Diamond FAQ (for older cards)	**ftp://sunsite.unc.edu/pub/Linux/X11/Diamond.FAQ**
Diamond Disgruntled Users Page	**http://gladstone.uoregon.edu/~trenton/diamond/** (for older cards)

SVGALIB (Graphics for Console)

- VGA
- EGA
- ARK Logic ARK1000PV/2000PV
- ATI VGA Wonder
- ATI Mach32
- Cirrus 542x, 543x
- OAK OTI-037/67/77/87
- S3 (limited support)
- Trident TVGA8900/9000
- Tseng ET3000/ET4000/W32

XFree86 3.1.2, Accelerated

- ATI Mach8
- ATI Mach32 (16 bpp—does not work with all Mach32 cards)
- ATI Mach64 (16/32 bpp)
- Cirrus Logic 5420, 542x/5430 (16 bpp), 5434 (16/32 bpp), 62x5
- IBM 8514/A
- IBM XGA, XGA-II

- IIT AGX-010/014/015/016
- Oak OTI-087
- S3 911, 924, 801, 805, 928, 864, 964, Trio32, Trio64, 868, 968
- See Appendix A of this HOWTO for a list of supported S3 cards
- Tseng ET4000/W32/W32i/W32p
- Weitek P9000 (16/32 bpp)
- Diamond Viper VLB/PCI
- Orchid P9000
- Western Digital WD90C31/33

XFree86 3.1.1, Unaccelerated

- ARK Logic ARK1000PV/VL, ARK2000PV
- ATI VGA Wonder series
- Avance Logic AL2101/2228/2301/2302/2308/2401
- Chips & Technologies 65520/65530/65540/65545
- Cirrus Logic 6420/6440
- Compaq AVGA
- Genoa GVGA
- MCGA (320 × 200)
- MX MX68000/MX68010
- NCR 77C22, 77C22E, 77C22E+
- Oak OTI-067, OTI-077
- RealTek RTG3106
- Trident TVGA8800, TVGA8900, TVGA9xxx (no support for TGUI chipsets)
- Tseng ET3000, ET4000AX
- VGA (standard VGA, 4-bit, slow)
- Video 7/Headland Technologies HT216-32
- Western Digital/Paradise PVGA1, WD90C00/10/11/24/30/31/33

Monochrome

- Hercules mono
- Hyundai HGC-1280
- Sigma LaserView PLUS
- VGA mono

Others

- EGA (ancient, from c. 1992)—**ftp://ftp.funet.fi/pub/OS/Linux/BETA/Xega/**
- ET4000/W32 and ICS5341 GenDAC—**ftp://sunsite.unc.edu/pub/Linux/X11/ X-servers/**
- Trident TGUI9440—**ftp://sunsite.unc.edu/pub/Linux/X11/X-servers/**

Works in Progress

- Compaq QVision
- Number Nine Imagine 128

I don't know when support for these cards will be finished, so please don't ask me. If you want support for these cards now, get Accelerated-X.

Commercial X Servers

Commercial X servers provide support for cards not supported by XFree86, and might give better performances for cards that are supported by XFree86. In general, they support many more cards than XFree86, so here I'll list only cards that aren't supported by Xfree86. Contact the vendors directly or check the Commercial HOWTO for more info. Commercial HOWTO sites are listed in Appendix B, "The Linux HOWTO Index."

App

C

Accelerated-X 1.2

- Chips & Technologies 82C45x, 82C48x, F655xx
- Compaq QVision 2000
- Matrox MGA-I, MGA-II
- Number Nine I-128
- Weitek P9100

$199, X Inside, Inc.—**info@xinside.com**

Accel-X supports most cards in 16- and 32-bpp modes and also supports 24-bit packed pixel modes for cards that have these modes, including ATI Mach32, Mach64 ($1280 \times 1024@24bpp$), ET4000/W32p, S3-866/868/968, and more. Accel-X also supports other input hardware, like graphics tablets and touchscreens.

Accel-X also supports XVideo (Xv) extensions (on Matrox Comet, Marvel-II, and SPEA ShowTime Plus), PEX, and XIE.

Metro-X 2.3.2

$199, Metro Link—**sales@metrolink.com**. Metro-X supports more boards than XFree but less than Accel-X; however, I don't have much more information as I can't seem to view the PostScript files they sent me. Mail them directly for more info.

NOTE   The commercial distribution of Red Hat Linux includes a single-user license for Metro-Link's Metro-X server. The distribution included with this book does not include this product. ■

Controllers (Hard Drive)

Linux will work with standard IDE, MFM, and RLL controllers. When you're using MFM/RLL controllers, it is important to use ext2fs and the bad block checking options when formatting the disk.

Enhanced IDE (EIDE) interfaces are supported, with up to two IDE interfaces and up to four hard drives and/or CD-ROM drives. Linux will detect these EIDE interfaces:

- CMD-640
- DTC 2278D
- FGI/Holtek HT-6560B
- RZ1000
- Triton (82371FB) IDE (with busmaster DMA)

ESDI controllers that emulate the ST-506 (MFM/RLL/IDE) interface will also work. The bad block checking comment also applies to these controllers. Generic 8-bit XT controllers also work.

Controllers (SCSI)

It is important to pick a SCSI controller carefully. Many cheap ISA SCSI controllers are designed to drive CD-ROMs rather than hard drives. Such low-end SCSI controllers are no better than IDE. See the SCSI HOWTO and look at performance figures before buying an SCSI card.

▶ **See** /usr/doc/HOWTO/SCSI-HOWTO.gz

Supported

- AMI Fast Disk VLB/EISA (BusLogic compatible)
- Adaptec AVA-1505/1515 (ISA) (Adaptec 152x compatible)
- Adaptec AHA-1510/152x (ISA) (AIC-6260/6360)
- Adaptec AHA-154x (ISA) (all models)
- Adaptec AHA-174x (EISA) (in enhanced mode)
- Adaptec AHA-274x (EISA)/284x (VLB) (AIC-7770)
- Adaptec AHA-2940/3940 (PCI) (AIC-7870) (since 1.3.6)
- Always IN2000
- BusLogic (ISA/EISA/VLB/PCI) (all models)
- DPT PM2001, PM2012A (EATA-PIO)
- DPT Smartcache (EATA-DMA) (ISA/EISA/PCI) (all models)
- DTC 329x (EISA) (Adaptec 154x compatible)

- Future Domain TMC-16x0, TMC-3260 (PCI)

- Future Domain TMC-8xx, TMC-950

- Media Vision Pro Audio Spectrum 16 SCSI (ISA)

- NCR 5380 generic cards

- NCR 53c400 (Trantor T130B) (use generic NCR 5380 SCSI support)

- NCR 53c406a (Acculogic ISApport / Media Vision Premium 3D SCSI)

- NCR 53c7x0, 53c8x0 (PCI)

- Qlogic/Control Concepts SCSI/IDE (FAS408) (ISA/VLB/PCMCIA) does not work with PCI (different chipset). PCMCIA cards must boot DOS to init card.

- Seagate ST-01/ST-02 (ISA)

- SoundBlaster 16 SCSI-2 (Adaptec 152x compatible) (ISA)

- Trantor T128/T128F/T228 (ISA)

- UltraStor 14F (ISA), 24F (EISA), 34F (VLB)

- Western Digital WD7000 SCSI

Others

Processor	Site
AMD AM53C974, AM79C974 (PCI) (Compaq, Zeos onboard SCSI)	**ftp://sunsite.unc.edu/pub/Linux/ kernel/patches/scsi/AM53C974- 0.3.tgz**
Adaptec ACB-40xx SCSI-MFM/	**ftp://sunsite.unc.edu/pub/Linux/ kernel/patches/scsi/ RLL bridgeboardadaptec-40XX.tar.gz**
Adaptec AHA-2940 (PCI) (AIC-7870)	**ftp://remus.nrl.navy.mil/pub/Linux/**
Adaptec APA-1460 SlimSCSI	**ftp://cb-iris.stanford.edu/pub/ pcmcia/(PCMCIA)**
Acculogic ISApport/MV Premium 3D SCSI (NCR 53c406a)	**ftp://sunsite.unc.edu/pub/Linux/ kernel/patches/scsi/ncr53c406- 0.10.patch.gz**
Always AL-500	**ftp://sunsite.unc.edu/pub/Linux/ kernel/patches/scsi/al500_0.1.tar.gz**
Iomega PC2/2B	**ftp://sunsite.unc.edu/pub/Linux/ kernel/patches/scsi/iomega_pc2- 1.1.x.tar.gz**
New Media Bus Toaster PCMCIA	**ftp://lamont.ldeo.columbia.edu/pub/ linux/bus_toaster-1.5.tgz**

continues

App
C

continued

Processor	Site
Ricoh GSI-8	**ftp://tsx-11.mit.edu/pub/linux/ ALPHA/scsi/gsi8.tar.gz**
Trantor T130B (NCR 53c400)	**ftp://sunsite.unc.edu/pub/Linux/ kernel/patches/scsi/53c400.tar.gz**

Unsupported

- Parallel port SCSI adapters
- Non-Adaptec-compatible DTC boards (327x, 328x)

Controllers (I/O)

Any standard serial/parallel/joystick/IDE combo cards. Linux supports 8250, 16450, 16550, and 16550A UARTs. Cards that support non-standard IRQs (IRQ > 9) can be used.

See National Semiconductor's Application Note AN-493 by Martin S. Michael. Section 5.0 describes in detail the differences between the NS16550 and NS16550A. Briefly, the NS16550 had bugs in the FIFO circuits, but the NS16550A (and later) chips fixed those. However, there were very few NS16550s produced by National, long ago, so these should be very rare.

Many of the "16550" parts in modern boards are from the many manufacturers of compatible parts, which may not use the National "A" suffix. Also, some multiport boards use 16552, 16554, or various other multiport or multifunction chips from National or other suppliers (generally, in a dense package soldered to the board, not a 40-pin DIP). Don't worry about it unless you encounter a very old 40-pin DIP National NS16550 (no "A") chip loose or in an old board, in which case treat it as a 16450 (no FIFO) rather than a 16550A.—Zhahai Stewart at **zstewart@hisys.com**.

Unintelligent Controllers (Multiport) Supported

- AST FourPort and clones
- Accent Async-4
- Arnet Multiport-8 (8 port)
- Bell Technologies HUB6
- Boca BB-1004, 1008 (4, 8 port)—no DTR, DSR, and CD
- Boca BB-2016 (16 port)
- Boca IO/AT66 (6 port)
- Boca IO 2×4 (4S/2P)—works with modems, but uses 5 IRQs
- Computone ValuePort (4, 6, 8 port) (AST FourPort compatible)
- DigiBoard PC/X (4, 8, 16 port)
- Comtrol Hostess 550 (4, 8 port)

- SIIG I/O Expander 4S (4 port, uses 4 IRQs)
- PC-COMM 4-port
- STB 4-COM
- Twincom ACI/550
- Usenet Serial Board II

Non-intelligent cards usually come in two varieties: one using standard com port addresses and using 4 IRQs, and another that's AST FourPort compatible and uses a selectable block of addresses and a single IRQ. (Addresses and IRQs are set by using setserial.) If you're getting one of these cards, be sure to check which standard it conforms to; prices are no indication.

Intelligent Controllers (Multiport) Supported

- Cyclades Cyclom-8Y/16Y (8, 16 port) (ISA/PCI)
- Stallion EasyIO (ISA) / EasyConnection 8/32 (ISA/MCA)
- Stallion EasyConnection 8/64 / ONboard (ISA/EISA/MCA) / Brumby / Stallion (ISA)

App
C

Others

Controller	Site
Comtrol RocketPort (8/16/32 port)	**ftp://tsx-11.mit.edu/pub/linux/ packages/comtrol/**
DigiBoard COM/Xi— Contact Simon Park	**si@wimpol.demon.co.uk** (e-mail address)
DigiBoard PC/Xe (ISA) and PC/Xi (EISA)	**ftp://ftp.digibd.com/drivers/linux/**
Hayes ESP8	contact Dennis Boylan at **dennis@lan.com**
Moxa C218 (8 port) / C320(8/16/24/ expandable)	**<ftp://ftp.moxa.com.tw/drivers/ c-218-320/32 linux/>**
Specialix SIO/XIO (modular, 4 to 32 ports)	**ftp://sunsite.unc.edu/pub/Linux/ kernel/patches/serial/sidrv0_5.taz**
Stallion Technologies EasyIO/	**ftp://sunsite.unc.edu/pub/Linux/ kernel/patches/EasyConnection 8/ 32serial/stallion-0.1.9.tar.gz**

Network Adapters

Ethernet adapters vary greatly in performance. In general, the newer the design, the better the adapter performs. Some very old cards like the 3C501 are useful only because they can be found in junk heaps for $5 a pop. Be careful with clones—not all are good clones, and bad clones often cause erratic lockups under Linux. Read the Ethernet HOWTO for detailed descriptions of various cards. (See Appendix B, "The Linux HOWTO Index," for the Ethernet HOWTO site address.)

Supported Ethernet

- 3Com 3C501—Avoid like the plague
- 3Com 3C503, 3C505, 3C507, 3C509/3C509B (ISA)/3C579 (EISA)
- AMD LANCE (79C960)/PCnet-ISA/PCI (AT1500, HP J2405A, NE1500/NE2100)
- AT&T GIS WaveLAN
- Allied Telesis AT1700
- Ansel Communications AC3200 EISA
- Apricot Xen-II
- Cabletron E21xx
- DEC DE425 (EISA)/DE434/DE435 (PCI)
- DEC DEPCA and EtherWORKS
- HP PCLAN (27245 and 27xxx series)
- HP PCLAN PLUS (27247B and 27252A)
- HP 10/100VG PCLAN (ISA/EISA/PCI)
- Intel EtherExpress
- Intel EtherExpress Pro
- NE2000/NE1000 (be careful with clones)
- New Media Ethernet
- Racal-Interlan NI5210 (i82586 Ethernet chip)
- Racal-Interlan NI6510 (am7990 lance chip). Doesn't work with more than 16MB of RAM.
- PureData PDUC8028, PDI8023
- SEEQ 8005
- SMC Ultra
- Schneider & Koch G16
- Western Digital WD80x3
- Zenith Z-Note/IBM ThinkPad 300 built-in adapter

Pocket and Portable Adapters

- AT-Lan-Tec/RealTek parallel port adapter
- D-Link DE600/DE620 parallel port adapter

Slotless

- SLIP/CSLIP/PPP (serial port)
- EQL (serial IP load balancing)
- PLIP (parallel port)—Using LapLink or bi-directional cable

ARCnet

- Works with all ARCnet cards

Token Ring

- IBM Tropic chipset cards

Amateur Radio (AX.25)

- Ottawa PI/PI2
- Most generic 8530-based HDLC boards

Others

Adapter	Site
Ethernet 3Com Vortex Ethercards (3C590, 3C595 (100 mbps)) (PCI)	http://cesdis.gsfc.nasa.gov/pub/linux/drivers/vortex.html
DEC 21040/21140 "Tulip"/SMC PCI EtherPower 10/100	http://cesdis.gsfc.nasa.gov/linux/drivers/tulip.html

ISDN

Check out the Linux ISDN WWW page at:

http://www.ix.de/ix/linux/linux-isdn.html

ISDN Card	Site
3Com Sonix Arpeggio	ftp://sunsite.unc.edu/pub/Linux/kernel/patches/network/sonix.tgz
Combinet EVERYWARE 1000 ISDN	ftp://sunsite.unc.edu/pub/Linux/patches/network/combinet1000isdn-1.02.tar.gz
Diehl SCOM card	ftp://sunsite.unc.edu/pub/Linux/kernel/patches/network/isdndrv-0.1.1.tar.gz
ICN ISDN card	ftp://ftp.franken.de/pub/isdn4linux/
Teles ISDN card	ftp://ftp.franken.de/pub/isdn4linux/

ISDN cards that emulate standard modems or common Ethernet adapters don't need any special drivers to work.

PCMCIA Cards

See Appendix B at the end of this HOWTO for a complete list.

App
C

ATM

- Efficient Networks ENI155P-MF 155 mbps ATM adapter—**http://lrcwww.epfl.ch/ linux-atm/**

Frame Relay

- Sangoma S502 56K Frame Relay card—**ftp://ftp.sovereign.org/pub/wan/fr/**

Load Balancing

- eql (load balancing driver)—**ftp://sunsite.unc.edu/pub/Linux/system/Network/ serial/eql-1.2.tar.gz**

Unsupported

- Xircom adapters (PCMCIA and parallel port) are not supported.

Sound Cards—Supported

- 6850 UART MIDI
- Adlib (OPL2)
- Audio Excell DSP16
- ATI Stereo F/X (Sound Blaster compatible)
- Aztech Sound Galaxy NX Pro
- Crystal CS4232 (PnP) based cards
- ECHO-PSS (Orchid SW32, Cardinal DSP16, and so on)
- Ensoniq SoundScape (boot DOS to initialize card)
- Gravis Ultrasound
- Gravis Ultrasound 16-bit sampling daughterboard
- Gravis Ultrasound MAX
- Logitech SoundMan Games (SBPro, 44kHz stereo support)
- Logitech SoundMan Wave (SBPro/MPU-401) (OPL4)
- Logitech SoundMan 16 (PAS-16 compatible)
- Microsoft Sound System (AD1848)
- MPU-401 MIDI
- MediaTrix AudioTriX Pro
- Media Vision Premium 3D (Jazz16) (SBPro compatible)
- Media Vision Pro Sonic 16 (Jazz)
- Media Vision Pro Audio Spectrum 16
- OAK OTI-601D cards (Mozart)
- OPTi 82C928/82C929 cards (MAD16/MAD16 Pro)
- SoundBlaster

■ SoundBlaster Pro

■ SoundBlaster 16 family

■ Sound Galaxy NX Pro

■ Turtle Beach Wavefront cards (Maui, Tropez)

■ WaveBlaster (and other SB16 daughterboards)

Others

Card	Site
MPU-401 MIDI (intelligent mode)	**ftp://sunsite.unc.edu/pub/Linux/ kernel/sound/mpu401.0.11a.tar.gz**
PC speaker/Parallel port DAC	**ftp://ftp.informatik.hu-berlin.de/ pub/os/linux/hu-sound/**
Turtle Beach MultiSound/Tahiti/ Monterey	**ftp://ftp.cs.colorado.edu/users/ mccreary/archive/tbeach/multisound/**

Unsupported

The ASP chip on the SoundBlaster 16 series and AWE32 is not supported. AWE32's onboard E-mu MIDI synthesizer is not supported. Nathan Laredo (**laredo@gnu.ai.mit.edu**) is willing to write AWE32 drivers if you send him a complimentary card. He is also willing to write drivers for almost any hardware if you send him free samples of your hardware.

SoundBlaster 16 cards with DSP 4.11 have a hardware bug that causes hung/stuck notes. The problem can happen with either Wave Blaster daughterboards or MIDI devices attached to the MIDI port. There is no known fix.

Hard Drives

All hard drives should work if the controller is supported (from the SCSI HOWTO). All direct-access SCSI devices with a block size of 256, 512, or 1,024 bytes should work. Other block sizes will not work (but often this can be fixed by changing the block and/or sector size using the MODE SELECT SCSI command).

Large IDE (EIDE) drives work fine with newer kernels. The boot partition must lie in the first 1024 cylinders due to PC BIOS limitations.

Some Conner CFP1060S drives may have problems with Linux and `ext2fs`. The symptoms are inode errors during `e2fsck` and corrupt file systems. Conner released a fix for this problem; contact Conner at 1-800-4CONNER (USA) or +44-1294-315333 (Europe). (Conner merged with Seagate Technologies in February 1996.) Have the microcode version (found on the drive label, 9WA1.6x) handy when you call.

Certain Micropolis drives have problems with Adaptec and BusLogic cards; contact the manu-facturers for firmware upgrades if you suspect problems.

■ Multiple device driver (RAID-0)—**ftp://sweet-smoke.ufr-info-p7.ibp.fr/public/Linux/**

Tape Drives—Supported

■ SCSI tape drives (from the SCSI HOWTO). Drives using both fixed- and variable-length blocks smaller than the driver buffer length (set to 32KB in the distribution sources) are supported. Virtually all drives should work. (Please send e-mail if you know of any incompatible drives.)

■ QIC-02

■ QIC-117, QIC-40/80 drives (Ftape)—**ftp://sunsite.unc.edu/pub/Linux/kernel/tapes**. Most tape drives using the floppy controller should work. Check the Ftape HOWTO for details. Various dedicated QIC-80 controllers (such as Colorado FC-10 and Iomega Tape Controller II) are also supported.

  ▶ **See** /usr/doc/HOWTO/Ftape-HOWTO.gz

Unsupported

■ Emerald and Tecmar QIC-02 tape controller cards. Chris Ulrich (**insom@math.ucr.edu**)

■ Drives that connect to the parallel port (for example, Colorado Trakker)

■ Some high-speed tape controllers (such as Colorado TC-15/FC-20)

■ Irwin AX250L/Accutrak 250 (not QIC-80)

■ IBM Internal Tape Backup Unit (not QIC-80)

■ COREtape Light

CD-ROM Drives Supported

■ SCSI CD-ROM drives (from the CD-ROM HOWTO). Any SCSI CD-ROM drive with a block size of 512 or 2048 bytes should work under Linux; this includes the vast majority of CD-ROM drives on the market.

■ EIDE (ATAPI) CD-ROM drives

■ Aztech CDA268, Orchid CDS-3110, Okano/Wearnes CDD-110

■ Goldstar R420

■ LMS Philips CM 206

■ Matsushita/Panasonic, Creative Labs, Longshine, Kotobuki (SBPCD)

■ Mitsumi

■ Optics Storage Dolphin 8000AT

■ Sanyo H94A

- Sony CDU31A/CDU33A
- Sony CDU-535/CDU-531
- Teac CD-55A SuperQuad

Others

CD-ROM Drive	Site
GoldStar R420	ftp://ftp.gwdg.de/pub/linux/cdrom/drivers/goldstar/
LMS/Philips CM 205/225/202	ftp://sunsite.unc.edu/pub/Linux/kernel/patches/cdrom/lmscd0.3d.tar.gz
LMS Philips CM 206	ftp://sunsite.unc.edu/pub/Linux/kernel/patches/cdrom/cm206.0.22b.tar.gz
Mitsumi (alternate drivers)	ftp://ftp.gwdg.de/pub/linux/cdrom/drivers/mitsumi/
Mitsumi (module)	ftp://ftp.gwdg.de/pub/linux/cdrom/drivers/mitsumi-1.2.x/
NEC CDR-35D (old)	ftp://sunsite.unc.edu/pub/Linux/kernel/patches/cdrom/linux-neccdr35d.patch
Sony SCSI multisession CD-XA	ftp://tsx-11.mit.edu/pub/linux/patches/sony-multi-0.00.tar.gz
Teac CD-55A SuperQuad	ftp://ftp.gwdg.de/pub/linux/cdrom/develop/teac/

App

C

Notes

PhotoCD (XA) is supported.

All CD-ROM drives should work similarly for reading data. There are various compatibility problems with audio CD-playing utilities (especially with some NEC drives). Some alpha drivers do not have audio support yet.

Early (single-speed) NEC CD-ROM drives may have trouble with currently available SCSI controllers.

Removable Drives

All SCSI drives should work if the controller is supported, including optical drives, WORM, CD-ROM, floptical, and others. Iomega Bernoulli and Zip drives work fine, and so do SyQuest drives.

Linux supports both 512 and 1024 bytes/sector disks. There's a problem with MS-DOS filesystems on 1024 bytes/sector disks on some kernels (fixed in 1.1.75).

■ Parallel port Zip drives—**ftp://gear.torque.net/pub/**

Removable drives work like floppies: just `fdisk`/`mkfs` and mount the disks. Linux provides drive locking if your drives support it. `mtools` can also be used if the disks are in MS-DOS format.

CD-ROM drives require special software to work. Read the CD-R Mini-HOWTO.

▶ **See** /usr/doc/HOWTO/mini/CD-WRiter

Mice

■ Microsoft serial mouse

■ Mouse Systems serial mouse

■ Logitech Mouseman serial mouse

■ Logitech serial mouse

■ ATI XL Inport busmouse

■ C&T 82C710 (QuickPort) (Toshiba, TI Travelmate)

■ Microsoft busmouse

■ Logitech busmouse

■ PS/2 (auxiliary device) mouse

Others

Mouse	Site
Sejin J-mouse	**ftp://sunsite.unc.edu/pub/Linux/kernel/patches/console/jmouse.1.1.70-jmouse.tar.gz**
MultiMouse—Use multiple mouse devices as a single mouse	**ftp://sunsite.unc.edu/pub/Linux/system/Misc/MultiMouse-1.0.tgz**

Notes

Touchpad devices like Alps Glidepoint also work, as long as they're compatible with another mouse protocol.

Newer Logitech mice (except the Mouseman) use the Microsoft protocol, and all three buttons work. Even though Microsoft's mice have only two buttons, the protocol allows three buttons. The mouse port on the ATI Graphics Ultra and Ultra Pro use the Logitech busmouse protocol. (See the Busmouse HOWTO for details.)

▶ **See** /usr/doc/HOWTO/Busmouse-HOWTO.gz

Modems

All internal modems or external modems are connected to the serial port. A small number of modems come with DOS software that downloads the control program at runtime. These modems normally can be used by loading the program under DOS and doing a warm boot. Such modems are probably best avoided, since you won't be able to use them with non-PC hardware in the future. PCMCIA modems should work with the PCMCIA drivers. Fax/modems need appropriate fax software to operate.

- Digicom Connection 96+/14.4+: DSP code downloading program—**ftp://sunsite.unc.edu/pub/Linux/system/Serial/smdl-linux.1.02.tar.gz**
- ZyXEL U-1496 series: ZyXEL 1.4, modem/fax/voice control program—**ftp://sunsite.unc.edu/pub/Linux/system/Serial/ZyXEL-1.4.tar.gz**

Printers and Plotters

Any printer or plotter connected to the parallel or serial port should work.

- HP LaserJet 4 series: free-lj4, printing modes control program—**ftp://sunsite.unc.edu/pub/Linux/system/Printing/free-lj4-1.1p1.tar.gz**
- BiTronics parallel port interface—**ftp://sunsite.unc.edu/pub/Linux/kernel/misc/bt-ALPHA-0.0.1.tar.gz**

Ghostscript

Many Linux programs output PostScript files. Non-PostScript printers can emulate PostScript Level 2 by using Ghostscript.

- Ghostscript—**ftp://ftp.cs.wisc.edu/pub/ghost/aladdin/**

Ghostscript-supported printers:

- Apple Imagewriter
- C Itoh M8510
- Canon BubbleJet BJ10e, BJ200
- Canon LBP-8II, LIPS III
- DEC LA50/70/75/75plus
- DEC LN03, LJ250
- Epson 9-pin, 24-pin, LQ series, Stylus, AP3250
- HP 2563B
- HP DesignJet 650C

App

C

- HP DeskJet/Plus/500
- HP DeskJet 500C/520C/550C/1200C color
- HP LaserJet/Plus/II/III/4
- HP PaintJet/XL/XL300 color
- IBM Jetprinter color
- IBM Proprinter
- Imagen ImPress
- Mitsubishi CP50 color
- NEC P6/P6+/P60
- Okidata MicroLine 182
- Ricoh 4081
- SPARCprinter
- StarJet 48 inkjet printer
- Tektronix 4693d color 2/4/8-bit
- Tektronix 4695/4696 inkjet plotter
- Xerox XES printers (2700, 3700, 4045, and so on)

Others:

- Canon BJC600 and Epson ESC/P color printers—**ftp://petole.imag.fr/pub/postscript/**

Scanners

Scanner	Site
A4 Tech AC 4096	**ftp://ftp.informatik.hu-berlin.de/pub/local/linux/ac4096.tgz**
Fujitsu SCSI-2 scanners—Contact Dr. G.W. Wettstein	**greg%wind.UUCP@plains.nodak.edu**
Genius GS-B105G	**ftp://tsx-11.mit.edu/pub/linux/ALPHA/scanner/gs105-0.0.1.tar.gz**
Genius GeniScan GS4500	**ftp://tsx-11.mit.edu/pub/linux/ALPHA/scanner/handheld scannergs4500-1.3.tar.gz**
HP ScanJet, ScanJet Plus	**ftp://ftp.ctrl- c.liu.se/unix/linux/wingel/**
HP ScanJet II series SCSI	**ftp://sunsite.unc.edu/pub/Linux/apps/graphics/scanners/hpscanpbm-0.3a.tar.gz**

Scanner	Site
Logitech Scanman 32/256	**ftp://tsx-11.mit.edu/pub/linux/ALPHA/ scanner/logiscan-0.0.2.tar.gz**
Mustek M105 handheld scanner with GI1904 interface	**ftp://tsx-11.mit.edu/pub/linux/ALPHA/ scanner/scan-driver-0.1.8.tar.gz**
UMAX SCSI scanners —Contact Craig Johnston	**mkshenk@u.washington.edu**

Other Hardware

- VESA Power Savings Protocol (DPMS) monitors

Support for power savings is included in the Linux kernel. Just use `setterm` to enable support.

Joysticks

- Joystick driver—**ftp://sunsite.unc.edu/pub/Linux/kernel/patches/console/ joystick-0.7.2.tgz**
- Joystick driver (module)—**ftp://sunsite.unc.edu/pub/Linux/kernel/patches/ console/joyfixed.tgz**

Video Capture Boards

Video Board	Site
FAST Screen Machine II	**ftp://sunsite.unc.edu/pub/Linux/apps/ video/ScreenMachineII_1.1.tgz**
ProMovie Studio	**ftp://sunsite.unc.edu/pub/Linux/apps/ video/PMS-grabber.tgz**
VideoBlaster, Rombo Media Pro+	**ftp://sunsite.unc.edu/pub/Linux/apps/ video/vid_src.gz**
WinVision video capture card	**ftp://sunsite.unc.edu/pub/Linux/apps/ video/fgrabber-1.0.tgz**
VT1500 TV	**ftp://sunsite.unc.edu/pub/Linux/apps/ video/vt1500-1.0.5.tgz**

Uninterruptible Power Supplies (UPSs)

- APC SmartUPS—**ftp://sunsite.unc.edu/pub/Linux/system/UPS/apcd-0.1.tar.gz**
- UPSs with RS-232 monitoring port (unipower package)—**ftp://sunsite.unc.edu/pub/ Linux/system/UPS/unipower-1.0.0.tgz**
- Various other UPSs are supported—read the UPS HOWTO (see Appendix B, "The Linux HOWTO Index," for the UPS HOWTO site address)

Data Acquisition

The Linux Lab Project site collects drivers for hardware dealing with data acquisition; they also maintain some mailing lists dealing with the subject. I have no experience with data acquisition, so please check the site for more details.

- Linux Lab Project—**ftp://koala.chemie.fu-berlin.de/pub/linux/LINUX-LAB/**
- CED 1401
- DBCC CAMAC
- IEEE-488 (GPIB, HPIB) boards
- Keithley DAS-1200
- National Instruments AT-MIO-16F / Lab-PC+
- Analog Devices RTI-800/815 ADC/DAC board—contact Paul Gortmaker (**gpg109@anu.edu.au**)

Miscellaneous

Device	Site
HP IEEE-488 (HP-IB) interface	**ftp://beaver.chemie.fu-berlin.de/pub/ linux/IEEE488/**
Maralu chip-card reader/writer	**ftp://ftp.thp.uni-koeln.de/pub/linux/ chip/**
Mattel Powerglove	**ftp://sunsite.unc.edu/pub/Linux/apps/ linux-powerglove.tgz**
Reveal FM Radio card	**ftp://magoo.uwsuper.edu/pub/fm-radio/**
Videotext cards	**ftp://sunsite.unc.edu/pub/Linux/apps/ video/videoteXt-0.4.tar.gz**

Related Sources of Information

Information	Site
Cameron Spitzer's hardware FAQ archive	**ftp://rahul.net/pub/cameron/PC-info/**
Computer hardware and software vendor phone numbers	**http://mtmis1.mis.semi.harris.com/ comp_ph1.html**
Guide to computer vendors	**http://www.ronin.com/SBA/**
System optimization information	**http://www.dfw.net/~sdw/**

Acknowledgments

Thanks to all the authors and contributors of other HOWTOs, since many things here are shamelessly stolen from their works! To Zane Healy and Ed Carp, the original authors of this list; and to everyone else who sent in updates and feedback. Special thanks to Eric Boerner and lilo (the person, not the program) for the sanity checks. Thanks also to Dan Quinlan for the original SGML conversion.

Appendix A: S3 Cards Supported by XFree86 3.1.2

- CHIPSET RAMDACCLOCKCHIP BPP CARD
- 801/805 AT&T 20C49016Actix GE 32
- Orchid Fahrenheit 1280+
- 801/805 AT&T 20C490 ICD2061A 16STB PowerGraph X.24
- 805 S3 GENDAC16Miro 10SD VLB/PCI SPEA Mirage VLB
- 805 SS2410ICD2061A 8 Diamond Stealth 24 VLB
- 928 AT&T 20C49016Actix Ultra
- 928 Sierra SC15025ICD2061A 32ELSA Winner 1000 ISA/VLB/EISA
- 928 Bt485 ICD2061A 32STB Pegasus VL
- 928 Bt485 SC1141216SPEA Mercury VLB
- 928 Bt485 ICD2061A 32#9 GXE Level 10/11/12
- 928 Ti3020ICD2061A 32#9 GXE Level 14/16
- 864 AT&T 20C498 ICS249432Miro 20SD (BIOS 1.x)
- 864 AT&T 20C498/ICD2061A/32ELSA Winner 1000 PRO VLB/PCI
- STG1700 ICS9161MIRO 20SD (BIOS 2.x)
- 864 STG1700 ICD2061A 32Actix GE 64 VLB
- 864 AT&T 20C498/ICS259516SPEA Mirage P64 DRAM (BIOS 3.x)
- AT&T 21C498
- 864 S3 86C716 SDAC 32ELSA Winner 1000 PRO Miro 20SD (BIOS 3.x) SPEA Mirage P64 DRAM (BIOS 4.x)
- Diamond Stealth 64 DRAM
- 864 ICS5342 ICS534232Diamond Stealth 64 DRAM (some)
- 864 AT&T 20C490 ICD2061A 32#9 GXE64
- 864 AT&T 20C498-13ICD2061A 32#9 GXE64 PCI
- 964 AT&T 20C505 ICD2061A 32Miro Crystal 20SV PCI
- 964 Bt485 ICD2061A 32Diamond Stealth 64
- 964 Bt9485ICS9161A 32SPEA Mercury 64

App
C

- 964 Ti3020ICD2061A 8 ELSA Winner 2000 PRO PCI
- 964 Ti3025Ti3025 32#9 GXE64 Pro VLB/PCI Miro Crystal 40SV
- 764 (Trio64) 32SPEA Mirage P64 (BIOS 5.x)
- Diamond Stealth 64 DRAM #9 GXE64 Trio64 STB PowerGraph 64

Appendix B: Supported PCMCIA Cards

These cards are supported by David Hinds' PCMCIA package, and this list is taken from his Web page.

Ethernet Cards

- 3Com 3c589, 3c589
- Accton EN2212
- EtherCardCNet CN30BC
- EthernetD-Link DE-650EFA
- InfoExpress SPT
- EFA 205 10baseTEP-210
- Ethernet Farallon
- EtherwaveGVC NIC-2000P
- Ethernet ComboHYPERTEC
- HyperEnetIBM CreditCard
- Ethernet AdapterIC-Card
- EthernetKatron PE-520
- EthernetKingston KNE-PCM/MLANEED
- EthernetLinksys
- EtherCardMaxtech PCN2000
- EthernetNetwork General "Sniffer"
- New Media
- EthernetNovell/National NE4100
- InfoMoverProteon
- EthernetPreMax PE-200
- EthernetRPTI EP400
- EthernetSocket Communications Socket EA LAN AdapterThomas-Conrad
- EthernetVolktek Ethernet

Modem Cards

All modem cards should work.

Memory Cards

■ New Media SRAMEpson 2MB SRAMIntel Series 2 and Series 2+ Flash

SCSI Adapters

■ Qlogic FastSCSI PCMCIANew Media Bus Toaster SCSIAdaptec APA-1460 SlimSCSI

Unsupported

■ Xircom ethernet and ethernet/modem cards

■ Canon/Compaq PCMCIA floppy drive

App

C

The GNU General Public License

What exactly is GNU? Many believe GNU software is public domain, and some believe GNU software is shareware. Neither is true. Basically, GNU software is copyrighted software that authors have granted the permission to distribute under certain conditions. Those conditions include the provision to provide source code, and that no part of the software may be placed under a copyright that restricts the further distribution of the software—that is, you can't use source code copyrighted under the GNU License within your program without making your source code freely available.

Although the GNU copyright specifies that you must make your source code available, it doesn't mean you have to give your program away for free; you can charge a fee for your program, but that fee MUST include the source code for both the GNU portions and YOUR portion. You can't charge a fee for the executable part of the program and then another fee for the source code—one price for both. Thus, you can't withhold or charge extra for what you might consider proprietary source code. This is the main objection many software executives have with using GNU software within their programs—they don't want to make their source code available to their competitors.

But the concept of GNU goes further, and perhaps the best source to explain this concept is Richard Stallman, the patriarch of the GNU philosophy. Stallman is a founder and proponent of the Free Software Foundation (FSF). He believes very strongly that all software should be free and that computer systems should be open for use by anyone. The fact that such programs as Linux and emacs are freely available matches his philosophy. Anyone can take them for their own use. Users are also encouraged to make modifications and share those changes with others.

N O T E   The GNU License is sometimes referred to as the *GNU copyleft*, as a play on the word *copyright*. GNU is also a play on words—*GNU's Not UNIX.* ■

What does all this have to do with Linux? Well, the various components of Linux are distributed under GNU's General Public License. Thus, Linux is neither in the public domain nor is it shareware; Linus Torvalds and the others retain copyright to their work under the GPL. The rest of this appendix is the GPL as published by the Free Software Federation. ■

ON THE WEB

The Web site for the Free Software Foundation is **http://www.fsf.org**.

The GNU License

Version 2, June 1991

Copyright© 1989, 1991 Free Software Foundation, Inc. 675 Mass Ave, Cambridge, MA 02139 USA

Everyone is permitted to copy and distribute verbatim copies of this license document, but changing it is not allowed.

Preamble

The licenses for most software are designed to take away your freedom to share and change it. By contrast, the GNU General Public License is intended to guarantee your freedom to share and change free software—to make sure the software is free for all its users. This General Public License applies to most of the Free Software Foundation's software and to any other program whose authors commit to using it. (Some other Free Software Foundation software is covered by the GNU Library General Public License instead.) You can apply it to your programs, too.

When we speak of free software, we are referring to freedom, not price. Our General Public Licenses are designed to make sure that you have the freedom to distribute copies of free software (and charge for this service if you wish), that you receive source code or can get it if you want it, that you can change the software or use pieces of it in new free programs; and that you know you can do these things.

To protect your rights, we need to make restrictions that forbid anyone to deny you these rights or to ask you to surrender the rights. These restrictions translate to certain responsibilities for you if you distribute copies of the software, or if you modify it.

For example, if you distribute copies of such a program, whether gratis or for a fee, you must give the recipients all the rights that you have. You must make sure that they, too, receive or can get the source code. And you must show them these terms so they know their rights.

We protect your rights with two steps: (1) copyright the software, and (2) offer you this license which gives you legal permission to copy, distribute and/or modify the software.

Also, for each author's protection and ours, we want to make certain that everyone understands that there is no warranty for this free software. If the software is modified by someone else and passed on, we want its recipients to know that what they have is not the original, so that any problems introduced by others will not reflect on the original authors' reputations.

Finally, any free program is threatened constantly by software patents. We wish to avoid the danger that redistributors of a free program will individually obtain patent licenses, in effect making the program proprietary. To prevent this, we have made it clear that any patent must be licensed for everyone's free use or not licensed at all.

The precise terms and conditions for copying, distribution and modification follow.

GNU General Public License Terms and Conditions for Copying, Distribution, and Modification

0. This License applies to any program or other work which contains a notice placed by the copyright holder saying it may be distributed under the terms of this General Public License. The "Program," below, refers to any such program or work, and a "work based on the Program" means either the Program or any derivative work under copyright law: that is to say, a work containing the Program or a portion of it, either verbatim or with modifications and/or translated into another language. (Hereinafter, translation is included without limitation in the term "modification.") Each licensee is addressed as "you."

Activities other than copying, distribution and modification are not covered by this License; they are outside its scope. The act of running the Program is not restricted, and the output from the Program is covered only if its contents constitute a work based on the Program (independent of having been made by running the Program). Whether that is true depends on what the Program does.

1. You may copy and distribute verbatim copies of the Program's source code as you receive it, in any medium, provided that you conspicuously and appropriately publish on each copy an appropriate copyright notice and disclaimer of warranty; keep intact all the notices that refer to this License and to the absence of any warranty; and give any other recipients of the Program a copy of this License along with the Program.

You may charge a fee for the physical act of transferring a copy, and you may at your option offer warranty protection in exchange for a fee.

2. You may modify your copy or copies of the Program or any portion of it, thus forming a work based on the Program, and copy and distribute such modifications or work under the terms of Section 1 above, provided that you also meet all of these conditions:

   a) You must cause the modified files to carry prominent notices stating that you changed the files and the date of any change.

   b) You must cause any work that you distribute or publish, that in whole or in part contains or is derived from the Program or any part thereof, to be licensed as a whole at no charge to all third parties under the terms of this License.

   c) If the modified program normally reads commands interactively when run, you must cause it, when started running for such interactive use in the most ordinary way, to print or display an announcement including an appropriate copyright notice and a notice that there is no warranty (or else, saying that you provide a warranty) and that users may redistribute the program under these conditions, and telling the user how to view a copy of this License. (Exception: if the Program itself is interactive but does not normally print such an announcement, your work based on the Program is not required to print an announcement.)

   These requirements apply to the modified work as a whole. If identifiable sections of that work are not derived from the Program, and can be reasonably considered independent and separate works in themselves, then this License, and its terms, do not apply to those sections when you distribute them as separate works. But when you distribute the same sections as part of a whole which is a work based on the Program, the distribution of the whole must be on the terms of this License, whose permissions for other licensees extend to the entire whole, and thus to each and every part regardless of who wrote it.

   Thus, it is not the intent of this section to claim rights or contest your rights to work written entirely by you; rather, the intent is to exercise the right to control the distribution of derivative or collective works based on the Program.

   In addition, mere aggregation of another work not based on the Program with the Program (or with a work based on the Program) on a volume of a storage or distribution medium does not bring the other work under the scope of this License.

3. You may copy and distribute the Program (or a work based on it, under Section 2) in object code or executable form under the terms of Sections 1 and 2 above, provided that you also do one of the following:

   a) Accompany it with the complete corresponding machine-readable source code, which must be distributed under the terms of Sections 1 and 2 above on a medium customarily used for software interchange; or,

   b) Accompany it with a written offer, valid for at least three years, to give any third party, for a charge no more than your cost of physically performing source distribution, a complete machine-readable copy of the corresponding source code, to be distributed under the terms of Sections 1 and 2 above on a medium customarily used for software interchange; or,

c) Accompany it with the information you received as to the offer to distribute corresponding source code. (This alternative is allowed only for noncommercial distribution and only if you received the program in object code or executable form with such an offer, in accord with Subsection b above.)

The source code for a work means the preferred form of the work for making modifications to it. For an executable work, complete source code means all the source code for all modules it contains, plus any associated interface definition files, plus the scripts used to control compilation and installation of the executable. However, as a special exception, the source code distributed need not include anything that is normally distributed (in either source or binary form) with the major components (compiler, kernel, and so on) of the operating system on which the executable runs, unless that component itself accompanies the executable.

If distribution of executable or object code is made by offering access to copy from a designated place, then offering equivalent access to copy the source code from the same place counts as distribution of the source code, even though third parties are not compelled to copy the source along with the object code.

4. You may not copy, modify, sublicense, or distribute the Program except as expressly provided under this License. Any attempt otherwise to copy, modify, sublicense or distribute the Program is void, and will automatically terminate your rights under this License. However, parties who have received copies, or rights, from you under this License will not have their licenses terminated so long as such parties remain in full compliance.

5. You are not required to accept this License, since you have not signed it. However, nothing else grants you permission to modify or distribute the Program or its derivative works. These actions are prohibited by law if you do not accept this License. Therefore, by modifying or distributing the Program (or any work based on the Program), you indicate your acceptance of this License to do so, and all its terms and conditions for copying, distributing or modifying the Program or works based on it.

6. Each time you redistribute the Program (or any work based on the Program), the recipient automatically receives a license from the original licensor to copy, distribute or modify the Program subject to these terms and conditions. You may not impose any further restrictions on the recipients' exercise of the rights granted herein. You are not responsible for enforcing compliance by third parties to this License.

7. If, as a consequence of a court judgment or allegation of patent infringement or for any other reason (not limited to patent issues), conditions are imposed on you (whether by court order, agreement or otherwise) that contradict the conditions of this License, they do not excuse you from the conditions of this License. If you cannot distribute so as to satisfy simultaneously your obligations under this License and any other pertinent obligations, then as a consequence you may not distribute the Program at all. For example, if a patent license would not permit royalty-free redistribution of the Program by all those who receive copies directly or indirectly through you, then the only way you could satisfy both it and this License would be to refrain entirely from distribution of the Program.

If any portion of this section is held invalid or unenforceable under any particular circumstance, the balance of the section is intended to apply and the section as a whole is intended to apply in other circumstances.

It is not the purpose of this section to induce you to infringe any patents or other property right claims or to contest validity of any such claims; this section has the sole purpose of protecting the integrity of the free software distribution system, which is implemented by public license practices. Many people have made generous contributions to the wide range of software distributed through that system in reliance on consistent application of that system; it is up to the author/donor to decide if he or she is willing to distribute software through any other system, and a licensee cannot impose that choice.

This section is intended to make thoroughly clear what is believed to be a consequence of the rest of this License.

8. If the distribution and/or use of the Program is restricted in certain countries either by patents or by copyrighted interfaces, the original copyright holder who places the Program under this License may add an explicit geographical distribution limitation excluding those countries, so that distribution is permitted only in or among countries not thus excluded. In such case, this License incorporates the limitation as if written in the body of this License.

9. The Free Software Foundation may publish revised and/or new versions of the General Public License from time to time. Such new versions will be similar in spirit to the present version, but may differ in detail to address new problems or concerns.

   Each version is given a distinguishing version number. If the Program specifies a version number of this License which applies to it and "any later version," you have the option of following the terms and conditions either of that version or of any later version published by the Free Software Foundation. If the Program does not specify a version number of this License, you may choose any version ever published by the Free Software Foundation.

10. If you wish to incorporate parts of the Program into other free programs whose distribution conditions are different, write to the author to ask for permission. For software which is copyrighted by the Free Software Foundation, write to the Free Software Foundation; we sometimes make exceptions for this. Our decision will be guided by the two goals of preserving the free status of all derivatives of our free software and of promoting the sharing and reuse of software generally.

NO WARRANTY

11. BECAUSE THE PROGRAM IS LICENSED FREE OF CHARGE, THERE IS NO WARRANTY FOR THE PROGRAM, TO THE EXTENT PERMITTED BY APPLICABLE LAW. EXCEPT WHEN OTHERWISE STATED IN WRITING THE COPYRIGHT HOLDERS AND/OR OTHER PARTIES PROVIDE THE PROGRAM "AS IS" WITHOUT WARRANTY OF ANY KIND, EITHER EXPRESSED OR IMPLIED, INCLUDING, BUT NOT LIMITED TO, THE IMPLIED WARRANTIES OF MERCHANTABILITY AND FITNESS FOR A PARTICULAR PURPOSE. THE ENTIRE RISK AS TO THE QUALITY AND

PERFORMANCE OF THE PROGRAM IS WITH YOU. SHOULD THE PROGRAM PROVE DEFECTIVE, YOU ASSUME THE COST OF ALL NECESSARY SERVICING, REPAIR OR CORRECTION.

12. IN NO EVENT UNLESS REQUIRED BY APPLICABLE LAW OR AGREED TO IN WRITING WILL ANY COPYRIGHT HOLDER, OR ANY OTHER PARTY WHO MAY MODIFY AND/OR REDISTRIBUTE THE PROGRAM AS PERMITTED ABOVE, BE LIABLE TO YOU FOR DAMAGES, INCLUDING ANY GENERAL, SPECIAL, INCIDENTAL OR CONSEQUENTIAL DAMAGES ARISING OUT OF THE USE OR INABILITY TO USE THE PROGRAM (INCLUDING BUT NOT LIMITED TO LOSS OF DATA OR DATA BEING RENDERED INACCURATE OR LOSSES SUSTAINED BY YOU OR THIRD PARTIES OR A FAILURE OF THE PROGRAM TO OPERATE WITH ANY OTHER PROGRAMS), EVEN IF SUCH HOLDER OR OTHER PARTY HAS BEEN ADVISED OF THE POSSIBILITY OF SUCH DAMAGES.

END OF TERMS AND CONDITIONS

How to Apply These Terms to Your New Programs

If you develop a new program, and you want it to be of the greatest possible use to the public, the best way to achieve this is to make it free software which everyone can redistribute and change under these terms.

To do so, attach the following notices to the program. It is safest to attach them to the start of each source file to most effectively convey the exclusion of warranty; and each file should have at least the "copyright" line and a pointer to where the full notice is found.

```
<one line to give the program's name and a brief idea of what it does.>
Copyright (C) 19yy  <name of author>
```

This program is free software; you can redistribute it and/or modify it under the terms of the GNU General Public License as published by the Free Software Foundation; either version 2 of the License, or (at your option) any later version.

This program is distributed in the hope that it will be useful, but WITHOUT ANY WARRANTY; without even the implied warranty of MERCHANTABILITY or FITNESS FOR A PARTICULAR PURPOSE. See the GNU General Public License for more details.

You should have received a copy of the GNU General Public License along with this program; if not, write to the Free Software Foundation, Inc., 675 Mass Ave, Cambridge MA 02139 USA.

Also add information on how to contact you by electronic and paper mail.

If the program is interactive, make it output a short notice like this when it starts in an interactive mode:

```
Gnomovision version 69, Copyright (C) 19yy name of author
Gnomovision comes with ABSOLUTELY NO WARRANTY; for details type 'show w'.
This is free software, and you are welcome to redistribute it
under certain conditions; type 'show c' for details.
```

App
D

The hypothetical commands 'show w' and 'show c' should show the appropriate parts of the General Public License. Of course, the commands you use may be called something other than 'show w' and 'show c;' they could even be mouse-clicks or menu items—whatever suits your program.

You should also get your employer (if you work as a programmer) or your school, if any, to sign a "copyright disclaimer" for the program, if necessary. Here is a sample; alter the names:

```
Yoyodyne, Inc., hereby disclaims all copyright interest in the program
'Gnomovision' (which makes passes at compilers) written by James Hacker.

<signature of Ty Coon>, 1 April 1989
Ty Coon, President of Vice
```

This General Public License does not permit incorporating your program into proprietary programs. If your program is a subroutine library, you may consider it more useful to permit linking proprietary applications with the library. If this is what you want to do, use the GNU Library General Public License instead of this License.

The Caldera Open Linux Lite CD-ROM

Linux evolves constantly, whether it's a new kernel release from Linus Torvalds or a new distribution. Things change so quickly, in fact, that a book tends to lag behind because of the production step involved. Thus, the need for this appendix. During the production of this edition, the editorial group at Que pursued Caldera for a copy of its distribution for this edition—and succeeded! Unfortunately, the distribution wasn't received in time to integrate coverage of it into the book, so we've included this brief appendix to cover Caldera's product—Open Linux Lite.

Like Red Hat and Slackware, Open Linux Lite is a complete distribution of a multiuser, multitasking operating system based on the Linux 2.0 kernel. The third CD-ROM accompanying this book contains a *lite* edition—that is, a non-commercial version—of Caldera's Open Linux distribution. The version on the CD-ROM is a subset of Caldera's commercial Open Linux Base product. Table E.1 illustrates the differences between Caldera's commercial product and the accompanying CD-ROM. Some products aren't supplied, such as Netscape Navigator, whereas other products are available, but only with a 30-day trial offer.

Table E.1 Open Linux Base vs. Open Linux Lite

Component	Open Linux Base (Official)	Open Linux Lite (CD-ROM)
Linux OS and utilities	Yes	Yes
System Admin and installation tools	Yes	Yes
250-page manual	Yes	No
Technical support	Yes	No
Netscape Navigator	Yes	No
Looking Glass Desktop	Yes	Yes (30-day trial)
CrispLite Graphical Editor	Yes	Yes (30-day trial)

ON THE WEB

For more information on Caldera's product line, visit the company's Web site at **http://www.caldera.com**. ▪

N O T E Caldera doesn't supply Netscape Navigator for Linux with Open Linux Lite. You can download the Linux version of Navigator from **ftp://sunsite.unc.edu/pub/packages/infosystems/WWW/clients/Netscape**. ▪

Installing Open Linux Lite

Caldera made arrangements with Red Hat to use its distribution, so many installation procedures are the same for Caldera and Red Hat. You should be able to use Chapter 3, "Installing Red Hat," to help you install Open Linux Lite. Your system must have the following components to successfully install Open Linux Lite:

- An 80386 or above Intel-based PC (Caldera doesn't support other processors at this time)
- A 3 1/2-inch floppy drive
- At least 8M of RAM
- About 250M of disk space
- A mouse and video card supported by XFree86
    - ▶ **See** "Video Cards," **p. 700**

To briefly recap, you need to partition your hard drive, create the boot floppy, and then install and configure the system.

▶ **See** "Partitioning Your Hard Drive," **p. 46**

The boot image is located on the CD-ROM in the file \col_10\bppt-disk\Install.img. To create the boot disk, insert a blank diskette and type the following at the prompt (this assumes that your CD-ROM is drive D):

```
d:\col_10\tools\rawrite3
```

Unlike other installation programs, Open Linux Lite's installation program should automatically detect your hard drive and other hardware. If not, you may need to use another diskette called the *modules disk*. To create the disk, simply repeat the preceding command and use the \col_10\bootdisk\Modules.img file located on the CD-ROM.

Using This Book with Red Hat, Slackware, and Caldera Open Linux Lite

Although Caldera's distribution is based on Red Hat's distribution, for parts of the installation you may have to use the online documentation to install Open Linux Lite. After you install Open Linux Lite, however, you'll find the rest of the book very useful in showing how to use Linux. Table E.2 lists which chapters are useful for Red Hat (R), Slackware (S), Caldera (C), Linux (L), and UNIX (U).

Table E.2   Chapters Useful for Each Distribution

Chapter	Title	Useful With...
1	"Understanding Linux"	R,S,C
2	"Overview of Features"	R,S,L
3	"Installing Red Hat"	R,L
4	"Installing Slackware 96"	S,L
5	"Running Linux Applications"	R,S,C,L
6	"Installing the X Windows System"	R,S,C,L
7	"Using X Windows"	R,S,C,L
8	"Understanding Systems Administration"	R,S,C,L,U
9	"Booting and Shutting Down"	R,S,C,L,U
10	"Managing User Accounts"	R,S,C,L,U
11	"Backing Up Data"	R,S,C,L,U
12	"Improving System Security"	R,S,C,L,U
13	"Upgrading and Installing Software"	R,L
14	"Managing File Systems"	R,S,C,L,U

continues

App
E

Table E.2 **Continued**

Chapter	Title	Useful With...
15	"Understanding the File and Directory System"	R,S,C,L,U
16	"Managing Files and Directories"	R,S,C,L,U
17	"Understanding Linux Shells"	R,S,C,L,U
18	"Managing Multiple Processes"	R,S,C,L,U
19	"Using the *vi* Editor"	R,S,C,L,U
20	"Using the *emacs* Editor"	R,S,C,L,U
21	"Printing"	R,S,C,L
22	"Understanding the TCP/IP Protocol Suite"	R,S,C,L,U
23	"Configuring a TCP/IP Network"	R,S,C,L,U
24	"Configuring Domain Name Service"	S,R,L,U
25	"Using SLIP and PPP"	R,S,C,L
26	"Understanding the Internet"	R,S,C,L,U
27	"Accessing the Network with *telnet*, *ftp*, and the *r*- Commands"	R,S,C,L,U
28	"Surfing the Internet with the World Wide Web"	R,S,C,L,U
29	"Using Electronic Mail"	R,S,C,L,U
30	"Surviving Usenet News"	R,S,C,L,U
31	"Creating Web Documents with HTML"	R,S,C,L,U
32	"Getting Started with Apache"	R,S,C,L
33	"Configuring Apache"	R,S,C,L
34	"Managing an Internet Web Server"	R,S,C,L,U

Index

Symbols

A

Y-Z

QUE'S SPECIAL OFFER!
ORDER FORM

1-800-800-6613
Tel: +1-520-526-9565
Fax: +1-520-526-9573
E-Mail: info@infomagic.com
Web: www.infomagic.com

InfoMagic
11950 N. Highway 89, Flagstaff AZ 86004

FIRST NAME:	LAST NAME:

ADDRESS

CITY	STATE
ZIP	COUNTRY

TEL, FAX or E-MAIL:

CD-ROMS & BOOKS available direct from InfoMagic, Inc.:	PRICE	QTY	AMOUNT
LINUX Developers Resource 6 CD Set - RedHat,Debian, Slackware, Metro-X & more!	$ 17.50		
LINUX Installation & Getting Started Guide 250 pg manual by Matt Welsh	$ 12.50		
LINUX Network Administrators Guide 350 pg manual by Olaf Kirch	$ 18.50		
RUNNING LINUX - 600 page manual	$ 24.95		
LINUX T-Shirt , (circle size) M L XL XXL	$ 15.00		
LINUX Journal Subscription - USA the only monthly magazine for Linux! 1yr = 12 issues	$ 22.00		
LINUX Journal Subscription - CANADA	$ 27.00		
LINUX Journal Subscription - OVERSEAS	$ 32.00		
MOO-TIFF 2 CD Set for LINUX-Graphical User Interface for PC's running LINUX	$ 99.00		
WORKGROUP SERVER (high performance file and printing services to PC and MAC clients using Linux)	$ 75.00		
WORKGROUP SERVER (with one year support contract)	$ 499.00		
UNIFIX LINUX 2.0 (Posix certified)	$ 80.00		

Sub-Total	
5.5% Sales Tax (Arizona Residents ONLY)	
Shipping	
TOTAL	

SHIPPING: $ 5.00 - US Mail
$10.00 - International AirMail
Ship rates are per order up to 2 items.

PAYMENT:

☐ MC/VISA	☐ AMEX	☐ **Check or Money Order Enclosed**

Int'l checks MUST be in U.S. funds and drawn on a U.S. Bank

Acct No. _____ Exp: _____

Name of
Cardholder _____

Signature _____

Complete and Return this Card
for a *FREE* Computer Book Catalog

Thank you for purchasing this book! You have purchased a superior computer book written expressly for your needs. To continue to provide the kind of up-to-date, pertinent coverage you've come to expect from us, we need to hear from you. Please take a minute to complete and return this self-addressed, postage-paid form. In return, we'll send you a free catalog of all our computer books on topics ranging from word processing to programming and the internet.

Mr. ☐ Mrs. ☐ Ms. ☐ Dr. ☐

Name (first) ☐☐☐☐☐☐☐☐☐☐☐☐☐☐ (M.I.) ☐ (last) ☐☐☐☐☐☐☐☐☐☐☐☐☐☐☐

Address ☐☐☐☐☐☐☐☐☐☐☐☐☐☐☐☐☐☐☐☐☐☐☐☐☐☐☐☐☐☐

☐☐☐☐☐☐☐☐☐☐☐☐☐☐☐☐☐☐☐☐☐☐☐☐☐☐☐☐☐☐

City ☐☐☐☐☐☐☐☐☐☐☐☐☐ State ☐☐ Zip ☐☐☐☐☐ ☐☐☐☐

Phone ☐☐☐ ☐☐☐ ☐☐☐☐ Fax ☐☐☐ ☐☐☐ ☐☐☐☐

Company Name ☐☐☐☐☐☐☐☐☐☐☐☐☐☐☐☐☐☐☐☐☐☐☐☐☐☐

E-mail address ☐☐☐☐☐☐☐☐☐☐☐☐☐☐☐☐☐☐☐☐☐☐☐☐☐☐

1. Please check at least (3) influencing factors for purchasing this book.

Front or back cover information on book .... ☐
Special approach to the content .... ☐
Completeness of content .... ☐
Author's reputation .... ☐
Publisher's reputation .... ☐
Book cover design or layout .... ☐
Index or table of contents of book .... ☐
Price of book .... ☐
Special effects, graphics, illustrations .... ☐
Other (Please specify): _____ ☐

2. How did you first learn about this book?

Saw in Macmillan Computer Publishing catalog .... ☐
Recommended by store personnel .... ☐
Saw the book on bookshelf at store .... ☐
Recommended by a friend .... ☐
Received advertisement in the mail .... ☐
Saw an advertisement in: _____ ☐
Read book review in: _____ ☐
Other (Please specify): _____ ☐

3. How many computer books have you purchased in the last six months?

This book only .... ☐   3 to 5 books .... ☐
books .... ☐   More than 5 .... ☐

4. Where did you purchase this book?

Bookstore .... ☐
Computer Store .... ☐
Consumer Electronics Store .... ☐
Department Store .... ☐
Office Club .... ☐
Warehouse Club .... ☐
Mail Order .... ☐
Direct from Publisher .... ☐
Internet site .... ☐
Other (Please specify): _____ ☐

5. How long have you been using a computer?

☐ Less than 6 months   ☐ 6 months to a year
☐ 1 to 3 years   ☐ More than 3 years

6. What is your level of experience with personal computers and with the subject of this book?

	With PCs	With subject of book
New	☐	☐
Casual	☐	☐
Accomplished	☐	☐
Expert	☐	☐

Source Code ISBN: 0-7897-1132-x

7. Which of the following best describes your job title?

Administrative Assistant ☐
Coordinator ☐
Manager/Supervisor ☐
Director ☐
Vice President ☐
President/CEO/COO ☐
Lawyer/Doctor/Medical Professional ☐
Teacher/Educator/Trainer ☐
Engineer/Technician ☐
Consultant ☐
Not employed/Student/Retired ☐
Other (Please specify): _____ ☐

8. Which of the following best describes the area of the company your job title falls under?

Accounting ☐
Engineering ☐
Manufacturing ☐
Operations ☐
Marketing ☐
Sales ☐
Other (Please specify): _____ ☐

9. What is your age?

Under 20 ☐
21-29 ☐
30-39 ☐
40-49 ☐
50-59 ☐
60-over ☐

10. Are you:

Male ☐
Female ☐

11. Which computer publications do you read regularly? (Please list)

_____
_____
_____
_____
_____
_____
_____
_____
_____
_____

Comments: _____
_____
_____

Fold here and scotch-tape to mail

Check out Que® Books on the World Wide Web
http://www.quecorp.com

As the biggest software release in computer history, Windows 95 continues to redefine the computer industry. Click here for the latest info on our Windows 95 books

Make computing quick and easy with these products designed exclusively for new and casual users

Examine the latest releases in word processing, spreadsheets, operating systems, and suites

The Internet, The World Wide Web, CompuServe®, America Online®, Prodigy® —it's a world of ever-changing information. Don't get left behind!

Find out about new additions to our site, new bestsellers and hot topics

In-depth information on high-end topics: find the best reference books for databases, programming, networking, and client/server technologies

A recent addition to Que, Ziff-Davis Press publishes the highly-successful *How It Works* and *How to Use* series of books, as well as *PC Learning Labs Teaches* and *PC Magazine* series of book/disc packages

Stay on the cutting edge of Macintosh® technologies and visual communications

Find out which titles are making headlines

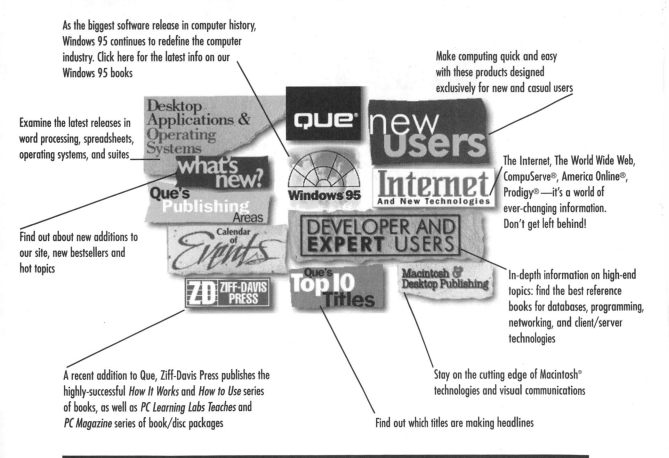

With 6 separate publishing groups, Que develops products for many specific market segments and areas of computer technology. Explore our Web Site and you'll find information on best-selling titles, newly published titles, upcoming products, authors, and much more.

- Stay informed on the latest industry trends and products available
- Visit our online bookstore for the latest information and editions
- Download software from Que's library of the best shareware and freeware

MACMILLAN COMPUTER PUBLISHING USA

A VIACOM COMPANY

Technical Support:

If you need assistance with the information in this book or with a CD/Disk accompanying the book, please access the Knowledge Base on our Web site at **http://www.superlibrary.com/general/support**. Our most Frequently Asked Questions are answered there. If you do not find the answer to your questions on our Web site, you may contact Macmillan Technical Support **(317) 581-3833** or e-mail us at **support@mcp.com**.